GENERAL MOTORS | METRO/SPRINT
1985-93 REPAIR MANUAL

President	Dean F. Morgantini, S.A.E.
Vice President–Finance	Barry L. Beck
Vice President–Sales	Glenn D. Potere
Executive Editor	Kevin M. G. Maher, A.S.E.
Production Manager	Ben Greisler, S.A.E.
Production Assistant	Melinda Possinger
Project Managers	George B. Heinrich III, A.S.E., S.A.E., Will Kessler, A.S.E., S.A.E., James R. Marotta, S.T.S., Richard Schwartz, Todd W. Stidham
Schematics Editor	Christopher G. Ritchie
Editor	James R. Marotta, S.T.S.

CHILTON™ *Automotive Books*

PUBLISHED BY **W. G. NICHOLS, INC.**

Manufactured in USA
© 1993 Chilton Book Company
1020 Andrew Drive
West Chester, PA 19380
ISBN 0-8019-8424-6
Library of Congress Catalog Card No. 92-054899
7890123456 7654321098

Contents

Contents

7 DRIVE TRAIN

8 SUSPENSION AND STEERING

9 BRAKES

10 BODY AND TRIM

GLOSSARY

MASTER INDEX

SAFETY NOTICE

Proper service and repair procedures are vital to the safe, reliable operation of all motor vehicles, as well as the personal safety of those performing repairs. This manual outlines procedures for servicing and repairing vehicles using safe, effective methods. The procedures contain many NOTES, CAUTIONS and WARNINGS which should be followed along with standard procedures to eliminate the possibility of personal injury or improper service which could damage the vehicle or compromise its safety.

It is important to note that the repair procedures and techniques, tools and parts for servicing motor vehicles, as well as the skill and experience of the individual performing the work vary widely. It is not possible to anticipate all of the conceivable ways or conditions under which vehicles may be serviced, or to provide cautions as to all of the possible hazards that may result. Standard and accepted safety precautions and equipment should be used when handling toxic or flammable fluids, and safety goggles or other protection should be used during cutting, grinding, chiseling, prying, or any other process that can cause material removal or projectiles.

Some procedures require the use of tools specially designed for a specific purpose. Before substituting another tool or procedure, you must be completely satisfied that neither your personal safety, nor the performance of the vehicle will be endangered.

Although information in this manual is based on industry sources and is complete as possible at the time of publication, the possibility exists that some vehicle manufacturers made later changes which could not be included here. While striving for total accuracy, W. G. Nichols, Inc. cannot assume responsibility for any errors, changes or omissions that may occur in the compilation of this data.

PART NUMBERS

Part numbers listed in this reference are not recommendations by Chilton for any product by brand name. They are references that can be used with interchange manuals and aftermarket supplier catalogs to locate each brand supplier's discrete part number.

SPECIAL TOOLS

Special tools are recommended by the vehicle manufacturer to perform their specific job. Use has been kept to a minimum, but where absolutely necessary, they are referred to in the text by the part number of the tool manufacturer. These tools can be purchased, under the appropriate part number, from your local dealer or regional distributor, or an equivalent tool can be purchased locally from a tool supplier or parts outlet. Before substituting any tool for the one recommended, read the SAFETY NOTICE at the top of this page.

ACKNOWLEDGMENTS

W. G. Nichols, Inc. expresses appreciation to General Motors Corp. for their generous assistance.

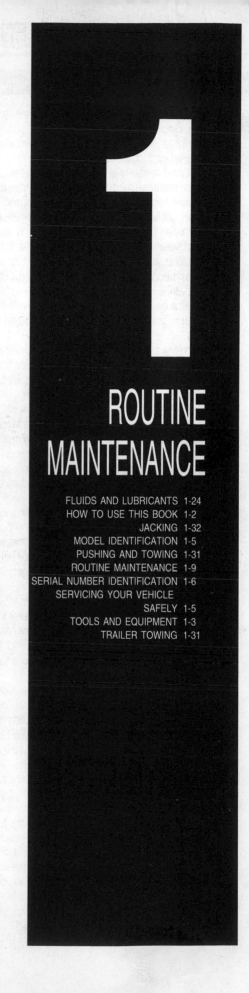

1

ROUTINE MAINTENANCE

HOW TO USE THIS BOOK

Chilton's Total Care Care Manual for 1985-93 Chevrolet Sprint and Geo Metro is intended to help you learn more about the inner working of your vehicle and save you money in it's upkeep and operation.

The first two sections will be the most used, since they contain maintenance and tune-up information and procedures. Studies have shown that a properly tuned and maintained vehicle can get at least 10% better gas mileage than an out-of-tune vehicle. Other sections deal with the more complex systems of your vehicle. Operating systems from engine through brakes are covered to the extent that the average do-it-yourselfer becomes mechanically involved. This book will give you detailed instructions to help you perform minor to major repairs on your vehicle that in turn will save you money, give you personal satisfaction and help you avoid expensive repair bills.

A secondary purpose of this book is a reference for owners who want to understand their vehicle and/or their mechanics better. In this case, no tools at all are required.

Before removing any bolts, read through the entire procedure. This will give you the overall view of what tools and supplies will be required. There is nothing more frustrating than having to walk to the bus stop on Monday morning because you were short one bolt on Sunday afternoon. So read ahead and plan ahead. Each operation should be approached logically and all procedures thoroughly understood before attempting any work.

All sections contain adjustments, maintenance, removal/installation and repair or overhaul procedures. When repair is not considered practical, we tell you how to remove the part and then how to install the new or rebuilt replacement. In this way, you at least save the labor costs. Backyard repair of some components is just not practical.

Two basic mechanic's rules should be mentioned: One, the left-side of the vehicle or engine is the driver's side. Conversely, the right-side of the vehicle means the passenger's side. Secondly, most screws and bolts are removed by turning them counterclockwise and tightened by turning them clockwise.

Safety is always the most important rule. Constantly be aware of the dangers involved in working on a vehicle and take the proper precautions. (See the section in this section, Servicing Your Vehicle Safely and the SAFETY NOTICE on the acknowledgment page). Pay attention to the instructions provided.

There are 3 common mistakes in mechanical work:

1. Incorrect order of assembly, disassembly or adjustment: When taking something apart or putting it together, doing things in the wrong order usually costs extra time, however, it CAN break something. Read the entire procedure before beginning disassembly. Do everything in the order in which the instructions say you should do it, even if you can't immediately see a reason for it. When you're taking something apart that is very intricate (for example, a carburetor), you might want to draw (or take) a picture of how it looks when assembled at one point, in order to make sure you get everything back in its proper position. (We will supply exploded views whenever possible). When making adjustments, especially tune-up adjustments, do them in order. Often, one adjustment affects another and you cannot expect satisfactory results unless each adjustment is made only when it cannot be changed by any other.

2. Overtorquing (or undertorquing): While it is more common for overtorquing to cause damage, undertorquing can cause a fastener to vibrate loose causing serious damage. Especially, when dealing with aluminum parts, pay attention to torque specifications and utilize a torque wrench during assembly. If a torque figure is not available, remember that by using the right tool for the job, you will probably not have to strain yourself to get a fastener tight enough. The pitch of most threads is so slight that the tension you put on the wrench will be multiplied many times (in actual force) on the fastener you are tightening. A good example of how critical torque is can be seen in the case of spark plug installation, especially where you are putting the plug into an aluminum cylinder head. Too little torque can fail to crush the gasket, causing leakage of combustion gases and consequent overheating of the plug and engine parts. Too much torque can damage the threads or distort the plug, which changes the spark gap.

➡**There are many commercial products available for ensuring that fasteners won't come loose, even if they are not torqued just right (a very common brand is Loctite®). If you're worried about getting something together tight enough to hold but loose enough to avoid mechanical damage during assembly, one of these products might offer substantial insurance. Read the label on the package and make sure the product is compatible with the components involved before choosing one.**

3. Crossthreading: Crossthreading occurs when a part such as a bolt is screwed into a nut or casting at the wrong angle. It is more likely to occur if access is difficult. To help prevent crossthreading, clean and lubricate the fasteners, then start threading with the part to be installed going straight in. Start the bolt or spark plug with your fingers. If you encounter resistance, unscrew the part and start over again at a different angle until it can be inserted and turned several turns without much effort. Keep in mind that many parts, especially spark plugs, use tapered threads so that gentle turning will automatically bring the part you're threading to the proper angle if you don't force it or resist a change in angle. Don't put a wrench on the part until it's been turned a couple of turns by hand. If you suddenly encounter resistance, and the part has not been fully seated, don't force it. Pull it back out and make sure it's clean and threading properly.

➡**Always take your time and be patient. Once you have some experience working on your vehicle, it will become an enjoyable hobby.**

TOOLS AND EQUIPMENT

▶ **See Figure 1**

Naturally, without the proper tools and equipment, it is impossible to properly service your vehicle. It would be impossible to catalog each tool that you would need to perform each and every operation in this book. It would also be unwise for the amateur to rush out and buy an expensive set of tools on the theory that he may need one or more of them at sometime.

The best approach is to proceed slowly, gathering a good quality set of tools that are used most frequently. Don't be misled by the low cost of bargain tools. It is far better to spend a little more for better quality. Forged wrenches, 6 or 12 point sockets and fine tooth ratchets are by far preferable to their less expensive counterparts. As any good mechanic can tell you, there are few worse experiences than trying to work on a vehicle with bad tools. Your monetary savings will be far outweighed by frustration and mangled knuckles.

Begin accumulating tools that are used most frequently; those associated with routine maintenance and tune-up.

In addition to the normal assortment of screwdrivers and pliers you should have the following tools for routine maintenance jobs:

1. SAE and Metric wrenches and sockets in sizes from $\frac{1}{8}$-$\frac{3}{4}$″ (6-19mm) and a spark plug socket $\frac{13}{16}$″ or $\frac{5}{8}$″ depending on plug type).

➡**If possible, buy various length socket drive extensions. One break in this department is that the metric sockets available in the U.S. will all fit the ratchet handles and extensions you may already have ($\frac{1}{4}$″, $\frac{3}{8}$″ and $\frac{1}{2}$″ drive).**

2. Jackstands, for support
3. Oil filter wrench
4. Oil filler spout, for pouring oil
5. Grease gun, for chassis lubrication
6. Hydrometer, for checking the battery
7. A container for draining oil
8. Many rags for wiping up inevitable spills.
9. A quality floor jack.

In addition to the above items there are several others that are not absolutely necessary but handy to have around. These include oil dry (kitty litter is a good substitute), a transmission funnel and the usual supply of lubricants, antifreeze and fluids, although these can be purchased as needed. This is a basic list for routine maintenance but only your personal needs and desires can accurately determine your list of tools.

The second list of tools is for tune-ups. While the tools involved here are slightly more sophisticated, they need not be outrageously expensive. There are several inexpensive tach/dwell meters on the market that are every bit as good for the average mechanic as an expensive professional model. Just be sure that the meter reads 1,200-1,500 rpm on the tach scale and that it works on 3, 4, 6 and 8 cylinder engines. A basic list of tune-up equipment should include:

10. Tach/dwell meter.
11. Spark plug wrench.
12. Timing light (a DC light that works from the vehicle's battery is best, although an AC light that plugs into 110V house current will suffice at some sacrifice in brightness).
13. Wire spark plug gauge/adjusting tools.
14. Set of feeler gauges.

There are several other tools that, in time, you will find you can't live without. These include:

15. A compression gauge. The screw-in type is slower to use but eliminates the possibility of a faulty reading due to escaping pressure.
16. A manifold vacuum gauge.
17. A test light, volt/ohm meter.
18. An induction meter. This is used for determining whether or not there is current in a wire. These are handy for use if a wire is broken somewhere in a wiring harness.

As a final note, you will probably find a torque wrench necessary for all but the most basic work. The beam type models are perfectly adequate, although the newer click type are more precise.

➡**Special tools are occasionally necessary to perform a specific job or are recommended to make a job easier. Their use has been kept to a minimum. When a special tool is indicated, it will be referred to by manufacturer's part number, and, where possible, an illustration of the tool will be provided so that an equivalent tool may be used. Special tools may be purchased through your local Chevrolet dealer or directly from the tool manufacturers. A list of tool manufacturers and their addresses follows:**

In the United States, contact:
Service Tool Division Kent-Moore Corporation 29784 Little Mack Roseville, MI 48066-2298
In Canada, contact:
Kent-Moore of Canada, Ltd. 2395 Cawthra Mississauga Ontario, Canada L5A 3P2.

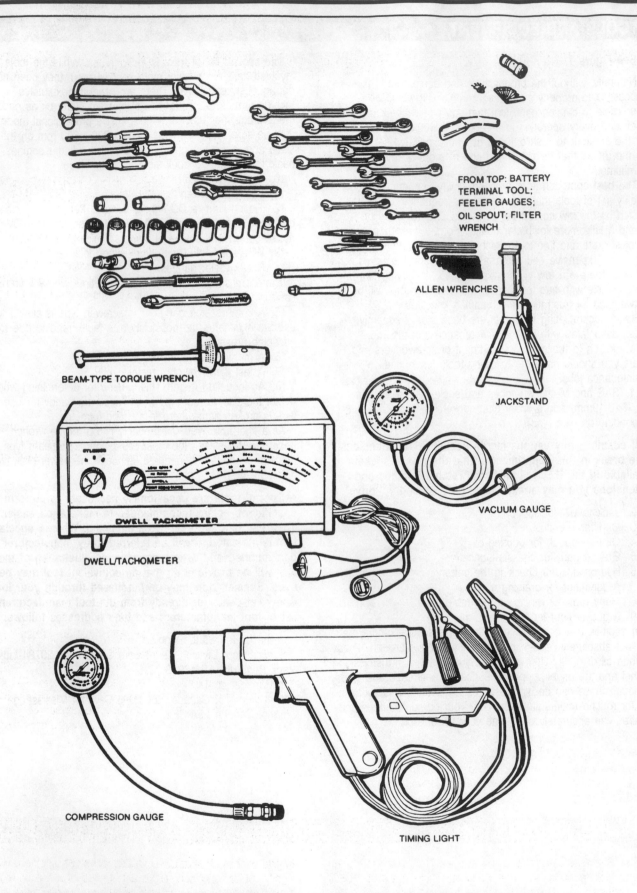

FROM TOP: BATTERY TERMINAL TOOL; FEELER GAUGES; OIL SPOUT; FILTER WRENCH

ALLEN WRENCHES

JACKSTAND

BEAM-TYPE TORQUE WRENCH

DWELL/TACHOMETER

VACUUM GAUGE

COMPRESSION GAUGE

TIMING LIGHT

Fig. 1 The tools and equipment shown here will handle the majority of the maintenance on your vehicle.

SERVICING YOUR VEHICLE SAFELY

It is virtually impossible to anticipate all of the hazards involved with automotive maintenance and service but care and common sense will prevent most accidents.

The rules of safety for mechanics range from 'don't smoke around gasoline," to 'use the proper tool for the job." The trick to avoiding injuries is to develop safe work habits and take every possible precaution.

Do's

• Do keep a fire extinguisher and first aid kit within easy reach.

• Do wear safety glasses or goggles when cutting, drilling, grinding or prying, even if you have 20/20 vision. If you wear glasses for the sake of vision, then they should be made of hardened glass that can serve also as safety glasses or wear safety goggles over your regular glasses.

• Do shield your eyes whenever you work around the battery. Batteries contain sulfuric acid. In case of contact with the eyes or skin, flush the area with water or a mixture of water and baking soda, then get medical attention immediately.

• Do use safety stands for any under vehicle service. Jacks are for raising the vehicle. Safety stands are for making sure the vehicle stays raised until you want it to come down. Whenever the vehicle is raised, block the wheels remaining on the ground and set the parking brake.

• Do use adequate ventilation when working with any chemicals. Like carbon monoxide, the asbestos dust resulting from brake lining wear can be poisonous in sufficient quantities.

• Do disconnect the negative battery cable when working on the electrical system. The primary ignition system can contain up to 40,000 volts.

• Do follow the manufacturer's instructions when working with potentially hazardous materials. Both brake fluid and antifreeze are poisonous if taken internally.

• Do properly maintain your tools. Loose hammer heads, mushroomed punches/chisels, frayed or poorly grounded electrical cords, excessively worn screwdrivers, spread wrenches (open end), cracked sockets, slipping ratchets and/or faulty droplight sockets cause accidents.

• Do use the proper size and type of tool for the job being done.

• Do pull on a wrench handle rather than push on it and adjust your stance to prevent a fall.

• Do be sure that adjustable wrenches are tightly adjusted on the nut or bolt and pulled so that the face is on the side of the fixed jaw.

• Do select a wrench or socket that fits the nut or bolt. The wrench or socket should sit straight, not cocked.

• Do strike squarely with a hammer — avoid glancing blows.

• Do set the parking brake and block the drive wheels if the work requires that the engine be running.

Don't's

• Don't run an engine in a garage or anywhere else without proper ventilation — EVER! Carbon monoxide is poisonous. It takes a long time to leave the body and can build up a deadly supply of it in your system by simply breathing in a little every day. You may not realize you are slowly poisoning yourself. Always use power vents, windows, fans or open the garage doors.

• Don't work around moving parts while wearing a necktie or other loose clothing. Short sleeves are much safer than long, loose sleeves and hard-toed shoes with neoprene soles protect your toes and give a better grip on slippery surfaces. Jewelry such as watches, fancy belt buckles, beads or body adornment or any kind is not safe working around a vehicle. Long hair should be tied back or hidden under a hat.

• Don't use pockets for tool boxes. A fall or bump can drive a screwdriver deep into your body. Even a wiping cloth hanging from the back pocket can wrap around a spinning shaft or fan.

• Don't smoke when working around gasoline, cleaning solvent or other flammable material.

• Don't smoke when working around the battery. When the battery is being charged, it gives off explosive hydrogen gas.

• Don't use gasoline to wash your hands. There are excellent soaps available. Gasoline may contain lead, and lead can enter the body through a cut, accumulating in the body until you are very ill. Gasoline also removes all the natural oils from the skin so that bone dry hands will suck up oil and grease.

• Don't attempt to service the air conditioning system unless you are equipped with the necessary tools and training. In most states it is now illegal to discharge refrigerant into the atmosphere due to the harmful effects Freon (R-12) has on the ozone layer. Most states now require that an approved recovery system be used to consume the discharged Freon and that the operator be licensed to operate the equipment.

MODEL IDENTIFICATION

The Chevrolet Sprint (1985-88) and the Geo Metro (1989-93) are very similar vehicles. The standard engine is a 1.0L SOHC 3-cylinder engine backed by either a 5-speed manual or 3-speed automatic transaxle.

Several variations of the Sprint/Metro have been built during the model run. In 1987, a turbocharged version of the 1.0L engine was made available. The turbocharged engine provided significant gains in horsepower and torque over the normally aspirated engine, while still providing fuel efficiency and driveability. It also introduced Electronic Fuel Injection (EFI) to the Sprint/Metro line-up. EFI has been used exclusively since 1988.

The other major variation on the Sprint/Metro line was the introduction of the convertible in 1990.

SERIAL NUMBER IDENTIFICATION

Vehicle

♦ **See Figures 2 and 3**

The vehicle identification number plate is located on the left upper instrument panel and is visible from the outside of the vehicle. A great deal of information about your vehicle can be extracted by the code numbers that make up this 17 digit number. Model and body style information, along with year of production and engine size are also listed on this plate. The engine code is in the 8th position. The 10th digit indicates the model year: F for 1985, G for 1986, H for 1987, J for 1988, K for 1989, L for 1990, M for 1991, N for 1992, and P for 1993.

Engine

♦ **See Figure 4**

Engines are stamped with an engine identification serial number which identifies the model year, engine displacement and engine type.

Fig. 2 Vehicle identification plate location

VEHICLE IDENTIFICATION CHART

It is important for servicing and ordering parts to be certain of the vehicle and engine identification. The VIN (vehicle identification number) is a 17 digit number visible through the windshield on the driver's side of the dash and contains the vehicle and engine identification codes. The tenth digit indicates model year and the eighth digit indicates engine code. It can be interpreted as follows:

Engine Code							Model Year	
Code	Liters	Cu. In. (cc)	Cyl.	Fuel Sys.	Eng. Mfg.		Code	Year
M	1.0	61 (1000)	3	2 bbl	Suzuki		F	1985
5	1.0	61 (1000)	3	2 bbl	Suzuki		G	1986
5	1.0	61 (1000)	3	2 bbl	Suzuki		H	1987
2	1.0	61 (1000)	3	EFI①	Suzuki		J	1988
5	1.0	61 (1000)	3	2 bbl	Suzuki		K	1989
2	1.0	61 (1000)	3	EFI①	Suzuki		L	1990
5	1.0	61 (1000)	3	EFI	Suzuki		M	1991
5	1.0	61 (1000)	3	EFI	Suzuki		N	1992
6	1.0	61 (1000)	3	EFI	Suzuki		P	1993
6	1.0	61 (1000)	3	EFI	Suzuki			
6	1.0	61 (1000)	3	EFI	Suzuki			

2 bbl—2 bbl carburetor
EFI—Electronic Fuel Injection
① Turbo

ENGINE IDENTIFICATION

Year	Model	Engine Displacement Liters (cc)	Engine Series (ID/VIN)	Fuel System	No. of Cylinders	Engine Type
1985	Sprint	1.0 (1000)	M	2 bbl	3	SOHC
1986	Sprint	1.0 (1000)	5	2 bbl	3	SOHC
1987	Sprint	1.0 (1000)	5	2 bbl	3	SOHC
1987	Sprint	1.0 (1000)	2	EFI①	3	SOHC
1988	Sprint	1.0 (1000)	5	2 bbl	3	SOHC
1988	Sprint	1.0 (1000)	2	EFI①	3	SOHC
1989	Metro	1.0 (1000)	5	EFI	3	SOHC
1990	Metro	1.0 (1000)	5	EFI	3	SOHC
1991	Metro	1.0 (1000)	6	EFI	3	SOHC
1992	Metro	1.0 (1000)	6	EFI	3	SOHC
1993	Metro	1.0 (1000)	6	EFI	3	SOHC

2 bbl—2 bbl carburetor
EFI—Electronic Fuel Injection
SOHC—Single Overhead Cam

Fig. 3 The vehicle identification number is also stamped into the firewall.

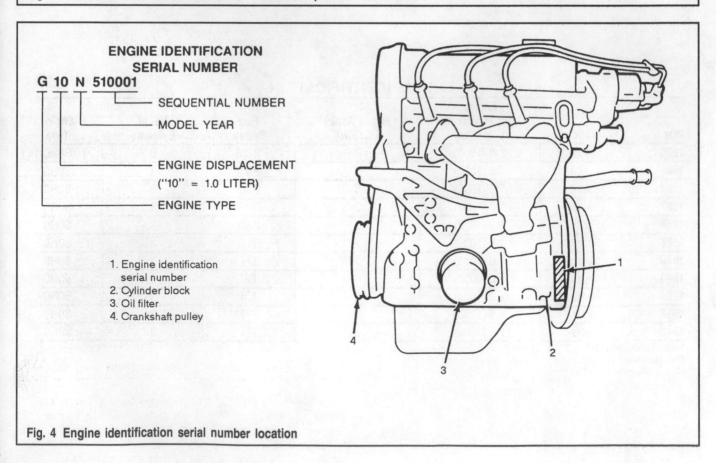

**ENGINE IDENTIFICATION
SERIAL NUMBER**

G 10 N 510001

— SEQUENTIAL NUMBER

— MODEL YEAR

— ENGINE DISPLACEMENT
("10" = 1.0 LITER)

— ENGINE TYPE

1. Engine identification
   serial number
2. Cylinder block
3. Oil filter
4. Crankshaft pulley

Fig. 4 Engine identification serial number location

Transaxle

▶ **See Figure 5**

Transaxles are stamped with a transaxle identification serial number which identifies the model year, transaxle serial number and transaxle type.

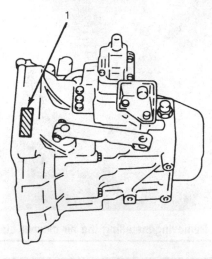

TRANSAXLE IDENTIFICATION NUMBER PLATE LOCATION

MANUAL TRANSAXLE

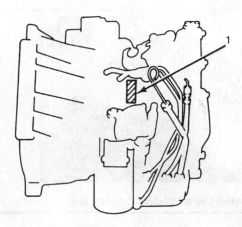

N 100001 ——————— (M/T)
N 700001 ——————— (A/T)

Serial Number
Model Year (Refer to VIN Designation)

AUTOMATIC TRANSAXLE

1. Transaxle identification number plate

Fig. 5 Transaxle identification number location

ROUTINE MAINTENANCE

Air Cleaner

Replace the cleaner element every 30,000 miles (50,000 km). Replace more often under dusty conditions. Replace the crankcase vent filter if so equipped.

REMOVAL & INSTALLATION

▶ **See Figures 6, 7, 8, 9 and 10**

1. Loosen and remove the air cleaner wing nut.
2. Unlatch the 4 upper air cleaner case clamps, as required.
3. Remove the air cleaner upper case and remove the air cleaner element.
   To install:
4. Inspect all hoses leading to the air cleaner. Replace the hoses if cracked or damaged.

Fig. 6 Loosening the air cleaner assembly wing nut

5. Clean the inside of the air cleaner base of debris and install a new element. Ensure the recess in the air cleaner element fits properly into the air cleaner base.
6. Install the upper air cleaner case.
7. Latch the upper air cleaner case clamps, as required.
8. Install and tighten the air cleaner wind nut.

Fig. 7 Loosening the air cleaner assembly spring clamps

Fig. 8 Removing the air cleaner upper case

Fig. 10 Removing/installing the air cleaner element

Fig. 9 Air cleaner element in lower case

Fig. 11 Fuel pump relay is located at the lower left side of the relay box — fuel injected engine.

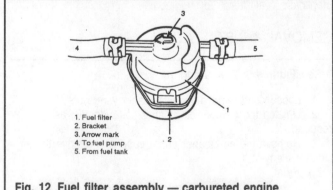

1. Fuel filter
2. Bracket
3. Arrow mark
4. To fuel pump
5. From fuel tank

Fig. 12 Fuel filter assembly — carbureted engine

Fuel Filter

Replace the fuel filter element every 30,000 miles (50,000 km). Replace more often under dusty conditions. The fuel filter is located in the engine compartment on carbureted and turbocharged models, and at the left side of the fuel tank on fuel injection models.

FUEL SYSTEM PRESSURE RELIEF

▶ See Figure 11

On fuel injected and turbocharged vehicles, it is necessary to relieve the fuel system pressure prior to servicing the fuel filter.

✳✳CAUTION

If the pressure in the fuel tank is not released prior to system service, the fuel in the tank may be forced out through the fuel hoses during servicing.

1. Place the gearshift selector in **NEUTRAL** on manual transaxle equipped vehicles or in **PARK** on automatic transaxle equipped vehicles.
2. Remove the fuel pump relay from the main fuse box in the engine compartment.
3. Start the engine and allow it to stall.
4. Crank the engine 2-3 times for approximately 3 seconds each time to ensure fuel pressure dissipation with fuel lines.
5. Remove the fuel filler cap to release fuel vapor pressure in the fuel tank. Reinstall the cap.
6. Install the fuel pump relay.
7. The fuel system components are now ready to be serviced.

FILTER REMOVAL & INSTALLATION

▶ See Figures 12, 13, 14 and 15

1. Relieve the fuel system pressure. Disconnect the negative battery cable.

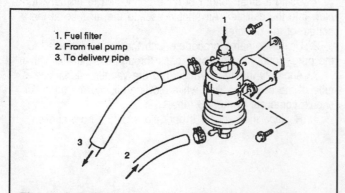

1. Fuel filter
2. From fuel pump
3. To delivery pipe

Fig. 13 Fuel filter assembly — turbocharged engine

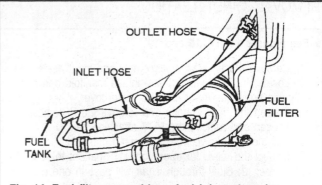

Fig. 14 Fuel filter assembly — fuel injected engine

Fig. 15 Fuel filter assembly as shown from under vehicle — fuel injected engine

2. As required, raise and support the vehicle safely.

✳✳CAUTION

A small amount of fuel may be released after the fuel hose is disconnected. In order to reduce the chance of personal injury, cover the fitting to be disconnected with a shop rag.

3. Label and disconnect all fuel lines from the fuel filter.
4. Remove the bolts from the fuel filter mounting bracket and remove the fuel filter.
   To install:
5. Inspect the fuel lines surrounding the filter and replace as necessary if damaged.
6. Install the new fuel filter and tighten the bracket bolts securely.
7. Install the fuel lines and tighten the clamps securely.
8. Lower the vehicle and connect the negative battery cable.
9. Start the vehicle. It may take a few seconds to prime the fuel system.
10. Check for fuel system leaks and repair as necessary.

PCV Valve

Inspect the PCV system for proper operation every 30,000 miles (50,000 km). If the engine is idling rough, check for a clogged PCV valve or plugged hose.

REMOVAL & INSTALLATION

▶ **See Figures 16, 17, 18 and 19**

1. Remove the air cleaner assembly and lay it aside.
2. Locate the PCV valve at the intake manifold between the throttle body/carburetor and the valve cover.
3. Loosen the hose clamps and remove the PCV hose.
4. Loosen and remove the PCV attaching bar.
5. Pull the PCV valve from the intake manifold.
6. Inspect the valve for operation: (1) Shake it to see if the valve is free; (2) Blow through it (air will pass in one direction only).

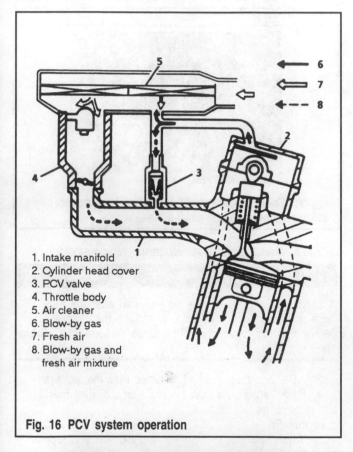

1. Intake manifold
2. Cylinder head cover
3. PCV valve
4. Throttle body
5. Air cleaner
6. Blow-by gas
7. Fresh air
8. Blow-by gas and fresh air mixture

Fig. 16 PCV system operation

Fig. 17 Removing the PCV hose

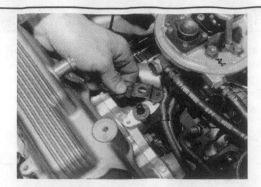

Fig. 18 Removing the PCV attaching bar

Fig. 19 Removing the PCV valve

7. To install, reverse the removal procedures.

Evaporative Emission System

Inspect the evaporative emission system, including the charcoal canister, for proper operation every 30,000 miles (50,000 km). Replace any worn, plugged or collapsed hoses or damaged seals. Clean or replace the canister as needed.

FUNCTIONAL TEST

▶ **See Figure 20**

1. Using a small length of hose connected to the tank tube, blow into the canister. Air should escape the air tube at the bottom of the canister.
2. Using the same procedure with the hose connected to the purge tube, no air should pass through the canister valve.
3. Apply 20 in. Hg of vacuum to the vacuum signal line tube of the canister valve, while blowing air into the tube. Air should come out of the TB tube.
4. Replace the canister if operations differs from above.

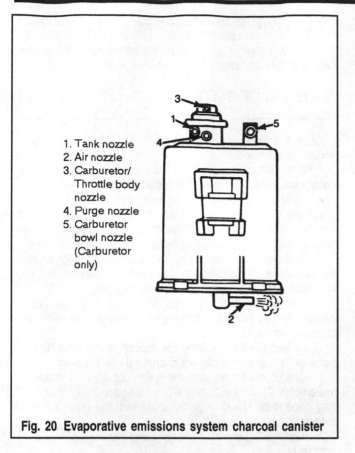

1. Tank nozzle
2. Air nozzle
3. Carburetor/
   Throttle body
   nozzle
4. Purge nozzle
5. Carburetor
   bowl nozzle
   (Carburetor
   only)

Fig. 20 Evaporative emissions system charcoal canister

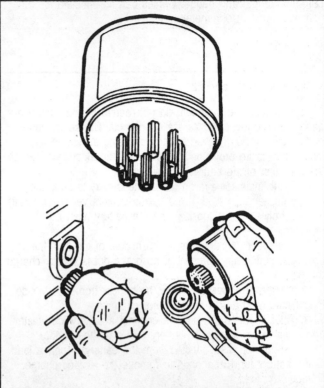

Fig. 21 Special tools are available for cleaning the posts and clamps on side terminal batteries.

REMOVAL & INSTALLATION

1. Label and disconnect the charcoal canister vent hoses.
2. Remove the canister-to-bracket bolt.
3. Lift the canister from the bracket.
4. To install, reverse the removal procedures.

Battery

All Sprint/Metro models have a Maintenance Free battery as standard equipment, eliminating the need for fluid level checks and the possibility of specific gravity tests. Never-the-less, the battery does require some attention.

✳✳CAUTION

Keep flames or sparks away from the battery. It gives off explosive hydrogen gas. The battery electrolyte contains sulfuric acid. If you should get any on your skin or in your eyes, flush the affected areas with plenty of clear water. If it lands in your eyes, seek medical help immediately.

GENERAL MAINTENANCE

▶ See Figure 21

At least once a year, the battery terminals and the cable clamps should be cleaned. Remove the side terminal bolts and the cables, negative cable first. Clean the cable clamps and

the battery terminals with a wire brush until all corrosion, grease, etc. is removed and the metal is shiny. It is especially important to clean the inside of the clamp thoroughly. A small deposit of foreign material or oxidation will prevent a sound electrical connection and inhibit either starting or charging. Special tools are available for cleaning side terminal clamps and terminals.

Before installing the cables, loosen the battery hold-down clamp, remove the battery and check the battery tray. Clear it of any debris and check it for soundness. Rust should be wire brushed away and the metal given a coat of anti-rust paint. Replace the battery and tighten the hold-down clamp securely but be careful not to overtighten, which will crack the battery case.

➡**Surface coatings on battery cases can actually conduct electricity which will cause a slight voltage drain, so make sure the battery case is clean. Batteries can be cleaned using a paste made from mixture of baking soda and water. Spread the paste on any corrosion, wait a few minutes, and rinse with water. Finish the job by cleaning metal parts with a wire brush.**

After the clamps and terminals are clean, reinstall the cables, negative cable last. Give the clamps and terminals a thin external coat of nonmetallic grease after installation, to retard corrosion.

Cables

Check the cables at the same time that the terminals are cleaned. If the cable insulation is cracked, broken or the ends are frayed, the cable should be replaced with a new one of the same length and gauge. Cables can be checked for continuity with an ohmmeter.

TESTING

▶ **See Figures 22 and 23**

Maintenance free batteries, do not require normal attention as far as fluid level checks are concerned. The sealed top battery cannot be checked for charge using a hydrometer, since there is no provision for access to the electrolyte. Check the condition of the battery as follows:

1. If the indicator eye on top of the battery is dark, the battery has enough fluid. If the eye is lit (light yellow or bright), the electrolyte fluid is too low and the battery must be replaced.

2. If a green dot appears in the middle of the eye, the battery is sufficiently charged. If no green dot is visible, charge the battery.

3. It may be necessary to tip the battery from side-to-side to get the green dot to appear after charging.

4. After charging the battery, connect a battery load tester and a voltmeter across the battery terminals (the battery cables should be disconnected from the battery). Apply a load to the battery for 15 seconds to remove the surface charge. Remove the load.

5. Wait 15 seconds to allow the battery to recover. Apply the load again for 15 seconds while reading the voltage. Remove the load.

6. Check the results against the chart. If the battery voltage is at or above the specified voltage for the temperature listed, the battery is good. It the voltage falls below what's listed, the battery should be replaced.

CHARGING OF BATTERY

When it is necessary to charge a battery several cautions should be observed.
• Do not charge an extremely cold battery. The battery may not accept current for several hours after charging has begun.
• The charging area should be well ventilated.
• If the battery feels hotter than 125°F during charging, or if violent gassing or spewing of electrolyte through the vent holes occurs, discontinue charging or reduce the charging rate.

1. Batteries with a built-in hydrometer showing a green dot do not require charging unless they have just been discharged by cranking the engine or leaving the lights on.

2. Connect the battery charger cables to the positive and negative battery terminals. Make sure all charger connections are clean and tight.

3. Charge the battery using the charge setting for 12V DC batteries that gives the highest charge rate to the battery.

4. Charge the battery until the green dot appears in the hydrometer. Check the battery every half-hour. The battery may need to be tipped or gently shaken for the green dot to appear.

5. Test the battery after charging and replace as necessary.

BATTERY REPLACEMENT

▶ **See Figure 24**

1. Disconnect the negative battery cable from the negative battery terminal.

2. Disconnect the positive battery cable from the positive battery terminal.

3. Remove the hold down nuts and battery retainer from the brackets.

4. Carefully lift the battery from the engine compartment.
To install:

5. Clean the battery tray and terminal ends of all corrosion.

6. Install the battery in the engine compartment and position in the tray.

7. Install the battery retainer and tighten nuts to 71 inch lbs. (8 Nm).

8. Install the positive battery cable on the positive battery terminal and tighten the nut to 11 ft. lbs. (15 Nm).

9. Install the negative battery cable on the negative battery terminal and tighten the nut to 11 ft. lbs. (15 Nm).

Belts

INSPECTION

Check the drive belts every 30,000 miles (50,000 km) or 24 months for evidence of cracking, fraying or incorrect tension.

Fig. 22 Maintenance free batteries contain their own built in hydrometer.

Temperature (°F)	Minimum Voltage
70 or above	9.6
60	9.5
50	9.4
40	9.3
30	9.1
20	8.9
10	8.7
0	8.5

Fig. 23 Battery minimum voltage specifications

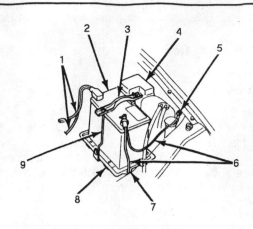

1. Positive battery cable
2. Battery
3. Battery retainer
4. Fuse and relay box
5. Body ground bolt
6. Negative battery cable
7. Harness retainer
8. Battery carrier
9. Battery hold down
   bracket

Fig. 24 Battery, cables, carrier and hold down brackets

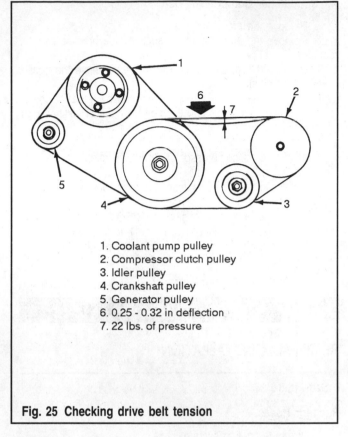

1. Coolant pump pulley
2. Compressor clutch pulley
3. Idler pulley
4. Crankshaft pulley
5. Generator pulley
6. 0.25 - 0.32 in deflection
7. 22 lbs. of pressure

Fig. 25 Checking drive belt tension

Determine the belt tension at a point halfway between the pulleys by using a GM Belt Tension Gauge No. BT-33-95-ACBN or equivalent. If tension is found to be too much or too little, perform the tension adjustments.

ADJUSTMENT

▶ **See Figure 25**

- It is better to have belts too loose than too tight. Overly tight belts will lead to bearing failure, particularly in the water pump and alternator. However, loose belts place an extremely high impact load on the driven components due to the whipping action of the belt.
- A GM Belt Tension Gauge No. BT-33-95-ACBN or equivalent is required for tensioning accessory drive belts.

1. If the belt is cold, operate the engine (at idle speed) for 15 minutes; the belt will seat itself in the pulleys allowing the belt fibers to relax or stretch. If the belt is hot, allow it to cool, until it is warm to the touch.
2. Loosen the component-to-mounting bracket bolts.
3. Using a GM Belt Tension Gauge or equivalent, place the tension gauge at the center of the belt between the longest span.
4. Applying belt tension pressure on the component, adjust the drive belt tension to the correct specifications.
5. While holding the correct tension on the component, tighten the component-to-mounting bracket bolt.
6. When the belt tension is correct, remove the tension gauge.

REMOVAL & INSTALLATION

Generator/Coolant Pump Belt

1. Remove the air cleaner assembly.
2. Remove the air compressor suction pipe bracket, as required.
3. Raise and support the vehicle safely. Remove the right lower splash shield.
4. Remove the air compressor drive belt by releasing the tensioner pulley and removing the belt from the crankshaft and compressor pulleys.
5. Lower the generator cover plate, then lower the vehicle.
6. Loosen the adjusting bolt on the upper generator mounting bracket and remove the coolant pump/generator drive belt from the vehicle.

To install:

7. Install the the coolant pump/generator drive belt on the pulleys.
8. Raise and support the vehicle safely. Install the lower generator cover plate and tighten bolts to 89 inch lbs. (10 Nm).
9. Install the air compressor drive belt by releasing the tensioner pulley.
10. Install the right lower splash shield and lower the vehicle.
11. Adjust the drive belt tension to 0.25-0.35 in. and tighten the upper generator adjustment bolt to 17 ft. lbs. (23 Nm).
12. Install the air compressor suction pipe bracket, as required.
13. Install the air cleaner assembly.

Air Conditioner Compressor Belt

1. Remove the air cleaner assembly.
2. Remove the air compressor suction pipe bracket, as required.
3. Raise and support the vehicle safely. Remove the right lower splash shield.
4. Remove the air compressor drive belt by releasing the tensioner pulley and removing the belt from the crankshaft and compressor pulleys.

To install:

5. Install the air compressor drive belt by releasing the tensioner pulley.
6. Install the right lower splash shield and lower the vehicle.
7. Adjust the drive belt tension to 0.25-0.35 in. and tighten the upper generator adjustment bolt to 17 ft. lbs. (23 Nm).
8. Install the air compressor suction pipe bracket, as required.
9. Install the air cleaner assembly.

Hoses

REMOVAL & INSTALLATION

▶ See Figure 26

Radiator Hoses

1. Drain the cooling system.

✳✳CAUTION

When draining the coolant, keep in mind that cats and dogs are attracted by the ethylene glycol antifreeze, and are quite likely to drink any that is left in an uncovered container or in puddles on the ground. This will prove fatal in sufficient quantity. Always drain the coolant into a sealable container. Coolant should be reused unless it is contaminated or several years old.

2. Remove the upper radiator hose by releasing the hose clamps at the thermostat outlet and radiator.

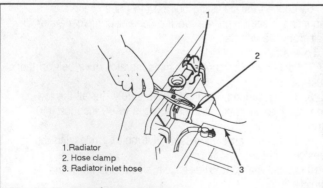

1. Radiator
2. Hose clamp
3. Radiator inlet hose

Fig. 26 Radiator hose removal

To install:

3. Install the upper radiator hose and tighten the clamps securely.
4. Fill the cooling system with a 50/50 mixture of antifreeze and water.

Heater Hoses

1. Drain the cooling system.
2. Remove the heater core inlet hose by releasing the hose clamps at the bulkhead and at the intake manifold.
3. Remove the heater core outlet hose by releasing the hose clamps at the bulkhead and the coolant pump inlet pipe running along the top of the transaxle. Remove the hose from the vehicle.

To install:

4. Install the heater core outlet hose to the bulkhead fitting and coolant pump inlet pipe and secure with hose clamps.
5. Install the heater core inlet hose to bulkhead fitting and intake manifold. Secure with hose clamps.
6. Fill the cooling system with a 50/50 mixture of antifreeze and water.

Air Conditioning System

SAFETY WARNINGS

- R-12 refrigerant is a chlorofluorocarbon which, when released into the atmosphere, contributes to the depletion of the ozone layer in the upper atmosphere. Ozone filters out harmful radiation from the sun.
- Consult the laws in your area before servicing the air conditioning system. In some states it is illegal to perform repairs involving refrigerant unless the work is done by a certified technician.
- Avoid contact with a charged refrigeration system, even when working on another part of the air conditioning system or truck. If a heavy tool comes into contact with a section of copper tubing or a heat exchanger, it can easily cause the relatively soft material to rupture.
- When it is necessary to apply force to a fitting which contains refrigerant, as when checking that all system couplings are securely tightened, use a wrench on both parts of the fitting involved, if possible. This will avoid putting torque on the refrigerant tubing. It is recommended that tube or line wrenches be used when tightening these flare nut fittings.
- DO NOT attempt to discharge the system by merely loosening a fitting. Precise control is possible only when using the service gauges with an approved recovery station.
- Always completely discharge the system before painting the truck (if the paint is to be baked on), or before welding anywhere near the refrigerant lines.

➡**Any repair work to an air conditioning system should be left to a professional. DO NOT, under any circumstances, attempt to loosen or tighten any fittings or perform any work other than that outlined here.**

SYSTEM INSPECTION

▶ **See Figure 27**

Checking For Oil Leaks

Refrigerant leaks show up as oily areas on the various components because the compressor oil is transported around the entire system along with the refrigerant. Look for oily spots on all the hoses and lines, especially on the hose and tubing connections. If there are oily deposits, the system may have a leak, have it checked by a qualified technician.

➡ **A small area of oil at the front of the compressor is normal and no cause for concern.**

Keep The Condenser Clear

Periodically inspect the front of the condenser for bent fins or foreign material (dirt, buts, leaves, etc.). If any cooling fins are bent, straighten them carefully with needle-nose pliers. You can remove any debris with a stiff bristle brush or hose.

Operate The A/C System Periodically

A lot of A/C problems can be avoided by simply running the air conditioner at least once a week regardless of the season. Simply let the system run for at least 5 minutes a week (even in the winter) and you'll keep the internal parts lubricated as well as preventing the hoses from hardening.

Leak Testing the System

There are several methods of detecting leaks in an air conditioning system; among them, the most popular is the electronic leak detector.

An Electronic Leak Detector No. J-26934 H-10B or equivalent, is a small portable electronic device with an extended probe. With the unit activated, the probe is passed along those components of the system which contain refrigerant. If a leak is detected, the unit will sound an alarm signal or activate a display signal depending on the manufacturer's design. It is advisable to follow the manufacturer's instructions as the design and function of the detection may vary significantly.

REFRIGERANT LEVEL CHECKS

▶ **See Figure 28**

A simple test to determine if the air conditioning system refrigerant level is correct can be made by observing the sight glass at the top of the receiver/dryer.

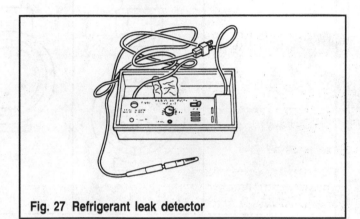

Fig. 27 Refrigerant leak detector

Amount of refrigerant / Check item	Almost no refrigerant	Insufficient	Suitable	Too much refrigerant
Temperature of high pressure and low pressure pipes.	Almost no difference between high pressure and low pressure side temperature.	High pressure side is warm and low pressure side is fairly cold.	High pressure side is hot and low pressure side is cold.	High pressure side is abnormally hot.
State in sight glass.	Bubbles flow continuously. Bubbles will disappear and something like mist will flow when refrigerant is nearly gone.	The bubbles are seen at intervals of 1 — 2 seconds.	Almost transparent. Bubbles may appear when engine speed is raised and lowered.	No bubbles can be seen.
			No clear difference exists between these two conditions.	
Pressure of system.	High pressure side is abnormally low.	Both pressure on high and low pressure sides are slightly low.	Both pressures on high and low pressure sides are normal.	Both pressures on high and low pressure sides are abnormally high.
Repair.	Stop compressor and conduct an overall check.	Check for gas leakage, repair as required, replenish and charge system.		Discharge refrigerant from service valve of low pressure side.

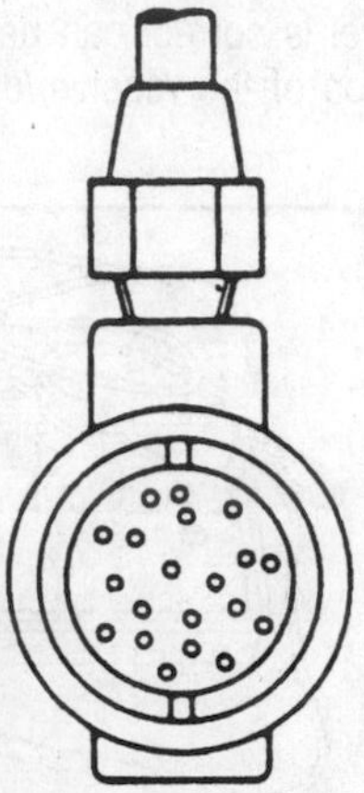

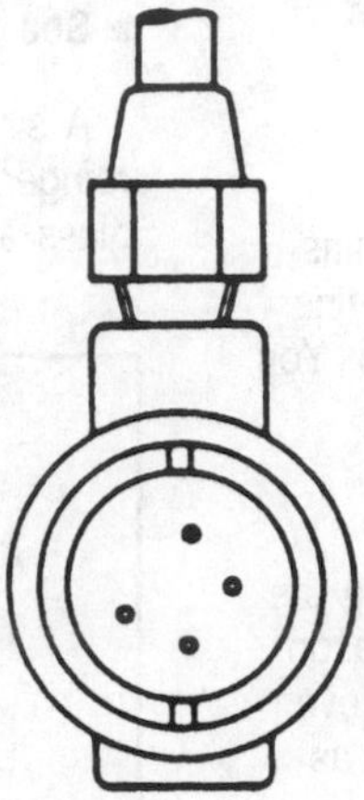

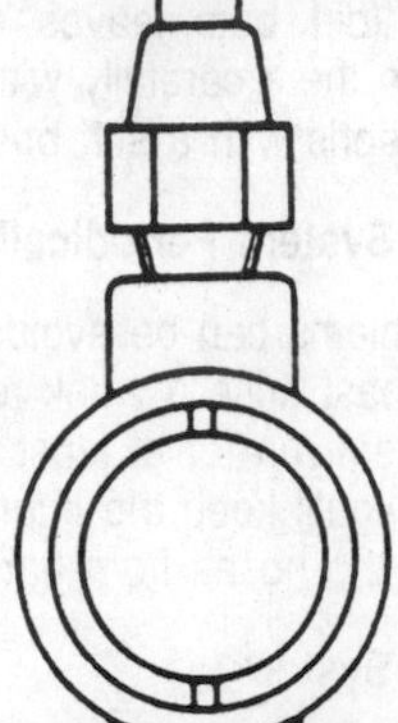

Fig. 28 Refrigerant level check at sight glass

1. Start the engine and run at fast idle (1,500 rpm).
2. Set the air conditioning controls for maximum cold and fastest blower speed.
3. Check the sight glass for the presence of bubbles.
4. Feel the high pressure side pipe leading from the compressor to the condenser and the low pressure side pipe leading from the receiver/dryer to the compressor.
5. If there are no bubbles, the high pressure side pipe is warm and the low pressure side pipe is cold, the system is functioning correctly.
6. If there are no bubbles and the high pressure side pipe is abnormally hot, there may be too much refrigerant in the system. Consult a certified air conditioning technician.
7. If bubbles can be seen at 1-2 second intervals, the high pressure side pipe is warm and the low pressure side pipe is

fairly cold, there is an insufficient amount of refrigerant in the system. Leak test the system prior to having a certified air conditioning technician refill it with refrigerant.
8. If bubbles flow continuously and there is almost no difference between the high pressure side pipe and the low pressure side pipe temperature, the refrigerant in the system is almost empty. Have a certified air conditioning technician conduct an overall check of the system, repair components and refill the system with refrigerant.

➡**Lack of refrigerant can allow moisture to enter the system and cause major damage.**

GAUGE SETS

▶ **See Figures 29, 30, 31 and 32**

Most of the service work performed in air conditioning requires the use of a two gauge set. The gauges on the set monitor the high (head) pressure side and the low (suction) side of the system.

The low side gauge records both pressure and vacuum. Vacuum readings are calibrated from 0-30 in. Hg, and the pressure graduations read from 0-60 psi. The high side gauge measures pressure from 0-600 psi.

Both gauges are threaded into a manifold that contains two hand shut-off valves. Proper manipulation of these valves and

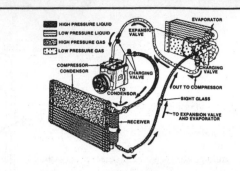

Fig. 32 Basic components of the air conditioning system and the flow of refrigerant.

the use of the attached test hoses allow the user to perform the following services:

- Test high and low side pressures.
- Remove air, moisture and/or contaminated refrigerant.
- Purge the system of refrigerant.
- Charge the system with refrigerant.

The manifold valves are designed so they have no direct effect on the gauge readings but serve only to provide for or cut off the flow of refrigerant through the manifold. During all testing and hook-up operations, the valves are kept in a closed position to avoid disturbing the refrigeration system. The valves are opened ONLY to allow refrigerant to be purged into a refrigerant recovery station or to charge the air conditioning system.

When purging the system, the center service fitting hose is connected to the refrigerant recovery station and both valves are cracked (opened) slightly. This allows the refrigerant pressure to force the entire contents of the system out through the center hose. During charging, the center service fitting hose is connected to the refrigerant storage container, the valve on the high side of the manifold is closed and the valve on the low side is cracked (opened). Under these conditions, the low pressure in the evaporator will draw refrigerant from the relatively warm refrigerant storage container into the system.

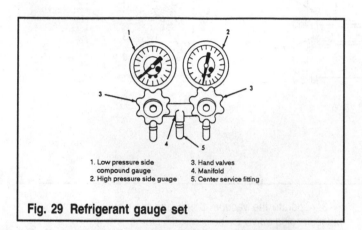

1. Low pressure side compound gauge
2. High pressure side guage
3. Hand valves
4. Manifold
5. Center service fitting

Fig. 29 Refrigerant gauge set

DISCHARGING THE SYSTEM

▶ **See Figure 33**

When any refrigeration system component except the pressure cycling switch is replaced, all of the refrigerant in the system must be completely discharged and recovered by using an approved air conditioning refrigerant recovery system. The system must always be discharged at the low pressure side service fitting to control the loss of refrigerant oil. Oil loss will occur if the high pressure side service fitting is used.

1. With the ignition switch **OFF**, remove the protective cap from the low pressure side service fitting.

2. The refrigerant recovery station should be connected following the manufacturer's instructions.

3. With the low pressure side of the refrigeration system fully discharged, the high pressure side service fitting should be check for any remaining pressure.

4. If refrigerant under pressure remains in the high pressure side of the system, an attempt should be made to

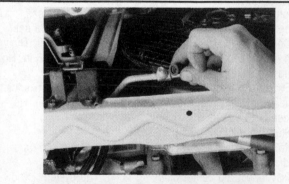

Fig. 30 High pressure side service port location

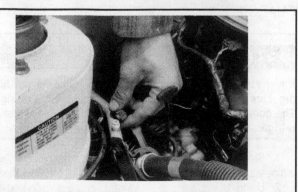

Fig. 31 Low pressure side service port location

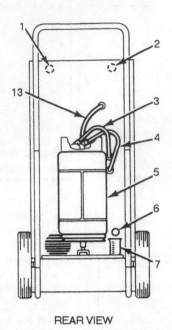
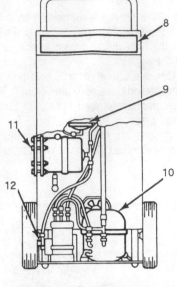

1. Accumulator pressurizing valve
2. Oil drain valve
3. Vapor hose
4. Liquid hose
5. Tank
6. Oil drain
7. Oil drain measured container
8. Control panel
9. Accumulator oil separator
10. Compressor
11. Filter dryer
12. Refrigerant pump
13. Air purge hose

REAR VIEW

FRONT CUT-AWAY VIEW

Fig. 33 Refrigerant recovery and recycling center

discharge the high pressure side of the system by using the same procedure as used for the low pressure side service fitting.

➡**Noticeable residual pressure in the system indicates a restriction in the high pressure side of the system. The cause for this pressure must be diagnosed and corrected before evacuating and charging the system.**

5. When the system is completely discharged and the refrigerant stored in the recovery tank, the technician should measure and record the amount of refrigerant oil that was collected in the recovery system accumulator.

6. If the measured amount of oil is 0.5 fl. oz or more, the same amount of new refrigerant oil must be added to the system, plus any quantity in the removed parts.

7. To add oil, the refrigerant system low pressure side (suction) hose should be disconnected at the receiver/dryer and the correct quantity of oil should be poured into the hose.

EVACUATING

Before charging any system it is necessary to purge the refrigerant and draw out the trapped moisture with a suitable vacuum pump. Failure to do so will result in ineffective charging and possible damage to the system.

1. Connect the high pressure hose to the compressor delivery hose and the low pressure hose to the compressor suction hose.

2. Connect the center hose of the gauge set to a vacuum pump.

3. Operate the vacuum pump and then open the low pressure side valve of the manifold gauge set.

4. If the system if functioning properly, there will be an indication on the high pressure gauge. When this happens, open the high pressure side valve of the manifold gauge set.

5. Operate the vacuum pump for at least 10 minutes. The vacuum gauge should show a vacuum no lower than 28 in. Hg providing no leakage exists. If a leak exists, repair it.

6. Evacuation should be carried out for at least 15 minutes. Continue evacuating until the vacuum gauge reads 28 in. Hg, then close both valves.

7. Stop the vacuum pump. Observe the low pressure gauge to determine if the vacuum is holding. A vacuum drop may indicate a leak.

8. Disconnect the center charging hose. The system is now ready for charging.

CHARGING

✳✳CAUTION

Never attempt to charge the system by opening the high pressure side valve while the compressor is operating. The compressor accumulating pressure can burst the refrigerant container, causing severe personal injury.

1. Start the engine and allow it to reach operating temperature. Position the A/C control lever in the **OFF** position.

2. Using 14 oz. cans of refrigerant, in the inverted position, allow about a 1/2 lb. of refrigerant to enter the system through the low pressure side service fitting.

3. After 1/2 lb. of refrigerant enters the system, position the A/C control lever in the **ON** position (the compressor will engage) and the blower motor on **HI** speed; this operation will draw the remainder of the refrigerant into the system.

➡**To speed up the operation, position a fan in front of the condenser; the lowering of the condenser temperature will allow refrigerant to enter the system faster.**

4. When the system is charged, turn off the refrigerant source and allow the engine to run for 30 seconds to clear the lines and gauges.

5. With the engine running, remove the hose adapter from the low pressure side service fitting (unscrew the hose quickly to prevent refrigerant from escaping).

❊❊CAUTION

Never remove the gauge line from the adapter when the line is connected to the system; always remove the line adapter from the service fitting first.

6. Replace the protective caps and turn the engine off.

7. Using a leak detector, inspect the A/C system for leaks. If a leak is present, repair it.

Windshield Wipers

▶ **See Figure 34**

For maximum effectiveness and longest element life, the windshield and wiper blades should be kept clean. Dirt, tree sap, road tar and so on will cause streaking, smearing and

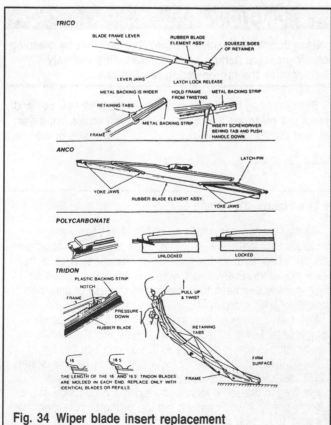

TRICO
ANCO
POLYCARBONATE
TRIDON

Fig. 34 Wiper blade insert replacement

blade deterioration if left on the glass. It is advisable to wash the windshield carefully with a commercial glass cleaner at least once a month. Wipe off the rubber blades with the wet rag afterwards. Do not attempt to move the wipers by hand. Damage to the motor and drive mechanism will result.

If the blades are found to be cracked, broken or torn, they should be replaced immediately. Replacement intervals will vary with usage, although ozone deterioration usually limits blade life to about one year. If the wiper pattern is smeared or streaked, or if the blade chatters across the glass, the elements should be replaced. It is easiest and most sensible to replace the elements in pairs.

There are basically three different types of refills, which differ in their method of replacement. One type has two release buttons, approximately 1/3 of the way up from the ends of the blade frame. Pushing the buttons down releases a lock and allows the rubber filler to be removed from the frame. The new filler slides back into the frame and locks in place.

The second type of refill has two metal tabs which are unlocked by squeezing them together. The rubber filler can then be withdrawn from the frame jaws. A new refill is installed by inserting the refill into the front frame jaws and sliding it rearward to engage the remaining frame jaws. There are usually four jaws. Be certain when installing that the refill is engaged in all of them. At the end of its travel, the tabs will lock into place on the front jaws of the wiper blade frame.

The third type is a refill made from polycarbonate. The refill has a simple locking device at one end which flexes downward out of the groove into which the jaws of the holder fit, allowing easy release. By sliding the new refill through all the jaws and pushing through the slight resistance when it reaches the end of its travel, the refill will lock into position.

Regardless of the type of refill used, make sure that all of the frame jaws are engaged as the refill is pushed into place and locked. The metal blade holder and frame will scratch the glass if allowed to touch it.

Tires and Wheels

Tire rotation is recommended at approximately 6,000 mile intervals. A tire pressure check should be performed at regular intervals to obtain maximum tire wear.

TIRE ROTATION

▶ **See Figure 35**

The pattern of tire rotation you use depends on whether or not your car has a usable spare. Depending on the manufacturer, a cross-switched (from one side of the car to the other) rotation pattern may be recommended. Check your owners manual for more specific recommendation.

Snow tires sometimes have directional arrows molded into the side of the carcass. The arrow shows the direction of rotation. They will wear very rapidly if the rotation is reversed. Studded tires will lose their studs if their rotational direction is reversed.

➡**Mark the wheel position or direction of rotation on all tires prior to removing them.**

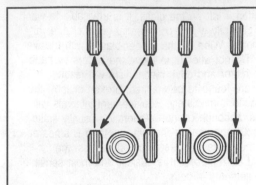

Fig. 35 Tire rotation patterns

TIRE DESIGN

For maximum satisfaction, tires should be used in sets of five. Mixing of different types (radial, bias-belted, fiberglass belted) should be avoided. Conventional bias tires are constructed so that the cords run bead to bead at an angle. Alternate plies run at an opposite angle. This type of construction gives rigidity to both tread and side wall. Bias belted tires are similar in construction to conventional bias ply tires. Belts run at an angle and also at a 90° angle to the bead, as in radial tires. Tread life is improved considerably over the conventional bias tire. The radial tire differs in construction, but instead of the carcass running at an angle of 90° to each other they run at an angle of 90° to the bead. This gives the tread a great deal of rigidity and the side wall a great deal of flexibility (which accounts for the characteristic bulge associated with radial tires).

INFLATION PRESSURE

▶ See Figure 36

Tire inflation is the most ignored item of auto maintenance. Gasoline mileage can drop as much as .8% for every 1 pound per square inch (psi) of under inflation.

Two items should be a permanent fixture in every glove compartment: a tire pressure gauge and a tread depth gauge. Check the tire air pressure (including the spare) regularly with a pocket type gauge. Kicking the tires won't tell you a thing, and the gauge on the service station air hose is notoriously inaccurate.

The tire pressures recommended for your car are usually found on the right door jam or in the owner's manual. Ideally, inflation pressure should be checked when the tires are cool. When the air becomes heated it expands and the pressure increases. Every 10° rise (or drop) in temperature means a difference of 1 psi, which also explains why the tire appears to lose air on a very cold night. When it is impossible to check the tires cold, allow for pressure build-up due to heat. If the hot pressure exceeds the cold pressure by more than 15 psi, reduce your speed, load or both. Otherwise internal heat is created in the tire. When the heat approaches the temperature

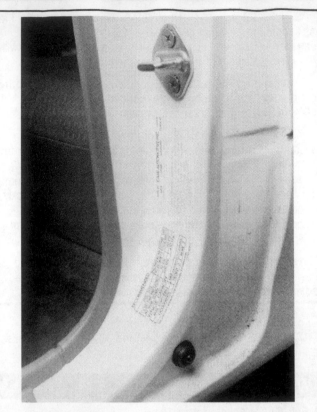

Fig. 36 Tire information sticker on the right door jam

at which the tire was cured, during manufacture, the tread can separate from the body.

❋❋CAUTION

Never counteract excessive pressure build-up by bleeding off air pressure (letting some air out). This will only further raise the tire operating temperature.

Before starting a long trip with lots of luggage, you can add about 2-4 psi to the tires to make them run cooler, but never exceed the maximum inflation pressure on the side of the tire.

TREAD DEPTH

▶ See Figures 37, 38 and 39

All tires made since 1968, have 7 built-in tread wear indicator bars that show up as ½" wide smooth bands across the tire when 1/16" of tread remains. The appearance of tread wear indicators means that the tires should be replaced. In fact, many states have laws prohibiting the use of tires with less than 1/16" tread.

You can check your own tread depth with an inexpensive gauge or by using a Lincoln head penny. Slip the Lincoln penny into several tread grooves. If you can see the top of Lincoln's head in 2 adjacent grooves, the tires have less than 1/16" tread left and should be replaced. You can measure snow tires in the same manner by using the tails side of the Lincoln penny. If you can see the top of the Lincoln memorial, it's time to replace the snow tires.

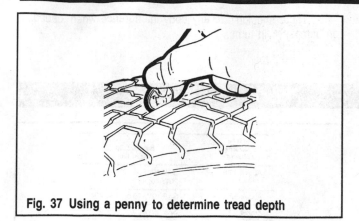

Fig. 37 Using a penny to determine tread depth

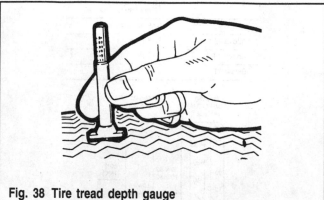

Fig. 38 Tire tread depth gauge

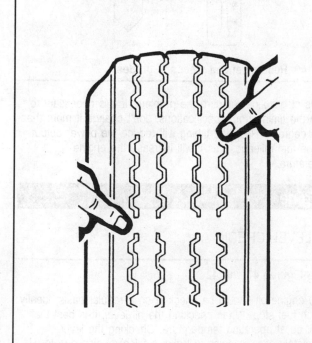

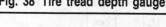

Fig. 39 Replace a tire that shows the built-in tread wear indicators

CARE OF SPECIAL WHEELS

If you have invested money in mag, aluminum alloy or sport wheels, special precautions should be taken to make sure your investment is not wasted, and that your special wheels look good for the lifetime of the car.

Special wheels are easily scratched and/or damaged. Occasionally check the rim for cracks, damage or air leaks. If any of these conditions are found, replace the wheel. In order to prevent this type of damage, and the costly replacement of a special wheel, observe the following precautions:

• Take special care not to damage the wheels during removal, installation, balancing etc. After removal of the wheels from the car, place them on a rubber mat or other protective surface.

• While the vehicle is being driven, be careful not to drive over sharp obstacles or allow the wheels to contact the shoulder of the road.

• When washing, use a mild detergent and water. Avoid using cleansers with abrasives, or hard brushes. And a little polish after washing will help your wheels keep that new look.

• If possible, remove your special wheels from the car during the winter months, and replace them with regular steel rims. Salt and sand that is applied to the roadways for snow removal during these months can do severe damage to special wheels.

• Make sure that the recommended lug nut torque is never exceeded, or you may crack your wheels. And never use snow chains with special wheels.

• If you intend to store the wheels, lay them flat on a protective surface and cover them. Do not stack them on top of each other and do not place anything else, except a protective cover, on them.

TIRE STORAGE

Store the tires at the proper inflation pressure if they are mounted on wheels. Keep them in a cool dry place, laid on their sides. If the tires are stored in the garage or basement, do not let them stand on a concrete floor. Set them on strips of wood.

BUYING NEW TIRES

When buying new tires, give some though to the following points, especially if you are considering a switch to larger tires or a different profile series:

1. All four tires must be of the same construction type. This rule cannot be violated. Radial, bias, and bias-belted tires must not be mixed.

2. The wheels should be the correct width for the tire. Tire dealers have charts of tire and rim compatibility. A mismatch will cause sloppy handling and rapid tire wear. The tread width should match the rim width (inside bead to inside bead) within an inch. For radial tires, the rim width should be 80% or less of the tire (not tread) width.

3. The height (mounted diameter) of the new tires can change speedometer accuracy, engine speed at a given road

speed, fuel mileage, acceleration, and ground clearance. Tire manufacturers furnish full measurement specifications.

4. The spare tire should be usable, at least for short distance and low speed operation, with the new tires.

5. There shouldn't be any body interference when loaded, on bumps, or in turns.

FLUIDS AND LUBRICANTS

Fluid Disposal

Used fluids such as engine oil, transmission fluid, antifreeze and brake fluid are hazardous wastes and must be disposed of properly. Before draining any fluids, consult with the local authorities; in many areas, waste oil, etc. is being accepted as a part of recycling programs. A number of service stations and auto parts stores are also accepting waste fluids for recycling.

Be sure of the recycling center's policies before draining any fluids, as many will not accept different fluids that have been mixed together, such as oil and antifreeze.

Fuel and Engine Oil Recommendations

ENGINE OIL

▶ See Figure 40

Use ONLY SG or SG/CD rated oils of the recommended viscosity. Under the classification system developed by the American Petroleum Institute, the SG rating designates the highest quality oil for use in passenger vehicles. In addition, oils labeled Energy Conserving or Fuel Saving are recommended due to their superior lubricating qualities (less friction — easier engine operation) and fuel saving characteristics.

Pick oil viscosity with regard to the anticipated temperatures during the period before your next oil change. Using the accompanying chart, choose the oil viscosity for the lowest expected temperature. You will be assured of easy cold starting and sufficient engine protection.

FUEL

Your vehicle is designed to operate on unleaded fuel. Fuel should be selected for the brand and octane which performs best with your engine. Judge a gasoline by its ability to prevent spark knock (pinging) and general all-weather performance.

Use of a fuel too low in octane will result in spark knock (pinging). Since many factors affect operating efficiency, such as altitude, terrain, air temperature and humidity, knocking may result even though the recommended fuel is being used. If persistent knocking occurs, it may be necessary to switch to a slightly higher grade of fuel. Continuous or heavy knocking may result in engine damage.

Fuel requirement can change with time, due to carbon buildup in the engine, which changes the compression ratio. If your engine knocks, pings or runs on, switch to a higher grade of fuel and check the ignition timing. Sometimes changing

Lowest Air Temperature Anticipated	Multiviscosity Engine Oil
Above 40°F	SAE 10W-30, 40, 50 or 20W-40, 50
Above 32°F	SAE 10W-30 or 10W-40
Above 0°F	SAE 10W-30 or 10W-40
Below 0°F	SAE 5W-20 or 5W-30
	Single-Viscosity Engine Oil
Above 40°F	SAE 30 or 40
Above 32°F	SAE 20W-20
Above 0°F	SAE 20
Below 0°F	SAE 10W

Fig. 40 Recommended viscosity grades

brands of gasoline will cure the problem. If it is necessary to retard the timing from specifications, don't change it more than a few degrees. Retarded timing will reduce the power output and the fuel mileage, plus it will increase the engine temperature.

Engine

OIL LEVEL CHECK

▶ See Figures 41 and 42

The engine oil should be checked on a regular basis, ideally at each fuel stop. When checking the oil level, it is best that the oil be at operating temperature. Checking the level immediately after stopping will give a false reading due to oil left in the upper part of the engine. Be sure that the vehicle is resting on a level surface, allowing time for the oil to drain back into the crankcase.

1. Open the hood and locate the dipstick. Remove it from the tube (located on right side of the engine compartment).

2. Wipe the dipstick with a clean rag.

Fig. 41 The correct oil level should be between the 'ADD" and 'FULL" level on the dipstick

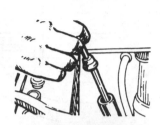

Fig. 42 The oil level is checked with the dipstick. When checking oil level, note the color and smell of the oil. Oil that is black or has a gas smell indicates a need for engine service.

3. Insert the dipstick fully into the tube and remove it again.

➡**When checking oil level, note the color and smell of the oil. Oil that is black or has a gas smell indicates a need for engine service.**

4. Hold the dipstick horizontally and read the oil level. The level should be between the FULL and ADD marks.

5. If the oil level is at or below the ADD mark, oil should be added as necessary. Oil is added through the capped opening on the valve cover(s) on gasoline engines. Refer to the 'Engine Oil and Fuel Recommendations" in this Section for the proper viscosity oil to use.

6. Replace the dipstick and check the level after adding oil. Be careful not to overfill the crankcase. Approximately one quart of oil will raise the level from ADD to FULL.

OIL AND FILTER CHANGE

▶ **See Figures 43 and 44**

Engine oil should be changed every 7,500 miles. The oil change and filter replacement interval should be cut in half under conditions such as:
- Driving in dusty conditions.
- Extensive or prolonged idling.
- Extensive short trip operation in freezing temperatures (when the engine is not thoroughly warmed-up).
- Frequent long runs at high speed and high ambient temperatures.

Fig. 43 Oil filter location — as seen from under the vehicle.

To change the oil, the vehicle should be on a level surface and the engine should be at operating temperature. This is to ensure that the foreign matter will be drained away along with the oil and not left in the engine to form sludge. You should have available a container that will hold a minimum of 8 quarts of liquid, a wrench to fit the old drain plug, a spout for pouring in new oil and a rag or two, which you will always need. If the filter is being replaced, you will also need a band wrench or filter wrench to fit the end of the filter.

When you have finished this job, you will notice that you now possess four or five quarts of dirty oil. The best thing to do with it is to pour it into plastic jugs, such as milk or antifreeze containers. Then, locate a service station where you can pour it into their used oil tank for recycling.

✳✳CAUTION

Pouring used motor oil into a storm drain not only pollutes the environment, it violates Federal law. Dispose of waste oil properly.

1. Position the vehicle on a level surface, raise and support the vehicle safely. Slide a drain pan under the oil drain plug.

2. From under the vehicle, loosen, but do not remove the oil drain plug. Cover your hand with a rag or glove and slowly unscrew the drain plug.

✳✳CAUTION

The engine oil will be HOT. Keep your arms, face and hands clear of the oil as it drains out.

3. Remove the plug and let the oil drain into the pan. Do not drop the plug into the drain pan.

4. When all of the oil has drained, clean off the drain plug and reinstall it into pan. Torque the drain plug to 26 ft.lb. (35 Nm).

5. Using an oil filter wrench, loosen the oil filter.

6. Cover your hand with a rag and spin the filter off by hand; turn it slowly.

7. Coat the rubber gasket on a new filter with a light film of clean engine oil. Screw the filter onto the mounting stud and tighten it according to the directions on the filter (usually hand-tight one turn past the point where the gasket contacts the mounting base); DO NOT overtighten the filter.

8. Refill the engine with the specified amount of clean engine oil.

Fig. 44 Adding engine oil through the filler hole in the rocker cover.

9. Run the engine for several minutes, checking for leaks. Check the level of the oil and add oil if necessary.

Manual Transaxle

FLUID RECOMMENDATIONS

When adding fluid or refilling the manual transaxle always use GL-5, 80W or 80W/90 weight gear oil.

LEVEL CHECK

▶ See Figures 45 and 46

With Oil Level Gauge

1. Drive the vehicle to bring the transmission up to operating temperature.
2. With the engine stopped, remove the oil level gauge front the side case of the transaxle.
3. Check the color and smell of the oil. If it is black in color or smells burnt, further transmission service is needed.
4. Wipe off oil level gauge with clean cloth.
5. Fit the oil level gauge to the transaxle side case so that the threads rest on top of the case.
6. Remove the gauge and check oil level. The level should be between **FULL** and **LOW** level line.
7. If the level is below **LOW** mark, add oil until the proper level is reached.

With Oil Level/Filler Plug

1. Drive the vehicle to bring the transmission up to operating temperature.
2. Raise and support the vehicle safely.
3. Remove the transaxle oil level/filler plug.
4. Check the color and smell of the oil. If it is black in color or smells burnt, further transmission service is needed.
5. Transaxle oil level should be even with the bottom of the plug hole. If oil level is low, adjust oil level accordingly.
6. Install transaxle oil level/filler plug and tighten to 40 ft. lbs. (54 Nm).
7. Lower the vehicle.

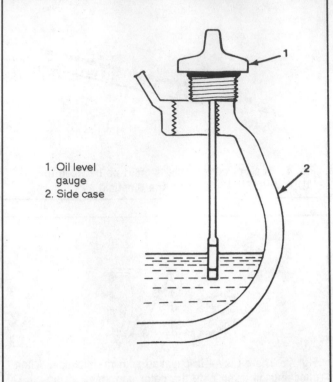

1. Oil level gauge
2. Side case

Fig. 45 Manual transaxle oil level check — with level gauge

DRAIN AND REFILL

▶ See Figure 46

1. Raise and support the vehicle safely.
2. Place a drain pan under transaxle.
3. Remove transaxle oil level/filler plug or oil level gauge.
4. Remove transaxle drain plug using a 10mm hex socket or wrench and drain oil.
5. Check the color and smell of the oil. If it is black in color or smells burnt, further transmission service is be needed.
6. Apply Loctite® pipe sealant, or equivalent to the threaded portion of the transaxle drain plug.
7. Install transaxle drain plug an tighten to 21 ft. lbs. (28 Nm).

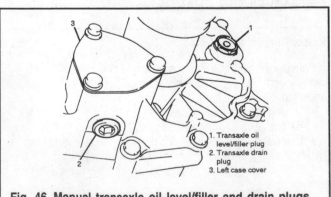

1. Transaxle oil level/filler plug
2. Transaxle drain plug
3. Left case cover

Fig. 46 Manual transaxle oil level/filler and drain plugs

8. Remove drain pan from under transaxle and lower vehicle.

9. Properly dispose of used oil.

Automatic Transaxle

FLUID RECOMMENDATIONS

When adding fluid or refilling the automatic transaxle always use Dexron® II automatic transmission fluid.

LEVEL CHECK

▶ **See Figures 47 and 48**

1. Drive the vehicle to bring the transmission up to operating temperature.

2. Place vehicle on a level surface.

3. With the engine running at idle, run the selector lever through each range and return to the **P** position.

4. Remove the fluid level indicator from the transmission filler tube and wipe clean.

5. Reinsert fluid level indicator into filler tube making sure it is seated in its original position.

6. Remove the indicator and check the fluid level. The level should be between the **FULL HOT** and **LOW HOT** marks.

7. If the level is below the **LOW HOT** mark, add fluid as necessary to bring the fluid level to the **FULL HOT** mark.

Fig. 47 Automatic transaxle dipstick location

Fig. 48 Fluid level should be between the cold notches if checking with the transaxle cold or between the hot notches if checking with the transaxle at normal operating temperature.

8. Check the color and smell of the fluid. If it is brown in color (transmission fluid is usually red) or smells burnt, further transmission service is be needed.

9. Reinsert fluid level indicator into filler tube making sure it is seated in its original position.

DRAIN AND REFILL

▶ **See Figure 49**

1. Raise and support the vehicle safely.

2. Place a drain pan or suitable container under the transaxle pan.

3. Remove the transaxle drain plug and drain the fluid.

4. Lower the vehicle.

5. Fill the transaxle with fluid and check fluid level.

PAN AND FILTER SERVICE

1. Raise and support the vehicle safely.

2. Place a drain pan or suitable container under the transaxle pan.

3. Remove the transaxle drain plug and drain the fluid.

4. Remove the 15 transaxle pan bolts and carefully lower the pan. Take note of the location of the 2 bolts with cross-recesses in their heads.

➡ **Do not attempt to pry the pan away from the transaxle. Doing so will damage the gasket mating surfaces. If the pan is frozen, use a mallet and a wood block to lightly tap it free.**

To install:

5. Inspect the bottom of the pan for large pieces of metal or other foreign matter. A small amount of clutch material in the pan is normal. However, if large amounts of clutch material, metal shavings or other foreign matter are present, further transaxle service is necessary.

6. Clean the fluid filter screen with solvent and dry thoroughly. If the screen mesh is damaged, replace it.

7. Clean the transaxle fluid pan magnet and the bottom of the pan.

8. Using a gasket scraper remove the gasket. Install the new transaxle pan gasket.

Fig. 49 Automatic transaxle fluid drain plug — as seen from under the vehicle

9. Install the fluid filter screen to the valve body making sure the solenoid wire clamp is in the correct position. Tighten fluid filter screen bolts to 53 inch lbs. (6 Nm).

10. Using a new gasket, install the pan and 15 pan bolts. Apply Loctite®, or equivalent, to the threaded portion of the 2 cross-recess bolts.

11. Tighten pan bolts to 53 inch lbs. (6 Nm) in a criss-cross pattern.

12. Install the transaxle drain plug and tighten to 17 ft. lbs. (23 Nm).

13. Lower the vehicle.

14. Fill the transaxle with fluid and check the fluid level.

Cooling System

▶ See Figures 50 and 51

FLUID RECOMMENDATIONS

The cooling system should be filled with a 50/50 mixture of good quality ethylene glycol antifreeze and water.

LEVEL CHECK

The coolant level should be checked at regular intervals, or if the temperature gauge registers abnormally hot. The coolant

Fig. 50 Engine coolant reservoir tank

Fig. 51 Radiator drain plug — as seen from under the vehicle

level should be between the **FULL** and **LOW** marks on the coolant reservoir tank. Add coolant to the reservoir tank as required to maintain proper coolant level.

At 15,000 mile (25,000 km) intervals the cooling system should be checked for leaks or damage. Also the proper level and freeze protection of the antifreeze should be checked. It is important to maintain the proper level of protection against freezing and loss of coolant from boiling. Inexpensive antifreeze testers are available to measure the degree of protection provided by the cooling system.

DRAIN AND REFILL

1. With the engine cold, remove the radiator cap. Turn the cap slowly to the left until it reaches a stop. Wait until pressure is relieved, then press down on cap and continue to rotate to the left.

2. Open the radiator drain plug to drain the coolant. Drain the coolant into a suitable container.

❊❊CAUTION

When draining the coolant, keep in mind that cats and dogs are attracted by the ethylene glycol antifreeze, and are quite likely to drink any that is left in an uncovered container or in puddles on the ground. This will prove fatal in sufficient quantity. Always drain the coolant into a sealable container. Coolant should be reused unless it is contaminated or several years old.

3. Add a a 50/50 mixture of good quality ethylene glycol antifreeze and water to the radiator and reservoir tank. Fill the radiator to the base of the filler neck and the reservoir tank to the **FULL** mark.

4. Run the engine, with the radiator cap removed, until the upper radiator hose is hot.

5. With the engine idling, add coolant to the radiator until the level reaches the bottom of the filler neck. Install the radiator cap.

DRAIN, FLUSH AND REFILL

The cooling system should be drained, flushed and refilled with fresh coolant every 2 years or 30,000 miles (48,000 km). This operation should be performed with the engine cold.

1. With the engine cold, remove the radiator cap. Turn the cap slowly to the left until it reaches a stop. Wait until pressure is relieved, then press down on cap and continue to rotate to the left.

2. With the radiator cap removed, run the engine until the upper radiator hose is hot (this shows that the thermostat is open and the coolant is flowing through the system).

❊❊CAUTION

Care should be taken as the antifreeze will be extremely hot.

3. Stop the engine and open the radiator drain plug to drain the coolant. Drain the coolant into a suitable container.

✳✳CAUTION

When draining the coolant, keep in mind that cats and dogs are attracted by the ethylene glycol antifreeze, and are quite likely to drink any that is left in an uncovered container or in puddles on the ground. This will prove fatal in sufficient quantity. Always drain the coolant into a sealable container. Coolant should be reused unless it is contaminated or several years old.

4. Close the drain plug. Add water until the system is filled and run the engine until the upper radiator hose is hot again.

5. Repeat Steps 3 and 4 until the drained liquid is nearly colorless.

6. Drain the system and close the radiator drain plug tightly.

7. Disconnect the hose from the water reservoir tank. Remove the tank and pour out any coolant. Clean the inside of the tank, then reinstall.

8. Add a a 50/50 mixture of good quality ethylene glycol antifreeze and water to the radiator and reservoir tank. Fill the radiator to the base of the filler neck and the reservoir tank to the **FULL** mark.

9. Run the engine, with the radiator cap removed, until the upper radiator hose is hot.

10. With the engine idling, add coolant to the radiator until the level reaches the bottom of the filler neck. Install the radiator cap.

Master Cylinder

At least twice a year the brake master cylinder reservoir should be checked for the proper fluid level. A low fluid level can indicate worn disc brake pads. A large loss in fluid may indicate a problem or leak in the system. Have it serviced immediately.

FLUID RECOMMENDATIONS

Use only heavy-duty Delco Supreme 11 or DOT 3 brake fluid.

LEVEL CHECK

▶ **See Figure 52**

The brake master cylinder reservoir is made of translucent plastic so that the fluid level may be checked without removing the cap. If the fluid level in the master cylinder reservoir falls below the **MIN** line molded on the side of the reservoir, add brake fluid to bring the level up to the **MAX** line.

Clean the top of the reservoir off before removing the cap to prevent dirt from entering the master cylinder. Pour the fluid

Fig. 52 Brake master cylinder reservoir

slowly to prevent air bubbles from forming. Reinstall the cap immediately.

✳✳CAUTION

Brake fluid damages paint. It also absorbs moisture from the air; never leave a container or the master cylinder uncovered any longer than necessary. All parts in contact with the brake fluid (master cylinder, hoses, plunger assemblies and etc.) must be kept clean, since any contamination of the brake fluid will adversely affect braking performance.

Windshield Washer

FLUID RECOMMENDATION

Use a generally available solvent and water solution. During the winter months, ensure the grade of solution used is freeze resistant.

LEVEL CHECK

Check the level of the windshield washer solution in the translucent reservoir tank is full at the same time the oil is being checked.

Chassis Greasing

Under normal conditions regular chassis greasing should be performed at 7,500 mile (12,500 km) intervals or at least once a year. If a component is replaced, or a dust boot or seal is damaged or leaking, the component will have to be removed, repacked with grease, and a new boot or seal installed.

Body Lubrication

Body lubrication should be performed at regularly scheduled intervals. Apply multipurpose chassis grease to the hood hinges, lock and striker, the door hinges, latch and striker, and the trunk hinges and striker. Use grease sparingly on the door and trunk strikers, as they may come into contact with clothing.

The clutch, brake, and accelerator linkages should be lubricated at regular intervals, with multipurpose chassis grease. Working inside the car, apply a small amount of grease to the pedal pivots and linkage. Working under the hood, grease all pivoting and sliding parts of the accelerator and brake linkages.

Use powdered graphite to lubricate the door key lock cylinders and trunk key lock cylinders. Do not use oil or grease to lubricate the insides of lock cylinders.

Use silicone lubricant to preserve the rubber weather stripping around the doors and trunk. This will prevent the rubber stripping from sticking to the painted surfaces of the body and also prevent the rubber from dry rotting.

Rear Wheel Bearings

Rear wheel bearings should be repacked with a high quality axle bearing grease every time the rear brake drum is removed.

REMOVAL, PACKING AND INSTALLATION

▶ See Figures 53, 54, 55, 56 and 57

1. Raise and support the vehicle safely.
2. Remove the rear wheel and tire assembly.
3. Using a prybar, remove the spindle nut dust cap.
4. Unstake and remove the spindle nut and washer.
5. Tap on the brake drum/hub assembly gently with a hammer to break it loose.
6. Remove the brake drum/hub assembly from the spindle.

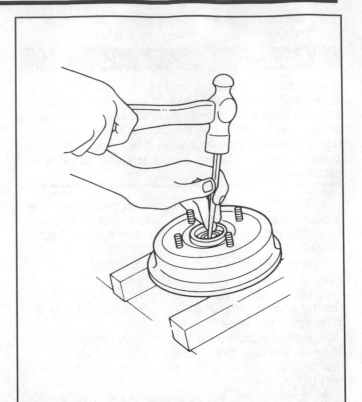

Fig. 54 Removing the inner wheel bearing from the rear brake drum/hub.

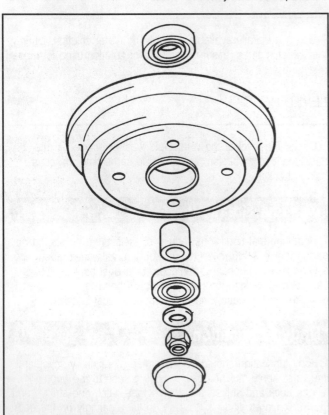

Fig. 53 Rear brake drum/hub and bearing assembly.

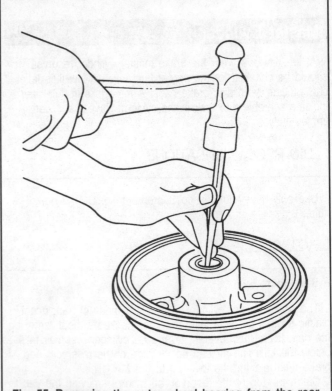

Fig. 55 Removing the outer wheel bearing from the rear brake drum/hub.

7. Place the brake drum/hub assembly on wood blocks on a clean workbench.

8. Drive the inner bearing out from the outboard side of the brake drum/hub assembly using a hammer and punch. The bearing spacer can be moved from side to side to facilitate

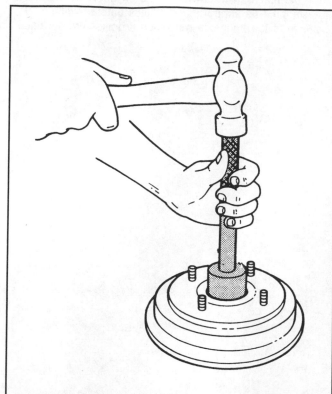

Fig. 56 Installing the outer wheel bearing on the rear brake drum/hub.

placement of the punch working around the perimeter of the inner bearing by moving this spacer.

9. Remove the bearing spacer.

10. Drive the outer bearing out from the inboard side of the brake drum/hub assembly using a hammer and punch working around the perimeter of the bearing.

To install:

11. Check both bearings for signs of wear, corrosion and contamination by dirt or water. If any of these conditions exist, replace the bearings.

12. Liberally grease the bearings with a high quality axle bearing grease.

13. Install the outer bearing to the outboard side of the brake drum/hub assembly using Rear Wheel Bearing Installer J34842, or equivalent. Use the proper side of the tool for the bearing diameter.

➡**The outer and inner bearing cartridges differ in size. The outer cartridge is smaller in diameter than the inner one.**

14. Install the bearing spacer to the brake drum/hub with the inner lip toward the outer bearing. The assembly will not fit on the knuckle spindle if the spacer lip is toward the inner bearing.

15. Install the outer bearing to the outboard side of the brake drum/hub assembly using Rear Wheel Bearing Installer J34842, or equivalent. Use the proper side of the tool for the bearing diameter.

16. Install the brake drum on the knuckle spindle.

17. Install the washer and spindle nut, then tighten the nut to 41 ft. lbs. (55 Nm) for vehicles through 1991, or to 74 ft. lbs. (100 Nm) for 1992-93 vehicles.

18. Stake the spindle nut in place with a blunt punch.

19. Install the spindle nut cap and rear wheel and tire assembly. Lower the vehicle.

TRAILER TOWING

The vehicles covered in this manual were designed primarily to carry passengers. These vehicles are not recommended for trailer towing. Factory hitches are not available and aftermarket hitches should not be installed.

PUSHING AND TOWING

Pushing

Chevrolet/Geo vehicles with manual transmissions can be push started. To push start, make sure that both bumpers are in reasonable alignment. Turn the ignition switch ON and engage High gear. Depress the clutch pedal. When a speed of about 10 mph is reached, slightly depress the gas pedal and slowly release the clutch. The engine should start.

➡**Automatic transmission equipped vehicles cannot be started by pushing.**

Towing

Two styles of towing are recommended, either a car carrier or a wheel lift tow truck.

➡**A sling type tow truck should never be used to tow the vehicle as it will damage the front or rear bumper fascia or the fog lamps.**

When towing the vehicle, have the ignition switch turned to the **LOCK** position. The steering wheel should be clamped in a straight ahead position using a device designed for towing services. Do not use the vehicle's steering column lock. The transaxle should be in the **N** position and the parking brake released.

For front towing hookup using a wheel lift tow truck, attach wheel straps to both front wheels. Attach safety chains to the front tie down brackets.

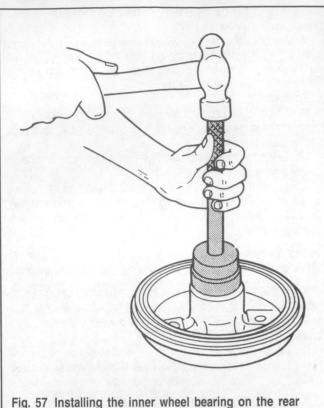

Fig. 57 Installing the inner wheel bearing on the rear brake drum/hub.

For rear towing hookup using a wheel lift tow truck, attach wheel straps to both rear wheels. Dollies are required under the front wheels when the vehicle is equipped with an automatic transaxle. Attach safety chains to the rear tie down brackets.

➡On automatic transaxle equipped vehicles, never tow from the rear with the front wheels on the road. The front wheels must be supported on dollies before towing. Damage to the transaxle will result if dollies are not used.

JACKING

▶ **See Figures 58, 59 and 60**

For lifting a vehicle with equipment other than original equipment jack, various lift points have been established and are recommended.

➡When jacking a vehicle at the frame side rails or other established lift points, be certain that lift pads do not contact the catalytic converter, brake pipes or cables or fuel pipes/hoses. Such contact may result in damage or unsatisfactory vehicle performance.

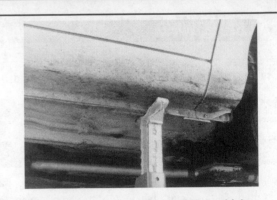

Fig. 59 Support point at the front of the vehicle.

The center line of gravity on front wheel drive vehicles is further forward than on rear wheel drive vehicles. Therefore, whenever removing major components from the rear of a front wheel drive vehicle supported on a hoist, it is mandatory to

Fig. 58 Jacking point at the rear of the vehicle.

Fig. 60 Support point at the rear of the vehicle.

support the vehicle in such a way that reduces the likelihood of the vehicle tipping forward.

✳✳CAUTION

To help avoid personal injury when a vehicle is on a jack, provide additional support for the vehicle at the end from which components are being removed. This will reduce the possibilities of the vehicle falling off of the jack.

When supporting a vehicle with jackstands, the supports should be placed under the body side rail pinch welds or a similar strong, stable structure.

ITEM NO.	TO BE SERVICED	WHEN TO PERFORM Miles (kilometers) or Months, Whichever Occurs First	The services shown in this schedule up to 48,000 miles (80 000 km) are to be performed after 48,000 miles at the same intervals															
		MILES (000)	3	6	9	12	15	18	21	24	27	30	33	36	39	42	45	48
		KILOMETERS (000)	5	10	15	20	25	30	35	40	45	50	55	60	65	70	75	80
1	Engine Oil & Oil Filter Change*	Every 3,000 Miles (5 000 km) or 3 Months	•	•	•	•	•	•	•	•	•	•	•	•	•	•	•	•
2	Chassis Lubrication	Every Other Oil Change		•		•		•		•		•		•		•		•
3	Carburetor Choke Inspection*	At 6,000 Miles (10 000 km), then every 30,000 Miles (50 000 km)		•								•†						
4	Engine Idle Speed Inspection*	At 6,000 Miles (10 000 km), then every 15,000 Miles (25 000 km)		•			•					•					•	
5	Valve Lash Inspection*	Every 15,000 Miles (25 000 km)					•					•					•	
6	Water Pump Belt Inspection*	Every 30,000 Miles (50 000 km) or 24 Months										•†						
7	Cooling System Service*	See Explanation of Scheduled Maintenance Services																
8	Fuel Cut System Inspection*	Every 30,000 Miles (50 000 km) or 24 Months										•						
9	Transaxle Service	Every 30,000 Miles (50 000 km) or 24 Months										•						
10	Fuel Filter Replacement	Every 30,000 Miles (50 000 km)										•						
11	Spark Plug Replacement*	Every 30,000 Miles (50 000 km)										•†						
12	PCV System Inspection*	Every 30,000 Miles (50 000 km) or 24 Months										•						
13	Air Cleaner Element Replacement*	Every 30,000 Miles (50 000 km) or 24 Months										•						
14	Oxygen Sensor Inspection*	Every 30,000 Miles (50 000 km)										•						
15	Pulse Air Control System Inspection*	Every 30,000 Miles (50 000 km) or 24 Months										•						
16	Spark Plug Wires & Distributor Inspection*	Every 30,000 Miles (50 000 km) or 24 Months										•						
17	Fuel Tank, Cap & Lines — Inspection	Every 15,000 Miles (25 000 km) or 12 Months					•					•					•	
18	Thermostatically Controlled Air Cleaner*	Every 30,000 Miles (50 000 km) or 12 Months										•						

Fig. 61 Maintenance interval chart, 1985-88 vehicles-Normal usage

ITEM NO.	TO BE SERVICED	WHEN TO PERFORM Miles (kilometers) or Months, Whichever Occurs First	The services shown in this schedule up to 45,000 miles (75 000 km) are to be performed after 45,000 miles at the same intervals					
		MILES (000)	7.5	15	22.5	30	37.5	45
		KILOMETERS (000)	12.5	25	37.5	50	62.5	75
1	Engine Oil & Oil Filter Change*	Every 7,500 Miles (12 500 km) or 12 Months	•	•	•	•	•	•
2	Chassis Lubrication	Every 7,500 Miles (12 500 km) or 12 Months	•	•	•	•	•	•
3	Carburetor Choke Inspection*	Every 30,000 Miles (50 000 km) or 24 Months				•†		
4	Engine Idle Speed Inspection*	At 7,500 Miles (12 500 km), then at 15,000 Mile (25 000 km) intervals	•	•		•		•
5	Valve Lash Inspection*	Every 15,000 Miles (25 000 km)		•		•		•
6	Water Pump Belt Inspection*	Every 30,000 Miles (50 000 km) or 24 Months				•†		
7	Cooling System Service*	See Explanation of Scheduled Maintenance Services						
8	Fuel Cut System Inspection*	Every 30,000 Miles (50 000 km) or 24 Months				•		
9	Transaxle Service	Every 30,000 Miles (50 000 km) or 24 Months				•		
10	Fuel Filter Replacement	Every 30,000 Miles (50 000 km)				•		
11	Spark Plug Replacement*	Every 30,000 Miles (50 000 km)				•†		
12	PCV System Inspection*	Every 30,000 Miles (50 000 km) or 24 Months				•		
13	Air Cleaner Element Replacement*	Every 30,000 Miles (50 000 km) or 24 Months				•		
14	Oxygen Sensor Inspection*	Every 30,000 Miles (50 000 km)				•		
15	Pulse Air Control System Inspection*	Every 30,000 Miles (50 000 km) or 24 Months				•		
16	Spark Plug Wires & Distributor Inspection*	Every 30,000 Miles (50 000 km) or 24 Months				•		
17	Fuel Tank, Cap & Lines — Inspection	Every 15,000 Miles (25 000 km) or 12 Months		•		•		•
18	Thermostatically Controlled Air Cleaner*	Every 30,000 Miles (50 000 km) or 12 Months				•		

FOOTNOTES:

* An Emission Control Service

† In California, these are the minimum Emission Control Maintenance Services an owner must perform according to the California Air Resources Board. General Motors, however, urges that all Emission Control Maintenance Services shown above be performed. To maintain your other new car warranties, all services shown in this section should be performed.

Fig. 62 Maintenance interval chart, 1985-88 vehicles-Severe usage

TO BE SERVICED	WHEN TO PERFORM MILES (KILOMETERS) OR MONTHS WHICHEVER OCCURS FIRST	THE SERVICES SHOWN IN THIS SCHEDULE UP TO 60,000 MILES (100 000 km) ARE TO BE PERFORMED AFTER 60,000 MILES (100 000 km) AT THE SAME INTERVALS																			
		MILES (000)	3	6	9	12	15	18	21	24	27	30	33	36	39	42	45	48	51	54	57	60
		KILOMETERS (000)	5	10	15	20	25	30	35	40	45	50	55	60	65	70	75	80	85	90	95	100
ENGINE OIL & OIL FILTER CHANGE*	EVERY 3,000 mi. (5 000 km) OR 3 mos.		•	•	•	•	•	•	•	•	•	•	•	•	•	•	•	•	•	•	•	•
CHASSIS LUBRICATION	EVERY OTHER OIL CHANGE			•		•		•		•		•		•		•		•		•		•
THROTTLE BODY MOUNT BOLT TORQUE*	AT 6,000 mi. (10 000 km) ONLY			•																		
TIRE & WHEEL INSPECTION AND ROTATION	AT 6,000 mi. (10 000 km) AND THEN EVERY 15,000 mi. (25 000 km)			•				•				•				•				•		
ENGINE ACCESSORY DRIVE BELT(S) INSPECTION*	AT 30,000 mi. (50 000 km) OR 24 mos.										•											•
COOLING SYSTEM SERVICE*											•											•
TRANSAXLE SERVICE	SEE EXPLANATION FOR SERVICE INTERVAL																					
SPARK PLUG REPLACEMENT*	EVERY 30,000 mi. (50 000 km)										•											•
SPARK PLUG (SECONDARY) WIRE INSPECTION*	EVERY 60,000 mi. (100 000 km) OR 60 mos.																					•
EGR SYSTEM INSPECTION* ††	EVERY 30,000 mi. (50 000 km) OR 36 mos.										•											•
AIR CLEANER & PCV INLET FILTER REPLACEMENT*											•											•
ENGINE TIMING CHECK*	EVERY 30,000 mi. (50 000 km)										•											•
FUEL TANK, CAP & PIPES/HOSES INSPECTION* ††	EVERY 15,000 mi. (25 000 km) OR 15 mos.					•					•					•						•
PCV SYSTEM INSPECTION	EVERY 60,000 mi. (100 000 km)																					•

FOOTNOTES:
* AN EMISSION CONTROL SERVICE
†† THE U.S. ENVIRONMENTAL AGENCY HAS DETERMINED THAT THE FAILURE TO PERFORM THIS MAINTENANCE ITEM WILL NOT NULLIFY THE EMISSION WARRANTY OR LIMIT RECALL LIABILITY PRIOR TO THE COMPLETION OF VEHICLE USEFUL LIFE. GENERAL MOTORS, HOWEVER, URGES THAT ALL RECOMMENDED MAINTENANCE SERVICES BE PERFORMED AT THE INDICATED INTERVALS AND THE MAINTENANCE BE RECORDED IN SECTION E OF THE OWNER'S MAINTENANCE SCHEDULE.

Fig. 63 Maintenance interval chart, 1989-93 vehicles and all turbocharged vehicles-Normal usage

TO BE SERVICED	WHEN TO PERFORM MILES (KILOMETERS) OR MONTHS WHICHEVER OCCURS FIRST	THE SERVICES SHOWN IN THIS SCHEDULE UP TO 60,000 MILES (100 000 km) ARE TO BE PERFORMED AFTER 60,000 MILES (100 000 km) AT THE SAME INTERVALS							
	MILES (000)	7.5	15	22.5	30	37.5	45	52.5	60
	KILOMETERS (000)	12.54	25	37.5	50	62.5	75	87.5	100
ENGINE OIL CHANGE*	EVERY 7,500 mi. (12 500 km) OR 7.5 mos.	•	•	•	•	•	•	•	•
OIL FILTER CHANGE*	EVERY 7,500 mi. (12 500 km) OR 7.5 mos.	•	•	•	•	•	•	•	•
CHASSIS LUBRICATION	EVERY 7,500 mi. (12 500 km) OR 12 mos.	•	•	•	•	•	•	•	•
THROTTLE BODY MOUNT BOLT TORQUE*	AT 7,500 mi. (12 500 km) ONLY	•							
TIRE & WHEEL INSPECTION AND ROTATION	AT 7,500 mi. (12 500 km) AND THEN EVERY 15,000 mi. (25 000 km)	•		•		•		•	
ENGINE ACCESSORY DRIVE BELT(S) INSPECTION*	EVERY 30,000 mi. (50 000 km) OR 24 mos.				•				•
COOLING SYSTEM SERVICE*	EVERY 30,000 mi. (50 000 km) OR 24 mos.				•				•
TRANSAXLE SERVICE	SEE EXPLANATION FOR SERVICE INTERVAL								
SPARK PLUG REPLACEMENT*	EVERY 30,000 mi. (50 000 km)				•				•
SPARK PLUG (SECONDARY) WIRE INSPECTION*	EVERY 60,000 mi. (100 000 km) OR 60 mos.								•
EGR SYSTEM INSPECTION* ††	EVERY 30,000 mi. (50 000 km) OR 36 mos.				•				•
AIR CLEANER & PCV INLET FILTER REPLACEMENT*	EVERY 30,000 mi. (50 000 km) OR 36 mos.				•				•
ENGINE TIMING CHECK*	EVERY 30,000 mi. (50 000 km) OR 36 mos.				•				•
FUEL TANK, CAP & PIPES/HOSES INSPECTION* ††	EVERY 15,000 mi. (25 000 km) OR 15 mos.		•		•		•		•
PCV SYSTEM INSPECTION*	EVERY 60,000 mi. (100 000 km)								•

FOOTNOTES:

* AN EMISSION CONTROL SERVICE

†† THE U.S. ENVIRONMENTAL AGENCY HAS DETERMINED THAT THE FAILURE TO PERFORM THIS MAINTENANCE ITEM WILL NOT NULLIFY THE EMISSION WARRANTY OR LIMIT RECALL LIABILITY PRIOR TO THE COMPLETION OF VEHICLE USEFUL LIFE. GENERAL MOTORS, HOWEVER, URGES THAT ALL RECOMMENDED MAINTENANCE SERVICES BE PERFORMED AT THE INDICATED INTERVALS AND THE MAINTENANCE BE RECORDED IN SECTION E OF THE OWNER'S MAINTENANCE SCHEDULE.

Fig. 64 Maintenance interval chart, 1989-93 vehicles and all turbocharged vehicles-Severe usage

CAPACITIES

Year	Model	Engine ID/VIN	Engine Displacement Liters (cc)	Engine Crankcase with Filter	Transmission (pts.) 4-Spd	5-Spd	Auto.	Transfer Case (pts.)	Drive Axle Front (pts.)	Rear (pts.)	Fuel Tank (gal.)	Cooling System (qts.)
1985	Sprint	M	1.0 (1000)	3.5	—	4.8	—	—	—	—	8.3	4.5
1986	Sprint	5	1.0 (1000)	3.5	—	4.8	9.5	—	—	—	8.3	4.5
1987	Sprint	5	1.0 (1000)	3.5	—	4.8	9.5	—	—	—	8.3	4.5
1988	Sprint	5	1.0 (1000)	3.5	—	4.8	9.5	—	—	—	8.3	4.5
1989	Metro	5	1.0 (1000)	3.7	—	4.8	9.6	—	—	—	8.7	4.5
1990	Metro	5	1.0 (1000)	3.7	—	5.0	10.4	—	—	—	10.0	4.2
1991	Metro	6	1.0 (1000)	3.7	—	5.0	10.4	—	—	—	10.6	4.2
1992	Metro	6	1.0 (1000)	3.7	—	5.0	10.4	—	—	—	10.6	4.2
1993	Metro	6	1.0 (1000)	3.7	—	5.0	10.4	—	—	—	10.6	4.2

TORQUE SPECIFICATIONS

Component	U.S.	Metric
Component Standard Metric		
Alternator		
Adjustment bolt	17 ft. lbs.	23 Nm
Lower cover plate	89 inch lbs.	10 Nm
Battery		
Cable nut	11 ft. lbs.	15 Nm
Hold down nut	71 inch lbs.	8 Nm
Manual Transaxle		
Oil level filler plug	40 ft. lbs.	54 Nm
Drain plug	21 ft. lbs.	28 Nm
Automatic Transaxle		
Drain plug	17 ft. lbs.	23 Nm
Filter screen screw	53 inch lbs.	6 Nm
Fluid pan bolts	53 inch lbs.	6 Nm
Rear spindle nut		
Through 1991	41 ft. lbs.	55 Nm
1992-93	74 ft. lbs.	100 Nm

2

ENGINE PERFORMANCE AND TUNE-UP

TUNE-UP PROCEDURES

▶ **See Figure 1**

In order to extract the full measure of performance and economy from your engine it is essential that it is properly tuned at regular intervals. A regular tune-up will keep your truck's engine running smoothly and will prevent the annoying breakdowns and poor performance associated with an untuned engine.

A complete tune-up should be performed every 30,000 miles. This interval should be halved if the vehicle is operated under severe conditions such as prolonged idling, start-and-stop driving, or if starting or running problems are noticed. It is assumed that the routine maintenance described in Section 1 has been kept up, as this will have a decided effect on the results of a tune-up. All of the applicable steps of a tune-up should be followed in order, as the result is a cumulative one.

If the specifications on the underhood tune-up sticker in the engine compartment disagree with the Tune-Up Specifications chart in this Section, the figures on the sticker must be used. The sticker often reflects changes made during the production run.

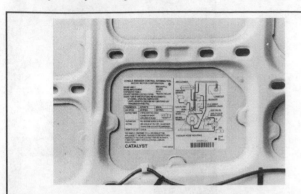

Fig. 1 Vehicle emission control information label

GASOLINE ENGINE TUNE-UP SPECIFICATIONS

Year	Engine ID/VIN	Engine Displacement Liters (cc)	Spark Plugs Gap (in.)	Ignition Timing (deg.) MT	AT	Fuel Pump (psi)	Idle Speed (rpm) MT	AT	Valve Clearance In.	Ex.
1985	M	1.0 (1000)	0.039–0.043	10B	6B	3.5	750	850	0.006	0.008
1986	5	1.0 (1000)	0.039–0.043	10B	6B	3.5	750	850	0.006	0.008
1987	5	1.0 (1000)	0.039–0.043	10B	6B	3.5	750②	850	0.006	0.008
1987	2	1.0 (1000)	0.039–0.043	12B	—	25–35	750	—	0.006	0.008
1988	5	1.0 (1000)	0.039–0.043	10B	6B	3.5	750②	850	0.006	0.008
1988	2	1.0 (1000)	0.039–0.043	12B	—	25–35	750	—	0.006	0.008
1989	5	1.0 (1000)	0.039–0.043	6B	6B①	25–31	700	750	Hyd.	Hyd.
1990	5	1.0 (1000)	0.039–0.043	6B	6B①	25–31	750③	850	Hyd.	Hyd.
1991	6	1.0 (1000)	0.039–0.043	6B	6B①	23–31	800④	850	Hyd.	Hyd.
1992	6	1.0 (1000)	0.039–0.043	5B	5B①	23–31	800④	850	Hyd.	Hyd.
1993	6	1.0 (1000)	0.039–0.043	5B	5B①	23–31	800	850	Hyd.	Hyd.

NOTE: The lowest cylinder pressure should be within 75% of the highest cylinder pressure reading. For example, if the highest cylinder is 134 psi, the lowest should be 101. Engine should be at normal operating temperature with throttle valve in the wide open position.
The underhood specifications sticker often reflects tune-up specification changes in production. Sticker figures must be used if they disagree with those in this chart.
NOTE: From 1989–93, a spare fuse must be inserted into the switch terminal in the fuse box prior to measuring idle speed.
B—Before Top Dead Center
① Electronic Spark Control Ignition: Jumper
   check connector terminals
   Conventional Spark Control Ignition: Disconnect
   vacuum line at gas filter and plug line

② ER model—700 rpm
③ LSi model—700 rpm
④ XFi model—700 rpm
   All convertible models—850 rpm

Spark Plugs

Normally, a set of spark plugs requires replacement about every 30,000 miles (50,000 km). Any vehicle which is subjected to severe conditions will need more frequent plug replacement.

Under normal operation, the plug gap increases about 0.001" (0.0254mm) for every 1,000-2,000 miles. As the gap increases, the plug's voltage requirement also increases. It requires a greater voltage to jump the wider gap and about 2-3 times as much voltage to fire a plug at high speeds than at idle.

When you are removing the spark plugs, work on one at a time. Don't start by removing the plug wires all at once, for unless you number them, they may become mixed up. Take a minute before you begin and number the wires with tape. The best location for numbering the wires is at the distributor cap and the spark plug boot.

Once removed, inspect all spark plugs carefully. Worn or dirty spark plugs will provide satisfactory performance at idle speed but under more demanding operating conditions, they will frequently misfire. Misfiring spark plugs should be suspected from a number of symptoms. These symptoms include poor fuel economy, power loss, loss of speed, hard starting and generally poor engine performance. Spark plugs may misfire due to carbon fouling, an excessive spark plug gap, a broken insulator, bridged electrodes or a damaged spark plug wire or boot.

Fouled spark plugs are indicated by black carbon deposits on electrodes. These black deposits are usually the result of slow-speed driving and short runs in which sufficient operating temperature is seldom achieved. Worn pistons, rings, faulty ignition, over-rich air/fuel mixture, and the incorrect spark plug heat range will also result in carbon deposits.

Carbon deposits on the spark plug insulator tip may become conductive and cause the high voltage arc to track along the tip to some point where it arcs to join the spark plug shell. This arc then ignites the air/fuel mixture later than normal which, in effect, retards ignition timing. Heavy carbon deposits may be conductive to the extent that the arc path now becomes a shunt path to the spark plug shell. This condition prevents the high voltage from arcing and igniting the air/fuel mixture. Once arc tracking occurs, the spark plug may be permanently damaged and must be replaced.

Excessive electrode wear, on low mileage spark plugs usually indicates that the engine is operating at speed consistently higher than those for which the engine was designed or that the spark plug's heat range is too high. Electrode wear may also be the result of spark plug overheating caused by combustion gases leaking past the threads. Electrode wear can become excessive to the point that the high voltage no longer arcs across the electrodes.

Heat range is a term used to describe the cooling characteristics of spark plugs. Plugs with longer nosed insulators take a longer time to dissipate heat than plugs with shorter nosed insulators. These are termed 'hot' or 'cold' plugs, respectively. It is generally advisable to use the factory recommended plugs. However, in conditions of extremely hard use (cross-country driving in summer) going to the next cooler heat range may be advisable. If most driving is done in the city or over short distances, go to the next hotter heat range plug to eliminate fouling.

Broken or cracked insulators are usually the result of improper installation. Broken lower insulators often result from improper gapping and are usually visible immediately. When gapping a spark plug, always make the gap adjustment by bending the ground electrode. Spark plugs with broken insulators must always be replaced.

Damaged spark plug wires and/or boots cause a similar condition to that of a cracked insulator. The high voltage arc flashes through the wire or boot and grounds on the spark plug shell or the engine.

Spark plugs are protected by an insulating boot comprised of heat resistant material which covers the spark plug terminal and extends downward over a portion of the spark plug insulator. These boots prevent the flashover that causes engine misfiring.

REMOVAL & INSTALLATION

▶ See Figures 2, 3, 4, 5, 6, 7 and 8

➡This engine has aluminum cylinder heads. Allow the engine to cool before removing spark plugs. Removing the plugs from an engine at operating temperature may damage the spark plug threads in the cylinder head.

1. Disconnect the negative battery cable.
2. Twist the spark plug boot ½ turn and remove the boot from the plug. DO NOT pull on the wire itself as this will damage wire.
3. Remove the spark plug from the cylinder head using the proper size spark plug socket.

Fig. 2 Spark plug location at the front of the engine

Fig. 3 Removing the spark plug wires from the retainer

Fig. 4 Removing the spark plug boot from the spark plug

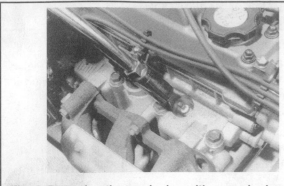

Fig. 5 Removing the spark plug with a spark plug socket

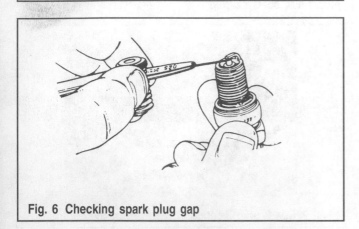

Fig. 6 Checking spark plug gap

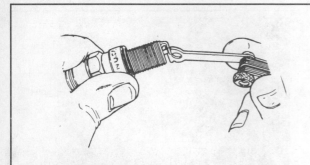

Fig. 7 Bending the side electrode to adjust spark plug gap

Fig. 8 Ensure the spark plug hole area is clean prior to installing the new spark plug

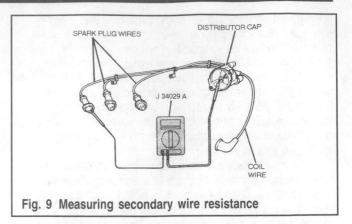

Fig. 9 Measuring secondary wire resistance

4. If removing the plug is difficult, drip some penetrating oil on the plug threads, allow it to work, then remove the plug. Also, be sure that the socket is straight on the plug.

To install:

5. Inspect spark plugs for electrode wear, carbon deposits and insulator damage.

6. Check the spark plug. The ground electrode (the L-shaped wire connected to the body of the plug) must be parallel to the center electrode and the specified size wire gauge (see Tune-Up Specifications) should pass through the gap with a slight drag.

➡Always check the gap on the new plugs, they are not always set correctly at the factory.

7. Wire gapping tools usually have a bending tool attached. Use that to adjust the side electrode until the proper distance is obtained. DO NOT use a flat feeler gauge when measuring the gap, because the reading will be inaccurate.

8. Set new spark plug gap to 0.039-0.043 in. (1.0-1.1 mm).

9. Using a drop of oil, install the spark plug in the cylinder head and tighten to 21 ft. lbs. (20 Nm).

10. Using dielectric grease on the spark plug boot, install the ignition wires on their respective plugs. Make sure you feel them click into place.

11. Connect the negative battery cable.

Spark Plug Wires

▶ **See Figure 9**

Every 15,000 miles, visually inspect the spark plug wires for burns, cuts or breaks in the insulation. Check the spark plug boots and the nipples on the distributor cap and coil. Replace any damaged wiring.

Every 30,000 miles or so, the resistance of the wires should be checked with an ohmmeter. Wires with excessive resistance will cause misfiring and may make the engine difficult to start in damp weather. Generally, the useful life of the spark plug wires is 30,000-45,000 miles.

To check spark plug wire resistance, remove the distributor cap, leaving the wires in place. Connect one lead of an ohmmeter to an electrode within the cap; connect the other lead to the corresponding spark plug terminal (remove it from the spark plug for this test). Replace any wire which shows a resistance over 3-6.7 ohms per foot.

REMOVAL & INSTALLATION

1. Disconnect the negative battery cable.
2. Remove the coil wire from the ignition coil. Gripping the boot firmly, turn the boot ½ turn and disconnect the wire.
3. Remove the spark plug wire retainers from the engine.
4. Label and remove the spark plug wires from the spark plugs. Gripping the boot firmly, turn the boot ½ turn and disconnect the wire.
5. Remove the screws retaining the distributor cap.
6. Remove the distributor cap and wires as an assembly.
7. Measure the resistance between the distributor cap terminals and the spark plug wire terminals using an ohmmeter. If the resistance is greater than 3-6.7 ohms per foot of spark plug wire, replace the wire.

➡If one or more wires show a resistance out of specification, it is recommended that the entire set of wires be replaced.

8. Remove the spark plug wire from the distributor and replace it with one of the correct length.
To install:
9. Install the new spark plug wire to the distributor cap after coating the inside of the boots with dielectric grease.
10. Install the distributor cap to the distributor and secure with screws.
11. Install the spark plug wires to the spark plugs. Ensure that the spark plug boots are coated inside with dielectric grease.
12. Reposition the spark plug wires and install the wire retainers on the engine.
13. Connect the coil wire to the ignition coil.
14. Connect the negative battery cable.

FIRING ORDER

▶ **See Figure 10**

➡To avoid confusion, label and remove the spark plug wires one at a time, for replacement.

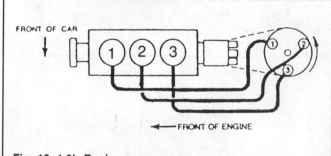

Fig. 10 1.0L Engine
Engine Firing Order: 1–3–2
Distributor Rotation: Counterclockwise

ELECTRONIC IGNITION

General Information

DESCRIPTION AND OPERATION

▶ **See Figures 11, 12 and 13**

Conventional Spark Control Ignition System

A conventional electronic ignition system with vacuum/centrifugal spark control is used on carbureted 1985-88 Chevrolet Sprint and 1989-91 Geo Metro LSi models.

The basic components of this ignition system are the ignition coil, the distributor, the spark plugs and spark plug wiring. The distributor consists of a signal generator (signal rotor and pick-up coil), igniter, rotor, ignition module, vacuum advancer and centrifugal advancer.

When the distributor shaft rotates, a fluctuating magnetic field is generated due to changes in the air gap between the pick-up coil and signal rotor. As a result, an alternating current (AC) voltage is induced in the pick-up coil. This induced AC voltage peaks when a ridge on the signal rotor is adjacent to the ridge on the pick-up coil. When the voltage peaks, the igniter breaks the circuit to ground from the negative side of the coil primary winding. With the circuit broken, the magnetic field in the ignition coil, which has been generated by the electrical current passing through it, collapses. The high voltage induced by the collapsing field is then forced to find a ground through the secondary coil wire, the distributor cap, the rotor, the spark plug wire and finally across the spark plug air gap to the engine block.

Spark timing is mechanically controlled by a vacuum advance system which uses engine manifold vacuum and a centrifugal advance mechanism.

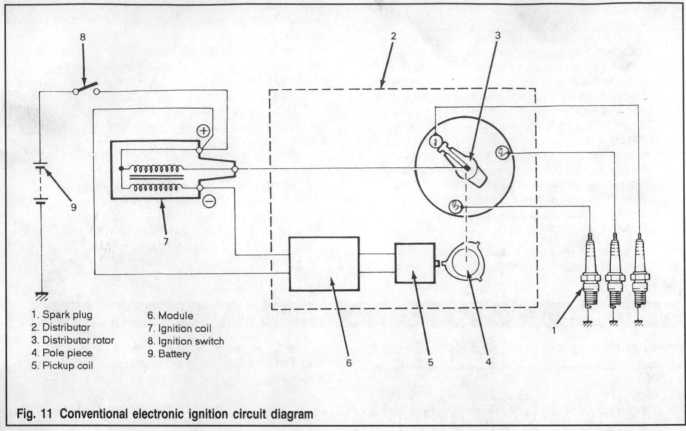

1. Spark plug
2. Distributor
3. Distributor rotor
4. Pole piece
5. Pickup coil
6. Module
7. Ignition coil
8. Ignition switch
9. Battery

Fig. 11 Conventional electronic ignition circuit diagram

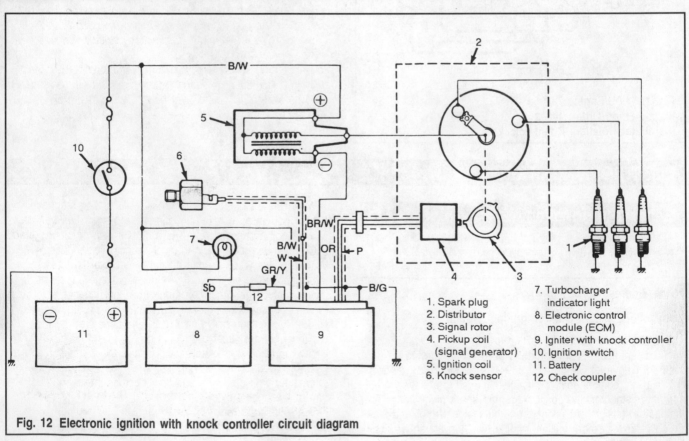

1. Spark plug
2. Distributor
3. Signal rotor
4. Pickup coil (signal generator)
5. Ignition coil
6. Knock sensor
7. Turbocharger indicator light
8. Electronic control module (ECM)
9. Igniter with knock controller
10. Ignition switch
11. Battery
12. Check coupler

Fig. 12 Electronic ignition with knock controller circuit diagram

Electronic Ignition System With Knock Controller

An electronic ignition system with knock controller is used on turbocharged 1987-88 Chevrolet Sprint vehicles only.

This system functions in much the same manner as a conventional electronic ignition system except it utilizes an igniter with knock controller which electrically controls the ignition timing based on signal received from a knock sensor. The system ensures that optimum ignition timing is always obtained for best engine output and drive train protection. When there is no knocking, the ignition system operates in the same way as an ordinary ignition system. When knocking occurs, the system can retard the ignition timing up to 12°, according to the degree of knocking.

The distributor uses a rotor, signal generator, vacuum advance unit and centrifugal advancer. The vacuum advance unit controls the ignition timing as follows. The throttle body bore and surge tank internal pressure is delivered into the vacuum advance unit through hoses. When the pressure is negative (vacuum), it moves the breaker clockwise (in reverse direction to rotor rotation) to advance the ignition timing. On the other hand, the positive pressure causes the breaker to move counterclockwise to retard the ignition timing.

The igniter with knock controller is located at the left side of the engine compartment. It has two main circuits, one serving as a fully transistorized igniter and the other as a knock controller. Based on the engine speed and signals from the Electronic Control Module (ECM) and knock sensor, the knock controller gives the igniter an instruction to retard the ignition timing so that engine knocking is suppressed.

The controller also has a fail safe circuit built-in. It give an instruction to retard ignition timing by a certain amount if the knock sensor fails or a short or open circuit occurs in the output leads.

The knock sensor is located on the cylinder block at the intake manifold side. It detects engine vibration and converts it into an electrical signal which is transmitted to the igniter.

Electronic Spark Control (ESC) Ignition System

An electronic spark control ignition system is used on 1989-91 Geo Metro Base and XFi models, and all 1992-93 Geo Metro models.

The ignition circuit consists of the battery, distributor, ignition switch spark plugs, primary and secondary wiring. The ESC system is monitored and controlled by the engine control module (ECM). The distributor used in this system consists of a signal generator (signal rotor and pick-up coil), and rotor. The igniter is located in the ECM.

All spark timing changes in the distributor are performed electronically by the ECM. After receiving signals indicating engine speed, manifold vacuum, coolant temperature and other engine functions, the ECM selects the most appropriate timing setting from memory and signals the distributor to change the timing accordingly. No vacuum or mechanical advance mechanisms are used.

The ECM controls a driver to ground which is connected to negative side from the coil's primary circuit. When this ground is interrupted, the field around the primary coil collapses and a high voltage is induced in the secondary coil. The high voltage induced in the secondary coil is then forced to find a ground through the coil wire, distributor cap, rotor, spark plug wire and across the spark plug air gap to the engine block.

Diagnosis and Testing

IGNITION COIL TESTING

▶ **See Figures 14 and 15**

1. Check for spark at each spark plug with a spark plug tester. If no spark is detected, proceed to Step 2. If spark is only detected on some spark plugs, check for a faulty distributor cap or rotor. Also check the spark plugs and wires. Replace as needed.
2. Check for voltage at the ignition coil positive terminal with a voltmeter. If battery voltage is detected, proceed to Step 3. If battery voltage is not detected, repair the open in the wiring between the battery and the ignition coil.
3. Disconnect the connector on the negative coil wire. Check ignition coil resistance. If resistance is within specification, proceed to Step 4. If resistance is not within specification, replace the coil.
   a. Measure the resistance between the positive and negative terminals. Resistance should be 1.08-1.32 ohms electronic ignition with knock control and 1.33-1.55 ohms for all others.
   b. Measure the resistance between the positive/negative terminals and the coil high tension wire terminal. Resistance should be 11.6-15.8 kilo-ohms for electronic ignition with knock control and 10.7-14.5 kilo-ohms for all others.
4. On Conventional and ESC ignitions, check the resistance of the noise filter and condenser with an ohmmeter. If the resistance is 2.0-2.5 ohms for both units, proceed to Step 5. If the resistance is not within specification, replace both units as a set.
5. On Conventional ignitions, check the continuity of the brown/white wire between the ignition coil negative terminal and the distributor. If continuity exists, replace the pick-up coil and igniter. If continuity does not exist, repair the open in the wire.

KNOCK CONTROL SYSTEM TESTING

▶ **See Figure 16**

1. Start the engine and allow it to reach normal operating temperature.
2. Depress the accelerator pedal rapidly and race engine. The **TURBO** light should illuminate on the dash. If not, inspect the lamp wiring and the lamp.
3. Connect a tachometer and check for proper idle speed.
4. Connect a timing light and check for proper ignition timing.
5. Disconnect the check coupler of the igniter. If ignition timing changes, replace the, replace the knock sensor and recheck the timing.

➡ **The check coupler is located near the knock controller and has gray/yellow lead wires.**

6. With the check coupler disconnected, disconnect the knock sensor wire at the coupler. If ignition timing does not retard, replace the igniter with knock controller.

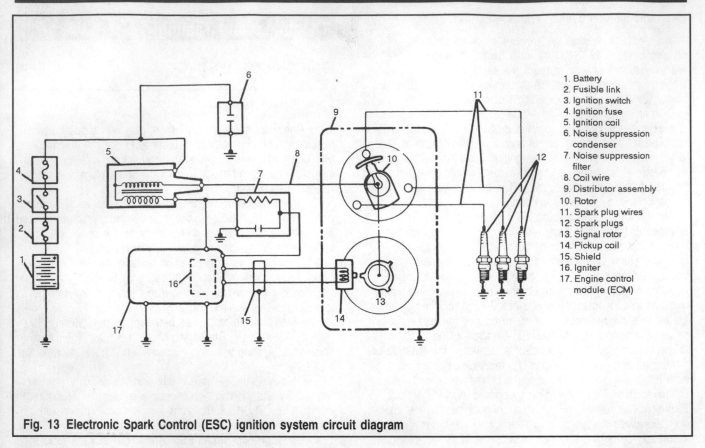

1. Battery
2. Fusible link
3. Ignition switch
4. Ignition fuse
5. Ignition coil
6. Noise suppression condenser
7. Noise suppression filter
8. Coil wire
9. Distributor assembly
10. Rotor
11. Spark plug wires
12. Spark plugs
13. Signal rotor
14. Pickup coil
15. Shield
16. Igniter
17. Engine control module (ECM)

Fig. 13 Electronic Spark Control (ESC) ignition system circuit diagram

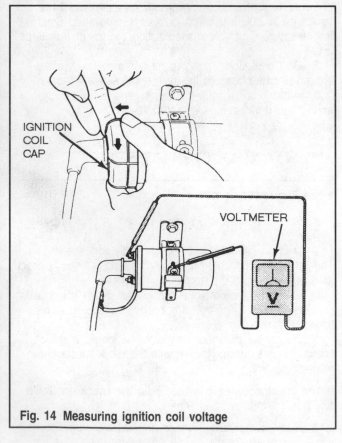

Fig. 14 Measuring ignition coil voltage

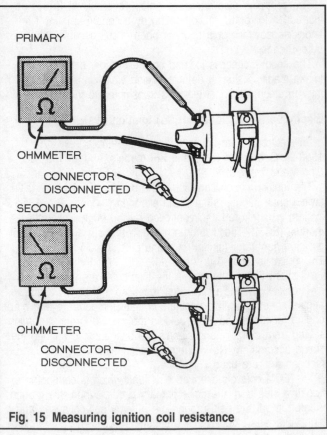

Fig. 15 Measuring ignition coil resistance

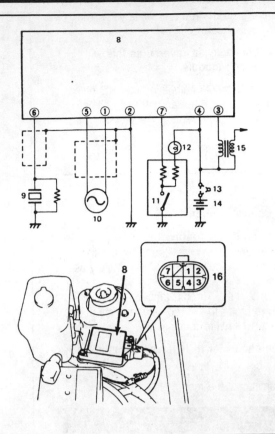

1. Orange wire
2. Black/Green wire
3. Brown/White wire
4. Black/White wire
5. Pink wire
6. White wire
7. Gray/Yellow wire
8. Igniter with knock sensor
9. Knock sensor
10. Pickup coil (signal generator)
11. Electronic control unit (ECM)
12. Turbo indicator light
13. Ignition switch
14. Battery
15. Ignition coil
16. Terminals viewed from wire harness side

Fig. 16 Knock controller circuit diagram

7. With the knock sensor coupler disconnected, connect check coupler. If timing is not restored to normally quickly, replace the igniter with knock controller.

8. Repeat Step 6 with the check coupler disconnected and connecting the knock sensor coupler. If timing is not restored to normally quickly, replace the igniter with knock controller.

9. Reconnect each coupler and check to ensure that ignition timing is set to specification.

CENTRIFUGAL ADVANCE TESTING

1. Remove the distributor cap.
2. Rotate the rotor counter-clockwise.
3. Release rotor, it should spring back.
4. Replace distributor if centrifugal advance fails this test.

VACUUM ADVANCE TESTING

1. Remove the distributor cap.
2. Remove the vacuum hoses.
3. Connect a vacuum pump to the outside vacuum hose on the distributor.
4. Apply 15 in. Hg of vacuum, the pick-up coil should move.
5. Repeat the same test with the inside vacuum hose.
6. On electronic ignition with knock control, connect a regulated air source to the nipple at the small vacuum chamber on the advance unit. When air pressure is applied, the pick-up coil should move.

➡ **Never apply more than 18 psi of air pressure to the advance unit.**

7. If the pick-up coil does not move replace the vacuum advance unit.

PICK-UP COIL TESTING

◆ See Figure 17

1. Remove the dust cover from the module.
2. Disconnect the red and white wires from the module.

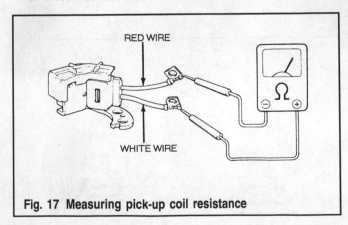

RED WIRE

WHITE WIRE

Fig. 17 Measuring pick-up coil resistance

3. Connect an ohmmeter to the red and white wires and measure the generator resistance.

➡ **Do not connect the ohmmeter in reverse as this will damage the pick-up coil and module.**

4. Pick-up coil resistance should be within 900-1100 ohms on electronic ignition with knock control and 130-190 ohms on all others. If not within specification, replace the pick-up coil.

IGNITION MODULE TESTING

▶ **See Figure 18**

Conventional Spark Control Ignition

1. Remove the dust cover from the module.
2. Disconnect the red and white wires from the module.
3. Connect an ohmmeter, a bulb and a 12 volt battery as shown in the illustration.
4. Set the ohmmeter to the 1-10 ohm range.
5. Touch the negative probe to the red wire terminal and the positive probe to the white wire terminal.

➡ **Do not connect the ohmmeter in reverse as this will damage the module.**

6. If the bulb is illuminated, the module is good.

Adjustments

PICK-UP COIL AIR GAP ADJUSTMENT

▶ **See Figure 19**

1. Remove the distributor cap and rotor.
2. Using a nonmagnetic thickness gauge, measure the air gap between the pole piece tooth and pick-up coil.
3. Air gap should be 0.009-0.015 in. (0.2-0.4 mm). If the gap is out of specification, adjust it.
4. Remove the module and loosen the screws securing pick-up coil. Using a screw driver, move the generator pick-up coil and adjust the gap to specification.
5. After adjustment tighten screws and recheck gap. Install module, rotor and distributor cap.

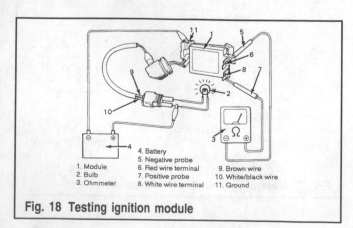

1. Module	
2. Bulb	
3. Ohmmeter	
4. Battery	
5. Negative probe	
6. Red wire terminal	
7. Positive probe	9. Brown wire
8. White wire terminal	10. White/black wire
	11. Ground

Fig. 18 Testing ignition module

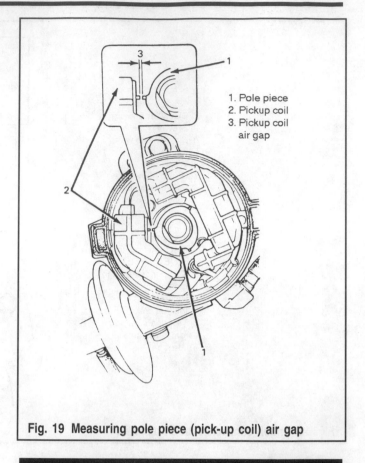

1. Pole piece
2. Pickup coil
3. Pickup coil air gap

Fig. 19 Measuring pole piece (pick-up coil) air gap

Component Replacement

IGNITION COIL REPLACEMENT

1. Disconnect the negative battery cable.
2. Remove the coil wire from the coil by gripping the boot firmly. Turn the boot ½ turn while removing the coil wire.
3. Remove the coil cap by turning clockwise and pushing forward. Remove the coil electrical connector.
4. Remove the the coil by loosening the clamp screw.
To install:
5. Install the coil into the clamp and tighten the clamp screw securely.
6. Install the coil electrical connector.
7. Install the coil wire by pressing the boot on firmly.
8. Connect the negative battery cable.

DISTRIBUTOR REPLACEMENT

▶ **See Figure 20**

1. Disconnect the negative battery cable.
2. Disconnect the wiring harness at the distributor and the vacuum line at the distributor vacuum advance unit.
3. Remove the distributor cap.

➡ **Mark the distributor body in reference to where the rotor is pointing. Mark the distributor hold-down bracket and cylinder head for a reinstallation location point.**

4. Remove the hold-down bolt and the distributor from the cylinder head. Do not rotate the engine after the distributor has been removed.

To install:

5. If the engine was not rotated proceed as follows:

a. Align the reference marks on the distributor housing to the distributor hold-down bracket.

b. Install the distributor into the offset slot in the camshaft, then the hold-down bolt.

c. Connect vacuum hoses and electrical connectors to the distributor.

d. Install the distributor cap, then connect the battery negative cable. Check and/or adjust the ignition timing.

6. If the engine was rotated while the distributor was removed, place the engine on TDC of the compression stroke to obtain the proper ignition timing.

a. Remove the No. 1 spark plug.

b. Place thumb over the spark plug hole. Crank the engine slowly until compression is felt. It will be easier to have someone rotate the engine by hand, using a wrench on the crankshaft pulley.

c. Align the timing mark on the crankshaft pulley with the **0** degrees mark on the timing scale attached to the front of the engine. This places the engine at TDC of the compression stroke.

d. Turn the distributor shaft until the rotor points to the No. 1 spark plug tower on the cap.

e. Install the distributor into the engine. Be sure to align the distributor-to-engine block mark made earlier.

f. Install the No. 1 spark plug. Connect all vacuum hoses and electrical connectors to the distributor.

g. Install distributor cap, then connect the battery negative cable.

h. Check and/or adjust ignition timing.

PICK-UP COIL REPLACEMENT

▶ **See Figures 21, 22 and 23**

Except Electronic Ignition With Knock Control

1. Disconnect the negative battery cable.

2. Remove the distributor and place it in a suitable holding device.

3. Remove the distributor cap if not already removed.

4. Remove the rotor by pulling upward with a twist.

5. Remove the pick-up coil and module dust covers.

6. Disconnect the wires from the pick-up coil.

7. Remove the pick-up coil attaching screws.

8. Remove the pick-up coil.

To install:

9. Install the pick-up coil. Adjust the pole piece air gap to specification and tighten the attaching screws to 44 inch lbs. (5 Nm).

10. Connect the pick-up coil wires.

11. Install the dust covers.

12. Install the rotor

13. Install the distributor cap.

14. Install the distributor.

15. Connect the negative battery cable.

16. Start the engine and adjust the ignition timing to specification.

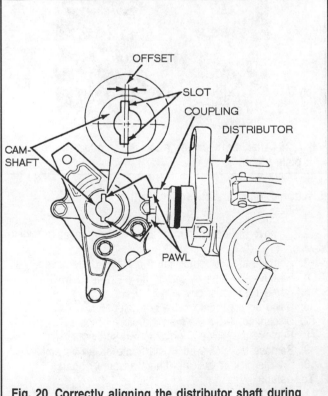

Fig. 20 Correctly aligning the distributor shaft during installation.

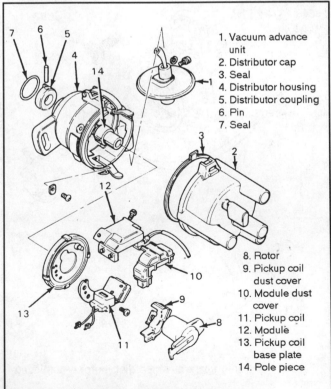

Fig. 21 Conventional spark control distributor — exploded view

1. Vacuum advance unit
2. Distributor cap
3. Seal
4. Distributor housing
5. Distributor coupling
6. Pin
7. Seal
8. Rotor
9. Pickup coil dust cover
10. Module dust cover
11. Pickup coil
12. Module
13. Pickup coil base plate
14. Pole piece

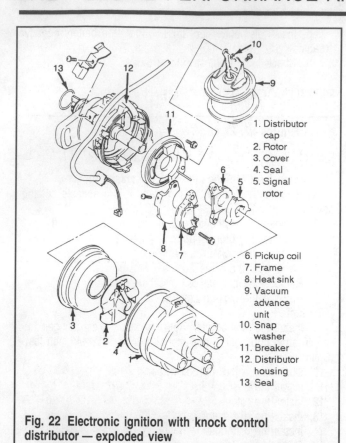

1. Distributor cap
2. Rotor
3. Cover
4. Seal
5. Signal rotor
6. Pickup coil
7. Frame
8. Heat sink
9. Vacuum advance unit
10. Snap washer
11. Breaker
12. Distributor housing
13. Seal

Fig. 22 Electronic ignition with knock control distributor — exploded view

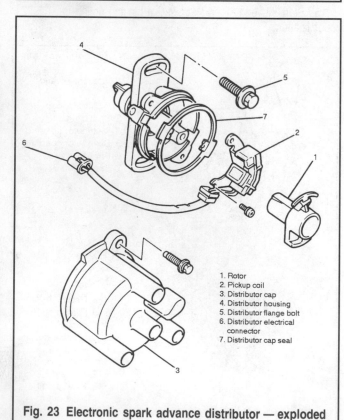

1. Rotor
2. Pickup coil
3. Distributor cap
4. Distributor housing
5. Distributor flange bolt
6. Distributor electrical connector
7. Distributor cap seal

Fig. 23 Electronic spark advance distributor — exploded view

Fig. 24 Loosening the distributor cap attaching screws

Fig. 25 Carefully remove the distributor cap taking care not to stretch the ignition wires or damage the rotor

Fig. 26 After the distributor cap is removed the rotor is in plain sight

Electronic Ignition With Knock Control

1. Disconnect the negative battery cable.
2. Remove the distributor and place it in a suitable holding device.
3. Remove the distributor cap if not already removed.
4. Remove the rotor by pulling upward with a twist.
5. Remove the dust cover.
6. Using a puller remove the pole piece.
7. Disconnect the wires from the pick-up coil.
8. Remove the pick-up coil attaching screws.
9. Remove the pick-up coil and frame as an assembly.
10. Pry the pick-up coil and frame assembly apart.

To install:

11. Joint the pick-up coil and frame assemblies and install.

12. Install the pick-up coil. Adjust the pole piece air gap and tighten the pick-up coil attaching screws to 44 inch lbs. (5 Nm).

13. Connect the pick-up coil wires.

14. Install the pole piece using an appropriate driver.

15. Install the dust cover. Install the rotor

16. Install the distributor cap.

17. Install the distributor.

18. Connect the negative battery cable.

19. Start the engine and adjust the ignition timing to specification.

CAP AND ROTOR REPLACEMENT

▶ **See Figures 24, 25, 26, 27 and 28**

1. Disconnect the negative battery cable.

2. Disconnect the ignition coil high tension wire at the coil.

3. Loosen and remove the 2 distributor cap attaching screws.

4. Carefully remove the distributor cap. Take care not to stretch the high tension spark plug cables or damage the rotor.

5. Remove the rotor by pulling with a slight twist.

To install:

6. Inspect the condition of the distributor cap. If the cap shows signs of cracks, broken pieces, carbon tracking, charred or eroded terminals, or a worn or damaged rotor button, replace it.

Fig. 27 The rotor is removed by pulling with a slight twist

7. Inspect the condition of the distributor rotor. If the rotor shows signs of cracks, broken pieces, a charred or eroded tip, physical contact of the tip with the cap or insufficient spring tension, replace it.

8. Apply a light coating of dielectric grease to the distributor cap terminals and rotor tip.

9. Install the rotor by aligning the flat on the rotor and shaft. Push the rotor until it bottoms on the shaft.

10. Check the condition of the distributor cap gasket and replace as necessary.

11. Install the distributor cap and tighten the attaching screws securely.

12. Reinstall the coil high tension wire at the coil.

IGNITION MODULE REPLACEMENT

▶ **See Figure 21**

Conventional Spark Control Ignition

1. Disconnect the negative battery cable.

2. Remove the distributor and place it in a suitable holding device.

3. Remove the distributor cap if not already removed.

4. Remove the rotor by pulling upward with a twist.

5. Remove the pick-up coil and module dust covers.

6. Disconnect the wires from the ignition module.

7. Remove the module attaching screws from the outside of the distributor housing.

8. Remove the ignition module.

To install:

9. Install the ignition module. As necessary, adjust the pole piece air gap to specification and tighten the attaching screws to 44 inch lbs. (5 Nm).

10. Connect the ignition module wires.

11. Install the dust covers.

12. Install the rotor

13. Install the distributor cap.

14. Install the distributor.

15. Connect the negative battery cable.

16. Start the engine and adjust the ignition timing to specification.

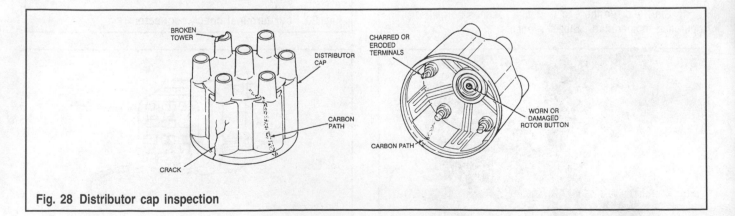

Fig. 28 Distributor cap inspection

IGNITION TIMING

Service Precautions

When connecting the tachometer in the following procedures, be sure not to ground the tachometer terminal. Grounding the tachometer could result in damage to the igniter or ignition coil.

Be sure that the tachometer being used is compatible with the ignition system before installation. Incompatible equipment installation could cause damage to the ignition system.

Before setting timing, make sure the headlights, heater fan, engine cooling fan and any other electrical equipment is turned off. If any current drawing systems are operating, the idle up system, if equipped, will operate and cause the idle speed to be higher than normal.

Timing

INSPECTION AND ADJUSTMENT

Sprint

▶ **See Figure 29**

1. Start and run the engine until it reaches normal operating temperature. Stop the engine.

2. Connect a tachometer to the negative terminal of the ignition coil. Connect a timing light to the No. 1 spark plug wire. Refer to the underhood sticker.

3. Check and/or adjust the idle speed to specification.

4. Aim the timing light at the timing marks and check the timing.

5. To adjust the ignition timing, loosen the distributor hold-down bolt and rotate the distributor until the correct timing marks are aligned.

6. Tighten the distributor hold-down bolt to 11 ft. lbs. (15 Nm) and recheck the timing.

Metro

CONVENTIONAL SPARK CONTROL IGNITION

1. Start and run the engine until it reaches normal operating temperature. Stop the engine.

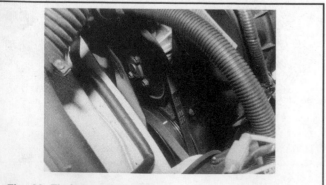

Fig. 29 Timing mark location

2. Connect a tachometer to the negative terminal of the ignition coil. Connect a timing light to the No. 1 spark plug wire. Refer to the underhood sticker.

3. Check and/or adjust the idle speed to specification.

4. Disconnect the vacuum line at the intake manifold gas filter and plug the gas filter.

5. Aim the timing light at the timing marks and check the timing.

6. To adjust the ignition timing, loosen the distributor hold-down bolt and rotate the distributor until the correct timing marks are aligned.

7. Tighten the distributor hold-down bolt to 11 ft. lbs. (15 Nm) and recheck the timing.

8. Reconnect the vacuum line at the gas filter. The timing should advance. If not, check for a vacuum leak or check the vacuum centrifugal advance mechanism for proper operation.

ELECTRONIC SPARK CONTROL (ESC) IGNITION

▶ **See Figures 30 and 31**

1. Start and run the engine until it reaches normal operating temperature. Stop the engine.

2. Connect a tachometer to the negative terminal of the ignition coil. Connect a timing light to the No. 1 spark plug wire. Refer to the underhood sticker.

3. Check and/or adjust the idle speed to specification.

4. On vehicles equipped with the electronic spark control (ESC) ignition, remove the diagnostic check connector, located

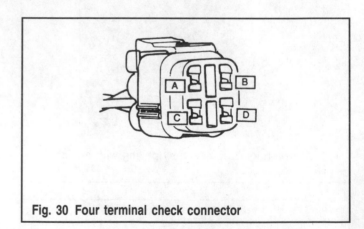

Fig. 30 Four terminal check connector

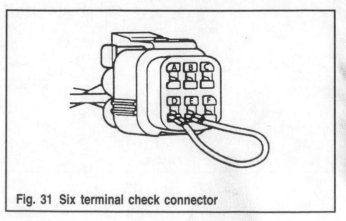

Fig. 31 Six terminal check connector

next to the ignition coil, and insert a fused jumper wire between appropriate terminals.

    a. With a 4 terminal connector, hold the connector with the locking tab at the top and jumper the lower two terminals (C and D).

    b. With a 6 terminal connector, hold the connector with the locking tab at the top and jumper the two terminals at the lower left (D and E).

    5. Aim the timing light at the timing marks and check the timing.

6. To adjust the ignition timing, loosen the distributor hold-down bolt and rotate the distributor until the correct timing marks are aligned.

7. Tighten the distributor hold-down bolt to 11 ft. lbs. (15 Nm) and recheck the timing.

8. Remove the diagnostic check connector jumper. Remove the timing light and tachometer.

VALVE LASH

Valve Lash

INSPECTION AND ADJUSTMENT

▶ **See Figures 32 and 33**

Sprint

➡**Always check the valve lash with the engine cold.**

1. Remove the air cleaner and cylinder head cover.
2. Rotate crankshaft clockwise and align timing notch on crankshaft pulley with the **0** mark on the timing tab.
3. Remove the distributor cap and check if the rotor is positioned correctly (pointing toward the No. 1 cylinder terminal on the cap).

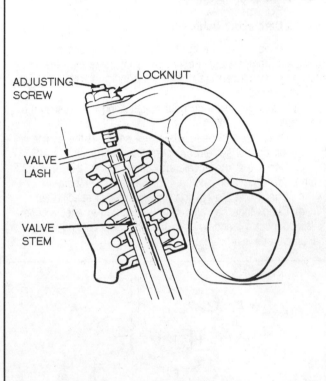

Fig. 33 Slide the thickness gauge between the adjusting screw and the valve tip. It should be a snug fit.

4. If the engine is not positioned correctly, rotate 360 degrees and align the timing notch with the **0** mark again.
5. Using a thickness gauge, check the intake and exhaust valve of the No. 1 cylinder. Slide the gauge between the adjusting screw and the valve tip. It should be a snug fit.
6. If the valve lash is out of specification, adjust it by loosening the locknut and turning the adjusting screw. Tighten the locknut to 11-13 ft. lbs. (15-19 Nm).
7. Rotate the engine 240 degrees and align the timing notch on the pulley with the left attaching bolt of the timing belt outside cover. Check and adjust the valve lash for No. 3 cylinder.
8. Rotate the engine 240 degrees and align the timing notch on the pulley with the right attaching bolt of the timing belt outside cover. Check and adjust the valve lash for No. 2 cylinder.

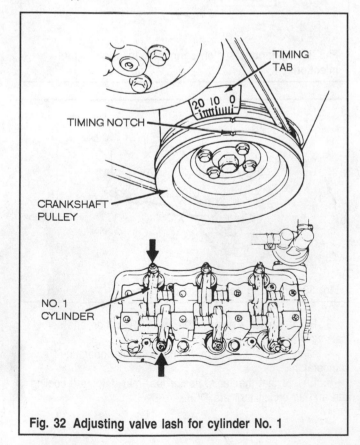

Fig. 32 Adjusting valve lash for cylinder No. 1

9. Install the distributor cap, cylinder head cover and air cleaner. Tighten the cylinder head cover bolts to 48 inch lbs. (5 Nm).

Metro

The Metro engine is equipped hydraulic valve lash adjusters which require no adjustment. If a tapping noise is noticed at idle, inspect the valve train components for excessive wear.

IDLE SPEED AND MIXTURE

Idle Speed

ADJUSTMENT

♦ See Figures 34, 35, 36, 37 and 38

1985-88 Carbureted Vehicles

The cooling fan runs and stops automatically according to the coolant temperature. For this reason, make sure that the cooling fan is not running before performing idle speed check and adjustment.

1. Confirm the following prior to checking or adjusting the idle speed.

   a. Check that the lead wires and hoses of the engine emission control system are connected correctly.

   b. Check that the accelerator cable has 0.12-0.20 in. (3-5 mm) free-play when engine is at operating temperature.

   c. Check that the ignition timing is within specification.

   d. Check that the valve lash is adjusted to specification.

2. Connect a tachometer to the engine according to the manufacturer's instructions.

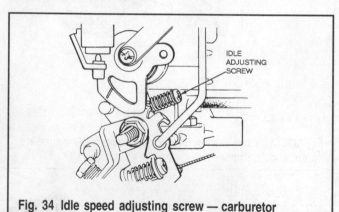

Fig. 34 Idle speed adjusting screw — carburetor

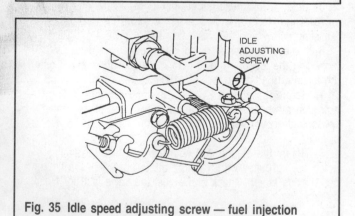

Fig. 35 Idle speed adjusting screw — fuel injection

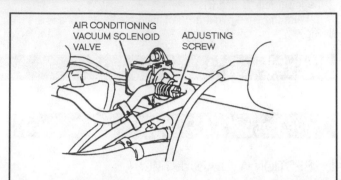

Fig. 36 Air conditioning vacuum solenoid valve adjusting screw — fuel injection

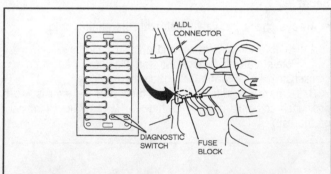

Fig. 37 Diagnostic switch connector location — fuel injection

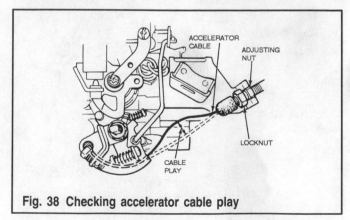

Fig. 38 Checking accelerator cable play

3. Place transaxle gear shift lever in **N** position and set parking brake.

4. Start engine and warm engine to normal operating temperature.

5. Ensure that the lights, heater fan, rear defogger, cooling fan and air conditioner are **OFF**.

6. Check the idle speed. If not within specifications, adjust by turning the idle adjusting screw on the carburetor.

7. If idle speed can not be adjusted to specification by turning the adjusting screw, it can be due to a faulty return of the throttle valve or some other mechanical reason. Determine the cause and repair.

8. After idle adjustment, check idle-up system for proper operation.

9. Stop engine and check to ensure that accelerator cable has some play. If not, adjust cable.

1987-93 Fuel Injected Vehicles

1. Confirm the following prior to checking or adjusting the idle speed.

   a. Check that the lead wires and hoses of the engine emission control system are connected correctly.

   b. Check that the accelerator cable has 0.12-0.20 in. (3-5 mm) free-play when engine is at operating temperature.

   c. Check that the ignition timing is within specification.

2. Place automatic transaxle gear shift lever in **P** position or manual transaxle gear shift lever in **NEUTRAL** position and set parking brake.

3. Ensure that the lights, heater fan, rear defogger, cooling fan and air conditioner are **OFF**.

4. Ensure that air cleaner is installed correctly.

5. Connect a tachometer according to the manufacturer's instructions.

6. Remove cover on idle speed adjusting screw.

7. Start engine and warm engine to normal operating temperature.

8. Install a spare fuse into the **DIAG SW** connector in the fuse block under the left side of the dash.

9. Check and adjust idle speed to specification. Turn idle speed screw in to decrease idle and out to increase idle.

10. If equipped with air conditioning, check and adjust the air conditioner idle speed vacuum solenoid valve.

11. With idle speed correct, turn air conditioner **ON**.

12. Check that engine idle is within specification or slightly higher. If not, adjust air conditioner vacuum solenoid valve adjusting screw to obtain correct idle.

13. Turn air conditioner **OFF** and check that idle speed is within specifications.

➡**On some vehicles, a slightly higher idle setting on the vacuum solenoid valve may be needed to maintain proper idle characteristics with the air conditioning system operating.**

14. After adjusting idle speed remove the spare fuse from the connector.

Idle-Up System

ADJUSTMENT

▸ **See Figure 39**

1985-88 Carbureted Vehicles

The cooling fan runs and stops automatically according to the coolant temperature. For this reason, make sure that the

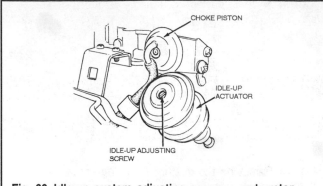

Fig. 39 Idle-up system adjusting screw — carburetor

cooling fan is not running before performing idle-up system check and adjustment.

MANUAL TRANSAXLE

1. Start the engine and allow it to reach operating temperature.

2. Run the engine at idle and check to see that the idle-up screw moves when the lights are turned **ON**.

3. Ensure that the heater fan, rear defogger, engine cooling fan and air conditioner are all **OFF**.

4. Turn the lights **ON** and check that the idle speed is within specification or slightly higher. If not, adjust by turning the adjusting screw on the back of the idle-up solenoid.

5. After adjustment, repeat Step 2 and check for idle-up screw movement.

AUTOMATIC TRANSAXLE

1. Start the engine and allow it to reach operating temperature.

2. Run the engine at idle, apply the parking brake and block drive wheels.

3. Ensure that the heater fan, rear defogger, engine cooling fan and air conditioner are all **OFF**.

4. With the brake pedal depressed, shift drive selector lever into **D** and check to see that the idle-up screw moves down.

5. Check that the idle speed is within specification or slightly higher. If not, adjust by turning the adjusting screw on the back of the idle-up solenoid.

6. After adjustment, repeat Step 4 and check for idle-up screw movement.

Idle Mixture

ADJUSTMENT

▸ **See Figures 40 and 41**

1985-88 Carbureted Vehicles

The carburetor has been calibrated at the factory and should not normally need adjustment. For this reason, the mixture adjustment should never be changed from original factory setting. However if during diagnosis, the check indicates the carburetor to be the cause of a performance complaint or

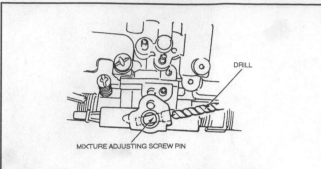

Fig. 40 Removing the mixture adjusting screw pin — carburetor

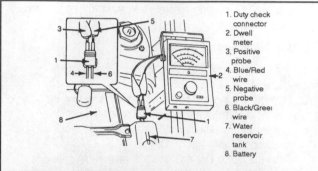

1. Duty check connector
2. Dwell meter
3. Positive probe
4. Blue/Red wire
5. Negative probe
6. Black/Green wire
7. Water reservoir tank
8. Battery

Fig. 41 Connecting dwell meter to duty check connector — carburetor

emission failure, or if the carburetor is being overhauled, the idle mixture can be adjusted using the following procedure.

1. Confirm the following prior to checking or adjusting the idle speed.

   a. Check that the lead wires and hoses of the engine emission control system are connected correctly.

   b. Check that the accelerator cable has some play.

   c. Check that the ignition timing is within specification.

   d. Check that the valve lash is adjusted to specification.

   e. Check that the idle-up actuator does not operate.

   f. Check that the cooling fan is not operating.

2. If not already done, remove the carburetor from the intake manifold and remove the mixture adjusting screw cover pin. This can be done by drilling the pin out using a 4-4.5 mm drill bit, then using a punch to remove the pin. Reinstall the carburetor and air cleaner.

3. Place gear shift lever in **N** position, set the parking brake and block the drive wheels.

4. Start the engine and allow it to reach operating temperature.

5. Remove the coupler on the duty check connector located in the engine compartment. Connect a dwell meter to the connector with the positive probe on the blue/red wire and the negative probe on the black/green wire.

6. Set dwell meter to 6-cylinder position and make sure indicator moves.

7. Check idle speed and adjust to specification as necessary.

8. Run engine at idle speed and adjust mixture adjusting screw slowly, in small increments, allowing time for dwell to stabilize. Adjust until a dwell of 21-27° is obtained.

9. If dwell is too high, back screw out. If dwell is too low, turn screw in.

10. Recheck idle speed and adjust as necessary.

11. If adjustment can not be made because dwell meter indicator does not deflect, check the feedback system for proper operation.

12. Install a new mixture adjusting screw pin.

1987-93 Fuel Injected Vehicles

The function of the electronic fuel injection system is to deliver the correct amount of fuel to the engine under all operating conditions. Fuel delivery is controlled by the engine control module (ECM) and can not be adjusted. If a fuel delivery problem is indicated, individual component inspection and electronic control system diagnosis must be performed to determine the proper corrective action.

TORQUE SPECIFICATIONS

Component	U.S.	Metric
Coil Pick-up Attaching bolt	44 inch lbs.	5 Nm
Cylinder Head Cover Attaching Bolt	48 inch lbs.	5 Nm
Distributor Hold down bolt	11 ft. lbs.	15 Nm
Rocker Arm Locknut	11-13 ft. lbs.	15-19 Nm
Spark Plug	21 ft. lbs.	20 Nm

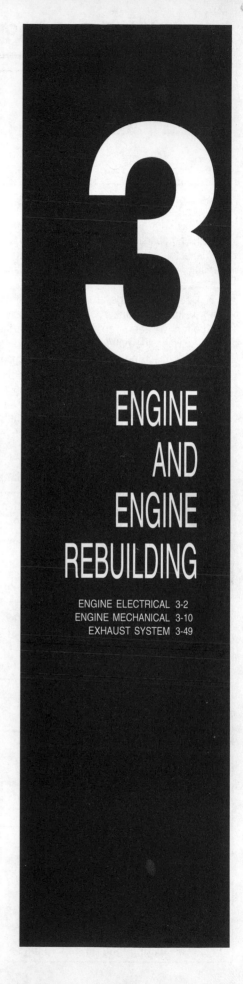

3

ENGINE AND ENGINE REBUILDING

ENGINE ELECTRICAL

Ignition Coil

TESTING

▶ **See Figures 1 and 2**

1. Check for spark at each spark plug with a spark plug tester. If no spark is detected, proceed to Step 2. If spark is only detected on some spark plugs, check for a faulty distributor cap or rotor. Also check the spark plugs and wires. Replace as needed.

2. Check for voltage at the ignition coil positive terminal with a voltmeter. If battery voltage is detected, proceed to Step 3. If battery voltage is not detected, repair the open in the wiring between the battery and the ignition coil.

3. Disconnect the connector on the negative coil wire. Check ignition coil resistance. If resistance is within specification, proceed to Step 4. If resistance is not within specification, replace the coil.

   a. Measure the resistance between the positive and negative terminals. Resistance should be 1.08-1.32 ohms for electronic ignition with knock control and 1.33-1.55 ohms for all others.

   b. Measure the resistance between the positive/negative terminals and the coil high tension wire terminal. Resistance should be 11.6-15.8 kilo-ohms for electronic ignition with knock control and 10.7-14.5 kilo-ohms for all others.

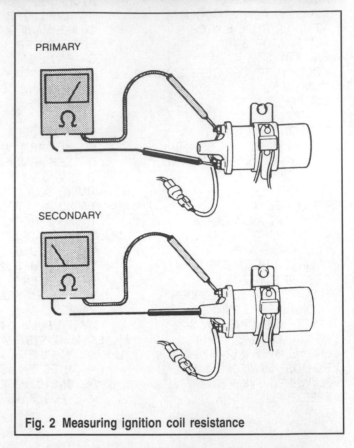

Fig. 2 Measuring ignition coil resistance

4. On Conventional and ESC ignitions, check the resistance of the noise filter and condenser with an ohmmeter. If the resistance is 2.0-2.5 ohms for both units, proceed to Step 5. If the resistance is not within specification, replace both units as a set.

5. On Conventional ignitions, check the continuity of the brown/white wire between the ignition coil negative terminal and the distributor. If continuity exists, replace the pickup coil and igniter. If continuity does not exist, repair the open in the wire.

REMOVAL & INSTALLATION

▶ **See Figure 3**

1. Disconnect the negative battery cable.

2. Remove the coil wire from the coil by gripping the boot firmly. Turn the boot ½ turn while removing the coil wire.

3. Remove the coil cap by turning clockwise and pushing forward. Remove the coil electrical connector.

4. Remove the the coil by loosening the clamp screw.

To install:

5. Install the coil into the clamp and tighten the clamp screw securely.

6. Install the coil electrical connector.

7. Install the coil wire by pressing the boot on firmly.

8. Connect the negative battery cable.

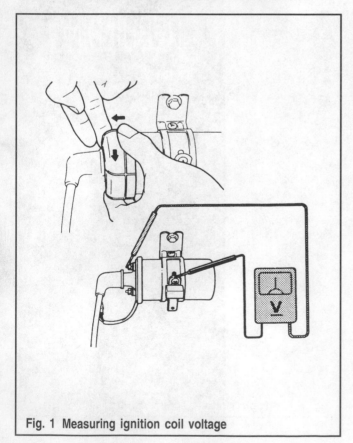

Fig. 1 Measuring ignition coil voltage

Fig. 3 Ignition coil location

Ignition Module

TESTING

Conventional Spark Control Ignition

1. Remove the dust cover from the module.
2. Disconnect the red and white wires from the module.
3. Connect an ohmmeter, a bulb and a 12 volt battery as shown in the illustration.
4. Set the ohmmeter to the 1-10 ohm range.
5. Touch the negative probe to the red wire terminal and the positive probe to the white wire terminal.

➡**Do not connect the ohmmeter in reverse as this will damage the module.**

6. If the bulb is illuminated, the module is assumed good.

REMOVAL & INSTALLATION

1. Disconnect the negative battery cable.
2. Remove the distributor and place it in a suitable holding device.
3. Remove the distributor cap if not already removed.
4. Remove the rotor by pulling upward with a twist.
5. Remove the pickup coil and module dust covers.
6. Disconnect the wires from the ignition module.
7. Remove the module attaching screws from the outside of the distributor housing.
8. Remove the ignition module.
To install:
9. Install the ignition module. As necessary, adjust the pole piece air gap to specification and tighten the attaching screws to 44 inch lbs.. (5 Nm).
10. Connect the ignition module wires.
11. Install the dust covers.
12. Install the rotor
13. Install the distributor cap.
14. Install the distributor.
15. Connect the negative battery cable.
16. Start the engine and adjust the ignition timing to specification.

Distributor

REMOVAL & INSTALLATION

▶ **See Figures 4 and 5**

1. Disconnect the negative battery cable.
2. Disconnect the wiring harness at the distributor and the vacuum line at the distributor vacuum advance unit.
3. Remove the distributor cap.

➡**Mark the distributor body in reference to where the rotor is pointing. Mark the distributor hold-down bracket and cylinder head for a reinstallation location point.**

4. Remove the hold-down bolt and the distributor from the cylinder head. Do not rotate the engine after the distributor has been removed.
To install:
5. If the engine was not rotated proceed as follows:
   a. Align the reference marks on the distributor housing to the distributor hold-down bracket.
   b. Install the distributor into the offset slot in the camshaft, then the hold-down bolt.
   c. Connect vacuum hoses and electrical connectors to the distributor.
   d. Install the distributor cap, then connect the battery negative cable. Check and/or adjust the ignition timing.

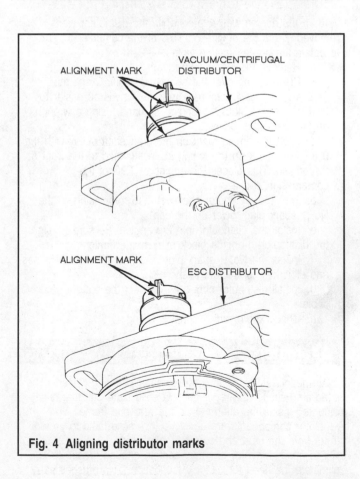

Fig. 4 Aligning distributor marks

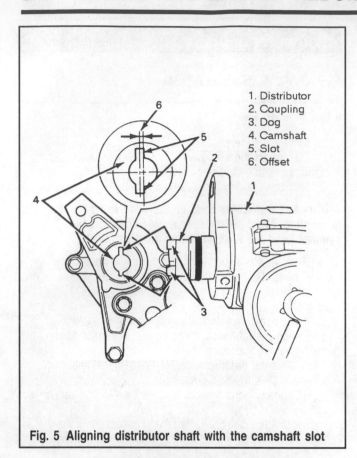

1. Distributor
2. Coupling
3. Dog
4. Camshaft
5. Slot
6. Offset

Fig. 5 Aligning distributor shaft with the camshaft slot

6. If the engine was rotated while the distributor was removed, place the engine on TDC of the compression stroke to obtain the proper ignition timing.

a. Remove the No. 1 spark plug.

b. Place thumb over the spark plug hole. Crank the engine slowly until compression is felt. It will be easier to have someone rotate the engine by hand, using a wrench on the crankshaft pulley.

c. Align the timing mark on the crankshaft pulley with the **0** degrees mark on the timing scale attached to the front of the engine. This places the engine at TDC of the compression stroke.

d. Turn the distributor shaft until the rotor points to the No. 1 spark plug tower on the cap.

e. Install the distributor into the engine. Be sure to align the distributor-to-engine block mark made earlier.

f. Install the No. 1 spark plug. Connect all vacuum hoses and electrical connectors to the distributor.

g. Install distributor cap, then connect the battery negative cable.

h. Check and/or adjust ignition timing.

Alternator

All models utilize an integral regulator charging system. The integrated circuit (IC) regulator is a solid state unit that is mounted inside the alternator to the rear end frame. All regulator components are enclosed in a solid mold to protect them from the heat and corrosive elements.

The alternator rotor bearings contain enough grease to eliminate the need for periodic lubrication. Two brushes carry current through two slip rings to the field coil, mounted on the rotor. Under normal conditions, this arrangement is capable of providing long periods for attention-free service.

Stator windings are assembled inside a laminated core that forms part of the alternator drive end frame. A rectifier bridge, that contains six diodes, is connected to the stator windings. These diodes electrically change stator AC voltage into DC voltage. The DC voltage is then transmitted to the alternator output terminal.

Two neutral diodes are utilized to smooth out voltage fluctuations caused by varying alternator speeds. A capacitor (condenser), mounted in the regulator, protects the rectifier bridge and neutral diodes. This capacitor also suppresses radio interference noise.

ALTERNATOR PRECAUTIONS

To prevent damage to the on-board computer, alternator and regulator, the following precautionary measures must be taken when working with the electrical system.

• Never reverse the battery connections. Always check the battery polarity visually. This is to be done before any connections are made to be sure that all of the connections correspond to the battery ground polarity.

• Booster batteries for starting must be connected properly. Make sure that the positive cable of the booster battery is connected to the positive terminal of the battery that is getting the boost. This applies to both negative and ground cables.

• Make sure the ignition switch is OFF when connecting or disconnecting any electrical component, especially on trucks equipped with an on-board computer control system.

• Disconnect the battery cables before using a fast charger; the charger has a tendency to force current through the diodes in the opposite direction for which they were designed. This burns out the diodes.

• Never use a fast charger as a booster for starting the vehicle.

• Never disconnect the voltage regulator while the engine is running.

• Do not ground the alternator output terminal.

• Do not attempt to polarize an alternator.

REMOVAL & INSTALLATION

▶ See Figures 6 and 7

1. Disconnect the negative battery cable.

2. Remove other components as necessary to gain access to the alternator.

3. Label and disconnect the alternator's electrical connectors.

4. Remove the alternator brace bolt and the drive belt.

5. Support the alternator while removing the mounting bolts, then remove the alternator.

To install:

6. Install the alternator and loosely tighten the mounting bolts.

7. Install the drive belt and tension to obtain a deflection of ¼ inch on the longest span of the belt.

8. Tighten the alternator drive belt adjuster bolt to 17 ft. lbs.. (23 Nm).

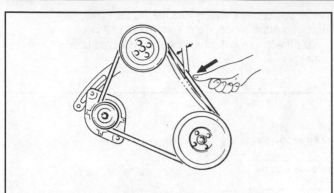

Fig. 6 Adjusting alternator drive belt tension

Fig. 7 The alternator is located next to the water pump at the front of the engine

9. Reconnect the electrical connector and tighten nut to 71 inch lbs.. (8 Nm).

10. Connect the negative battery cable.

Battery

The battery is the first link in the chain of mechanisms which work together to provide cranking of the engine. In most modern vehicles, the battery is a lead-acid electrochemical device consisting of six 2 volt (2V) subsections connected in series so the unit is capable of producing approximately 12V of electrical pressure.

Each subsection (cell) consists of a series of positive and negative plates held a short distance apart in a solution of sulfuric acid and water. The two types of plates are of dissimilar metals. A chemical reaction takes place which produces current flow from the battery, when it's positive and negative terminals are connected to an electrical appliance such as a lamp or motor. The continued transfer of electrons would eventually convert the sulfuric acid in the electrolyte to water and make the two plates identical in chemical composition.

As electrical energy is removed from the battery, it's voltage output tends to drop. Thus, measuring battery voltage and battery electrolyte composition are two ways of checking the ability of the unit to supply power. During the starting of the engine, electrical energy is removed from the battery. However, if the charging circuit is in good condition and the operating conditions are normal, the power removed from the battery will be replaced by the alternator which will force electrons back

into the battery, reversing the normal flow and restoring the battery to it's original chemical state.

Additional procedures covering basic testing and maintenance of the battery are covered in Section 1 of this manual.

REMOVAL & INSTALLATION

▶ **See Figure 8**

1. Disconnect the negative battery terminal, then the positive battery terminal.
2. Remove the battery hold-down retainer.
3. Remove the battery from the vehicle.

To install:

4. Inspect the battery, the cables and the battery carrier for damage.
5. Install the battery in the vehicle and tighten the battery hold down retainer to 71 inch lbs.. (8 Nm).
6. Install the negative batter cable, then the positive battery cable. Tighten terminal nuts to 11 ft. lbs.. (15 Nm).

Starter

Four types of starter motor are utilized depending upon the vehicle transaxle and assembly plant location. Manual transaxle equipped vehicles utilize a conventional starter motor which consists of a yoke, an armature assembly, an overrunning clutch assembly, a solenoid, a commutator end cover, a brush holder and a pinion drive lever. Automatic transaxle equipped vehicles utilize a reduction type starter motor which has, in addition to the components found on conventional starter motors, a reduction gear and shock absorber assembly.

In the basic circuit, the solenoid windings are energized when the ignition switch is turn to the **START** position and the clutch start/neutral safety switch is closed. The resulting plunger and shift lever movement causes the pinion to engage the engine flywheel ring gear. This movement also causes the starter solenoid contacts to close.

With the contacts closed, the starter solenoid provides a closed circuit between the battery positive terminal and the starter motor. Because the starter motor is permanently grounded to the engine block, the circuit is complete and cranking occurs as soon as the starter solenoid contacts are closed.

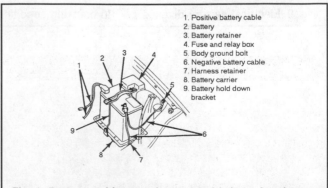

1. Positive battery cable
2. Battery
3. Battery retainer
4. Fuse and relay box
5. Body ground bolt
6. Negative battery cable
7. Harness retainer
8. Battery carrier
9. Battery hold down bracket

Fig. 8 Battery, cables, carrier and hold down brackets

When the engine starts, the pinion is designed to overrun and protect the armature from excessive speed until the ignition switch is released from the **START** position. With the ignition switch released, a return spring in the solenoid assembly forces the starter solenoid contacts open, breaks the circuit between the battery and the starter motor, and disengages the pinion. To prevent prolonged overrun, the ignition switch should be immediately released upon engine start-up.

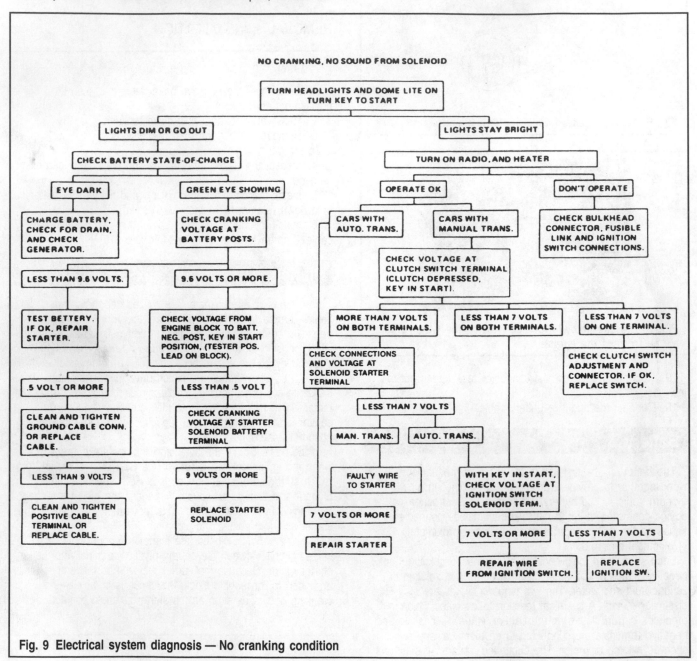

Fig. 9 Electrical system diagnosis — No cranking condition

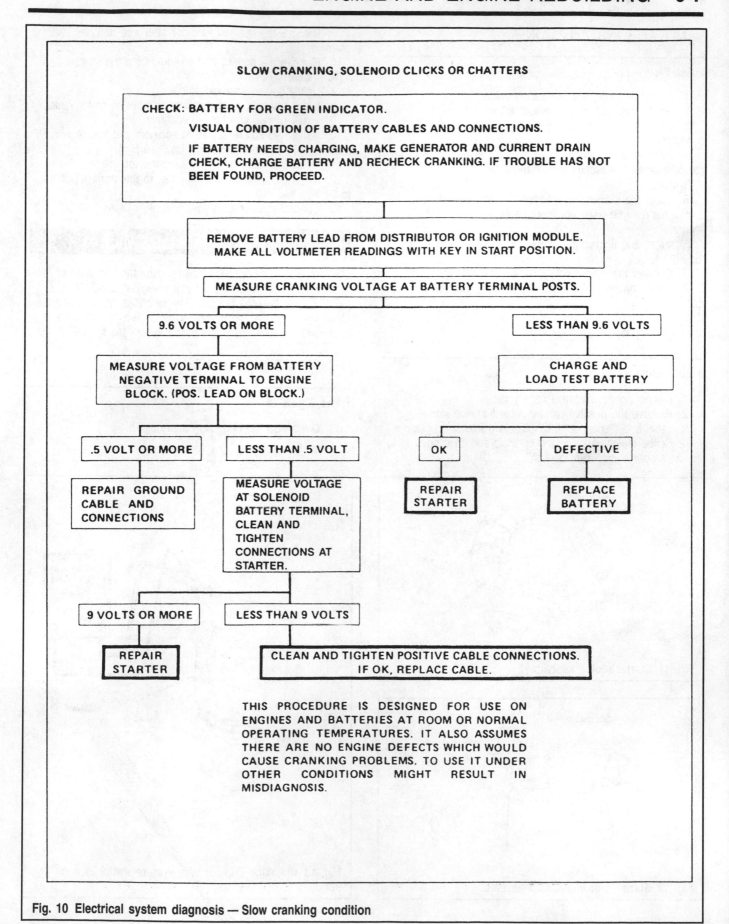

Fig. 10 Electrical system diagnosis — Slow cranking condition

REMOVAL & INSTALLATION

▶ **See Figure 11**

1. Disconnect the negative battery cable.
2. Raise and support the vehicle safely.
3. Label and disconnect the starter solenoid electrical connector.
4. Remove the mounting bolts from the starter motor, then carefully lower the assembly from the vehicle.

To install:

5. Install the starter motor assembly complete with any shims that may be used between the engine block and the starter.
6. Install and tighten the starter mounting bolts to 17 ft. lbs.. (23 Nm).
7. Connect the starter solenoid electrical connector.
8. Lower the vehicle and connect the negative battery cable.

SOLENOID REPLACEMENT

▶ **See Figure 12**

1. Disconnect the negative battery cable.
2. Remove the positive battery cable from the starter.
3. Label and disconnect the solenoid electrical connectors.
4. Scribe matchmarks on the solenoid and drive housing to ensure proper solenoid installation.

5. Remove the nut and field coil lead wire from the solenoid.
6. Remove the screws and solenoid from the starter.

To install:

7. Lightly grease solenoid plunger.
8. Install solenoid to starter aligning housing matchmarks.
9. Install screws and tighten securely.
10. Install field coil lead wire to solenoid and secure with retaining nut. Tighten to 89 inch lbs.. (10 Nm).
11. Install the solenoid electrical connector.
12. Install the positive battery cable. to the starter. Tighten to 89 inch lbs.. (10 Nm).
13. Connect the negative battery cable.

Radiator Fan Thermostat Switch

A temperature switch is used to control the operation of the radiator fan. The switch closes (continuity) at 208-215°F (98-102°C) to turn the fan ON. The switch is closed when the coolant temperature (no continuity) when the coolant temperature is 199-206°F (93-97°C) to turn the fan OFF.

REMOVAL & INSTALLATION

▶ **See Figure 13**

1. Disconnect the negative battery cable.

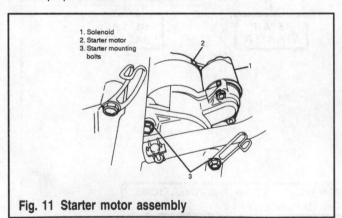

1. Solenoid
2. Starter motor
3. Starter mounting bolts

Fig. 11 Starter motor assembly

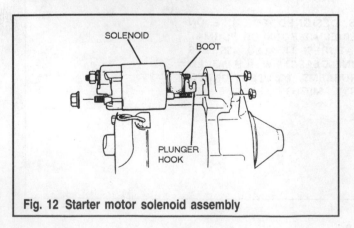

SOLENOID

BOOT

PLUNGER HOOK

Fig. 12 Starter motor solenoid assembly

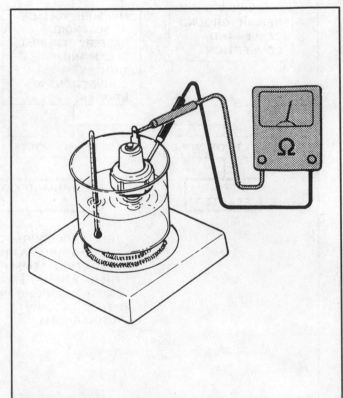

Fig. 13 Checking coolant temperature switches and senders

2. Drain the cooling system below the level of the thermostat housing.

3. Disconnect the radiator fan thermostat switch electrical connector.
4. Remove the switch from the thermostat housing.
To install:
5. Coat the thermostat switch with sealant and install in the thermostat housing.
6. Connect the radiator fan thermostat switch electrical connector.
7. Fill the cooling system.
8. Connect the negative battery cable.

Air Conditioning Coolant Temperature Switch

An engine coolant temperature switch is used to shut down air conditioning system when engine coolant reaches 226°F (108°C). Compressor operation will not be initiated until coolant temperature drops below the specified range. The switch is located on the left side of the throttle body below the air cleaner assembly.

REMOVAL & INSTALLATION

▶ **See Figure 13**

1. Disconnect the negative battery cable.
2. Drain the cooling system below the level of the thermostat housing.
3. Disconnect the air conditioning coolant temperature switch electrical connector.
4. Remove the switch from the thermostat housing.
To install:
5. Coat the thermostat switch with sealant and install in the thermostat housing.
6. Connect the air conditioning coolant temperature switch electrical connector.
7. Fill the cooling system.
8. Connect the negative battery cable.

Coolant Temperature Sending Unit

The coolant temperature sending unit is located in the thermostat housing next to the radiator fan thermostat switch. This unit activates the coolant temperature gage in the instrument cluster.

REMOVAL & INSTALLATION

▶ **See Figures 13 and 14**

1. Disconnect the negative battery cable.
2. Drain the cooling system below the level of the thermostat housing.
3. Disconnect the coolant temperature sending unit electrical connector.
4. Remove the sending unit from the thermostat housing.
To install:
5. Coat the sending unit with sealant and install in the thermostat housing.
6. Connect the coolant temperature sending unit electrical connector.
7. Fill the cooling system.
8. Connect the negative battery cable.

Oil Pressure Switch

REMOVAL & INSTALLATION

▶ **See Figure 15**

1. Disconnect the negative battery cable.
2. Drain the engine oil
3. Disconnect the oil pressure switch electrical connector.
4. Remove the switch from the cylinder block.

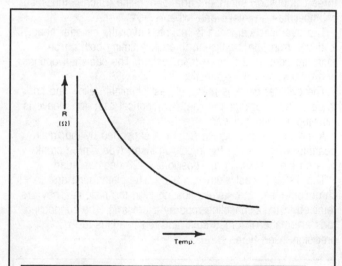

Temperature	Resistance
50°C (122° F)	133.9 〜 178.9 Ω
80°C (176° F)	47.5 〜 56.8 Ω
100°C (212° F)	26.2 〜 29.3 Ω

Fig. 14 Coolant temperature sender resistance values

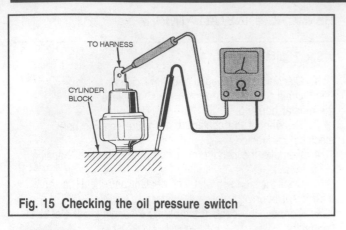

Fig. 15 Checking the oil pressure switch

6. Connect the oil pressure switch electrical connector.
7. Fill the engine with oil.
8. Connect the negative battery cable.

To install:

5. Coat the sending unit with sealant and install in the cylinder block

ENGINE MECHANICAL

Description

▶ **See Figure 16**

The engine is a water-cooled, in-line three cylinder, four stroke cycle gasoline unit with a direct acting type overhead camshaft (OHC) valve configuration.

The cylinder head is made of cast aluminum alloy and has three combustion chambers arranged in-line. Each combustion chamber has an intake and exhaust port.

The overhead camshaft is mounted over the cylinder head. It is driven from the crankshaft through a timing belt; no push rods are used in the valve train system. The camshaft opens and closes the valves directly.

The cylinder block is made of cast aluminum alloy and has three cylinder arranged in-line. A cylindrical cast iron sleeve is installed in each cylinder.

A monoblock casting crankshaft is supported by four main bearings which are of the precision insert type. Three crank pins on the crankshaft are positioned 120 degrees apart.

The piston is cast aluminum alloy. The piston pins are chromium steel and have a floating fit in the pistons. They are retained in the connecting rods by a press fit. The connecting rods are made of forged steel and rod bearings are of precision insert type.

Fig. 16 Overall view of the engine compartment

Engine Overhaul Tips

Most engine overhaul procedures are fairly standard. In addition to specific parts replacement procedures and complete specifications for your individual engine, this Section also is a guide to acceptable rebuilding procedures. Examples of standard rebuilding practice are shown and should be used along with specific details concerning your particular engine.

The choice of a competent, reliable machinist is one of the most important decisions faced by the home mechanic. In most instances it is more profitable for the home mechanic to remove, clean and inspect components, buy the necessary parts and deliver these to a shop for actual machine work. Competent and accurate machine shop services will ensure maximum performance, reliability and engine life. Choose your machinist carefully. If the engine is not machined properly, engine failure will result within a short time period after installation.

Disassembly, assembly, and the majority of inspection procedures presented in this Section are well within the scope of the home mechanic. By following the procedures outlined, the home mechanic will be able to save money, while providing him/her self with the gratification of a job well done.

TOOLS

The tools required for an engine overhaul or parts replacement will depend on the depth of your involvement. With a few exceptions, they will be the tools found in a mechanic's tool kit (see Section 1). More in-depth work will require any or all of the following:
- A dial indicator (reading in thousandths) mounted on a universal base
- Micrometers and telescope gauges
- Jaw and screw-type pullers
- Scraper
- Valve spring compressor
- Ring groove cleaner

- Piston ring expander and compressor
- Ridge reamer
- Cylinder hone or glaze breaker
- Plastigage®
- Engine stand

Use of most of these tools is illustrated in this Section. Many can be rented for a one-time use from a local parts jobber or tool supply house specializing in automotive work. However, the purchase of quality tools is never a bad decision.

Occasionally, the use of special tools is called for. See the information on Special Tools and Safety Notice in the front of this book before substituting another tool.

INSPECTION TECHNIQUES

Procedures and specifications are given in this Section for inspecting, cleaning and assessing the wear limits of most major components. Other procedures such as Magnaflux® and Zyglo® can be used to locate material flaws and stress cracks.

Magnaflux® is a magnetic process applicable only to ferrous materials. The component to be inspected is magnetized. Fine dust is sprinkled over the component and collects along the crack line. Careful inspection and an eye for problem areas are necessary qualities for a Magnaflux® technician.

The Zyglo® process coats the material with a fluorescent dye penetrant and can be used on any material. The dye is developed and then the component is placed under a black light. Cracks will show as bright lines. Careful inspection and an eye for problem areas are also necessary for this type of inspection.

PRECAUTIONS

- Never hot tank aluminum parts (the caustic hot tank solution will eat the aluminum.
- Remove all aluminum parts (identification tag, etc.) from engine parts prior to the tanking.
- Always coat threads lightly with engine oil or anti-seize compounds before installation, to prevent seizure.
- Never over-torque bolts or spark plugs especially in aluminum for you may strip the threads.
- When assembling the engine, any parts that will have frictional contact must be prelubed to provide lubrication at initial start-up. Any product specifically formulated for this purpose can be used, but engine oil is not recommended as a prelube.
- When semi-permanent (locked, but removable) installation of bolts or nuts is desired, threads should be cleaned and coated with Loctite® or equivalent non-hardening sealant.

REPAIRING DAMAGED THREADS

▶ **See Figures 17, 18, 19, 20 and 21**

Several methods of repairing damaged threads are available. Heli-Coil® (shown here), Keenserts® and Microdot® are among the most widely used. All involve basically the same principle — drilling out stripped threads, tapping the hole and

installing a pre-wound insert — making welding, plugging and oversize fasteners unnecessary.

Two types of thread repair inserts are usually supplied — a standard type for most Inch Coarse, Inch Fine, Metric Course and Metric Fine thread sizes and a spark lug type to fit most spark plug port sizes. Consult the individual manufacturer's catalog to determine exact applications.

Typical thread repair kits will contain a selection of pre-wound threaded inserts, a tap (corresponding to the outside diameter threads of the insert) and an installation tool. Spark plug inserts usually differ because they require a tap equipped with pilot threads and a combined reamer/tap section. Most manufacturers also supply blister-packed thread repair inserts separately in addition to a master kit containing a variety of taps and inserts plus installation tools.

Before effecting a repair to a threaded hole, remove any snapped, broken or damaged bolts or studs. Penetrating oil can be used to free frozen threads; the offending item can be removed with locking pliers or with a screw or stud extractor. After the hole is clear, the thread can be repaired, as follows:

CHECKING ENGINE COMPRESSION

A noticeable lack of engine power, excessive oil consumption and/or poor fuel mileage measured over an extended period are all indicators of internal engine wear. Worn piston rings, scored or worn cylinder bores, blown head gaskets, sticking or burnt valves and worn valve seats are all possible culprits here. A check of each cylinder's compression will help you locate the problems.

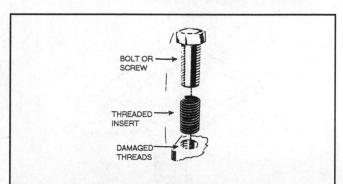

Fig. 17 Using a thread insert to repair a damaged hole is a quick and easy fix to a difficult problem

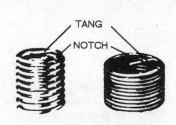

Fig. 18 Standard thread repair insert (left) and the spark plug repair insert (right) are identified by size and thread count

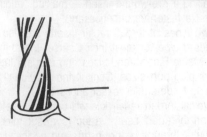

Fig. 19 Using the specified drill bit, enlarge the damaged hole to accept the insert. Drill completely through the hole or to the bottom of a blind hole.

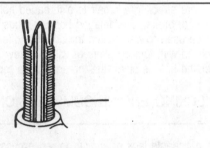

Fig. 20 With the supplied tapping bit, tap the hole to receive the thread insert. Keep the tap well oiled and back it out frequently to avoid clogging the threads

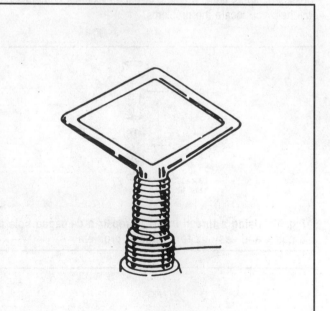

Fig. 21 Screw the threaded insert onto the installation tool until the tang engages the slot. Screw the insert into the tapped hole until it is ¼-½ turn below the top surface. After installation, break off the tang with a hammer and punch

As mentioned in Section 1, a screw-in type compression gauge is more accurate than the type you simply hold against the spark plug hole. Although the screw in type gauge takes slightly longer to use, it is worth the accuracy you gain.

1. Start the engine and allow it to reach normal operating temperature.

2. Stop the engine and remove all spark plugs.

3. Disconnect the high tension lead from the ignition coil.

4. Fully open the throttle, either by operating the throttle linkage by hand or by having an assistant hold the accelerator pedal to the floor.

5. Screw the compression gauge into the No. 1 spark plug hole until the fitting is snug.

➡**Be careful not to crossthread the plug hole. On aluminum cylinder heads use extra care, as the threads in these heads are easily damaged.**

6. Crank the engine through 4-5 compression strokes (complete revolutions) recording the highest reading on the compression gauge.

7. Repeat this procedure for each of the engine's cylinders. Compare the highest reading of each cylinder against the other cylinders. Note difference between each cylinder. The variance should be no more than 12-14 pounds.

8. If a cylinder is unusually low, pour a tablespoon of clean engine oil (30W) into the cylinder through the spark plug hole and repeat the compression test. If the compression rises after adding the oil, worn or damaged piston rings or cylinder bore should be suspected.

9. If the pressure remains low, the valves may not be seating properly (a valve job is needed), or the head gasket may be blown near that cylinder.

10. If compression in any two adjacent cylinders is low and if the addition of oil doesn't help the compression, there is leakage past the head gasket. Oil and coolant in the combustion chamber can result from this problem. There may be evidence of water droplets (sometimes seen as a milky white substance) on the engine dipstick when a head gasket has blown.

GENERAL ENGINE SPECIFICATIONS

Year	Engine ID/VIN	Engine Displacement Liters (cc)	Fuel System Type	Net Horsepower @ rpm	Net Torque @ rpm (ft. lbs.)	Bore × Stroke (in.)	Compression Ratio	Oil Pressure @ rpm
1985	M	1.0 (1000)	2 bbl	48 @ 5100	57 @ 3200	2.91 × 3.03	9.5:1	42–54 @ 3000
1986	5	1.0 (1000)	2 bbl	48 @ 5100	57 @ 3200	2.91 × 3.03	9.5:1	42–54 @ 3000
1987	5	1.0 (1000)	2 bbl	48 @ 5100	78 @ 3200	2.91 × 3.03	9.5:1	42–54 @ 3000
1987	2	1.0 (1000)	EFI①	70 @ 5100	107 @ 3500	2.91 × 3.03	8.3:1	42–60 @ 3000
1988	5	1.0 (1000)	2 bbl	48 @ 5100	78 @ 3200	2.91 × 3.03	9.5:1	42–54 @ 3000
1988	2	1.0 (1000)	EFI①	70 @ 5500	107 @ 3500	2.91 × 3.03	8.3:1	42–60 @ 3000
1989	5	1.0 (1000)	EFI	52 @ 5700	58 @ 3300	2.91 × 3.03	9.5:1	39 @ 4000
1990	5	1.0 (1000)	EFI	52 @ 5700	58 @ 3300	2.91 × 3.03	9.5:1	39 @ 4000
1991	6	1.0 (1000)	EFI	52 @ 5700	58 @ 3300	2.91 × 3.03	9.5:1	39 @ 4000
1992	6	1.0 (1000)	EFI	52 @ 5700	58 @ 3300	2.91 × 3.03	9.5:1	39 @ 4000
1993	6	1.0 (1000)	EFI	52 @ 5700	58 @ 3300	2.91 × 3.03	9.5:1	39 @ 4000

NOTE: Horsepower and torque are SAE net figures. They are measured at the rear of the transmission with all accessories installed and operating. Since the figures vary when a given engine is installed in different models, some are representative rather than exact.

2 bbl—2 bbl carburetor

EFI—Electronic Fuel Injection

① Turbo

VALVE SPECIFICATIONS

Year	Engine ID/VIN	Engine Displacement Liters (cc)	Seat Angle (deg.)	Face Angle (deg.)	Spring Test Pressure (lbs. @ in.)	Spring Installed Height (in.)	Stem-to-Guide Clearance (in.)		Stem Diameter (in.)	
							Intake	Exhaust	Intake	Exhaust
1985	M	1.0 (1000)	45	45	54.7–64.3 @ 1.63 in.	—	0.0008–0.0019	0.0014–0.0025	0.2742–0.2748	0.2737–0.2742
1986	5	1.0 (1000)	45	45	54.7–64.3 @ 1.63 in.	—	0.0008–0.0019	0.0014–0.0025	0.2742–0.2748	0.2737–0.2742
1987	5	1.0 (1000)	45	45	54.7–64.3 @ 1.63 in.	—	0.0008–0.0019	0.0014–0.0025	0.2742–0.2748	0.2737–0.2742
1988	5	1.0 (1000)	45	45	54.7–64.3 @ 1.63 in.	—	0.0008–0.0019	0.0014–0.0025	0.2742–0.2748	0.2737–0.2742
1989	5	1.0 (1000)	45	45	41.0–47.2 @ 1.28 in.	—	0.0008–0.0021	0.0014–0.0024	0.2148–0.2157	0.2146–0.2151
1990	5	1.0 (1000)	45	45	41.0–47.2 @ 1.28 in.	—	0.0008–0.0021	0.0014–0.0024	0.2148–0.2157	0.2146–0.2151
1991	6	1.0 (1000)	45	45	41.0–47.2 @ 1.28 in.	—	0.0008–0.0021	0.0014–0.0024	0.2148–0.2157	0.2146–0.2151
1992	6	1.0 (1000)	45	45	41.0–47.2 @ 1.28 in.	—	0.0008–0.0022	0.0018–0.0028	0.2148–0.2157	0.2142–0.2144
1993	6	1.0 (1000)	45	45	41.0–47.2 @ 1.28 in.	—	0.0008–0.0022	0.0018–0.0028	0.2148–0.2157	0.2142–0.2144

CAMSHAFT SPECIFICATIONS

All measurements given in inches.

Year	Engine ID/VIN	Engine Displacement Liters (cc)	Journal Diameter 1	2	3	4	Elevation In.	Ex.	Bearing Clearance	Camshaft End Play
1985	M	1.0 (1000)	1.737–1.738	1.737–1.738	1.737–1.738	1.737–1.738	1.472–1.476	1.472–1.476	0.002–0.003	0.0039
1986	5	1.0 (1000)	1.737–1.738	1.737–1.738	1.737–1.738	1.737–1.738	1.149–1.150	1.149–1.150	0.002–0.003	0.0039
1987	5	1.0 (1000)	1.737–1.738	1.737–1.738	1.737–1.738	1.737–1.738	1.149–1.150	1.149–1.150	0.002–0.003	0.0039
1988	5	1.0 (1000)	1.737–1.738	1.737–1.738	1.737–1.738	1.737–1.738	1.149–1.150	1.149–1.150	0.002–0.003	0.0039
1989	5	1.0 (1000)	1.022–1.023	1.179–1.180	1.179–1.180	—	1.560–1.566	1.560–1.566	0.0008–0.0024	0.0039
1990	5	1.0 (1000)	1.022–1.023	1.179–1.180	1.179–1.180	—	1.560–1.566	1.560–1.566	0.0008–0.0024	0.0039
1991	6	1.0 (1000)	1.022–1.023	1.179–1.180	1.179–1.180	—	1.560–1.566	1.560–1.566	0.0008–0.0024	0.0039
1992	6	1.0 (1000)	1.022–1.023	1.179–1.180	1.179–1.180	—	1.591–1.597 ①	1.591–1.597	0.0008–0.0024	0.0039
1993	6	1.0 (1000)	1.022–1.023	1.179–1.180	1.179–1.180	—	1.591–1.597 ①	1.591–1.597	0.0008–0.0024	0.0039

① XFI model: 1.560–1.566 in.
Intake and Exhaust

CRANKSHAFT AND CONNECTING ROD SPECIFICATIONS

All measurements are given in inches.

Year	Engine ID/VIN	Engine Displacement Liters (cc)	Crankshaft Main Brg. Journal Dia.	Main Brg. Oil Clearance	Shaft End-play	Thrust on No.	Connecting Rod Journal Diameter	Oil Clearance	Side Clearance
1985	M	1.0 (1000)	①	0.0008–0.0015	0.0044–0.0122	3	1.6529–1.6535	0.0012–0.0019	0.0039–0.0078
1986	5	1.0 (1000)	①	0.0008–0.0015	0.0044–0.0122	3	1.6529–1.6535	0.0012–0.0019	0.0039–0.0078
1987	5	1.0 (1000)	①	0.0008–0.0015	0.0044–0.0122	3	1.6529–1.6535	0.0012–0.0019	0.0039–0.0078
1988	5	1.0 (1000)	①	0.0008–0.0015	0.0044–0.0122	3	1.6529–1.6535	0.0012–0.0019	0.0039–0.0078
1989	5	1.0 (1000)	①	0.0008–0.0015	0.0044–0.0122	3	1.6529–1.6535	0.0012–0.0019	0.0039–0.0078
1990	5	1.0 (1000)	①	0.0008–0.0015	0.0044–0.0122	3	1.6529–1.6535	0.0012–0.0019	0.0039–0.0078
1991	6	1.0 (1000)	①	0.0008–0.0015	0.0044–0.0122	3	1.6529–1.6535	0.0012–0.0019	0.0039–0.0078
1992	6	1.0 (1000)	①	0.0008–0.0015	0.0044–0.0122	3	1.6529–1.6535	0.0012–0.0019	0.0039–0.0078
1993	6	1.0 (1000)	①	0.0008–0.0015	0.0044–0.0122	3	1.6529–1.6535	0.0012–0.0019	0.0039–0.0078

① Number on no. 1 cylinder counterweight
1: 1.7714–1.7716 in.
2: 1.7712–1.7714 in.
3: 1.7710–1.7712 in.

PISTON AND RING SPECIFICATIONS

All measurements are given in inches.

Year	Engine ID/VIN	Engine Displacement Liters (cc)	Piston Clearance	Ring Gap			Ring Side Clearance		
				Top Compression	Bottom Compression	Oil Control	Top Compression	Bottom Compression	Oil Control
1985	M	1.0 (1000)	0.0008–0.0015	0.0079–0.0129	0.0079–0.0137	0.0079–0.0275	0.0012–0.0027	0.0008–0.0023	—
1986	5	1.0 (1000)	0.0008–0.0015	0.0079–0.0129 ①	0.0079–0.0137	0.0079–0.0275	0.0012–0.0027	0.0008–0.0023	—
1987	5	1.0 (1000)	0.0008–0.0015	0.0079–0.0129 ①	0.0079–0.0137	0.0079–0.0275	0.0012–0.0027	0.0008–0.0023	—
1987	5	1.0 (1000) ②	0.0008–0.0015	0.0079–0.0119	0.0079–0.0119	0.0079–0.0237	0.0012–0.0030	0.0008–0.0023	—
1988	5	1.0 (1000)	0.0008–0.0015	0.0079–0.0129 ①	0.0079–0.0137	0.0079–0.0275	0.0012–0.0027	0.0008–0.0023	—
1988	5	1.0 (1000) ②	0.0008–0.0015	0.0079–0.0119	0.0079–0.0119	0.0079–0.0237	0.0012–0.0030	0.0008–0.0023	—
1989	5	1.0 (1000)	0.0008–0.0015	0.0079–0.0129 ①	0.0079–0.0137	0.0079–0.0275	0.0012–0.0027	0.0008–0.0023	—
1990	5	1.0 (1000)	0.0008–0.0015	0.0079–0.0129	0.0079–0.0137	0.0079–0.0275	0.0012–0.0027	0.0008–0.0023	—
1991	6	1.0 (1000)	0.0008–0.0015	0.0079–0.0129	0.0079–0.0137	0.0079–0.0275	0.0012–0.0027	0.0008–0.0023	—
1992	6	1.0 (1000)	0.0008–0.0015	0.0079–0.0118	0.0079–0.0118	0.0079–0.0236	0.0012–0.0027	0.0008–0.0023	—
1993	6	1.0 (1000)	0.0008–0.0015	0.0079–0.0118	0.0079–0.0118	0.0079–0.0236	0.0012–0.0027	0.0008–0.0023	—

① ER model: 0.0079–0.0157 in.
  The ER model has only 1 compression ring
② Turbo model

TORQUE SPECIFICATIONS

All readings in ft. lbs.

Year	Engine ID/VIN	Engine Displacement Liters (cc)	Cylinder Head Bolts	Main Bearing Bolts	Rod Bearing Bolts	Crankshaft Damper Bolts	Flywheel Bolts	Manifold		Spark Plugs	Lug Nut
								Intake	Exhaust		
1985	M	1.0 (1000)	46–50	36–41	24–26	47–54	41–47	18–28	18–28	18–20	29–50
1986	5	1.0 (1000)	46–50	36–41	24–26	47–54	41–47	18–28	18–28	18–20	29–50
1987	5	1.0 (1000)	46–50	36–41	24–26	47–54	41–47	18–28	18–28	18–20	29–50
1988	5	1.0 (1000)	46–50	36–41	24–26	47–54	41–47	18–28	18–28	18–20	29–50
1989	5	1.0 (1000)	54	40	26	81	45	17	17	18	44
1990	5	1.0 (1000)	54	40	26	81	45	17	17	18	44
1991	6	1.0 (1000)	54	40	26	81	45	17	17	18	44
1992	6	1.0 (1000)	54	40	26	81	45	17	17	18	44
1993	5	1.0 (1000)	54	40	26	81	45	17	17	18	44

Engine Assembly

REMOVAL & INSTALLATION

1. Relieve the fuel system pressure on fuel injected vehicles.

2. Using a scratch awl, scribe the hood hinge-to-hood outline, then, using an assistant remove the hood.

3. Disconnect the negative battery cable. Drain the cooling system.

✳✳CAUTION

When draining the coolant, keep in mind that cats and dogs are attracted by the ethylene glycol antifreeze, and are quite likely to drink any that is left in an uncovered container or in puddles on the ground. This will prove fatal in sufficient quantity. Always drain the coolant into a sealable container. Coolant should be reused unless it is contaminated or several years old.

4. Remove the air cleaner assembly. Remove the radiator assembly along with the cooling fan.

5. Disconnect and tag all necessary electrical connections.

6. Disconnect and tag all necessary vacuum lines.

7. Disconnect, tag and plug all necessary fuel lines.

8. Disconnect the heater inlet and outlet hoses.

9. Disconnect the following cables:

   a. The accelerator cable from the throttle body or carburetor.

   b. The clutch cable from the transaxle (for manual transaxle models).

   c. The gear select cable and the oil pressure control cable from the transaxle (for automatic transaxle models).

   d. The speedometer cable from the transaxle.

10. Raise and safely support the vehicle safely.

11. Disconnect the exhaust pipe from the exhaust manifold.

12. Disconnect the gear shift control shaft and the extension to the transaxle for (manual transaxle models).

13. Drain the engine oil and transaxle oil.

14. Remove the drive axles from the differential side gears of the transaxle. For the engine/transaxle removal, it is not necessary to remove the drive axle from the steering knuckle.

15. Remove the engine rear torque rod bracket from the transaxle (for automatic transaxle models).

16. Lower the vehicle.

17. Install a suitable chain hoist to the lifting device on the engine.

18. Remove the right side engine mounting from its bracket.

19. On vehicles equipped with a automatic transaxle, remove the transaxle rear mounting nut.

20. On vehicles equipped with a manual transaxle, remove the transaxle rear mounting from the body.

21. Remove the transaxle left side mounting bracket.

22. Lift the engine and transaxle assembly out from the vehicle. Separate the transaxle from the engine.

To install:

23. Install the transaxle to the engine, then a suitable hoist onto the engine lifting brackets.

24. Install engine and transaxle into vehicle and leave the hoist connected to the lifting device.

25. On vehicles equipped with a automatic transaxle, install the transaxle rear mounting nut.

26. On vehicles equipped with a manual transaxle, install the transaxle rear mounting from the body.

27. Install the transaxle left side mounting bracket.

28. Install the transaxle right side engine mounting to its bracket.

29. Tighten all the bolts and nuts.

30. Remove the lifting device.

31. To complete the installation procedure, reverse the removal procedure.

32. Adjust the clutch pedal free-play.

33. Adjust the gear select cable, and oil pressure control cable.

34. Adjust the accelerator cable play.

35. Refill the transaxle with the recommended fluid. Do the same for the engine oil and engine coolant.

36. Reconnect the negative battery cable. Start the engine and check for leakage of any kind. Make all necessary repairs and adjustments.

37. Torque the transaxle-to-engine bolts and nuts to 37 ft. lbs.. (50 Nm).

38. Torque the engine mounting nuts to 37 ft. lbs.. (50 Nm).

39. Torque the engine mounting left hand bracket bolts to 37 ft. lbs.. (50 Nm).

40. Torque the exhaust pipe to manifold bolts to 37 ft. lbs.. (50 Nm).

41. Torque the flywheel retaining bolts to 47 ft. lbs.. (64 Nm).

Rocker Arm (Valve) Cover

REMOVAL & INSTALLATION

▶ See Figures 22, 23, 24, 25, 26 and 27

1. Disconnect the negative battery cable.
2. Remove the air cleaner assembly.
3. Remove the spark plug wire retaining clips. Lay the spark plug wires aside.
4. Disconnect the PCV valve hose.
5. Remove the nuts and seal washers located under the nuts.
6. Remove the valve cover from the cylinder head.

Fig. 23 Removing the air cleaner-to-valve cover brace bolt

Fig. 24 Removing the PCV valve hose from the valve cover

Fig. 25 Removing the valve cover retaining nuts

Fig. 22 Overall view of the valve cover at the top of the engine.

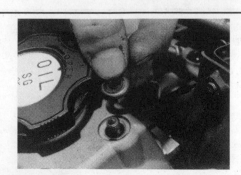

Fig. 26 Removing the valve cover seal washers. Always use new seal washers during installation

Fig. 27 When installing the valve cover gasket, place a small amount of silicone sealant at the corners of the valve cover

To install:

7. Apply a small amount of silicone sealant to the corners of the new valve cover gasket.

✳✳CAUTION

Be sure not to block the oil drain hole, located at the front of the cylinder head opening, with silicone sealant. This could cause excessive oil pressure with the cylinder head, resulting in a possible oil leak.

8. Install the new gasket.
9. Install the valve cover and secure with new seal washers and nuts. Tighten nuts to 44 inch lbs.. (5 Nm).
10. Install the spark plug wire retaining clips. Route the spark plug wires in their original position.
11. Install the air cleaner assembly.
12. Connect the negative battery cable.

Rocker Arms/Shafts

REMOVAL & INSTALLATION

1985-88 Sprint

▶ **See Figures 28, 29 and 30**

1. Disconnect the negative battery cable.
2. Remove the air cleaner and cylinder head cover.

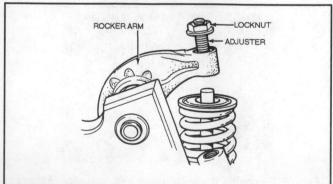

Fig. 28 Adjusting screw and locknut assembly

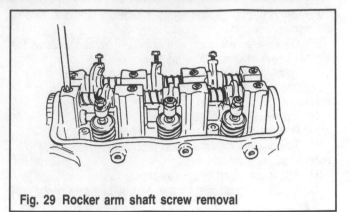

Fig. 29 Rocker arm shaft screw removal

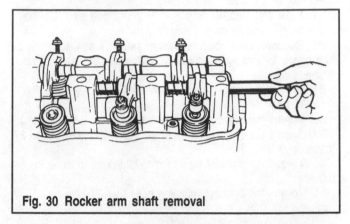

Fig. 30 Rocker arm shaft removal

3. Remove the distributor cap, then mark the position of the rotor and the distributor housing with the cylinder head. Remove the distributor and the case from the cylinder head.
4. After loosening all valve adjusting screw lock nuts, turn the adjusting screws back all the way to allow all rocker arms to move freely.

➡**Rocker arm shafts are of different sizes. Mark the intake and exhaust rocker arm shafts for installation reference.**

5. Remove the rocker shaft screws.
6. Remove the intake and exhaust rocker arm shafts, then the rocker arms and springs.

To install:

7. Apply engine oil to all rocker arms and rocker arm shafts.
8. Install rocker arms, springs and rocker arm shafts.

➡**Rocker arm shafts are of different sizes. Install the intake rocker arm shaft facing its stepped end to the camshaft pulley side. Install the exhaust rocker arm shaft facing its stepped end to the distributor side.**

9. Tighten rocker arm shaft bolts to 7-9 ft. lbs.. (9-12 Nm).
10. Install distributor and distributor cap, aligning them with the matchmarks make during removal.
11. Adjust the valve lash.
12. Install the cylinder head cover.
13. Install the air cleaner.
14. Connect the negative battery cable.
15. Start the engine and allow it to reach operating temperature. Check for leaks.

VALVE LASH ADJUSTMENT

1. Remove the air cleaner and cylinder head cover.
2. Rotate crankshaft clockwise and align timing notch on crankshaft pulley with the **0** mark on the timing tab.
3. Remove the distributor cap and check if the rotor is positioned correctly (pointing toward the No. 1 cylinder terminal on the cap).
4. If the engine is not positioned correctly, rotate 360 degrees and align the timing notch with the **0** mark again.
5. Using a thickness gauge, check the intake and exhaust valve of the No. 1 cylinder. Slide the gauge between the adjusting screw and the valve tip. It should be a snug fit.
6. If the valve lash is out of specification, adjust it by loosening the locknut and turning the adjusting screw. Tighten the locknut to 11-13 ft. lbs.. (15-19 Nm).
7. Rotate the engine 240 degrees and align the timing notch on the pulley with the left attaching bolt of the timing belt outside cover. Check and adjust the valve lash for No. 3 cylinder.
8. Rotate the engine 240 degrees and align the timing notch on the pulley with the right attaching bolt of the timing belt outside cover. Check and adjust the valve lash for No. 2 cylinder.
9. Install the distributor cap, cylinder head cover and air cleaner. Tighten the cylinder head cover bolts to 48 inch lbs.. (5 Nm).

Thermostat

REMOVAL & INSTALLATION

▶ **See Figure 31**

1. Disconnect the battery negative cable.
2. Drain cooling system to a level below the thermostat.
3. Remove the air cleaner.
4. Disconnect the electrical connectors at the thermostat cap.
5. Remove the inlet hose, cap mounting bolts and the thermostat from the thermostat housing.
6. Clean the gasket mounting surfaces. Ensure that the thermostat air bleed hose is clear.
To install:
7. Install thermostat into housing with the spring side down.

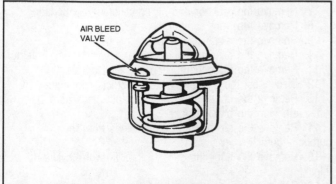

Fig. 31 Thermostat air bleed valve

8. Install the thermostat housing using a new gasket. Tighten bolts to 15 ft. lbs.. (20 Nm).
9. Install the inlet hose and tighten clap securely.
10. Fill cooling system.
11. Connect the battery negative cable. Start engine and check for leaks.

Intake Manifold

REMOVAL & INSTALLATION

▶ **See Figures 32 and 33**

1. On fuel injected models, relieve the fuel system pressure.
2. Disconnect the negative battery cable.
3. Drain the cooling system.

✱✱CAUTION

When draining the coolant, keep in mind that cats and dogs are attracted by the ethylene glycol antifreeze, and are quite likely to drink any that is left in an uncovered container or in puddles on the ground. This will prove fatal in sufficient quantity. Always drain the coolant into a sealable container. Coolant should be reused unless it is contaminated or several years old.

4. Remove the air cleaner assembly.
5. Label and disconnect all electrical connectors from the intake manifold.

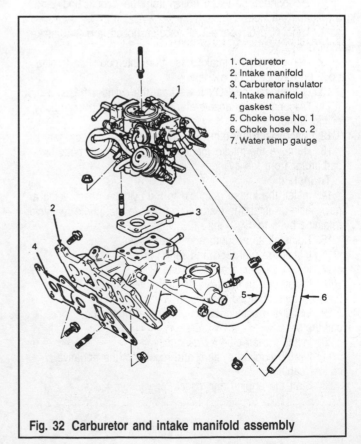

1. Carburetor
2. Intake manifold
3. Carburetor insulator
4. Intake manifold gaskest
5. Choke hose No. 1
6. Choke hose No. 2
7. Water temp gauge

Fig. 32 Carburetor and intake manifold assembly

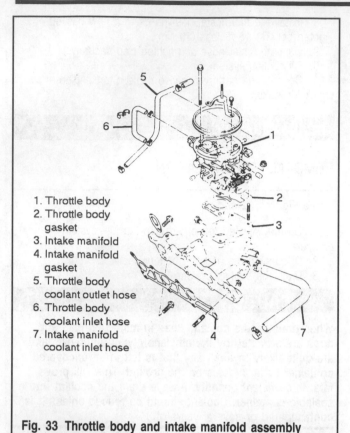

1. Throttle body
2. Throttle body gasket
3. Intake manifold
4. Intake manifold gasket
5. Throttle body coolant outlet hose
6. Throttle body coolant inlet hose
7. Intake manifold coolant inlet hose

Fig. 33 Throttle body and intake manifold assembly

6. Label and disconnect the fuel return and feed hoses from the throttle body or carburetor.
7. Disconnect the water hoses from the throttle body and the intake manifold.
8. Label and disconnect all vacuum hoses from the intake manifold.
9. Remove the air intake hose from intercooler to throttle body on turbocharged models.
10. Disconnect the PCV hose from the cylinder head cover.
11. Disconnect the accelerator cable from the throttle body or carburetor.
12. Disconnect any other lines and cables, as necessary.
13. Remove the intake manifold with the throttle body or carburetor from the cylinder head.

To install:
14. Install the intake manifold to the cylinder head, using a new gasket, install the clamps and tighten the intake manifold retaining bolts to 17 ft. lbs.. (23 Nm).
15. Reinstall all vacuum and water hoses.
16. Install the fuel feed and return hoses.
17. Install all electrical lead wires.
18. Install the air intake hose from intercooler to throttle body on turbocharged models.
19. Install the accelerator cable to the throttle body or carburetor.
20. Install the air cleaner assembly.
21. Fill the cooling system and reconnect the negative battery cable.
22. Start the engine and check for vacuum leaks.

Exhaust Manifold

REMOVAL & INSTALLATION

1. Disconnect the negative battery cable.
2. Remove the turbocharger assembly, as required.
3. Disconnect the oxygen sensor coupler.
4. Remove the exhaust pipe from the exhaust manifold.
5. Remove the manifold retaining bolts and remove the exhaust manifold and gaskets.

To install:
6. Install a new manifold gasket and torque the bolts to 17 ft. lbs.. (23 Nm).
7. Install the turbocharger assembly, as required.
8. Install the exhaust pipe and tighten bolts to 30-43 ft. lbs.. (40-60 Nm).
9. Reconnect the oxygen sensor coupler.
10. Connect the negative battery cable. Start the engine and check for leaks.

Turbocharger

REMOVAL & INSTALLATION

▶ See Figure 34

1. Disconnect the negative battery cable.
2. Drain the cooling system.

✳✳CAUTION

When draining the coolant, keep in mind that cats and dogs are attracted by the ethylene glycol antifreeze, and are quite likely to drink any that is left in an uncovered container or in puddles on the ground. This will prove fatal in sufficient quantity. Always drain the coolant into a sealable container. Coolant should be reused unless it is contaminated or several years old.

3. As required, remove the hood and front grille to gain access to components.
4. Remove the intercooler.
5. Remove the radiator hoses and fan motor electrical connector.
6. Remove the front upper member.
7. Remove the radiator and air conditioning condenser.
8. Remove the front bumper.
9. Remove the exhaust pipe bolts.
10. Remove the air conditioning compressor and lay it aside.
11. Remove the turbocharger top and side covers.
12. Disconnect the oxygen sensor electrical connector.
13. Remove the upper and lower exhaust pipes as a unit after removing the bracket bolt.
14. Remove the air inlet and outlet pipes from the turbocharger.
15. Remove the turbocharger oil pipes from the cylinder block.
16. Remove the turbocharger water pipes.
17. Unbolt and remove the turbocharger.

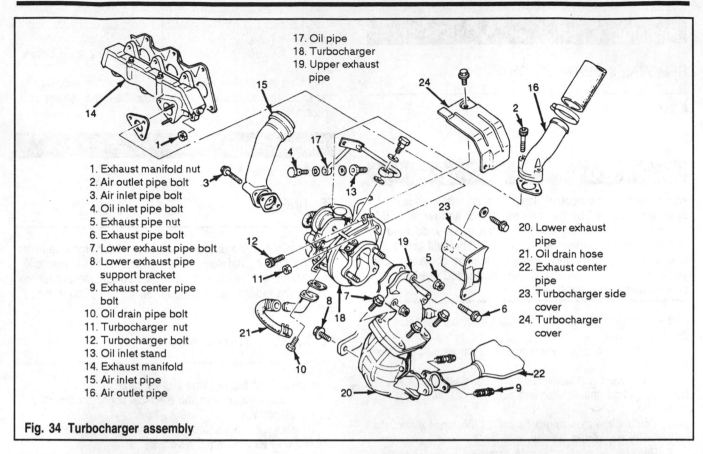

17. Oil pipe
18. Turbocharger
19. Upper exhaust pipe

1. Exhaust manifold nut
2. Air outlet pipe bolt
3. Air inlet pipe bolt
4. Oil inlet pipe bolt
5. Exhaust pipe nut
6. Exhaust pipe bolt
7. Lower exhaust pipe bolt
8. Lower exhaust pipe support bracket
9. Exhaust center pipe bolt
10. Oil drain pipe bolt
11. Turbocharger nut
12. Turbocharger bolt
13. Oil inlet stand
14. Exhaust manifold
15. Air inlet pipe
16. Air outlet pipe

20. Lower exhaust pipe
21. Oil drain hose
22. Exhaust center pipe
23. Turbocharger side cover
24. Turbocharger cover

Fig. 34 Turbocharger assembly

To install:

18. Turn the turbocharger by hand and check the blades for damage. Check the inside of the housing for oil deposits. If found, replace the turbocharger assembly.

19. Check the oil pipe orifices for clogs. If found clear the obstruction.

20. Install the air inlet pipe to the turbocharger using a new gasket. Tighten bolts to 6-8 ft. lbs.. (8-12 Nm).

21. Install the oil pipe to the turbocharger and air inlet pipe using a new gasket.

22. Install the turbocharger on the exhaust manifold using a new gasket. Tighten bolts to 13-20 ft. lbs.. (18-28 Nm).

23. Install the water hoses to the turbocharger and cylinder head.

24. Install the oil drain hose. Tighten to 3-5 ft. lbs.. (4-7 Nm).

25. Install the oil inlet pipe on the cylinder head using a new gasket. Tighten to 8-10 ft. lbs.. (11-15 Nm).

26. Install the air inlet tube clamp bolt to the cylinder head.

27. Install the air outlet pipe using a new gasket. Tighten bolt to 6-8 ft. lbs.. (8-12 Nm).

28. Install the upper and lower exhaust pipes. Tighten bolts to 18-25 ft. lbs.. (25-35 Nm) and nuts to 13-20 ft. lbs.. (18-28 Nm).

29. Install the lower exhaust pipe bracket bolt and tighten to 29-43 ft. lbs.. (40-60 Nm).

30. Install the turbocharger covers.

31. Connect the oxygen sensor electrical connector.

32. Install the air conditioning compressor and belt.

33. Install the front bumper, radiator and air conditioning condenser.

34. Connect the radiator fan motor electrical connector.

35. Install the radiator hoses, intercooler, front grille and hood.

36. Fill the engine with coolant and connect the negative battery cable.

37. Start the engine and allow it to reach normal operating temperature. Check for leaks.

Intercooler

REMOVAL & INSTALLATION

1. Remove the intercooler cover.
2. Remove the intercooler inlet and outlet hoses
3. Remove the intercooler.
4. Remove the relief valve from the intercooler.

To install:

5. Check the intercooler for cracks or damage. Blow air into the relief valve and confirm that air does not come through. Also push relief valve and check spring for setting and damage, and valve for looseness. If defective replace valve.

6. Install relief valve using new gasket. Install screws using Loctite® or equivalent.

7. Install intercooler.

8. Install inlet and outlet hoses.

9. Install intercooler cover.

Radiator

REMOVAL & INSTALLATION

▶ See Figure 35

1. Disconnect the battery negative cable.
2. Drain the cooling system.

✳✳CAUTION

When draining the coolant, keep in mind that cats and dogs are attracted by the ethylene glycol antifreeze, and are quite likely to drink any that is left in an uncovered container or in puddles on the ground. This will prove fatal in sufficient quantity. Always drain the coolant into a sealable container. Coolant should be reused unless it is contaminated or several years old.

3. Disconnect the cooling fan motor electrical connector and the air inlet hose.
4. Remove the upper, lower and reservoir tank hoses from the radiator.
5. If equipped with automatic transaxle, disconnect the oil cooler lines from the radiator and plug them to prevent oil spills.
6. Remove the mounting bolts and lift the radiator from the vehicle with the cooling fan attached.
7. Remove the cooling fan and shroud.

To install:

8. Install the cooling fan and shroud on the radiator. Tighten bolts to 89 inch lbs.. (10 Nm).
9. Place the radiator in the vehicle and install the mounting bolts. Tighten bolts to 89 inch lbs.. (10 Nm).
10. If equipped with automatic transaxle, connect the oil cooler lines to the radiator.
11. Install the upper, lower and reservoir tank hoses on the radiator.

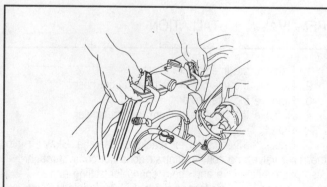

Fig. 35 Removing the radiator/cooling fan assembly

12. Connect the cooling fan motor electrical connector and the air inlet hose.
13. Fill the cooling system and connect the negative battery cable.
14. Start the engine, allow it to reach operating temperature and check the cooling system for leaks. Refill the system as necessary.

Electric Engine Fan

▶ See Figure 36

TESTING

Refer to the wiring diagrams in Section 6 for proper terminal identification. The radiator fan relay is located in the fuse and relay box on the left side of the engine compartment, near the battery. The radiator fan thermostat switch is located in the thermostat housing.

REMOVAL & INSTALLATION

1. Disconnect the negative battery cable.
2. Label and disconnect the electrical connector from the cooling fan motor.
3. Remove the fan shroud-to-radiator frame bolts and the fan/shroud assembly from the vehicle.
4. Remove the fan blade-to-motor nut, fan blade and washer.
5. Remove the fan-to-shroud bolts and the fan motor from the shroud.

To install:

6. Install the fan motor in the shroud.
7. Install the fan blade on the motor.
8. Install the fan shroud on the radiator and tighten bolts to 89 inch lbs.. (10 Nm).
9. Connect the fan motor electrical connector.
10. Connect the negative battery cable.
11. Test fan motor for proper operation.

Electric Air Conditioner Condenser Fan

TESTING

▶ See Figures 38 and 39

Refer to the wiring diagrams in Section 6 for proper terminal identification. The air conditioner condenser fan relay is located in the fuse and relay box on the left side of the engine compartment, near the battery.

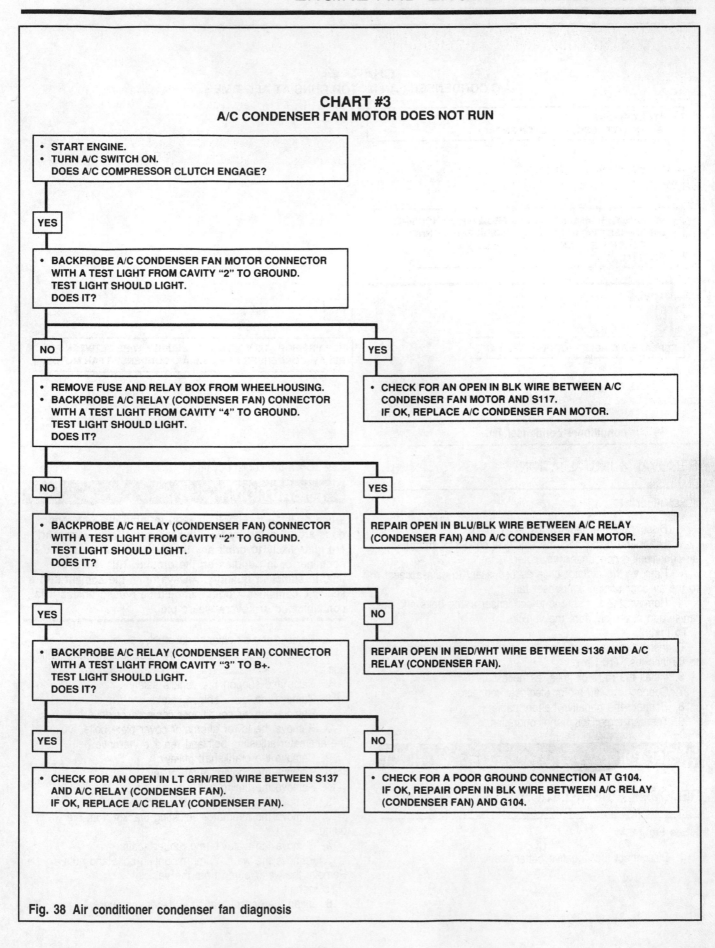

CHART #3
A/C CONDENSER FAN MOTOR DOES NOT RUN

- START ENGINE.
- TURN A/C SWITCH ON.
  DOES A/C COMPRESSOR CLUTCH ENGAGE?

YES

- BACKPROBE A/C CONDENSER FAN MOTOR CONNECTOR
  WITH A TEST LIGHT FROM CAVITY "2" TO GROUND.
  TEST LIGHT SHOULD LIGHT.
  DOES IT?

NO

YES

- REMOVE FUSE AND RELAY BOX FROM WHEELHOUSING.
- BACKPROBE A/C RELAY (CONDENSER FAN) CONNECTOR
  WITH A TEST LIGHT FROM CAVITY "4" TO GROUND.
  TEST LIGHT SHOULD LIGHT.
  DOES IT?

- CHECK FOR AN OPEN IN BLK WIRE BETWEEN A/C
  CONDENSER FAN MOTOR AND S117.
  IF OK, REPLACE A/C CONDENSER FAN MOTOR.

NO

YES

- BACKPROBE A/C RELAY (CONDENSER FAN) CONNECTOR
  WITH A TEST LIGHT FROM CAVITY "2" TO GROUND.
  TEST LIGHT SHOULD LIGHT.
  DOES IT?

REPAIR OPEN IN BLU/BLK WIRE BETWEEN A/C RELAY
(CONDENSER FAN) AND A/C CONDENSER FAN MOTOR.

YES

NO

- BACKPROBE A/C RELAY (CONDENSER FAN) CONNECTOR
  WITH A TEST LIGHT FROM CAVITY "3" TO B+.
  TEST LIGHT SHOULD LIGHT.
  DOES IT?

REPAIR OPEN IN RED/WHT WIRE BETWEEN S136 AND A/C
RELAY (CONDENSER FAN).

YES

NO

- CHECK FOR AN OPEN IN LT GRN/RED WIRE BETWEEN S137
  AND A/C RELAY (CONDENSER FAN).
  IF OK, REPLACE A/C RELAY (CONDENSER FAN).

- CHECK FOR A POOR GROUND CONNECTION AT G104.
  IF OK, REPAIR OPEN IN BLK WIRE BETWEEN A/C RELAY
  (CONDENSER FAN) AND G104.

Fig. 38 Air conditioner condenser fan diagnosis

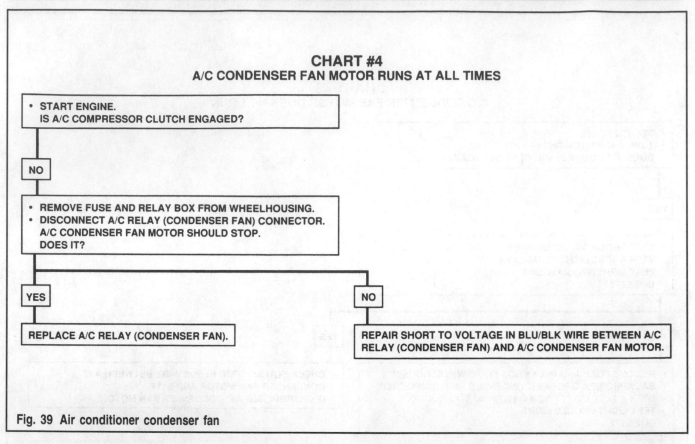

CHART #4
A/C CONDENSER FAN MOTOR RUNS AT ALL TIMES

- START ENGINE.
  IS A/C COMPRESSOR CLUTCH ENGAGED?

NO

- REMOVE FUSE AND RELAY BOX FROM WHEELHOUSING.
- DISCONNECT A/C RELAY (CONDENSER FAN) CONNECTOR.
  A/C CONDENSER FAN MOTOR SHOULD STOP.
  DOES IT?

YES

NO

REPLACE A/C RELAY (CONDENSER FAN).

REPAIR SHORT TO VOLTAGE IN BLU/BLK WIRE BETWEEN A/C RELAY (CONDENSER FAN) AND A/C CONDENSER FAN MOTOR.

Fig. 39 Air conditioner condenser fan

REMOVAL & INSTALLATION

▶ **See Figure 40**

1. Disconnect the negative battery cable.
2. Label and disconnect the electrical connector from the air conditioning condenser fan motor.
3. Remove the radiator grille as necessary to gain access to the air conditioning condenser fan.
4. Remove the fan shroud-to-condenser frame bolts and the fan/shroud assembly from the vehicle.

To install:
5. Install the fan shroud on the condenser and tighten bolts to 89 inch lbs.. (10 Nm).
6. Install the radiator grille, as necessary.
7. Connect the fan motor electrical connector.
8. Connect the negative battery cable.
9. Test fan motor for proper operation.

Water Pump

REMOVAL & INSTALLATION

▶ **See Figure 41**

1. Disconnect the negative battery cable.

2. Drain the cooling system.

✳✳CAUTION

When draining the coolant, keep in mind that cats and dogs are attracted by the ethylene glycol antifreeze, and are quite likely to drink any that is left in an uncovered container or in puddles on the ground. This will prove fatal in sufficient quantity. Always drain the coolant into a sealable container. Coolant should be reused unless it is contaminated or several years old.

3. Remove the air cleaner assembly.
4. Loosen but do not remove the four coolant pump pulley bolts.
5. Raise and support the vehicle safely.
6. Remove the lower splash shield.
7. Remove the air conditioner compressor drive belt.
8. Remove the lower alternator cover plate bolts, loosen the alternator adjusting bolt and remove the drive belt.
9. Remove the crankshaft pulley.
10. Remove the coolant pump pulley.
11. Remove the timing belt.
12. Remove the oil level dipstick and guide tube.
13. Remove the alternator adjusting bracket from the water pump.
14. Remove the water pump rubber seals.
15. Remove the water pump mounting bolts and nuts. Remove the water pump from the vehicle.

To install:
16. Clean the gasket mating surfaces thoroughly.

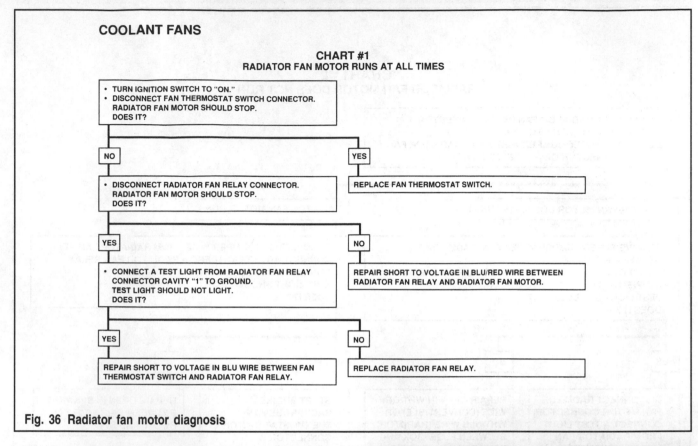

COOLANT FANS

CHART #1
RADIATOR FAN MOTOR RUNS AT ALL TIMES

- TURN IGNITION SWITCH TO "ON."
- DISCONNECT FAN THERMOSTAT SWITCH CONNECTOR. RADIATOR FAN MOTOR SHOULD STOP. DOES IT?

NO

YES

- DISCONNECT RADIATOR FAN RELAY CONNECTOR. RADIATOR FAN MOTOR SHOULD STOP. DOES IT?

REPLACE FAN THERMOSTAT SWITCH.

YES

NO

- CONNECT A TEST LIGHT FROM RADIATOR FAN RELAY CONNECTOR CAVITY "1" TO GROUND. TEST LIGHT SHOULD NOT LIGHT. DOES IT?

REPAIR SHORT TO VOLTAGE IN BLU/RED WIRE BETWEEN RADIATOR FAN RELAY AND RADIATOR FAN MOTOR.

YES

NO

REPAIR SHORT TO VOLTAGE IN BLU WIRE BETWEEN FAN THERMOSTAT SWITCH AND RADIATOR FAN RELAY.

REPLACE RADIATOR FAN RELAY.

Fig. 36 Radiator fan motor diagnosis

17. Check the water pump by hand for smooth operation. If the pump does not operate smoothly or is noisy, replace it.

18. Install the pump using a new gasket. Tighten bolts to 115 inch lbs.. (13 Nm).

19. Install new rubber seals.

20. Install the upper alternator adjusting bracket and tighten bolt to 17 ft. lbs.. (23 Nm).

21. Install the oil level dipstick and guide tube.

22. Install the timing belt.

23. Install the water pump pulley and leave the bolts hand tight.

24. Install the crankshaft pulley.

25. Install the water pump/alternator drive belt.

26. Install the lower alternator cover plate and tighten bolts to 89 inch lbs.. (10 Nm).

27. Install the air conditioner compressor drive belt by releasing the tensioner pulley and installing belt.

28. Install the lower splash shield and lower vehicle.

29. Tighten water pump pulley mounting bolts to 18 ft. lbs.. (24 Nm).

30. Adjust the water pump drive belt tension and tighten alternator adjustment bolt to 17 ft. lbs.. (23 Nm).

31. Install the air cleaner assembly.

32. Refill the cooling system.

33. Connect the negative battery cable.

34. Start the engine and allow it to reach operating temperature. Check for leaks and refill cooling system as necessary.

Cylinder Head

REMOVAL & INSTALLATION

▶ See Figures 42, 43 and 44

1. On fuel injected vehicles, relieve the fuel system pressure.

2. Disconnect the negative battery cable.

3. Drain the cooling system.

✳✳CAUTION

When draining the coolant, keep in mind that cats and dogs are attracted by the ethylene glycol antifreeze, and are quite likely to drink any that is left in an uncovered container or in puddles on the ground. This will prove fatal in sufficient quantity. Always drain the coolant into a sealable container. Coolant should be reused unless it is contaminated or several years old.

4. Label and disconnect all necessary electrical connectors.

5. Label and disconnect all necessary vacuum, fuel and water hoses.

6. Remove the intake manifold with the carburetor or throttle body installed.

7. Remove the exhaust manifold.

8. Remove the timing belt and belt tensioner.

9. Remove the distributor cap, then mark the position of the rotor and the distributor housing with the cylinder head. Remove the distributor and the case from the cylinder head.

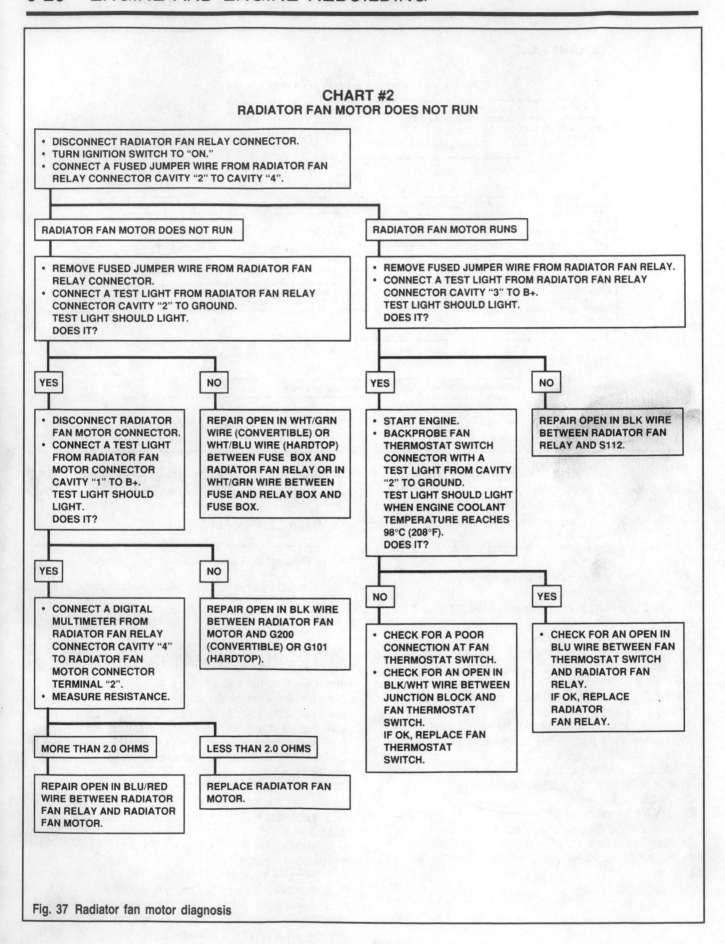

CHART #2
RADIATOR FAN MOTOR DOES NOT RUN

- DISCONNECT RADIATOR FAN RELAY CONNECTOR.
- TURN IGNITION SWITCH TO "ON."
- CONNECT A FUSED JUMPER WIRE FROM RADIATOR FAN RELAY CONNECTOR CAVITY "2" TO CAVITY "4".

RADIATOR FAN MOTOR DOES NOT RUN

- REMOVE FUSED JUMPER WIRE FROM RADIATOR FAN RELAY CONNECTOR.
- CONNECT A TEST LIGHT FROM RADIATOR FAN RELAY CONNECTOR CAVITY "2" TO GROUND. TEST LIGHT SHOULD LIGHT. DOES IT?

YES

- DISCONNECT RADIATOR FAN MOTOR CONNECTOR.
- CONNECT A TEST LIGHT FROM RADIATOR FAN MOTOR CONNECTOR CAVITY "1" TO B+. TEST LIGHT SHOULD LIGHT. DOES IT?

NO

REPAIR OPEN IN WHT/GRN WIRE (CONVERTIBLE) OR WHT/BLU WIRE (HARDTOP) BETWEEN FUSE BOX AND RADIATOR FAN RELAY OR IN WHT/GRN WIRE BETWEEN FUSE AND RELAY BOX AND FUSE BOX.

YES

- CONNECT A DIGITAL MULTIMETER FROM RADIATOR FAN RELAY CONNECTOR CAVITY "4" TO RADIATOR FAN MOTOR CONNECTOR TERMINAL "2".
- MEASURE RESISTANCE.

NO

REPAIR OPEN IN BLK WIRE BETWEEN RADIATOR FAN MOTOR AND G200 (CONVERTIBLE) OR G101 (HARDTOP).

MORE THAN 2.0 OHMS

REPAIR OPEN IN BLU/RED WIRE BETWEEN RADIATOR FAN RELAY AND RADIATOR FAN MOTOR.

LESS THAN 2.0 OHMS

REPLACE RADIATOR FAN MOTOR.

RADIATOR FAN MOTOR RUNS

- REMOVE FUSED JUMPER WIRE FROM RADIATOR FAN RELAY.
- CONNECT A TEST LIGHT FROM RADIATOR FAN RELAY CONNECTOR CAVITY "3" TO B+. TEST LIGHT SHOULD LIGHT. DOES IT?

YES

- START ENGINE.
- BACKPROBE FAN THERMOSTAT SWITCH CONNECTOR WITH A TEST LIGHT FROM CAVITY "2" TO GROUND. TEST LIGHT SHOULD LIGHT WHEN ENGINE COOLANT TEMPERATURE REACHES 98°C (208°F). DOES IT?

NO

REPAIR OPEN IN BLK WIRE BETWEEN RADIATOR FAN RELAY AND S112.

NO

- CHECK FOR A POOR CONNECTION AT FAN THERMOSTAT SWITCH.
- CHECK FOR AN OPEN IN BLK/WHT WIRE BETWEEN JUNCTION BLOCK AND FAN THERMOSTAT SWITCH. IF OK, REPLACE FAN THERMOSTAT SWITCH.

YES

- CHECK FOR AN OPEN IN BLU WIRE BETWEEN FAN THERMOSTAT SWITCH AND RADIATOR FAN RELAY. IF OK, REPLACE RADIATOR FAN RELAY.

Fig. 37 Radiator fan motor diagnosis

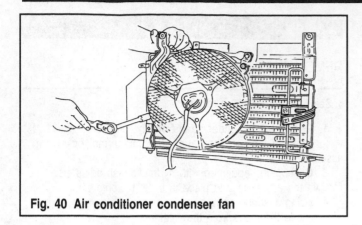

Fig. 40 Air conditioner condenser fan

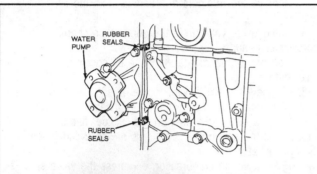

Fig. 41 Water pump assembly showing rubber seal location

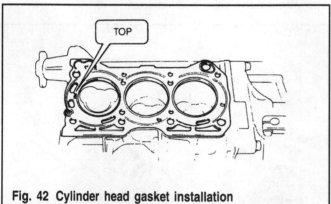

Fig. 42 Cylinder head gasket installation

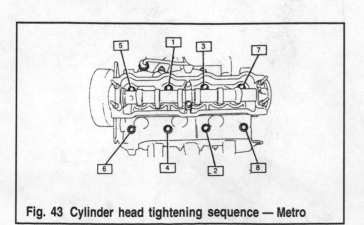

Fig. 43 Cylinder head tightening sequence — Metro

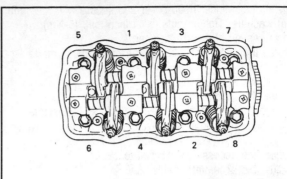

Fig. 44 Cylinder head tightening sequence — Sprint

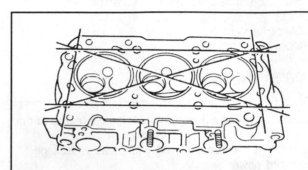

Fig. 45 Locations for measuring cylinder head gasket surface distortion

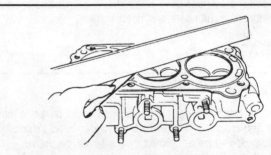

Fig. 46 Measuring the cylinder head surface with a straightedge and feeler gauge.

10. Remove the cylinder head cover.
11. Loosen and remove the cylinder head bolts in the reverse order of the tightening sequence.
12. Remove the cylinder head from the engine. Discard the cylinder head gasket.

To install:

13. Install the cylinder head gasket with the TOP indicator facing upward and to the crankshaft pulley side.
14. Install the cylinder head and eight cylinder head bolts. Lubricate the head bolts with engine oil prior to installation.
15. Tighten cylinder head bolts in the proper sequence to 54 ft. lbs.. (73 Nm). Repeat tighten sequence several times before reaching specified torque figure.
16. Install rubber seals between the water pump and the cylinder head.

17. Install the cylinder head cover and secure with nuts and new seal washers. Tighten nuts to 44 inch lbs.. (5 Nm).

18. Install timing belt and tensioner.

19. Install the distributor, aligning the matchmarks made during removal.

20. Install the intake manifold.

21. Install the exhaust manifold.

22. Connect all previously removed electrical connectors.

23. Connect all previously removed vacuum, fuel and water hoses.

24. Adjust the accessory drive belt tension.

25. Adjust the accelerator cable play.

26. Refill the cooling system.

27. Connect the negative battery cable.

28. Start the engine and allow it to reach operating temperature.

29. Check for leaks.

30. Make any necessary adjustments.

CLEANING AND INSPECTION

➡**Do not use any sharp edged tool to scrape carbon from the head. Be careful not to scuff or nick the metal surfaces when decarboning. This could lead to leakage and reduced power output.**

1. Disassemble the cylinder head, clean with solvent and air dry thoroughly. Remove all carbon from the combustion chambers.

2. Check the cylinder head for cracks in intake and exhaust ports, combustion chambers and head surface.

RESURFACING

♦ **See Figures 45 and 46**

All cylinder head resurfacing operations should be performed by a qualified machine shop; only the cylinder head inspection is recommended to be performed by the home mechanic.

1. Check the flatness of the cylinder head gasket surface. Using a straight edge and feeler gauge, check surface at a total of six locations.

2. If distortion exceeds the 0.0002 in. (0.05mm) limit at any location, resurfacing of the head is necessary.

3. If distortion cannot be brought within limits, replace the cylinder head.

➡**Leakage of combustion gases from this gasket joint is often due to a warped gasket surface. Leakage results in reduced power output.**

4. Check for distortion of the manifold seating faces. Using a straight edge and feeler gauge, check the seating faces of the intake and exhaust manifolds-to-cylinder head to determine whether these faces can be corrected or if the cylinder head must be replaced.

5. If measurement after any correction exceeds 0.004 in. (0.10mm), replace the cylinder head.

Valves

REMOVAL & INSTALLATION

♦ **See Figures 47, 48 and 49**

1. Remove the cylinder head from the engine.

2. Remove the camshaft and, as required, the rocker arm assemblies.

3. On engines equipped with hydraulic lash adjusters, remove the adjusters and place in order of removal.

4. Using a spring compressor, compress the valve springs and remove the locks from the retainers.

5. Remove the retainers and springs from the cylinder head.

6. Remove the valve from the combustion chamber side of the cylinder head.

7. Remove the valve seal from the cylinder head.

To install:

8. Lubricate the valve with engine oil and install from the combustion chamber side of the cylinder head.

9. Install a new valve seal on the cylinder head.

10. Install the springs and retainers on the cylinder head one cylinder at a time.

11. Using a spring compressor, compress the valve springs and install the locks in the retainers.

12. Once all cylinders are assembled, use a rubber hammer to hit each valve assembly on the retainer side. This will positively seat the locks in the retainer.

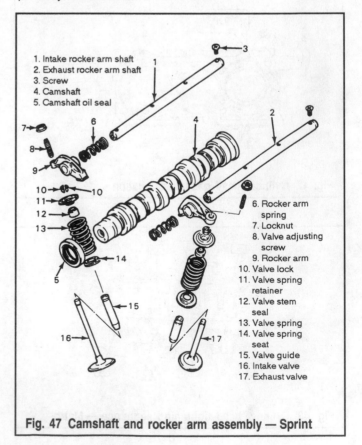

1. Intake rocker arm shaft
2. Exhaust rocker arm shaft
3. Screw
4. Camshaft
5. Camshaft oil seal
6. Rocker arm spring
7. Locknut
8. Valve adjusting screw
9. Rocker arm
10. Valve lock
11. Valve spring retainer
12. Valve stem seal
13. Valve spring
14. Valve spring seat
15. Valve guide
16. Intake valve
17. Exhaust valve

Fig. 47 Camshaft and rocker arm assembly — Sprint

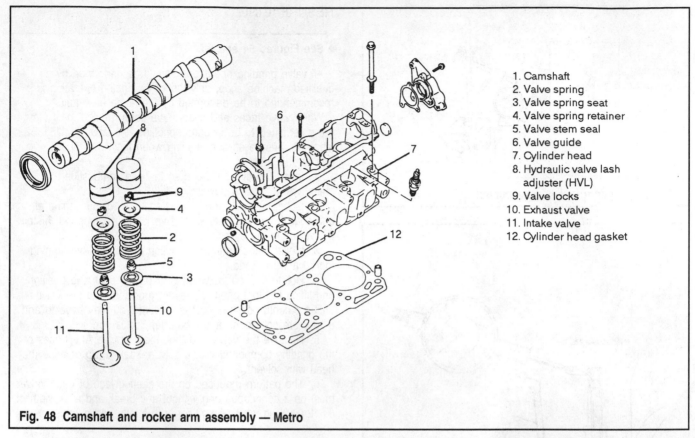

1. Camshaft
2. Valve spring
3. Valve spring seat
4. Valve spring retainer
5. Valve stem seal
6. Valve guide
7. Cylinder head
8. Hydraulic valve lash adjuster (HVL)
9. Valve locks
10. Exhaust valve
11. Intake valve
12. Cylinder head gasket

Fig. 48 Camshaft and rocker arm assembly — Metro

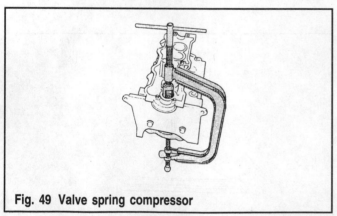

Fig. 49 Valve spring compressor

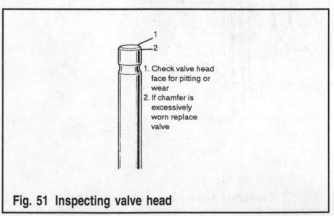

1. Check valve head face for pitting or wear
2. If chamfer is excessively worn replace valve

Fig. 51 Inspecting valve head

13. On engines equipped with hydraulic lash adjusters, lubricate and install the adjusters in their original positions.
14. Install the camshaft and, as required, the rocker arm assemblies.
15. Install the cylinder head on the engine.
16. Adjust valve lash as required.

INSPECTION

▶ **See Figures 50, 51, 52 and 53**

1. Check each valve for wear, burn or distortion at its face and stem and replace as necessary.

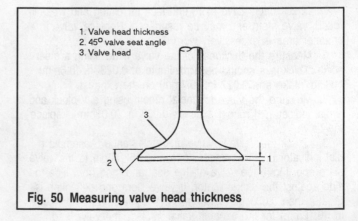

1. Valve head thickness
2. 45° valve seat angle
3. Valve head

Fig. 50 Measuring valve head thickness

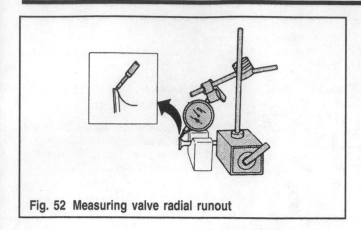

Fig. 52 Measuring valve radial runout

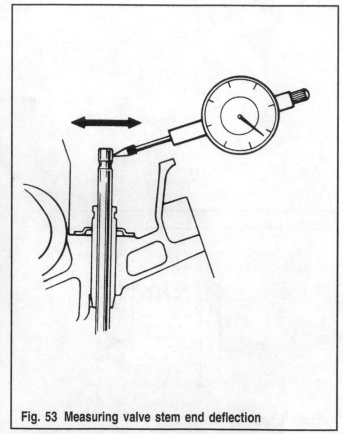

Fig. 53 Measuring valve stem end deflection

2. Check each valve stem end face for pitting and wear. If found, valve stem end may be resurfaced. Replace valve if chamfer area is excessively worn.

3. Measure the thickness of the valve head using a steel scale. Thickness should be a minimum of 0.023 in. (0.6mm) on the intake and 0.027 in. (0.7mm) on the exhaust.

4. Measure the valve for radial runout using a V-block and a dial indicator. If runout exceeds 0.003 in. (0.08mm), replace the valve.

5. Check the valve-to-valve guide clearance. Assemble a dial indicator on the cylinder head at a 45° angle to the valve stem end. Move the valve off the seat and then from side to side against the dial indicator. If valve stem end deflection is greater than 0.005 in. (0.14mm) for the intake valve, or 0.007 in. (0.18mm) for the exhaust valve, replace the valve and valve guide.

RESURFACING

▶ **See Figures 54 and 55**

All valve grinding operations should be performed by a qualified machine shop; only the valve lapping operation is recommended to be performed by the home mechanic.

When valve faces and seats have been refaced, or if they are determined to be in good condition, the valves MUST BE lapped to ensure efficient sealing when the valve closes against the seat.

1. Invert the cylinder head so that the combustion chambers are facing upward.

2. Lightly lubricate the valve stems with clean engine oil and coat the valve seats with valve lapping compound. Install the valves in the cylinder head as numbered.

3. Moisten and attach the suction cup of a valve lapping tool to a valve head.

4. Rotate the tool between your palms, changing position and lifting the tool often to prevent grooving. Lap the valve until a smooth polished seat is evident (you may have to add a bit more compound after some lapping is done).

5. Remove the valve and tool, then remove ALL traces of the grinding compound with a solvent-soaked rag or rinse the head with solvent.

6. The pattern produced on the seating face of each valve must be a continuous ring without any break and at a width of 0.512-0.590 in. (1.3-1.5mm) for both intake and exhaust valves.

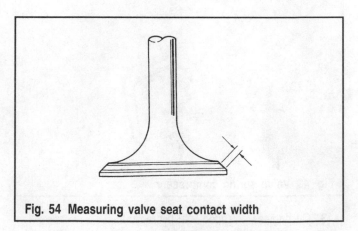

Fig. 54 Measuring valve seat contact width

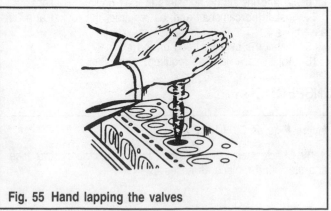

Fig. 55 Hand lapping the valves

Valve Stem Seals

REPLACEMENT

♦ **See Figures 56 and 57**

Head On Engine

When removing valve seals with the cylinder head on the engine, something must prevent the valve from dropping into the cylinder when the spring and retainer are removed. The method used most commonly is to fill the cylinder with compressed air.

1. Remove the camshaft and, as required, the rocker arm assemblies.

2. On engines equipped with hydraulic lash adjusters, remove the adjusters and place in order of removal.

3. Rotate the engine so that the piston in the cylinder being worked on is at TDC on the compression stroke (both valves closed).

4. Remove the spark plug and install an air adapter tool. Pressurize the cylinder head with compressed air.

5. Using a spring compressor, compress the valve springs and remove the locks from the retainers.

6. Remove the retainers and springs from the cylinder head.

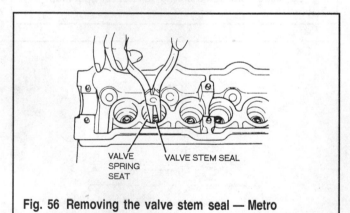

VALVE SPRING SEAT   VALVE STEM SEAL

Fig. 56 Removing the valve stem seal — Metro

Fig. 57 Removing the valve stem seal — Sprint

1. Valve stem oil seal
2. Prybar
3. Valve spring seat

7. Remove the valve seal from the cylinder head.
To install:
8. Lubricate the valve with engine oil and install the valve seal.

➠**Never reuse old valve seals. Always install new valve seals when the cylinder head is disassembled.**

9. Install the valve spring and retainer on the cylinder head.

10. Using a spring compressor, compress the valve spring and install the locks in the retainers.

11. Remove the air adapter hose and proceed to the next cylinder.

12. Once all cylinders are assembled, use a rubber hammer to hit each valve assembly on the retainer side. This will positively seat the locks in the retainer.

13. On engines equipped with hydraulic lash adjusters, lubricate and install the adjusters in their original positions.

14. Install the camshaft and, as required, the rocker arm assemblies.

15. Adjust valve lash as required.

Head Removed

1. Remove the cylinder head from the engine.

2. Remove the camshaft and, as required, the rocker arm assemblies.

3. On engines equipped with hydraulic lash adjusters, remove the adjusters and place in order of removal.

4. Using a spring compressor, compress the valve springs and remove the locks from the retainers.

5. Remove the retainers and springs from the cylinder head.

6. Remove the valve from the combustion chamber side of the cylinder head.

7. Remove the valve seal from the cylinder head.
To install:
8. Lubricate the valve with engine oil and install from the combustion chamber side for the cylinder head.

9. Install a new valve seal on the cylinder head.

➠**Never reuse old valve seals. Always install new valve seals when the cylinder head is disassembled.**

10. Install the springs and retainers on the cylinder head one cylinder at a time.

11. Using a spring compressor, compress the valve springs and install the locks in the retainers.

12. Once all cylinders are assembled, use a rubber hammer to hit each valve assembly on the retainer side. This will positively seat the locks in the retainer.

13. On engines equipped with hydraulic lash adjusters, lubricate and install the adjusters in their original positions.

14. Install the camshaft and, as required, the rocker arm assemblies.

15. Install the cylinder head on the engine.

16. Adjust valve lash as required.

Valve Springs

REMOVAL & INSTALLATION

▶ See Figures 47, 48, 49 and 58

1. Remove the cylinder head from the engine.
2. Remove the camshaft and, as required, the rocker arm assemblies.
3. On engines equipped with hydraulic lash adjusters, remove the adjusters and place in order of removal.
4. Using a spring compressor, compress the valve springs and remove the locks from the retainers.
5. Remove the retainers and springs from the cylinder head.

To install:

6. Install the springs and retainers on the cylinder head one cylinder at a time.

➡**Position the valve spring with the small pitch end facing the cylinder head.**

7. Using a spring compressor, compress the valve springs and install the locks in the retainers.
8. Once all cylinders are assembled, use a rubber hammer to hit each valve assembly on the retainer side. This will positively seat the locks in the retainer.
9. On engines equipped with hydraulic lash adjusters, lubricate and install the adjusters in their original positions.
10. Install the camshaft and, as required, the rocker arm assemblies.
11. Adjust valve lash as necessary.

INSPECTION

▶ See Figures 59, 60 and 61

1. With the valve spring removed from the cylinder head, measure the free length. Minimum free length is 1.5551 in. (39.5mm).
2. Using a valve spring tester, measure the spring tension at the specified height. Minimum tension is 36.6 lbs.. at 1.28 in.
3. Using a square, check valve spring squareness. Measure the clearance at the top if the spring. Maximum clearance is 0.079 in. (2.0mm).

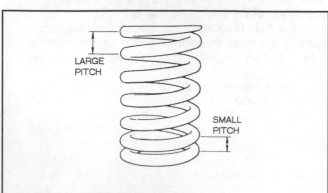

Fig. 58 Valve spring identification

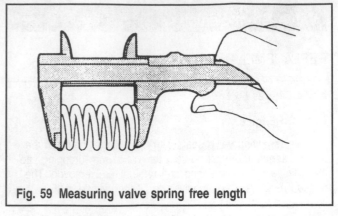

Fig. 59 Measuring valve spring free length

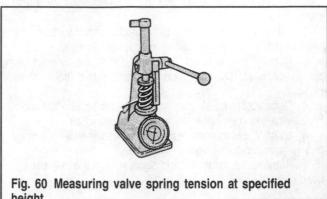

Fig. 60 Measuring valve spring tension at specified height

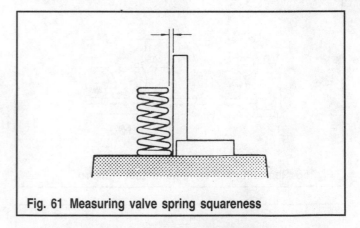

Fig. 61 Measuring valve spring squareness

4. If the valve spring does not meet specification, replace it. If two or more springs are out of specification, it is recommended that the entire set be replaced.

Valve Seat

REMOVAL & INSTALLATION

Valve seats are not replaceable. If the valve seat cannot be resurfaced to show the specified seat contact width, replace the cylinder head as an assembly.

Valve Guides

REMOVAL & INSTALLATION

▶ **See Figures 62 and 63**

1. Remove the cylinder head from the engine.
2. Remove the camshaft and, as required, the rocker arms.
3. Number and remove the valves from the engine.
4. Using a valve guide remover press the valve guide out from the combustion chamber side to the valve spring side of the cylinder head.

   To install:

→**Never reuse a valve guide once removed from the cylinder head.**

5. Ream the valve guide hole in the cylinder head to remove burrs.
6. Heat the cylinder head uniformly at a temperature of 176-212°F (80-100°C) so that the head will not be distorted during valve guide installation.
7. Install the valve guide into the cylinder head.
8. Drive the guide into the cylinder head until there is 0.45 in. (11.5mm) of the valve guide protruding from the top of the cylinder head.
9. Ream the valve guide bore to obtain the proper valve guide-to-valve clearance.
10. Reface the valves and valve seat as required.
11. Lubricate and install the valves.

12. Install the valve seals, springs, retainers, locks, lash adjusters (as required), and camshaft.
13. Install the cylinder head on the engine.
14. Adjust the valve lash as required.

Hydraulic Lash Adjusters (Valve Lifters)

REMOVAL & INSTALLATION

▶ **See Figures 64 and 65**

1. Remove the cylinder head cover.
2. Remove the distributor.
3. Remove the timing belt and tensioner.
4. Remove the camshaft.
5. Remove the HVL adjusters from the cylinder head.

   To install:

6. Pour engine oil through camshaft journal oil holes and check that oil comes out from oil holes in HVL adjuster bores.

→**Always replace the HVL adjusters in the order they were removed.**

7. Apply engine oil around adjuster and then install HVL adjusters in cylinder head.
8. Install the camshaft.
9. Install the timing belt and tensioner.
10. Install the distributor.
11. Install the cylinder head cover.
12. Make all necessary adjustments.

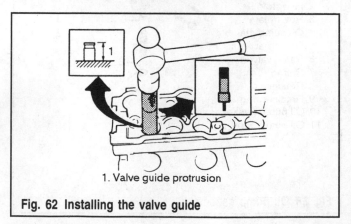

Fig. 62 Installing the valve guide

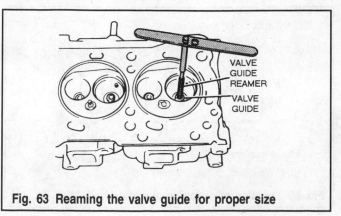

Fig. 63 Reaming the valve guide for proper size

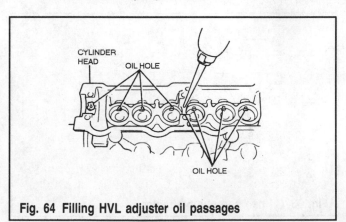

Fig. 64 Filling HVL adjuster oil passages

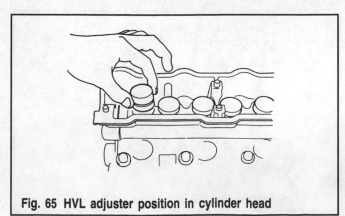

Fig. 65 HVL adjuster position in cylinder head

Oil Pan

REMOVAL & INSTALLATION

▶ **See Figures 66 and 67**

1. Remove the negative battery cable.
2. Raise and support the vehicle safely.
3. Drain the engine oil.
4. Remove the flywheel dust cover.
5. Remove the exhaust pipe at the exhaust manifold.
6. Remove the oil pan bolts, the pan and the oil pump strainer.

To install:

7. Clean the oil pan and oil pump strainer screen. Clean the gasket mating surfaces.
8. Install the oil pump strainer with a new seal. Secure with bolt and tighten to 97 inch lbs.. (11 Nm).
9. Apply a continuous bead of RTV sealant to the engine oil pan and install. Tighten the oil pan bolts to 9 ft. lbs.. (11 Nm).
10. Install the oil pan drain plug with a new gasket and tighten to 26 ft. lbs.. (35 Nm).
11. Install the exhaust pipe at the exhaust manifold.
12. Install the flywheel dust cover.
13. Lower the vehicle and fill the engine with oil.
14. Connect the negative battery cable, start the engine and check for proper oil pressure.

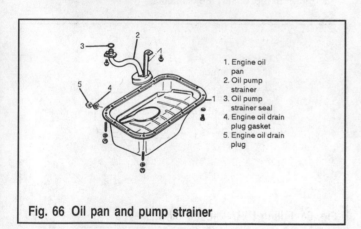

1. Engine oil pan
2. Oil pump strainer
3. Oil pump strainer seal
4. Engine oil drain plug gasket
5. Engine oil drain plug

Fig. 66 Oil pan and pump strainer

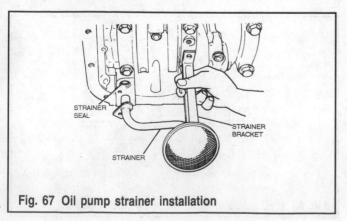

Fig. 67 Oil pump strainer installation

Oil Pump

REMOVAL

▶ **See Figures 68 and 69**

1. Remove the negative battery cable.
2. Raise and support the vehicle safely.
3. Drain the engine oil.
4. Remove the water pump belt, pulley, alternator, alternator bracket and air conditioning mounting bracket, if equipped.
5. Remove the crankshaft pulley, timing belt outside cover, timing belt and tensioner.

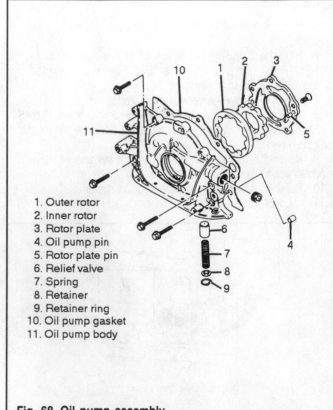

1. Outer rotor
2. Inner rotor
3. Rotor plate
4. Oil pump pin
5. Rotor plate pin
6. Relief valve
7. Spring
8. Retainer
9. Retainer ring
10. Oil pump gasket
11. Oil pump body

Fig. 68 Oil pump assembly

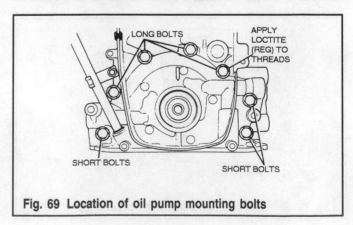

Fig. 69 Location of oil pump mounting bolts

6. Disconnect the engine oil level gauge.

7. Remove the crankshaft timing belt gear and timing belt guide. With the crankshaft locked, remove the crankshaft timing belt pulley bolt.

8. Remove the oil pan bolts, oil pan, oil strainer fixing bolt and the oil strainer assembly.

9. Remove the oil pump bolts and the oil pump assembly.

INSPECTION

▶ **See Figures 70 and 71**

1. Inspect the oil seal lip for damage and replace as necessary.

2. Inspect the outer and inner rotors, rotor plate and oil pump body for excessive wear or damage. Replace as necessary.

3. Measure the radial clearance between the outer rotor and case using a feeler gauge. If clearance exceeds 0.0122 in. (0.310mm), replace the outer rotor or case.

4. Measure the side clearance using a straight edge and feeler gauge. If clearance exceeds 0.0059 in. (0.15 mm), replace the oil pump case.

OVERHAUL

1. Remove the bolt and guide tube from the oil pump. Discard the seal.

2. Remove the screws and rotor plate from the pump body.

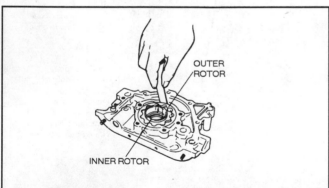

Fig. 70 Measuring oil pump rotor radial clearance

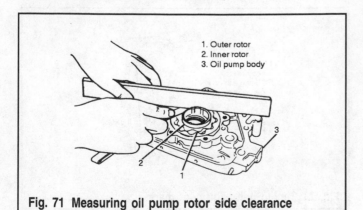

Fig. 71 Measuring oil pump rotor side clearance

3. Remove the outer and inner rotors from the pump body.

4. Inspect the pump and rotors. Measure clearances and replace components as necessary.

5. Clean and dry all disassembled parts.

6. Apply a thin coat of engine oil to inner and outer rotors, oil seal lip portion and inside surfaces of oil pump body.

7. Assemble outer and inner rotors to pump body.

8. Install rotor plate and secure with screws.

9. Check to be sure that rotors turn freely by hand.

10. Install guide seal and guide tube to oil pump. Tighten bolt to 97 inch lbs.. (11 Nm).

INSTALLATION

1. Clean the gasket mating surfaces thoroughly.

2. Lubricate the oil pump with fresh engine oil.

3. Using new gaskets and sealant, install the oil pump on the engine.

➡**Take care not to damage the front seal on the crankshaft snout.**

4. Apply Loctite® pipe sealant or equivalent to the oil pump bolts and install. Tighten to 97 inch lbs.. (11 Nm).

➡**After tightening the oil pump seal may bulge out. If it does, trim the edge with a sharp knife, making sure the edge is smooth and flush with the cylinder block.**

5. Install the rubber seal between the oil pump and coolant pump.

6. Install the crankshaft timing belt gear and timing belt guide. With the crankshaft locked, tighten the pulley bolt to 81 ft. lbs.. (110 Nm).

7. Install the engine oil level gauge.

8. Install the oil strainer and oil pan.

9. Install the timing belt, tensioner and outside cover.

10. Install the water pump belt, pulley, alternator, alternator bracket and air conditioning mounting bracket, if equipped.

11. Lower the vehicle and fill the engine with oil.

12. Connect the negative battery cable, start the engine and check for proper oil pressure. Check for leaks.

Crankshaft Pulley

REMOVAL & INSTALLATION

▶ **See Figure 72**

1. Disconnect the negative battery cable.

2. Raise and support the vehicle safely.

3. Remove the clips and right side splash shield.

4. Remove the lower generator cover plate.

5. Remove the alternator and, as required, air conditioner drive belt.

➡**It is not necessary to remove the crankshaft timing gear bolt in the center of the pulley to remove the pulley.**

6. Remove the crankshaft pulley bolts and crankshaft pulley.

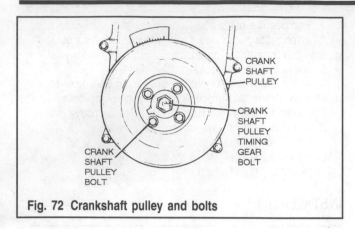

Fig. 72 Crankshaft pulley and bolts

To install:

7. Install the crankshaft pulley. Fit the keyway on the pulley to the key on crankshaft timing gear. Tighten pulley bolts to 97 ft. lbs.. (11 Nm).

8. Install the generator drive belt and lower generator cover plate. Tighten cover plate bolts to 89 inch lbs.. (10 Nm).

9. Install the air conditioner drive belt, as required.

10. Install the right side splash shield and secure with clips.

11. Lower the vehicle and connect the negative battery cable.

Timing Belt Front Cover

REMOVAL & INSTALLATION

▶ **See Figure 73**

1. Disconnect the negative battery cable.
2. Raise and support the vehicle safely.
3. Remove the clips and right side splash shield.
4. Remove the lower generator cover plate.
5. Remove the alternator and, as required, air conditioner drive belt.
6. Remove the water pump pulley.

➡**It is not necessary to remove the crankshaft timing gear bolt in the center of the pulley to remove the pulley.**

7. Remove the crankshaft pulley bolts and crankshaft pulley.

8. Remove the 7 bolts and 1 nut from the timing belt outside cover.

9. Remove the timing belt outside cover.

To install:

10. Clean seal mating surfaces thoroughly.

11. Using a new seal, install timing belt cover and tighten bolts and nut to 97 inch lbs.. (11 Nm).

12. Install the crankshaft pulley and water pump pulley.

13. Install and tension the alternator and, as required, air conditioner drive belt.

14. Install the lower generator cover plate. Tighten bolts to 89 inch lbs.. (10 Nm).

15. Install the clips and right side splash shield.

16. Lower the vehicle and connect the negative battery cable.

Timing Belt

REMOVAL & INSTALLATION

▶ **See Figures 73, 74 and 75**

➡Timing belts must always be handled carefully and kept completely free of dirt, grease, fluids and lubricants. This includes any accidental contact from spillage, fingerprints, rags, etc. These same precautions apply to the pulleys and contact surfaces on which the belt rides. The belt must never be crimped, twisted or bent. Never use tools to pry or wedge the belt into place. Such actions will damage the structure of the belt and possibly cause breakage.

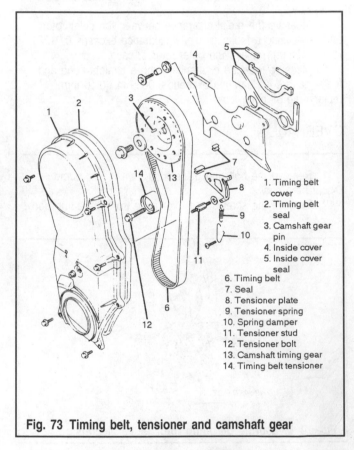

1. Timing belt cover
2. Timing belt seal
3. Camshaft gear pin
4. Inside cover
5. Inside cover seal
6. Timing belt
7. Seal
8. Tensioner plate
9. Tensioner spring
10. Spring damper
11. Tensioner stud
12. Tensioner bolt
13. Camshaft timing gear
14. Timing belt tensioner

Fig. 73 Timing belt, tensioner and camshaft gear

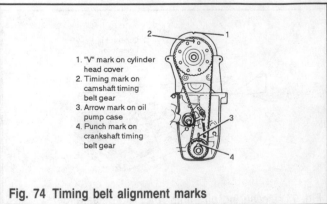

1. "V" mark on cylinder head cover
2. Timing mark on camshaft timing belt gear
3. Arrow mark on oil pump case
4. Punch mark on crankshaft timing belt gear

Fig. 74 Timing belt alignment marks

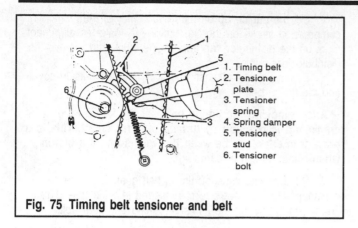

1. Timing belt
2. Tensioner plate
3. Tensioner spring
4. Spring damper
5. Tensioner stud
6. Tensioner bolt

Fig. 75 Timing belt tensioner and belt

1. Disconnect the negative battery cable.
2. Raise and safely support the vehicle.
3. Remove the 4 crankshaft pulley bolts and remove the crankshaft pulley.

➡It is not necessary to loosen the crankshaft timing belt pulley bolt at the center.

4. Remove the timing belt cover.
5. Align the 4 timing marks by turning the crankshaft.
6. Remove the timing belt tensioner, tensioner plate, tensioner spring, spring damper and timing belt.

➡After the timing belt is removed, never turn the camshaft or crankshaft independently. If turned, interference may occur among the pistons, and valves and parts related to the pistons and valves may be damaged.

7. Inspect the timing belt for wear or cracks and replace as necessary. Check the tensioner for smooth rotation.
   To install:
8. Install the tensioner plate to the tensioner.
9. Insert the lug of the tensioner plate into the hole of the tensioner.
10. Install the tensioner, tensioner plate and spring. Do not tighten the tensioner bolt and stud, make the bolt hand tight only.

➡Be sure that plate movement is installed in the proper direction that causes the same directional movement of the tensioner inner race. If no movement between the plate and inner race occurs remove the tensioner and plate again and reinsert the plate lug into the tensioner hole.

11. Check that the timing mark on the camshaft timing pulley is aligned with the **V** mark on the cylinder head cover. If not align the 2 marks by turning the camshaft by be careful not to turn it more than the allowable range.
12. Check that the punch mark on the crankshaft timing belt pulley is aligned with the arrow mark on the oil pump case. If not align the 2 marks by turning the camshaft by be careful not to turn it more than the allowable range.
13. With the 4 marks aligned, install the timing belt on the 2 pulleys in such a way that the arrow marks on the belt (if so equipped) coincide with the rotating direction of the crankshaft. In this state the No. 1 piston is at top dead center of its compression stroke.
14. Install the tensioner spring and spring damper. To allow the belt to be free of any slack, turn the crankshaft 2 rotations

clockwise after installing the tensioner spring and damper. After removing the belt slack, first tighten the tensioner stud to 8 ft. lbs.. (11 Nm) and then the tensioner bolt to 20 ft. lbs.. (27 Nm).

➡As a final check, confirm that both sets of timing marks are aligned properly.

15. Ensure that the seal is between the water pump and the oil pump case. Install the timing belt outside cover. Torque the timing belt cover bolts to 8 ft. lbs.. (11 Nm).
16. Install the crankshaft pulley. Fit the keyway on the pulley to the key on the crank timing belt pulley and tighten the 4 bolts to 8 ft. lbs.. (11 Nm).
17. Lower the vehicle and install the negative battery cable.

Timing Sprockets

REMOVAL & INSTALLATION

▶ **See Figures 73, 74, 75 and 76**

1. Disconnect the battery negative cable.
2. Remove the timing belt cover and timing belt.

➡After the timing belt is removed, never turn the camshaft or crankshaft independently. If turned, interference may occur among the pistons, and valves and parts related to the pistons and valves may be damaged.

3. Using a 0.39 in. (10mm) inserted into the camshaft, hold the camshaft sprocket and remove the retaining bolt, camshaft sprocket, alignment pin and inside cover.
4. Using a suitable spanner wrench, remove the crankshaft pulley bolt and the crankshaft pulley.
   To install:
5. Install the crankshaft sprocket, aligning the keyway with the key. Tighten the crankshaft sprocket bolt to 81 ft. lbs.. (110 Nm).
6. Install the camshaft sprocket and tighten the bolt to Torque the camshaft bolt to 44 ft. lbs.. (60 Nm). Remove the locking rod.
7. Align the 'V' mark on the timing belt cover with the timing mark on the camshaft sprocket and the arrow mark on the engine block with the punch mark on the crankshaft timing sprocket.
8. Install the timing belt and cover.

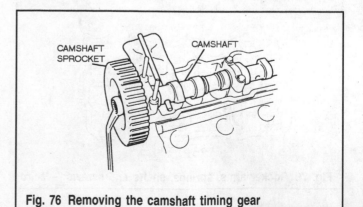

CAMSHAFT SPROCKET   CAMSHAFT

Fig. 76 Removing the camshaft timing gear

9. Connect the negative battery cable.

Camshaft and Bearings

REMOVAL & INSTALLATION

Sprint

▶ **See Figures 77, 78 and 79**

1. Disconnect the negative battery cable.
2. Remove the air cleaner assembly.
3. Remove the cylinder head cover assembly.

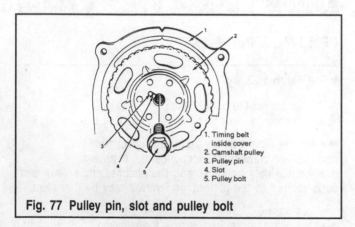

1. Timing belt inside cover
2. Camshaft pulley
3. Pulley pin
4. Slot
5. Pulley bolt

Fig. 77 Pulley pin, slot and pulley bolt

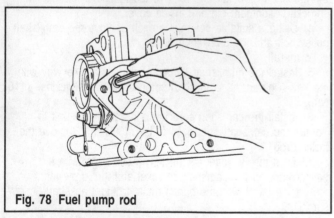

Fig. 78 Fuel pump rod

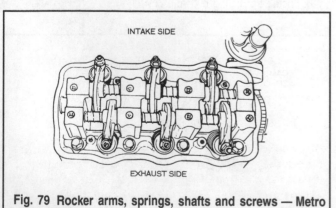

INTAKE SIDE

EXHAUST SIDE

Fig. 79 Rocker arms, springs, shafts and screws — Metro

4. Set the engine up on top dead center of the compression stroke on the No. 1 cylinder. Make an alignment mark on the distributor cap and engine block and remove the distributor assembly.
5. Remove the crankshaft pulley, timing belt outside cover and the timing belt.

➡**After removing the timing belt, set the key on the crankshaft in position by turning the crankshaft. This is to prevent interference between the valves and the piston when reinstalling the camshaft.**

6. Remove the camshaft timing belt gear. Lock the camshaft with a proper size rod inserted into the hole 0.39 in. (10mm) in it. Loosen the camshaft timing belt gear bolt.

➡**The mating surface of the cylinder head and cover must not be damaged in this work. So, put a clean shop cloth between the rod and mating surfaces and use care not to bump the rod against the mating surfaces hard when loosening.**

7. Remove the fuel pump and fuel pump rod. Remove the camshaft from the cylinder head.

To install:

8. Apply engine oil to lobes and journals on camshaft and oil seal on cylinder head.
9. Install the camshaft into the cylinder head.
10. Install the timing belt inside cover and camshaft pulley. Fit pulley pin on camshaft into slot on camshaft pulley. Tighten the pulley bolt to 41-46 ft. lbs.. (55-64 Nm).
11. Install the fuel pump rod, gasket and fuel pump to the cylinder head.
12. Apply engine oil to rocker arms and rocker arm shafts.

➡**The two rocker arm shafts are different. To distinguish between the two, the dimensions of their stepped ends differ. The intake rocker arm step measures 0.55 in. (14mm). The exhaust rocker arm step measures 0.59 in. (15mm).**

13. Install the intake rocker arm shaft facing its stepped end to camshaft pulley side, and the exhaust rocker arm shaft facing its stepped end to distributor side.
14. Install rocker arms, springs and rocker arm shafts. Tighten the rocker arm shaft screws to 7-9 ft. lbs.. (9-12 Nm).
15. Install the distributor.
16. Install the belt tensioner, timing belt, outside cover, crankshaft pulley and water pump belt.
17. Adjust the intake and exhaust valves.
18. Install the cylinder head cover and air cleaner.
19. Connect the negative battery cable.
20. Adjust the ignition timing.

Metro

▶ **See Figures 76, 80, 81, 82 and 83**

1. Disconnect the negative battery cable.
2. Remove the air cleaner assembly.
3. Remove the cylinder head cover assembly.
4. Set the engine up on top dead center of the compression stroke on the No. 1 cylinder. Make an alignment mark on the distributor cap and engine block and remove the distributor assembly.

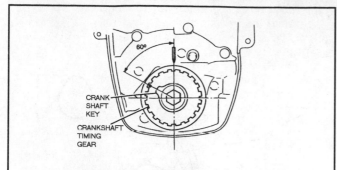

Fig. 80 Position of the crankshaft key for camshaft removal

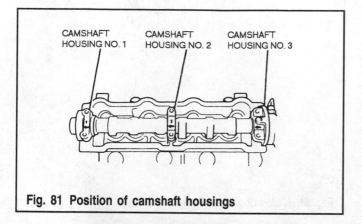

Fig. 81 Position of camshaft housings

Fig. 82 Removing the valve cover to expose the camshaft — Metro

Fig. 83 The camshaft is held in place by three bearing caps — Metro

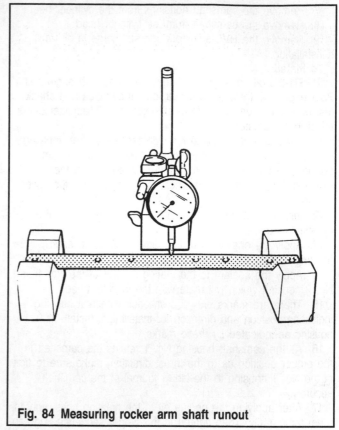

Fig. 84 Measuring rocker arm shaft runout

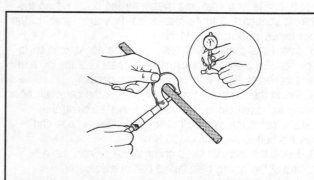

Fig. 85 Measuring rocker arm shaft and rocker arm bore to determine clearance

5. Remove the crankshaft pulley, timing belt outside cover and the timing belt.

➡After removing the timing belt, set the key on the crankshaft in position by turning the crankshaft. This is to prevent interference between the valves and the piston when reinstalling the camshaft.

6. Remove the camshaft timing belt gear. Lock the camshaft with a proper size rod inserted into the hole 0.39 in. (10mm) in it. Loosen the camshaft timing belt gear bolt.

➡The mating surface of the cylinder head and cover must not be damaged in this work. So, put a clean shop cloth between the rod and mating surfaces and use care not to bump the rod against the mating surfaces hard when loosening.

7. Remove the camshaft housings from the cylinder head.

8. Remove the camshaft from the cylinder head.

9. Remove the HVL adjusters and submerge in oil until reinstallation.

To install:

10. Fill the oil passage in the cylinder head with engine oil. Pour engine oil through camshaft journal oil holes and check that engine oil comes out from oil holes in HVL adjuster bores. Install HVL adjusters.

11. Install the camshaft to the cylinder head. After applying engine oil to the camshaft journal and all around the cam, position the camshaft into the cylinder head so that the camshaft timing belt gear pin hole in camshaft is at the lower position.

12. Install the camshaft housing to the camshaft and the cylinder head.

13. Apply the engine oil to the sliding surface of each housing against the camshaft journal.

14. Apply the sealant to the mating surface of the No. 1 and No. 3 housing which will mate with the cylinder head.

15. There are marks provided on each camshaft housing indicating position and direction for installation. Install the housing as indicated by these marks.

16. As the camshaft housing No. 1 retains the camshaft in the proper position as to the thrust direction, make sure to first fit the No. 1 housing to the No. 1 journal of the camshaft securely.

17. After applying the engine oil to the housing bolts, tighten them temporarily. Then tighten in the proper sequence. Tighten the bolts a little at a time and evenly among bolts, repeat the tightening sequence 3 to 4 times before they are tighten to the proper torque of 8 ft. lbs.. (11 Nm).

18. Install the camshaft oil seal. After applying engine oil to the oil seal lip, press-fit the camshaft oil seal until the oil seal surface becomes flush with the housing surfaces.

19. Install the camshaft timing belt gear to the camshaft after installing the dwell pin to the camshaft. While locking the camshaft, install the camshaft pulley and retaining bolt and torque the bolt to 44 ft. lbs.. (60 Nm).

20. Install the cylinder head cover to the cylinder head.

21. Install the timing belt, timing belt outside cover, crankshaft pulley, coolant pump pulley and coolant pump belt.

22. Install the distributor assembly into the engine.

23. Install the air cleaner assembly and reinstall the negative battery cable.

24. Adjust the ignition timing.

INSPECTION

▶ **See Figures 84, 85, 86, 87 and 88**

1. On Sprint models, inspect the adjusting screw and rocker arm. If the tip of the adjusting screw is badly worn, replace the screw. The arm must be replaced if its cam riding face is badly worn.

2. On Sprint models, inspect the rocker arm shaft runout. Using V-blocks and a dial gauge, check runout. If runout exceeds the limit, replace the rocker arm shaft.

3. On Sprint models, inspect rocker arm-to-rocker arm shaft clearance. Using a micrometer and bore gauge, measure the rocker shaft diameter and rocker arm inside diameter. The

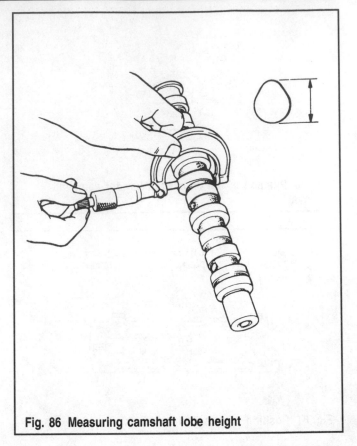

Fig. 86 Measuring camshaft lobe height

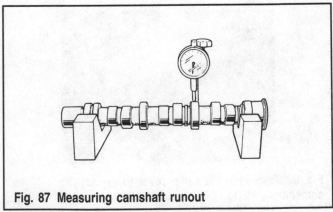

Fig. 87 Measuring camshaft runout

difference between the reading is the clearance. If clearance exceeds the limit, replace the shaft and/or rocker arm.

4. Inspect camshaft wear. Using a micrometer, measure the height of the lobe. If the height measurement is less than the limit, replace the camshaft.

5. Inspect the camshaft runout. Hold the camshaft between two V-blocks and measure the runout by using a dial gauge. If the runout exceeds the limit, replace the camshaft.

6. Inspect camshaft journal wear. Measure the journal diameter in two directions at four places to obtain four readings on each journal and measure the journal bores in the cylinder head with a bore gauge. Subtract the journal diameter measurement from the journal bore measurement to determine the journal clearance. If journal clearance exceeds the limit, replace the camshaft, and as necessary, the cylinder head.

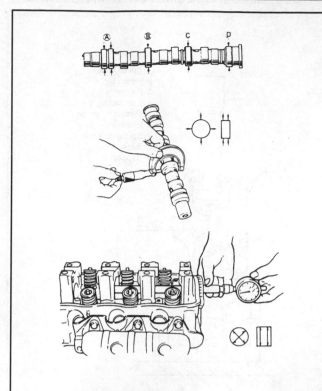

Fig. 88 Measuring camshaft journal diameter and cylinder head camshaft bore to determine clearance

Pistons and Connecting Rods

→This procedure assumes that the engine has already been partially disassembled, including removing the cylinder head and oil pan to allow access to the internal components. It is recommended that the engine be removed to facilitate servicing.

REMOVAL

1. Remove the engine from the vehicle.
2. Remove the intake manifold and the cylinder head(s).
3. Remove the oil pan and the oil pump assembly.
4. Stamp the cylinder number on the machined surfaces of the bolt bosses on the connecting rod and cap for identification when reinstalling.
5. If the pistons are to be removed from the connecting rod, mark the cylinder number on the piston with a silver pencil or quick drying paint for proper cylinder identification and cap to rod location.
6. Examine the cylinder bore above the ring travel. If a ridge exists, remove it with a ridge reamer before attempting to remove the piston and rod assembly.
7. Remove the connecting rod bearing cap and bearing.
8. Install a ⅜ inch rubber guide hose over the rod bolt threads; this will prevent damage to the bearing journal and rod bolt threads.

9. Remove the rod and piston assembly through the top of the cylinder bore; remove the other rod and piston assemblies in the same manner.
10. Clean and inspect all components.

CLEANING AND INSPECTION

Use a piston ring expanding tool, remove the piston rings from the pistons; any other method (screwdriver blades, pliers, etc.) usually results in the rings being bent, scratched or distorted and/or the piston itself being damaged.

Pistons

Clean the varnish from the piston skirts and pins with a cleaning solvent. Clean the ring grooves with a ring cleaner and make sure that the oil ring holes and slots are clean.

→Do not wire brush any part of the piston.

Inspect the piston for cracked ring lands, scuffed or damaged skirts, eroded areas at the top of the piston. Inspect the grooves for nicks of burrs that might cause the rings to hang up. Replace the pistons that are damaged or show signs of excessive wear.

Measure the piston skirt perpendicular to the piston pin at a point approximately ½ inch up from the bottom of the position. Use this figure when checking the piston clearance. If installing replacement pistons, follow the manufacturers recommendations on where to measure the piston. After measuring, mark the pistons with a felt-tip pen for assembly reference.

Cylinder Bores

Using a telescoping gauge or an inside micrometer, measure the diameter of the cylinder bore, perpendicular (90°) to the piston pin, at 1-2½″ below the surface of the cylinder block.

The difference between the piston outside diameter and the cylinder bore inside diameter is the piston clearance. If clearance exceeds specifications, the cylinder block must be bored to the next standard oversize and new pistons installed. If the clearance is within specifications or slightly below, finish honing is all that is necessary

→Boring or honing of the cylinder block should be performed by a reputable machine shop with the proper equipment. In some cases, clean-up honing can be done with the cylinder block in the vehicle, but most excessive honing and all cylinder boring MUST BE done with the block stripped and removed from the vehicle.

Connecting Rods

Wash the connecting rods in cleaning solvent and dry with compressed air. Check for twisted or bent rods and inspect for nicks or cracks. Replace the connecting rods that are damaged.

RIDGE REMOVAL AND HONING

Prior to removing the piston and rod assemblies, an inspection must be made to determine if a ridge exists at the top of the cylinder bore, above the travel of the piston.

1. Use a dial bore gauge or inside micrometer to measure the difference between the ridge at the top of the bore and the portion of the bore where the piston travels.

2. If a ridge exists, it must be removed using a ridge reamer.

3. Place the piston at the bottom of its bore and cover it with a rag.

4. Cut the ridge away using a ridge reamer, exercising extreme care to avoid cutting too deeply.

5. Remove the rag and remove the cuttings that remain on the piston.

6. Using a hammer handle or a wooden bar, force the pistons out through the top of the cylinder block.

➡ **Boring or honing of the cylinder block should be performed by a reputable machine shop with the proper equipment. In some cases, clean-up honing can be accomplished by the do-it-yourselfer, however, most boring or honing operations should be left to an experienced machine shop.**

PISTON PIN REPLACEMENT

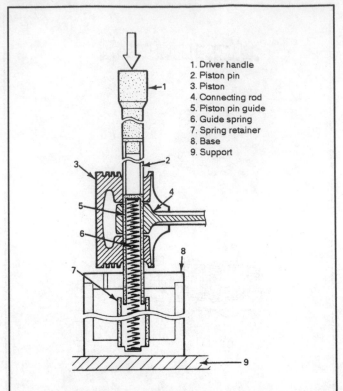

1. Driver handle
2. Piston pin
3. Piston
4. Connecting rod
5. Piston pin guide
6. Guide spring
7. Spring retainer
8. Base
9. Support

Fig. 89 Piston pin replacement using a piston pin tool — Non-turbocharged engine

Non-Turbocharged Engine

▶ **See Figures 89 and 90**

The piston pins on non-turbocharged engines are held in place by an interference fit with the connecting rod. A special tool, Piston Pin Remover/Installer J-34838, must be used to prevent damage to the piston when removing the pin.

1. Fit the piston and connecting rod assembly into the piston pin remover so that the arrow mark on the piston head faces upward.

2. Place the piston pin remover and piston assembly into a press and press the piston pin out of the connecting rod.

To install:

3. After applying engine oil to piston pin holes in piston and connecting rod, fit connecting rod to piston with the dot on the connecting rod facing you and the arrow on the piston facing to the right.

4. Fit the piston and connecting rod assembly into the piston pin remover so that the arrow mark on the piston head faces upward.

5. Place the piston pin remover and piston assembly into a press and press the piston pin through the piston and connecting rod.

6. Press the piston pin until the line marked on the driver handle is flush with the flat surface of the piston.

Turbocharged Engine

▶ **See Figures 90, 91 and 92**

The piston pins on turbocharged engines are of the full floating type and are held in place by circlips at the ends of the pin. Special tools are not needed to remove the piston pin.

1. Use a ring expander to remove the piston rings.

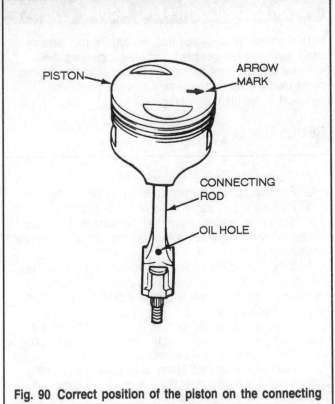

PISTON

ARROW MARK

CONNECTING ROD

OIL HOLE

Fig. 90 Correct position of the piston on the connecting rod

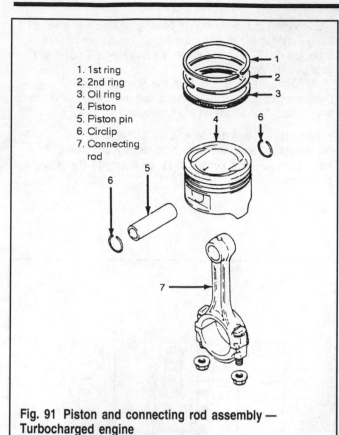

1. 1st ring
2. 2nd ring
3. Oil ring
4. Piston
5. Piston pin
6. Circlip
7. Connecting rod

Fig. 91 Piston and connecting rod assembly — Turbocharged engine

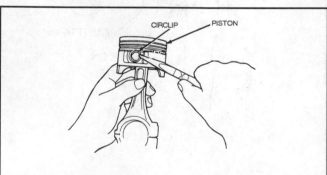

CIRCLIP   PISTON

Fig. 92 Removing the piston pin circlip with needle-nose pliers

2. Use needle-nose pliers to remove the circlip from one end of the piston.

3. Remove the piston pin and separate the piston from the connecting rod.

4. Remove the circlip from the opposite side of the piston.

To install:

5. Measure the inside diameter of the piston pin bore in the connecting rod. Inside diameter should be 0.7481-0.7485 in. (19.003-19.011mm).

6. Measure the outside diameter of the piston pin. Outside diameter should measure 0.7478-0.7481 in. (18.995-19.000mm).

7. The difference between the measurements is the piston pin-to-bore clearance. Clearance should be 0.0001-0.0006 in. (0.003-0.016mm).

8. Install the circlip at one end of the piston.

➡**Always use new circlips when reinstalling piston pins.**

9. Join the piston and connecting rod with the dot on the piston facing upward and the arrow on the piston facing the right.

10. Install the piston pin after lubricating with oil.

11. Install the circlip on the other end of the piston. Ensure that the circlip is fitted in piston groove securely.

12. Move the piston around to ensure it does not bind.

PISTON RING REPLACEMENT

◆ **See Figures 93, 94 and 95**

1. Use a ring expander to remove the piston rings. Take care not to scratch the piston during ring removal.

2. Compress the piston ring into a cylinder (one at a time).

3. Squirt some clean oil into the cylinder so that the ring and the top 2″ (51mm) of the cylinder wall are coated.

4. Using an inverted piston, push the ring approximately 1 inch(25.4mm) below the top of the cylinder.

5. Using a feeler gauge, measure the ring gap and compare it to the specifications. If ring gap is smaller than specifications, it may be filed to enlarge the gap. Although, this is rarely necessary if the correct rings are used.

6. Carefully remove the ring from the cylinder.

7. Check the pistons to see that the ring grooves and oil return holes have been properly cleaned.

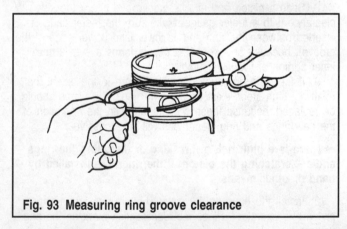

Fig. 93 Measuring ring groove clearance

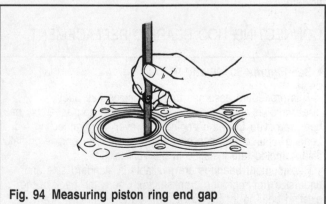

Fig. 94 Measuring piston ring end gap

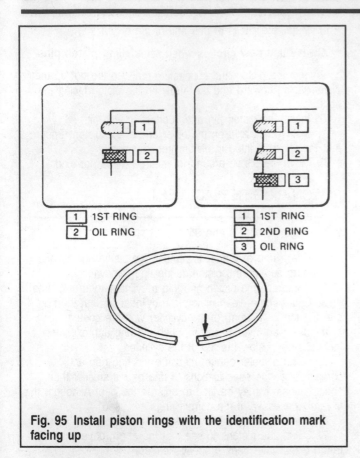

Fig. 95 Install piston rings with the identification mark facing up

8. Slide a piston ring into its groove and check the side clearance with a feeler gauge. Make sure the feeler gauge is inserted between the ring and its lower land (lower edge of the groove), because any wear that occurs forms a step at the inner portion of the lower land.

9. If the piston grooves have been worn to the extent that relatively high steps exist on the lower land, the piston should be replaced, because these will interfere with the operation of the new rings and ring clearances will be excessive.

➡**There is a high risk of breaking or distorting the rings and/or scratching the piston, if the rings are installed by hand or other means.**

10. Install the rings on the piston, bottom ring first, using a piston ring expander. Place the identification mark on the ring upward.

CONNECTING ROD BEARING REPLACEMENT

◆ **See Figures 90, 96 and 97**

This procedure assumes that the engine has been disassembled and the connecting rod and piston assembly has been removed from the engine. However, the connecting rod bearing replacement can be performed with the engine partially disassembled and installed in the vehicle.

Replacement bearings are available in standard size and undersize (for reground crankshafts). Check the back of the existing bearing inserts to determine the undersize, if any, of the existing bearings.

Connecting rod-to-crankshaft bearing clearance is checked using Plastigage® at either the top or the bottom of each crank journal. The Plastigage® has a range of 0.001-0.003″ (0.0254-0.0762mm).

1. Remove the rod cap from the connecting rod. Completely clean the bearing shell and the crank journal. Blow any oil from the oil hole in the crankshaft.

➡**Plastigage® will dissolve in oil or solvent. The components being checked must be dry and completely free of dirt, oil and solvent prior to checking the bearing clearance.**

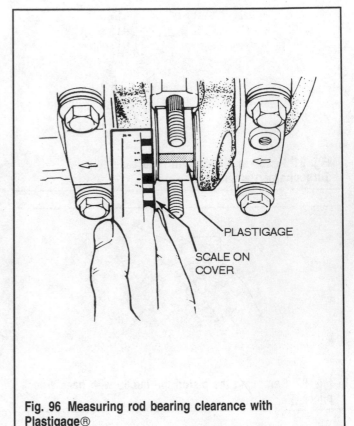

Fig. 96 Measuring rod bearing clearance with Plastigage®

Fig. 97 Bearing undersize is stamped into the back of the insert

2. Lightly lubricate the cylinder wall and install the piston and connecting rod assembly in the cylinder with the upper bearing insert in place.

➥**The piston rings do not have to be installed for this step as the assembly will be removed prior to finally assembly.**

3. Place the Plastigage® lengthwise along the bottom center of the lower bearing shell, then install the cap with the shell and torque nuts to 24-26 ft. lbs.. (33-35 Nm).

➥**Do not turn the crankshaft with the Plastigage® on the bearing.**

4. Remove the bearing cap with the shell. The flattened Plastigage® will be found sticking to either the bearing shell or the crank journal. Do not remove the Plastigage® until measuring it with the scale on the package.

5. Use the scale printed on the Plastigage® envelope to measure the flattened material at its widest point. The number within the scale which most closely corresponds to the width of the Plastigage® indicates the bearing clearance in thousandths of an inch.

6. Compare the measurement to specifications and replace the bearing if clearance is not within range. However, if the bearing is within specification and in good condition, bearing replacement is not necessary.

7. If the crankshaft is in good condition, install new standard size bearings and check the clearance again. If clearance is not within specification, undersize bearings are available.

8. After all measurements have been made, remove the piston and connecting rod assembly.

INSTALLATION

▶ **See Figures 90, 98, 99, 100, 101, 102 and 103**

This procedure assumes the crankshaft has already been Installed in the engine. The crankshaft must be installed in the engine prior to installing the piston and connecting rod assemblies.

During installation, lubricate all moving components with oil. When the engine is first started, oil pressure will take time to build. The oil used to lubricate the engine during the first few seconds of operation must be placed on moving surfaces during installation.

1. Install the piston rings on the piston using a ring expander.

2. Install the upper rod bearing insert on the connecting rod.

3. Position the piston rings as shown in the illustration and install the ring compressor. Install rubber boots over the rod bolts, as required.

4. Install the piston into its cylinder with the arrow facing the crankshaft pulley side of the engine. The dot on the connecting rod should be facing upward.

5. Tap the piston into place using a wooden hammer handle. Remove the rubber boot, install the rod cap so that

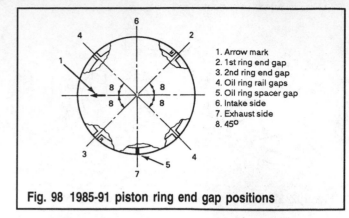

Fig. 98 1985-91 piston ring end gap positions

1. Arrow mark
2. 1st ring end gap
3. 2nd ring end gap
4. Oil ring rail gaps
5. Oil ring spacer gap
6. Intake side
7. Exhaust side
8. 45°

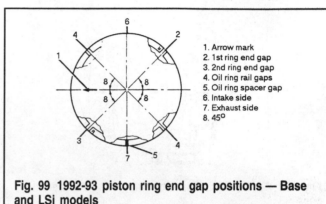

Fig. 99 1992-93 piston ring end gap positions — Base and LSi models

1. Arrow mark
2. 1st ring end gap
3. 2nd ring end gap
4. Oil ring rail gaps
5. Oil ring spacer gap
6. Intake side
7. Exhaust side
8. 45°

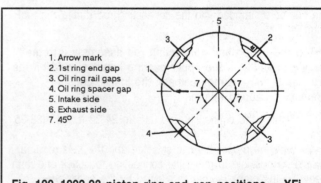

Fig. 100 1992-93 piston ring end gap positions — XFi models

1. Arrow mark
2. 1st ring end gap
3. Oil ring rail gaps
4. Oil ring spacer gap
5. Intake side
6. Exhaust side
7. 45°

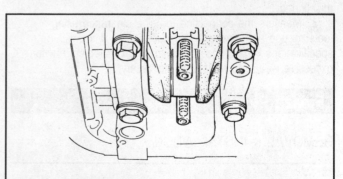

Fig. 101 Install guide hoses on the connecting rod bolts to avoid damaging the crankshaft journals

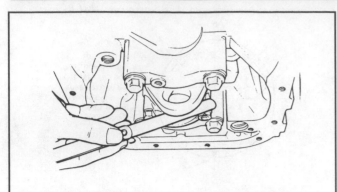

Fig. 102 Measuring connecting rod side clearance

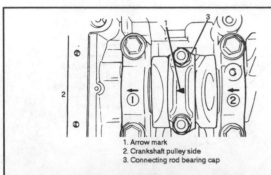

1. Arrow mark
2. Crankshaft pulley side
3. Connecting rod bearing cap

Fig. 103 Correct installation of connecting rod bearing caps

the numbers stamped into the connecting rod during removal align.

➡**Tap the piston and connecting rod assembly into the engine carefully. If the upper bearing insert should hit the crankshaft hard, it may damage the insert, causing premature bearing failure.**

6. Tighten the connecting rod nuts to 24-26 ft. lbs.. (33-35 Nm).

7. With the proper bearing selected and the nuts torqued, it should be possible to move the connecting rod back and forth freely on the crank journal as allowed by the specified connecting rod end clearance. If the rod cannot be moved, either the rod bearing is too far undersize or the rod is misaligned.

8. Measure the connecting rod side clearance using a feeler gauge and compare to specifications. If not within specifications inspect the crankshaft and connecting rod for excessive wear and replace as necessary.

Freeze Plugs

REMOVAL & INSTALLATION

1. Remove the negative battery cable.

2. Drain the cooling system.

✳✳CAUTION

When draining the coolant, keep in mind that cats and dogs are attracted by the ethylene glycol antifreeze, and are quite likely to drink any that is left in an uncovered container or in puddles on the ground. This will prove fatal in sufficient quantity. Always drain the coolant into a sealable container. Coolant should be reused unless it is contaminated or several years old.

3. Drill a small hole in the leaking freeze plug and allow the coolant to drain.

4. Remove any components that restrict access to the freeze plug.

5. Using a chisel, tap the bottom edge of the freeze plug to cock it in the bore. Remove the plug using pliers.

6. An alternate method is to drill an $\frac{1}{8}''$ hole in the plug and remove it using a dent puller.

7. Clean the freeze plug hole and using an appropriate driver tool or socket, install the freeze plug into the hole. Coat the freeze plug with sealer before installation.

8. Fill the engine with coolant, install the negative battery cable, start the engine and check for leaks.

Rear Main Seal

REMOVAL & INSTALLATION

▶ **See Figure 104**

1. Disconnect the negative battery cable.
2. Raise and support the vehicle safely.
3. Remove the transaxle from the vehicle.
4. On manual transaxle equipped models, remove the pressure plate assembly and clutch disc.
5. Mark the flywheel-to-engine position.
6. Remove the flywheel retaining bolts and flywheel from the crankshaft.
7. Remove the rear main seal attaching bolts.

➡**It may be necessary to loosen the oil pan bolts to allow clearance for rear main seal removal.**

8. Remove the rear main seal.

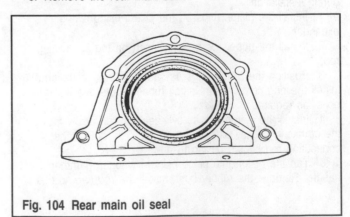

Fig. 104 Rear main oil seal

To install:

9. Lubricate and install the rear main seal.

10. Apply Loctite® sealant, or equivalent, to the flywheel retaining bolt threads.

11. Install the flywheel and secure with retaining bolts. Tighten bolts to 41-47 ft. lbs.. (56-64 Nm).

12. On manual transaxle equipped vehicles, install the pressure plate and clutch disc.

13. Install the transaxle.

Crankshaft and Main Bearings

REMOVAL & INSTALLATION

▶ **See Figures 103, 105, 106 and 107**

This procedure assumes that the engine has been removed from the vehicle and disassembled. However, it is possible to remove the crankshaft with the engine in the vehicle.

1. Remove the flywheel and mount the engine onto a workstand.

2. Rotate the crankshaft, until the timing marks on the sprockets align with each other, then remove the timing belt and timing sprocket from the crankshaft.

3. Drain the oil, remove the oil pan and oil pump.

4. Inspect the connecting rods and bearing caps for identification numbers. If there are none, mark them for reassembly purposes.

5. Remove the connecting rod nuts and caps, then store them in the order of removal. Place short pieces of rubber

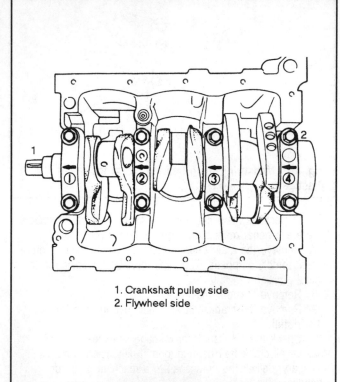

1. Crankshaft pulley side
2. Flywheel side

Fig. 106 Main bearing cap installation with arrows facing crankshaft pulley side of engine

hose on the connecting rod studs to prevent damaging the crankshaft bearing surfaces.

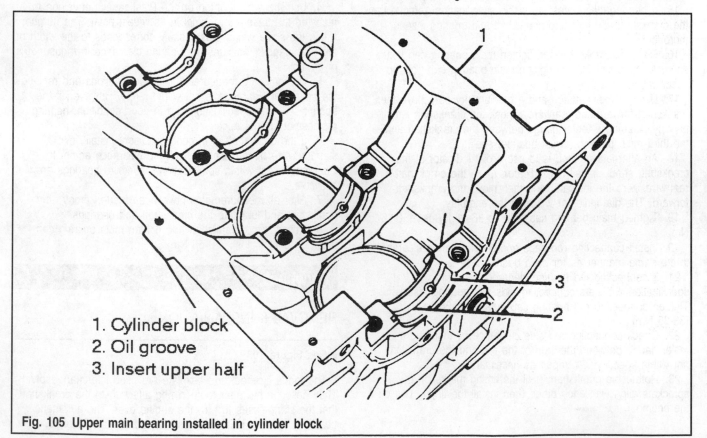

1. Cylinder block
2. Oil groove
3. Insert upper half

Fig. 105 Upper main bearing installed in cylinder block

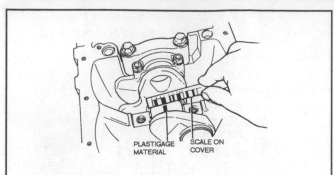

Fig. 107 Measuring main bearing clearance using Plastigage®

6. Inspect the main bearing caps for identification numbers. If there are none, mark them for reassembly purposes.

7. Remove the main bearing caps and store them in order, for reassembly purposes. The caps must be reinstalled in their original position.

8. Remove the rear main seal.

9. Remove the crankshaft and main bearing inserts.

To install:

10. Check the crankshaft for damage or excessive wear. Measure all crankshaft bearing journal dimensions and, as necessary, deliver the crankshaft to a machine shop for regrinding.

11. Using solvent, clean all of the parts and dry thoroughly.

12. Install the upper bearing inserts into the engine.

13. Carefully install the crankshaft and main caps with new lower inserts.

14. Check crankshaft bearing clearance using Plastigage®.

15. If bearing clearances are within specification, remove the the crankshaft and lubricate crankshaft and bearing inserts thoroughly.

16. Reinstall crankshaft and tighten main bearing cap bolts snug. At this point, do not tighten main bearing cap bolts to specification.

17. Using a feeler gauge and a medium pry bar, move the crankshaft forward-and-rearward. Check the crankshaft end-play by inserting a feeler gauge between the crankshaft and the third main bearing (thrust bearing) shell.

18. An alternate method is to use a dial indicator at the crankshaft snout. Install the indicator, move the crankshaft rearward, zero the indicator and then move the crankshaft forward. The dial indicator will read the end-play.

19. Tighten main bearing cap bolts to 36-41 ft. lbs.. (50-56 Nm).

20. Install connecting rod caps and check bearing clearance in the same manner as for main bearing inserts.

21. If connecting rod bearing clearance is within specification, lubricate connecting rods and bearing inserts. Tighten connecting rod bearing cap nuts to 24-26 ft. lbs.. (33-35 Nm).

22. Check connecting rod side clearance by inserting a feeler gauge between the side of the rod and the crankshaft. If not within specification, repair as necessary.

23. Rotate the crankshaft, until the timing marks on the sprockets align with each other, then install the timing belt on the engine.

CLEANING, INSPECTION AND BEARING REPLACEMENT

♦ **See Figures 105, 106 and 107**

Replacement bearings are available in standard size and undersize (for reground crankshafts). Check the back of the existing bearing inserts to determine the undersize, if any, of the existing bearings.

Connecting rod-to-crankshaft bearing clearance is checked using Plastigage® at either the top or the bottom of each crank journal. The Plastigage® has a range of 0.001-0.003 inch(0.0254-0.0762mm).

1. Remove the crankshaft main bearing cap. Completely clean the bearing shell and the crank journal. Blow any oil from the oil hole in the crankshaft.

➡**Plastigage® will dissolve in oil or solvent. The components being checked must be dry and completely free of dirt, oil and solvent prior to checking the bearing clearance.**

2. Place the Plastigage® lengthwise along the center of the crankshaft journal, then install the cap with the shell and torque nuts to 36-41 ft. lbs.. (50-56 Nm).

➡**Do not turn the crankshaft with the Plastigage® on the bearing.**

3. Remove the bearing cap with the shell. The flattened Plastigage® will be found sticking to either the bearing shell or the crank journal. Do not remove the Plastigage® until measuring it with the scale on the package.

4. Use the scale printed on the Plastigage® envelope to measure the flattened material at its widest point. The number within the scale which most closely corresponds to the width of the Plastigage® indicates the bearing clearance in thousandths of an inch.

5. Compare the measurement to specifications and replace the bearing if clearance is not within range. However, if the bearing is within specification and in good condition, bearing replacement is not necessary.

6. If the crankshaft is in good condition, install new standard size bearings and check the clearance again. If clearance is not within specification, undersize bearings are available.

7. After all measurements have been made, remove the crankshaft and lubricate the crankshaft and bearings.

8. Reinstall the crankshaft and tighten main bearing cap bolts to 36-41 ft. lbs.. (50-56 Nm).

Flywheel

REMOVAL & INSTALLATION

♦ **See Figure 108**

The terms flywheel and flexplate are used interchangeably. They describe the gear toothed ring attached to the crankshaft that the starter uses to turn the engine over. The automatic transaxle flywheel is sometimes referred to as a flexplate.

On manual transaxle equipped vehicles, the flywheel is the mounting point and friction surface for the clutch disc and pressure plate. On automatic transaxle equipped vehicles, the flywheel is the attaching point for the torque converter.

The flywheel and ring gear are machined from one piece of metal and cannot be separated. If gear teeth are damaged, the flywheel must be replaced as an assembly.

1. Disconnect the negative battery cable. Raise and support the vehicle safely.

2. Remove the transaxle from the vehicle.

3. On manual transaxle equipped vehicles, inspect the flywheel/pressure plate assembly for match marks. If no mark exists, mark the flywheel and the pressure plate for installation reference.

➡**The flywheel is balanced and must be replaced in the same position to ensure trouble free operation of the engine.**

4. On manual transaxle equipped vehicles, loosen the clutch-to-flywheel bolts, evenly (one turn at a time), until the spring tension is relieved, then remove the retaining bolts, the pressure plate and the clutch assembly.

✳✳CAUTION

The clutch driven disc contains asbestos, which has been determined to be a cancer causing agent. Never clean clutch surfaces with compressed air! Avoid inhaling any

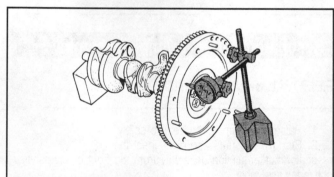

Fig. 108 Measuring flywheel runout — manual transaxle shown

dust from any clutch surface! When cleaning clutch surfaces, use a commercially available brake cleaning fluid.

5. Check the flywheel face for runout using a dial indicator. If runout exceeds 0.0078 in. (0.2mm), resurface the flywheel prior to installation.

6. Remove the flywheel-to-crankshaft bolts and the flywheel from the engine.

To install:

7. On manual transaxle equipped vehicles, clean the clutch disc (use a stiff brush), the pressure plate and the flywheel of all dirt, oil and grease.

8. Inspect the flywheel, the pressure plate and the clutch disc for scoring, cracks, heat checking and/or other defects.

9. If flywheel resurfacing is needed sent the flywheel to an experienced machine shop.

➡**When the flywheel is removed, it is a good idea to replace the rear main oil seal, the pilot bushing and/or the clutch plate (as necessary).**

10. Install the flywheel on the crankshaft and align the matchmarks.

11. Apply Loctite® sealant, or equivalent, to the flywheel retaining bolt threads.

12. Install the flywheel retaining bolts and tighten to 41-47 ft. lbs.. (56-64 Nm).

13. On manual transaxle equipped vehicles, position a clutch disc aligner tool in the pilot bushing (to support the clutch disc), then assemble the clutch disc (the damper springs facing the transaxle) and pressure plate. Align the matchmarks made during removal and install the retaining bolts into the flywheel.

14. Tighten the pressure plate-to-flywheel bolts to 17 ft. lbs.. (23 Nm) gradually and evenly (to prevent clutch plate distortion). Then remove the alignment tool.

15. On manual transaxle equipped vehicles, lubricate the pilot bushing and the clutch release lever.

16. Install the transaxle, lower the vehicle and connect the negative battery cable.

17. On manual transaxle equipped vehicles, adjust the clutch linkage.

EXHAUST SYSTEM

▶ **See Figure 109**

Periodic maintenance of the exhaust system is not required. However, if the vehicle is raised for other service, it is advisable to check the general condition of the catalytic converter, pipes and muffler.

Check the complete exhaust system and nearby body areas for broken, damaged, missing or incorrectly positioned parts, open seams, holes, loose connections or other deterioration that could permit exhaust fumes to seep into the passenger compartment. Dust or water in the rear compartment may indicate a problem in one of these areas. Any faulty areas should be corrected immediately.

The exhaust system consists of an exhaust manifold, heat shield, front pipe/catalytic converter assembly and a resonator/muffler/tailpipe assembly. Various flexible rubber hangers suspend the system along the underside of the vehicle.

✳✳CAUTION

Be very careful when working on or near the catalytic converter! External temperatures can reach 1,500°F and more, causing severe burns! Removal or installation should be performed only on a cold exhaust system.

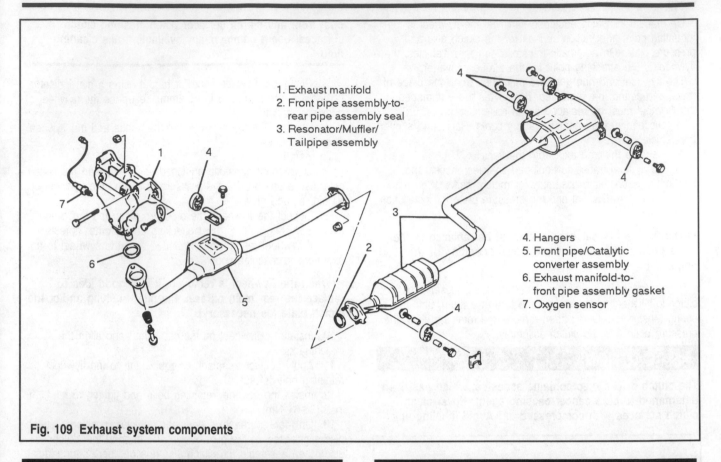

1. Exhaust manifold
2. Front pipe assembly-to-rear pipe assembly seal
3. Resonator/Muffler/Tailpipe assembly

4. Hangers
5. Front pipe/Catalytic converter assembly
6. Exhaust manifold-to-front pipe assembly gasket
7. Oxygen sensor

Fig. 109 Exhaust system components

Front Pipe/Catalytic Converter Assembly

REMOVAL & INSTALLATION

1. Raise and support the vehicle safely.
2. Remove two bolts and disconnect the front pipe/catalytic converter assembly from the exhaust manifold.
3. Remove two nuts and disconnect the front pipe/catalytic converter assembly from the resonator/muffler/tailpipe assembly.
4. Remove the hanger supporting the catalytic converter and remove the front pipe/catalytic converter assembly from the vehicle.
   To install:
5. Clean the gasket mating surfaces thoroughly.
6. Install the front pipe/catalytic converter assembly to the vehicle and support catalytic converter with hanger.
7. Connect the front pipe/catalytic converter assembly with a new gasket to the resonator/muffler/tailpipe assembly. Secure with two nuts by do not tighten fully.
8. Connect the front pipe/catalytic converter assembly with a new gasket to the exhaust manifold. Secure with two bolts by do not tighten fully.
9. Align all system components properly to prevent any noise or vibrations before tightening fasteners.
10. Tighten resonator/muffler/tailpipe assembly nuts to 26 ft. lbs.. (35 Nm) and front pipe/catalytic converter assembly bolts to 37 ft. lbs.. (50 Nm). Tighten catalytic converter hanger bolts to 11 ft. lbs.. (15 Nm).
11. Lower vehicle. Start the engine and check for leaks.

Resonator/Muffler/Tailpipe Assembly

REMOVAL & INSTALLATION

1. Raise and support the vehicle safely.
2. Remove two nuts and disconnect the resonator/muffler/tailpipe assembly from the front pipe/catalytic converter assembly.
3. Remove the bolt and hanger from the pipe at the resonator.
4. Remove the three bolts and hangers from the muffler.
5. Remove the resonator/muffler/tailpipe assembly from the vehicle.
   To install:
6. Clean the gasket mating surfaces thoroughly.
7. Install the resonator/muffler/tailpipe assembly to the vehicle and secure muffler with three hangers. Do not tighten hanger bolts fully.
8. Connect the resonator/muffler/tailpipe assembly, with a new gasket, to the front pipe/catalytic converter assembly and secure with two nuts. Do not tighten bolts fully.
9. Connect the hanger tot he pipe at the resonator and secure with one bolt. Do not tighten bolt fully.
10. Align all system components properly to prevent any noise or vibrations before tightening fasteners.
11. Tighten resonator/muffler/tailpipe assembly nuts to 26 ft. lbs.. (35 Nm) and all hanger bolts to 11 ft. lbs. (15 Nm).
12. Lower vehicle. Start the engine and check for leaks.

ENGINE REBUILDING SPECIFICATIONS CHART

Component	U.S.	Metric
Camshaft:		
Camshaft Journal Diameter		
1985-88	1.737-1.738 in.	44.119-44.145 mm
1989-93		
Journal No. 1	1.022-1.023 in.	25.958-25.984 mm
Journal No. 2-3	1.179-1.180 in.	29.946-29.972 mm
Camshaft Lobe Height:		
1985-88	1.472-1.476 in.	37.388-37.490 mm
1989-91	1.560-1.566 in.	39.624-39.776 mm
1992-93		
Base and LSi	1.591-1.597 in.	40.411-40.563 mm
Xfi	1.560-1.566 in.	39.624-39.776 mm
Camshaft Bearing Clearance:		
1985-88	0.0020-0.0030 in.	0.0508-0.0762 mm
1989-93	0.0008-0.0024 in.	0.0203-0.0609 mm
Camshaft Runout	0.0039 in. limit	0.0990 mm limit
Crankshaft:		
Main Bearing Journal Diameter:		
Number on No. 1 Cylinder Counterweight:		
No. 1:	1.7714-1.7716 in.	44.993-44.998 mm
No. 2:	1.7712-1.7714 in.	44.988-44.993 mm
No. 3:	1.7710-1.7712 in.	44.983-44.988 mm
Main Bearing Oil Clearance	0.0008-0.0015 in.	0.0203-0.0381 mm
Crankshaft Endplay	0.0044-0.0122 in.	0.1117-0.3098 mm
Thrust Bearing Number	3	3
Connecting Rod:		
Journal Diameter	1.6529-1.6535 in.	41.983-41.998 mm
Side Clearance	0.0039-0.0078 in.	0.0990-0.1981 mm
Rod Bearing Oil Clearance	0.0012-0.0019 in.	0.0304-0.0482 mm
Valves:		
Seat Angle	45 deg	45 deg
Face Angle	45 deg	45 deg
Valve Spring Test Pressure:		
1985-88	54.7-64.3 lbs. @ 1.63 in.	24.83-29.19 kg @ 41.40 mm
1989-93	41.0-47.2 lbs. @ 1.28 in.	18.61-21.42 kg @ 32.51 mm
Valve Stem-to-Guide Clearance:		
Intake:		
1985-88	0.0008-0.0019 in.	0.0203-0.0482 mm
1989-91	0.0008-0.0021 in.	0.0203-0.0533 mm
1992-93	0.0008-0.0022 in.	0.0203-0.0558 mm
Exhaust:		
1985-88	0.0014-0.0025 in.	0.0355-0.0635 mm
1989-91	0.0014-0.0024 in.	0.0355-0.0600 mm
1992-93	0.0018-0.0028 in.	0.0457-0.0711 mm
Valve Stem Diameter		
Intake:		
1985-88	0.2742-0.2748 in.	6.964-6.979 mm
1989-93	0.2148-0.2157 in.	5.455-5.478 mm
Exhaust:		
1985-88	0.2737-0.2742 in.	6.951-6.964 mm
1989-91	0.2146-0.2151 in.	5.450-5.463 mm
1992-93	0.2142-0.2144 in.	5.440-5.445 mm

ENGINE REBUILDING SPECIFICATIONS CHART

Component	U.S.	Metric
Piston and Ring:		
Piston-to-Cylinder Clearance	0.0008-0.0015 in.	0.0203-0.0381 mm
Piston Ring End Gap:		
1st Ring:		
1985-91	0.0079-0.0129 in.	0.0200-0.3276 mm
1987-88 Turbo	0.0079-0.0119 in.	0.0200-0.3022 mm
1992-93	0.0079-0.0118 in.	0.0200-0.2997 mm
2nd Ring:		
1985-91	0.0079-0.0137 in.	0.0200-0.3479 mm
1987-88 Turbo	0.0079-0.0119 in.	0.0200-0.3022 mm
1992-93	0.0079-0.0118 in.	0.0200-0.2997 mm
Oil Control:		
1987-88 Turbo	0.0079-0.0237 in.	0.0200-0.6019 mm
1985-91	0.0079-0.0275 in.	0.0200-0.6985 mm
1992-93	0.0079-0.0236 in.	0.0200-0.5994 mm
Piston Ring Side Clearance:		
1st Ring	0.0008-0.0023 in.	0.0203-0.0584 mm
2nd Ring	0.0008-0.0023 in.	0.0203-0.0584 mm

TORQUE SPECIFICATIONS

Component	U.S.	Metric
Alternator:		
Drive Belt Adjuster	17 ft. lbs.	23 Nm
Electrical Connector Nut	71 inch lbs.	8 Nm
Lower Cover	89 inch lbs.	10 Nm
Battery:		
Hold Down	71 inch lbs.	8 Nm
Terminal	11 ft. lbs.	15 Nm
Camshaft:		
Sprocket	44 ft. lbs.	60 Nm
Bearing Cap	8 ft. lbs.	11 Nm
Catalytic Converter:		
Hanger Bolts	11 ft. lbs.	15 Nm
Connecting Rod	24-26 ft. lbs.	33-35 Nm
Cooling Fan	89 inch lbs.	10 Nm
Crankshaft Pulley:		
Center Bolt	81 ft. lbs.	110 Nm
Outside Bolts	8 ft. lbs.	11 Nm
Cylinder Head	54 ft. lbs.	73 Nm
Cylinder Head Cover	44 inch lbs.	5 Nm
Distributor		
Ignition Module	44 inch lbs.	5 Nm
Engine Mounts	37 ft. lbs.	50 Nm
Engine Left Hand Bracket	37 ft. lbs.	50 Nm
Exhaust Manifold	17 ft. lbs.	23 Nm
Exhaust Pipe:		
Front Assembly Nuts	26 ft. lbs.	35 Nm
Front Assembly Bolts	37 ft. lbs.	50 Nm
Rear Assembly Bolts	26 ft. lbs.	35 Nm
Lower Bracket	29-43 ft. lbs.	40-60 Nm
Hanger Bolts	11 ft. lbs.	15 Nm
Flywheel-to-Crankshaft	47 ft. lbs.	64 Nm
Intake Manifold	17 ft. lbs.	23 Nm
Main Bearing Cap	36-41 ft. lbs.	50-56 Nm
Oil Pump	97 inch lbs.	11 Nm
Oil Pump Strainer	97 inch lbs.	11 Nm
Oil Pan	9 ft. lbs.	11 Nm
Oil Pan Drain Plug	26 ft. lbs.	35 Nm
Oil Dipstick Tube	97 inch lbs.	11 Nm
Pressure Plate	17 ft. lbs.	23 Nm
Radiator Bolts	89 inch lbs.	10 Nm
Rocker Arm:		
Shaft Bolts	7-9 ft. lbs.	9-12 Nm
Adjusting Locknut	11-13 ft. lbs.	15-19 Nm
Starter:		
Mounting Bolt	17 ft. lbs.	23 Nm
Solenoid Terminal Nut	89 inch lbs.	10 Nm
Thermostat Housing	15 ft. lbs.	20 Nm

TORQUE SPECIFICATIONS

Component	U.S.	Metric
Timing Belt:		
Cover	97 inch lbs.	11 Nm
Tensioner Stud	8 ft. lbs.	11 Nm
Tensioner Bolt	20 ft. lbs.	27 Nm
Transaxle-to-Engine	37 ft. lbs.	50 Nm
Turbocharger:		
Mounting bolt	13-20 ft. lbs.	18-28 Nm
Exhaust Pipe Bolts	30-43 ft. lbs.	40-60 Nm
Air Inlet Pipe Clamp	6-8 ft. lbs.	8-12 Nm
Air Outlet Pipe Clamp	6-8 ft. lbs.	8-12 Nm
Oil Drain Hose	3-5 ft. lbs.	4-7 Nm
Oil Inlet Pipe	8-10 ft. lbs.	11-15 Nm
Water Pump:		
Mounting Bolts	115 inch lbs.	13 Nm
Pulley Bolts	18 ft. lbs.	24 Nm

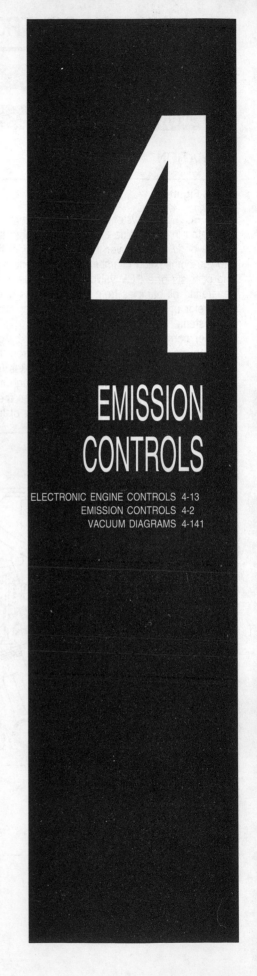

4

EMISSION CONTROLS

EMISSION CONTROLS

PCV Valve System

OPERATION

▶ **See Figure 1**

The PCV valve system is designed to force blow-by gases generated in the engine crankcase back into the carburetor or throttle body, then deliver them together with the fuel mixture into the combustion chambers. This system is a closed type and consists of a PCV valve in the cylinder head cover for separating oil particles from blow-by gases and a hose to the carburetor or throttle body. The air cleaner allows fresh air into the system.

Under normal operating conditions blow-by gases passing between the piston rings and fuel vapor from the fuel tank are mixed with the ambient temperature supplies from the air cleaner. This mixture is then drawn through the PCV valve into the intake manifold for burning. When the engine is operating with the throttle wide open, part of the blow-by

generated is drawn directly into the air cleaner via a hose in the cylinder head cover.

INSPECTION

The PCV system should be inspected every 60,000 miles (100,000 km). Check the PCV valve for blockage or deterioration. Clean the valve and hoses with carburetor cleaner and dry with compressed air. Check the mounting grommet and hoses for deterioration and leakage; replace as necessary.

PCV Valve

1. Run the engine at idle.
2. Place a finger over the end of the PCV valve to check for vacuum. If there is no vacuum, check for clogged valve.
3. If the engine is idling rough, this may be caused by a clogged valve or plugged hoses. Never adjust idle speed without checking the PCV valve first.
4. Turn the engine OFF and remove the valve. Shake the valve and listen for a rattle of the needle inside the valve. If the valve does not rattle, replace the valve.

REMOVAL & INSTALLATION

▶ **See Figures 2 and 3**

PCV Valve

1. Remove the PCV hose from the air cleaner assembly and from the PCV valve.
2. Loosen the screws holding the PCV valve retaining bracket, as required.
3. Remove the PCV valve from the intake manifold.
4. Installation is the reverse of removal.

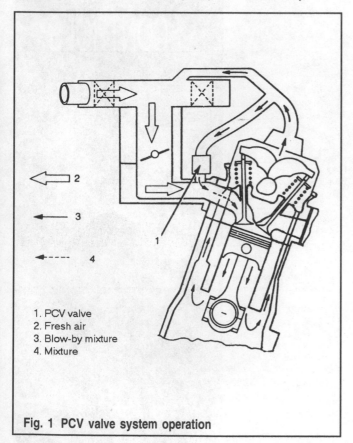

1. PCV valve
2. Fresh air
3. Blow-by mixture
4. Mixture

Fig. 1 PCV valve system operation

Fig. 2 Removing the PCV valve from the intake manifold

Fig. 3 Removing the crankcase ventilation hose from the cylinder head cover

EVAPORATIVE EMISSION CONTROL SYSTEM

OPERATION

▶ **See Figures 4, 5, 6, 7, 8 and 9**

The basic evaporative emission control system used on all fuel injected vehicles is the charcoal canister storage method. This method transfers fuel vapor from the fuel tank and, if equipped, the carburetor bowl, to an activated carbon storage device. This canister stores the vapors in activated charcoal when the vehicle is not running. When the engine is started, the fuel vapor is purged from the carbon element by intake air flow and consumed in the normal combustion process.

Carbureted Engines

Carbureted vehicles use a switch vent solenoid operated by the ignition switch and the Electronic Control Module (ECM). The switch vent prevents the fuel vapor in the float chamber of the carburetor from flowing out into the atmosphere.

When the ignition switch is in the OFF position, or when cranking the engine, the vent tube is closed by the solenoid valve and allows the fuel vapor to flow from the float chamber into the vapor storage canister. When the engine is operating, the solenoid receives an electrical signal from the ECM to keep the inner vent tube open. As a result, the vapor passes

through the tube into the carburetor and is drawn into the engine.

Fuel Injected Engines

Fuel injected vehicles use a vacuum operated canister purge control valve. The canister purge control valve prevents the vapor in the fuel tank from flowing out into the atmosphere.

Certain conditions must be satisfied for the canister purge to occur. When the engine is running, the coolant temperature is operational and the throttle valve is at any position other than idle, the canister purge control valve will receive ported vacuum. As a result, fuel vapor in the canister is sucked into the intake manifold through the purge control valve and purge line.

When coolant temperature is below normal (cold start), the vacuum signal is interrupted by a bimetal vacuum switching valve and ported vacuum is not applied to the purge control valve. In this condition, the canister is not purged.

A 2-way check valve is also used to keep pressure in the fuel tank constant. When the pressure in the fuel tank becomes positive and reaches its specified value, it opens the valve to let the vapor flow to the charcoal canister. If a vacuum develops in the fuel tank, it opens the valve to let air flow into the tank.

SERVICE

The evaporative emissions system should be inspected at least once a year. Inspect the canister for internal damage or clogging. Clean with compressed air, as necessary. Inspect the fuel tank, cap and evaporative emission hoses for damage or leaks. Replace hoses as necessary.

Canister Purge Control Valve

1. Using a small length of vacuum hose connected to the tank tube, blow into the canister. Air should escape the air tube at the bottom of the canister.

✳✳CAUTION

The fuel vapor in the canister may be harmful. Care should be taken not to inhale the vapor.

2. Using a small length of vacuum hose connected to the purge tube, blow into the canister. No air should pass through the valve.
3. Apply 20 in. Hg of vacuum to the vacuum signal line tube of the valve, while blowing air into purge tube. Air should come out of the throttle body (TB) tube.
4. If the valve fails to function as specified, replace the canister.

Switch Vent Solenoid Valve

1. Disconnect the canister hose from the carburetor bowl nozzle of the canister, and connect a new hose to the pipe connecting with the solenoid.

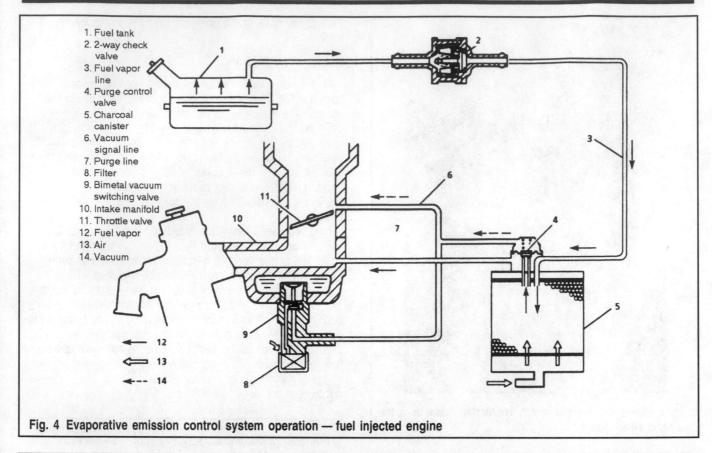

1. Fuel tank
2. 2-way check valve
3. Fuel vapor line
4. Purge control valve
5. Charcoal canister
6. Vacuum signal line
7. Purge line
8. Filter
9. Bimetal vacuum switching valve
10. Intake manifold
11. Throttle valve
12. Fuel vapor
13. Air
14. Vacuum

Fig. 4 Evaporative emission control system operation — fuel injected engine

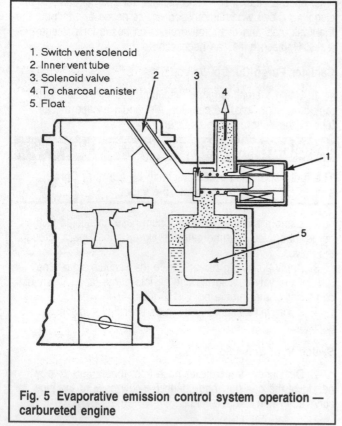

1. Switch vent solenoid
2. Inner vent tube
3. Solenoid valve
4. To charcoal canister
5. Float

Fig. 5 Evaporative emission control system operation — carbureted engine

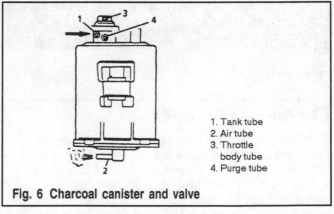

1. Tank tube
2. Air tube
3. Throttle body tube
4. Purge tube

Fig. 6 Charcoal canister and valve

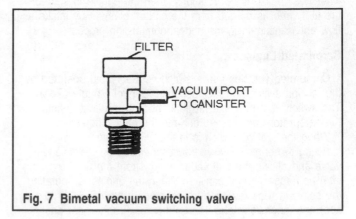

FILTER

VACUUM PORT TO CANISTER

Fig. 7 Bimetal vacuum switching valve

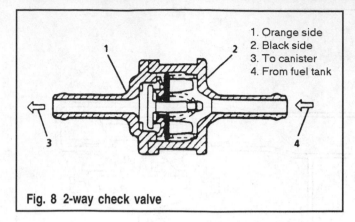

1. Orange side
2. Black side
3. To canister
4. From fuel tank

Fig. 8 2-way check valve

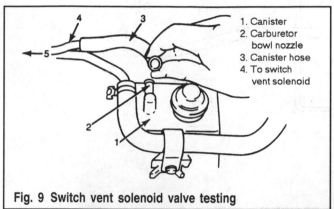

1. Canister
2. Carburetor bowl nozzle
3. Canister hose
4. To switch vent solenoid

Fig. 9 Switch vent solenoid valve testing

2. Blow air into the new hose with the ignition switch in the **OFF** and **ON** positions. Air should not pass through the solenoid valve.

✳✳CAUTION

The fuel vapor in the canister and float chamber may be harmful. Care should be taken not to inhale the vapor.

3. Start the engine and run at idle speed. Check the solenoid valve as before. Air should not pass through the solenoid.
4. If the valve fails to function as specified, replace the canister.

Bi-Metal Vacuum Switching Valve

1. Remove the vacuum hoses from the VSV.
2. Connect a length of hose to the valve with the engine cold.
3. Blow into the valve, air should not pass through the valve.
4. Start the engine and allow to reach 140°F (60°C).
5. Blow air into the valve, air should pass through the valve.
6. If the valve fails to function as specified, replace it.

2-Way Check Valve

1. Remove the valve and blow hard into the BLACK side of the valve. Air should pass through the valve.
2. Blow lightly into the ORANGE side of the valve, air should pass through.

3. If the valve fails to function as specified, replace it.

REMOVAL & INSTALLATION

Charcoal Canister

1. Label and disconnect all vacuum lines from the canister.
2. As required, disconnect the electrical connector from the canister.
3. Loosen the canister mounting bracket and remove the canister.
4. Inspect and replace vacuum lines as necessary.
5. Installation is the reverse of removal.

Bi-Metal Vacuum Switching Valve

1. Label and disconnect all vacuum lines from the valve.
2. Remove the valve attaching screw, as required.
3. Remove the valve.
4. Inspect and replace vacuum lines as necessary.
5. Installation is the reverse of removal.

2-Way Check Valve

The valve may be located either in the engine compartment or near the fuel tank at the rear of the vehicle.
1. Raise and support the vehicle safely, as required.
2. Locate the check valve.

➡**The valve must be replaced in the same position. Take note which way the valve is removed.**

3. Label and disconnect the hoses from the valve.
4. Remove the valve.
5. Installation is the reverse of removal.

Exhaust Gas Recirculation System

OPERATION

▶ **See Figures 10, 11, 12, 13, 14 and 15**

The EGR system lowers combustion temperatures in the combustion chamber to reduce NOx (Oxides of Nitrogen) emissions. The exhaust gases are drawn from the cylinder head exhaust port into the intake manifold riser portion through the passages in the cylinder head, the intake manifold and the EGR valve.

The diaphragm mounted in the EGR modulator is operated by the back pressure of the exhaust gas on carbureted engines, or by the Engine Control Module (ECM) on fuel injected engines, to open and close the valve. By this opening and closing action the EGR modulator controls the vacuum transmitted to the EGR valve.

Under low load condition such as low speed driving, the exhaust pressure is low. In this state, the diaphragm in the EGR modulator is pushed down by the spring force and the modulator valve opens to allow the air into the vacuum passage from the outside.

As a result, the vacuum transmitted to the EGR valve becomes less and so does the opening of the EGR valve. Thus, less exhaust gas is recirculated to the intake manifold.

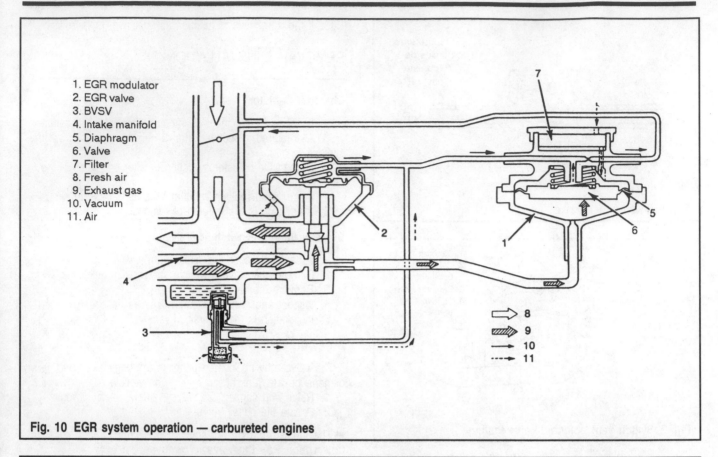

1. EGR modulator
2. EGR valve
3. BVSV
4. Intake manifold
5. Diaphragm
6. Valve
7. Filter
8. Fresh air
9. Exhaust gas
10. Vacuum
11. Air

→ 8
↗ 9
→ 10
⇢ 11

Fig. 10 EGR system operation — carbureted engines

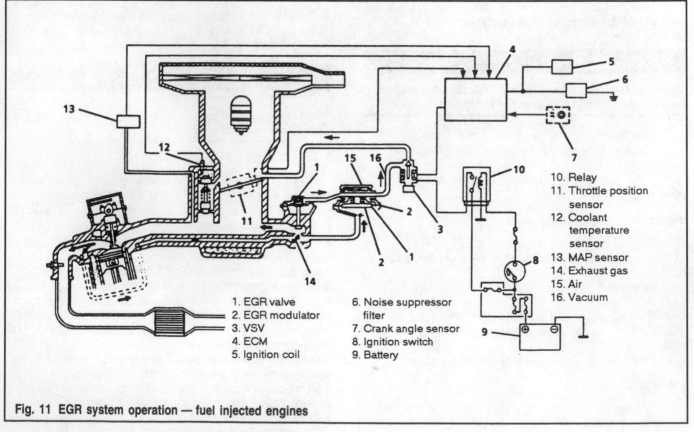

1. EGR valve
2. EGR modulator
3. VSV
4. ECM
5. Ignition coil
6. Noise suppressor filter
7. Crank angle sensor
8. Ignition switch
9. Battery
10. Relay
11. Throttle position sensor
12. Coolant temperature sensor
13. MAP sensor
14. Exhaust gas
15. Air
16. Vacuum

Fig. 11 EGR system operation — fuel injected engines

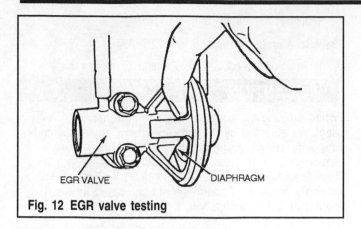

Fig. 12 EGR valve testing

EGR VALVE   DIAPHRAGM

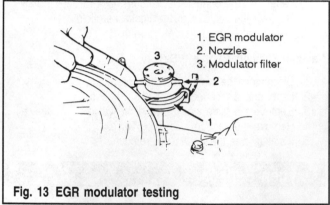

1. EGR modulator
2. Nozzles
3. Modulator filter

Fig. 13 EGR modulator testing

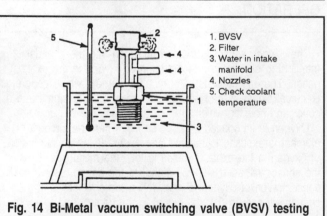

1. BVSV
2. Filter
3. Water in intake manifold
4. Nozzles
5. Check coolant temperature

Fig. 14 Bi-Metal vacuum switching valve (BVSV) testing

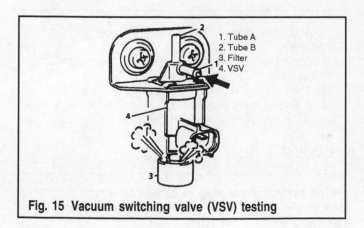

1. Tube A
2. Tube B
3. Filter
4. VSV

Fig. 15 Vacuum switching valve (VSV) testing

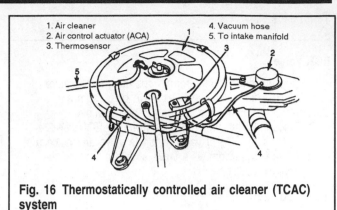

1. Air cleaner
2. Air control actuator (ACA)
3. Thermosensor
4. Vacuum hose
5. To intake manifold

Fig. 16 Thermostatically controlled air cleaner (TCAC) system

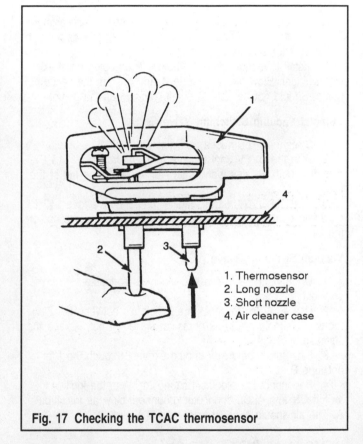

1. Thermosensor
2. Long nozzle
3. Short nozzle
4. Air cleaner case

Fig. 17 Checking the TCAC thermosensor

Under a high load condition such as high speed driving, the exhaust pressure is high. By the high exhaust pressure, the diaphragm in the modulator is pushed up and closes its valve. As the air does not enter the vacuum passage in this state, the vacuum transmitted to the EGR valve becomes larger and so does the opening of the EGR valve. Thus, a larger amount of exhaust gas is recirculated to the intake manifold.

When coolant temperature is low, the vacuum passage of the EGR valve is opened to the air through the bi-metal vacuum switching valve (BVSV) on carbureted vehicles, or the vacuum switching valve (VSV) on fuel injected vehicles. In this state, because vacuum is not transmitted to the EGR valve, it remains closed.

On the other hand, when the coolant temperature is normal, the BVSV or VSV is closed. So the EGR valve opens and closes in accordance with the EGR modulator operation.

TESTING

EGR Valve

1. Run the engine until normal operating temperature.
2. Place a finger on the EGR valve diaphragm and accelerate the engine, the diaphragm should move.
3. Disconnect the vacuum hose from the EGR valve.
4. Apply 10 in. Hg of vacuum to the valve and place a finger on the diaphragm. The valve should move and the engine should stall.

EGR Modulator

1. Check the filter for contamination and damage. Clean using compressed air.
2. Remove the modulator and plug the nozzle with a finger. Blow air into another nozzle and check that air passes through to the air filter side freely.
3. Install a vacuum pump to nozzle **P** and plug nozzle **Q** with a finger. Blow air into nozzle **A** and operate the vacuum pump. Should not be able to obtain vacuum on the pump.

Bi-metal Vacuum Switching Valve (BVSV)

1. Disconnect the hoses from the valve.
2. With the BVSV cool (engine temperature below 113°F) blow into both nozzles individually. Air should come out of the filter.
3. With the BVSV warm (engine temperature above 140°F) blow into both nozzles individually. Air should not come out of the filter.

Vacuum Switching Valve (VSV)

1. Disconnect the hoses and electrical connectors from the solenoid.
2. Use a DVOM to check the resistance between the 2 terminals; should be 33-39 ohms resistance. If not, replace the solenoid.
3. Blow into tube **A**, air should exhaust through the filter, not tube **B**.
4. Reconnect the electrical connector. With the ignition switch **ON** and ALDL connector grounded, blow air into tube **A**. The air should exhaust from tube **B**.

REMOVAL & INSTALLATION

EGR Valve

1. Allow the engine to cool prior to removing the EGR valve
2. Disconnect the EGR valve vacuum hose.
3. Remove the EGR valve retaining bolts.
4. Remove the EGR valve.
5. When installing the valve use a new gasket.
6. Installation is the reverse of removal.

EGR Modulator

1. Remove the air cleaner assembly.
2. Label and disconnect the modulator vacuum hoses.
3. Remove the modulator.

4. Installation is the reverse of removal.

Bi-Metal Vacuum Switching Valve (BVSV)

1. Drain engine coolant below the level of the valve.

❋❋CAUTION

When draining the coolant, keep in mind that cats and dogs are attracted by the ethylene glycol antifreeze, and are quite likely to drink any that is left in an uncovered container or in puddles on the ground. This will prove fatal in sufficient quantity. Always drain the coolant into a sealable container. Coolant should be reused unless it is contaminated or several years old.

2. Label and disconnect the vacuum hoses from the valve.
3. Remove the valve from the intake manifold.
4. Installation is the reverse of removal.

Vacuum Switching Valve (VSV)

1. Disconnect the valve electrical connector.
2. Label and disconnect the vacuum hoses.
3. Remove the fasteners the hold the valve to the firewall.
4. Remove the vacuum switching valve.
5. Installation is the reverse of removal.

Oxygen Sensor

OPERATION

The oxygen sensor is located threaded into the exhaust manifold to detect the concentration of oxygen in the exhaust gases. The unit consists of a zirconia element which generates electrical signal, a lead wire which draws out the signal and a cover and housing which protects the element from damage.

Oxygen is introduced into the sensor when the zirconia element is exposed to the exhaust gases. If the concentration of oxygen in the exhaust gases is low, the mixture is rich and the sensor will send a 1 volt signal to the control unit. If the concentration of oxygen is high, the mixture is lean and the sensor will send a 0.1 volt signal to the control unit.

SERVICE

1. Start the engine and allow it to reach operating temperature.
2. Connect an analog voltmeter between the oxygen sensor electrical connector and ground.
3. The voltmeter should deflect between 0-0.8 volts.
4. If reading is not as specified, refer to "Electronic Engine Controls" in this Section for further diagnosis.

REMOVAL & INSTALLATION

➡**The oxygen sensor may be difficult to remove at temperatures above 120°F. Care should be taken not to burn yourself on a hot exhaust manifold.**

1. Start the engine and allow it to reach operating temperature. Stop the engine.

2. Disconnect the oxygen sensor electrical connector.

3. Remove the oxygen sensor from the exhaust manifold.

4. Installation is the reverse of removal. Tighten oxygen sensor to 30 ft. lbs. (41 Nm).

Catalytic Converter

OPERATION

This system reduces Oxides of Nitrogen (NOx) and oxidizes Hydrocarbons (HC) and Carbon Monoxide (CO). In order for the converter to function properly the air/fuel ratio of the fuel system must be constantly maintained 14.7:1.

SERVICE

Check to be sure a light can be seen through the catalytic converter when removed. If not, replace the converter. This unit is usually covered under the 5/50 emissions warranty.

1. Carefully remove the oxygen sensor. Install an exhaust back pressure tester or equivalent, in place of the oxygen sensor.

2. With the engine at normal operating temperature, observe the tester reading on the gauge. The reading should not exceed ¼ psi (18.6 kPa).

3. Accelerate the engine to 2000 rpm and observe the gauge. The reading should not exceed 3 psi (20.7 kPa).

4. If the back pressure at either rpm exceeds specifications, an exhaust system restriction is indicated.

5. Inspect the entire system for a collapsed pipe, heat distress or internal muffler failure. If there are no obvious reasons for excessive back pressure, a restricted catalytic converter should be suspected.

REMOVAL & INSTALLATION

The catalytic converter is an integral part of the front exhaust pipe assembly. If the converter requires replacement, the front pipe assembly must be replaced as a unit.

1. Raise and support the vehicle safely.

2. Remove two bolts and disconnect the front pipe/catalytic converter assembly from the exhaust manifold.

3. Remove two nuts and disconnect the front pipe/catalytic converter assembly from the resonator/muffler/tailpipe assembly.

4. Remove the hanger supporting the catalytic converter and remove the front pipe/catalytic converter assembly from the vehicle.

To install:

5. Clean the gasket mating surfaces thoroughly.

6. Install the front pipe/catalytic converter assembly to the vehicle and support catalytic converter with hanger.

7. Connect the front pipe/catalytic converter assembly with a new gasket to the resonator/muffler/tailpipe assembly. Secure with two nuts by do not tighten fully.

8. Connect the front pipe/catalytic converter assembly with a new gasket to the exhaust manifold. Secure with two bolts by do not tighten fully.

9. Align all system components properly to prevent any noise or vibrations before tightening fasteners.

10. Tighten resonator/muffler/tailpipe assembly nuts to 26 ft. lbs. (35 Nm) and front pipe/catalytic converter assembly bolts to 37 ft. lbs. (50 Nm). Tighten catalytic converter hanger bolts to 11 ft. lbs. (15 Nm).

11. Lower vehicle. Start the engine and check for leaks.

Thermostatically Controlled Air Cleaner (TCAC) System

OPERATION

▶ **See Figures 16 and 17**

This system consists of the Air Control Actuator (ACA), and the thermosensor. The TCAC system controls the temperature of intake air by mixing warm, preheated air, and cold air to help improve fuel vaporization and engine warm-up characteristics. The thermosensor senses the inside temperature of the air cleaner, and opens and closes its valve. The vacuum from the carburetor is transmitted to the ACA diaphragm when the thermosensor's valve is closed and not transmitted when open. A damper is linked to the ACA diaphragm and opens or closes the warm air duct according to the movement of the ACA diaphragm.

When the engine is started during cold weather, the thermosensor is closed because the temperature of the intake air in the air cleaner is low. therefore, the vacuum is transmitted to the ACA diaphragm, which then pulls up the damper to open the warm air duct fully. As the engine is warmed up, the temperature of the intake air coming into the air cleaner from the warm air duct rises and the thermosensor starts opening. As a result, vacuum to the ACA diaphragm decreases, and the damper pushed down by the spring force closes the warm air duct opening. In this state warm air and cold air are mixed together and enter the air cleaner.

When the engine is operating at high rpm and under high load condition, the temperature of the air coming from the warm air duct rises very high, causing the thermosensor opening to become even larger and the damper opening smaller due to the decreased vacuum. That is, the warm air amount decreases and the cold air amount increases. When throttle valve is fully opened, the damper closes the warm air duct due to very small vacuum applied to the ACA diaphragm.

SERVICE

System Inspection

1. Check vacuum hoses for connection, deterioration or damage. Replace as necessary.

2. Remove warm air hose from warm air duct, when air cleaner is cool.

3. Make sure that damper closes warm air duct with engine stopped. Perform this check by touching damper with your finger through warm air duct.

4. Start and run engine at idle. Damper should fully open warm air duct immediately.

Air Control Actuator (ACA)

1. Disconnect vacuum hose from ACA.
2. Make sure that damper opens fully when more than 7 in. Hg of vacuum is applied to the ACA.

Thermosensor

1. Remove air cleaner cap and air cleaner case.
2. Disconnect 2 vacuum hoses from thermosensor.
3. Measure the temperature around the thermosensor.
4. Close the long nozzle with your finger and then blow air into the short nozzle. If the measured temperature is above 104°F (40°C), air should come out of thermosensor. If the measured temperature is below 77°F (25°C), air should not come out.
5. After checking, connect 2 vacuum hoses to thermosensor, and reinstall air cleaner case and cap.

REMOVAL & INSTALLATION

Air Control Actuator (ACA)

1. Disconnect vacuum hose from ACA.
2. Disconnect the heated air tube from the air cleaner.
3. Remove the attaching bolt from the air cleaner.
4. Lift the ACA and unhook the rod from the trap door.
5. Remove the ACA.
6. Installation is the reverse of removal.

Thermosensor

1. Remove air cleaner cap and air cleaner case.
2. Disconnect 2 vacuum hoses from thermosensor.
3. Remove the thermosensor attaching clip.
4. Remove the thermosensor.
5. Installation is the reverse of removal.

Hot Idle Compensator (HIC)

OPERATION

The hot idle compensator is provided in the air cleaner. When the engine room temperature and intake air temperature rise abnormally high, the air/fuel mixture tends to become rich due to the decreased intake air amount, and as a result, the idling becomes unstable.

In order to avoid this unstable idling of the engine, the HIC opens and allows air to flow into the intake manifold when intake air temperature rises abnormally high. Thus, the intake air amount can be increased at idling to obtain the stable idling.

INSPECTION

▶ See Figure 18

1. Remove the air cleaner cap and case.
2. Remove the vacuum hose from the HIC.
3. Check temperature around HIC with thermometer.
4. If temperature is below 113°F (45°C), air should not come out of the HIC when air is blown into HIC nozzle. If temperature is above 149°F (65°C), air should come out of the HIC.
5. After checking, connect vacuum hose to HIC and then reinstall air cleaner case and cap.

REMOVAL & INSTALLATION

HIC Valve

1. Remove air cleaner cap and air cleaner case.
2. Disconnect 2 vacuum hoses from thermosensor.
3. Remove the thermosensor attaching clip.
4. Remove the thermosensor.
5. Installation is the reverse of removal.

Pulse Air Control System

This system serves to reduce Hydrocarbon (HC), and Carbon Monoxide (CO) emission by supplying secondary air into the exhaust manifold when the engine coolant temperature is low or during deceleration. The thermal switch mounted in the intake operates according to the engine coolant temperature. This switch is connected to the ECM and the ECM to the Three Way Solenoid Valve (TWSV). When the TWSV receives an electrical signal from the ECM, it opens its inner valve to transmit vacuum from the intake manifold to the secondary air valve.

When the engine coolant temperature is low, the thermal switch is **ON**. Then the TWSV receives a signal from the ECM, and opens the valve. Thus the TWSV transmits vacuum to the secondary air valve to opens its valve.

In the secondary air valve, there is a reed valve. When the exhaust gas pressure is low, the reed valve opens and lets the air flow from the air cleaner into the exhaust manifold, when the secondary air valve opens. When the exhaust gas pressure is high, the reed valve closes by the high exhaust

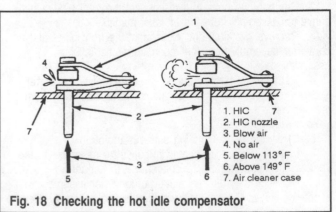

1. HIC
2. HIC nozzle
3. Blow air
4. No air
5. Below 113° F
6. Above 149° F
7. Air cleaner case

Fig. 18 Checking the hot idle compensator

gas pressure and prevents backflow of the exhaust gas. Thus, the pulsating secondary air is supplied to the exhaust manifold.

When the coolant temperature is normal, the thermal switch is **OFF**, this system does not operate. During deceleration, the ECM sends an electrical signal to the TWSV to operate the secondary air valve, even though the thermal switch is **OFF**. Thus the Hydrocarbon (HC), and Carbon Monoxide (CO) emission can be reduced even during deceleration.

INSPECTION

System Operation
▶ **See Figures 19 and 20**

Check hoses and pipe for cracks, kinks, damage or loose connections. Also, check lead wire of Three Way Solenoid Valve (TWSV) for loose connections. If above checks are satisfactory, then check system for operation according to the following procedures:

1. Disconnect secondary air hose from air cleaner when engine is cold.
2. Start cold engine and run it at idle. In this state, check to be sure that air is drawn into hose (bubbling sound is heard from inside of hose).
3. Warm up engine to normal operating temperature.
4. With engine warm, make sure air is not drawn into hose during idling (no bubbling sound is heard). Depress accelerator pedal until engine revolution increases to over 3000 rpm and

release pedal quickly. Air is drawn into hose during deceleration (bubbling sound is heard).

5. Disconnect coupler of thermal switch and connect terminals on wire harness side with lead wire to short. In this state, make sure air is drawn into hose during idling (bubbling sound is heard).
6. After checking, connect air hose to air cleaner and coupler of thermal switch.

Three Way Solenoid Valve (TWSV)

1. Label and disconnect 2 vacuum hoses from TWSV.
2. Blow into nozzle 1. Air should come out of 3 and not out of 2.
3. Disconnect coupler and connect 12 volt source to TWSV terminals. In this state, blow into nozzle 1. Air should come out of nozzle 2.
4. After checking, connect 2 vacuum hoses to TWSV.

Secondary Air Valve

1. Remove the secondary air valve with air pipe.
2. While applying vacuum to diaphragm of secondary air valve, blow into air hose. Air should come out of air pipe. Blow into air pipe. No air should come out of air hose.
3. Reinstall secondary air valve with air pipe.

REMOVAL & INSTALLATION

Three Way Solenoid Valve (TWSV)

1. Label and disconnect the solenoid valve vacuum hoses.
2. Disconnect the solenoid valve electrical connector.
3. Remove the attaching screws, then remove the solenoid valve.
4. Installation is the reverse of removal.

Secondary Air Valve

1. Disconnect the vacuum hose.
2. Disconnect the air hose.
3. Disconnect the air pipe.
4. Remove the secondary air valve.
5. Installation is the reverse of removal.

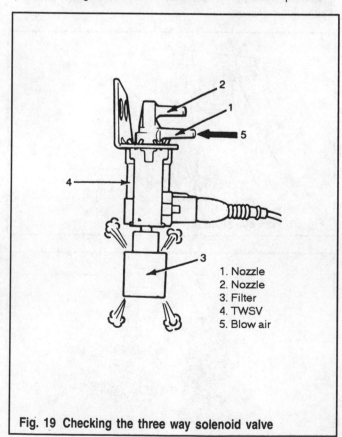

1. Secondary air valve
2. Vacuum hose
3. Air hose
4. Air pipe

Fig. 20 Checking the secondary air valve

1. Nozzle
2. Nozzle
3. Filter
4. TWSV
5. Blow air

Fig. 19 Checking the three way solenoid valve

Idle Up System

OPERATION

The ECM sends an electric signal to the Three Way Solenoid Valve (TWSV). Receiving the signal, the TWSV opens its inner valve and transmits the manifold vacuum to the idle-up diaphragm. As the diaphragm moves down by the vacuum, the idle-up adjusting screw and adjusting rod also move down and push the throttle lever to open the throttle valve a little for the idle-up state.

On manual transmission equipped vehicles, this system operates at idle and compensates for engine loads as a result of electrical loads for lights, cooling fan, rear defogger or heater fan.

On automatic transmission equipped vehicles, this system operates when the selector lever is shifted into **D**, **2**, **L** or **R** range and vehicle speed is below 15 mph. The system also operates when the temperature of the oxygen sensor is low and the sensor is not satisfactorily activated.

ADJUSTMENT

The idle-up actuator operates even when cooling fan is running. Therefore, idle-up adjustment must be performed when cooling fan is not running.

Manual Transaxle

1. Warm engine to normal operating temperature.
2. While running engine at idle speed, check to ensure that idle up adjusting screw moves down when lights are turned **ON**.
3. With lights turned **ON** check engine rpm. Be sure that heater fan, rear defogger, engine cooling fan and air conditioner are **OFF**.
4. Engine rpm should be at specified idle speed or 50 rpm higher. If not, adjust using idle up adjusting screw located at top of idle up solenoid.
5. Check idle up system as described above with the heater fan, rear defogger, engine cooling fan and air conditioner are all operated separately.

Automatic Transaxle

1. Warm engine to normal operating temperature.
2. While running engine at idle speed, check to ensure that idle up adjusting screw moves down when brake pedal is depressed and shift selector lever is moved to **D** range. All accessories should be **OFF**.
3. Check engine rpm. Engine rpm should be at specified idle speed or 50 rpm higher. If not, adjust using idle up adjusting screw located at top of idle up solenoid.

Fuel Cut System

OPERATION

The fuel cut solenoid valve is provided in the primary flow system of the carburetor to open and close the fuel passage. Turning the ignition switch **OFF** cuts off the electric current to the solenoid, the solenoid then closes the fuel passage. Thus, this system contributes to prevent engine run-on. Also, during deceleration and provided that the coolant temperature is normal, the engine rpm is greater than 2000, the clutch switch is **OFF** (clutch pedal is not depressed) and the idle switch is **ON** (primary throttle valve is closed).

SERVICE

▶ See Figures 21 and 22

System Inspection

1. Make sure that fuel cut solenoid valve makes a clicking sound when ignition switch is turned to **ON** or **OFF** without cranking the engine.
2. Warm up the engine to normal operating temperature.
3. With clutch engaged (manual transaxle), increase engine speed to 3000-4000 rpm. Under these conditions, check to be sure that engine rpm changes when idle micro switch lever on carburetor is moved.

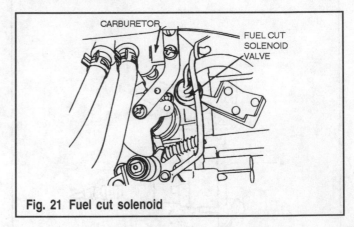

Fig. 21 Fuel cut solenoid

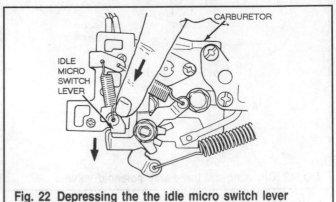

Fig. 22 Depressing the the idle micro switch lever

4. Perform the same check with clutch disengaged (clutch pedal depressed). Engine rpm should not change.

ELECTRONIC ENGINE CONTROLS

Computer Controlled Emission Control System

◆ See Figure 23

DESCRIPTION

This system is a feedback system that is used on all 1985-86 carbureted engines. A similar system with increased diagnostic capability is used on 1987-88 carbureted engines. The systems consist of an Electronic Control Module (ECM), oxygen sensor and a feedback carburetor.

The oxygen sensor mounted on the exhaust manifold monitors the exhaust gas air/fuel ratio and sends signals to the ECM. The ECM processes the oxygen sensor signal and controls carburetor air/fuel ratio by operating the mixture control solenoid in the carburetor. Thus the signal of the exhaust gas air/fuel ratio sensed by the oxygen sensor is fed back to the ECM and the carburetor air/fuel ratio is controlled.

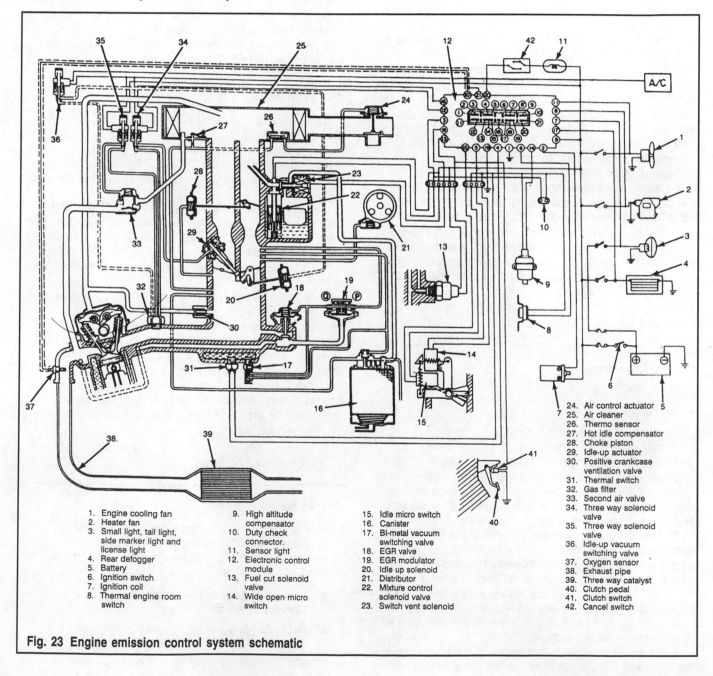

1. Engine cooling fan
2. Heater fan
3. Small light, tail light, side marker light and license light
4. Rear defogger
5. Battery
6. Ignition switch
7. Ignition coil
8. Thermal engine room switch
9. High altitude compensator
10. Duty check connector.
11. Sensor light
12. Electronic control module
13. Fuel cut solenoid valve
14. Wide open micro switch
15. Idle micro switch
16. Canister
17. Bi-metal vacuum switching valve
18. EGR valve
19. EGR modulator
20. Idle up solenoid
21. Distributor
22. Mixture control solenoid valve
23. Switch vent solenoid
24. Air control actuator
25. Air cleaner
26. Thermo sensor
27. Hot idle compensator
28. Choke piston
29. Idle-up actuator
30. Positive crankcase ventilation valve
31. Thermal switch
32. Gas filter
33. Second air valve
34. Three way solenoid valve
35. Three way solenoid valve
36. Idle-up vacuum switching valve
37. Oxygen sensor
38. Exhaust pipe
39. Three way catalyst
40. Clutch pedal
41. Clutch switch
42. Cancel switch

Fig. 23 Engine emission control system schematic

Electronic Control Module (ECM)

The ECM controls the pulse air control system, fuel cut system, idle-up system and bowl vent system, as well as the feedback system. The ECM is located inside the instrument panel under the left side of the dash.

The ECM sensed parameters are as follows:

• Exhaust oxygen concentration is sensed by the oxygen sensor installed in the exhaust manifold.

• Engine coolant temperature is sensed by the thermal switch installed on the intake manifold.

• Throttle position is sensed by the micro-switches (wide open switch and idle switch) installed on the carburetor.

• Engine speed is computed by the ECM based on the electrical signal received from the ignition system.

• Clutch engagement on manual transmission vehicles is sensed by the clutch switch located above the clutch pedal. The switch turns ON when the clutch pedal is depressed and OFF when released.

• The ECM senses electric loads of the headlights, engine cooling fan, rear defogger and heater fan.

• Altitude compensation. When the vehicle is at high altitude and the feedback system does not function, the air/fuel mixture becomes richer because of low air density. To compensate for the richer air/fuel mixture at high altitude, the high altitude compensator is ON by sensing the barometric pressure and sends a signal to the ECM. Following the signal, the ECM controls the mixture control solenoid in the carburetor, thus compensating the air/fuel mixture.

• Engine compartment temperature compensation. Sensing the air temperature in the engine compartment the switch sends an electric signal to the ECM to compensate the air/fuel ratio of the fuel mixture. When air temperature in the engine compartment is low, the switch operates to make the mixture right. When the air temperature in the engine compartment is high, the switch stops operating and the air/fuel ratio of the mixture is not controlled.

SYSTEM DIAGNOSIS

Feedback System

1985-86 VEHICLES

▶ See Figure 24

The feedback system uses a SENSOR lamp in the instrument panel to warn the driver of possible system problems. The sensor light will automatically flash at 30,000 mile intervals if the system is in proper working order.

Should the fuel consumption increase by an excessive amount, the engine stalls or is hard to start, the feedback system should be checked using the procedure below.

1. Turn **ON** the cancel switch, located at the left side of the dash in the fuse box.

2. Turn the ignition switch **ON** without running the engine. At this time the SENSOR light should illuminate but not flash. If the light does not flash, check the electric circuit of the light, the light for a burned bulb and the lead wire for shorts.

3. After the light illuminates, start the engine and warm it up to normal operating temperature.

4. When engine is warm, run engine at 1500-2000 rpm. In this state and with the cancel switch ON, the SENSOR light

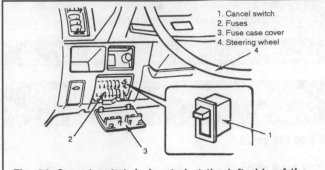

1. Cancel switch
2. Fuses
3. Fuse case cover
4. Steering wheel

Fig. 24 Cancel switch is located at the left side of the dash in the fuse box.

should flash. Flashing of the light proves that the system is functioning properly.

5. If the light does not flash, it can be caused by a defective feedback system component.

6. After making sure that the SENSOR light flashes, turn the cancel switch **OFF**. The light should not stay illuminated.

7. Stop the engine.

1987-88 VEHICLES

1. Turn the ignition key **ON**. The CHECK ENGINE light should illuminate but not flash.

2. Reach under the dash and turn the diagnosis switch **ON**. If the CHECK ENGINE light remains ON steady or goes out, the ECM is defective or poor contact exists between the ECM wires.

3. If the CHECK ENGINE light flashes, codes are stored in the system. Record the flashes and check the diagnostic code list. (Refer to 'Diagnostic Trouble Codes-Feedback System' in this Section for more information.)

4. Turn the diagnosis switch **OFF** after all codes have been recorded.

5. Stored fault codes may be erased from memory at any time by removing power from the ECM for at least 30 seconds. This time period must be increased as the temperature drops. It may be necessary to clear stored codes during diagnosis to check for any recurrence during a test drive, but the stored codes must be written down when retrieved. The codes may still be required for subsequent troubleshooting. Whenever a repair is complete, the stored codes must be erased and the vehicle test driven to confirm correct operation and repair.

COMPONENT TESTING

Oxygen Sensor

1. Warm the engine to normal operating temperature.

2. Disconnect the connector of the oxygen sensor.

3. Connect a voltmeter between the sensor side terminal and ground.

➡**Never apply voltage to the oxygen sensor as it may cause damage to the sensor.**

4. While keeping the engine running at 1500-2000 rpm, push the lever on the wide open micro switch down and ensure the reading on the voltmeter is about 0.8 volts.

5. With the engine running at 1000-1500 rpm, disconnect the vacuum hose at the intake manifold under the wide open switch. Ensure the reading on the voltmeter is about zero volts.

6. After checking, reconnect the vacuum hose to the intake manifold and connector to the oxygen sensor.

Idle Micro Switch

▶ **See Figures 25 and 26**

1. Warm the engine to normal operating temperature.
2. Disconnect the micro switch connector and connect an ohmmeter to the top two terminals.
3. Run the engine at idle and make sure that the reading is zero.
4. After connecting a tachometer to the engine, increase engine rpm gradually from idle speed and make sure that engine rpm is between 1500-2400 rpm when ohmmeter indicates infinity. If it is not within specified range, make adjustment by bending lever. Bend lever down when engine rpm is below specification and up when over specification.

Wide Open Throttle Switch

▶ **See Figures 27, 28 and 29**

1. Remove air cleaner and carburetor
2. Connect an ohmmeter to wide open micro switch terminals and check for resistance. Resistance should be infinity.
3. Open throttle valve gradually until the ohmmeter indicates zero ohms. Then, using a vernier caliper, measure

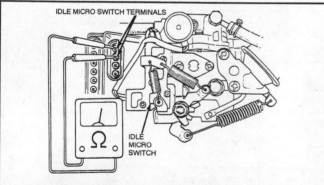

Fig. 25 Checking the idle micro switch

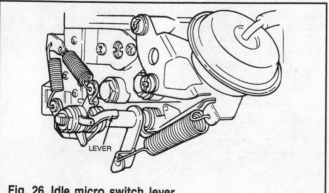

Fig. 26 Idle micro switch lever

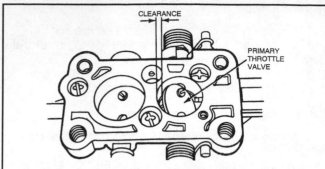

Fig. 28 Checking clearance between throttle valve and carburetor bore

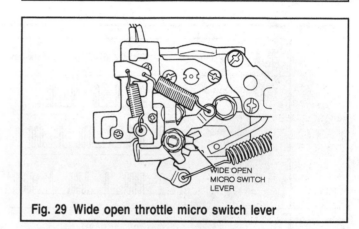

Fig. 29 Wide open throttle micro switch lever

the clearance between throttle valve and carburetor bore. Clearance should be within 0.29-0.33 in. (7.2-8.4mm). If the clearance is out of specification, make adjustment by bending the wide open micro switch lever.

Mixture Control Solenoid Valve

1. Remove the cap of the duty check connector located in the engine compartment behind the water reservoir tank and the battery. Connect the terminals with a jumper wire.
2. Turn Ignition **ON** and **OFF** repeatedly without starting the engine.
3. Touch the carburetor body near the mixture control solenoid valve and make sure that carburetor makes small vibrations according to the operation of the ignition switch.

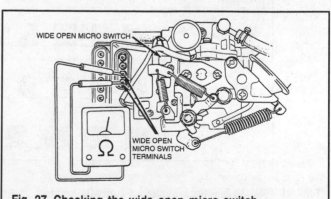

Fig. 27 Checking the wide open micro switch

Thermal Switch

1. Disconnect the thermal switch electrical connector.
2. With coolant temperature below 86°F (30°C), check that there is continuity between the terminals.
3. With coolant temperature above 116°F (46°C), check that there is no continuity between the terminals.

Thermal Engine Compartment Switch

1. Disconnect switch connector and connect ohmmeter between terminals on switch side.
2. With atmospheric temperature is 44°F (7°C) ohmmeter should read zero ohms.
3. With atmospheric temperature is 67°F (19°C) ohmmeter should read infinity.

High Altitude Compensator

1. Disconnect the compensator electrical connector and connect an ohmmeter between the terminals.
2. At an altitude above 4000 feet, the ohmmeter should read zero ohms.
3. At an altitude below 4000 feet, the ohmmeter should read infinity.

Diagnostic Trouble Codes-Feedback System

▶ See Figure 30

Diagnosis Code No.	System	"CHECK ENGINE" light flashing condition	Trouble
12	Ignition		This code indicates that the diagnosis system functions properly.
13	Oxygen sensor		• Oxygen sensor or its circuit faulty. • ECM faulty.
14	Coolant temp. sensor		• Coolant temp. sensor or its circuit faulty. • ECM faulty.
21	Throttle position switches		• Idle/Wide open micro switches or its circuit faulty. • ECM faulty.
23	Intake air temp. sensor		• Intake air temperature sensor or its circuit faulty. • ECM faulty.
32	Ambient pressure sensor		Ambient pressure sensor (provided in ECM) faulty.
51	ECM		ECM faulty.
52	Fuel cut solenoid		• Fuel cut solenoid or its circuit faulty. • ECM faulty.
53	Second air solenoid		• Second air three-way solenoid or its circuit faulty. • ECM faulty
54	Mixture control solenoid		• Mixture control solenoid or its circuit faulty. • ECM faulty.
55	Bowl vent solenoid		• Bowl vent solenoid or its circuit faulty. • ECM faulty.

Fig. 30 1987-88 feedback system diagnostic codes

Electronic Fuel Injection (EFI) Turbo System

♦ See Figures 31 and 32

DESCRIPTION

The EFI Turbo system is used only on 1987-88 turbocharged Sprint vehicles. The system, namely the electronic control type fuel injection system, consists of an ECM, an in-tank type electric fuel pump, a pressure regulator, fuel injectors, a turbocharger, a throttle position sensor, an intake air temperature sensor, a coolant temperature sensor, an oxygen sensor, an airflow meter and others.

Electronic Control Module (ECM)

The ECM is required to maintain the exhaust emissions at acceptable levels. The module is a small, solid state computer which receives signals from many sources and sensors; it uses these data to make judgments about operating conditions and then control output signals to the fuel and emission systems to match the current requirements.

Inputs are received from many sources to form a complete picture of engine operating conditions. Some inputs are simply Yes or No messages, such as that from the Park/Neutral switch; the vehicle is either in gear or in Park/Neutral; there are no other choices. Other data is sent in quantitative input, such as engine RPM or coolant temperature. The ECM is pre-programmed to recognize acceptable ranges or combinations of signals and control the outputs to control emissions while providing good driveability and economy. The ECM also

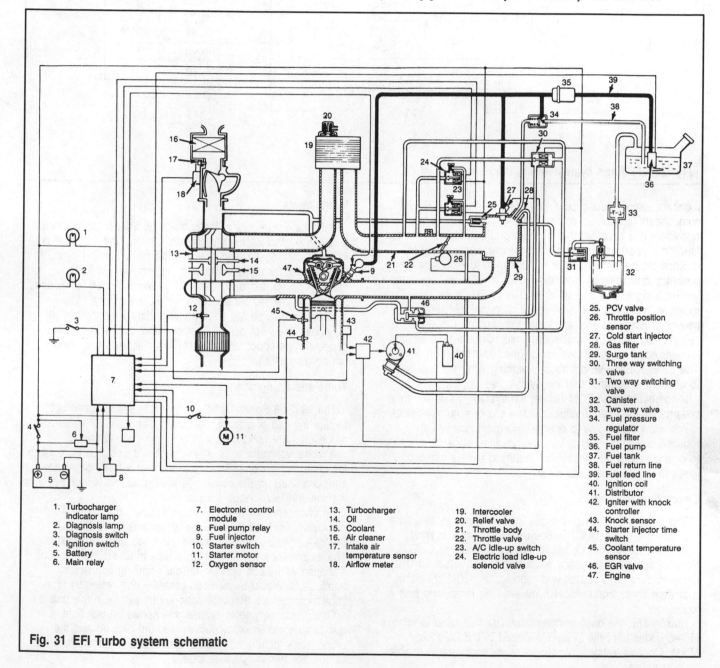

25. PCV valve
26. Throttle position sensor
27. Cold start injector
28. Gas filter
29. Surge tank
30. Three way switching valve
31. Two way switching valve
32. Canister
33. Two way valve
34. Fuel pressure regulator
35. Fuel filter
36. Fuel pump
37. Fuel tank
38. Fuel return line
39. Fuel feed line
40. Ignition coil
41. Distributor
42. Igniter with knock controller
43. Knock sensor
44. Starter injector time switch
45. Coolant temperature sensor
46. EGR valve
47. Engine

1. Turbocharger indicator lamp
2. Diagnosis lamp
3. Diagnosis switch
4. Ignition switch
5. Battery
6. Main relay

7. Electronic control module
8. Fuel pump relay
9. Fuel injector
10. Starter switch
11. Starter motor
12. Oxygen sensor

13. Turbocharger
14. Oil
15. Coolant
16. Air cleaner
17. Intake air temperature sensor
18. Airflow meter

19. Intercooler
20. Relief valve
21. Throttle body
22. Throttle valve
23. A/C idle-up switch
24. Electric load idle-up solenoid valve

Fig. 31 EFI Turbo system schematic

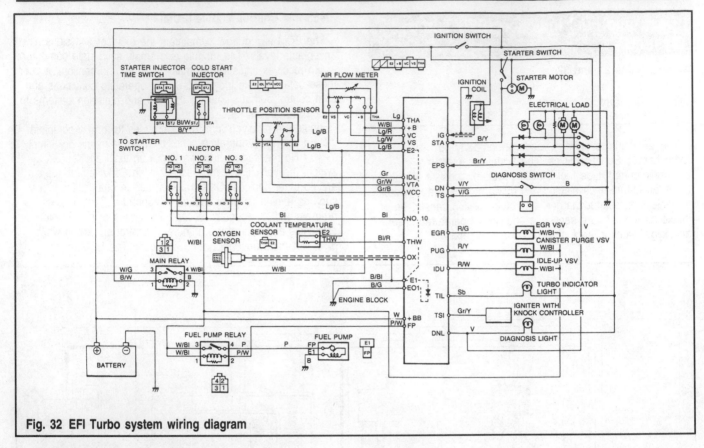

Fig. 32 EFI Turbo system wiring diagram

monitors some output circuits, making sure that the components function as commanded. For proper engine operation, it is essential that all input and output components function properly and communicate properly with the ECM.

Since the control module is programmed to recognize the presence and value of electrical inputs, it will also note the lack of a signal or a radical change in values. It will, for example, react to the loss of signal from the vehicle speed sensor or note that engine coolant temperature has risen beyond acceptable (programmed) limits. Once a fault is recognized, a numeric code is assigned and held in memory. The CHECK ENGINE dashboard warning lamp will illuminate to advise the operator that the system has detected a fault.

In the event of an ECM failure, the system will default to a pre-programmed set of values. These are compromise values which allow the engine to operate, although possibly at reduced efficiency. This is variously known as the default, limp-in or back-up mode. Driveability is almost always affected when the ECM enters this mode.

Check Engine Lamp

The primary function of the dash warning lamp is to advise the operator that a fault has been detected, and, in most cases, a code stored. Under normal conditions, the CHECK ENGINE lamp will illuminate when the ignition is turned **ON**. Once the engine is started and running, the ECM will perform a system check and extinguish the warning lamp if no fault is found.

Additionally, the dash warning lamp must be used to retrieve stored codes after the system is placed in the Diagnostic Mode. Codes are transmitted as a series of flashes with short or long pauses.

Intermittents

If a fault occurs intermittently, such as a loose connector pin breaking contact as the vehicle hits a bump, the ECM will note the fault as it occurs and energize the dash warning lamp. If the problem self-corrects, as with the terminal pin again making contact, the dash lamp will extinguish after 10 seconds but a code will remain stored in the ECM memory.

When an unexpected code appears during diagnostics, it may have been set during an intermittent failure that self-corrected; the codes are still useful in diagnosis and should not be discounted.

Tools and Equipment

The 1987-88 Sprint Turbo fuel injection system does not require the use of a scan tool during diagnosis. All diagnostic procedures are conducted with common shop tools.

A digital voltmeter with 10-mega-ohm impedance is required for testing all systems. This type of meter will not place an additional load on the circuit it is testing; this is extremely important in low voltage circuits.

An ohmmeter will also be required during diagnosis. A particularly useful tool is the digital multimeter, such as J 34029-A or equivalent, combining the volt and ohm meters. The multimeter must be of high quality in all respects and be equipped with leads suitable for back-probing connector terminals. It should be handled carefully and protected from impact or damage. Replace batteries frequently in the unit.

Other necessary tools include an unpowered test light, a quality tachometer with inductive (clip-on) pick up and the proper tools for releasing GM's Metri-Pack, Weather Pack and Micro-Pack terminals as necessary.

DIAGNOSIS

Diagnosis of a driveability and/or emissions problems requires attention to detail and following the diagnostic procedures in the correct order. Resist the temptation to perform any repairs before performing the preliminary diagnostic steps. In many cases this will shorten diagnostic time and often cure the problem without electronic testing.

The proper troubleshooting procedure for these vehicles is as follows:

Visual/Physical Underhood Inspection

This is possibly the most critical step of diagnosis. A detailed examination of connectors, wiring and vacuum hoses can often lead to a repair without further diagnosis. Performance of this step relies on the skill of the technician performing it; a careful inspector will check the undersides of hoses as well as the integrity of hard-to-reach hoses blocked by the air cleaner or other component. Wiring should be checked carefully for any sign of strain, burning, crimping, or terminal pull-out from a connector. Checking connectors at components or in harnesses is required; usually, pushing them together will reveal a loose fit.

Diagnostic Circuit Check

This step is used to check that the on-board diagnostic system is working correctly. A system which is faulty or shorted may not yield correct codes when placed in the Diagnostic Mode. Performing this test confirms that the diagnostic system is not failed and is able to communicate through the dash warning lamp.

If the diagnostic system is not operating correctly, or if a problem exists without the dash warning lamp being lit, refer to the specific 'A' Diagnostic Charts. These charts cover such conditions as Engine Cranks but Will Not Run or No CHECK ENGINE Light.

Diagnostic Trouble Codes-EFI Turbo System

READING CODES

▶ See Figure 33

Once the integrity of the system is confirmed, enter the Diagnostic Mode and read any stored codes. Once the

Diagnostic Mode is engaged, the dash warning lamp should begin to flash.

The Sprint uses a Code 12 to indicate that no other codes are stored. If a fault is in memory, it will be broadcast as soon as the system enters Diagnostic Mode. The codes are stored and transmitted in numeric order from lowest to highest; each fault code is transmitted 3 times before moving to the next.

➡The order of codes in the memory does not indicate the order of occurrence.

Record each code transmitted for later reference. Once all codes have been sent, the memory may need to be cleared during diagnostics. If there are no codes stored, but a driveability or emissions problem is evident, inspection of individual components is necessary.

To retrieve codes from the ECM:

1. When the ignition switch is turned ON with the engine not running the CHECK ENGINE light illuminates. This indicates the circuit of the CHECK ENGINE light is functioning properly.

2. If the EFI system is functioning properly, the CHECK ENGINE light should go out when the engine is started.

3. If a malfunction exists in the signal to the ECM when the engine is running, the CHECK ENGINE light remains illuminated as long as the malfunction exists.

4. If a malfunction in the input signal to the ECM is detected even once, it will be kept in the ECM memory in the form of a diagnostic code.

5. The memorized code will be stored until the power from the battery to the ECM is disconnected. Therefore, after correcting the problem area, erase the ECM memory by disconnecting the negative battery cable for 20 seconds or longer.

6. When the diagnosis switch, located under the left side of the instrument panel, to the right of the steering column, is turned ON, the CHECK ENGINE light flashes to indicate the diagnostic code in the ECM memory.

7. When the ECM is damaged, the CHECK ENGINE light will remain ON instead of flashing codes.

8. The CHECK ENGINE light flashing pattern of each diagnostic code represents a 2-digit number. The diagnostic code repeats until the switch is turned OFF.

9. If two or more areas are involved the CHECK ENGINE light indicates each code corresponding to the area of trouble three times and in the increasing order of the code numbers. After all codes are displayed, the sequence is repeated.

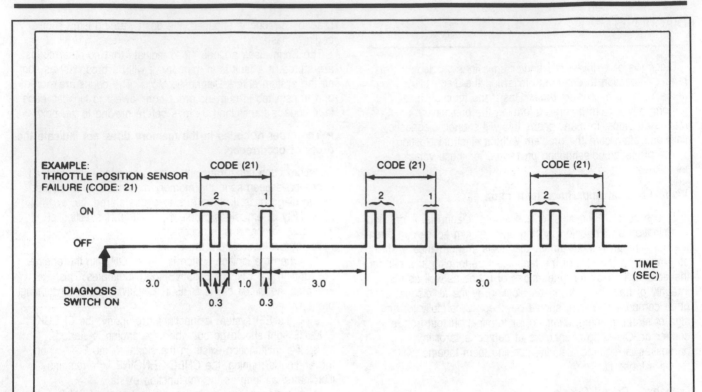

DIAGNOSTIC CODE		MALFUNCTION AREA	DIAGNOSIS
NO.	MODE		
12		Normal	This code appears when none of the other codes (13 to 41) are identified
13		Oxygen Sensor	Open circuit in Oxygen sensor signal (only lean indication)
14		Coolant temperature sensor	Open circuit in coolant temperature sensor signal
15		Coolant temperature sensor	Short circuit in coolant temperature sensor signal
21		Throttle position sensor	Open circuit in throttle position sensor signal
22		Throttle position sensor	Short circuit in throttle position sensor signal
23		Intake air temperature sensor	Open circuit in intake air temperature sensor signal
25		Intake air temperature sensor	Short circuit in intake air temperature sensor signal
31		Turbocharger	Abnormally high super charged pressure
33		Air flow meter	Open or short circuit in air flow meter signal
41		Ignition signal	No signal from ignition coil for two seconds with engine starter switch turned ON
ON		ECM	ECM failure

Fig. 33 1987-88 EFI turbo diagnostic codes

CIRCUIT/COMPONENT DIAGNOSIS AND REPAIR

Using the appropriate chart(s) based on the Diagnostic Circuit Check, the fault codes and scan tool data will lead to diagnosis and checking of a particular circuit or component. It is important to note that the fault code indicates a fault or loss of signal in an ECM-controlled system, not necessarily in the specific component. Detailed procedures to isolate the problem are included in each code chart; these procedures must be followed accurately to insure timely and correct repair. Following the procedure will also insure that only truly faulty components are replaced.

CLEARING CODES

Stored fault codes may be erased from memory at any time by removing power from the ECM for at least 30 seconds. This time period must be increased as the temperature drops. It may be necessary to clear stored codes during diagnosis to check for any recurrence during a test drive, but the stored codes must be written down when retrieved. The codes may still be required for subsequent troubleshooting. Whenever a repair is complete, the stored codes must be erased and the vehicle test driven to confirm correct operation and repair.

➡The ignition switch must be OFF any time power is disconnected or restored to the ECM. Severe damage may result if this precaution is not observed.

Removing the TAIL LAMP fuse from the under dash fuse box will interrupt power to the ECM without blanking other memories within the vehicle. The pink, 30 amp main fuse may be removed from the underhood fuse holder on the right front fender apron, but this will also disconnect power to the clock and the radio.

COMPONENT TESTING

Electronic Control Module (ECM)
▶ See Figure 34

The ECM is grounded to the surge tank. A loose ground may hinder proper operation of the ECM. Check to make sure that it is properly and securely grounded. The ECM is located under the left side of the dash to the left of the steering column.
1. Turn the ignition switch OFF.
2. Disconnect the left coupler from the ECM by pushing the lockdown.
3. Check for continuity between each terminal of the Black/Green lead wire and Black/Blue lead wire and ground with an ohmmeter.
4. After checking, connect the coupler to the ECM securely.

Airflow Meter
▶ See Figure 35

1. Turn the ignition switch OFF.

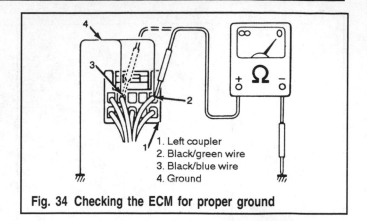

1. Left coupler
2. Black/green wire
3. Black/blue wire
4. Ground

Fig. 34 Checking the ECM for proper ground

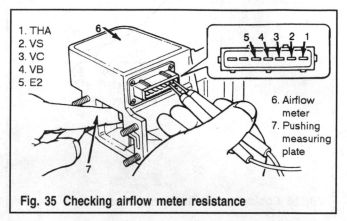

1. THA
2. VS
3. VC
4. VB
5. E2
6. Airflow meter
7. Pushing measuring plate

Fig. 35 Checking airflow meter resistance

2. Disconnect the airflow meter connector.
3. Check for resistance between the terminals of the airflow meter with an ohmmeter as described in the illustration.

Oxygen Sensor

1. Warm the engine to normal operating temperature.
2. Disconnect the connector of the oxygen sensor.
3. Connect a voltmeter between the sensor side terminal and ground.

➡Never apply voltage to the oxygen sensor as it may cause damage to the sensor.

4. With the engine running at 3000 rpm, check that the voltage from oxygen sensor exceeds 0.7 volts.
5. With the engine idling, check that the voltage from oxygen sensor is zero volts.
6. After checking, reconnect oxygen sensor connector.

Coolant Temperature Sensor
▶ See Figure 36

1. Disconnect electrical connector from coolant temperature sensor.
2. Using an ohmmeter, check resistance between the sensor terminals.
3. With engine cold, resistance should be approximately 2000 ohms.
4. With engine at normal operating temperature, resistance should be less than 500 ohms.

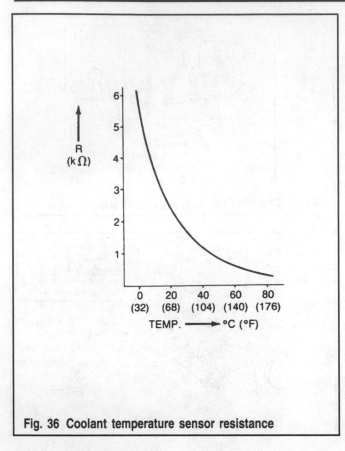

Fig. 36 Coolant temperature sensor resistance

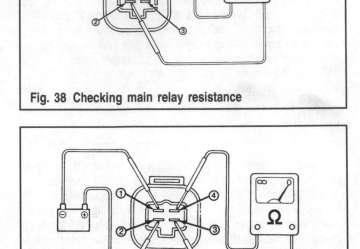

Fig. 38 Checking main relay resistance

Fig. 39 Checking main relay operation

Starter Injector Time Switch

1. Disconnect electrical connector from coolant temperature sensor.

2. Using an ohmmeter, check resistance between the sensor terminals.

3. With coolant temperature lower than 66°F (19°C), resistance should be 34-39 ohms.

4. With coolant temperature higher than 77°F (25°C), resistance should be 68-78 ohms.

Main Relay

▶ See Figures 37, 38 and 39

The main relay and fuel pump relay sit side by side on a bracket at the shock tower. The main relay has Black, Black/White, White/Blue and White/Green lead wires.

1. Check that main relay makes a sound when the ignition switch is turned **ON**.

2. With ignition switch **ON**, check for battery voltage between the top and bottom two terminals.

3. Check that there is continuity between terminals 3 and 4 when the battery is connected to terminals 1 and 2.

Ignition Signal

▶ See Figure 40

➡ **This inspection should only be performed when the vehicle fails to start.**

1. With the ignition switch **OFF**, disconnect the right connector from the ECM.

2. Check for battery voltage at the White lead wire when the ignition switch is **ON**.

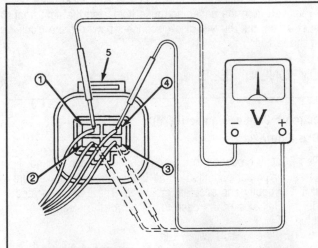

1. BLACK LEAD WIRE
2. BLACK/WHITE LEAD WIRE
3. WHITE/GREEN LEAD WIRE
4. WHITE/BLUE LEAD WIRE
5. MAIN RELAY

Terminal	Voltage
②—①	Battery voltage (Approx. 12V)
③—①	Battery voltage (Approx. 12V)
④—①	Battery voltage (Approx. 12V)

Fig. 37 Checking main relay voltage

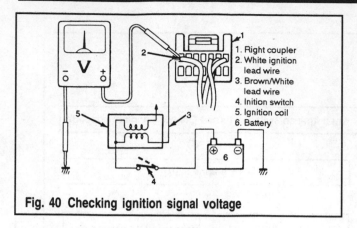

Fig. 40 Checking ignition signal voltage

1. Right coupler
2. White ignition lead wire
3. Brown/White lead wire
4. Inition switch
5. Ignition coil
6. Battery

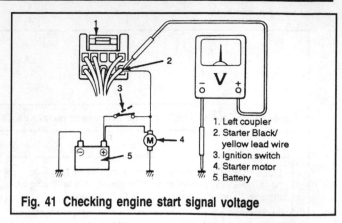

Fig. 41 Checking engine start signal voltage

1. Left coupler
2. Starter Black/yellow lead wire
3. Ignition switch
4. Starter motor
5. Battery

3. If battery voltage is not detected, check ignition coil and circuit.

4. Connect ECM coupler after ensuring that ignition switch is **OFF**.

Engine Start Signal
♦ **See Figure 41**

1. With ignition **OFF**, remove the left coupler from the ECM.

2. Check for battery voltage at the Black/Yellow wire when the starter motor is turning.

3. If battery voltage is not detected, check starter motor and circuit.

4. Connect ECM coupler after ensuring that ignition switch is **OFF**.

Fuel Cut Check

1. Warm the engine to normal operating temperature.

2. While listening to the sound of the injectors using a mechanics scope, increase engine speed to 3000 rpm.

3. Check to make sure that sound of injectors stops when throttle is closed suddenly and is not heard again when engine speed is increased to less than 1900 rpm.

4. If injector operation sound does not disappear, check throttle position sensor.

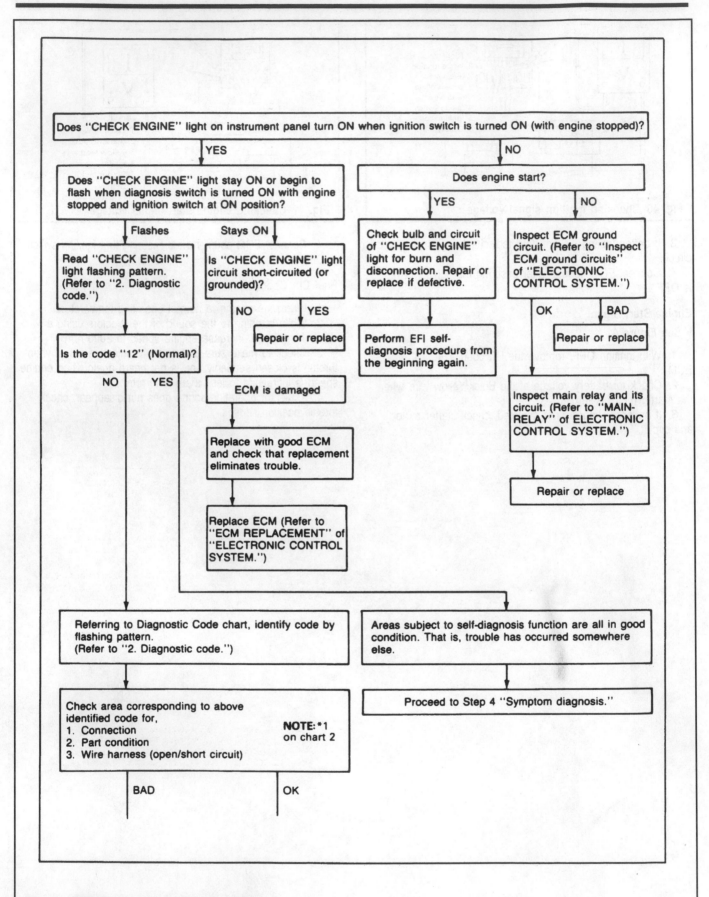

Fig. 42 1987-88 EFI turbo diagnostic chart

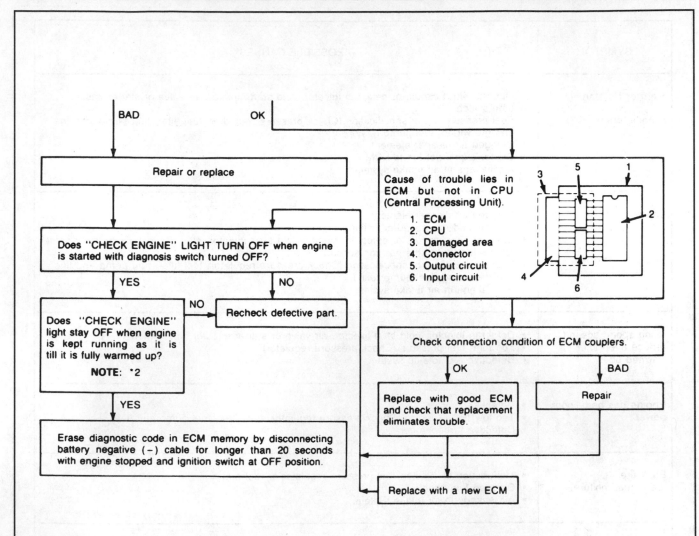

NOTE:

*1. If an intermittent fault occured, the ECM keeps that fault in memory and indicates the diagnostic code corresponding to the fault. As such a case is possible, be sure to execute each check very carefully. Also, note that disconnecting power from battery to ECM will erase the memory.

*2. When the trouble has occurred in the area of the oxygen sensor, warm up the engine fully, run at the 3rd, 4th, or 5th gear position and when the engine speed has risen to 2,000 rpm, depress the accelerator pedal fully for more than 2 seconds. And then stop the car and engine and with the ignition switch at ON position, operate the diagnosis switch.

CAUTION:
To minimize the chance of personal injury or property damage, select a safe place to operate the vehicle when performing this operation.

Fig. 43 1987-88 EFI turbo diagnostic chart

SYMPTOM	POSSIBLE CAUSES
Hard or No starting (Engine cranks OK)	• Open or short circuit, or defect in injector, cold start injector, air valve or starter injector time switch • Fuel pressure out of specification (Check pressure regulator, fuel filter, fuel pump and line and the wiring, fuel pump relay.) • Clogged air cleaner element. • Starter signal not fed to ECM • Air leakage in air intake system.
Improper engine idling	• Clogged air cleaner element • Maladjusted idle speed adjusting screw. • Open or short circuit, or defect in injector, cold start injector, starter injector time switch, idle switch (in throttle position sensor) • Fuel pressure out of specification (Check pressure regulator, fuel filter, fuel pump and line and the wiring, fuel pump relay) • Air leakage in air intake system.
Idling speed doesn't reduce even after warmed up	• Defect in injector, cold start injector, air valve or starter injector time switch • Too high fuel pressure (Check pressure regulator) • Defective A/C idle-up system
Engine has no or poor power	• Defective injector • Too low fuel pressure (Check pressure regulator, fuel filter, fuel pump and line) • Defective turbocharger
Back fire (Lean fuel mixture)	• Malfunction of injector, fuel pressure regulator or fuel pump • Clogged fuel filter • Air leakage in air intake system.
After fire (Rich fuel mixture)	• Malfunction of injector, cold start injector, starter injector time switch, or fuel pressure regulator
Knocking	• Knock sensor, knock controller and their wiring defective.
No idle-up even when one of lights, heater fan, rear defogger (if equipped), cooling fan, and brake light is turned ON or when air conditioner is operated	• Idle-up VSV and its wiring defective or its hose leaking or clogged
Excessive hydrocarbons (HC) emission (Rich or lean fuel mixture)	• Malfunction of injector, cold start injector, starter injector time switch • Fuel pressure is too high or low (pressure regulator, fuel filter, fuel pump) • Malfunction of feedback control (oxygen sensor) • Insufficient warming up • Leakage at air intake system • Defective catalyzer

Fig. 44 1987-88 EFI turbo diagnostic chart

SYMPTOM	POSSIBLE CAUSES
Excessive carbon monoxide (CO) emission Rich fuel mixture	• Leaky injector nozzle • Malfunction of injector, cold start injector, starter injector time switch • Fuel pressure is too high (pressure regulator) • Malfunction of feedback control (oxygen sensor) • Insufficient warming up • Defective catalyzer
Excessive oxides of nitrogen (NOx) emission (Lean fuel mixture)	• Clogged or defective injector • Fuel pressure is too low (pressure regulator, fuel filter, fuel pump) • Malfunction of feedback control (oxygen sensor) • Leakage at air intake system • Leakage at exhaust system

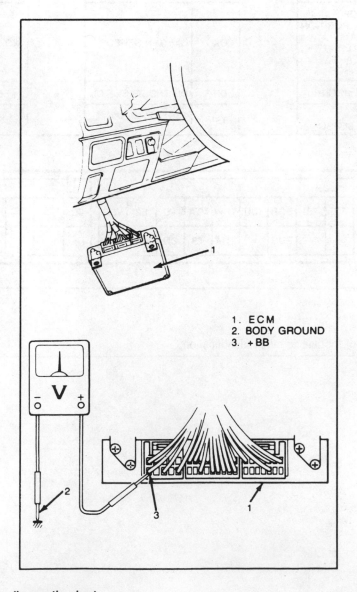

1. ECM
2. BODY GROUND
3. +BB

Fig. 45 1987-88 EFI turbo diagnostic chart

ECM TERMINAL

COUPLER	SYMBOL	TERMINAL	COUPLER	SYMBOL	TERMINAL	COUPLER	SYMBOL	TERMINAL
14 PIN	DNL	DIAGNOSIS LIGHT "CHECK ENGINE"	18 PIN	THW	COOLANT TEMP. SENSOR	18 PIN	THA	INLET AIR TEMP. SENSOR
	FP	FUEL PUMP RELAY		IDU	IDLE UP VSV		PUG	EVAPO PURGE VALVE VSV
	IDL	IDLE SWITCH		EGR	EGR VALVE VSV	10 PIN	E01	ENGINE BLOCK GROUND
	IG	IGNITION COIL $\ominus$		TSI	EXTERNAL ECU		E1	ENGINE BLOCK GROUND
	EPS	ELECTRIC LOAD SWITCH		TIL	TURBO LAMP		+B	MAIN RELAY
18 PIN	VCC	THROTTLE POSITION SENSOR		VC	AIR FLOW METER		STA	STARTER SWITCH
	E2	GROUND OF THROTTLE POSITION SENSOR, AIR FLOW METER AND COOLANT TEMP. SENSOR		OX	OXYGEN SENSOR		NO. 10	INJECTOR
	VS	AIR FLOW METER		DN	DIAGNOSIS SWITCH		+BB	BATTERY $\oplus$
	VTA	THROTTLE POSITION SENSOR		TS	TEST TERMINAL			

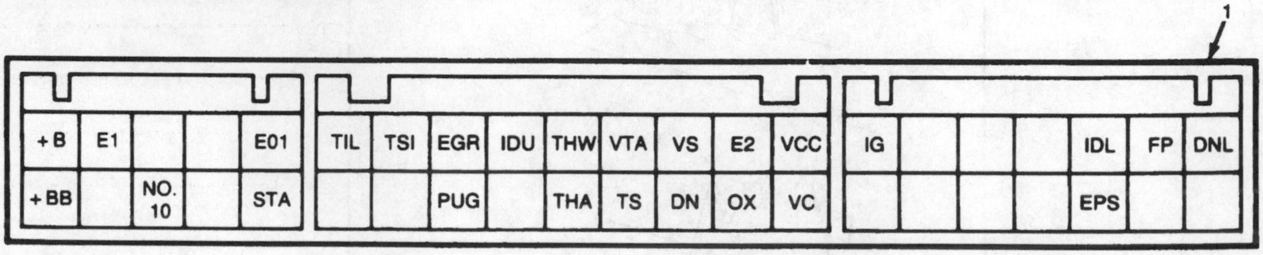

+B	E1			E01		TIL	TSI	EGR	IDU	THW	VTA	VS	E2	VCC		IG				IDL	FP	DNL
+BB		NO. 10		STA				PUG		THA	TS	DN	OX	VC						EPS		

1. ECM

Fig. 46 1987-88 EFI turbo control module terminal identification

		VOLTAGE AT ECM WIRING COUPLER TERMINALS	
TERMINAL	**STANDARD VOLTAGE (V)**	**CONDITION**	
DNL	1 - 2	IG S/W ON	
	10 - 14	Idling with engine fully warmed up	
FP	0 - 1	IG S/W ON	During about 4 seconds after IG S/W turned ON
	10 - 14		After the about 4 seconds
IDL	0 - 0.5	IG S/W ON	Accelerator pedal released
EPS	0 - 0.5	IG S/W ON	
	9 - 13		Head light, heater fan switch, rear defogger, stop light or cooling fan motor is turned ON
IG	10 - 14	IG S/W ON	
VCC	APPROX. 5	IG S/W ON	
VC	6.4 - 9.0	IG S/W ON	
VS	1.4 - 2.0	IG S/W ON	
DN	10 - 14	IG S/W ON	
VTA	0 - 1	IG S/W ON	Accelerator pedal released
	APPROX. 5	IG S/W ON	Accelerator pedal fully depressed
THW	APPROX. 2.4	IG S/W ON	Coolant temperature 20°C (68°F)
	APPROX. 0.6	IG S/W ON	Coolant temperature 80°C (176°F)
THA	APPROX. 2.4	IG S/W ON	Intake air temperature 20°C (68°F)
IDU	1 - 3	IG S/W ON	
EGR	10 - 14	IG S/W ON	
PUG	10 - 14	IG S/W ON	
TSI	10 - 14	IG S/W ON	
TIL	10 - 14	IG S/W ON	
STA	0 - 0.5	IG S/W ON	
	10 - 14	Starter switch turned ON with clutch pedal fully depressed	
NO. 10	10 - 14	IG S/W ON	
+ B	10 - 14	IG S/W ON	
+ BB	10 - 14	IG S/W ON and OFF	

Fig. 47 1987-88 EFI turbo control module terminal voltages

Electronic Fuel Injection (EFI) System

▶ **See Figure 48**

DESCRIPTION

The Electronic Fuel Injection (EFI) system is used on 1989-93 Geo Metro vehicles. The system, namely the electronic control type fuel injection system, consists of an ECM, an in-tank type electric fuel pump, a pressure regulator, fuel injectors, a manifold absolute pressure sensor, a throttle position sensor, an intake air temperature sensor, a coolant temperature sensor, an oxygen sensor, a vehicle speed sensor, a crankshaft angle sensor and others

Electronic Control Module (ECM)

The ECM is required to maintain the exhaust emissions at acceptable levels. The module is a small, solid state computer which receives signals from many sources and sensors; it uses these data to make judgments about operating conditions and then control output signals to the fuel and emission systems to match the current requirements.

Inputs are received from many sources to form a complete picture of engine operating conditions. Some inputs are simply Yes or No messages, such as that from the Park/Neutral switch; the vehicle is either in gear or in Park/Neutral; there are no other choices. Other data is sent in quantitative input, such as engine RPM or coolant temperature. The ECM is pre-programmed to recognize acceptable ranges or combinations of signals and control the outputs to control emissions while providing good driveability and economy. The ECM also

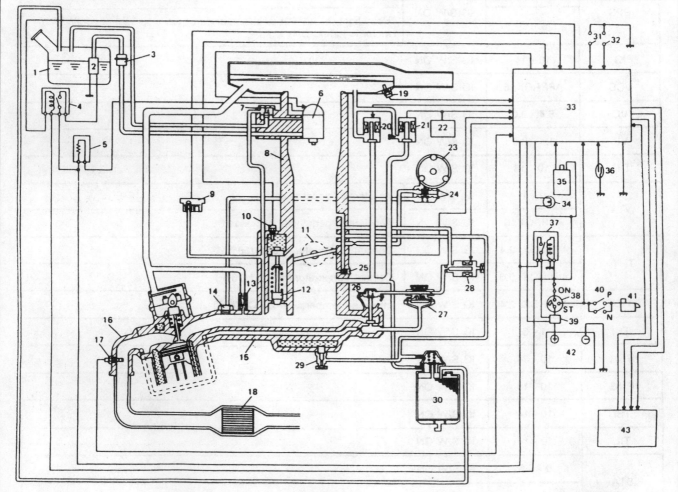

1. Fuel tank	10. Coolant temperature sensor	19. Manifold air temperature sensor	25. Idle speed adjusting screw	35. Ignition coil
2. Fuel pump	11. Throttle position sensor	20. Idle speed control solenoid	29. Bimetal vacuum switching valve	36. Speed sensor
3. Fuel filter	12. Air valve	21. Air conditioner vacuum switching valve	30. Charcoal canister	37. Main relay
4. Fuel pump relay	13. PCV valve	22. Air conditioner amplifier	31. Diagnosis switch terminal	38. Main switch
5. Fuel injector resistor	14. Gas filter	23. Distributor	32. Test switch terminal	39. Main fuse
6. Fuel injector	15. Intake manifold	24. Vacuum advancer	33. Electronic control module	40. Shift switch
7. Fuel pressure regulator	16. Exhaust manifold		34. Check engine light	41. Starter magnetic switch
8. Throttle body	17. Oxygen sensor			42. Battery
9. Manifold absolute pressure sensor	18. Three-way catalyst			43. Automatic transmission control module

Fig. 48 EFI system schematic

monitors some output circuits, making sure that the components function as commanded. For proper engine operation, it is essential that all input and output components function properly and communicate properly with the ECM.

Since the control module is programmed to recognize the presence and value of electrical inputs, it will also note the lack of a signal or a radical change in values. It will, for example, react to the loss of signal from the vehicle speed sensor or note that engine coolant temperature has risen beyond acceptable (programmed) limits. Once a fault is recognized, a numeric code is assigned and held in memory. The CHECK ENGINE dashboard warning lamp will illuminate to advise the operator that the system has detected a fault.

In the event of an ECM failure, the system will default to a pre-programmed set of values. These are compromise values which allow the engine to operate, although possibly at reduced efficiency. This is variously known as the default, limp-in or back-up mode. Driveability is almost always affected when the ECM enters this mode.

Check Engine Lamp

The primary function of the dash warning lamp is to advise the operator that a fault has been detected, and, in most cases, a code stored. Under normal conditions, the CHECK ENGINE lamp will illuminate when the ignition is turned **ON**. Once the engine is started and running, the ECM will perform a system check and extinguish the warning lamp if no fault is found.

Additionally, the dash warning lamp must be used to retrieve stored codes after the system is placed in the Diagnostic Mode. Codes are transmitted as a series of flashes with short or long pauses.

Intermittents

If a fault occurs intermittently, such as a loose connector pin breaking contact as the vehicle hits a bump, the ECM will note the fault as it occurs and energize the dash warning lamp. If the problem self-corrects, as with the terminal pin again making contact, the dash lamp will extinguish after 10 seconds but a code will remain stored in the ECM memory.

When an unexpected code appears during diagnostics, it may have been set during an intermittent failure that self-corrected; the codes are still useful in diagnosis and should not be discounted.

Tools and Equipment

The 1989-91 Metro fuel injection system does not require the use of a scan tool during diagnosis. All diagnostic procedures are conducted with common shop tools. The 1992-93 Metro fuel injection uses a scan tool to read the data stream during diagnosis and is required in certain diagnostic tests. However, the diagnostic codes can be read without the use of the scan tool.

A digital voltmeter with 10-mega-ohm impedance is required for testing all systems. This type of meter will not place an additional load on the circuit it is testing; this is extremely important in low voltage circuits.

An ohmmeter will also be required during diagnosis. A particularly useful tool is the digital multimeter, such as J 34029-A or equivalent, combining the volt and ohm meters. The multimeter must be of high quality in all respects and be

equipped with leads suitable for back-probing connector terminals. It should be handled carefully and protected from impact or damage. Replace batteries frequently in the unit.

Other necessary tools include an unpowered test light, a quality tachometer with inductive (clip-on) pick up and the proper tools for releasing GM's Metri-Pack, Weather Pack and Micro-Pack terminals as necessary.

SYSTEM DIAGNOSIS

◆ See Figures 49 and 50

Diagnosis of a driveability and/or emissions problems requires attention to detail and following the diagnostic procedures in the correct order. Resist the temptation to perform any repairs before performing the preliminary diagnostic steps. In many cases this will shorten diagnostic time and often cure the problem without electronic testing.

The proper troubleshooting procedure for these vehicles is as follows:

Visual/Physical Underhood Inspection

This is possibly the most critical step of diagnosis. A detailed examination of connectors, wiring and vacuum hoses can often lead to a repair without further diagnosis. Performance of this step relies on the skill of the technician performing it; a careful inspector will check the undersides of hoses as well as the integrity of hard-to-reach hoses blocked by the air cleaner or other component. Wiring should be checked carefully for any sign of strain, burning, crimping, or terminal pull-out from a connector. Checking connectors at components or in harnesses is required; usually, pushing them together will reveal a loose fit.

Diagnostic Circuit Check

This step is used to check that the on-board diagnostic system is working correctly. A system which is faulty or shorted may not yield correct codes when placed in the Diagnostic Mode. Performing this test confirms that the diagnostic system is not failed and is able to communicate through the dash warning lamp.

If the diagnostic system is not operating correctly, or if a problem exists without the dash warning lamp being lit, refer to the specific 'A' diagnostic charts. These charts cover such conditions as Engine Cranks but Will Not Run or No CHECK ENGINE Light.

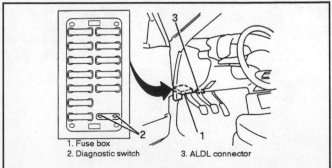

1. Fuse box
2. Diagnostic switch
3. ALDL connector

Fig. 49 Diagnostic switch location under the left side of the instrument panel

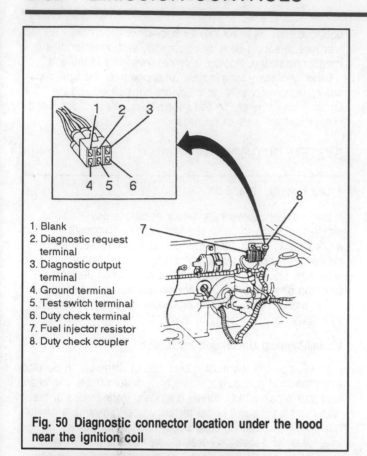

1. Blank
2. Diagnostic request terminal
3. Diagnostic output terminal
4. Ground terminal
5. Test switch terminal
6. Duty check terminal
7. Fuel injector resistor
8. Duty check coupler

Fig. 50 Diagnostic connector location under the hood near the ignition coil

Diagnostic Trouble Codes-EFI System

READING CODES

▶ **See Figure 51**

Once the integrity of the system is confirmed, enter the Diagnostic Mode and read any stored codes. Once the

Diagnostic Mode is engaged, the dash warning lamp should begin to flash.

The Metro uses Code 12 to indicate that no other codes are stored. If a fault is in memory, it will be broadcast as soon as the system enters Diagnostic Mode. The codes are stored and transmitted in numeric order from lowest to highest; each fault code is transmitted 3 times before moving to the next.

➡**The order of codes in the memory does not indicate the order of occurrence.**

Record each code transmitted for later reference. Once all codes have been sent, the memory may need to be cleared during diagnostics. If there are no codes stored, but a driveability or emissions problem is evident, refer A-Charts.

To retrieve codes from the ECM without the use of a scan tool:

1. Locate the diagnostic terminals at the bottom of the under dash fuse block.

2. Turn the ignition switch **ON** but do not start the engine.

3. Insert a spare fuse into the diagnostic terminals. This completes the ground circuit for the ECM diagnostic circuit. The CHECK ENGINE light should display Code 12 and/or any stored codes.

   a. An alternate diagnostic position is provided under the hood. The diagnostic connector is located next to the ignition coil.

   b. Use a jumper to connect the diagnostic switch terminal to the ground terminal.

4. Read the flashes of the CHECK ENGINE light to determine the codes. If the light flashes a Code 12, the system is functioning normally.

EXAMPLE: THROTTLE SWITCH (THROTTLE POSITION SENSOR FOR A/T) FAILURE (CODE: 21)

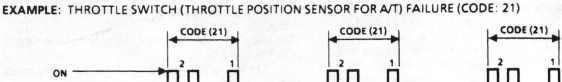
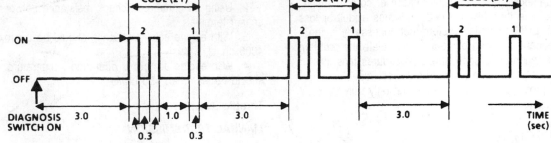

DIAGNOSTIC CODE		DIAGNOSTIC AREA	DIAGNOSIS
NO.	MODE		
12		Normal	This code appears when none of the other codes (Below codes) is identified.
13		Oxygen sensor	
14		Coolant temperature sensor	
15			
21		Throttle switch (M/T model only)	
21		Throttle position sensor (A/T model only)	
22			
23		Manifold air temperature sensor	Diagnose trouble according to "DIAGNOSTIC FLOW CHART" corresponding to each code No.
25			
24		Speed sensor	
31		Manifold absolute pressure sensor	
32			
41		Ignition signal	
42		Crank angle sensor (METRO model only) ★	
51		EGR system California Only (METRO model only) ★	★ Metro with ESA Ignition
ON		ECM	ECM failure

Fig. 51 1989-91 EFI diagnostic code table

CIRCUIT/COMPONENT DIAGNOSIS AND REPAIR

Using the appropriate chart(s) based on the Diagnostic Circuit Check, the fault codes and scan tool data will lead to diagnosis and checking of a particular circuit or component. It is important to note that the fault code indicates a fault or loss of signal in an ECM-controlled system, not necessarily in the specific component. Detailed procedures to isolate the problem are included in each code chart; these procedures must be followed accurately to insure timely and correct repair. Following the procedure will also insure that only truly faulty components are replaced.

CLEARING CODES

Stored fault codes may be erased from memory at any time by removing power from the ECM for at least 30 seconds. This time period must be increased as the temperature drops. It may be necessary to clear stored codes during diagnosis to check for any recurrence during a test drive, but the stored codes must be written down when retrieved. The codes may still be required for subsequent troubleshooting. Whenever a repair is complete, the stored codes must be erased and the vehicle test driven to confirm correct operation and repair.

➡**The ignition switch must be OFF any time power is disconnected or restored to the ECM. Severe damage may result if this precaution is not observed.**

Removing the TAIL LAMP fuse from the under dash fuse box will interrupt power to the ECM without blanking other memories within the vehicle. The pink, 30 amp main fuse may be removed from the underhood fuse holder on the right front fender apron, but this will also disconnect power to the clock and the radio.

COMPONENT TESTING

▶ **See Figure 52**

Oxygen Sensor

1. Warm the engine to normal operating temperature.
2. Disconnect the connector of the oxygen sensor.
3. Connect a voltmeter between the sensor side terminal and ground.

➡**Never apply voltage to the oxygen sensor as it may cause damage to the sensor.**

4. With the engine running at 1200 rpm, check that the voltage from oxygen sensor varies between 0-0.9 volts.

5. After checking, reconnect oxygen sensor connector.

Coolant Temperature Sensor

1. Disconnect electrical connector from coolant temperature sensor.
2. Using an ohmmeter, check resistance between the sensor terminals.
3. With engine cold, resistance should be approximately 4000 ohms.
4. With engine at normal operating temperature, resistance should be less than 450 ohms.

Throttle Switch

MANUAL TRANSMISSION

1. Turn the ignition switch **ON**.
2. Backprobe the throttle switch connector LT GRN/WHT wire.
3. Voltage should be 4 volts.
4. Turn the ignition switch **OFF** and disconnect the throttle switch.
5. Turn the ignition switch **ON** and measure the voltage at the LT GRN/WHT wire terminal at the throttle switch connector.
6. Voltage should be 4 volts.
7. If switch is within specifications, check switch adjustment.

Throttle Position Sensor

1. Using a digital voltmeter, backprobe the throttle position sensor LT GRN/YEL wire.
2. Voltage should vary between 0.49-0.59 volts at closed throttle and 4.5-5.5 volts at wide open throttle.
3. If sensor is not within specifications, check for faulty connections or shorts.

Manifold Air Temperature Sensor

1. Disconnect the sensor electrical connector.
2. Measure the resistant between the connector terminals.
3. Resistance should be approximately 3400 ohms when the air temperature is 70°F (20°C).
4. If resistance is not within specification, check for faulty connections or shorts.

Crankshaft Angle Sensor

1. Disconnect the sensor electrical connector.
2. Check resistance between the sensor terminals.
3. Resistance should be 140-180 ohms.
4. If resistance is not within specification, check sensor air gap.

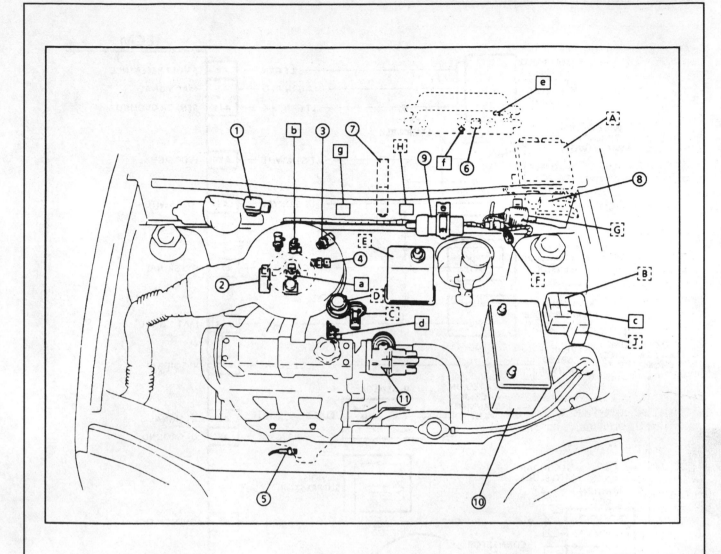

INFORMATION SENSORS

1. MAP
2. TS or TPS
3. MAT
4. CTS
5. Oxygen sensor
6. Speed sensor
7. A/T control module (For A/T model)
8. Passenger compartment fuse block (Diagnosis switch terminal)
9. Ignition coil
10. Battery
11. Distributor

CONTROLLED DEVICES

a: Fuel injector
b: ISC solenoid valve
c: Fuel pump relay
d: EGR VSV*
e: "CHECK ENGINE" light
f: Shift Light (For M/T model)
g: A/C VSV (If equipped)

NOT ECM CONNECTED

A: ECM
B: EFI main relay
C: EGR modulator*
D: EGR valve*
E: Canister
F: Monitor coupler
G: Injector resistor
H: A/C Amplifier
J: Engine compartment relay/fuse block

* CALIFORNIA ONLY

Fig. 52 1989-91 EFI COMPONENT LOCATIONS

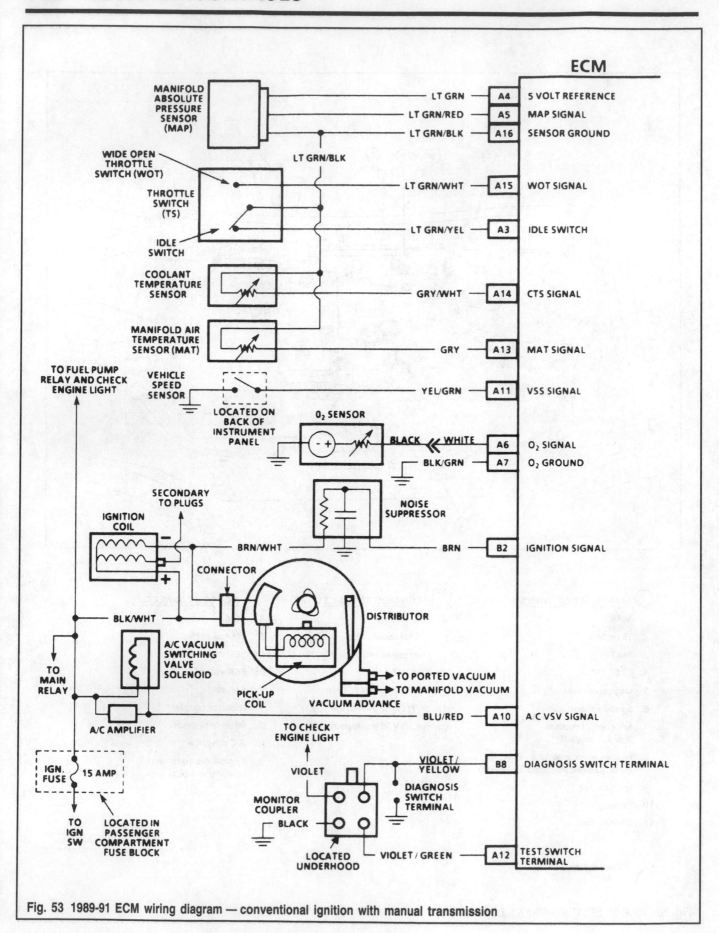

Fig. 53 1989-91 ECM wiring diagram — conventional ignition with manual transmission

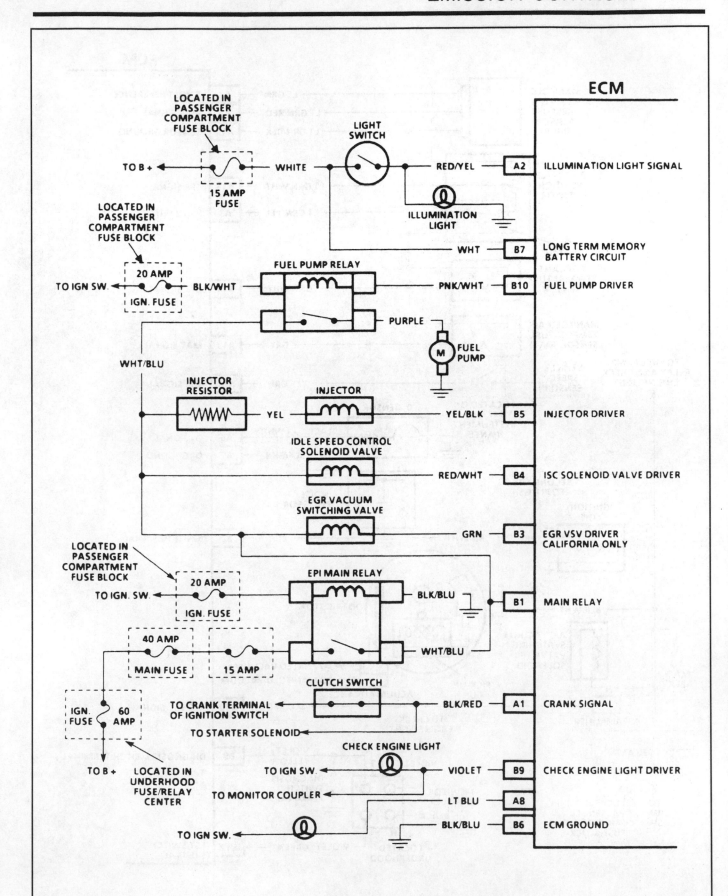

Fig. 54 1989-91 ECM wiring diagram — conventional ignition with manual transmission

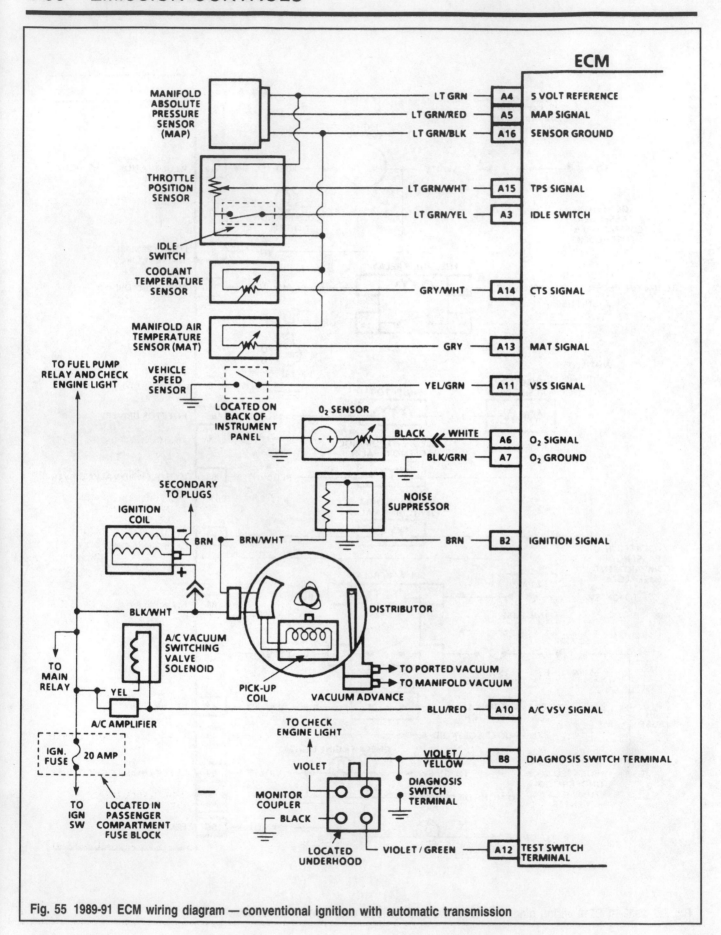

Fig. 55 1989-91 ECM wiring diagram — conventional ignition with automatic transmission

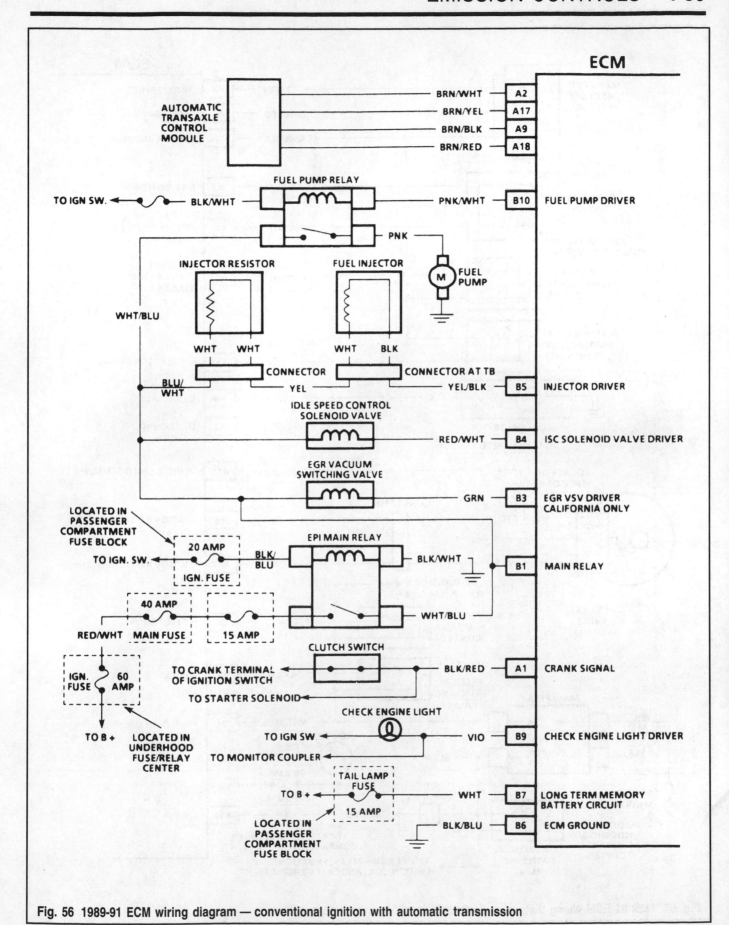

Fig. 56 1989-91 ECM wiring diagram — conventional ignition with automatic transmission

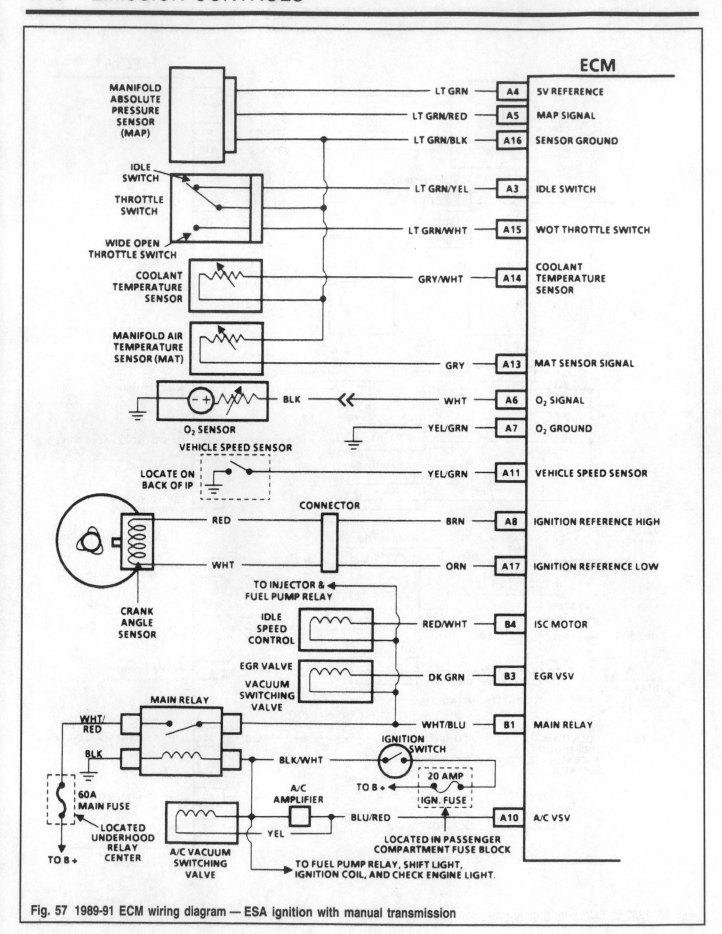

Fig. 57 1989-91 ECM wiring diagram — ESA ignition with manual transmission

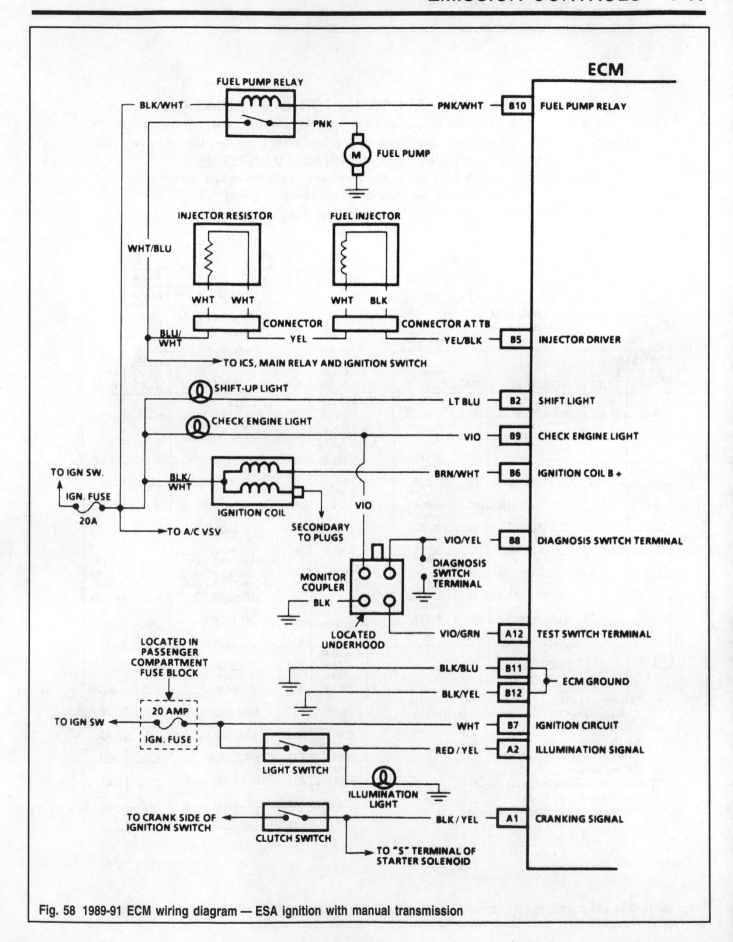

Fig. 58 1989-91 ECM wiring diagram — ESA ignition with manual transmission

FUEL INJECTION ECM CONNECTOR IDENTIFICATION

The following ECM voltage charts are for use with a digital voltmeter to further aid in diagnosis. The voltages you get may vary due to low battery charge or other reasons, but they should be very close.

THE FOLLOWING CONDITIONS MUST BE MET BEFORE TESTING:

- Engine at operating temperature • Engine idling (for "Engine Run" column)
- Test terminal not grounded (except where noted)
- All voltages shown "B + " indicates battery or charging voltage

1	2	3	4	5	6
7	8	9	10	11	12

BACKVIEW ECM CONNECTOR B

1	2	3	4	5	6	7	8	9
10	11	12	13	14	15	16	17	18

BACKVIEW ECM CONNECTOR A

| VOLTAGE | | | | |
KEY "ON"	ENG. RUN	CIRCUIT	PIN	WIRE COLOR
B +	B +	MAIN RELAY	B1	
		NOT USED	B2	
B +	B +	EGR DRIVER	B3	GREEN
0*	ON * OFF B +	ISC SOLENOID	B4	RED/ WHITE
B +	B +	INJECTOR DRIVER	B5	YELLOW/ BLACK
0*	0*	ECM GROUND	B6	BLACK/ BLUE
B +	B +	LONG TERM BATTERY FEED	B7	WHITE
4 - 5	4 - 5	DIAGNOSIS SWITCH TERMINAL	B8	VIOLET/ YELLOW
0*	B +	CHECK ENGINE LIGHT	B9	VIOLET
B + ③	0*	FUEL PUMP	B10	PINK/ WHITE
		NOT USED	B11	
		NOT USED	B12	

0* Less than .5 volts.
① Varies between 6-5 volt with drive wheels turning.
② Varies.
③ B + for first 2 seconds.
④ 0 volts at wide open throttle.
⑤ Off idle position.
⑥ Varies with engine temperature
⑦ B + with light switch "ON"
⑧ Voltage present only during cranking.

| WIRE COLOR | PIN | CIRCUIT | VOLTAGE | | |
			KEY "ON"	ENG. RUN	
BLACK/ YELLOW	A1	CRANK SIGNAL	6-12V	0V	⑧
RED/ YELLOW	A2	ILLUMINATION LIGHT SIGNAL			⑦
LT GREEN/ YELLOW	A3	IDLE SWITCH SIGNAL	4-5V	4-5V	⑤
LT GREEN	A4	5V REFERENCE	5V	5V	
LT GREEN/ RED	A5	MAP SIGNAL	3 - 5	3 - 5	②
WHITE	A6	O2 SIGNAL	.35 - .45	.1 - .9	
BLACK/ GREEN	A7	O2 GROUND	0*	0*	
LT BLUE	A8	UPSHIFT IND. LAMP LIGHTING SW "OFF"	2-3V	IDLE 10-14V	
		UPSHIFT IND. LAMP LIGHTING SW "ON"	6-7V	IDLE 10-14V	
	A9	NOT USED			
BLUE/ RED	A10	A/C SIGNAL	ON * OFF B +	ON * OFF B +	
YELLOW/ GREEN	A11	VSS SIGNAL			①
VIOLET/ GREEN	A12	TEST SWITCH TERMINAL	4 - 5	4 - 5	
GRAY	A13	MAT SIGNAL	2V	2V	②
GRAY/ WHITE	A14	CTS SIGNAL	.45	.45	⑥
LT GREEN/ WHITE	A15	WOT SIGNAL	4 - 5	4 - 5	④
LT GREEN/ BLACK	A16	SENSOR GROUND	0*	0*	
	A17	NOT USED			
	A18	NOT USED			

Fig. 59 1989-91 EFI control module terminal identification — conventional ignition with manual transmission

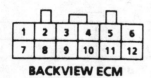

BACKVIEW ECM CONNECTOR B

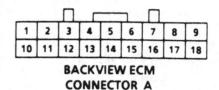

BACKVIEW ECM CONNECTOR A

VOLTAGE		CIRCUIT	PIN	WIRE COLOR
KEY "ON"	ENG. RUN			
B+	B+	MAIN RELAY	B1	WHITE/BLUE
B+	⑤	IGNITION SIGNAL	B2	
B+	B+	EGR DRIVER	B3	GREEN
0*	ON* OFF B+	ISC SOLENOID	B4	RED/WHITE
B+	B+	INJECTOR DRIVER	B5	YELLOW/BLACK
0*	0*	ECM GROUND	B6	BLACK/BLUE
B+	B+	LONG TERM BATTERY FEED	B7	WHITE
4-5	4-5	DIAGNOSIS SWITCH TERMINAL	B8	VIOLET/YELLOW
0*	B+	CHECK ENGINE LIGHT	B9	VIOLET
B+ ⑥	0*	FUEL PUMP RELAY	B10	PINK/WHITE
		NOT USED	B11	
		NOT USED	B12	

0* Less than .5 volts.
① Varies from .60 to battery voltage depending on position of drive wheels.
② Varies.
③ Varies with temperature.
⑤ B+ for first 2 seconds.
⑥ California only
⑦ Varies with throttle position.

WIRE COLOR	PIN	CIRCUIT	VOLTAGE		
			KEY "ON"	ENG. RUN	
BLACK/RED	A1	CRANK SIGNAL	6-12V	0*	⑦
BRN/WHT	A2	TRANSAXLE	.2-.4V		
LT GREEN/YELLOW	A3	IDLE SWITCH	0*	0*	
LT GREEN	A4	5V REFERENCE	5.0	5.0	
LT GREEN/RED	A5	MAP SIGNAL	3-5	4.1	②
WHITE	A6	O_2 SIGNAL	0*	0-1	
BLACK/GREEN	A7	O_2 GROUND	0*	0*	
	A8	NOT USED			
BROWN/BLACK	A9	TRANSAXLE	.2-.4V	.2-.4V	
BLUE/RED	A10	A/C SIGNAL	ON* OFF B+	ON* OFF B+	
YELLOW/GREEN	A11	VSS SIGNAL	0*	4-5	①
VIOLET/GREEN	A12	TEST SWITCH TERMINAL	4-5	4-5	
GRAY	A13	MAT SIGNAL	2.0	2.0	③
GRAY/WHITE	A14	CTS SIGNAL	.45	.45	③
LT GREEN/WHITE	A15	TPS SIGNAL			②
LT GREEN/BLACK	A16	SENSOR GROUND	0*	0*	
BROWN/YELLOW	A17	TRANSAXLE	.2-.4V	.2-.4V	
BROWN/RED	A18	TRANSAXLE	.2-.4V	.2-.4V	

Fig. 60 1989-91 EFI control module terminal identification — conventional ignition with automatic transmission

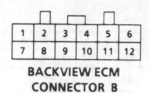

BACKVIEW ECM CONNECTOR B

BACKVIEW ECM CONNECTOR A

VOLTAGE				
KEY "ON"	ENG. RUN	CIRCUIT	PIN	WIRE COLOR
B+	B+	MAIN RELAY	B1	WHITE/ BLUE
6 - 7V	B+	UPSHIFT IND. LIGHT LIGHTING SW "ON"	B2	LT BLUE
2 - 3V	B+	UPSHIFT IND. LIGHT LIGHTING SW "OFF"		
B+	B+	EGR VSV	B3	GREEN
.9 - 1.5V	⑤	ISC	B4	RED/ WHITE
B+	B+	INJECTOR	B5	YELLOW/ BLACK
B+	B+	IGNITION COIL	B6	BROWN/ WHITE
B+	B+	LONG TERM BATTERY CIRCUIT	B7	WHITE
4 - 5	4 - 5	DIAGNOSIS SWITCH TERMINAL	B8	VIOLET/ YELLOW
12 - 2V	B+	CHECK ENGINE LIGHT	B9	VIOLET
B+	0*	FUEL PUMP RELAY	B10	PINK/ WHITE
0*	0*	ECM GROUND	B11	BLACK/ BLUE
0*	0*	IGNITION GROUND	B12	BLACK/ YELLOW

⑥

WIRE COLOR	PIN	CIRCUIT	VOLTAGE	
			KEY "ON"	ENG. RUN
BLACK/ YELLOW	A1	CRANKING SIGNAL	0*	0*
RED/ YELLOW	A2	ILLUMINATION LIGHT SIGNAL	0*	0*
LT GREEN/ YELLOW	A3	IDLE SWITCH	0*	0*
LT GREEN	A4	5V REFERENCE	5.0	5.0
LT GREEN/ RED	A5	MAP SIGNAL	3 - 5	②
WHITE	A6	O₂ SIGNAL	0*	.45 - 1
YELLOW/ GREEN	A7	O₂ GROUND	0*	0*
BROWN	A8	CRANK ANGLE SENSOR POSITIVE	.4 - .8	.4 - .8
	A9	NOT USED		
BLUE/ RED	A10	A/C SIGNAL	ON * OFF B+	ON * OFF B+
YELLOW/ GREEN	A11	VSS SIGNAL	0*	4 - 5
VIOLET/ GREEN	A12	TEST TERMINAL	4 - 5	4 - 5
GREEN	A13	MAT SIGNAL	2.0	2.0
GREEN/ WHITE	A14	CTS SIGNAL	.45	.45
LT GREEN/ WHITE	A15	WOT SIGNAL	4 - 5	4 - 5
LT GREEN/ BLACK	A16	SENSOR GROUNDS	0*	0*
TAN	A17	CRANK ANGLE SENSOR NEGATIVE	.4 - .8	.4 - .8
	A18	NOT USED		

★ ②
① ③ ③ ④

0* Less than .5 volts.
★ Will be 6 - 7 volts with light switch "ON".
① Varies as front wheels are being turned.
② Varies.
③ Varies with temperature.
④ 0 volt at wide open throttle.
⑤ Varies with load (eg: A/C)
⑥ California only

Fig. 61 1989-91 EFI control module terminal identification — ESA ignition with manual transmission

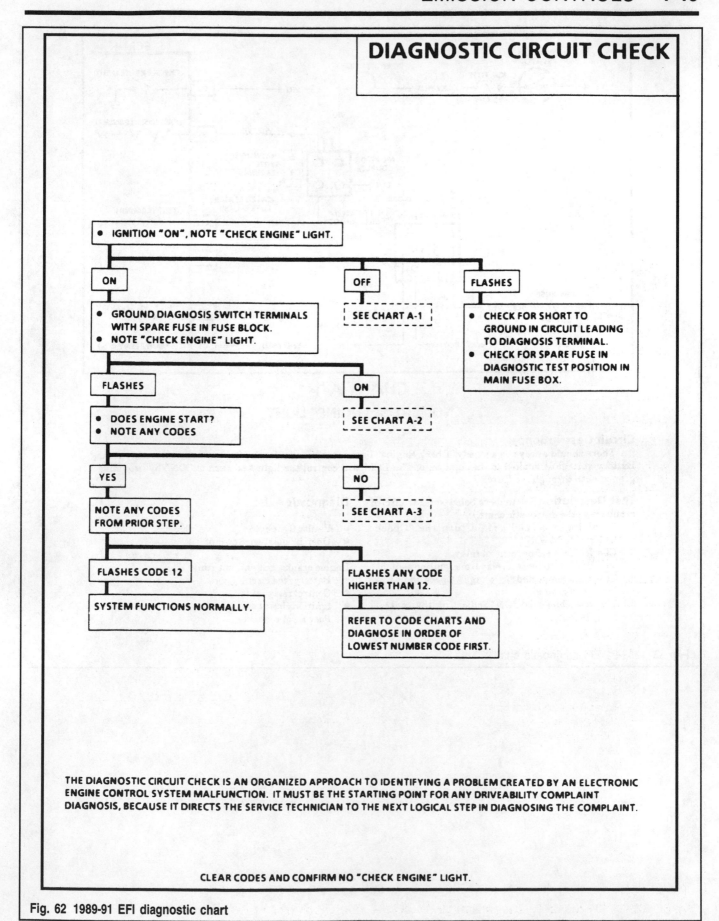

DIAGNOSTIC CIRCUIT CHECK

- IGNITION "ON", NOTE "CHECK ENGINE" LIGHT.

ON

- GROUND DIAGNOSIS SWITCH TERMINALS WITH SPARE FUSE IN FUSE BLOCK.
- NOTE "CHECK ENGINE" LIGHT.

OFF

SEE CHART A-1

FLASHES

- CHECK FOR SHORT TO GROUND IN CIRCUIT LEADING TO DIAGNOSIS TERMINAL.
- CHECK FOR SPARE FUSE IN DIAGNOSTIC TEST POSITION IN MAIN FUSE BOX.

FLASHES

- DOES ENGINE START?
- NOTE ANY CODES

ON

SEE CHART A-2

YES

NOTE ANY CODES FROM PRIOR STEP.

NO

SEE CHART A-3

FLASHES CODE 12

SYSTEM FUNCTIONS NORMALLY.

FLASHES ANY CODE HIGHER THAN 12.

REFER TO CODE CHARTS AND DIAGNOSE IN ORDER OF LOWEST NUMBER CODE FIRST.

THE DIAGNOSTIC CIRCUIT CHECK IS AN ORGANIZED APPROACH TO IDENTIFYING A PROBLEM CREATED BY AN ELECTRONIC ENGINE CONTROL SYSTEM MALFUNCTION. IT MUST BE THE STARTING POINT FOR ANY DRIVEABILITY COMPLAINT DIAGNOSIS, BECAUSE IT DIRECTS THE SERVICE TECHNICIAN TO THE NEXT LOGICAL STEP IN DIAGNOSING THE COMPLAINT.

CLEAR CODES AND CONFIRM NO "CHECK ENGINE" LIGHT.

Fig. 62 1989-91 EFI diagnostic chart

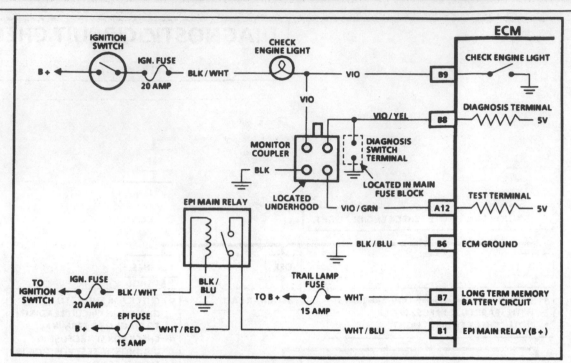

CHART A-1
NO "CHECK ENGINE" LIGHT

Circuit Description:

There should always be a steady "Check Engine" light when the ignition is "ON" and engine is not running. Battery voltage is applied to the light bulb. The ECM will control the light and turn it "ON" by providing a ground path through the ECM.

Test Description: Numbers below refer to circled numbers on the diagnostic chart.

1. Providing a ground should turn the "Check Engine" light "ON".
2. Checks for B+ from control relay.
3. Verifies B+ to control relay from ignition switch.
4. Test light connected to voltage. Check the ECM for a good ground.
5. The test should be "ON" indicating the control relay is faulty.

Diagnostic Aids:

- Faulty light bulb
- Open in violet wire circuit

Engine cranks, but will not run
- Battery feed circuit open
- Control relay faulty
- Ignition circuit open
- Poor ECM connects

Fig. 63 1989-91 EFI diagnostic chart

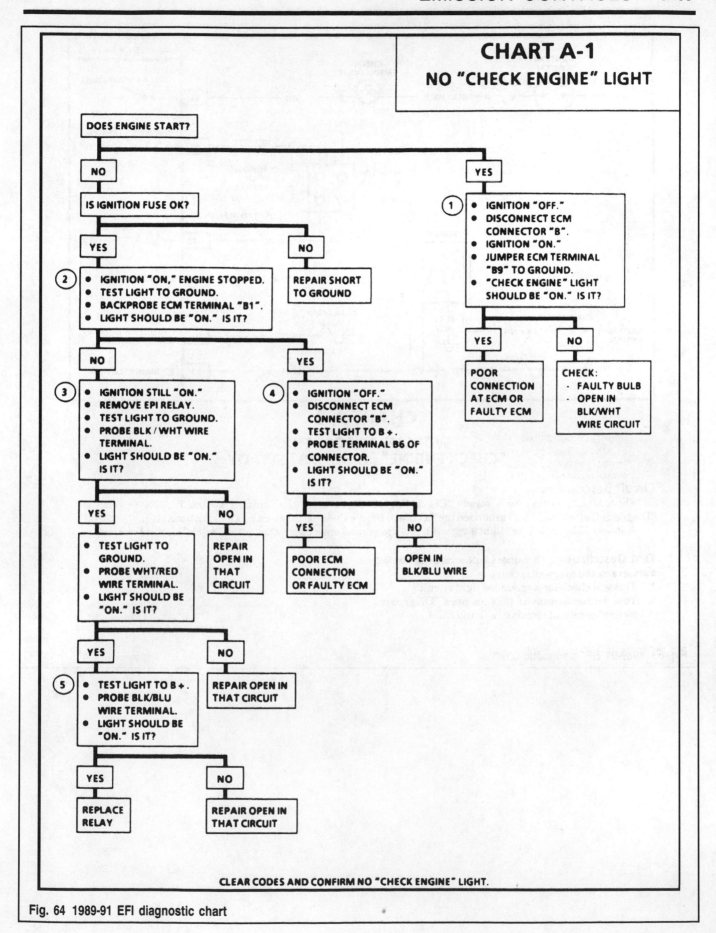

CHART A-1
NO "CHECK ENGINE" LIGHT

DOES ENGINE START?

NO — YES

IS IGNITION FUSE OK?

YES — NO

(1)
- IGNITION "OFF."
- DISCONNECT ECM CONNECTOR "B".
- IGNITION "ON."
- JUMPER ECM TERMINAL "B9" TO GROUND.
- "CHECK ENGINE" LIGHT SHOULD BE "ON." IS IT?

YES — NO

POOR CONNECTION AT ECM OR FAULTY ECM

CHECK:
- FAULTY BULB
- OPEN IN BLK/WHT WIRE CIRCUIT

(2)
- IGNITION "ON," ENGINE STOPPED.
- TEST LIGHT TO GROUND.
- BACKPROBE ECM TERMINAL "B1".
- LIGHT SHOULD BE "ON." IS IT?

REPAIR SHORT TO GROUND

NO — YES

(3)
- IGNITION STILL "ON."
- REMOVE EPI RELAY.
- TEST LIGHT TO GROUND.
- PROBE BLK / WHT WIRE TERMINAL.
- LIGHT SHOULD BE "ON." IS IT?

(4)
- IGNITION "OFF."
- DISCONNECT ECM CONNECTOR "B".
- TEST LIGHT TO B +.
- PROBE TERMINAL B6 OF CONNECTOR.
- LIGHT SHOULD BE "ON." IS IT?

YES — NO

POOR ECM CONNECTION OR FAULTY ECM

OPEN IN BLK/BLU WIRE

YES — NO

- TEST LIGHT TO GROUND.
- PROBE WHT/RED WIRE TERMINAL.
- LIGHT SHOULD BE "ON." IS IT?

REPAIR OPEN IN THAT CIRCUIT

YES — NO

(5)
- TEST LIGHT TO B +.
- PROBE BLK/BLU WIRE TERMINAL.
- LIGHT SHOULD BE "ON." IS IT?

REPAIR OPEN IN THAT CIRCUIT

YES — NO

REPLACE RELAY

REPAIR OPEN IN THAT CIRCUIT

CLEAR CODES AND CONFIRM NO "CHECK ENGINE" LIGHT.

Fig. 64 1989-91 EFI diagnostic chart

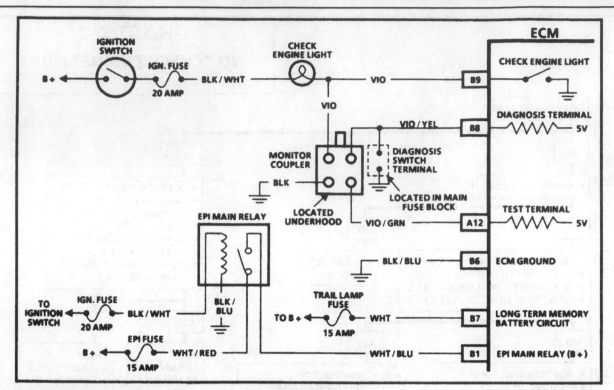

CHART A-2

WON'T FLASH CODE 12
"CHECK ENGINE" LIGHT "ON" STEADY

Circuit Description:

There should always be a steady "Check Engine" light when the ignition switch is "ON". With the "Diagnosis Switch" terminal grounded the ECM will flash a Code 12, followed by any additional trouble code(s).

A steady "Check Engine" light suggests a short to ground or an open "Diagnosis Switch" circuit terminal.

Test Description: Numbers below refer to circled numbers on the diagnostic chart.

1. This will check for a grounded light circuit.
2. This will determine if it is an open "Diagnosis Switch" terminal circuit or a faulty ECM.

Fig. 65 1989-91 EFI diagnostic chart

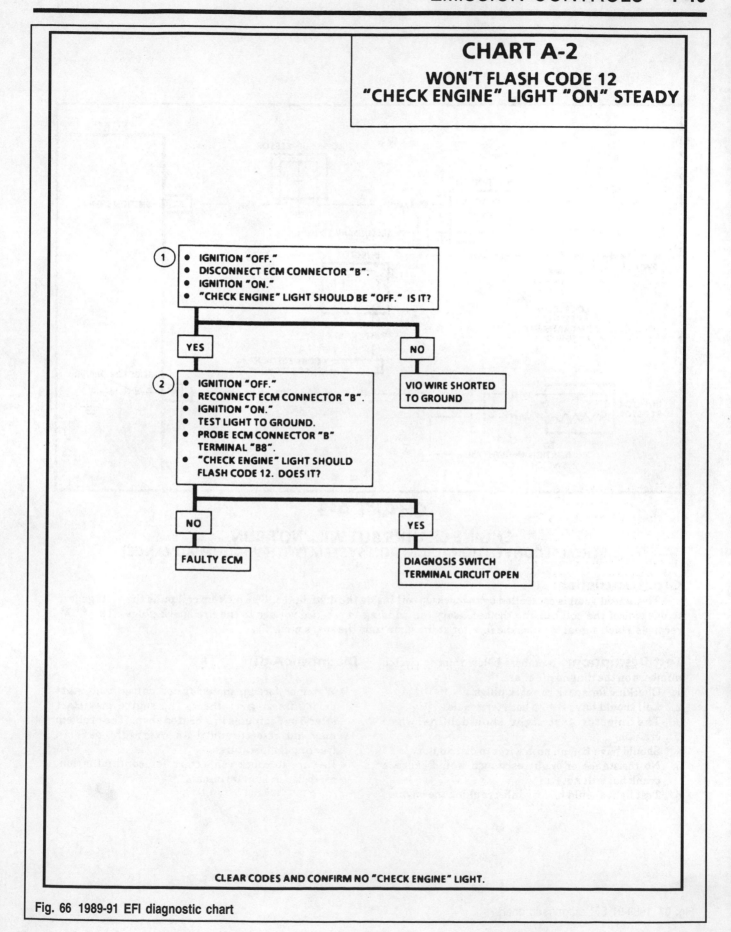

CHART A-2
WON'T FLASH CODE 12
"CHECK ENGINE" LIGHT "ON" STEADY

1
● IGNITION "OFF."
● DISCONNECT ECM CONNECTOR "B".
● IGNITION "ON."
● "CHECK ENGINE" LIGHT SHOULD BE "OFF." IS IT?

YES

NO

VIO WIRE SHORTED TO GROUND

2
● IGNITION "OFF."
● RECONNECT ECM CONNECTOR "B".
● IGNITION "ON."
● TEST LIGHT TO GROUND.
● PROBE ECM CONNECTOR "B" TERMINAL "B8".
● "CHECK ENGINE" LIGHT SHOULD FLASH CODE 12. DOES IT?

NO

YES

FAULTY ECM

DIAGNOSIS SWITCH TERMINAL CIRCUIT OPEN

CLEAR CODES AND CONFIRM NO "CHECK ENGINE" LIGHT.

Fig. 66 1989-91 EFI diagnostic chart

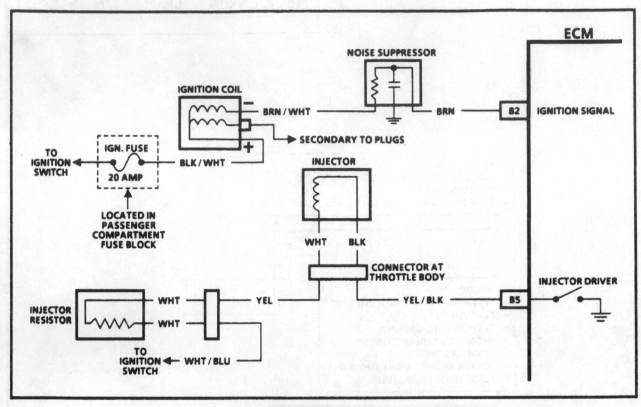

CHART A-3

ENGINE CRANKS BUT WILL NOT RUN
METRO LSI CONVENTIONAL IGNITION SYSTEM (WITH VACUUM ADVANCE)

Circuit Description:

The ignition coil is controlled by the pick-up coil inside the distributor. The pick-up coil pulls the voltage low to one side of the coil causing the secondary coil winding to produce voltage to the fire spark plugs. The ECM receives a tach signal to pulse the injector at the same time the spark plugs fired.

Test Description: Numbers below refer to circled numbers on the diagnostic chart.

1. Checking for spark to spark plugs.
2. Coil should have B+ to both terminals.
3. The injector test light should blink when cranking.
4. Should have B+ on both wires to distributor.
5. No resistance or high resistance would cause a crank but will not run.
6. Test light should blink while cranking the engine.

Diagnostic Aids:

• Water or foreign material can cause a no start during freezing weather. The engine may start after 5 or 6 minutes in a heated shop. The problem may nut re-occur until an overnight park in freezing temperatures.

• Be sure to check connectors for contamination, corrosion or bent terminals.

Fig. 67 1989-91 EFI diagnostic chart

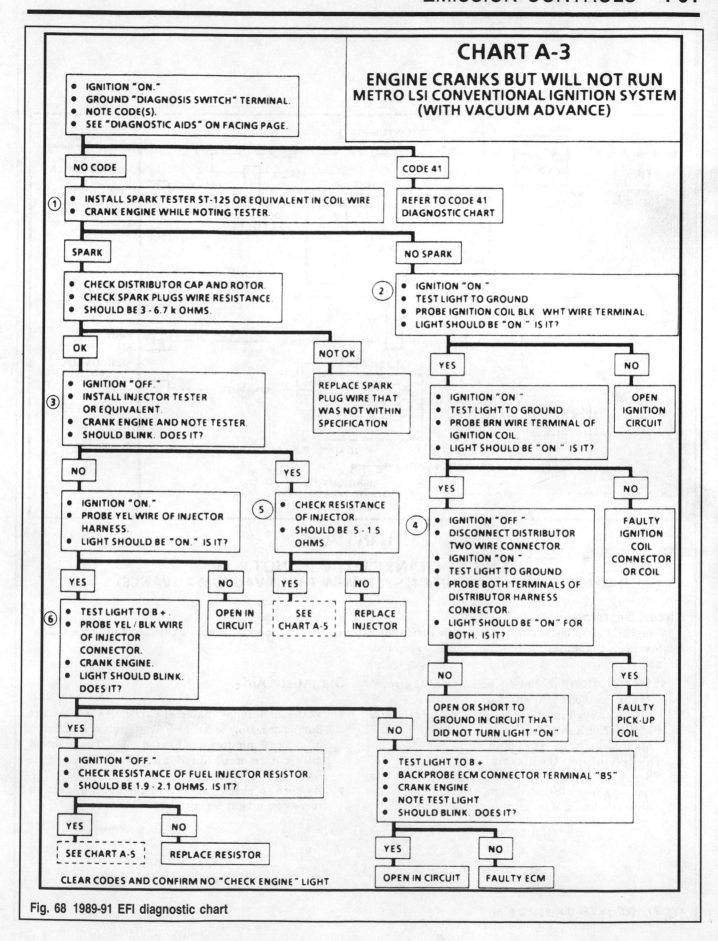

CHART A-3

ENGINE CRANKS BUT WILL NOT RUN
METRO LSI CONVENTIONAL IGNITION SYSTEM
(WITH VACUUM ADVANCE)

- IGNITION "ON."
- GROUND "DIAGNOSIS SWITCH" TERMINAL.
- NOTE CODE(S).
- SEE "DIAGNOSTIC AIDS" ON FACING PAGE.

NO CODE

① • INSTALL SPARK TESTER ST-125 OR EQUIVALENT IN COIL WIRE
   • CRANK ENGINE WHILE NOTING TESTER.

CODE 41

REFER TO CODE 41 DIAGNOSTIC CHART

SPARK

- CHECK DISTRIBUTOR CAP AND ROTOR.
- CHECK SPARK PLUGS WIRE RESISTANCE.
- SHOULD BE 3 - 6.7 k OHMS.

NO SPARK

② • IGNITION "ON."
   • TEST LIGHT TO GROUND
   • PROBE IGNITION COIL BLK WHT WIRE TERMINAL.
   • LIGHT SHOULD BE "ON " IS IT?

OK

③ • IGNITION "OFF."
   • INSTALL INJECTOR TESTER OR EQUIVALENT.
   • CRANK ENGINE AND NOTE TESTER.
   • SHOULD BLINK. DOES IT?

NOT OK

REPLACE SPARK PLUG WIRE THAT WAS NOT WITHIN SPECIFICATION

YES

- IGNITION "ON "
- TEST LIGHT TO GROUND.
- PROBE BRN WIRE TERMINAL OF IGNITION COIL.
- LIGHT SHOULD BE "ON " IS IT?

NO

OPEN IGNITION CIRCUIT

NO

- IGNITION "ON."
- PROBE YEL WIRE OF INJECTOR HARNESS.
- LIGHT SHOULD BE "ON." IS IT?

YES

⑤ • CHECK RESISTANCE OF INJECTOR.
   • SHOULD BE .5 - 1.5 OHMS.

YES

④ • IGNITION "OFF "
   • DISCONNECT DISTRIBUTOR TWO WIRE CONNECTOR.
   • IGNITION "ON"
   • TEST LIGHT TO GROUND
   • PROBE BOTH TERMINALS OF DISTRIBUTOR HARNESS CONNECTOR.
   • LIGHT SHOULD BE "ON" FOR BOTH. IS IT?

NO

FAULTY IGNITION COIL CONNECTOR OR COIL

YES

⑥ • TEST LIGHT TO B + .
   • PROBE YEL / BLK WIRE OF INJECTOR CONNECTOR.
   • CRANK ENGINE.
   • LIGHT SHOULD BLINK. DOES IT?

NO

OPEN IN CIRCUIT

YES

SEE CHART A-5

NO

REPLACE INJECTOR

NO

OPEN OR SHORT TO GROUND IN CIRCUIT THAT DID NOT TURN LIGHT "ON"

YES

FAULTY PICK-UP COIL

YES

- IGNITION "OFF."
- CHECK RESISTANCE OF FUEL INJECTOR RESISTOR.
- SHOULD BE 1.9 - 2.1 OHMS. IS IT?

NO

- TEST LIGHT TO B +
- BACKPROBE ECM CONNECTOR TERMINAL "B5".
- CRANK ENGINE.
- NOTE TEST LIGHT
- SHOULD BLINK. DOES IT?

YES

SEE CHART A-5

NO

REPLACE RESISTOR

YES

OPEN IN CIRCUIT

NO

FAULTY ECM

CLEAR CODES AND CONFIRM NO "CHECK ENGINE" LIGHT

Fig. 68 1989-91 EFI diagnostic chart

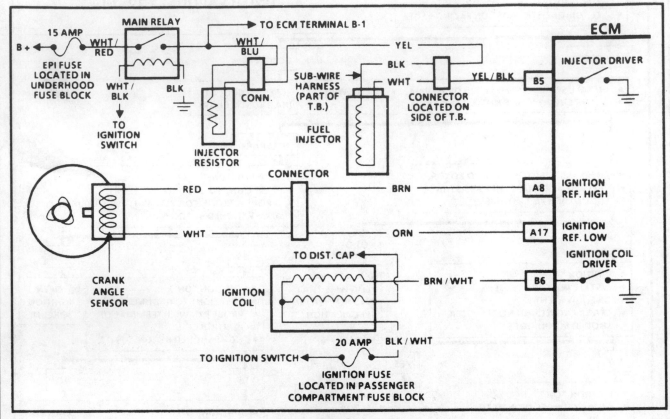

CHART A-3

ENGINE CRANKS BUT WILL NOT RUN
METRO WITH ESA IGNITION SYSTEM (WITHOUT VACUUM ADVANCE)

Circuit Description:

The ECM supplies voltage to a module inside the distributor. The module supplies this voltage to the crank angle sensor, the sensor toggles this voltage to ground.

Test Description: Numbers below refer to circled numbers on the diagnostic chart.
1. Open in either fuse could be the cause of a 'Crank But Will Not Run'.
2. This will check the spark plug wire for opens.
3. This test inspects the injector.
4. This will determine if the ignition coil is supplying spark to distributor.
5. This tests the ECM toggling of the ignition coil.

Diagnostic Aids:

- Water or foreign material can cause a no start during freezing weather. The engine may start after 5 or 6 minutes in a heated shop. The problem may not re-occur until an overnight park in freezing temperatures.
- Be sure to check connectors for contamination, corrosion or bent terminals.

Fig. 69 1989-91 EFI diagnostic chart

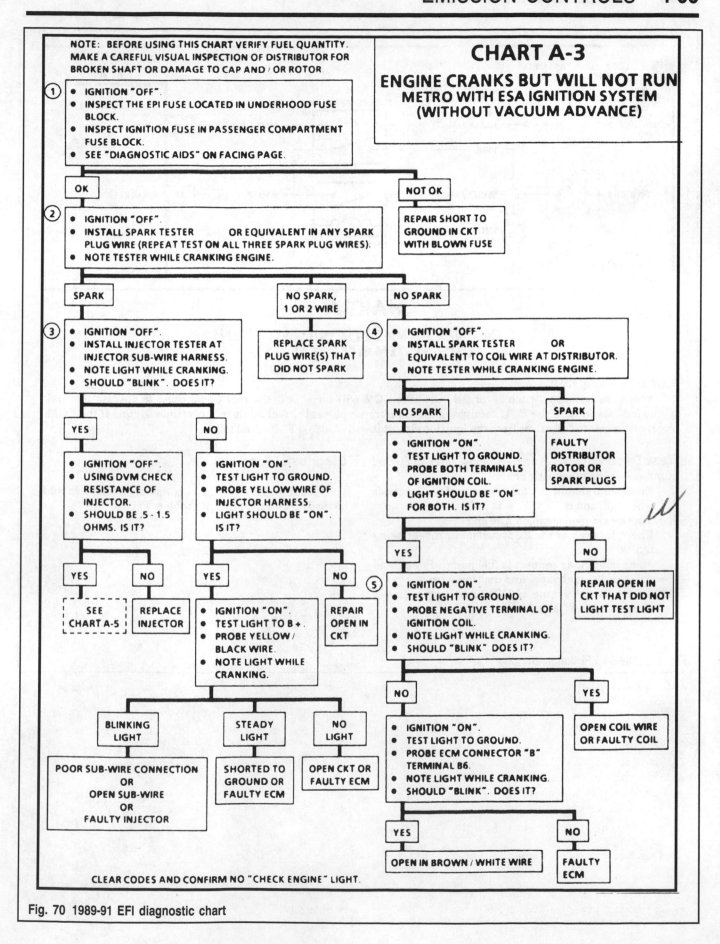

CHART A-3
ENGINE CRANKS BUT WILL NOT RUN
METRO WITH ESA IGNITION SYSTEM
(WITHOUT VACUUM ADVANCE)

NOTE: BEFORE USING THIS CHART VERIFY FUEL QUANTITY. MAKE A CAREFUL VISUAL INSPECTION OF DISTRIBUTOR FOR BROKEN SHAFT OR DAMAGE TO CAP AND / OR ROTOR.

① • IGNITION "OFF".
• INSPECT THE EPI FUSE LOCATED IN UNDERHOOD FUSE BLOCK.
• INSPECT IGNITION FUSE IN PASSENGER COMPARTMENT FUSE BLOCK.
• SEE "DIAGNOSTIC AIDS" ON FACING PAGE.

OK

NOT OK
REPAIR SHORT TO GROUND IN CKT WITH BLOWN FUSE

② • IGNITION "OFF".
• INSTALL SPARK TESTER OR EQUIVALENT IN ANY SPARK PLUG WIRE (REPEAT TEST ON ALL THREE SPARK PLUG WIRES).
• NOTE TESTER WHILE CRANKING ENGINE.

SPARK

NO SPARK, 1 OR 2 WIRE
REPLACE SPARK PLUG WIRE(S) THAT DID NOT SPARK

NO SPARK

③ • IGNITION "OFF".
• INSTALL INJECTOR TESTER AT INJECTOR SUB-WIRE HARNESS.
• NOTE LIGHT WHILE CRANKING.
• SHOULD "BLINK". DOES IT?

④ • IGNITION "OFF".
• INSTALL SPARK TESTER OR EQUIVALENT TO COIL WIRE AT DISTRIBUTOR.
• NOTE TESTER WHILE CRANKING ENGINE.

NO SPARK
• IGNITION "ON".
• TEST LIGHT TO GROUND.
• PROBE BOTH TERMINALS OF IGNITION COIL.
• LIGHT SHOULD BE "ON" FOR BOTH. IS IT?

SPARK
FAULTY DISTRIBUTOR ROTOR OR SPARK PLUGS

YES
• IGNITION "OFF".
• USING DVM CHECK RESISTANCE OF INJECTOR.
• SHOULD BE .5 - 1.5 OHMS. IS IT?

NO
• IGNITION "ON".
• TEST LIGHT TO GROUND.
• PROBE YELLOW WIRE OF INJECTOR HARNESS.
• LIGHT SHOULD BE "ON". IS IT?

YES

NO
REPAIR OPEN IN CKT THAT DID NOT LIGHT TEST LIGHT

YES
SEE CHART A-5

NO
REPLACE INJECTOR

YES
• IGNITION "ON".
• TEST LIGHT TO B +.
• PROBE YELLOW / BLACK WIRE.
• NOTE LIGHT WHILE CRANKING.

NO
REPAIR OPEN IN CKT

⑤ • IGNITION "ON".
• TEST LIGHT TO GROUND.
• PROBE NEGATIVE TERMINAL OF IGNITION COIL.
• NOTE LIGHT WHILE CRANKING.
• SHOULD "BLINK" DOES IT?

BLINKING LIGHT

STEADY LIGHT

NO LIGHT

POOR SUB-WIRE CONNECTION OR OPEN SUB-WIRE OR FAULTY INJECTOR

SHORTED TO GROUND OR FAULTY ECM

OPEN CKT OR FAULTY ECM

NO
• IGNITION "ON".
• TEST LIGHT TO GROUND.
• PROBE ECM CONNECTOR "B" TERMINAL B6.
• NOTE LIGHT WHILE CRANKING.
• SHOULD "BLINK". DOES IT?

YES
OPEN COIL WIRE OR FAULTY COIL

YES
OPEN IN BROWN / WHITE WIRE

NO
FAULTY ECM

CLEAR CODES AND CONFIRM NO "CHECK ENGINE" LIGHT.

Fig. 70 1989-91 EFI diagnostic chart

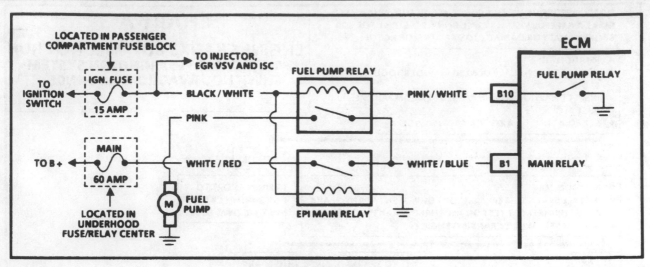

CHART A-5

ENGINE CRANKS BUT WILL NOT RUN
(FUEL SYSTEM ELECTRICAL TEST)

Circuit Description:

When the ignition switch is turned "ON" the ECM will turn "ON" the fuel pump relay to operate the fuel pump for 2 seconds. If the ECM receives ignition reference pulses the fuel pump will continue to run. If the ECM receives no reference pulses from the ignition circuit it will shut "OFF" the fuel pump.

Test Description: Numbers below refer to circled numbers on the diagnostic chart.

1. Fuel pump should run for approximately 2 seconds when ignition is "ON".
2. Test for an open between fuse and relay.
3. Check for open or the ECM fuel pump driver being faulty.
4. Jumpering relay connect to fuel pump. Power lead will test the fuel pump and the lead wire.
5. This will determine if ECM fuel pump driver circuit inside ECM is faulty.

Diagnostic Aids:

Visual inspection of wiring and connectors should be made if an intermittent problem exists.

Fig. 71 1989-91 EFI diagnostic chart

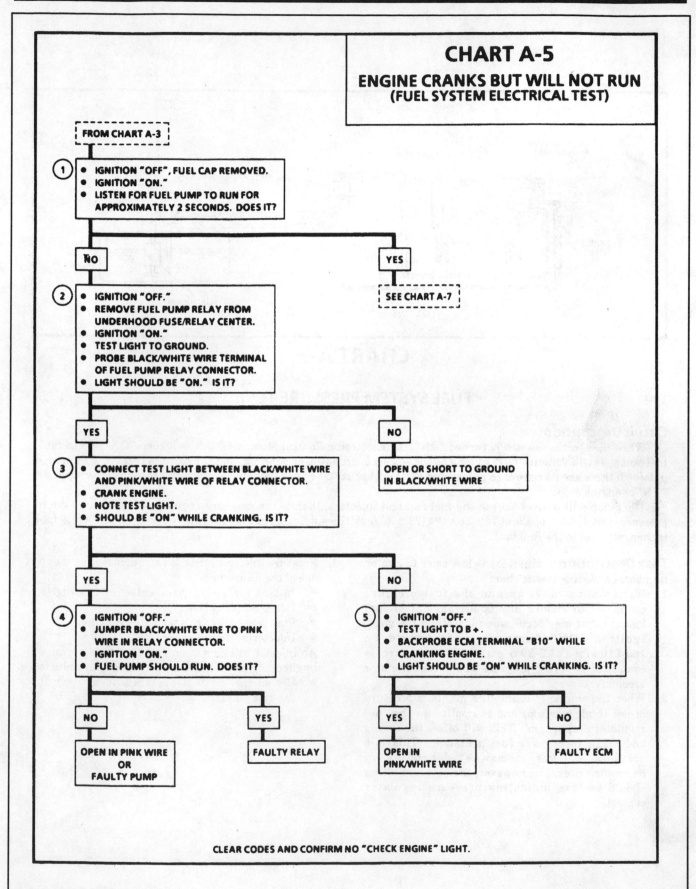

CHART A-5

ENGINE CRANKS BUT WILL NOT RUN
(FUEL SYSTEM ELECTRICAL TEST)

FROM CHART A-3

1
- IGNITION "OFF", FUEL CAP REMOVED.
- IGNITION "ON."
- LISTEN FOR FUEL PUMP TO RUN FOR APPROXIMATELY 2 SECONDS. DOES IT?

NO

YES

SEE CHART A-7

2
- IGNITION "OFF."
- REMOVE FUEL PUMP RELAY FROM UNDERHOOD FUSE/RELAY CENTER.
- IGNITION "ON."
- TEST LIGHT TO GROUND.
- PROBE BLACK/WHITE WIRE TERMINAL OF FUEL PUMP RELAY CONNECTOR.
- LIGHT SHOULD BE "ON." IS IT?

YES

NO

OPEN OR SHORT TO GROUND IN BLACK/WHITE WIRE

3
- CONNECT TEST LIGHT BETWEEN BLACK/WHITE WIRE AND PINK/WHITE WIRE OF RELAY CONNECTOR.
- CRANK ENGINE.
- NOTE TEST LIGHT.
- SHOULD BE "ON" WHILE CRANKING. IS IT?

YES

NO

4
- IGNITION "OFF."
- JUMPER BLACK/WHITE WIRE TO PINK WIRE IN RELAY CONNECTOR.
- IGNITION "ON."
- FUEL PUMP SHOULD RUN. DOES IT?

5
- IGNITION "OFF."
- TEST LIGHT TO B+.
- BACKPROBE ECM TERMINAL "B10" WHILE CRANKING ENGINE.
- LIGHT SHOULD BE "ON" WHILE CRANKING. IS IT?

NO

YES

YES

NO

OPEN IN PINK WIRE OR FAULTY PUMP

FAULTY RELAY

OPEN IN PINK/WHITE WIRE

FAULTY ECM

CLEAR CODES AND CONFIRM NO "CHECK ENGINE" LIGHT.

Fig. 72 1989-91 EFI diagnostic chart

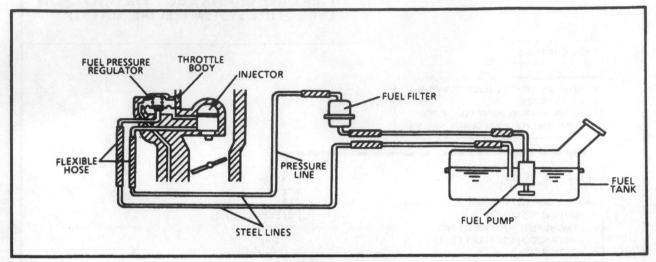

CHART A-7

FUEL SYSTEM PRESSURE TEST

Circuit Description:

When the ignition switch is turned "ON", the Electronic Control Module (ECM) will turn "ON" the in-tank fuel pump. It will remain "ON" as long as the engine is cranking or running, and the ECM is receiving reference pulses. If there are no reference pulses, the ECM will shut "OFF" the fuel pump in about 2 seconds after ignition "ON" or engine stops.

The pump will deliver fuel to the fuel rail and injectors, then to the pressure regulator, where the system pressure is controlled to about 160-210 kPa (23.2-30.5 psi) depending on engine operating conditions. Excess fuel is then returned to the fuel tank.

Test Description: Numbers below refer to circled numbers on the diagnostic chart.

1. Wrap a shop towel around the fuel pressure connector to absorb any small amount of fuel leakage that may occur when installing the gage. Ignition "ON" pump pressure should be 160-210 kPa (23.2-30.5 psi). This pressure is controlled by spring pressure within the regulator assembly.

2. When the engine is idling, the manifold pressure is low (high vacuum) and is applied to the fuel regulator diaphragm. This will offset the spring and result in a lower fuel pressure. This idle pressure will vary somewhat depending on barometric pressure, however, the pressure idling should be less indicating pressure regulator control.

3. Pressure that continues to fall quickly is caused by one of the following:
   - In-tank fuel pump check valve not holding.
   - Pump coupling hose.
   - Fuel pressure regulator valve leaking.
   - Injector(s) sticking open.

4. An injector sticking open can best be determined by checking for a fouled or saturated spark plug(s).
   - Pressurize the fuel system and observe for injector leaking.

Fig. 73 1989-91 EFI diagnostic chart

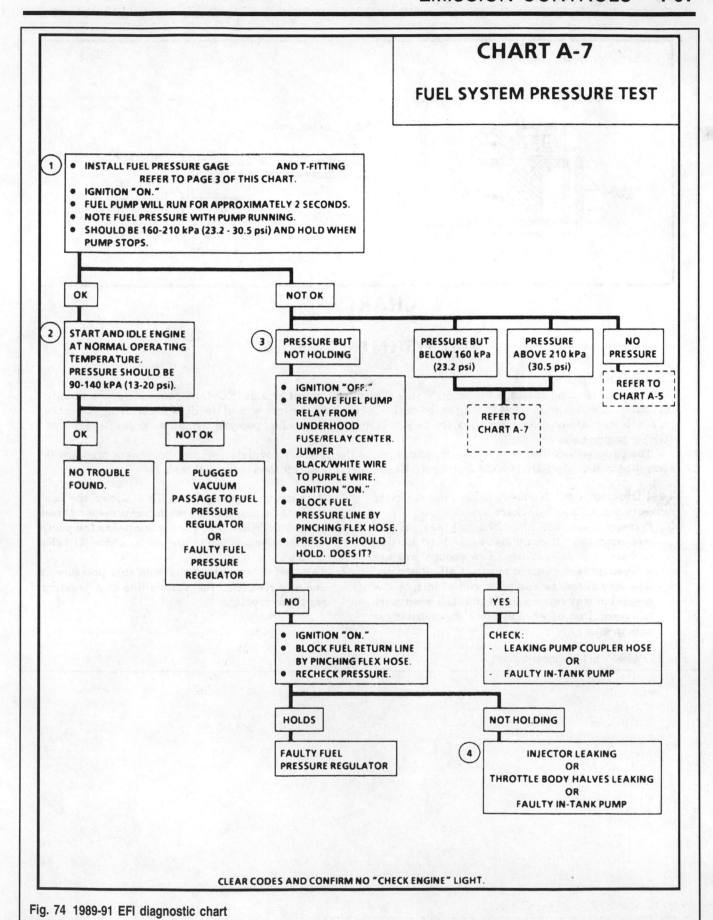

CHART A-7

FUEL SYSTEM PRESSURE TEST

1
- INSTALL FUEL PRESSURE GAGE   AND T-FITTING REFER TO PAGE 3 OF THIS CHART.
- IGNITION "ON."
- FUEL PUMP WILL RUN FOR APPROXIMATELY 2 SECONDS.
- NOTE FUEL PRESSURE WITH PUMP RUNNING.
- SHOULD BE 160-210 kPa (23.2 - 30.5 psi) AND HOLD WHEN PUMP STOPS.

OK

NOT OK

2 START AND IDLE ENGINE AT NORMAL OPERATING TEMPERATURE. PRESSURE SHOULD BE 90-140 kPa (13-20 psi).

3 PRESSURE BUT NOT HOLDING

PRESSURE BUT BELOW 160 kPa (23.2 psi)

PRESSURE ABOVE 210 kPa (30.5 psi)

NO PRESSURE

REFER TO CHART A-5

REFER TO CHART A-7

OK

NOT OK

NO TROUBLE FOUND.

PLUGGED VACUUM PASSAGE TO FUEL PRESSURE REGULATOR OR FAULTY FUEL PRESSURE REGULATOR

- IGNITION "OFF."
- REMOVE FUEL PUMP RELAY FROM UNDERHOOD FUSE/RELAY CENTER.
- JUMPER BLACK/WHITE WIRE TO PURPLE WIRE.
- IGNITION "ON."
- BLOCK FUEL PRESSURE LINE BY PINCHING FLEX HOSE.
- PRESSURE SHOULD HOLD. DOES IT?

NO

YES

- IGNITION "ON."
- BLOCK FUEL RETURN LINE BY PINCHING FLEX HOSE.
- RECHECK PRESSURE.

CHECK:
- LEAKING PUMP COUPLER HOSE OR
- FAULTY IN-TANK PUMP

HOLDS

NOT HOLDING

FAULTY FUEL PRESSURE REGULATOR

4 INJECTOR LEAKING OR THROTTLE BODY HALVES LEAKING OR FAULTY IN-TANK PUMP

CLEAR CODES AND CONFIRM NO "CHECK ENGINE" LIGHT.

Fig. 74 1989-91 EFI diagnostic chart

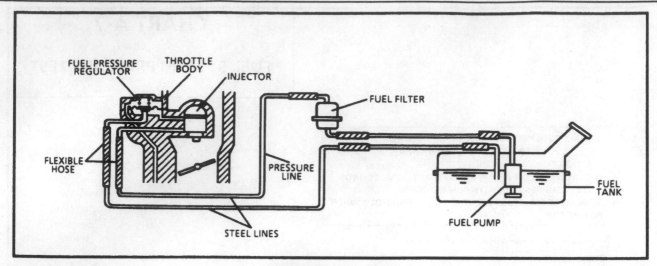

CHART A-7

FUEL SYSTEM PRESSURE TEST

Circuit Description:

When the ignition switch is turned "ON", the Electronic Control Module (ECM) will turn "ON" the in-tank fuel pump. It will remain "ON" as long as the engine is cranking or running, and the ECM is receiving reference pulses. If there are no reference pulses, the ECM will shut "OFF" the fuel pump in about 2 seconds after ignition "ON" or engine stops.

The pump will deliver fuel to the injector, then to the pressure regulator, where the system pressure is controlled to about 160-210 kPa (23.2-30.5 psi). Excess fuel is then returned to the fuel tank.

Test Description: Numbers below refer to circled numbers on the diagnostic chart.

5. Pressure below 160 kPa (23.2 psi) may cause a lean condition. It could also cause hard starting cold and poor driveability. Low enough pressure will cause the engine not to run at all. Restricted flow may allow the engine to run at idle, or low speeds but may cause a surge and stall when more fuel is required, as when accelerating or driving at high speeds.

6. Restricting the fuel return line allows the fuel pump to develop its maximum pressure (dead head pressure). When B+, volts is applied to the pump test terminal, pressure should be above 210 kPa (30.5 psi).

7. This test determines if the high fuel pressure is due to a restricted fuel return line or a pressure regulator problem.

Fig. 75 1989-91 EFI diagnostic chart

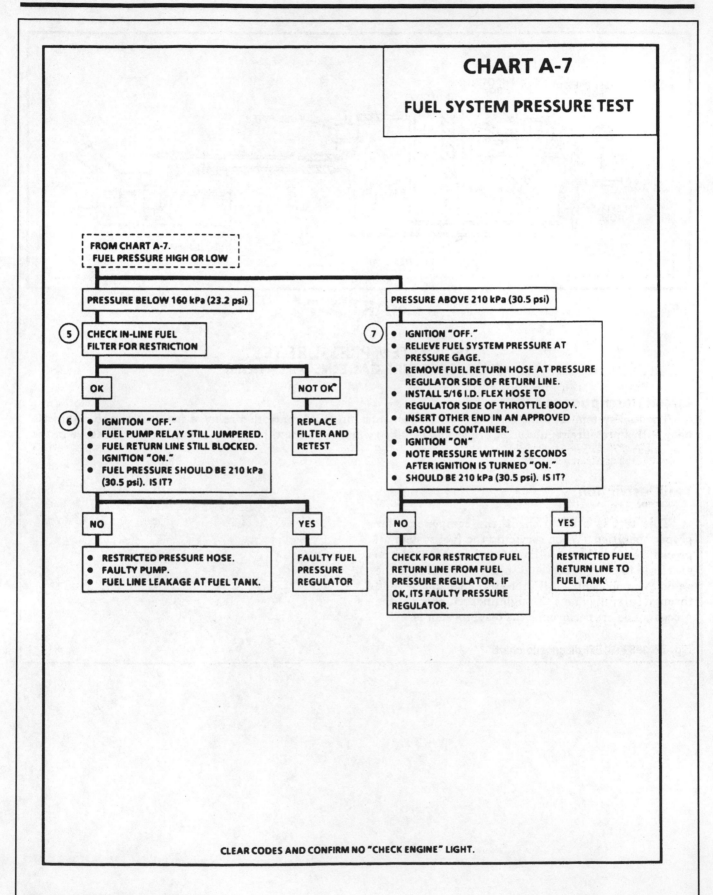

CHART A-7

FUEL SYSTEM PRESSURE TEST

FROM CHART A-7.
FUEL PRESSURE HIGH OR LOW

PRESSURE BELOW 160 kPa (23.2 psi)

⑤ CHECK IN-LINE FUEL FILTER FOR RESTRICTION

OK

NOT OK

⑥
- IGNITION "OFF."
- FUEL PUMP RELAY STILL JUMPERED.
- FUEL RETURN LINE STILL BLOCKED.
- IGNITION "ON."
- FUEL PRESSURE SHOULD BE 210 kPa (30.5 psi). IS IT?

REPLACE FILTER AND RETEST

NO

YES

- RESTRICTED PRESSURE HOSE.
- FAULTY PUMP.
- FUEL LINE LEAKAGE AT FUEL TANK.

FAULTY FUEL PRESSURE REGULATOR

PRESSURE ABOVE 210 kPa (30.5 psi)

⑦
- IGNITION "OFF."
- RELIEVE FUEL SYSTEM PRESSURE AT PRESSURE GAGE.
- REMOVE FUEL RETURN HOSE AT PRESSURE REGULATOR SIDE OF RETURN LINE.
- INSTALL 5/16 I.D. FLEX HOSE TO REGULATOR SIDE OF THROTTLE BODY.
- INSERT OTHER END IN AN APPROVED GASOLINE CONTAINER.
- IGNITION "ON"
- NOTE PRESSURE WITHIN 2 SECONDS AFTER IGNITION IS TURNED "ON."
- SHOULD BE 210 kPa (30.5 psi). IS IT?

NO

YES

CHECK FOR RESTRICTED FUEL RETURN LINE FROM FUEL PRESSURE REGULATOR. IF OK, ITS FAULTY PRESSURE REGULATOR.

RESTRICTED FUEL RETURN LINE TO FUEL TANK

CLEAR CODES AND CONFIRM NO "CHECK ENGINE" LIGHT.

Fig. 76 1989-91 EFI diagnostic chart

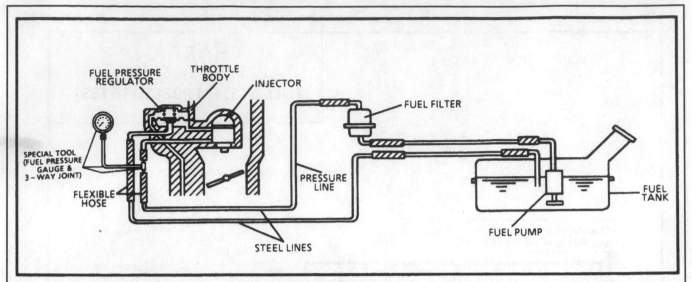

CHART A-7

FUEL SYSTEM PRESSURE TEST
(FUEL PRESSURE GAGE INSTALLATION)

Circuit Description:

The fuel system contains the following components: an ECM controlled relay, a fuel pump, and a throttle body with a pressure regulator. Care should be taken when servicing this system due to the high presure in the fuel lines.

Test Description:

This test is used to check the components for proper operation. When servicing the fuel system all procedures should be followed and care should be exercised to prevent personal injury or damage to the vehicles components. All procedures should be read through carefully and a through understanding of the procedure before performing the test procedures.

Fig. 77 1989-91 EFI diagnostic chart

CHART A-7

FUEL SYSTEM PRESSURE TEST
(FUEL PRESSURE GAGE INSTALLATION)

FUEL PRESSURE RELIEF PROCEDURE

CAUTION:
- To reduce the risk of fire and personal injury, it is necessary to relieve the fuel system pressure before servicing the fuel system.
- After relieving system pressure, a small amount of fuel may be released when servicing fuel lines or connections. In order to reduce the chance of personal injury, cover fuel line fittings with a shop towel before disconnecting, to catch any fuel that may leak out. Place the towel in an approved container when disconnect is completed.

FUEL PRESSURE GAGE INSTALLATION

1. Loosen fuel filler cap to relieve tank vapor pressure.
2. Place transaxle gear shift lever in Neutral for M/T models, or Park for A/T models. Set parking brake and block drive wheels.
3. Remove main fuse block cover and engine coolant reservoir from its bracket.
4. Remove screws holding underhood fuse/relay block.
5. Remove connector holding fuel pump relay and disconnect.
6. Start engine and run till it stalls, crank engine for 3 seconds to insure there is no fuel left in lines.
7. Disconnect negative battery cable.
8. Remove air cleaner assembly.
9. Disconnect fuel feed hose from throttle body.
10. Install fuel pressure gauge, and T-Fitting between fuel feed line and throttle body. Clamp securely to ensure that no leaks occur.
11. Reverse steps 3-4.

CLEAR CODES AND CONFIRM NO "CHECK ENGINE" LIGHT.

Fig. 78 1989-91 EFI diagnostic chart

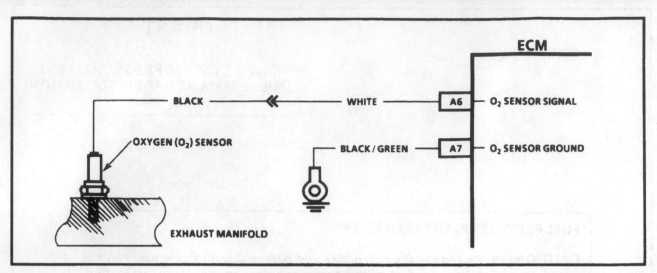

CODE 13

OXYGEN SENSOR CIRCUIT
(OPEN CIRCUIT)

Circuit Description:

The Oxygen (O_2) sensor produces a varying voltage as engine temperature rises to normal operation. This voltage varies from 0 to 900 mV. The signal will vary depending on the exhaust gases. If the voltage stays above 450 mV, this indicates a rich condition. If voltage remains below 450 mV and does not vary a lean condition is indicated.

The O_2 sensor acts like an "open circuit" and produces no voltage when below 360°C (600°F). An open sensor circuit causes the engine to operate in an "open loop" operation.

Test Description: Numbers below refer to circled numbers on the diagnostic chart.

1. Running the engine above 1200 rpm keeps the oxygen sensor hot, so that an accurate check of the sensor can be performed.
2. This will check the O_2 Sensor.
3. Voltage above 900 mV and not varying indicates a short to voltage on O_2 sensor circuit.

Diagnostic Aids:

Normal voltage varies between 0mV and 900mV. Code 13 will set if voltage is indicated low (0 volt) or high (900mV) all the time.

Fig. 79 1989-91 EFI diagnostic chart

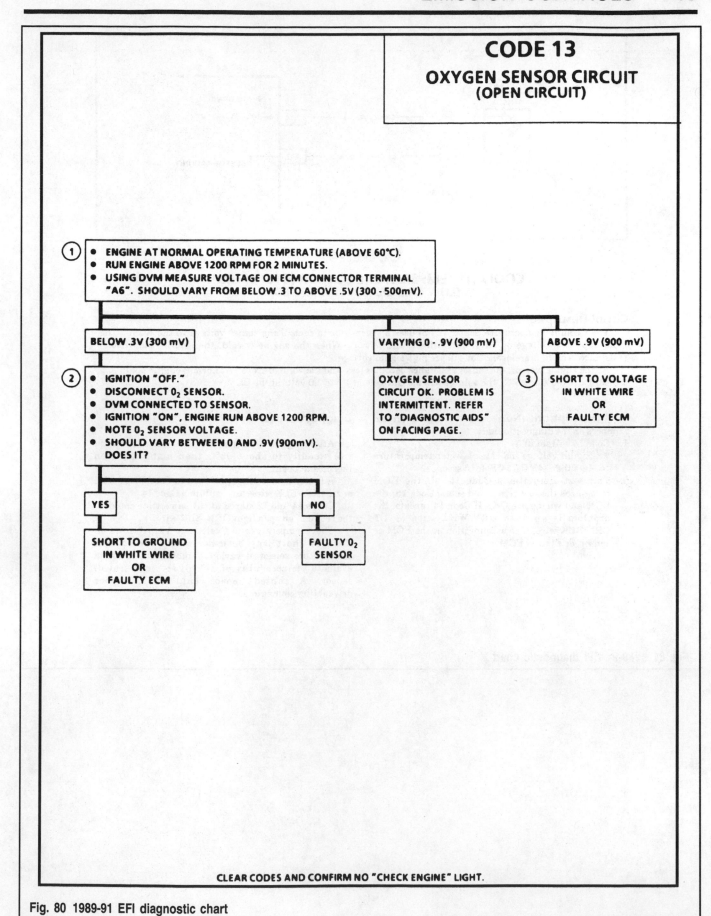

CODE 13
OXYGEN SENSOR CIRCUIT
(OPEN CIRCUIT)

① • ENGINE AT NORMAL OPERATING TEMPERATURE (ABOVE 60°C).
   • RUN ENGINE ABOVE 1200 RPM FOR 2 MINUTES.
   • USING DVM MEASURE VOLTAGE ON ECM CONNECTOR TERMINAL "A6". SHOULD VARY FROM BELOW .3 TO ABOVE .5V (300 - 500mV).

BELOW .3V (300 mV)   VARYING 0 - .9V (900 mV)   ABOVE .9V (900 mV)

② • IGNITION "OFF."   OXYGEN SENSOR   ③ SHORT TO VOLTAGE
   • DISCONNECT O₂ SENSOR.   CIRCUIT OK. PROBLEM IS   IN WHITE WIRE
   • DVM CONNECTED TO SENSOR. INTERMITTENT. REFER   OR
   • IGNITION "ON", ENGINE RUN TO "DIAGNOSTIC AIDS"   FAULTY ECM
     ABOVE 1200 RPM.   ON FACING PAGE.
   • NOTE O₂ SENSOR VOLTAGE.
   • SHOULD VARY BETWEEN 0 AND .9V (900mV).
     DOES IT?

YES   NO

SHORT TO GROUND   FAULTY O₂
IN WHITE WIRE   SENSOR
OR
FAULTY ECM

CLEAR CODES AND CONFIRM NO "CHECK ENGINE" LIGHT.

Fig. 80 1989-91 EFI diagnostic chart

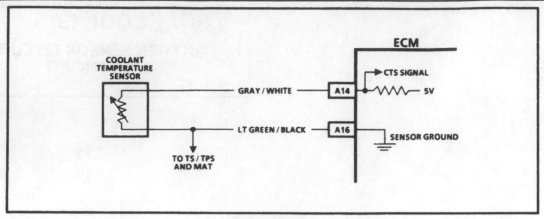

CODE 14

COOLANT TEMPERATURE SENSOR (CTS) CIRCUIT
(LOW TEMPERATURE INDICATED)

Circuit Description:

The Coolant Temperature Sensor (CTS) uses a thermistor to control the signal voltage to the ECM. The ECM applies a voltage on GRY/WHT wire to the sensor. When the engine is cold, the sensor (thermistor) resistance is high, therefore, ECM will see high signal voltage.

As the engine warms, the sensor resistance becomes less, and the voltage drops. At normal engine operating temperature (80°C to 95°C), the voltage will measure about 1.5 to 2.0 volts at the ECM.

Test Description: Numbers below refer to circled numbers on the diagnostic chart.
1. Code 14 will set if:
   - Signal voltage indicates a water temperature less than -48°C (-54°F) for 3 seconds.
2. This test simulates a Code 15. If the ECM recognizes the low signal and sets a Code 15, the ECM and wiring are OK. If Code 14 repeats, the problem is an open GRY/WHT wire or LT GRN/BLK wire, a poor connection at the ECM or sensor, or a faulty ECM.

Diagnostic Aids:

After engine is started the temperature should rise steadily to about 95°C then stabilize when thermostat opens.

A faulty connection, or an open in GRY/WHT wire or LT GRN/BLK wire can result in a Code 14.

Codes 14 and 22 stored at the same time could be the result of an open light GRN/BLK wire.

The "Temperature to Resistance Value" scale on Code 15 chart may be used to test the coolant temperature sensor at various temperature levels to evaluate the possibility of a "shifted" (mis-scaled) sensor. A "shifted" sensor could result in poor driveability complaints.

Fig. 81 1989-91 EFI diagnostic chart

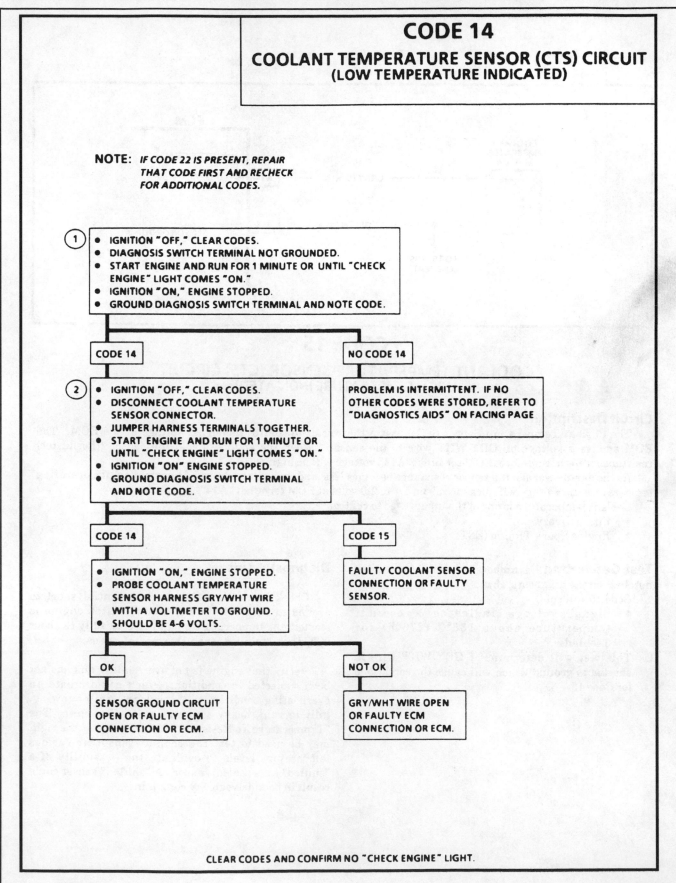

Fig. 82 1989-91 EFI diagnostic chart

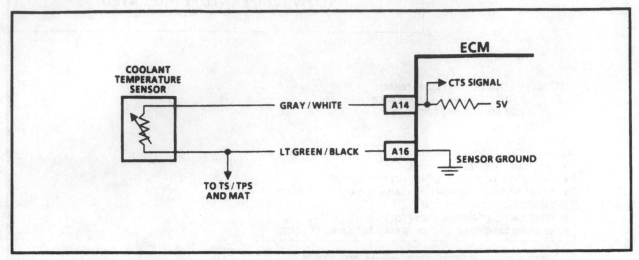

CODE 15

COOLANT TEMPERATURE SENSOR (CTS) CIRCUIT
(HIGH TEMPERATURE INDICATED)

Circuit Description:

The Coolant Temperature Sensor (CTS) uses a thermistor to control the signal voltage at the ECM. The ECM applies a voltage on GRY/WHT wire to the sensor. When the engine is cold the sensor (thermistor) resistance is high, therefore, ECM terminal "A14" voltage will be high.

As the engine warms, the sensor resistance becomes less, and the voltage drops. At normal engine operating temperature the voltage will measure about 1.5 to 2.0 volts at ECM terminal "A14".

Coolant temperature is one of the inputs used to control
- Fuel delivery
- Engine Spark Timing (EST)

Test Description: Numbers below refer to circled numbers on the diagnostic chart.
1. Code 15 will set if:
   - Signal voltage indicates a coolant temperature above 136°C (276°F) for 3 seconds.
2. This test will determine if GRY/WHT wire is shorted to ground which will cause the conditions for Code 15.

Diagnostic Aids:

Check harness routing for a potential short to ground in GRY/WHT wire circuit. After engine is started, the temperature should rise steadily to about 90°C then stabilize when thermostat opens.

Verify that engine is not overheating and has not been subjected to conditions which could create an overheating condition (i.e. overload, trailer towing, hilly terrain, heavy stop and go traffic, etc.). The "Temperature To Resistance Value" scale at the right may be used to test the coolant sensor at various temperature levels to evaluate the possibility of a "shifted" (mis-scaled) sensor. A "shifted" sensor could result in poor driveability complaints.

Fig. 83 1989-91 EFI diagnostic chart

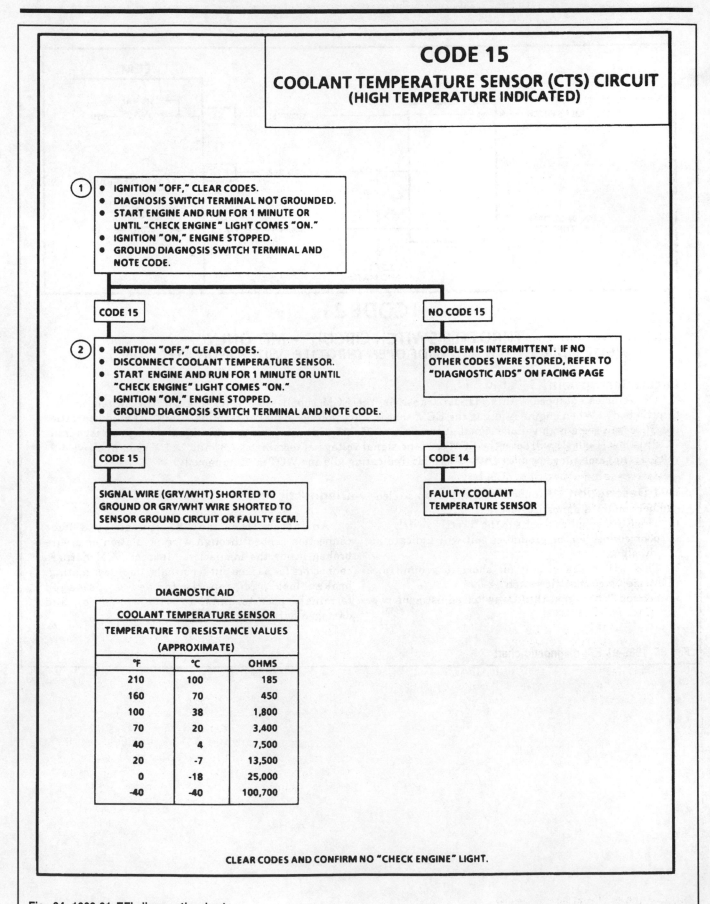

CODE 15

COOLANT TEMPERATURE SENSOR (CTS) CIRCUIT
(HIGH TEMPERATURE INDICATED)

1
- IGNITION "OFF," CLEAR CODES.
- DIAGNOSIS SWITCH TERMINAL NOT GROUNDED.
- START ENGINE AND RUN FOR 1 MINUTE OR UNTIL "CHECK ENGINE" LIGHT COMES "ON."
- IGNITION "ON," ENGINE STOPPED.
- GROUND DIAGNOSIS SWITCH TERMINAL AND NOTE CODE.

CODE 15

NO CODE 15

2
- IGNITION "OFF," CLEAR CODES.
- DISCONNECT COOLANT TEMPERATURE SENSOR.
- START ENGINE AND RUN FOR 1 MINUTE OR UNTIL "CHECK ENGINE" LIGHT COMES "ON."
- IGNITION "ON," ENGINE STOPPED.
- GROUND DIAGNOSIS SWITCH TERMINAL AND NOTE CODE.

PROBLEM IS INTERMITTENT. IF NO OTHER CODES WERE STORED, REFER TO "DIAGNOSTIC AIDS" ON FACING PAGE

CODE 15

CODE 14

SIGNAL WIRE (GRY/WHT) SHORTED TO GROUND OR GRY/WHT WIRE SHORTED TO SENSOR GROUND CIRCUIT OR FAULTY ECM.

FAULTY COOLANT TEMPERATURE SENSOR

DIAGNOSTIC AID

COOLANT TEMPERATURE SENSOR		
TEMPERATURE TO RESISTANCE VALUES (APPROXIMATE)		
°F	°C	OHMS
210	100	185
160	70	450
100	38	1,800
70	20	3,400
40	4	7,500
20	-7	13,500
0	-18	25,000
-40	-40	100,700

CLEAR CODES AND CONFIRM NO "CHECK ENGINE" LIGHT.

Fig. 84 1989-91 EFI diagnostic chart

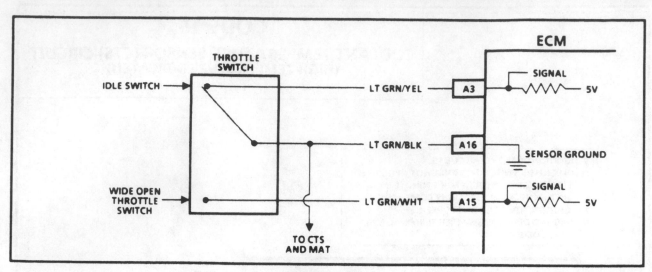

CODE 21

THROTTLE SWITCH CIRCUIT - M/T ONLY
(BOTH IDLE SWITCH AND WIDE OPEN THROTTLE SWITCH INDICATED "ON")

Circuit Description:

On vehicles equipped with a manual transaxle, the ECM supplies 4-5 volts to a throttle switch on the throttle body When engine is idling, the ECM senses a low voltage signal at terminal "A3." At slight throttle the ECM will see a high voltage signal at terminal "A3". At wide open throttle the signal voltage on terminal "A15" is low Code 21 will set if the ECM sees the signal voltage at terminals "A3" and "A15" remain above 4-9 volts, at the same time, for more than .3 seconds (indicating idle and WOT simultaneously).

Test Description: Numbers below refer to circled numbers on the diagnostic chart.

1   The ECM supplies 5 volts to the throttle switch A poor connection or ground circuit will indicate a low signal.
2   This will check circuit for short to ground or misadjusted throttle switch
3   Section "C2" checks throttle switch adjustment

Diagnostic Aids:

An intermittent may be caused by a poor connection rubbed through wire insulation or a wire broken inside the insulation. Inspect ECM harness connectors for backed out terminals, improper mating, broken locks, improperly formed or damaged terminals, poor terminal to wire connection and damaged harness.

Fig. 85 1989-91 EFI diagnostic chart

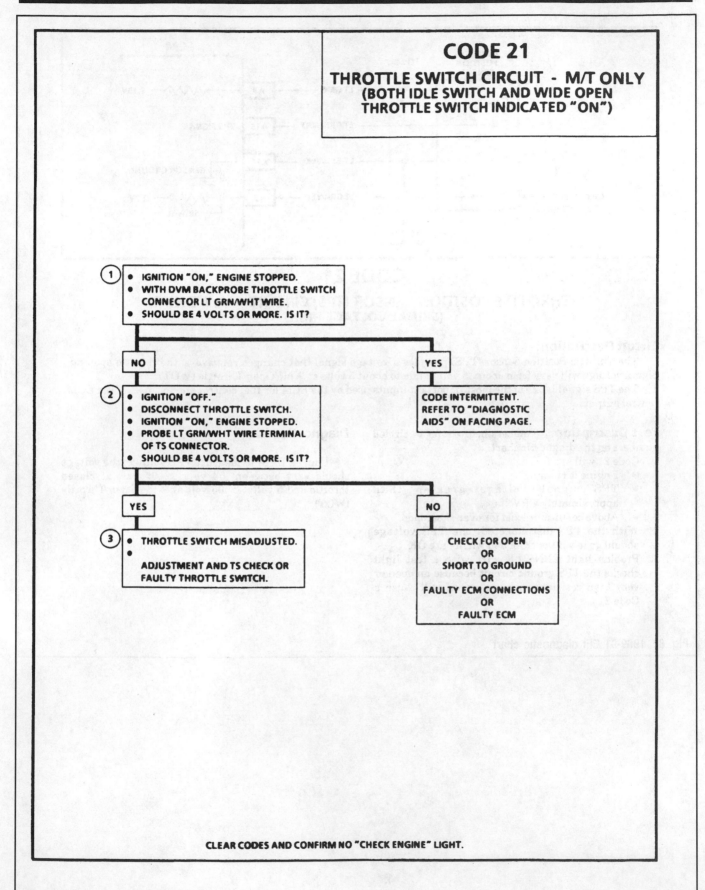

CODE 21

THROTTLE SWITCH CIRCUIT - M/T ONLY
(BOTH IDLE SWITCH AND WIDE OPEN
THROTTLE SWITCH INDICATED "ON")

1
- IGNITION "ON," ENGINE STOPPED.
- WITH DVM BACKPROBE THROTTLE SWITCH CONNECTOR LT GRN/WHT WIRE.
- SHOULD BE 4 VOLTS OR MORE. IS IT?

NO

YES

CODE INTERMITTENT. REFER TO "DIAGNOSTIC AIDS" ON FACING PAGE.

2
- IGNITION "OFF."
- DISCONNECT THROTTLE SWITCH.
- IGNITION "ON," ENGINE STOPPED.
- PROBE LT GRN/WHT WIRE TERMINAL OF TS CONNECTOR.
- SHOULD BE 4 VOLTS OR MORE. IS IT?

YES

NO

3
- THROTTLE SWITCH MISADJUSTED.

- ADJUSTMENT AND TS CHECK OR FAULTY THROTTLE SWITCH.

CHECK FOR OPEN
OR
SHORT TO GROUND
OR
FAULTY ECM CONNECTIONS
OR
FAULTY ECM

CLEAR CODES AND CONFIRM NO "CHECK ENGINE" LIGHT.

Fig. 86 1989-91 EFI diagnostic chart

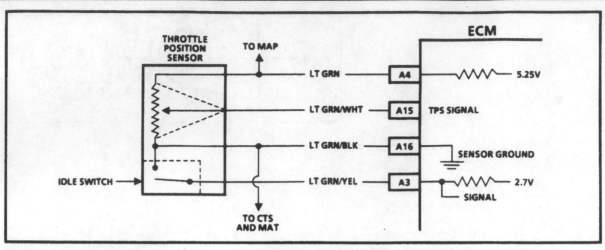

CODE 21
THROTTLE POSITION SENSOR (TPS) CIRCUIT - A/T ONLY
(SIGNAL VOLTAGE HIGH)

Circuit Description:

The Throttle Position Sensor (TPS) provides a voltage signal that changes relative to the throttle opening. Signal voltage will vary from about .5 volt at idle to about 5 volts at Wide Open Throttle (WOT).

The TPS signal is one of the most important inputs used by the ECM for fuel control and for most of the ECM control outputs.

Test Description: Numbers below refer to circled numbers on the diagnostic chart.

1. Code 21 will set if:
   - Engine is running.
   - TPS signal voltage greater than approximately 4.9 volts.
   - Above conditions exist for over .7 seconds.
2. With the TPS disconnected, the TPS voltage should go low if the ECM and wiring are OK.
3. Probing light GRN/BLK wire with a test light checks the TPS ground circuit because an open or very high resistance ground circuit will cause a Code 21.

Diagnostic Aids:

Using a DVM to measure TPS voltage, the voltage should vary between .54 volt ± .05 volt at closed throttle and 5 volts ± .05 volt at Wide Open Throttle (WOT).

Fig. 87 1989-91 EFI diagnostic chart

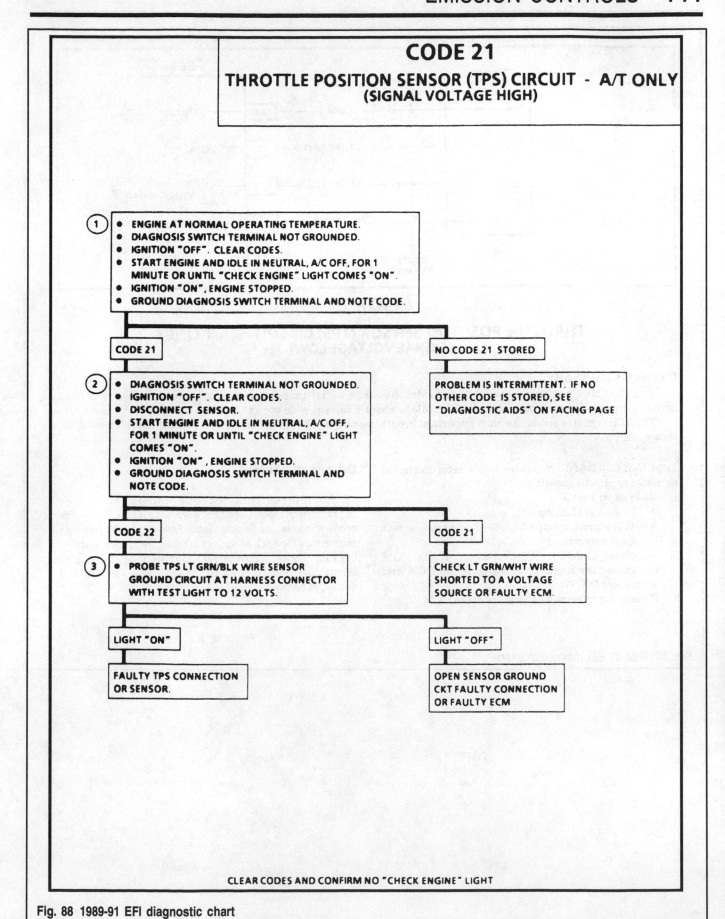

CODE 21
THROTTLE POSITION SENSOR (TPS) CIRCUIT - A/T ONLY
(SIGNAL VOLTAGE HIGH)

①
- ENGINE AT NORMAL OPERATING TEMPERATURE.
- DIAGNOSIS SWITCH TERMINAL NOT GROUNDED.
- IGNITION "OFF". CLEAR CODES.
- START ENGINE AND IDLE IN NEUTRAL, A/C OFF, FOR 1 MINUTE OR UNTIL "CHECK ENGINE" LIGHT COMES "ON".
- IGNITION "ON", ENGINE STOPPED.
- GROUND DIAGNOSIS SWITCH TERMINAL AND NOTE CODE.

CODE 21

NO CODE 21 STORED

②
- DIAGNOSIS SWITCH TERMINAL NOT GROUNDED.
- IGNITION "OFF". CLEAR CODES.
- DISCONNECT SENSOR.
- START ENGINE AND IDLE IN NEUTRAL, A/C OFF, FOR 1 MINUTE OR UNTIL "CHECK ENGINE" LIGHT COMES "ON".
- IGNITION "ON", ENGINE STOPPED.
- GROUND DIAGNOSIS SWITCH TERMINAL AND NOTE CODE.

PROBLEM IS INTERMITTENT. IF NO OTHER CODE IS STORED, SEE "DIAGNOSTIC AIDS" ON FACING PAGE

CODE 22

CODE 21

③
- PROBE TPS LT GRN/BLK WIRE SENSOR GROUND CIRCUIT AT HARNESS CONNECTOR WITH TEST LIGHT TO 12 VOLTS.

CHECK LT GRN/WHT WIRE SHORTED TO A VOLTAGE SOURCE OR FAULTY ECM.

LIGHT "ON"

LIGHT "OFF"

FAULTY TPS CONNECTION OR SENSOR.

OPEN SENSOR GROUND CKT FAULTY CONNECTION OR FAULTY ECM

CLEAR CODES AND CONFIRM NO "CHECK ENGINE" LIGHT

Fig. 88 1989-91 EFI diagnostic chart

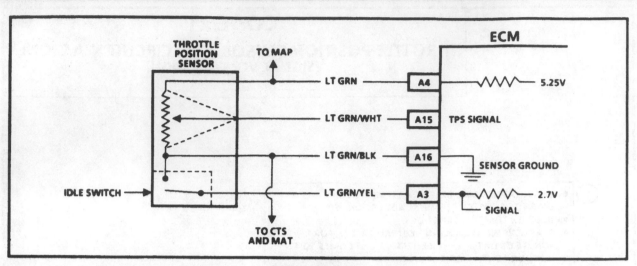

CODE 22

THROTTLE POSITION SENSOR (TPS) CIRCUIT - A/T ONLY
(SIGNAL VOLTAGE LOW)

Circuit Description:

The Throttle Position Sensor (TPS) provides a voltage signal that changes relative to the throttle blade. Signal voltage will vary from about .5 volt at idle to about 5 volts at wide open throttle.

The TPS signal is one of the most important inputs used by the ECM for fuel control and for most of the ECM control outputs.

Test Description: Numbers below refer to circled numbers on the diagnostic chart.

1. Code 22 will set if:
   - Engine is running.
   - TPS signal voltage is less than about .1 volt for .7 seconds.
2. Simulates Code 21: (high voltage). If the ECM recognizes the high signal voltage, the ECM and wiring are OK.
3. Checks for reference voltage from the ECM.

Diagnostic Aids:

An intermittent may be caused by a poor connection rubbed through wire insulation or a wire broken inside the insulation. Inspect ECM harness connectors for backed out terminals, improper mating, broken locks, improperly formed or damaged terminals, poor terminal to wire connection and damaged harness.

Fig. 89 1989-91 EFI diagnostic chart

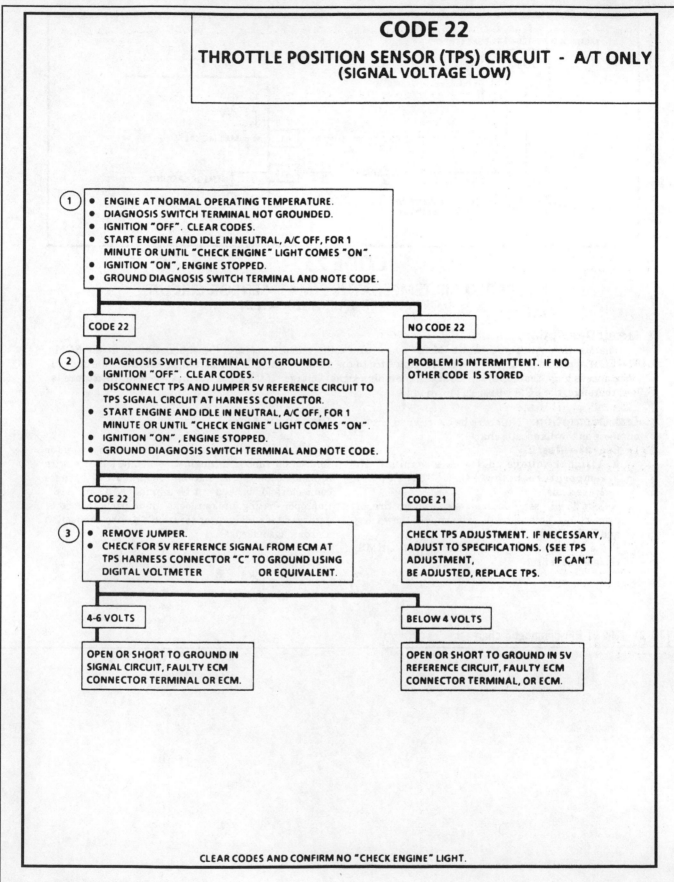

CODE 22
THROTTLE POSITION SENSOR (TPS) CIRCUIT - A/T ONLY
(SIGNAL VOLTAGE LOW)

①
- ENGINE AT NORMAL OPERATING TEMPERATURE.
- DIAGNOSIS SWITCH TERMINAL NOT GROUNDED.
- IGNITION "OFF". CLEAR CODES.
- START ENGINE AND IDLE IN NEUTRAL, A/C OFF, FOR 1 MINUTE OR UNTIL "CHECK ENGINE" LIGHT COMES "ON".
- IGNITION "ON", ENGINE STOPPED.
- GROUND DIAGNOSIS SWITCH TERMINAL AND NOTE CODE.

CODE 22

NO CODE 22

PROBLEM IS INTERMITTENT. IF NO OTHER CODE IS STORED

②
- DIAGNOSIS SWITCH TERMINAL NOT GROUNDED.
- IGNITION "OFF". CLEAR CODES.
- DISCONNECT TPS AND JUMPER 5V REFERENCE CIRCUIT TO TPS SIGNAL CIRCUIT AT HARNESS CONNECTOR.
- START ENGINE AND IDLE IN NEUTRAL, A/C OFF, FOR 1 MINUTE OR UNTIL "CHECK ENGINE" LIGHT COMES "ON".
- IGNITION "ON", ENGINE STOPPED.
- GROUND DIAGNOSIS SWITCH TERMINAL AND NOTE CODE.

CODE 22

CODE 21

③
- REMOVE JUMPER.
- CHECK FOR 5V REFERENCE SIGNAL FROM ECM AT TPS HARNESS CONNECTOR "C" TO GROUND USING DIGITAL VOLTMETER   OR EQUIVALENT.

CHECK TPS ADJUSTMENT. IF NECESSARY, ADJUST TO SPECIFICATIONS. (SEE TPS ADJUSTMENT,   IF CAN'T BE ADJUSTED, REPLACE TPS.

4-6 VOLTS

BELOW 4 VOLTS

OPEN OR SHORT TO GROUND IN SIGNAL CIRCUIT, FAULTY ECM CONNECTOR TERMINAL OR ECM.

OPEN OR SHORT TO GROUND IN 5V REFERENCE CIRCUIT, FAULTY ECM CONNECTOR TERMINAL, OR ECM.

CLEAR CODES AND CONFIRM NO "CHECK ENGINE" LIGHT.

Fig. 90 1989-91 EFI diagnostic chart

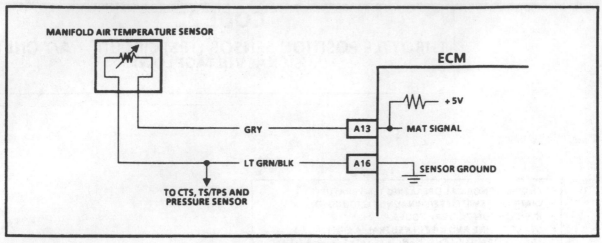

CODE 23
MANIFOLD AIR TEMPERATURE (MAT) SENSOR CIRCUIT
(LOW TEMPERATURE INDICATED)

Circuit Description:

The Manifold Air Temperature (MAT) sensor uses a thermistor to control the signal voltage at the ECM. The ECM applies a voltage (4-6 volts) on gray wire to the sensor. When the air is cold, the sensor (thermistor) resistance is high, therefore, the ECM will see a high signal voltage. If the air is warm, the sensor resistance is low, therefore, the ECM will see a low voltage.

Test Description: Numbers below refer to circled numbers on the diagnostic chart.

1. Code 23 will set if:
   - A signal voltage indicates a manifold air temperature below -48°C (-54.4°F) for 2.7 seconds.

   A Code 23 will set, due to an open sensor, wire, or connection. This test will determine if the wiring and ECM are OK.
2. If the resistance is greater than 25,000 OHMS, replace the sensor.

Diagnostic Aids:

An intermittent may be caused by a poor connection rubbed through wire insulation or a wire broken inside the insulation. Inspect ECM harness connectors for backed out terminals "A13" or "A16", improper mating, broken locks, improperly formed or damaged terminals, poor terminal to wire connection and damaged harness.

Fig. 91 1989-91 EFI diagnostic chart

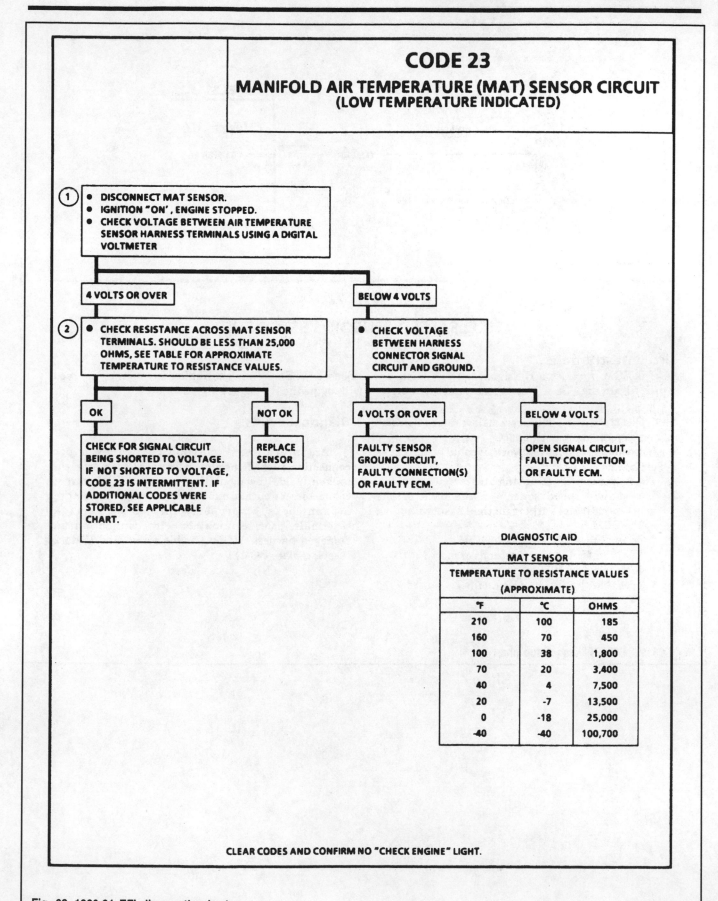

CODE 23
MANIFOLD AIR TEMPERATURE (MAT) SENSOR CIRCUIT
(LOW TEMPERATURE INDICATED)

1
- DISCONNECT MAT SENSOR.
- IGNITION "ON", ENGINE STOPPED.
- CHECK VOLTAGE BETWEEN AIR TEMPERATURE SENSOR HARNESS TERMINALS USING A DIGITAL VOLTMETER

4 VOLTS OR OVER

BELOW 4 VOLTS

2
- CHECK RESISTANCE ACROSS MAT SENSOR TERMINALS. SHOULD BE LESS THAN 25,000 OHMS, SEE TABLE FOR APPROXIMATE TEMPERATURE TO RESISTANCE VALUES.

- CHECK VOLTAGE BETWEEN HARNESS CONNECTOR SIGNAL CIRCUIT AND GROUND.

OK

NOT OK

4 VOLTS OR OVER

BELOW 4 VOLTS

CHECK FOR SIGNAL CIRCUIT BEING SHORTED TO VOLTAGE. IF NOT SHORTED TO VOLTAGE, CODE 23 IS INTERMITTENT. IF ADDITIONAL CODES WERE STORED, SEE APPLICABLE CHART.

REPLACE SENSOR

FAULTY SENSOR GROUND CIRCUIT, FAULTY CONNECTION(S) OR FAULTY ECM.

OPEN SIGNAL CIRCUIT, FAULTY CONNECTION OR FAULTY ECM.

DIAGNOSTIC AID

MAT SENSOR		
TEMPERATURE TO RESISTANCE VALUES (APPROXIMATE)		
°F	°C	OHMS
210	100	185
160	70	450
100	38	1,800
70	20	3,400
40	4	7,500
20	-7	13,500
0	-18	25,000
-40	-40	100,700

CLEAR CODES AND CONFIRM NO "CHECK ENGINE" LIGHT.

Fig. 92 1989-91 EFI diagnostic chart

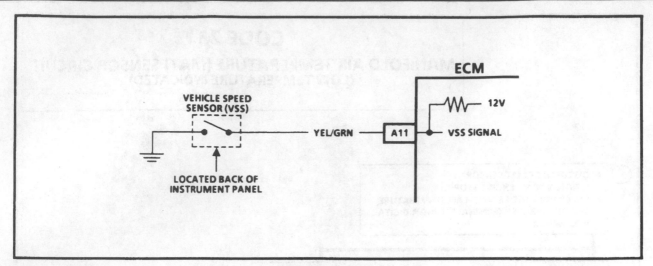

CODE 24
VEHICLE SPEED SENSOR (VSS) CIRCUIT

Circuit Description:

The ECM provides a B+ signal to the Vehicle Speed Sensor (VSS). While the vehicle is moving, the reed switch within the VSS will open and close, which in turn will toggle the B+ signal high and low.

Test Description: Numbers below refer to circled numbers on the diagnostic chart.

1. If speedometer does not work, it could be the cause of Code 24.
2. The ECM supplies B+ to the VSS.
3. The vehicle speed sensor on the back of the instrument panel will toggle the 12 volts supplied by the ECM.

   Code 24 will set if:
   - Fuel remains cut for 4 seconds or more.
   - RPM is below 4000.
   - Less than 1 mile / hr. (1.1 km/hr.) is sensed.

Diagnostic Aids:

An intermittent may be caused by a poor connection rubbed through wire insulation or a wire broken inside the insulation. Inspect ECM harness connectors for backed out terminals, improper mating, broken locks, improperly formed or damaged terminals, poor terminal to wire connection and damaged harness. If no trouble found and Code 24 resets, replace ECM.

Fig. 93 1989-91 EFI diagnostic chart

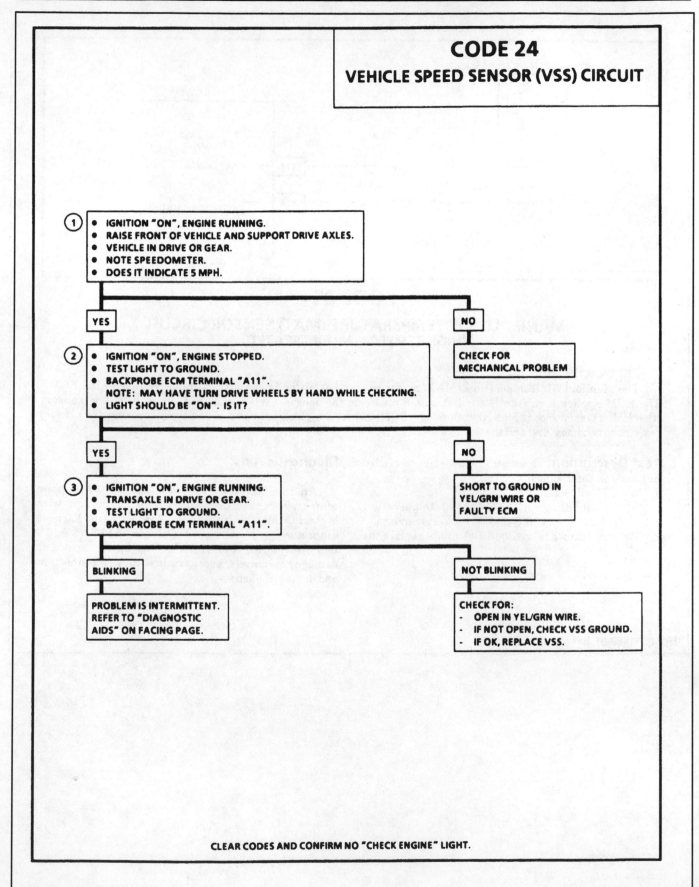

CODE 24
VEHICLE SPEED SENSOR (VSS) CIRCUIT

1
- IGNITION "ON", ENGINE RUNNING.
- RAISE FRONT OF VEHICLE AND SUPPORT DRIVE AXLES.
- VEHICLE IN DRIVE OR GEAR.
- NOTE SPEEDOMETER.
- DOES IT INDICATE 5 MPH.

YES

NO

2
- IGNITION "ON", ENGINE STOPPED.
- TEST LIGHT TO GROUND.
- BACKPROBE ECM TERMINAL "A11".
  NOTE: MAY HAVE TURN DRIVE WHEELS BY HAND WHILE CHECKING.
- LIGHT SHOULD BE "ON". IS IT?

CHECK FOR
MECHANICAL PROBLEM

YES

NO

3
- IGNITION "ON", ENGINE RUNNING.
- TRANSAXLE IN DRIVE OR GEAR.
- TEST LIGHT TO GROUND.
- BACKPROBE ECM TERMINAL "A11".

SHORT TO GROUND IN
YEL/GRN WIRE OR
FAULTY ECM

BLINKING

NOT BLINKING

PROBLEM IS INTERMITTENT.
REFER TO "DIAGNOSTIC
AIDS" ON FACING PAGE.

CHECK FOR:
- OPEN IN YEL/GRN WIRE.
- IF NOT OPEN, CHECK VSS GROUND.
- IF OK, REPLACE VSS.

CLEAR CODES AND CONFIRM NO "CHECK ENGINE" LIGHT.

Fig. 94 1989-91 EFI diagnostic chart

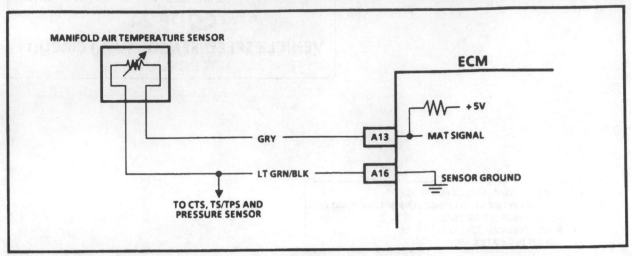

CODE 25
MANIFOLD AIR TEMPERATURE (MAT) SENSOR CIRCUIT
(HIGH TEMPERATURE INDICATED)

Circuit Description:

The Manifold Air Temperature (MAT) sensor uses a thermistor to control the signal voltage to the ECM. The ECM applies a voltage (4-6 volts) on GRY wire to the sensor. When manifold air is cold, the sensor (thermistor) resistance is high, therefore, the ECM will see a high signal voltage. As the air warms, the sensor resistance becomes less, and the voltage drops.

Test Description: Numbers below refer to circled numbers on the diagnostic chart.
1. Code 25 will set if :
   - Signal voltage indicates an air temperature greater than 136°C (277°F) for 2.7 seconds.
2. If the resistance is less than 100 ohm's, replace the sensor.

Diagnostic Aids:

An intermittent may be caused by a poor connection rubbed through wire insulation or a wire broken inside the insulation. Inspect ECM harness connectors for backed out terminals "A13" or "A16", improper mating, broken locks, improperly formed or damaged terminals, poor terminal to wire connection and damaged harness.

Fig. 95 1989-91 EFI diagnostic chart

CODE 25
MANIFOLD AIR TEMPERATURE (MAT) SENSOR CIRCUIT
(HIGH TEMPERATURE INDICATED)

1
- DISCONNECT MAT SENSOR.
- IGNITION "ON", ENGINE STOPPED.
- CHECK VOLTAGE BETWEEN AIR TEMPERATURE SENSOR HARNESS CONNECTOR TERMINALS USING A DIGITAL VOLTMETER

4 VOLTS OR OVER

BELOW 4 VOLTS

2
- CHECK RESISTANCE ACROSS MAT SENSOR TERMINALS. SHOULD BE MORE THAN 185 OHMS WITH WARM ENGINE. SEE TABLE FOR APPROXIMATE TEMPERATURE TO RESISTANCE VALUES.

GRAY WIRE SHORTED TO GROUND
OR
GRAY WIRE SHORTED TO SENSOR GROUND CIRCUIT
OR
FAULTY ECM

OK

NOT OK

INTERMITTENT FAULT IN SENSOR CIRCUIT OR CONNECTOR. IF ADDITIONAL CODES WERE STORED, USE APPLICABLE CHART.

REPLACE SENSOR

DIAGNOSTIC AID

MAT SENSOR		
TEMPERATURE TO RESISTANCE VALUES (APPROXIMATE)		
°F	°C	OHMS
210	100	185
160	70	450
100	38	1,800
70	20	3,400
40	4	7,500
20	-7	13,500
0	-18	25,000
-40	-40	100,700

CLEAR CODES AND CONFIRM NO "CHECK ENGINE" LIGHT.

Fig. 96 1989-91 EFI diagnostic chart

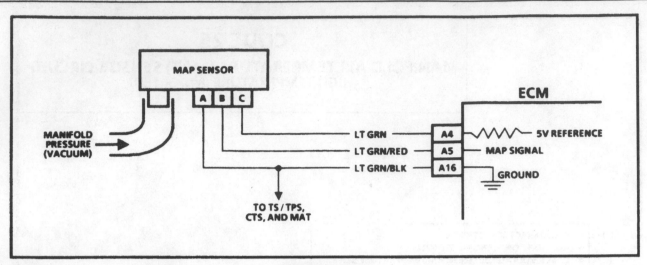

CODE 31

MANIFOLD ABSOLUTE PRESSURE (MAP) SENSOR CIRCUIT
(SIGNAL VOLTAGE LOW - HIGH VACUUM)

Circuit Description:

The Manifold Absolute Pressure (MAP) sensor responds to changes in manifold pressure (vacuum). The ECM receives this information as a signal voltage that will vary from about 1 to 1.5 volts at closed throttle idle, to 4 - 4.5 volts at wide open throttle.

If the MAP Sensor fails, the ECM will substitute a fixed MAP value to control fuel delivery.

Test Description: Numbers below refer to circled numbers on the diagnostic chart.

1. This step determines if Code 31 is the result of a hard failure or an intermittent condition.
   A Code 31 will set when:
   - MAP signal voltage is too low (less than 40mmHg) for .5 seconds.
2. Jumpering harness terminals "B" to "C", 5 volts to signal, will determine if the sensor is at fault, or if there is a problem with the ECM or wiring.

Diagnostic Aids:

An intermittent may be caused by a poor connection rubbed through wire insulation or a wire broken inside the insulation. Inspect ECM harness connectors for backed out terminals, improper mating, broken locks, improperly formed or damaged terminals, poor terminal to wire connection and damaged harness.

Fig. 97 1989-91 EFI diagnostic chart

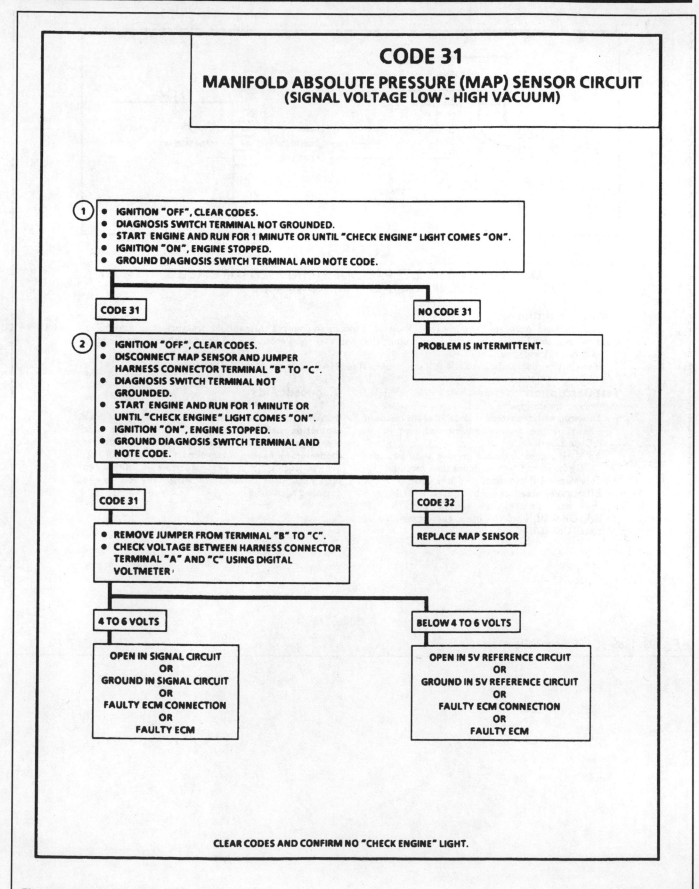

CODE 31
MANIFOLD ABSOLUTE PRESSURE (MAP) SENSOR CIRCUIT
(SIGNAL VOLTAGE LOW - HIGH VACUUM)

(1)
- IGNITION "OFF", CLEAR CODES.
- DIAGNOSIS SWITCH TERMINAL NOT GROUNDED.
- START ENGINE AND RUN FOR 1 MINUTE OR UNTIL "CHECK ENGINE" LIGHT COMES "ON".
- IGNITION "ON", ENGINE STOPPED.
- GROUND DIAGNOSIS SWITCH TERMINAL AND NOTE CODE.

CODE 31

NO CODE 31

(2)
- IGNITION "OFF", CLEAR CODES.
- DISCONNECT MAP SENSOR AND JUMPER HARNESS CONNECTOR TERMINAL "B" TO "C".
- DIAGNOSIS SWITCH TERMINAL NOT GROUNDED.
- START ENGINE AND RUN FOR 1 MINUTE OR UNTIL "CHECK ENGINE" LIGHT COMES "ON".
- IGNITION "ON", ENGINE STOPPED.
- GROUND DIAGNOSIS SWITCH TERMINAL AND NOTE CODE.

PROBLEM IS INTERMITTENT.

CODE 31

CODE 32

- REMOVE JUMPER FROM TERMINAL "B" TO "C".
- CHECK VOLTAGE BETWEEN HARNESS CONNECTOR TERMINAL "A" AND "C" USING DIGITAL VOLTMETER

REPLACE MAP SENSOR

4 TO 6 VOLTS

BELOW 4 TO 6 VOLTS

OPEN IN SIGNAL CIRCUIT
OR
GROUND IN SIGNAL CIRCUIT
OR
FAULTY ECM CONNECTION
OR
FAULTY ECM

OPEN IN 5V REFERENCE CIRCUIT
OR
GROUND IN 5V REFERENCE CIRCUIT
OR
FAULTY ECM CONNECTION
OR
FAULTY ECM

CLEAR CODES AND CONFIRM NO "CHECK ENGINE" LIGHT.

Fig. 98 1989-91 EFI diagnostic chart

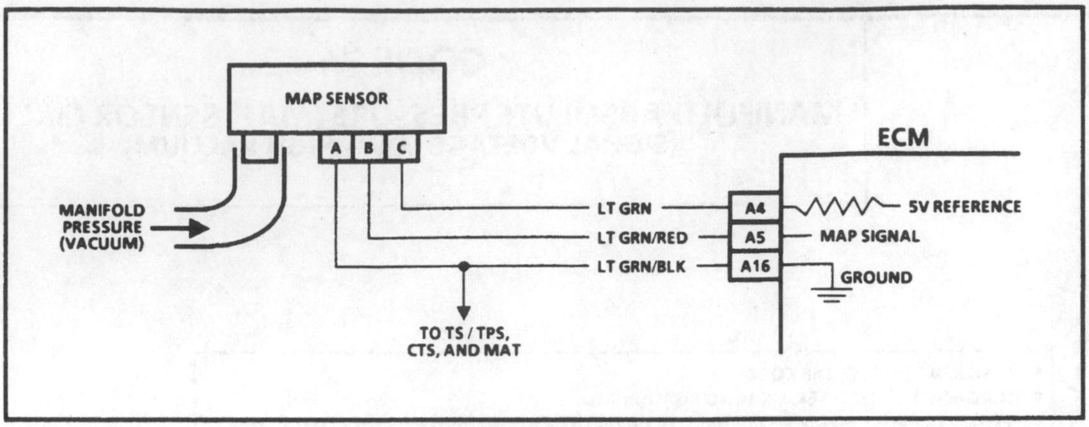

CODE 32

MANIFOLD ABSOLUTE PRESSURE (MAP) SENSOR CIRCUIT
(SIGNAL VOLTAGE HIGH - LOW VACUUM)

Circuit Description:

The Manifold Absolute Pressure (MAP) sensor responds to changes in manifold pressure (vacuum). The ECM receives this information as a signal voltage that will vary from about 1 to 1.5 volts at closed throttle idle, to 4 - 4.5 volts at wide open throttle.

If the MAP sensor fails, the ECM will substitute a fixed MAP value to control fuel delivery.

Test Description: Numbers below refer to circled numbers on the diagnostic chart.

1. This step will determine if Code 32 is the result of a hard failure or an intermittent condition.
   A Code 32 will set if:
   - MAP signal indicates greater than 940 mm Hg for more than .5 seconds (low vacuum).
2. This step simulates conditions for a Code 31. If the ECM recognizes the change, the ECM and the wire to pressure sensor are OK. If light GRN/ BLK wire is open, there may also be stored Code 25.

Diagnostic Aids:

An intermittent may be caused by a poor connection rubbed through wire insulation or a wire broken inside the insulation. Inspect ECM harness connectors for backed out terminals, improper mating, broken locks, improperly formed or damaged terminals, poor terminal to wire connection and damaged harness.

Fig. 99 1989-91 EFI diagnostic chart

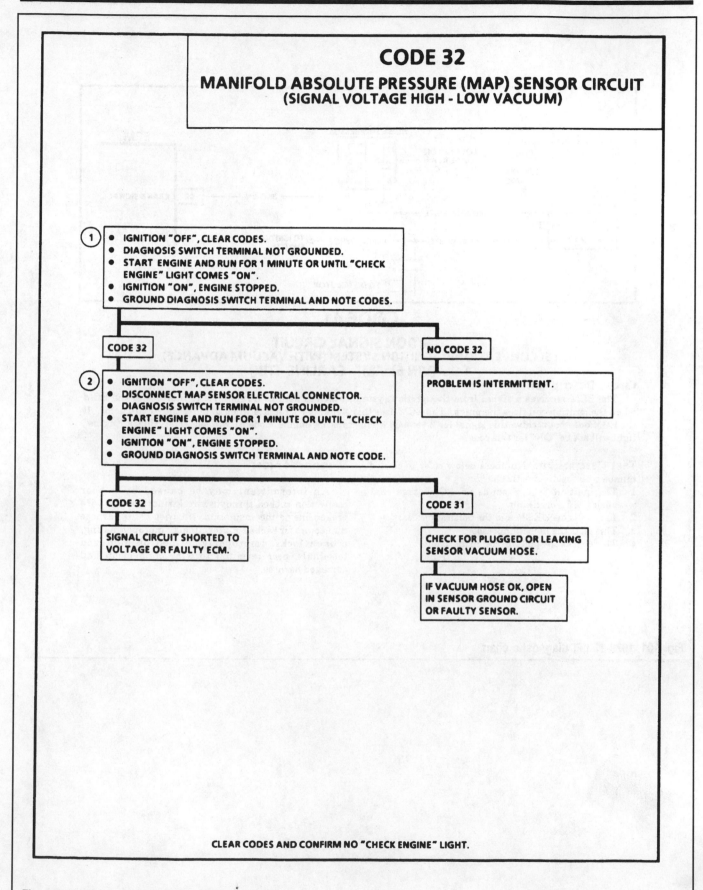

CODE 32

MANIFOLD ABSOLUTE PRESSURE (MAP) SENSOR CIRCUIT
(SIGNAL VOLTAGE HIGH - LOW VACUUM)

1
- IGNITION "OFF", CLEAR CODES.
- DIAGNOSIS SWITCH TERMINAL NOT GROUNDED.
- START ENGINE AND RUN FOR 1 MINUTE OR UNTIL "CHECK ENGINE" LIGHT COMES "ON".
- IGNITION "ON", ENGINE STOPPED.
- GROUND DIAGNOSIS SWITCH TERMINAL AND NOTE CODES.

CODE 32

NO CODE 32

PROBLEM IS INTERMITTENT.

2
- IGNITION "OFF", CLEAR CODES.
- DISCONNECT MAP SENSOR ELECTRICAL CONNECTOR.
- DIAGNOSIS SWITCH TERMINAL NOT GROUNDED.
- START ENGINE AND RUN FOR 1 MINUTE OR UNTIL "CHECK ENGINE" LIGHT COMES "ON".
- IGNITION "ON", ENGINE STOPPED.
- GROUND DIAGNOSIS SWITCH TERMINAL AND NOTE CODE.

CODE 32

CODE 31

SIGNAL CIRCUIT SHORTED TO VOLTAGE OR FAULTY ECM.

CHECK FOR PLUGGED OR LEAKING SENSOR VACUUM HOSE.

IF VACUUM HOSE OK, OPEN IN SENSOR GROUND CIRCUIT OR FAULTY SENSOR.

CLEAR CODES AND CONFIRM NO "CHECK ENGINE" LIGHT.

Fig. 100 1989-91 EFI diagnostic chart

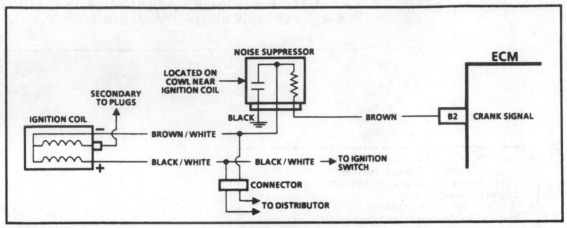

CODE 41

IGNITION SIGNAL CIRCUIT
LSI CONVENTIONAL IGNITION SYSTEM (WITH VACUUM ADVANCE)
1.0L (VIN 6) "M" CARLINE (TBI)

Circuit Description:

The ECM receives a signal from the ignition system, which is used as a reference to indicate to the ECM when the ignition coil fires the plugs. The ECM uses this signal to coordinate when to pulse the fuel injector. If the ECM does not receive this signal for 2 seconds when cranking engine, Code 41 will set. The "Check Engine" light will not be "ON" for this code.

Test Description: Numbers below refer to circled numbers on the diagnostic chart.

1. The Ignition System sends an AC voltage that varies while cranking.
2. This will check ECM and the noise suppressor.
3. This tests the noise suppressor.
4. This checks the pick-up coil in distributor.

Diagnostic Aids:

An intermittent may be caused by a poor connection rubbed through wire insulation or a wire broken inside the insulation. Inspect ECM harness connectors for backed out terminals, improper mating, broken locks, improperly formed or damaged terminals, poor terminal to wire connection and damaged harness.

Fig. 101 1989-91 EFI diagnostic chart

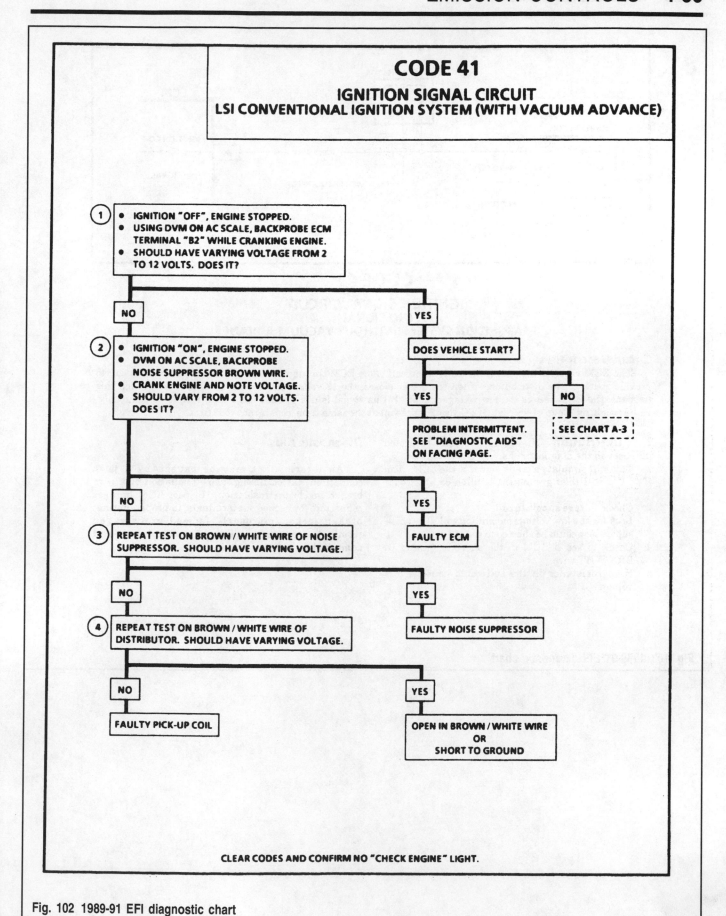

CODE 41
IGNITION SIGNAL CIRCUIT
LSI CONVENTIONAL IGNITION SYSTEM (WITH VACUUM ADVANCE)

1
- IGNITION "OFF", ENGINE STOPPED.
- USING DVM ON AC SCALE, BACKPROBE ECM TERMINAL "B2" WHILE CRANKING ENGINE.
- SHOULD HAVE VARYING VOLTAGE FROM 2 TO 12 VOLTS. DOES IT?

NO

YES

DOES VEHICLE START?

2
- IGNITION "ON", ENGINE STOPPED.
- DVM ON AC SCALE, BACKPROBE NOISE SUPPRESSOR BROWN WIRE.
- CRANK ENGINE AND NOTE VOLTAGE.
- SHOULD VARY FROM 2 TO 12 VOLTS. DOES IT?

YES

NO

PROBLEM INTERMITTENT. SEE "DIAGNOSTIC AIDS" ON FACING PAGE.

SEE CHART A-3

NO

YES

3 REPEAT TEST ON BROWN / WHITE WIRE OF NOISE SUPPRESSOR. SHOULD HAVE VARYING VOLTAGE.

FAULTY ECM

NO

YES

4 REPEAT TEST ON BROWN / WHITE WIRE OF DISTRIBUTOR. SHOULD HAVE VARYING VOLTAGE.

FAULTY NOISE SUPPRESSOR

NO

YES

FAULTY PICK-UP COIL

OPEN IN BROWN / WHITE WIRE
OR
SHORT TO GROUND

CLEAR CODES AND CONFIRM NO "CHECK ENGINE" LIGHT.

Fig. 102 1989-91 EFI diagnostic chart

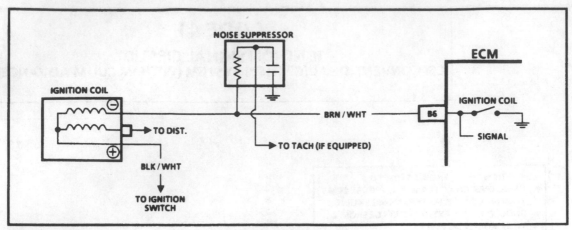

CODE 41

IGNITION SIGNAL CIRCUIT
(NO SIGNAL)
ESA IGNITION SYSTEM (WITHOUT VACUUM ADVANCE)

Circuit Description:

   The ECM receives a signal from the ignition coil. The ECM through the use of a driver, allows the coil to provide spark to the distributor. When the driver closes, the 12 volts from the coil is pulled low. When this happens, the ECM senses the low voltage signal. If this signal is not present more than 6 time continuously, while cranking, Code 41 will set. If a Code 42 is present at the same time, repair that code first.

Test Description: Numbers below refer to circled numbers on the diagnostic chart.
1. This will simulate a crank signal to the ECM. The ECM will then ground the ignition coil to create spark.
2. Check voltage supply to coil.
3. Look for the low voltage on ignition coil. The noise suppressor could be shorted to ground.
4. Check to see if ECM in the short to ground in BRN/WHT wire.
5. High resistance in the coil could cause a low voltage.

Diagnostic Aids:

   An intermittent may be caused by a poor connection rubbed through wire insulation or a wire broken inside the insulation. Inspect ECM harness connectors for backed out terminals, improper mating, broken locks, improperly formed or damaged terminals, poor terminal to wire connection and damaged harness.

Fig. 103 1989-91 EFI diagnostic chart

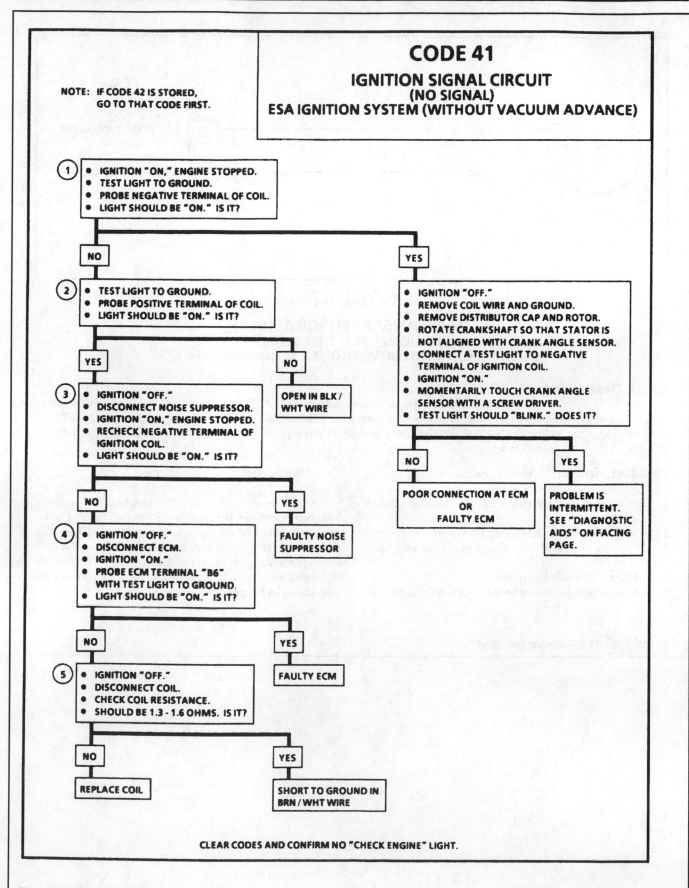

CODE 41

IGNITION SIGNAL CIRCUIT
(NO SIGNAL)
ESA IGNITION SYSTEM (WITHOUT VACUUM ADVANCE)

NOTE: IF CODE 42 IS STORED, GO TO THAT CODE FIRST.

1
- IGNITION "ON," ENGINE STOPPED.
- TEST LIGHT TO GROUND.
- PROBE NEGATIVE TERMINAL OF COIL.
- LIGHT SHOULD BE "ON." IS IT?

NO

YES

2
- TEST LIGHT TO GROUND.
- PROBE POSITIVE TERMINAL OF COIL.
- LIGHT SHOULD BE "ON." IS IT?

YES

NO

OPEN IN BLK / WHT WIRE

IGNITION "OFF." (YES column)
- IGNITION "OFF."
- REMOVE COIL WIRE AND GROUND.
- REMOVE DISTRIBUTOR CAP AND ROTOR.
- ROTATE CRANKSHAFT SO THAT STATOR IS NOT ALIGNED WITH CRANK ANGLE SENSOR.
- CONNECT A TEST LIGHT TO NEGATIVE TERMINAL OF IGNITION COIL.
- IGNITION "ON."
- MOMENTARILY TOUCH CRANK ANGLE SENSOR WITH A SCREW DRIVER.
- TEST LIGHT SHOULD "BLINK." DOES IT?

3
- IGNITION "OFF."
- DISCONNECT NOISE SUPPRESSOR.
- IGNITION "ON," ENGINE STOPPED.
- RECHECK NEGATIVE TERMINAL OF IGNITION COIL.
- LIGHT SHOULD BE "ON." IS IT?

NO

YES

NO

YES

POOR CONNECTION AT ECM OR FAULTY ECM

PROBLEM IS INTERMITTENT. SEE "DIAGNOSTIC AIDS" ON FACING PAGE.

FAULTY NOISE SUPPRESSOR

4
- IGNITION "OFF."
- DISCONNECT ECM.
- IGNITION "ON."
- PROBE ECM TERMINAL "B6" WITH TEST LIGHT TO GROUND.
- LIGHT SHOULD BE "ON." IS IT?

NO

YES

FAULTY ECM

5
- IGNITION "OFF."
- DISCONNECT COIL.
- CHECK COIL RESISTANCE.
- SHOULD BE 1.3 - 1.6 OHMS. IS IT?

NO

YES

REPLACE COIL

SHORT TO GROUND IN BRN / WHT WIRE

CLEAR CODES AND CONFIRM NO "CHECK ENGINE" LIGHT.

Fig. 104 1989-91 EFI diagnostic chart

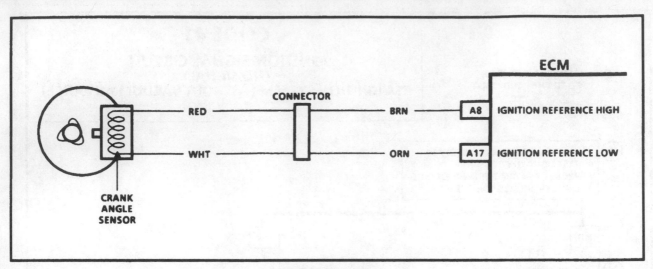

CODE 42

CRANK ANGLE SENSOR CIRCUIT
(NO SIGNAL FOR 2 SECONDS)
ESA IGNITION SYSTEM (WITHOUT VACUUM ADVANCE)

Circuit Description:

The ECM supplies 12 volts to the crank angle sensor at terminal "A8". As the stator inside the distributor passes the crank angle sensor, the 12 volts is pulled low. The ECM uses this signal (at terminal A17) in determining when to fire the the coil and the fuel injector. If this signal is not present during cranking, Code 42 will set. A Code 41 may also set.

Test Description: Numbers below refer to circled numbers on the diagnostic chart.

1. B+ is supplied by the ECM to the distributor module.
2. A short to voltage in BRN or TAN wires.
3. Checking the ECM for voltage on Terminals "A8" or "A17".
4. Looking for short to ground.
5. Improper air gap could be the cause of Code 42.

Diagnostic Aids:

An intermittent may be caused by a poor connection rubbed through wire insulation or a wire broken inside the insulation. Inspect ECM harness connectors for backed out terminals "A8" or "A17", improper mating, broken locks, improperly formed or damaged terminals, poor terminal to wire connection and damaged harness.

Fig. 105 1989-91 EFI diagnostic chart

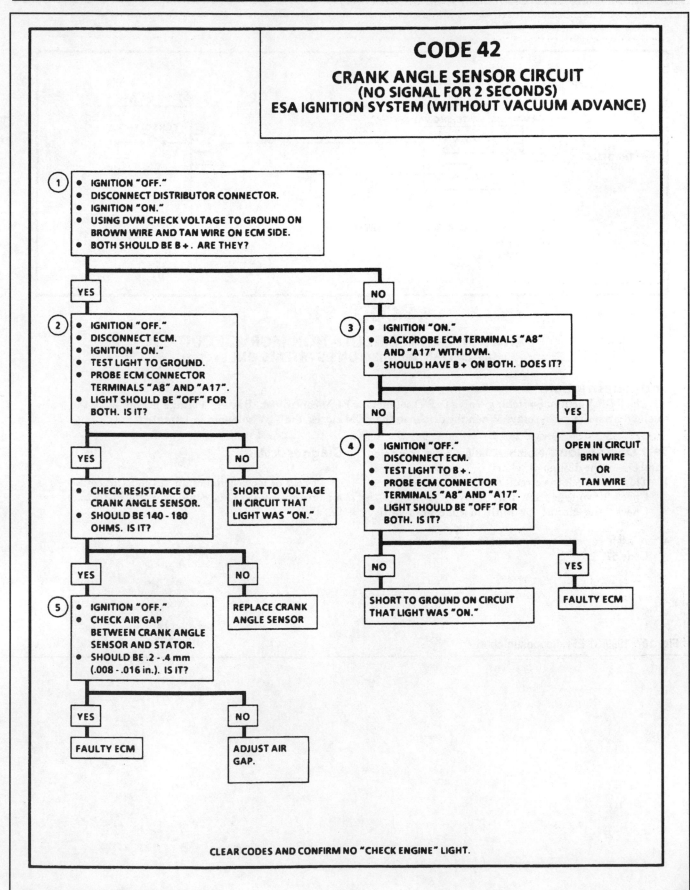

CODE 42

CRANK ANGLE SENSOR CIRCUIT
(NO SIGNAL FOR 2 SECONDS)
ESA IGNITION SYSTEM (WITHOUT VACUUM ADVANCE)

1
- IGNITION "OFF."
- DISCONNECT DISTRIBUTOR CONNECTOR.
- IGNITION "ON."
- USING DVM CHECK VOLTAGE TO GROUND ON BROWN WIRE AND TAN WIRE ON ECM SIDE.
- BOTH SHOULD BE B+. ARE THEY?

YES

2
- IGNITION "OFF."
- DISCONNECT ECM.
- IGNITION "ON."
- TEST LIGHT TO GROUND.
- PROBE ECM CONNECTOR TERMINALS "A8" AND "A17".
- LIGHT SHOULD BE "OFF" FOR BOTH. IS IT?

NO

3
- IGNITION "ON."
- BACKPROBE ECM TERMINALS "A8" AND "A17" WITH DVM.
- SHOULD HAVE B+ ON BOTH. DOES IT?

YES

- CHECK RESISTANCE OF CRANK ANGLE SENSOR.
- SHOULD BE 140 - 180 OHMS. IS IT?

NO

SHORT TO VOLTAGE IN CIRCUIT THAT LIGHT WAS "ON."

NO

4
- IGNITION "OFF."
- DISCONNECT ECM.
- TEST LIGHT TO B+.
- PROBE ECM CONNECTOR TERMINALS "A8" AND "A17".
- LIGHT SHOULD BE "OFF" FOR BOTH. IS IT?

YES

OPEN IN CIRCUIT BRN WIRE OR TAN WIRE

YES

5
- IGNITION "OFF."
- CHECK AIR GAP BETWEEN CRANK ANGLE SENSOR AND STATOR.
- SHOULD BE .2 - .4 mm (.008 - .016 in.). IS IT?

NO

REPLACE CRANK ANGLE SENSOR

NO

SHORT TO GROUND ON CIRCUIT THAT LIGHT WAS "ON."

YES

FAULTY ECM

YES

FAULTY ECM

NO

ADJUST AIR GAP.

CLEAR CODES AND CONFIRM NO "CHECK ENGINE" LIGHT.

Fig. 106 1989-91 EFI diagnostic chart

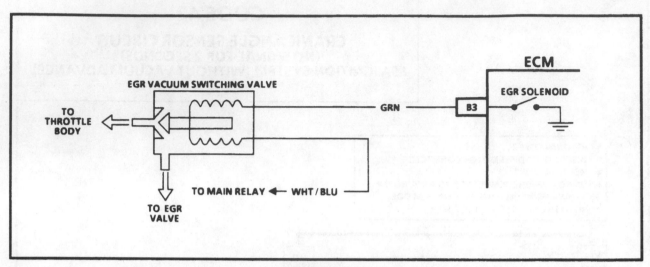

CODE 51

EXHAUST GAS RECIRCULATION (EGR) CIRCUIT
(CALIFORNIA EMISSIONS SYSTEMS ONLY)

Circuit Description:

The EGR Vacuum Switching Valve (VSV) solenoid is ECM controlled. Battery voltage is applied to the VSV solenoid from the main relay. When the driver in the ECM closes, the VSV solenoid is activated.

Test Description: Numbers below refer to circled numbers on the diagnostic chart.

1. This will check the circuit for a short to ground.
2. Check for voltage from main relay.
3. Checks the circuit for fault of code or a faulty ECM.
4. A high resistance in solenoid coil could cause a Code 51.

Diagnostic Aids:

A poor or loose connection at the ECM could cause an Intermittent. This could cause a code to be set falsely.

Fig. 107 1989-91 EFI diagnostic chart

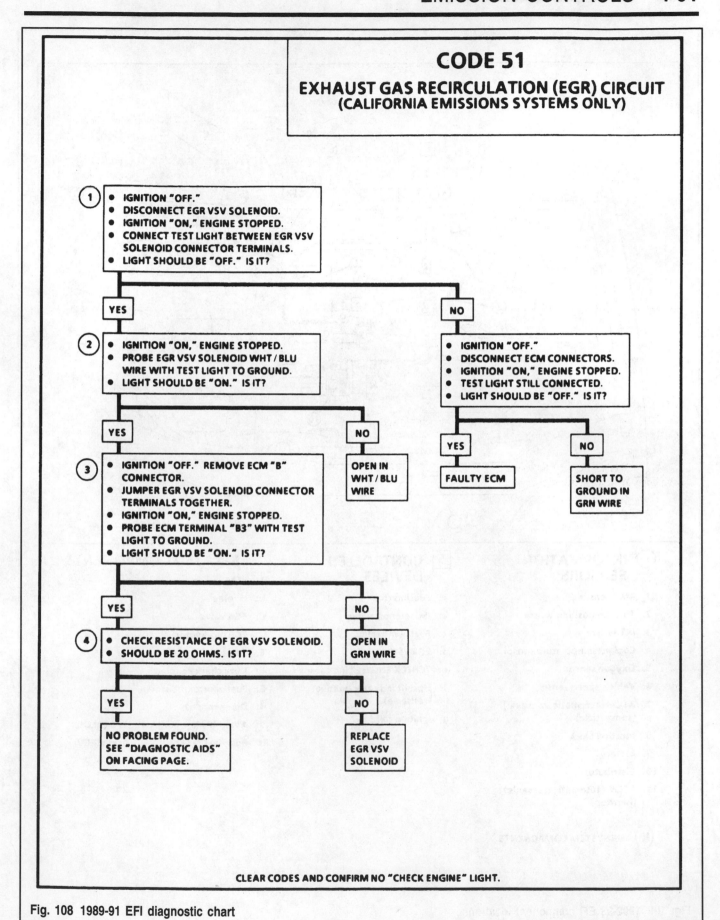

CODE 51
EXHAUST GAS RECIRCULATION (EGR) CIRCUIT
(CALIFORNIA EMISSIONS SYSTEMS ONLY)

1
- IGNITION "OFF."
- DISCONNECT EGR VSV SOLENOID.
- IGNITION "ON," ENGINE STOPPED.
- CONNECT TEST LIGHT BETWEEN EGR VSV SOLENOID CONNECTOR TERMINALS.
- LIGHT SHOULD BE "OFF." IS IT?

YES

NO

2
- IGNITION "ON," ENGINE STOPPED.
- PROBE EGR VSV SOLENOID WHT / BLU WIRE WITH TEST LIGHT TO GROUND.
- LIGHT SHOULD BE "ON." IS IT?

- IGNITION "OFF."
- DISCONNECT ECM CONNECTORS.
- IGNITION "ON," ENGINE STOPPED.
- TEST LIGHT STILL CONNECTED.
- LIGHT SHOULD BE "OFF." IS IT?

YES

NO

YES

NO

3
- IGNITION "OFF." REMOVE ECM "B" CONNECTOR.
- JUMPER EGR VSV SOLENOID CONNECTOR TERMINALS TOGETHER.
- IGNITION "ON," ENGINE STOPPED.
- PROBE ECM TERMINAL "B3" WITH TEST LIGHT TO GROUND.
- LIGHT SHOULD BE "ON." IS IT?

OPEN IN WHT / BLU WIRE

FAULTY ECM

SHORT TO GROUND IN GRN WIRE

YES

NO

4
- CHECK RESISTANCE OF EGR VSV SOLENOID.
- SHOULD BE 20 OHMS. IS IT?

OPEN IN GRN WIRE

YES

NO

NO PROBLEM FOUND. SEE "DIAGNOSTIC AIDS" ON FACING PAGE.

REPLACE EGR VSV SOLENOID

CLEAR CODES AND CONFIRM NO "CHECK ENGINE" LIGHT.

Fig. 108 1989-91 EFI diagnostic chart

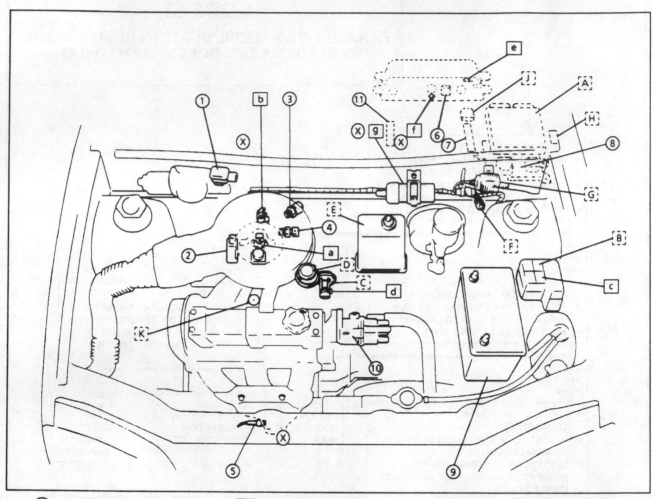

○ INFORMATION SENSORS

1. MAP sensor
2. Throttle position sensor
3. IAT sensor
4. Coolant temperature sensor
5. Oxygen sensor
6. Vehicle speed sensor
7. ATCM (automatic transaxle) (convertible)
8. Junction block
9. Battery
10. Distributor
11. ATCM (automatic transaxle) (hardtop)

Ⓧ SIR SYSTEM COMPONENTS

☐ CONTROLLED DEVICES

a: Fuel injector
b: ISC solenoid valve
c: Fuel pump relay
d: EGR VSV
e: "CHECK ENGINE" indicator
f: Upshift indicator (manual transaxle)
g: Ignition coil

⌐⌐ RELATED COMPONENTS

A: ECM
B: FI relay
C: EGR valve
D: EGR modulator
E: Canister
F: Duty check coupler
G: Fuel injector resistor
H: Diode module
J: Assembly line diagnostic link (ALDL)
K: Positive Crankcase Ventilation (PCV)

Fig. 109 1992-93 EFI component locations

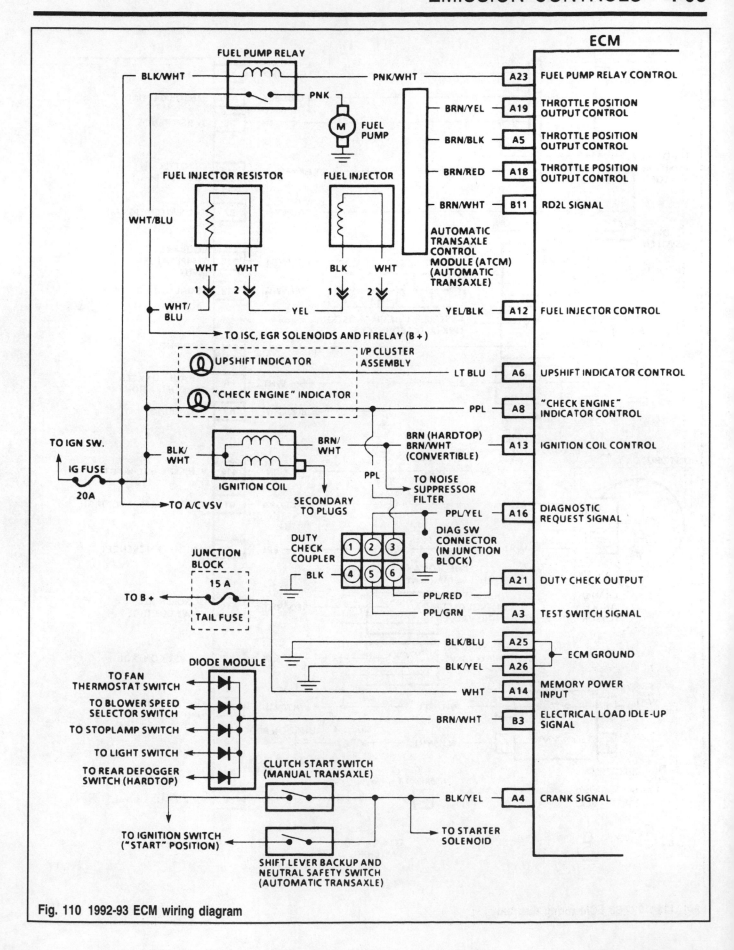

Fig. 110 1992-93 ECM wiring diagram

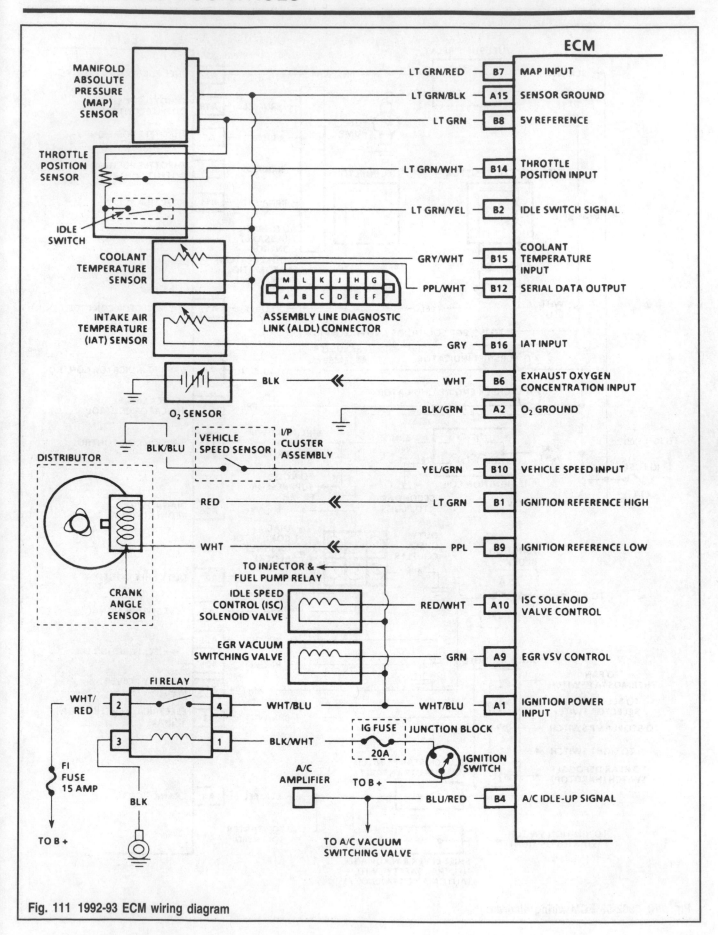

Fig. 111 1992-93 ECM wiring diagram

FUEL INJECTION ECM CONNECTOR IDENTIFICATION

The following ECM voltage charts are for use with a digital voltmeter to further aid in diagnosis. The voltages you get may vary due to low battery charge or other reasons, but they should be very close.

THE FOLLOWING CONDITIONS MUST BE MET BEFORE TESTING:

- Engine at operating temperature   • Engine idling (for "Engine Run" column)
- Test terminal not grounded (except where noted)
- All voltages shown "B +" indicate battery or charging voltage

A13	A12	A11	A10	A9	A8	A7	A6	A5	A4	A3	A2	A1
A26	A25	A24	A23	A22	A21	A20	A19	A18	A17	A16	A15	A14

B8	B7	B6	B5	B4	B3	B2	B1
B16	B15	B14	B13	B12	B11	B10	B9

BACKVIEW OF ECM CONNECTOR C1

PIN	WIRE COLOR	CIRCUIT	VOLTAGE KEY "ON"	VOLTAGE ENG. RUN
A1	WHT/BLU	IGNITION POWER INPUT	B +	B +
A2	BLK/GRN	O₂ GROUND	0*	0*
A3	PPL/GRN	TEST SWITCH SIGNAL	B +	B +
A4	BLK/YEL	CRANK SIGNAL	0* (8)	0*
A5	BRN/BLK	THROTTLE POSITION OUTPUT CONTROL (AUTOMATIC TRANSAXLE)	0-10V (9)	0-10V (9)
A6	LT BLU	UPSHIFT INDICATOR CONTROL (MANUAL TRANSAXLE)	(11)	B +
A7	—	NOT USED	—	—
A8	PPL	"CHECK ENGINE" INDICATOR CONTROL	1-2V	B +
A9	GRN	EGR VSV CONTROL	B +	B +
A10	RED/WHT	ISC SOLENOID VALVE CONTROL	1-1.5V	B +
A11	—	NOT USED	—	—
A12	YEL/BLK	FUEL INJECTOR CONTROL	B +	B +
A13	BRN (HARDTOP) BRN/WHT (CONVERTIBLE)	IGNITION COIL CONTROL	B +	B +
A14	WHT	MEMORY POWER INPUT	B +	B +
A15	LT GRN/BLK	SENSOR GROUND	0*	0*
A16	PPL/YEL	DIAGNOSTIC REQUEST SIGNAL	B +	B +
A17	—	NOT USED	—	—
A18	BRN/RED	THROTTLE POSITION OUTPUT CONTROL (AUTOMATIC TRANSAXLE)	0-10V (9)	0-10V (9)
A19	BRN/YEL	THROTTLE POSITION OUTPUT CONTROL (AUTOMATIC TRANSAXLE)	0-10V (9)	0-10V (9)
A20	—	NOT USED	—	—
A21	PPL/RED	DUTY CHECK OUTPUT	0*	0*
A22	—	NOT USED	—	—
A23	PNK/WHT	FUEL PUMP RELAY CONTROL	(3)	0*
A24	—	NOT USED	—	—
A25	BLK/BLU	ECM GROUND	0*	0*
A26	BLK/YEL	ECM GROUND	0*	0*

BACKVIEW OF ECM CONNECTOR C2

PIN	WIRE COLOR	CIRCUIT	VOLTAGE KEY "ON"	VOLTAGE ENG. RUN
B1	LT GRN	IGN REFERENCE HIGH	.4-.8V	.4-.8V
B2	LT GRN/YEL	IDLE SWITCH SIGNAL	(5)	(5)
B3	BRN/WHT	ELECTRICAL LOAD IDLE-UP SIGNAL	(7)	(7)
B4	BLU/RED	A/C IDLE-UP SIGNAL	(4)	(4)
B5	—	NOT USED	—	—
B6	WHT	EXHAUST OXYGEN CONCENTRATION INPUT	0*	.45-1V
B7	LT GRN/RED	MAP INPUT	3-4V	1-2V
B8	LT GRN	REFERENCE VOLTAGE (5V)	4-5V	4-5V
B9	PPL	IGNITION REFERENCE LOW	.4-.8V	.4-.8V
B10	YEL/GRN	VEHICLE SPEED INPUT	0-12V (1)	0-12V (1)
B11	BRN/WHT	RD2L SIGNAL (AUTOMATIC TRANSAXLE)	0-12V (2)	0-12V (2)
B12	PPL/WHT	SERIAL DATA OUTPUT	4-5V	4-5V
B13	—	NOT USED	—	—
B14	LT GRN/WHT	THROTTLE POSITION INPUT	.3-.6V (9)	.3-.6V (9)
B15	GRY/WHT	COOLANT TEMPERATURE INPUT	.4-.6V (6)	.4-.6V (6)
B16	GRY	IAT INPUT	1-3V (10)	1-3V (10)

(7) B + with light switch "ON" or with rear defogger "ON" or with blower motor "ON" or with radiator fan "ON" or with stoplamps "ON"

(8) Voltage present only during cranking.

(9) Varies with throttle position

(10) Varies with ambient temperature

(11) 1-2 volts with light switch "OFF" and 3-5 volts with light switch "ON"

0* Less than .5 volts.

(1) Varies as front wheels rotate

(2) 0 in "P" or "N", B + otherwise

(3) B + for first 2 seconds.

(4) B + with A/C switch "OFF" and 0V with A/C switch "ON"

(5) 0 volts at idle, B + otherwise

(6) Varies with engine temperature

Fig. 112 1992-93 ECM terminal identification

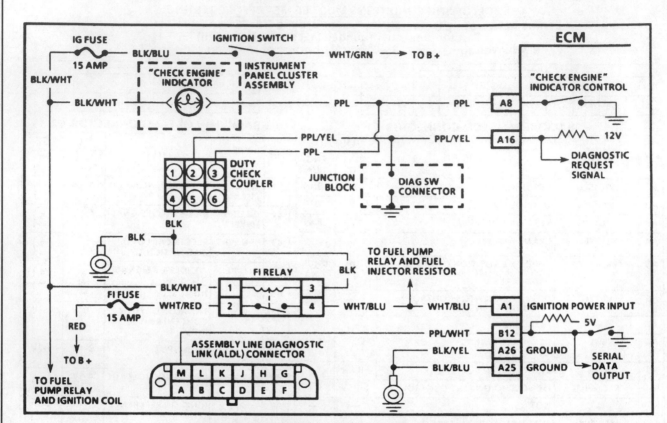

DIAGNOSTIC CIRCUIT CHECK

Circuit Description:

The Diagnostic Circuit Check is an organized approach to identifying a problem created by an electronic engine control system malfunction. It must be the starting point for any driveability complaint diagnosis, because it directs the service technician to the next logical step in diagnosing the complaint. Understanding the chart and using it correctly will reduce diagnostic time and prevent the unnecessary replacement of good parts.

Test Description: Number(s) below refer to circled number(s) on the diagnostic chart.

1. Checks the "CHECK ENGINE" indicator operation.
2. Checks to see if the ECM's self-diagnostic mode is operating.
3. Checks to see if the ECM's serial data output is operating.
4. Checks to see if vehicle will start.
5. Checks for any codes that are stored in the ECM's memory with the engine running.
6. Checks for any codes that are stored in the ECM's memory with the engine off.
7. Compares ECM's control data to typical data values.
8. Checks to see if codes are intermittent problems.

Fig. 113 1992-93 EFI diagnostic chart

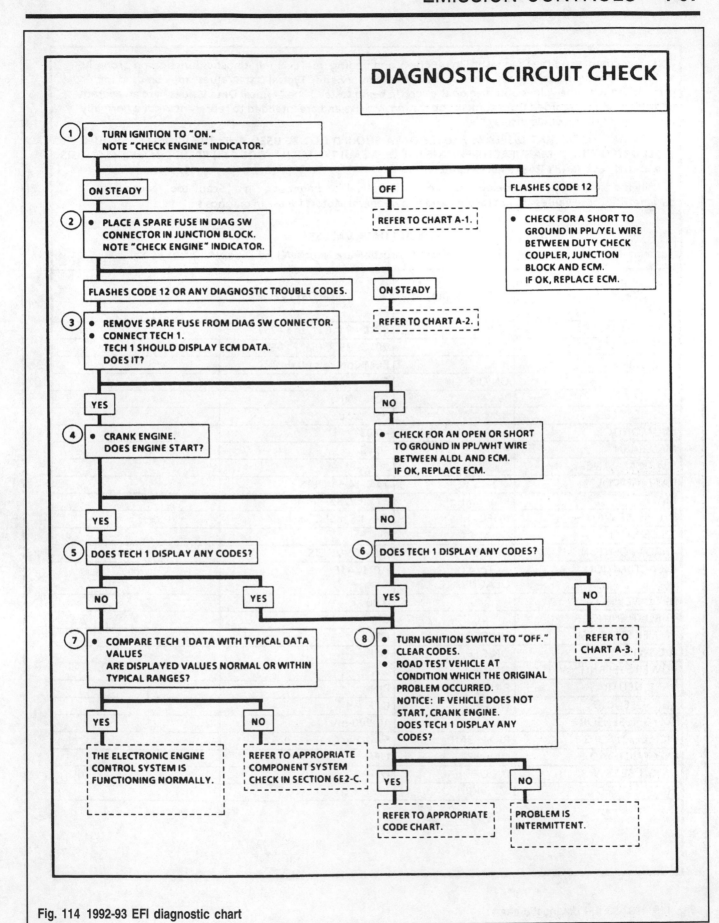

Fig. 114 1992-93 EFI diagnostic chart

If after completing the Diagnostic Circuit Check and finding the TECH 1 diagnostics functioning properly, and no diagnostic trouble codes stored in the ECM's memory, the "Typical Data Values" may be used for comparison with the values obtained on the vehicle being tested. The "Typical Data Values" are an average of display values recorded from normally operating vehicles and are intended to represent what a normally functioning system would display.

A "SCAN" TOOL THAT DISPLAYS FAULTY DATA SHOULD NOT BE USED AND THE PROBLEM SHOULD BE REPORTED TO THE MANUFACTURER. THE USE OF A FAULTY "SCAN" TOOL CAN RESULT IN MISDIAGNOSIS AND UNNECESSARY PARTS REPLACEMENT.

Only the parameters listed below are used in this manual for diagnosing . If a "Scan" tool reads other parameters, those values are not recommended by General Motors for use in diagnosis.

TECH 1 DATA VALUES

Idle/Upper Radiator Hose Hot/Closed Throttle/Park/Neutral/Closed Loop/Accessories off

"Scan" Position	Units Displayed	Typical Data Value	
COOLANT TEMP	°C/°F	80° C - 94° C (176° F - 201° F)	
INTAKE AIR TEMP	°C/°F	20° C - 35° C (68° F - 95° F)	
DESIRED IDLE	RPM	ECM Controls (varies)	
IDLE SWITCH	ON/OFF	ON	
ISC DUTY	%	10% - 50%	
ENGINE SPEED	RPM	850 ± 50	
M/C MONITOR	–	–0.03	
M/C LEARN	–	–0.03	
SPARK ADVANCE	°	20° - 28°	
BATT/IGN VOLTS	VOLTS	14.0-14.5 VOLTS	
MAP	kPa/mmHg	37 kPa/282 mmHg	
INJ. PULSE WIDTH	mSEC	1.0 - 1.7 mSEC	
IDLE SWITCH	ON/OFF	ON	
THROT POSITION	VOLTS	.45 - .65 VOLTS	
OX ACTIVATION	ACTIVATE/ DEACTIVATE	ACTIVATE	
M/C DWELL	–	0.00	
THROTTLE ANGLE	°	0°	
POWER STEER VSV	ON/OFF	OFF	
A/C SWITCH	ON/OFF	OFF	
POWER STEERNG SW	ON/OFF	OFF	
PARK/NEUTRAL	P-N/-R-DL	P-N	
EGR SOLENOID	ON/OFF	OFF	
OXYGEN SENSOR	mV	10-900-mV	
RICH/LEAN FLAG	RICH/LEAN	Switches	
ELECTRIC LOAD	ON/OFF	OFF	
INITIAL SET SW	ON/OFF	OFF	
ENGINE SPEED	MPH/KPH	0 MPH 0 KPH	

Fig. 115 1992-93 EFI diagnostic chart

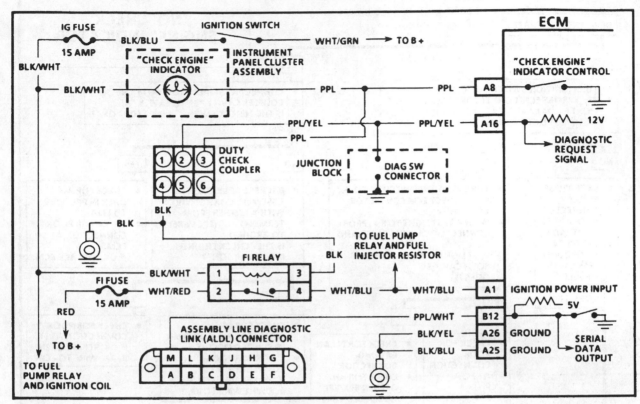

CHART A-1
NO "CHECK ENGINE" INDICATOR

Circuit Description:

There should always be a steady "CHECK ENGINE" indicator when the ignition switch is in the "ON" position and the engine is not running. Battery voltage is applied to the indicator bulb. The ECM will control the indicator and turn it "ON" by providing a ground path through the PPL wire to the ECM.

Test Description: Number(s) below refer to circled number(s) on the diagnostic chart.

1. Checks to see if ECM is receiving power.
2. Checks to see if ECM is faulty.
3. Checks for an open in WHT/BLU wire between FI relay and ECM.
4. Checks to see if ECM has a good ground.
5. Checks for an open in BLK/WHT wire to I/P and PPL wire to ECM.
6. Checks to see if FI relay switch is receiving power.
7. Checks to see if FI relay coil is receiving power.
8. Checks to see if FI relay or ECM is faulty, or an open in BLK wire between FI relay and ground.

Diagnostic Aids:

Be sure to check connectors for contamination, corrosion or bent terminals.

Fig. 116 1992-93 EFI diagnostic chart

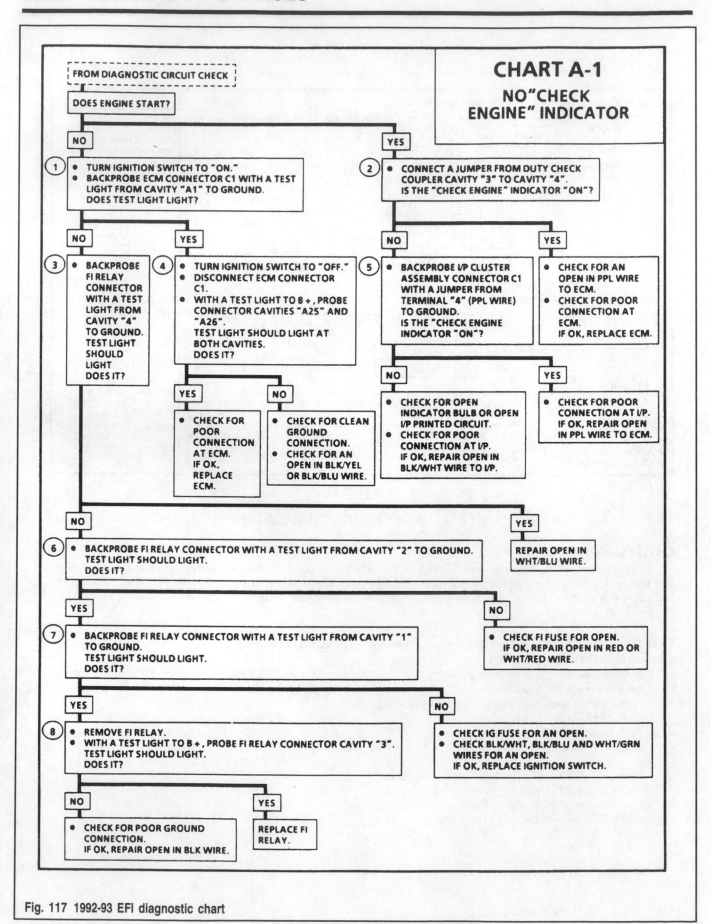

CHART A-1

NO "CHECK ENGINE" INDICATOR

FROM DIAGNOSTIC CIRCUIT CHECK

DOES ENGINE START?

NO

1.
• TURN IGNITION SWITCH TO "ON."
• BACKPROBE ECM CONNECTOR C1 WITH A TEST LIGHT FROM CAVITY "A1" TO GROUND. DOES TEST LIGHT LIGHT?

NO

3.
• BACKPROBE FI RELAY CONNECTOR WITH A TEST LIGHT FROM CAVITY "4" TO GROUND. TEST LIGHT SHOULD LIGHT DOES IT?

YES

4.
• TURN IGNITION SWITCH TO "OFF."
• DISCONNECT ECM CONNECTOR C1.
• WITH A TEST LIGHT TO B + , PROBE CONNECTOR CAVITIES "A25" AND "A26". TEST LIGHT SHOULD LIGHT AT BOTH CAVITIES. DOES IT?

YES
• CHECK FOR POOR CONNECTION AT ECM. IF OK, REPLACE ECM.

NO
• CHECK FOR CLEAN GROUND CONNECTION.
• CHECK FOR AN OPEN IN BLK/YEL OR BLK/BLU WIRE.

YES

2.
• CONNECT A JUMPER FROM DUTY CHECK COUPLER CAVITY "3" TO CAVITY "4". IS THE "CHECK ENGINE" INDICATOR "ON"?

NO

5.
• BACKPROBE I/P CLUSTER ASSEMBLY CONNECTOR C1 WITH A JUMPER FROM TERMINAL "4" (PPL WIRE) TO GROUND. IS THE "CHECK ENGINE INDICATOR "ON"?

NO
• CHECK FOR OPEN INDICATOR BULB OR OPEN I/P PRINTED CIRCUIT.
• CHECK FOR POOR CONNECTION AT I/P. IF OK, REPAIR OPEN IN BLK/WHT WIRE TO I/P.

YES
• CHECK FOR POOR CONNECTION AT I/P. IF OK, REPAIR OPEN IN PPL WIRE TO ECM.

YES
• CHECK FOR AN OPEN IN PPL WIRE TO ECM.
• CHECK FOR POOR CONNECTION AT ECM. IF OK, REPLACE ECM.

NO

6.
• BACKPROBE FI RELAY CONNECTOR WITH A TEST LIGHT FROM CAVITY "2" TO GROUND. TEST LIGHT SHOULD LIGHT. DOES IT?

YES
REPAIR OPEN IN WHT/BLU WIRE.

YES

7.
• BACKPROBE FI RELAY CONNECTOR WITH A TEST LIGHT FROM CAVITY "1" TO GROUND. TEST LIGHT SHOULD LIGHT. DOES IT?

NO
• CHECK FI FUSE FOR OPEN. IF OK, REPAIR OPEN IN RED OR WHT/RED WIRE.

YES

8.
• REMOVE FI RELAY.
• WITH A TEST LIGHT TO B + , PROBE FI RELAY CONNECTOR CAVITY "3". TEST LIGHT SHOULD LIGHT. DOES IT?

NO
• CHECK IG FUSE FOR AN OPEN.
• CHECK BLK/WHT, BLK/BLU AND WHT/GRN WIRES FOR AN OPEN. IF OK, REPLACE IGNITION SWITCH.

NO
• CHECK FOR POOR GROUND CONNECTION. IF OK, REPAIR OPEN IN BLK WIRE.

YES
REPLACE FI RELAY.

Fig. 117 1992-93 EFI diagnostic chart

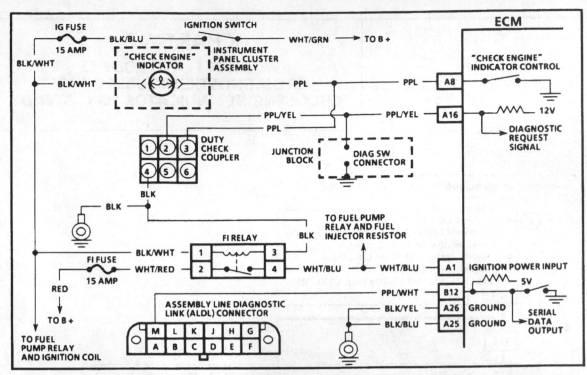

CHART A-2

WILL NOT FLASH CODE 12 OR
DIAGNOSTIC TROUBLE CODES
"CHECK ENGINE" INDICATOR "ON" STEADY

Circuit Description:

The "CHECK ENGINE" indicator will flash diagnostic trouble codes when either the diagnostic request terminal in the duty check coupler or the DIAG SW connector in the junction block is grounded.

Test Description: Number(s) below refer to circled number(s) on the diagnostic chart.

1. This will check for a grounded indicator circuit.
2. This will determine if it is an open diagnostic request terminal circuit or a faulty ECM.

Fig. 118 1992-93 EFI diagnostic chart

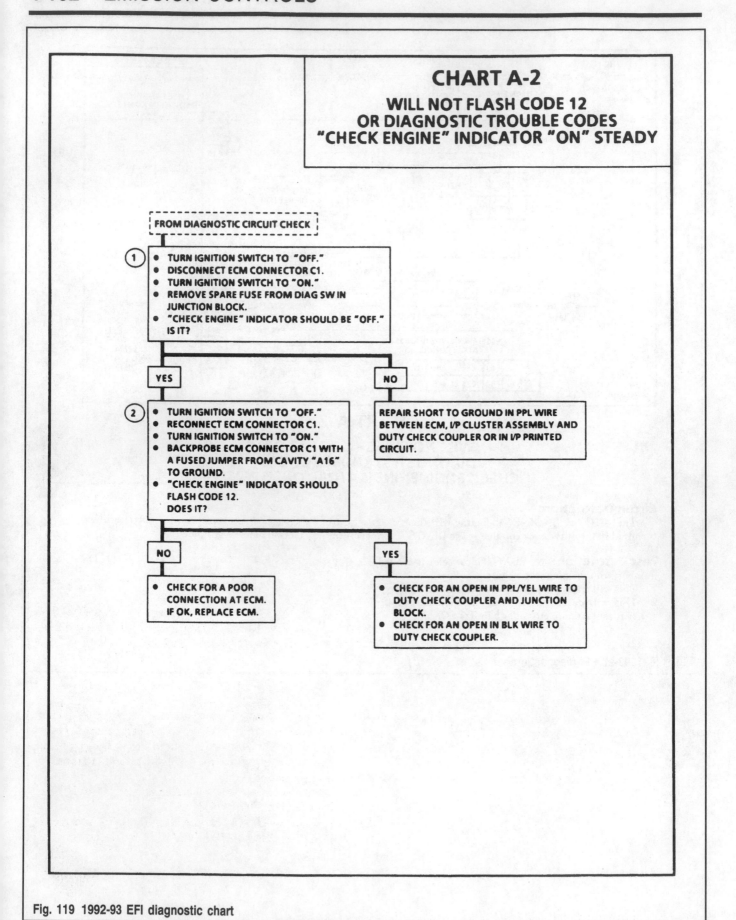

CHART A-2

WILL NOT FLASH CODE 12
OR DIAGNOSTIC TROUBLE CODES
"CHECK ENGINE" INDICATOR "ON" STEADY

FROM DIAGNOSTIC CIRCUIT CHECK

1
- TURN IGNITION SWITCH TO "OFF."
- DISCONNECT ECM CONNECTOR C1.
- TURN IGNITION SWITCH TO "ON."
- REMOVE SPARE FUSE FROM DIAG SW IN JUNCTION BLOCK.
- "CHECK ENGINE" INDICATOR SHOULD BE "OFF." IS IT?

YES

NO

2
- TURN IGNITION SWITCH TO "OFF."
- RECONNECT ECM CONNECTOR C1.
- TURN IGNITION SWITCH TO "ON."
- BACKPROBE ECM CONNECTOR C1 WITH A FUSED JUMPER FROM CAVITY "A16" TO GROUND.
- "CHECK ENGINE" INDICATOR SHOULD FLASH CODE 12. DOES IT?

REPAIR SHORT TO GROUND IN PPL WIRE BETWEEN ECM, I/P CLUSTER ASSEMBLY AND DUTY CHECK COUPLER OR IN I/P PRINTED CIRCUIT.

NO

YES

- CHECK FOR A POOR CONNECTION AT ECM. IF OK, REPLACE ECM.

- CHECK FOR AN OPEN IN PPL/YEL WIRE TO DUTY CHECK COUPLER AND JUNCTION BLOCK.
- CHECK FOR AN OPEN IN BLK WIRE TO DUTY CHECK COUPLER.

Fig. 119 1992-93 EFI diagnostic chart

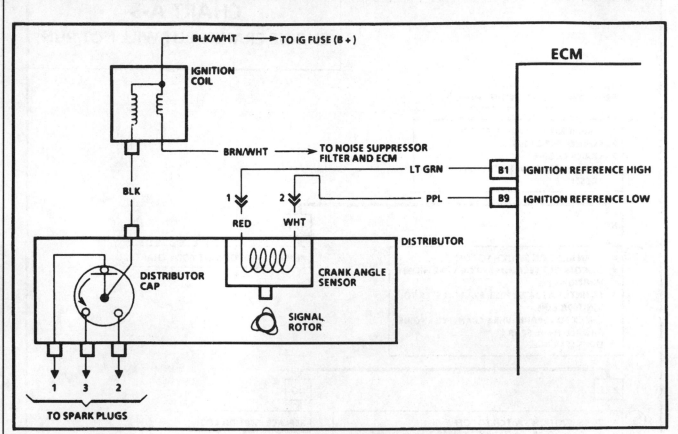

CHART A-3

ENGINE CRANKS BUT WILL NOT RUN

Circuit Description:

Before using this chart, battery condition, engine cranking speed and fuel quantity should be checked and verified as being OK.

When the ignition switch is turned to the "ON" or "START" positions, battery voltage is applied to the ignition coil. If the ignition coil's primary coil is being toggled to ground by the ECM, a high voltage is induced in the secondary windings of the ignition coil and is applied through the distributor to the spark plugs.

Test Description: Number(s) below refer to circled number(s) on the diagnostic chart.

1. Checks to see if any diagnostic trouble codes are stored in ECM's memory.
2. Checks for spark at ignition coil.
3. Checks for spark at distributor.
4. Checks for spark at spark plugs.

Diagnostic Aids:

- Water or foreign material can cause a no start during freezing weather. The engine may start after 5 or 6 minutes in a heated shop. The problem may not recur until an overnight park in freezing temperatures.
- Fuel Pressure: Low fuel pressure can result in a very lean air/fuel ratio.
- Fouled or damaged spark plugs will cause a "Engine Cranks But Will Not Run" condition.

Fig. 120 1992-93 EFI diagnostic chart

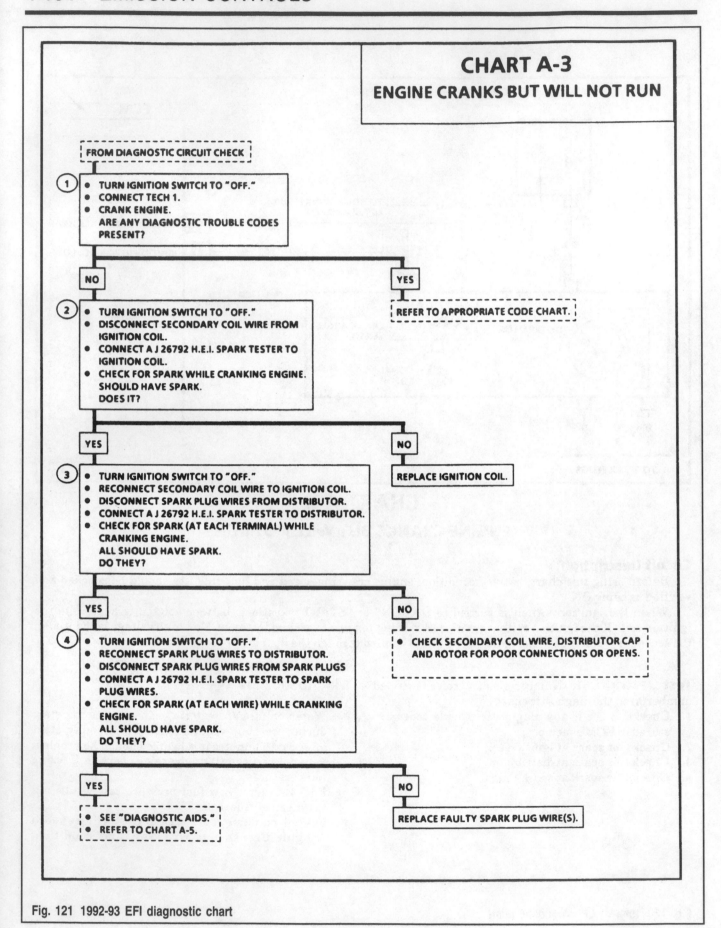

Fig. 121 1992-93 EFI diagnostic chart

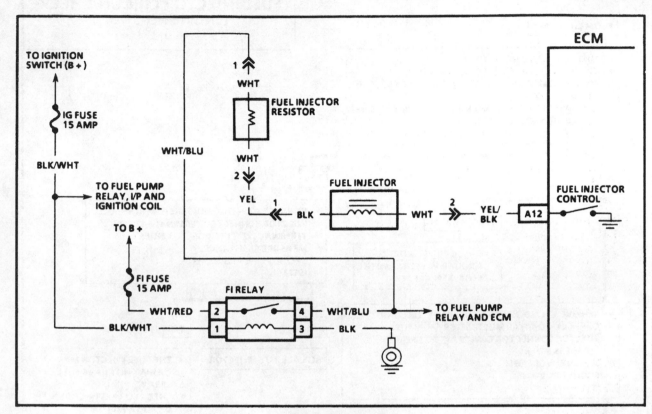

CHART A-5

FUEL INJECTOR CIRCUIT CHECK
(ENGINE NO-START)
1.0L (VIN 6) "M" CARLINE

Circuit Description:

When the solenoid coil of the fuel injector is energized by the engine control module (ECM), it will activate the plunger and pressurized fuel will be injected into the throttle body. The fuel pump will operate as long as the engine is cranking, and the ECM is receiving ignition reference pulses.

Test Description: Number(s) below refer to circled number(s) on the diagnostic chart.

1. Check to see if the ECM is controlling the fuel injector signals.
2. Checks the fuel injector for correct resistance.
3. Checks for voltage at fuel injector.
4. Checks for an open or short to ground in YEL/BLK wire, a faulty ECM or a faulty fuel injector.
5. Checks for an open or short to ground in YEL wire, and open in WHT/BLU wire or a faulty fuel injector resistor.

Diagnostic Aids:

- There may be fuel spray at the fuel injector, but it may not be enough to start the engine. If both the fuel injector and the circuit are OK, the fuel injector nozzle may be partly blocked.

Fig. 122 1989-91 EFI diagnostic chart

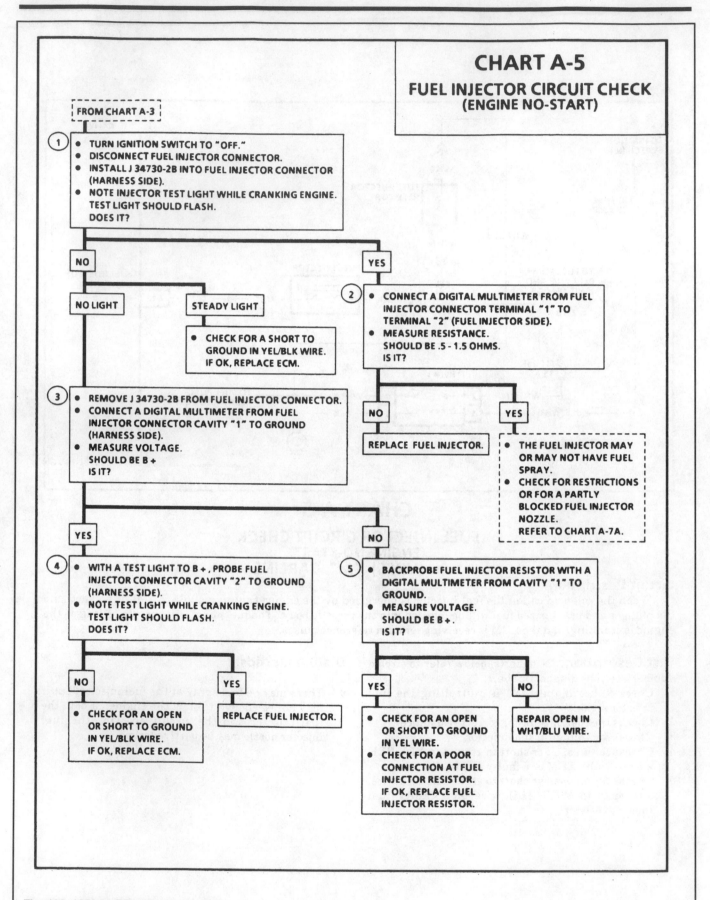

CHART A-5
FUEL INJECTOR CIRCUIT CHECK
(ENGINE NO-START)

FROM CHART A-3

1
- TURN IGNITION SWITCH TO "OFF."
- DISCONNECT FUEL INJECTOR CONNECTOR.
- INSTALL J 34730-2B INTO FUEL INJECTOR CONNECTOR (HARNESS SIDE).
- NOTE INJECTOR TEST LIGHT WHILE CRANKING ENGINE. TEST LIGHT SHOULD FLASH. DOES IT?

NO

YES

NO LIGHT

STEADY LIGHT

- CHECK FOR A SHORT TO GROUND IN YEL/BLK WIRE. IF OK, REPLACE ECM.

2
- CONNECT A DIGITAL MULTIMETER FROM FUEL INJECTOR CONNECTOR TERMINAL "1" TO TERMINAL "2" (FUEL INJECTOR SIDE).
- MEASURE RESISTANCE. SHOULD BE .5 - 1.5 OHMS. IS IT?

3
- REMOVE J 34730-2B FROM FUEL INJECTOR CONNECTOR.
- CONNECT A DIGITAL MULTIMETER FROM FUEL INJECTOR CONNECTOR CAVITY "1" TO GROUND (HARNESS SIDE).
- MEASURE VOLTAGE. SHOULD BE B + IS IT?

NO

YES

REPLACE FUEL INJECTOR.

- THE FUEL INJECTOR MAY OR MAY NOT HAVE FUEL SPRAY.
- CHECK FOR RESTRICTIONS OR FOR A PARTLY BLOCKED FUEL INJECTOR NOZZLE. REFER TO CHART A-7A.

YES

NO

4
- WITH A TEST LIGHT TO B + , PROBE FUEL INJECTOR CONNECTOR CAVITY "2" TO GROUND (HARNESS SIDE).
- NOTE TEST LIGHT WHILE CRANKING ENGINE. TEST LIGHT SHOULD FLASH. DOES IT?

5
- BACKPROBE FUEL INJECTOR RESISTOR WITH A DIGITAL MULTIMETER FROM CAVITY "1" TO GROUND.
- MEASURE VOLTAGE. SHOULD BE B + . IS IT?

NO

YES

YES

NO

- CHECK FOR AN OPEN OR SHORT TO GROUND IN YEL/BLK WIRE. IF OK, REPLACE ECM.

REPLACE FUEL INJECTOR.

- CHECK FOR AN OPEN OR SHORT TO GROUND IN YEL WIRE.
- CHECK FOR A POOR CONNECTION AT FUEL INJECTOR RESISTOR. IF OK, REPLACE FUEL INJECTOR RESISTOR.

REPAIR OPEN IN WHT/BLU WIRE.

Fig. 123 1989-91 EFI diagnostic chart

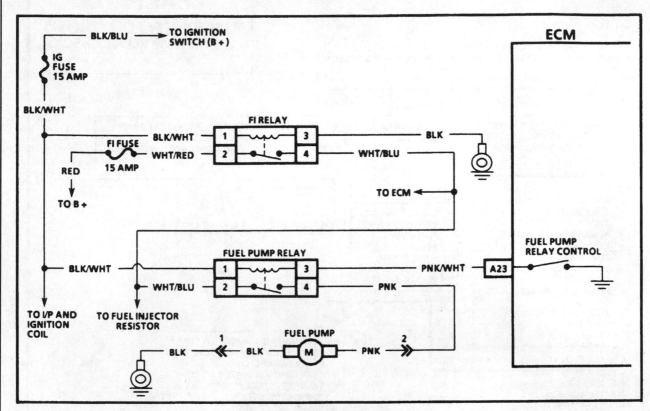

CHART A-7A

FUEL SYSTEM DIAGNOSIS
(FUEL PUMP RELAY CHECK)
1.0L (VIN 6) "M" CARLINE

Circuit Description:

When the ignition switch is turned to the "ON" position, the engine control module (ECM) will energize the fuel pump relay for 3 seconds, allowing for fuel pump operation. When the fuel pump relay is de-energized, the fuel pump stops operating. If the engine is being cranked, or is running, the fuel pump will continue to operate, as long as the ECM is receiving ignition reference pulses. If the ignition reference pulses are not detected, the fuel pump will stop after 3 seconds.

Test Description: Number(s) below refer to circled number(s) on the diagnostic chart.

1. Checks fuel pump operation with ignition switch in the "ON" position.
2. Checks fuel pump relay switch for power.
3. Checks for faulty ECM or improper fuel pressure.
4. Checks fuel pump circuit.
5. Checks for an open PNK wire.
6. Checks fuel pump relay coil for power.
7. Checks for faulty fuel pump or an open BLK wire.
8. Checks for faulty fuel pump relay.
9. Checks for faulty ECM or an open PNK/WHT wire.

Diagnostic Aids:

Visual inspection of wiring and connectors should be made if an intermittent problem exists.

Fig. 124 1992-93 EFI diagnostic chart

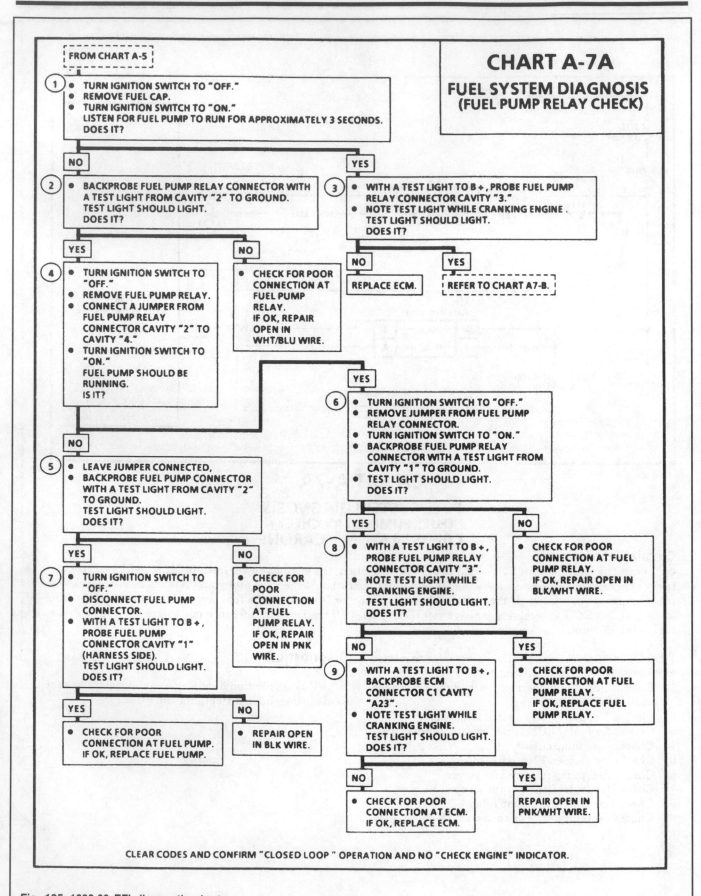

CHART A-7A

FUEL SYSTEM DIAGNOSIS
(FUEL PUMP RELAY CHECK)

FROM CHART A-5

1
- TURN IGNITION SWITCH TO "OFF."
- REMOVE FUEL CAP.
- TURN IGNITION SWITCH TO "ON."
  LISTEN FOR FUEL PUMP TO RUN FOR APPROXIMATELY 3 SECONDS.
  DOES IT?

NO | YES

2
- BACKPROBE FUEL PUMP RELAY CONNECTOR WITH A TEST LIGHT FROM CAVITY "2" TO GROUND.
  TEST LIGHT SHOULD LIGHT.
  DOES IT?

3
- WITH A TEST LIGHT TO B +, PROBE FUEL PUMP RELAY CONNECTOR CAVITY "3."
- NOTE TEST LIGHT WHILE CRANKING ENGINE .
  TEST LIGHT SHOULD LIGHT.
  DOES IT?

YES | NO

NO | YES

REPLACE ECM. | REFER TO CHART A7-B.

4
- TURN IGNITION SWITCH TO "OFF."
- REMOVE FUEL PUMP RELAY.
- CONNECT A JUMPER FROM FUEL PUMP RELAY CONNECTOR CAVITY "2" TO CAVITY "4."
- TURN IGNITION SWITCH TO "ON."
  FUEL PUMP SHOULD BE RUNNING.
  IS IT?

- CHECK FOR POOR CONNECTION AT FUEL PUMP RELAY.
  IF OK, REPAIR OPEN IN WHT/BLU WIRE.

YES

6
- TURN IGNITION SWITCH TO "OFF."
- REMOVE JUMPER FROM FUEL PUMP RELAY CONNECTOR.
- TURN IGNITION SWITCH TO "ON."
- BACKPROBE FUEL PUMP RELAY CONNECTOR WITH A TEST LIGHT FROM CAVITY "1" TO GROUND.
- TEST LIGHT SHOULD LIGHT.
  DOES IT?

NO

5
- LEAVE JUMPER CONNECTED,
- BACKPROBE FUEL PUMP CONNECTOR WITH A TEST LIGHT FROM CAVITY "2" TO GROUND.
  TEST LIGHT SHOULD LIGHT.
  DOES IT?

YES | NO

YES | NO

7
- TURN IGNITION SWITCH TO "OFF."
- DISCONNECT FUEL PUMP CONNECTOR.
- WITH A TEST LIGHT TO B +, PROBE FUEL PUMP CONNECTOR CAVITY "1" (HARNESS SIDE).
  TEST LIGHT SHOULD LIGHT.
  DOES IT?

- CHECK FOR POOR CONNECTION AT FUEL PUMP RELAY.
  IF OK, REPAIR OPEN IN PNK WIRE.

8
- WITH A TEST LIGHT TO B +, PROBE FUEL PUMP RELAY CONNECTOR CAVITY "3".
- NOTE TEST LIGHT WHILE CRANKING ENGINE.
  TEST LIGHT SHOULD LIGHT.
  DOES IT?

- CHECK FOR POOR CONNECTION AT FUEL PUMP RELAY.
  IF OK, REPAIR OPEN IN BLK/WHT WIRE.

YES | NO

NO | YES

CHECK FOR POOR CONNECTION AT FUEL PUMP. IF OK, REPLACE FUEL PUMP. | REPAIR OPEN IN BLK WIRE.

9
- WITH A TEST LIGHT TO B +, BACKPROBE ECM CONNECTOR C1 CAVITY "A23".
- NOTE TEST LIGHT WHILE CRANKING ENGINE.
  TEST LIGHT SHOULD LIGHT.
  DOES IT?

- CHECK FOR POOR CONNECTION AT FUEL PUMP RELAY.
  IF OK, REPLACE FUEL PUMP RELAY.

NO | YES

- CHECK FOR POOR CONNECTION AT ECM.
  IF OK, REPLACE ECM. | REPAIR OPEN IN PNK/WHT WIRE.

CLEAR CODES AND CONFIRM "CLOSED LOOP " OPERATION AND NO "CHECK ENGINE" INDICATOR.

Fig. 125 1992-93 EFI diagnostic chart

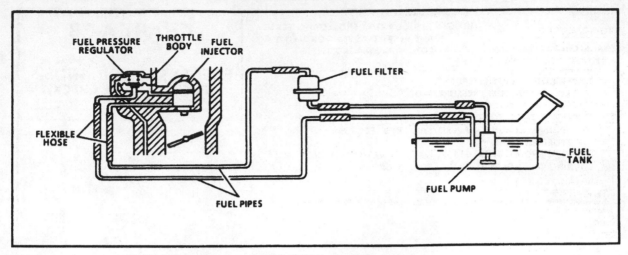

CHART A-7B

FUEL SYSTEM DIAGNOSIS
(FUEL PRESSURE CHECK)

Circuit Description:

When the ignition switch is turned "ON," the engine control module (ECM) will turn "ON" the in-tank fuel pump. It will remain "ON" as long as the engine is cranking or running and the ECM is receiving reference pulses. If there are no reference pulses, the ECM will shut "OFF" the fuel pump in about 3 seconds after ignition "ON" or engine stops.

The pump will deliver fuel to the fuel rail and injectors, then to the pressure regulator, where the system pressure is controlled to about 160-210 kPa (23-31 psi) depending on engine operating conditions. Excess fuel is then returned to the fuel tank.

Test Description: Number(s) below refer to circled number(s) on the diagnostic chart.
1. Checks to see if fuel system pressure is within specifications.
2. Checks fuel feed pipe and hose for leaks.
3. Checks for faulty fuel pump or a leaky fuel filter.
4. Checks for a leaky fuel injector, throttle body or for a faulty fuel pressure regulator.

Diagnostic Aids:

Improper fuel system pressure can result in one of the following conditions:
- Cranks, but will not run.
- Cuts out, may feel like ignition problem.
- Poor fuel economy, loss of power.
- Hard starts.

Fig. 126 1992-93 EFI diagnostic chart

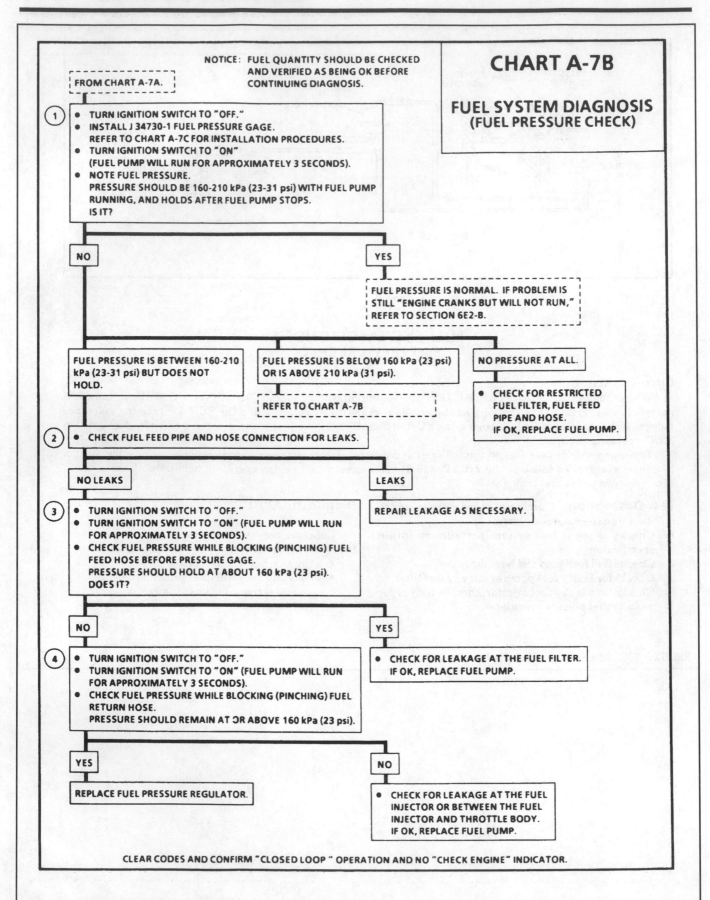

NOTICE: FUEL QUANTITY SHOULD BE CHECKED AND VERIFIED AS BEING OK BEFORE CONTINUING DIAGNOSIS.

FROM CHART A-7A.

CHART A-7B

FUEL SYSTEM DIAGNOSIS
(FUEL PRESSURE CHECK)

1
- TURN IGNITION SWITCH TO "OFF."
- INSTALL J 34730-1 FUEL PRESSURE GAGE. REFER TO CHART A-7C FOR INSTALLATION PROCEDURES.
- TURN IGNITION SWITCH TO "ON" (FUEL PUMP WILL RUN FOR APPROXIMATELY 3 SECONDS).
- NOTE FUEL PRESSURE. PRESSURE SHOULD BE 160-210 kPa (23-31 psi) WITH FUEL PUMP RUNNING, AND HOLDS AFTER FUEL PUMP STOPS. IS IT?

NO | **YES**

FUEL PRESSURE IS NORMAL. IF PROBLEM IS STILL "ENGINE CRANKS BUT WILL NOT RUN," REFER TO SECTION 6E2-B.

FUEL PRESSURE IS BETWEEN 160-210 kPa (23-31 psi) BUT DOES NOT HOLD.

FUEL PRESSURE IS BELOW 160 kPa (23 psi) OR IS ABOVE 210 kPa (31 psi).

REFER TO CHART A-7B

NO PRESSURE AT ALL.
- CHECK FOR RESTRICTED FUEL FILTER, FUEL FEED PIPE AND HOSE. IF OK, REPLACE FUEL PUMP.

2
- CHECK FUEL FEED PIPE AND HOSE CONNECTION FOR LEAKS.

NO LEAKS | **LEAKS**

3
- TURN IGNITION SWITCH TO "OFF."
- TURN IGNITION SWITCH TO "ON" (FUEL PUMP WILL RUN FOR APPROXIMATELY 3 SECONDS).
- CHECK FUEL PRESSURE WHILE BLOCKING (PINCHING) FUEL FEED HOSE BEFORE PRESSURE GAGE. PRESSURE SHOULD HOLD AT ABOUT 160 kPa (23 psi). DOES IT?

REPAIR LEAKAGE AS NECESSARY.

NO | **YES**

CHECK FOR LEAKAGE AT THE FUEL FILTER. IF OK, REPLACE FUEL PUMP.

4
- TURN IGNITION SWITCH TO "OFF."
- TURN IGNITION SWITCH TO "ON" (FUEL PUMP WILL RUN FOR APPROXIMATELY 3 SECONDS).
- CHECK FUEL PRESSURE WHILE BLOCKING (PINCHING) FUEL RETURN HOSE. PRESSURE SHOULD REMAIN AT OR ABOVE 160 kPa (23 psi).

YES | **NO**

REPLACE FUEL PRESSURE REGULATOR.

- CHECK FOR LEAKAGE AT THE FUEL INJECTOR OR BETWEEN THE FUEL INJECTOR AND THROTTLE BODY. IF OK, REPLACE FUEL PUMP.

CLEAR CODES AND CONFIRM "CLOSED LOOP" OPERATION AND NO "CHECK ENGINE" INDICATOR.

Fig. 127 1992-93 EFI diagnostic chart

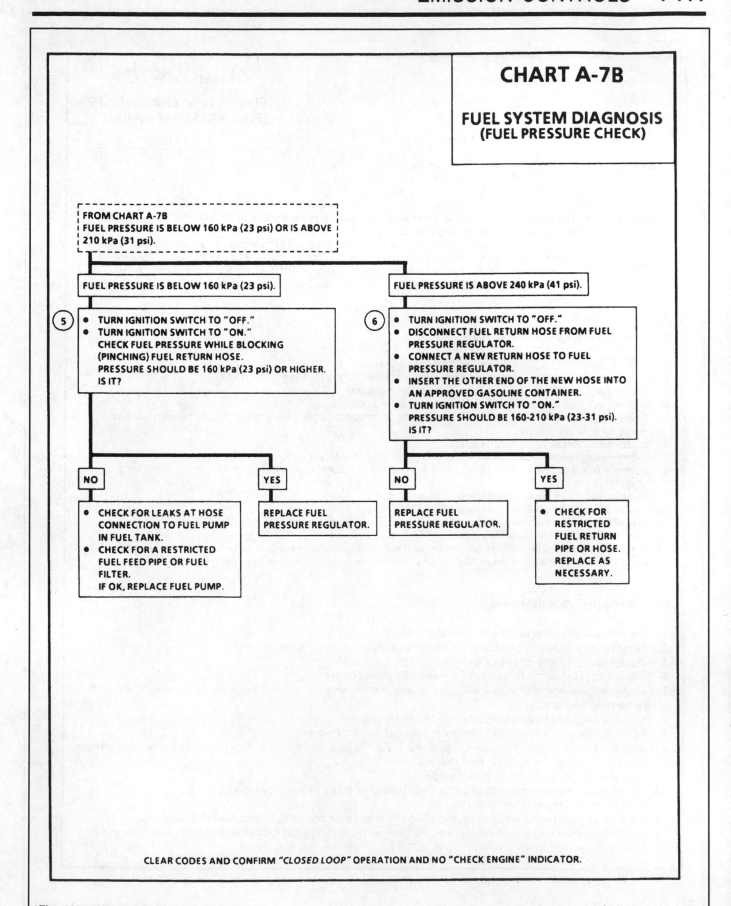

CHART A-7B

FUEL SYSTEM DIAGNOSIS
(FUEL PRESSURE CHECK)

FROM CHART A-7B
FUEL PRESSURE IS BELOW 160 kPa (23 psi) OR IS ABOVE 210 kPa (31 psi).

FUEL PRESSURE IS BELOW 160 kPa (23 psi).

⑤
- TURN IGNITION SWITCH TO "OFF."
- TURN IGNITION SWITCH TO "ON."
  CHECK FUEL PRESSURE WHILE BLOCKING (PINCHING) FUEL RETURN HOSE.
  PRESSURE SHOULD BE 160 kPa (23 psi) OR HIGHER. IS IT?

FUEL PRESSURE IS ABOVE 240 kPa (41 psi).

⑥
- TURN IGNITION SWITCH TO "OFF."
- DISCONNECT FUEL RETURN HOSE FROM FUEL PRESSURE REGULATOR.
- CONNECT A NEW RETURN HOSE TO FUEL PRESSURE REGULATOR.
- INSERT THE OTHER END OF THE NEW HOSE INTO AN APPROVED GASOLINE CONTAINER.
- TURN IGNITION SWITCH TO "ON."
  PRESSURE SHOULD BE 160-210 kPa (23-31 psi). IS IT?

NO

- CHECK FOR LEAKS AT HOSE CONNECTION TO FUEL PUMP IN FUEL TANK.
- CHECK FOR A RESTRICTED FUEL FEED PIPE OR FUEL FILTER.
  IF OK, REPLACE FUEL PUMP.

YES

REPLACE FUEL PRESSURE REGULATOR.

NO

REPLACE FUEL PRESSURE REGULATOR.

YES

- CHECK FOR RESTRICTED FUEL RETURN PIPE OR HOSE. REPLACE AS NECESSARY.

CLEAR CODES AND CONFIRM "CLOSED LOOP" OPERATION AND NO "CHECK ENGINE" INDICATOR.

Fig. 128 1992-93 EFI diagnostic chart

CHART A-7C
FUEL SYSTEM DIAGNOSIS
(FUEL PRESSURE GAGE)

Tools Required: J 34730-1   Fuel Pressure Gage
                       J 34730-75 Fuel Rail Adapter

CAUTION: • To reduce the risk of fire and personal injury, it is necessary to relieve the fuel system pressure before servicing the fuel system.
               • After relieving fuel system pressure, a small amount of fuel may be released when servicing fuel pipes, hoses or connections. To reduce the chance of personal injury and to catch any fuel that may leak out, cover fuel pipe fittings with a shop towel before disconnecting them. Place the shop towel in an approved container when disconnect is completed.

FUEL PRESSURE GAGE INSTALLATION:

1. Loosen fuel filler cap to relieve fuel tank pressure.
2. Remove fuse and relay box cover and engine coolant reservoir from its bracket.
3. Disconnect fuse and relay box from fender (two screws).
4. Disconnect fuel pump relay from fuse and relay box connector.
5. Crank engine and allow to stall. Crank engine for an additional 3 seconds to assure relief of any remaining fuel pressure.
6. Disconnect negative (-) battery cable.
7. Remove air cleaner assembly (one bolt, one nut and PCV hose).
8. Remove fuel feed hose from throttle body. Use a shop towel to catch any remaining fuel that may leak.
9. Install J 34730-75 Fuel Rail Adapter to throttle body.
10. Install J 34730-1 Fuel Pressure Gage to J 34730-75 Fuel Rail Adapter.
11. Install air cleaner assembly to throttle body (one bolt, one nut and PCV hose).
12. Reconnect negative (-) battery cable.
13. Install fuel pump relay into its connector and connect fuse and relay box to fender (two screws).
14. Install fuse and relay box cover and engine coolant reservoir to its bracket and tighten fuel filler cap.

FUEL PRESSURE GAGE REMOVAL:

1. Loosen fuel filler cap to relieve fuel tank pressure.
2. Remove fuse and relay box cover and engine coolant reservoir from its bracket.
3. Disconnect fuse and relay box from fender (two screws).
4. Disconnect fuel pump relay from fuse and relay box connector.
5. Crank engine and allow to stall. Crank engine for an additional 3 seconds to assure relief of any remaining fuel pressure.
6. Remove negative (-) battery cable.
7. Remover air cleaner assembly (one bolt, one nut and PCV hose).
8. Remove J 34730-1 Fuel Pressure Gage and J 34730-75 Fuel Rail Adapter from throttle body. Use a shop towel to catch any remaining fuel that may leak.
9. Reconnect fuel feed hose to throttle body.
10. Install air cleaner assembly to throttle body (one bolt, one nut and PCV hose).
11. Reconnect negative (-) battery cable.
12. Install fuel pump relay into its connector and connect fuse and relay box to fender (two screw).
13. Install fuse and relay box cover and engine coolant reservoir to its bracket and tighten fuel filler cap.
14. Turn ignition switch to "ON" and then to "OFF." Check for any fuel leaks.

Fig. 129 1992-93 EFI diagnostic chart

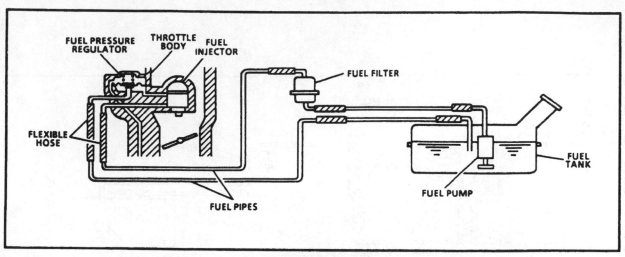

CHART A-7B

FUEL SYSTEM DIAGNOSIS
(FUEL PRESSURE CHECK)

Circuit Description:

When the ignition switch is turned "ON," the engine control module (ECM) will turn "ON" the in-tank fuel pump. It will remain "ON" as long as the engine is cranking or running and the ECM is receiving reference pulses. If there are no reference pulses, the ECM will shut "OFF" the fuel pump in about 3 seconds after ignition "ON" or engine stops.

The pump will deliver fuel to the injector, then to the pressure regulator, where the system pressure is controlled to about 160-210 kPa (23-31 psi). Excess fuel is then returned to the fuel tank.

Test Description: Number(s) below refer to circled number(s) on the diagnostic chart.

5. Checks for a restricted fuel feed pipe or fuel filter or a faulty fuel pressure regulator.

6. This determines if there is a restricted fuel return pipe or fuel pressure regulator.

Fig. 130 1992-93 EFI diagnostic chart

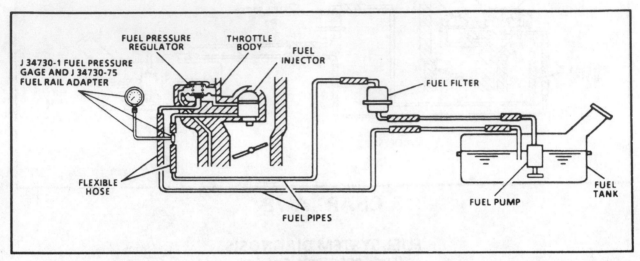

CHART A-7C

FUEL SYSTEM DIAGNOSIS
(FUEL PRESSURE GAGE)

Circuit Description:

The following procedure outlines the installation and removal of the fuel pressure gage. Make sure to observe all cautions while performing this procedure.

Fig. 131 1992-93 EFI diagnostic chart

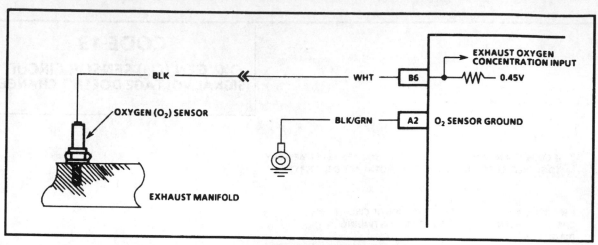

CODE 13

OXYGEN (O₂) SENSOR CIRCUIT
(SIGNAL VOLTAGE DOESN'T CHANGE)

Circuit Description:

The oxygen (O_2) sensor produces a varying voltage after the sensor is hot, above 360°C (600°F). This voltage varies from 0 to 900 mV. The signal will vary, depending on the exhaust gas oxygen content. After the sensor is hot, if the voltage stays above 450 mV for more than 10 seconds, this indicates a rich condition. If voltage remains below 450 mV for more than 10 seconds, a lean condition is indicated.

The O_2 sensor acts like an "open circuit" and produces no voltage when below 360°C (600°F). An open sensor circuit causes the fuel control system to operate in an "Open Loop" operation.

Test Description: Number(s) below refer to circled number(s) on the diagnostic chart.

1. O_2 sensor output voltage, at this step, should be fluctuating between 0-1 volt.

2. When the vacuum hose is removed from the MAP sensor, its output voltage will increase, and the ECM should interpret this as a high engine load. The ECM should increase the fuel injector pulse width, causing a rich A/F mixture. This should cause the O_2 sensor to generate a high output voltage, usually more than 0.900 volt (900 mV).

Diagnostic Aids:

Normal voltage varies between 0 mV and 900 mV.

A loose or intermittent oxygen sensor ground circuit could cause a Code 13. The grounding point at the engine is located on the rear of the intake manifold, on the lower right edge.

Fig. 132 1992-93 EFI diagnostic chart

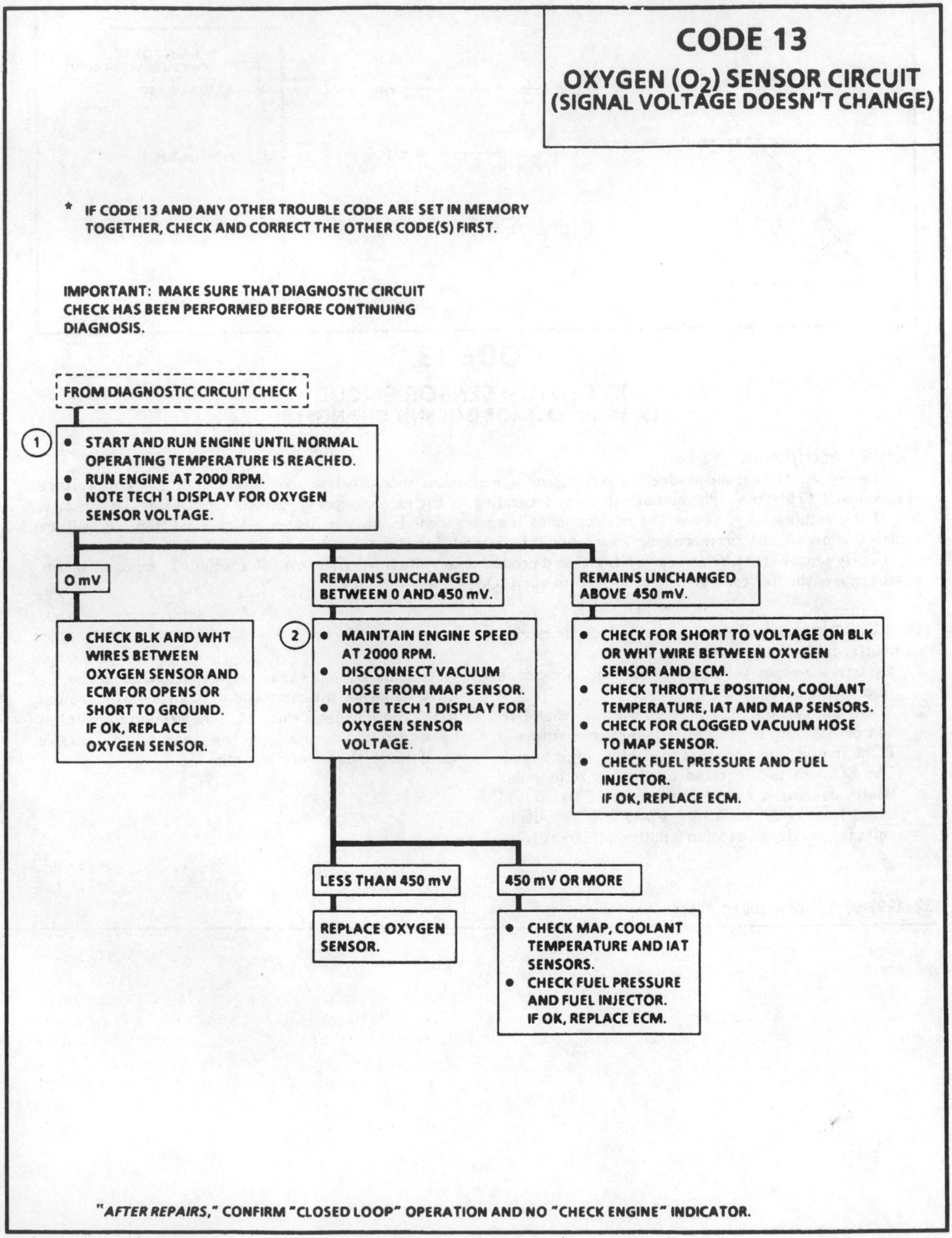

CODE 13
OXYGEN (O$_2$) SENSOR CIRCUIT
(SIGNAL VOLTAGE DOESN'T CHANGE)

*   IF CODE 13 AND ANY OTHER TROUBLE CODE ARE SET IN MEMORY TOGETHER, CHECK AND CORRECT THE OTHER CODE(S) FIRST.

IMPORTANT: MAKE SURE THAT DIAGNOSTIC CIRCUIT CHECK HAS BEEN PERFORMED BEFORE CONTINUING DIAGNOSIS.

FROM DIAGNOSTIC CIRCUIT CHECK

1
*   START AND RUN ENGINE UNTIL NORMAL OPERATING TEMPERATURE IS REACHED.
*   RUN ENGINE AT 2000 RPM.
*   NOTE TECH 1 DISPLAY FOR OXYGEN SENSOR VOLTAGE.

0 mV

REMAINS UNCHANGED BETWEEN 0 AND 450 mV.

REMAINS UNCHANGED ABOVE 450 mV.

*   CHECK BLK AND WHT WIRES BETWEEN OXYGEN SENSOR AND ECM FOR OPENS OR SHORT TO GROUND. IF OK, REPLACE OXYGEN SENSOR.

2
*   MAINTAIN ENGINE SPEED AT 2000 RPM.
*   DISCONNECT VACUUM HOSE FROM MAP SENSOR.
*   NOTE TECH 1 DISPLAY FOR OXYGEN SENSOR VOLTAGE.

*   CHECK FOR SHORT TO VOLTAGE ON BLK OR WHT WIRE BETWEEN OXYGEN SENSOR AND ECM.
*   CHECK THROTTLE POSITION, COOLANT TEMPERATURE, IAT AND MAP SENSORS.
*   CHECK FOR CLOGGED VACUUM HOSE TO MAP SENSOR.
*   CHECK FUEL PRESSURE AND FUEL INJECTOR. IF OK, REPLACE ECM.

LESS THAN 450 mV

450 mV OR MORE

REPLACE OXYGEN SENSOR.

*   CHECK MAP, COOLANT TEMPERATURE AND IAT SENSORS.
*   CHECK FUEL PRESSURE AND FUEL INJECTOR. IF OK, REPLACE ECM.

"*AFTER REPAIRS*," CONFIRM "CLOSED LOOP" OPERATION AND NO "CHECK ENGINE" INDICATOR.

Fig. 133 1992-93 EFI diagnostic chart

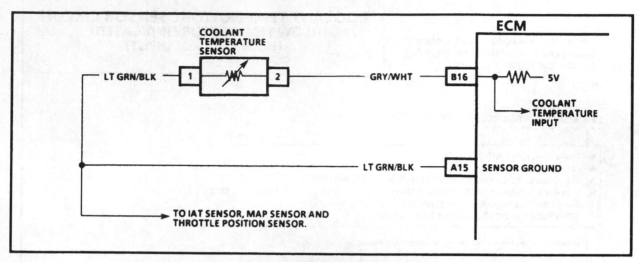

CODE 14

COOLANT TEMPERATURE SENSOR CIRCUIT
(LOW TEMPERATURE INDICATED)
(HIGH VOLTAGE INPUT)

Circuit Description:

The coolant temperature sensor is a thermistor (a variable resistor that changes along with coolant temperature) in series with a fixed resistor in the ECM. The ECM applies 5 volts to the sensor. The ECM monitors the voltage across the coolant temperature sensor and converts it into a temperature reading. When the engine is cold the coolant temperature sensor resistance is high, and when the engine is warm the coolant temperature sensor resistance is low. Therefore, when the engine is cold the ECM will receive a high voltage input, and when the engine is warm the ECM will receive a low voltage input.

Code 14 will set if the following condition is met for at least 3 seconds:

- Voltage input at the ECM indicates a coolant temperature below -48°C (-54°F).

Test Description: Number(s) below refer to circled number(s) on the diagnostic chart.

1. This test simulates Code 15. If the ECM stores Code 15, the ECM and its wiring are OK and the coolant temperature sensor is faulty. If Code 14 resets, the coolant temperature sensor is OK and the wiring to the ECM or the ECM if faulty.

2. This test determines whether there is an open in the GRY/WHT or LT GRN/BLK wires, a short to B+ in the GRY/WHT wire or a faulty ECM.

Diagnostic Aids:

After the engine is started the temperature should rise steadily to about 95°C (203°F) and stabilize when the thermostat opens.

Codes 14, 23 and 32 stored at the same time could be the result of an open LT GRN/BLK sensor ground wire.

When replacing the coolant temperature sensor the "Temperature to Resistance Value" scale on the diagnostic chart may be used to test the coolant temperature sensor at various temperature levels to evaluate the possibility of a "shifted" (mis-scaled) sensor. A "shifted" sensor could result in poor driveability complaints.

Fig. 134 1992-93 EFI diagnostic chart

IMPORTANT: MAKE SURE THAT DIAGNOSTIC CIRCUIT CHECK HAS BEEN PERFORMED BEFORE CONTINUING DIAGNOSIS.

CODE 14

COOLANT TEMPERATURE SENSOR CIRCUIT
(LOW TEMPERATURE INDICATED)
(HIGH VOLTAGE INPUT)

FROM DIAGNOSTIC CIRCUIT CHECK

1
- TURN IGNITION SWITCH TO "OFF."
- CLEAR CODES.
- DISCONNECT COOLANT TEMPERATURE SENSOR CONNECTOR.
- CONNECT A JUMPER FROM CONNECTOR CAVITY "1" TO CAVITY "2" (HARNESS SIDE).
- START ENGINE AND RUN FOR 1 MINUTE.
  DOES TECH 1 INDICATE CODE 14 OR CODE 15?

CODE 14

CODE 15

2
- TURN IGNITION SWITCH TO "OFF."
- REMOVE JUMPER FROM COOLANT TEMPERATURE SENSOR CONNECTOR.
- CONNECT A DIGITAL MULTIMETER FROM CONNECTOR CAVITY "2" TO GROUND.
- TURN IGNITION SWITCH TO "ON."
- MEASURE VOLTAGE.

- CHECK FOR POOR CONNECTION AT COOLANT TEMPERATURE SENSOR.
  IF OK, REPLACE COOLANT TEMPERATURE SENSOR.

4-6 VOLTS

0 VOLTS

MORE THAN 6 VOLTS

- CHECK FOR AN OPEN IN LT GRN/BLK WIRE.
- CHECK FOR A POOR CONNECTION AT ECM.
  IF OK, REPLACE ECM.

- CHECK FOR AN OPEN IN GRY/WHT WIRE.
- CHECK FOR POOR CONNECTION AT ECM.
  IF OK, REPLACE ECM.

- CHECK FOR A SHORT TO B + IN GRY/WHT WIRE.
  IF OK, REPLACE ECM.

DIAGNOSTIC AID

COOLANT TEMPERATURE SENSOR		
TEMPERATURE TO RESISTANCE VALUES (APPROXIMATE)		
°F	°C	OHMS
210	99	190
160	71	400
100	38	1,250
70	21	2,350
40	4	4,780
20	-7	8,100
0	-18	14,650

"AFTER REPAIRS," CONFIRM "CLOSED LOOP" OPERATION AND NO "CHECK ENGINE" INDICATOR.

Fig. 135 1992-93 EFI diagnostic chart

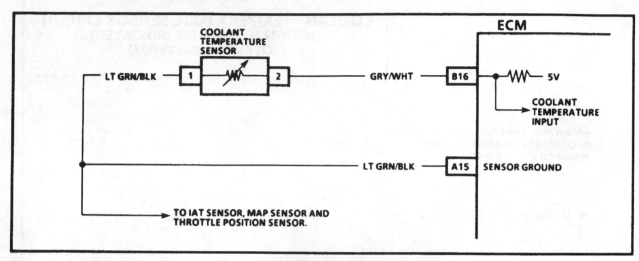

CODE 15

COOLANT TEMPERATURE SENSOR CIRCUIT
(HIGH TEMPERATURE INDICATED)
(LOW VOLTAGE INPUT)

Circuit Description:

The coolant temperature sensor is a thermistor (a variable resistor that changes along with coolant temperature) in a series with a fixed resistor in the ECM. The ECM applies 5 volts to the sensor. The ECM monitors the voltage across the coolant temperature sensor and converts it into a temperature reading. When the engine is cold the coolant temperature sensor resistance is high, and when the engine is warm the coolant temperature sensor resistance is low. Therefore, when the engine is cold the ECM will receive a high voltage input, and when the engine is warm the ECM will receive a low voltage input.

Code 15 will set if the following condition si met for a least 3 seconds:

- Voltage input at the ECM indicates a coolant temperature above 136°C (276°F).

Test Description: Number(s) below refer to circled number(s) on the diagnostic chart.

1. This test simulates Code 14. If the ECM stores Code 14, the ECM and its wiring are OK and the coolant temperature sensor is faulty. If Code 15 resets, the coolant temperature sensor is OK and the wiring to the ECM or the ECM is faulty.

Diagnostic Aids:

After the engine is started, the temperature should rise steadily to about 95°C (203°F) and stabilize when thermostat opens.

Verify that engine is not overheating and has not been subjected to conditions which could create an overheating condition (i.e., overload, trailer towing, hilly terrain, heavy stop and go traffic, etc.).

When replacing the coolant temperature sensor the "Temperature To Resistance Value" scale on diagnostic chart may be used to test the coolant temperature sensor at various temperature levels to evaluate the possibility of a "shifted" (mis-scaled) sensor. A "shifted" sensor could result in poor driveability complaints.

Fig. 136 1992-93 EFI diagnostic chart

CODE 15
COOLANT TEMPERATURE SENSOR CIRCUIT
(HIGH TEMPERATURE INDICATED)
(LOW VOLTAGE INPUT)

IMPORTANT: MAKE SURE THAT DIAGNOSTIC
CIRCUIT CHECK HAS BEEN PERFORMED
BEFORE CONTINUING DIAGNOSIS.

FROM DIAGNOSTIC CIRCUIT CHECK

1
- TURN IGNITION SWITCH TO "OFF."
- CLEAR CODES.
- DISCONNECT COOLANT TEMPERATURE SENSOR CONNECTOR.,
- START AND RUN ENGINE FOR 1 MINUTE. DOES TECH 1 INDICATE CODE 14 OR CODE 15?

CODE 14
- REPLACE COOLANT TEMPERATURE SENSOR.

CODE 15
- CHECK FOR SHORT TO GROUND IN GRY/WHT WIRE IF OK, REPLACE ECM.

DIAGNOSTIC AID

COOLANT TEMPERATURE SENSOR		
TEMPERATURE TO RESISTANCE VALUES (APPROXIMATE)		
°F	°C	OHMS
210	99	190
160	71	400
100	38	1,250
70	21	2,350
40	4	4,780
20	-7	8,100
0	-18	14,650

"AFTER REPAIRS," CONFIRM "CLOSED LOOP" OPERATION AND NO "CHECK ENGINE" INDICATOR.

Fig. 137 1992-93 EFI diagnostic chart

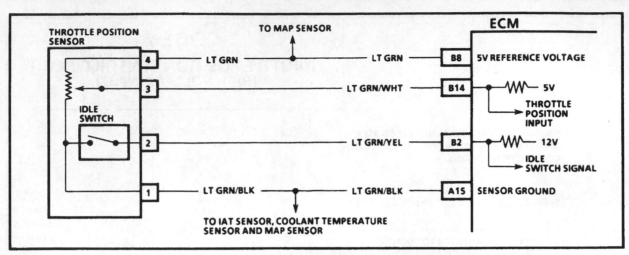

CODE 21
THROTTLE POSITION SENSOR CIRCUIT
(HIGH VOLTAGE INPUT)

Circuit Description:

The throttle position sensor has a potentiometer whose resistance changes along with the throttle valve position. The ECM provides a 5 volt reference voltage to the sensor. The ECM reads the voltage across the sensor and converts it into throttle position. When the sensor resistance decreases, indicating the throttle valve opening is increasing to wide open throttle, the voltage being monitored at the ECM increases. When the sensor resistances increases, indicating the throttle valve opening is decreasing to idle, the voltage being monitored at the ECM decreases.

Code 21 will set if the following condition is met for at least 2 seconds:

- High voltage input at the ECM indicated with the engine running at idle.

Test Description: Number(s) below refer to circled number(s) on the diagnostic chart.

1. Checks for an open or short to B+ in LT GRN/WHT wire or for a faulty ECM.
2. Checks for an open or short to B+ in LT GRN wire or for a faulty ECM.
3. Checks for a faulty ECM or a misadjusted or faulty throttle position sensor.

Diagnostic Aids:

Codes 21 and 22 stored at the same time could be the result of an open LT GRN wire.

Fig. 138 1992-93 EFI diagnostic chart

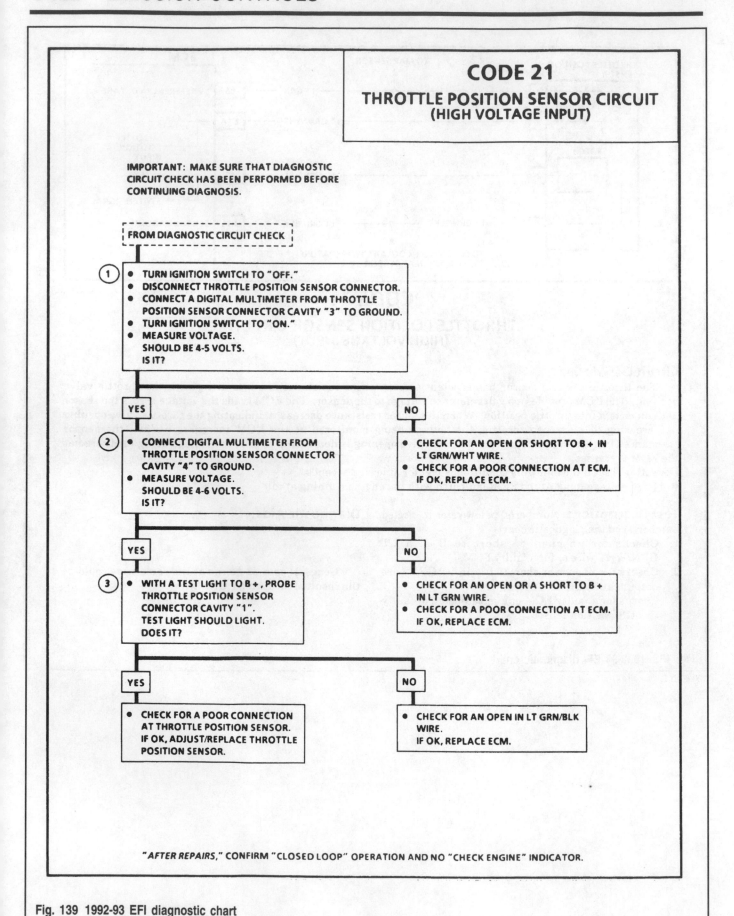

CODE 21
THROTTLE POSITION SENSOR CIRCUIT
(HIGH VOLTAGE INPUT)

IMPORTANT: MAKE SURE THAT DIAGNOSTIC CIRCUIT CHECK HAS BEEN PERFORMED BEFORE CONTINUING DIAGNOSIS.

FROM DIAGNOSTIC CIRCUIT CHECK

1
- TURN IGNITION SWITCH TO "OFF."
- DISCONNECT THROTTLE POSITION SENSOR CONNECTOR.
- CONNECT A DIGITAL MULTIMETER FROM THROTTLE POSITION SENSOR CONNECTOR CAVITY "3" TO GROUND.
- TURN IGNITION SWITCH TO "ON."
- MEASURE VOLTAGE.
  SHOULD BE 4-5 VOLTS.
  IS IT?

YES / NO

2
- CONNECT DIGITAL MULTIMETER FROM THROTTLE POSITION SENSOR CONNECTOR CAVITY "4" TO GROUND.
- MEASURE VOLTAGE.
  SHOULD BE 4-6 VOLTS.
  IS IT?

NO
- CHECK FOR AN OPEN OR SHORT TO B + IN LT GRN/WHT WIRE.
- CHECK FOR A POOR CONNECTION AT ECM. IF OK, REPLACE ECM.

YES / NO

3
- WITH A TEST LIGHT TO B + , PROBE THROTTLE POSITION SENSOR CONNECTOR CAVITY "1". TEST LIGHT SHOULD LIGHT. DOES IT?

NO
- CHECK FOR AN OPEN OR A SHORT TO B + IN LT GRN WIRE.
- CHECK FOR A POOR CONNECTION AT ECM. IF OK, REPLACE ECM.

YES / NO

- CHECK FOR A POOR CONNECTION AT THROTTLE POSITION SENSOR. IF OK, ADJUST/REPLACE THROTTLE POSITION SENSOR.

- CHECK FOR AN OPEN IN LT GRN/BLK WIRE. IF OK, REPLACE ECM.

"AFTER REPAIRS," CONFIRM "CLOSED LOOP" OPERATION AND NO "CHECK ENGINE" INDICATOR.

Fig. 139 1992-93 EFI diagnostic chart

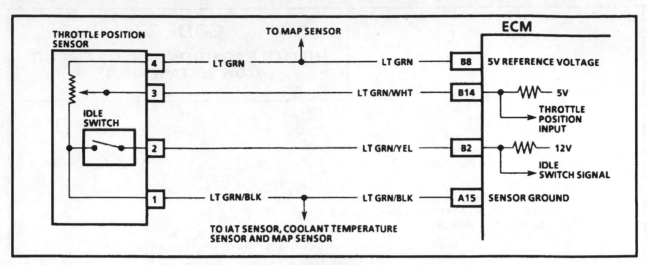

CODE 22

THROTTLE POSITION SENSOR CIRCUIT
(LOW VOLTAGE INPUT)

Circuit Description:

The throttle position sensor has a potentiometer whose resistance changes along with the throttle valve position. The ECM provides a 5 volt reference voltage to the sensor. The ECM reads the voltage across the sensor and converts it into throttle position. When the sensor resistance decreases, indicating the throttle valve opening is increasing to wide open throttle, the voltage being monitored at the ECM increases. When the sensor resistances increases, indicating the throttle valve opening is decreasing to idle, the voltage being monitored at the ECM decreases.

Code 22 will set if the following condition is met for at least 2 seconds:

- Low voltage input at the ECM indicated with the engine running off idle.

Test Description: Number(s) below refer to circled number(s) on the diagnostic chart.

1. Measures throttle position sensor signal voltage at sensor. Checks for short to ground in LT GRN/WHT wire.
2. Checks for reference voltage from the ECM.

Diagnostic Aids:

Codes 21 and 22 stored at the same time could be the result of an open LT GRN wire.

Fig. 140 1992-93 EFI diagnostic chart

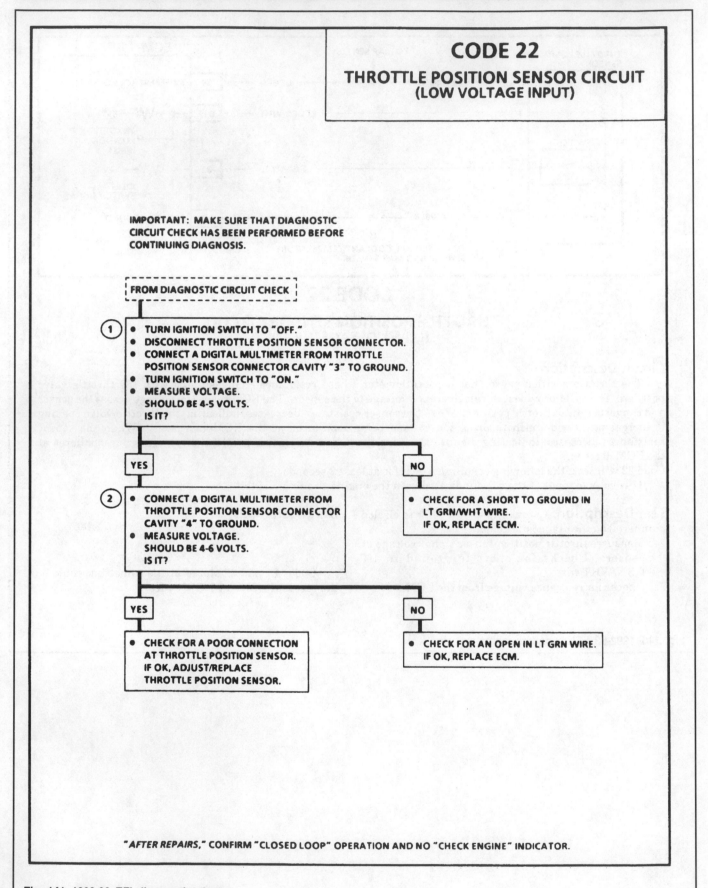

CODE 22
THROTTLE POSITION SENSOR CIRCUIT
(LOW VOLTAGE INPUT)

IMPORTANT: MAKE SURE THAT DIAGNOSTIC
CIRCUIT CHECK HAS BEEN PERFORMED BEFORE
CONTINUING DIAGNOSIS.

FROM DIAGNOSTIC CIRCUIT CHECK

1
- TURN IGNITION SWITCH TO "OFF."
- DISCONNECT THROTTLE POSITION SENSOR CONNECTOR.
- CONNECT A DIGITAL MULTIMETER FROM THROTTLE
  POSITION SENSOR CONNECTOR CAVITY "3" TO GROUND.
- TURN IGNITION SWITCH TO "ON."
- MEASURE VOLTAGE.
  SHOULD BE 4-5 VOLTS.
  IS IT?

YES

NO

2
- CONNECT A DIGITAL MULTIMETER FROM
  THROTTLE POSITION SENSOR CONNECTOR
  CAVITY "4" TO GROUND.
- MEASURE VOLTAGE.
  SHOULD BE 4-6 VOLTS.
  IS IT?

- CHECK FOR A SHORT TO GROUND IN
  LT GRN/WHT WIRE.
  IF OK, REPLACE ECM.

YES

NO

- CHECK FOR A POOR CONNECTION
  AT THROTTLE POSITION SENSOR.
  IF OK, ADJUST/REPLACE
  THROTTLE POSITION SENSOR.

- CHECK FOR AN OPEN IN LT GRN WIRE.
  IF OK, REPLACE ECM.

"AFTER REPAIRS," CONFIRM "CLOSED LOOP" OPERATION AND NO "CHECK ENGINE" INDICATOR.

Fig. 141 1992-93 EFI diagnostic chart

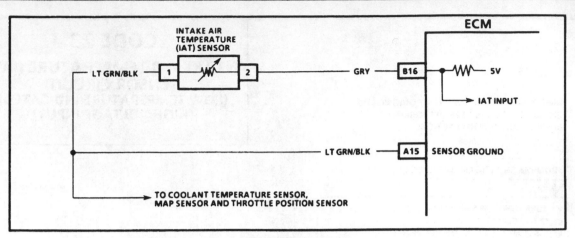

CODE 23
INTAKE AIR TEMPERATURE (IAT) SENSOR CIRCUIT
(LOW TEMPERATURE INDICATED)
(HIGH VOLTAGE INPUT)
1.0L (VIN 6) "M" CARLINE

Circuit Description:

The intake air temperature (IAT) sensor is a thermistor (a variable resistor that changes along with outside air temperature) in series with a fixed resistor in the ECM. The ECM applies 5 volts to the sensor. The ECM monitors the voltage across the IAT sensor and converts it into a temperature reading. When the outside air temperature is cold the IAT sensor resistance is high, and when the outside air temperature is warm the IAT sensor resistance is low. Therefore, when the air temperature is cold the ECM will receive a high voltage input, and when the air temperature is warm the ECM will receive a low voltage input.

Code 23 will set if the following condition is met for at least 3 seconds:

• Voltage input at the ECM indicates an air temperature below -48°C (-54°F).

Test Description: Number(s) below refer to circled number(s) on the diagnostic chart.

1. This test simulates Code 25. If the ECM stores Code 25, the ECM and its wiring are OK and the IAT sensor is faulty. If Code 23 resets, the IAT sensor is OK, and the wiring to the ECM or the ECM is faulty.

2. This test determines whether there is an open in the GRY or LT GRN/BLK wires, a short to B+ in the GRY wire or a faulty ECM.

Diagnostic Aids:

When replacing the IAT sensor the "Temperature to Resistance Value" scale on the diagnostic chart may be used to test the sensor at various temperature levels to evaluate the possibility of a "shifted"' (mis-scaled) sensor. A "shifted" sensor could result in poor driveability complaints.

Fig. 142 1989-91 EFI diagnostic chart

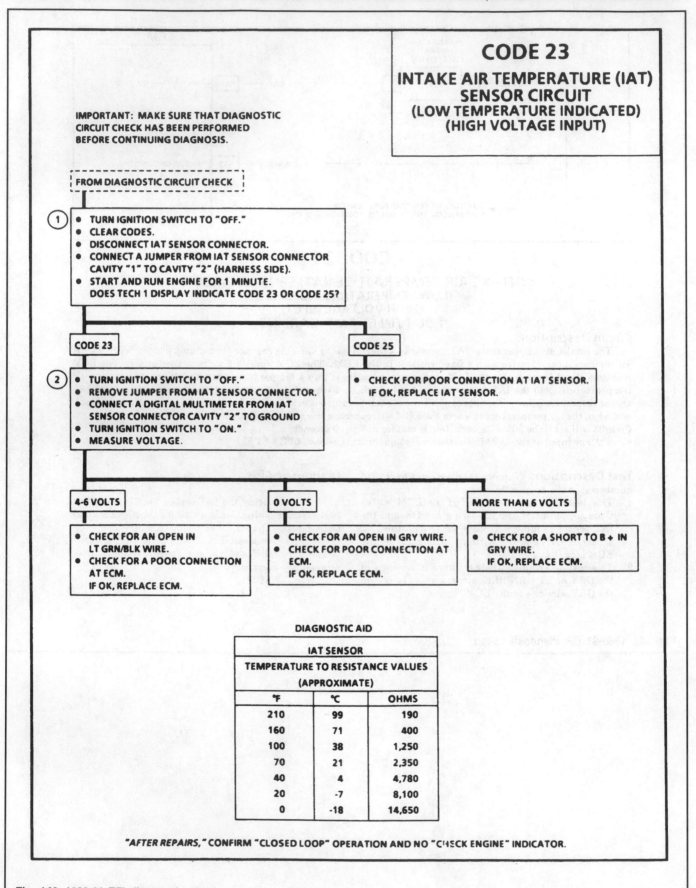

CODE 23
INTAKE AIR TEMPERATURE (IAT) SENSOR CIRCUIT
(LOW TEMPERATURE INDICATED)
(HIGH VOLTAGE INPUT)

IMPORTANT: MAKE SURE THAT DIAGNOSTIC CIRCUIT CHECK HAS BEEN PERFORMED BEFORE CONTINUING DIAGNOSIS.

FROM DIAGNOSTIC CIRCUIT CHECK

(1)
- TURN IGNITION SWITCH TO "OFF."
- CLEAR CODES.
- DISCONNECT IAT SENSOR CONNECTOR.
- CONNECT A JUMPER FROM IAT SENSOR CONNECTOR CAVITY "1" TO CAVITY "2" (HARNESS SIDE).
- START AND RUN ENGINE FOR 1 MINUTE. DOES TECH 1 DISPLAY INDICATE CODE 23 OR CODE 25?

CODE 23

CODE 25

(2)
- TURN IGNITION SWITCH TO "OFF."
- REMOVE JUMPER FROM IAT SENSOR CONNECTOR.
- CONNECT A DIGITAL MULTIMETER FROM IAT SENSOR CONNECTOR CAVITY "2" TO GROUND
- TURN IGNITION SWITCH TO "ON."
- MEASURE VOLTAGE.

- CHECK FOR POOR CONNECTION AT IAT SENSOR. IF OK, REPLACE IAT SENSOR.

4-6 VOLTS

0 VOLTS

MORE THAN 6 VOLTS

- CHECK FOR AN OPEN IN LT GRN/BLK WIRE.
- CHECK FOR A POOR CONNECTION AT ECM. IF OK, REPLACE ECM.

- CHECK FOR AN OPEN IN GRY WIRE.
- CHECK FOR POOR CONNECTION AT ECM. IF OK, REPLACE ECM.

- CHECK FOR A SHORT TO B + IN GRY WIRE. IF OK, REPLACE ECM.

DIAGNOSTIC AID

IAT SENSOR		
TEMPERATURE TO RESISTANCE VALUES (APPROXIMATE)		
°F	°C	OHMS
210	99	190
160	71	400
100	38	1,250
70	21	2,350
40	4	4,780
20	-7	8,100
0	-18	14,650

"AFTER REPAIRS," CONFIRM "CLOSED LOOP" OPERATION AND NO "CHECK ENGINE" INDICATOR.

Fig. 143 1989-91 EFI diagnostic chart

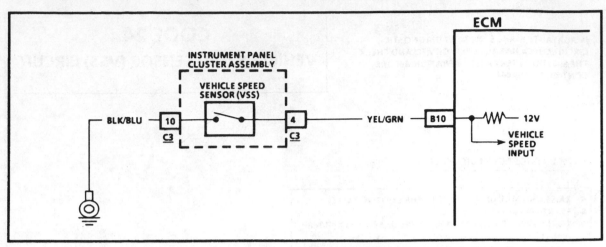

CODE 24
VEHICLE SPEED SENSOR (VSS) CIRCUIT
1.0L (VIN 6) "M" CARLINE

Circuit Description:

The ECM supplies 12 volts to the vehicle speed sensor (VSS). While the vehicle is moving, the reed switch within the VSS will open and close four times per each revolution of the speedometer cable. Because the reed switch opens and closes, the voltage at the ECM is toggled high and low. The ECM then converts this toggled high/low voltage into a vehicle speed that is displayed in kph and mph.

Code 24 will set if the following condition is met for at least 4 seconds:
- A constant voltage signal (either high of low) detected at the ECM with the engine running and the vehicle moving.

Test Description: Number(s) below refer to circled number(s) on the diagnostic chart.
1. Checks to see if problem is intermittent.
2. If the VSS is not receiving the 12 volts from the ECM, Code 24 will set. This step checks for an open in the YEL/GRN wire or a faulty ECM.
3. This checks for a poor ground connection, an open in the BLK wire or for a faulty VSS.

Diagnostic Aids:

If the speedometer cable is binding, Code 24 can be set. Make sure that the speedometer cable is free from any restrictions and that it has a secure connection to the I/P cluster assembly.

Fig. 144 1992-93 EFI diagnostic chart

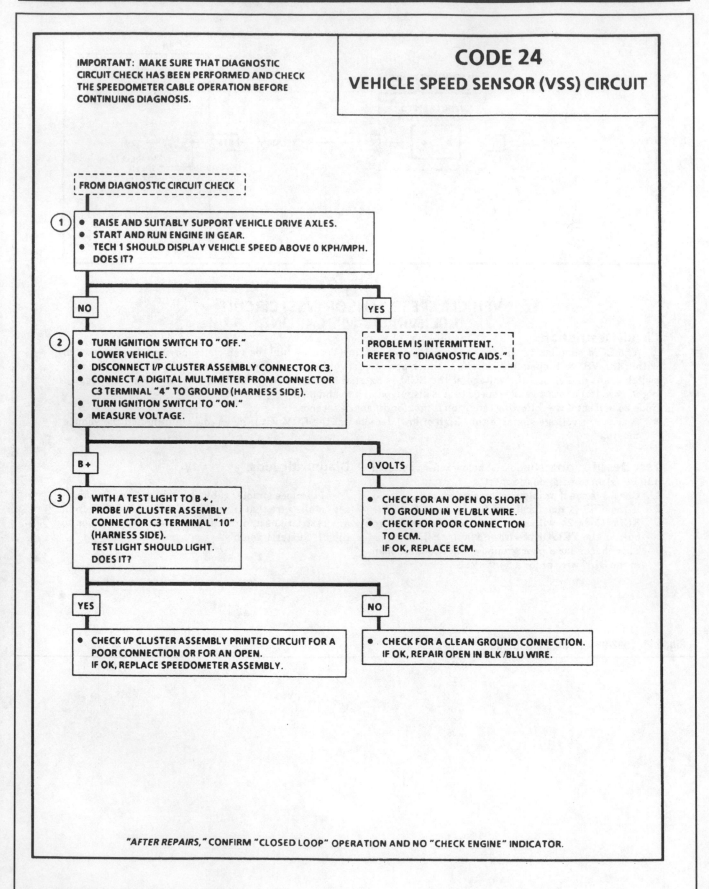

IMPORTANT: MAKE SURE THAT DIAGNOSTIC CIRCUIT CHECK HAS BEEN PERFORMED AND CHECK THE SPEEDOMETER CABLE OPERATION BEFORE CONTINUING DIAGNOSIS.

CODE 24
VEHICLE SPEED SENSOR (VSS) CIRCUIT

FROM DIAGNOSTIC CIRCUIT CHECK

1
- RAISE AND SUITABLY SUPPORT VEHICLE DRIVE AXLES.
- START AND RUN ENGINE IN GEAR.
- TECH 1 SHOULD DISPLAY VEHICLE SPEED ABOVE 0 KPH/MPH. DOES IT?

NO

YES

2
- TURN IGNITION SWITCH TO "OFF."
- LOWER VEHICLE.
- DISCONNECT I/P CLUSTER ASSEMBLY CONNECTOR C3.
- CONNECT A DIGITAL MULTIMETER FROM CONNECTOR C3 TERMINAL "4" TO GROUND (HARNESS SIDE).
- TURN IGNITION SWITCH TO "ON."
- MEASURE VOLTAGE.

PROBLEM IS INTERMITTENT.
REFER TO "DIAGNOSTIC AIDS."

B+

0 VOLTS

3
- WITH A TEST LIGHT TO B+, PROBE I/P CLUSTER ASSEMBLY CONNECTOR C3 TERMINAL "10" (HARNESS SIDE).
  TEST LIGHT SHOULD LIGHT. DOES IT?

- CHECK FOR AN OPEN OR SHORT TO GROUND IN YEL/BLK WIRE.
- CHECK FOR POOR CONNECTION TO ECM.
  IF OK, REPLACE ECM.

YES

NO

- CHECK I/P CLUSTER ASSEMBLY PRINTED CIRCUIT FOR A POOR CONNECTION OR FOR AN OPEN.
  IF OK, REPLACE SPEEDOMETER ASSEMBLY.

- CHECK FOR A CLEAN GROUND CONNECTION.
  IF OK, REPAIR OPEN IN BLK/BLU WIRE.

"AFTER REPAIRS," CONFIRM "CLOSED LOOP" OPERATION AND NO "CHECK ENGINE" INDICATOR.

Fig. 145 1992-93 EFI diagnostic chart

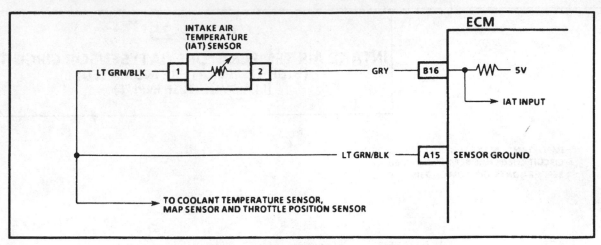

CODE 25

INTAKE AIR TEMPERATURE (IAT) SENSOR CIRCUIT
(HIGH TEMPERATURE INDICATED)
(LOW VOLTAGE INPUT)

Circuit Description:

The intake air temperature (IAT) sensor is a thermistor (a variable resistor that changes along with outside air temperature) in series with a fixed resistor in the ECM. The ECM applies 5 volts to the sensor. The ECM monitors the voltage across the IAT sensor and converts it into a temperature reading. When the outside air temperature is cold the IAT sensor resistance is high, and when the outside air temperature is warm the IAT sensor resistance is low. Therefore, when the air temperature is cold the ECM will receive a high voltage input, and when the air temperature is warm the ECM will receive a low voltage input.

Code 25 will set if the following condition is met for a least 3 seconds:
- Voltage input at the ECM indicates an air temperature above 136°C (277°F).

Test Description: Number(s) below refer to circled number(s) on the diagnostic chart.

1. This test simulates Code 23. If the ECM stores Code 23, the ECM and its wiring are OK and the IAT sensor is faulty. If Code 25 resets, the IAT sensor is OK, and the wiring to the ECM or the ECM is faulty.

Diagnostic Aids:

When replacing the IAT sensor the "Temperature to Resistance Value" scale on the diagnostic chart may be used to test the sensor at various temperature levels to evaluate the possibility of a "shifted" (mis-scaled) sensor. A "shifted" sensor could result in poor driveability complaints.

Fig. 146 1992-93 EFI diagnostic chart

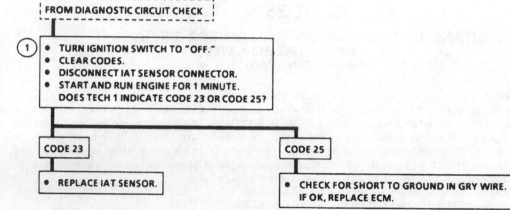

CODE 25
INTAKE AIR TEMPERATURE (IAT) SENSOR CIRCUIT
(HIGH TEMPERATURE INDICATED)
(LOW VOLTAGE INPUT)

IMPORTANT: MAKE SURE THAT DIAGNOSTIC
CIRCUIT CHECK HAS BEEN PERFORMED
BEFORE CONTINUING DIAGNOSIS.

FROM DIAGNOSTIC CIRCUIT CHECK

1
- TURN IGNITION SWITCH TO "OFF."
- CLEAR CODES.
- DISCONNECT IAT SENSOR CONNECTOR.
- START AND RUN ENGINE FOR 1 MINUTE.
  DOES TECH 1 INDICATE CODE 23 OR CODE 25?

CODE 23

- REPLACE IAT SENSOR.

CODE 25

- CHECK FOR SHORT TO GROUND IN GRY WIRE.
  IF OK, REPLACE ECM.

DIAGNOSTIC AID

IAT SENSOR		
TEMPERATURE TO RESISTANCE VALUES		
(APPROXIMATE)		
°F	°C	OHMS
210	99	190
160	71	400
100	38	1,250
70	21	2,350
40	4	4,780
20	-7	8,100
0	-18	14,650

"AFTER REPAIRS," CONFIRM "CLOSED LOOP" OPERATION AND NO "CHECK ENGINE" INDICATOR.

Fig. 147 1992-93 EFI diagnostic chart

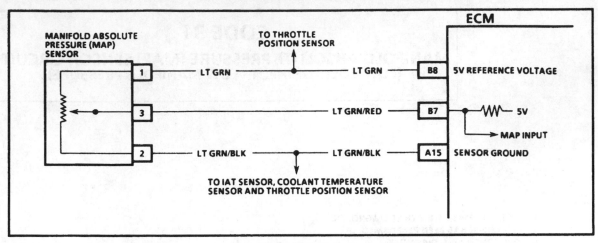

CODE 31
MANIFOLD ABSOLUTE PRESSURE (MAP) SENSOR CIRCUIT
(LOW VOLTAGE INPUT - LOW MANIFOLD PRESSURE)

Circuit Description:

The manifold absolute pressure (MAP) sensor measures the change in the intake manifold pressure (vacuum). The ECM applies 5 volts to the MAP sensor. The change in the pressure, that results from engine load and rpm changes, is converted into a voltage input that is monitored by the ECM. A low voltage reading at the ECM indicates low manifold pressure, and a high voltage reading at the ECM indicates high manifold pressure. Code 31 will set if the following condition is met for 0.2 seconds:

- Low voltage input at the ECM indicating intake manifold pressure below 40 mmHg.

Test Description: Number(s) below refer to circled number(s) on the diagnostic chart.

1. This step checks that the ECM is providing a 5 volt reference.
2. This step checks for the bias voltage to the MAP sensor which has a value between 4.5 and 4.9 volts. This step checks that value.

Diagnostic Aids:

Check for a clogged or pinched vacuum hose to MAP sensor.

An intermittent may be caused by a poor connection, rubbed through wire insulation, or a wire broken inside the insulation. Inspect ECM harness connectors for backed out terminals, improper mating, broken locks, improperly formed or damaged terminals, poor terminal to wire connection and damaged harness.

Fig. 148 1992-93 EFI diagnostic chart

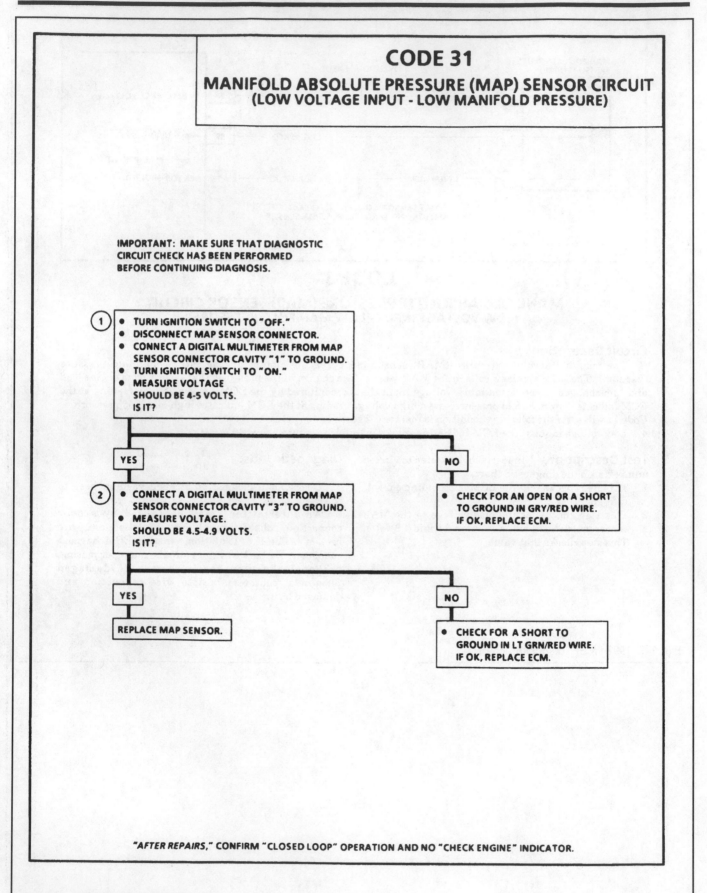

CODE 31
MANIFOLD ABSOLUTE PRESSURE (MAP) SENSOR CIRCUIT
(LOW VOLTAGE INPUT - LOW MANIFOLD PRESSURE)

IMPORTANT: MAKE SURE THAT DIAGNOSTIC
CIRCUIT CHECK HAS BEEN PERFORMED
BEFORE CONTINUING DIAGNOSIS.

1
- TURN IGNITION SWITCH TO "OFF."
- DISCONNECT MAP SENSOR CONNECTOR.
- CONNECT A DIGITAL MULTIMETER FROM MAP
  SENSOR CONNECTOR CAVITY "1" TO GROUND.
- TURN IGNITION SWITCH TO "ON."
- MEASURE VOLTAGE
  SHOULD BE 4-5 VOLTS.
  IS IT?

YES

NO

2
- CONNECT A DIGITAL MULTIMETER FROM MAP
  SENSOR CONNECTOR CAVITY "3" TO GROUND.
- MEASURE VOLTAGE.
  SHOULD BE 4.5-4.9 VOLTS.
  IS IT?

- CHECK FOR AN OPEN OR A SHORT
  TO GROUND IN GRY/RED WIRE.
  IF OK, REPLACE ECM.

YES

NO

REPLACE MAP SENSOR.

- CHECK FOR A SHORT TO
  GROUND IN LT GRN/RED WIRE.
  IF OK, REPLACE ECM.

"AFTER REPAIRS," CONFIRM *"CLOSED LOOP"* OPERATION AND NO *"CHECK ENGINE"* INDICATOR.

Fig. 149 1992-93 EFI diagnostic chart

CODE 32
MANIFOLD ABSOLUTE PRESSURE (MAP) SENSOR CIRCUIT
(HIGH VOLTAGE INPUT - HIGH MANIFOLD PRESSURE)

IMPORTANT: MAKE SURE THAT DIAGNOSTIC CIRCUIT CHECK HAS BEEN PERFORMED BEFORE CONTINUING DIAGNOSIS.

FROM DIAGNOSTIC CIRCUIT CHECK

(1)
- TURN IGNITION SWITCH TO "OFF."
- DISCONNECT MAP SENSOR CONNECTOR.
- TURN IGNITION SWITCH TO "ON."
- CONNECT A DIGITAL MULTIMETER FROM CONNECTOR CAVITY "3" TO GROUND (HARNESS SIDE).
- MEASURE VOLTAGE.

4.5-4.9 VOLTS

0 VOLTS

5 VOLTS OR MORE

(2)
- CONNECT A DIGITAL MULTIMETER FROM CONNECTOR CAVITY "2" TO CAVITY "3" (HARNESS SIDE).
- MEASURE VOLTAGE.

- CHECK FOR AN OPEN IN LT GRN/RED WIRE.
- CHECK FOR POOR CONNECTION AT ECM. IF OK, REPLACE ECM.

- CHECK FOR A SHORT TO VOLTAGE (5 VOLTS OR B +) IN LT GRN/RED WIRE. IF OK, REPLACE ECM.

4-5 VOLTS

0 VOLTS

- CHECK FOR A POOR CONNECTION AT MAP SENSOR. IF OK, REPLACE MAP SENSOR.

- CHECK FOR AN OPEN IN LT GRN/BLK WIRE.
- CHECK FOR A POOR CONNECTION AT ECM. IF OK, REPLACE ECM.

"AFTER REPAIRS," CONFIRM "CLOSED LOOP" OPERATION AND NO "CHECK ENGINE" INDICATOR.

Fig. 150 1992-93 EFI diagnostic chart

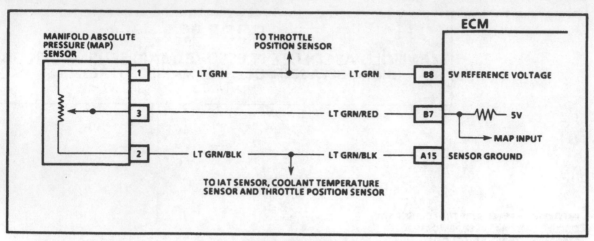

CODE 32

MANIFOLD ABSOLUTE PRESSURE (MAP) SENSOR CIRCUIT
(HIGH VOLTAGE INPUT - HIGH MANIFOLD PRESSURE)

Circuit Description:

The manifold absolute pressure (MAP) sensor measures the change in the intake manifold pressure (vacuum). The ECM applies 5 volts to the MAP sensor. The change in the pressure, that results from engine load and rpm changes, is converted into a voltage input that is monitored by the ECM. A low voltage reading at the ECM indicates low manifold pressure, and a high voltage reading at the ECM indicates high manifold pressure. Code 32 will set if the following condition is met for 0.2 seconds:

● High voltage input at the ECM indicating intake manifold pressure above 840 mmHg.

Test Description: Number(s) below refer to circled number(s) on the diagnostic chart.

1. This step checks the LT GRN/RED wire for an open, a short to voltage and a faulty ECM. Under normal conditions the LT GRN/RED wire should carry a little less than 5 volts. A short to 5 volts or B+ will cause Code 32 to set.

2. This step checks for an open LT GRN/BLK wire, poor connection at the MAP sensor or ECM and for a faulty MAP sensor or ECM.

Diagnostic Aids:

Check for a leaking vacuum hose to MAP sensor.

An intermittent may be caused by a poor connection, rubbed through wire insulation, or a wire broken inside the insulation. Inspect ECM harness connectors for backed out terminals, improper mating, broken locks, improperly formed or damaged terminals, poor terminal to wire connection and damaged harness.

Fig. 151 1992-93 EFI diagnostic chart

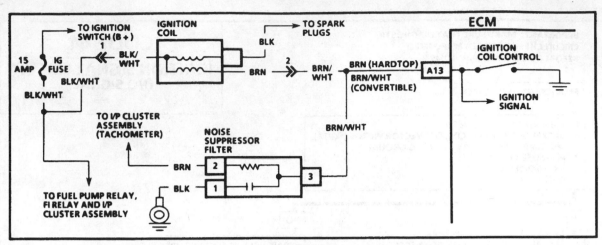

CODE 41

IGNITION SIGNAL CIRCUIT
(NO SIGNAL)

Circuit Description:

The engine control module (ECM) receives an ignition signal when the ignition switch is turned to the "ON" position. When the ignition switch is turned to the "START" position, this signal is toggled on and off through the ECM. As this signal is toggled on and off, so is the ignition coil, thus inducing a voltage in the secondary coil of the ignition coil. This induced voltage is then used to fire the spark plugs.

Code 41 will set if the following condition is met:

• Toggled ignition signal not present at the ECM within 3 seconds of cranking.

Test Description: Number(s) below refer to circled number(s) on the diagnostic chart.

1. This checks for power to the ignition coil.
2. This checks for a poor connection or for a faulty ignition coil.
3. This checks for a poor connection or for a faulty ECM.
4. This checks for a faulty noise suppressor filter.
5. This checks for an open or short to ground in wires between ignition coil, noise suppressor filter and ECM.

Diagnostic Aids:

An intermittent may be caused by a poor connection, rubbed through wire insulation, or a wire broken inside the insulation. Inspect ECM harness connectors for backed out terminals, improper mating, broken locks, improperly formed or damaged terminals, poor terminal to wire connection and damaged harness.

Fig. 152 1992-93 EFI diagnostic chart

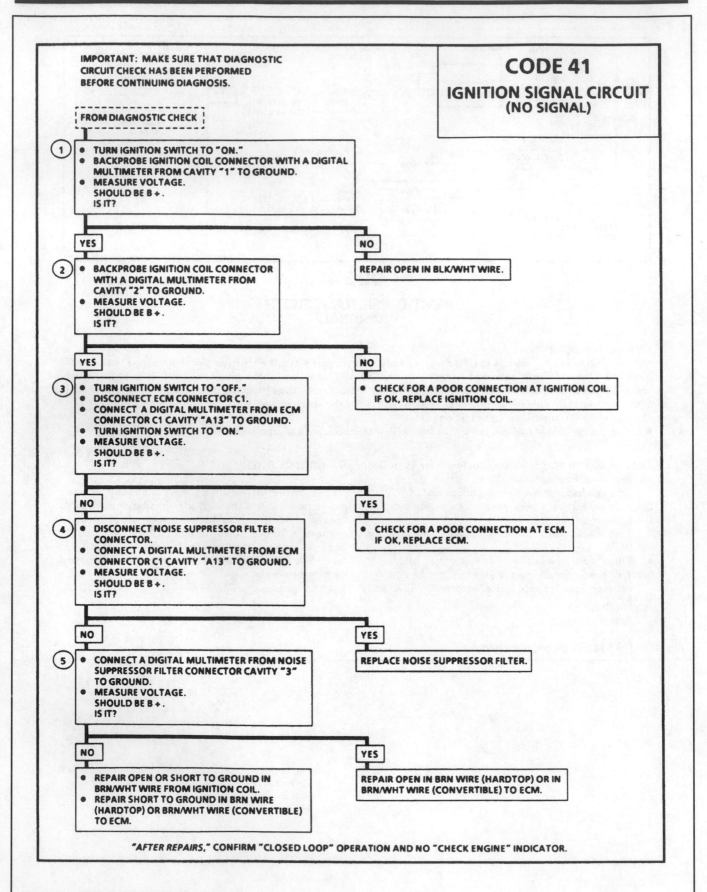

IMPORTANT: MAKE SURE THAT DIAGNOSTIC
CIRCUIT CHECK HAS BEEN PERFORMED
BEFORE CONTINUING DIAGNOSIS.

CODE 41

IGNITION SIGNAL CIRCUIT
(NO SIGNAL)

FROM DIAGNOSTIC CHECK

1
- TURN IGNITION SWITCH TO "ON."
- BACKPROBE IGNITION COIL CONNECTOR WITH A DIGITAL MULTIMETER FROM CAVITY "1" TO GROUND.
- MEASURE VOLTAGE. SHOULD BE B +. IS IT?

YES

NO

2
- BACKPROBE IGNITION COIL CONNECTOR WITH A DIGITAL MULTIMETER FROM CAVITY "2" TO GROUND.
- MEASURE VOLTAGE. SHOULD BE B +. IS IT?

REPAIR OPEN IN BLK/WHT WIRE.

YES

NO

3
- TURN IGNITION SWITCH TO "OFF."
- DISCONNECT ECM CONNECTOR C1.
- CONNECT A DIGITAL MULTIMETER FROM ECM CONNECTOR C1 CAVITY "A13" TO GROUND.
- TURN IGNITION SWITCH TO "ON."
- MEASURE VOLTAGE. SHOULD BE B +. IS IT?

- CHECK FOR A POOR CONNECTION AT IGNITION COIL. IF OK, REPLACE IGNITION COIL.

NO

YES

4
- DISCONNECT NOISE SUPPRESSOR FILTER CONNECTOR.
- CONNECT A DIGITAL MULTIMETER FROM ECM CONNECTOR C1 CAVITY "A13" TO GROUND.
- MEASURE VOLTAGE. SHOULD BE B +. IS IT?

- CHECK FOR A POOR CONNECTION AT ECM. IF OK, REPLACE ECM.

NO

YES

5
- CONNECT A DIGITAL MULTIMETER FROM NOISE SUPPRESSOR FILTER CONNECTOR CAVITY "3" TO GROUND.
- MEASURE VOLTAGE. SHOULD BE B +. IS IT?

REPLACE NOISE SUPPRESSOR FILTER.

NO

YES

- REPAIR OPEN OR SHORT TO GROUND IN BRN/WHT WIRE FROM IGNITION COIL.
- REPAIR SHORT TO GROUND IN BRN WIRE (HARDTOP) OR BRN/WHT WIRE (CONVERTIBLE) TO ECM.

REPAIR OPEN IN BRN WIRE (HARDTOP) OR IN BRN/WHT WIRE (CONVERTIBLE) TO ECM.

"AFTER REPAIRS," CONFIRM "CLOSED LOOP" OPERATION AND NO "CHECK ENGINE" INDICATOR.

Fig. 153 1992-93 EFI diagnostic chart

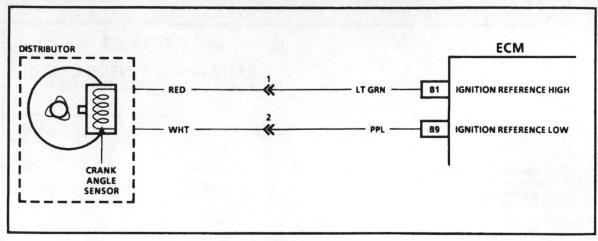

CODE 42

CRANK ANGLE SENSOR CIRCUIT
(NO SIGNAL FOR 3 SECONDS)

Circuit Description:

When the distributor shaft rotates, a fluctuating magnetic field is generated due to changes in the air gap between the crank angle sensor and distributor shaft signal rotor. As a result, a small alternating current (AC) voltage is induced in the crank angle sensor. This ignition reference signal is sent to the ECM on terminals "B1" and "B9," the ECM monitors the AC voltage between these two terminals. The ECM uses this signal in determining when to fire the ignition coil and the fuel injector.

Code 42 will set if the following condition is met for 3 seconds:

• No ignition reference signal at the ECM.

Test Description: Number(s) below refer to circled number(s) on the diagnostic chart.

1. Crank angle sensor contains a coil of very small wire. Its DC resistance is checked here.
2. When the distributor shaft turns, the crank angle sensor acts as an AC voltage signal generator. This checks for a proper AC signal voltage being produced.
3. After proving that the sensor is capable of generating the proper AC signal voltage, this step checks to see if this voltage is getting through to the ECM connector.

Diagnostic Aids:

A loose or damaged crank angle sensor could cause an intermittent code.

A misaligned crank angle sensor or improper air gap could result in Code 42 or intermittent "Cranks But Won't Run."

Fig. 154 1992-93 EFI diagnostic chart

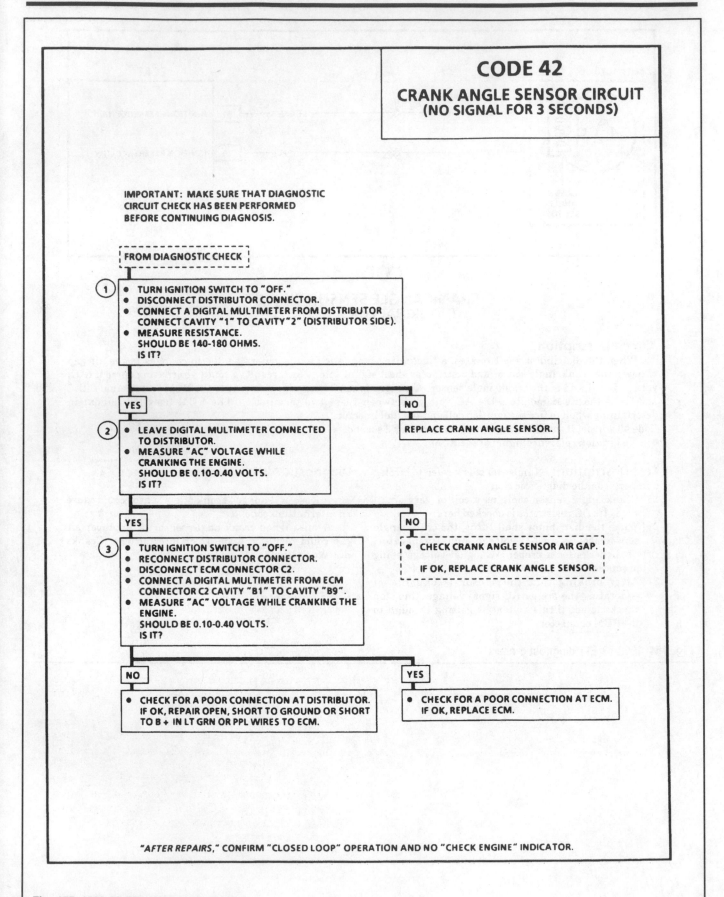

CODE 42
CRANK ANGLE SENSOR CIRCUIT
(NO SIGNAL FOR 3 SECONDS)

IMPORTANT: MAKE SURE THAT DIAGNOSTIC
CIRCUIT CHECK HAS BEEN PERFORMED
BEFORE CONTINUING DIAGNOSIS.

FROM DIAGNOSTIC CHECK

1
- TURN IGNITION SWITCH TO "OFF."
- DISCONNECT DISTRIBUTOR CONNECTOR.
- CONNECT A DIGITAL MULTIMETER FROM DISTRIBUTOR
  CONNECT CAVITY "1" TO CAVITY "2" (DISTRIBUTOR SIDE).
- MEASURE RESISTANCE.
  SHOULD BE 140-180 OHMS.
  IS IT?

YES | NO

2
- LEAVE DIGITAL MULTIMETER CONNECTED
  TO DISTRIBUTOR.
- MEASURE "AC" VOLTAGE WHILE
  CRANKING THE ENGINE.
  SHOULD BE 0.10-0.40 VOLTS.
  IS IT?

NO → REPLACE CRANK ANGLE SENSOR.

YES | NO

3
- TURN IGNITION SWITCH TO "OFF."
- RECONNECT DISTRIBUTOR CONNECTOR.
- DISCONNECT ECM CONNECTOR C2.
- CONNECT A DIGITAL MULTIMETER FROM ECM
  CONNECTOR C2 CAVITY "B1" TO CAVITY "B9".
- MEASURE "AC" VOLTAGE WHILE CRANKING THE
  ENGINE.
  SHOULD BE 0.10-0.40 VOLTS.
  IS IT?

NO →
- CHECK CRANK ANGLE SENSOR AIR GAP.

  IF OK, REPLACE CRANK ANGLE SENSOR.

NO | YES

- CHECK FOR A POOR CONNECTION AT DISTRIBUTOR.
  IF OK, REPAIR OPEN, SHORT TO GROUND OR SHORT
  TO B + IN LT GRN OR PPL WIRES TO ECM.

- CHECK FOR A POOR CONNECTION AT ECM.
  IF OK, REPLACE ECM.

"AFTER REPAIRS," CONFIRM *"CLOSED LOOP"* OPERATION AND NO *"CHECK ENGINE"* INDICATOR.

Fig. 155 1992-93 EFI diagnostic chart

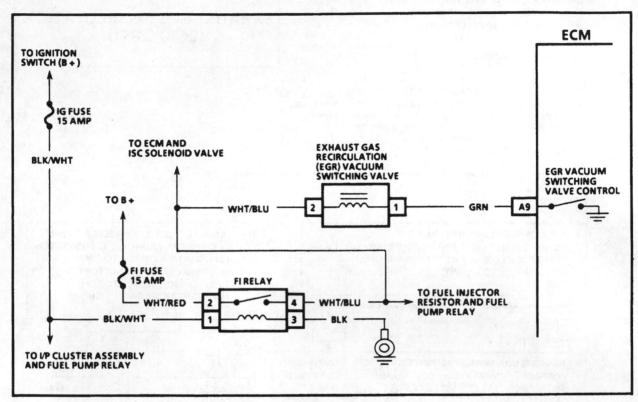

CODE 51
EXHAUST GAS RECIRCULATION (EGR) CIRCUIT

Circuit Description:

The EGR vacuum switching valve solenoid is ECM controlled. Battery voltage is applied to the VSV solenoid from the FI relay. When the driver in the ECM closes, the EGR vacuum switching valve solenoid is activated. Code 51 will set if the following conditions are met:
- System is operating in "closed loop" operation.
- MAP is less than a calibrated value.

Test Description: Number(s) below refer to circled number(s) on the diagnostic chart.

1. This will check the circuit for a short to ground.
2. Checks for voltage from FI relay.
3. Checks the circuit for a short to ground or a faulty ECM.
4. Checks the circuit for an open GRN wire.
5. A high resistance in the solenoid coil could cause a Code 51.

Diagnostic Aids:

A poor or loose connection at the ECM could cause an intermittent. This could cause a code to be set falsely.

Closely check all vacuum hoses to the throttle body and the EGR valve. Also check the MAP sensor vacuum hose for leaks or restrictions. In "closed loop" operation with EGR enabled, the ECM will periodically turn "OFF" the EGR VSV. If the corresponding manifold pressure change is less than a calibrated value, the ECM determines that a fault exists in the EGR system and sets a Code 51.

Fig. 156 1992-93 EFI diagnostic chart

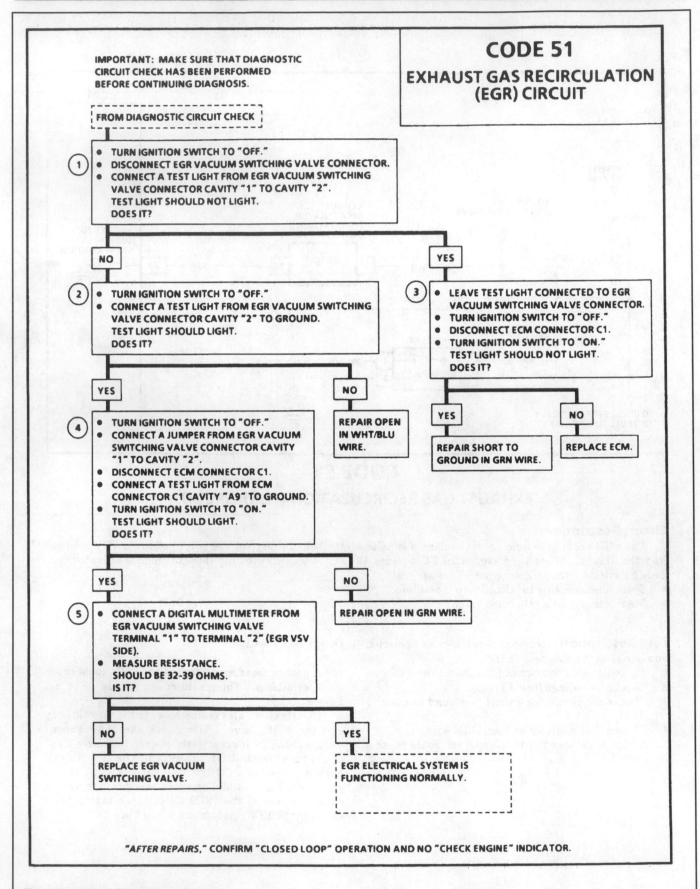

IMPORTANT: MAKE SURE THAT DIAGNOSTIC CIRCUIT CHECK HAS BEEN PERFORMED BEFORE CONTINUING DIAGNOSIS.

CODE 51

EXHAUST GAS RECIRCULATION (EGR) CIRCUIT

FROM DIAGNOSTIC CIRCUIT CHECK

1
- TURN IGNITION SWITCH TO "OFF."
- DISCONNECT EGR VACUUM SWITCHING VALVE CONNECTOR.
- CONNECT A TEST LIGHT FROM EGR VACUUM SWITCHING VALVE CONNECTOR CAVITY "1" TO CAVITY "2". TEST LIGHT SHOULD NOT LIGHT. DOES IT?

NO

YES

2
- TURN IGNITION SWITCH TO "OFF."
- CONNECT A TEST LIGHT FROM EGR VACUUM SWITCHING VALVE CONNECTOR CAVITY "2" TO GROUND. TEST LIGHT SHOULD LIGHT. DOES IT?

3
- LEAVE TEST LIGHT CONNECTED TO EGR VACUUM SWITCHING VALVE CONNECTOR.
- TURN IGNITION SWITCH TO "OFF."
- DISCONNECT ECM CONNECTOR C1.
- TURN IGNITION SWITCH TO "ON." TEST LIGHT SHOULD NOT LIGHT. DOES IT?

YES

NO

REPAIR OPEN IN WHT/BLU WIRE.

YES

NO

4
- TURN IGNITION SWITCH TO "OFF."
- CONNECT A JUMPER FROM EGR VACUUM SWITCHING VALVE CONNECTOR CAVITY "1" TO CAVITY "2".
- DISCONNECT ECM CONNECTOR C1.
- CONNECT A TEST LIGHT FROM ECM CONNECTOR C1 CAVITY "A9" TO GROUND.
- TURN IGNITION SWITCH TO "ON." TEST LIGHT SHOULD LIGHT. DOES IT?

REPAIR SHORT TO GROUND IN GRN WIRE.

REPLACE ECM.

YES

NO

REPAIR OPEN IN GRN WIRE.

5
- CONNECT A DIGITAL MULTIMETER FROM EGR VACUUM SWITCHING VALVE TERMINAL "1" TO TERMINAL "2" (EGR VSV SIDE).
- MEASURE RESISTANCE. SHOULD BE 32-39 OHMS. IS IT?

NO

YES

REPLACE EGR VACUUM SWITCHING VALVE.

EGR ELECTRICAL SYSTEM IS FUNCTIONING NORMALLY.

"AFTER REPAIRS," CONFIRM "CLOSED LOOP" OPERATION AND NO "CHECK ENGINE" INDICATOR.

Fig. 157 1992-93 EFI diagnostic chart

VACUUM DIAGRAMS

▶ See Figures 158, 159, 160, 161, 162, 163, 164, 165, 166, 167 and 168

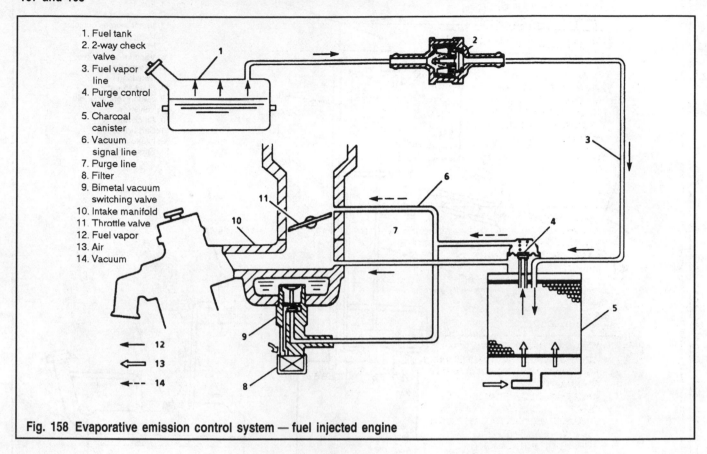

1. Fuel tank
2. 2-way check valve
3. Fuel vapor line
4. Purge control valve
5. Charcoal canister
6. Vacuum signal line
7. Purge line
8. Filter
9. Bimetal vacuum switching valve
10. Intake manifold
11. Throttle valve
12. Fuel vapor
13. Air
14. Vacuum

Fig. 158 Evaporative emission control system — fuel injected engine

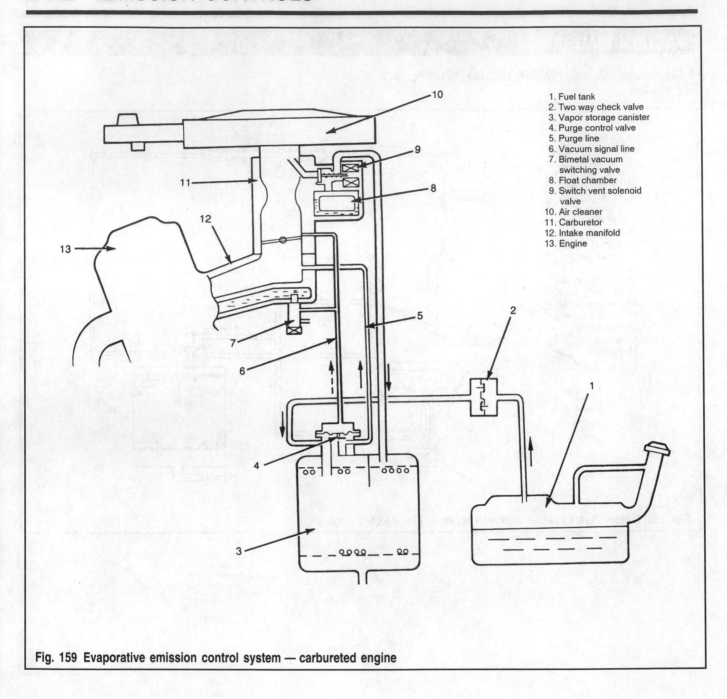

1. Fuel tank
2. Two way check valve
3. Vapor storage canister
4. Purge control valve
5. Purge line
6. Vacuum signal line
7. Bimetal vacuum switching valve
8. Float chamber
9. Switch vent solenoid valve
10. Air cleaner
11. Carburetor
12. Intake manifold
13. Engine

Fig. 159 Evaporative emission control system — carbureted engine

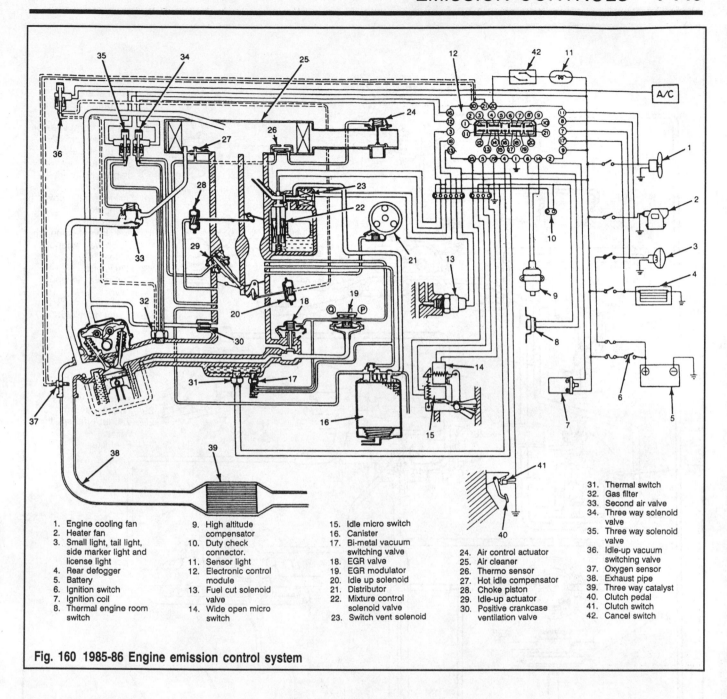

Fig. 160 1985-86 Engine emission control system

1. Engine cooling fan
2. Heater fan
3. Small light, tail light, side marker light and license light
4. Rear defogger
5. Battery
6. Ignition switch
7. Ignition coil
8. Thermal engine room switch
9. High altitude compensator
10. Duty check connector.
11. Sensor light
12. Electronic control module
13. Fuel cut solenoid valve
14. Wide open micro switch
15. Idle micro switch
16. Canister
17. Bi-metal vacuum switching valve
18. EGR valve
19. EGR modulator
20. Idle up solenoid
21. Distributor
22. Mixture control solenoid valve
23. Switch vent solenoid
24. Air control actuator
25. Air cleaner
26. Thermo sensor
27. Hot idle compensator
28. Choke piston
29. Idle-up actuator
30. Positive crankcase ventilation valve
31. Thermal switch
32. Gas filter
33. Second air valve
34. Three way solenoid valve
35. Three way solenoid valve
36. Idle-up vacuum switching valve
37. Oxygen sensor
38. Exhaust pipe
39. Three way catalyst
40. Clutch pedal
41. Clutch switch
42. Cancel switch

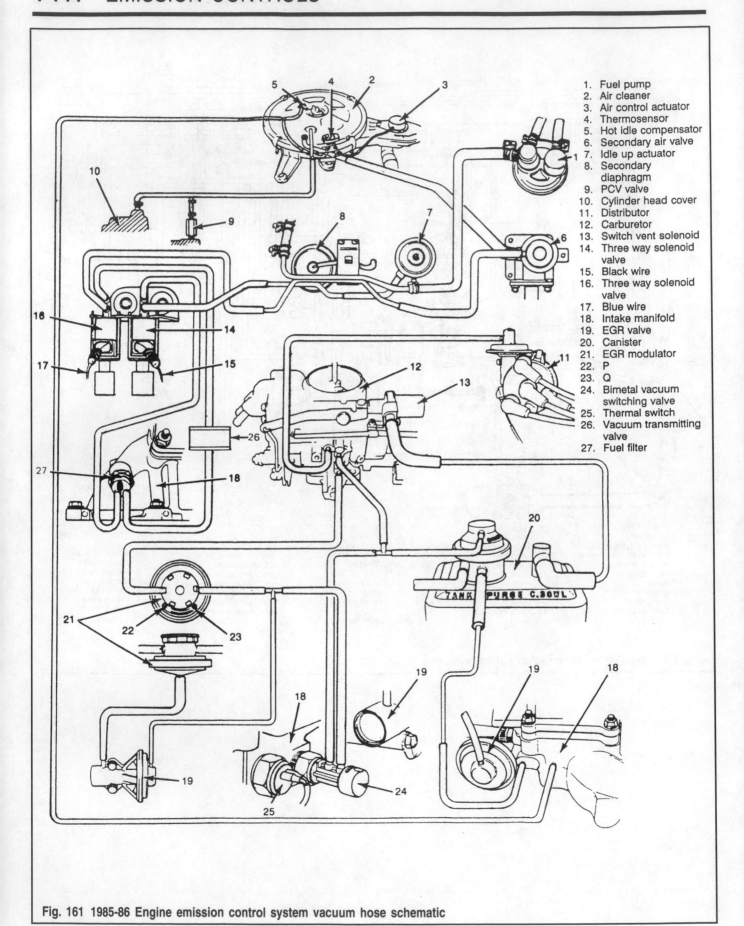

1. Fuel pump
2. Air cleaner
3. Air control actuator
4. Thermosensor
5. Hot idle compensator
6. Secondary air valve
7. Idle up actuator
8. Secondary diaphragm
9. PCV valve
10. Cylinder head cover
11. Distributor
12. Carburetor
13. Switch vent solenoid
14. Three way solenoid valve
15. Black wire
16. Three way solenoid valve
17. Blue wire
18. Intake manifold
19. EGR valve
20. Canister
21. EGR modulator
22. P
23. Q
24. Bimetal vacuum switching valve
25. Thermal switch
26. Vacuum transmitting valve
27. Fuel filter

Fig. 161 1985-86 Engine emission control system vacuum hose schematic

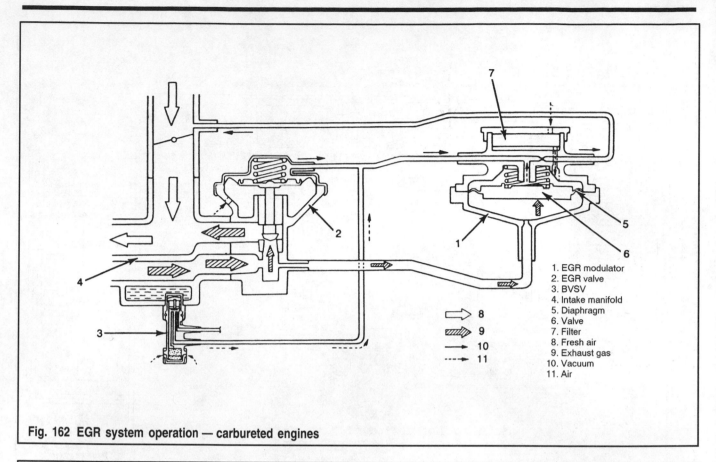

Fig. 162 EGR system operation — carbureted engines

1. EGR modulator
2. EGR valve
3. BVSV
4. Intake manifold
5. Diaphragm
6. Valve
7. Filter
8. Fresh air
9. Exhaust gas
10. Vacuum
11. Air

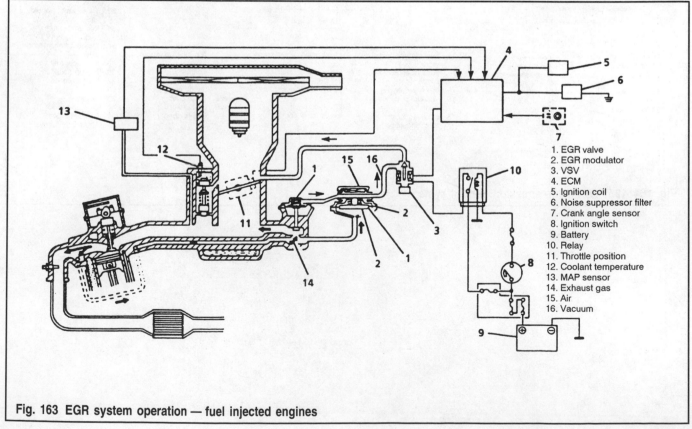

Fig. 163 EGR system operation — fuel injected engines

1. EGR valve
2. EGR modulator
3. VSV
4. ECM
5. Ignition coil
6. Noise suppressor filter
7. Crank angle sensor
8. Ignition switch
9. Battery
10. Relay
11. Throttle position
12. Coolant temperature
13. MAP sensor
14. Exhaust gas
15. Air
16. Vacuum

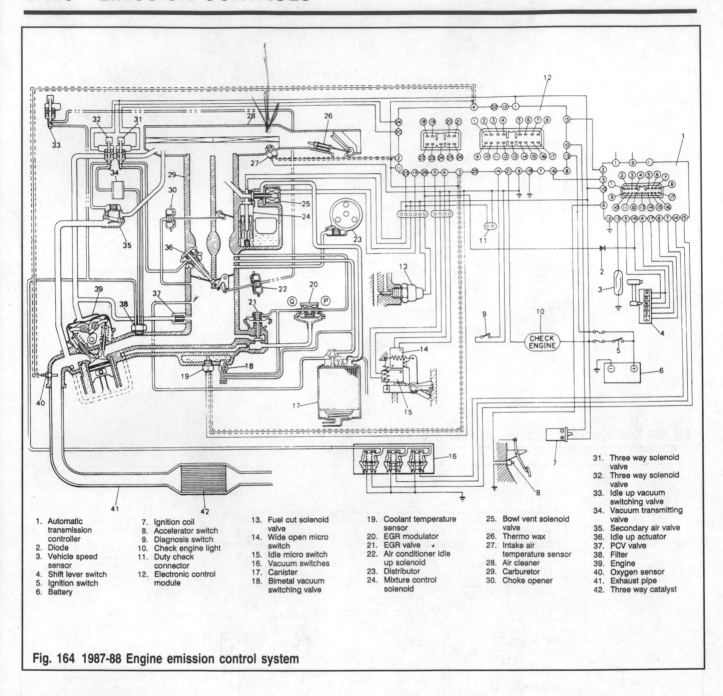

Fig. 164 1987-88 Engine emission control system

1. Automatic transmission controller
2. Diode
3. Vehicle speed sensor
4. Shift lever switch
5. Ignition switch
6. Battery

7. Ignition coil
8. Accelerator switch
9. Diagnosis switch
10. Check engine light
11. Duty check connector
12. Electronic control module

13. Fuel cut solenoid valve
14. Wide open micro switch
15. Idle micro switch
16. Vacuum switches
17. Canister
18. Bimetal vacuum switching valve

19. Coolant temperature sensor
20. EGR modulator
21. EGR valve
22. Air conditioner idle up solenoid
23. Distributor
24. Mixture control solenoid

25. Bowl vent solenoid valve
26. Thermo wax
27. Intake air temperature sensor
28. Air cleaner
29. Carburetor
30. Choke opener

31. Three way solenoid valve
32. Three way solenoid valve
33. Idle up vacuum switching valve
34. Vacuum transmitting valve
35. Secondary air valve
36. Idle up actuator
37. PCV valve
38. Filter
39. Engine
40. Oxygen sensor
41. Exhaust pipe
42. Three way catalyst

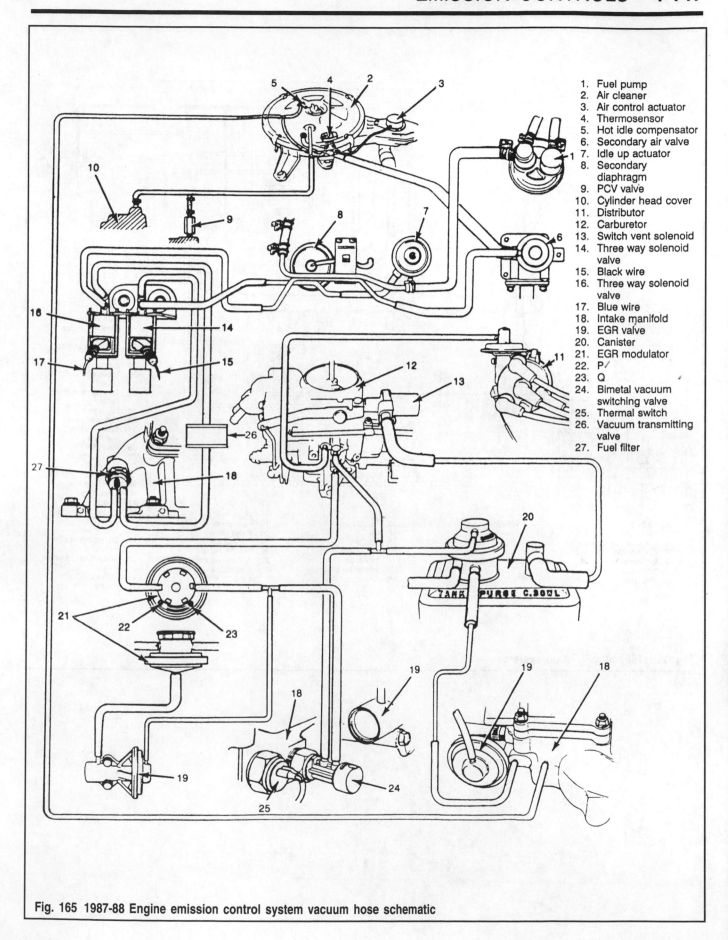

1. Fuel pump
2. Air cleaner
3. Air control actuator
4. Thermosensor
5. Hot idle compensator
6. Secondary air valve
7. Idle up actuator
8. Secondary diaphragm
9. PCV valve
10. Cylinder head cover
11. Distributor
12. Carburetor
13. Switch vent solenoid
14. Three way solenoid valve
15. Black wire
16. Three way solenoid valve
17. Blue wire
18. Intake manifold
19. EGR valve
20. Canister
21. EGR modulator
22. P
23. Q
24. Bimetal vacuum switching valve
25. Thermal switch
26. Vacuum transmitting valve
27. Fuel filter

Fig. 165 1987-88 Engine emission control system vacuum hose schematic

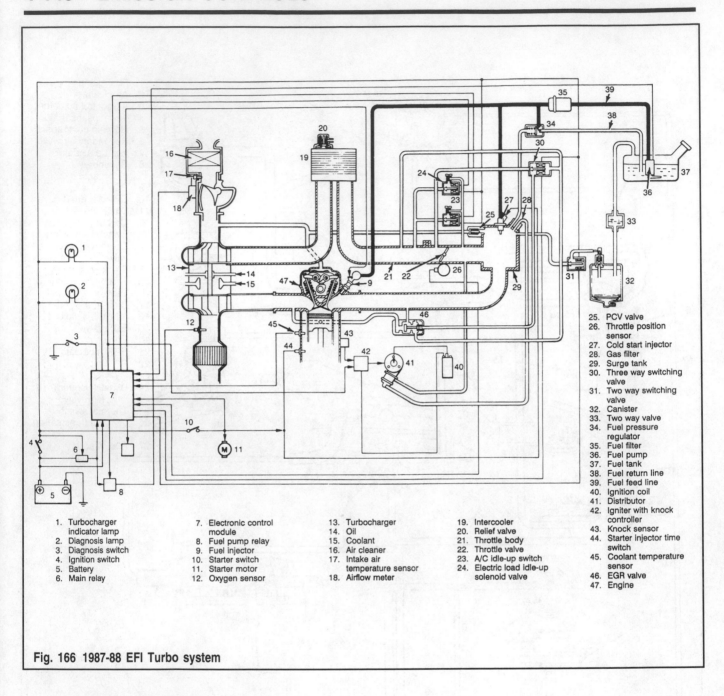

Fig. 166 1987-88 EFI Turbo system

1. Turbocharger indicator lamp
2. Diagnosis lamp
3. Diagnosis switch
4. Ignition switch
5. Battery
6. Main relay
7. Electronic control module
8. Fuel pump relay
9. Fuel injector
10. Starter switch
11. Starter motor
12. Oxygen sensor
13. Turbocharger
14. Oil
15. Coolant
16. Air cleaner
17. Intake air temperature sensor
18. Airflow meter
19. Intercooler
20. Relief valve
21. Throttle body
22. Throttle valve
23. A/C idle-up switch
24. Electric load idle-up solenoid valve
25. PCV valve
26. Throttle position sensor
27. Cold start injector
28. Gas filter
29. Surge tank
30. Three way switching valve
31. Two way switching valve
32. Canister
33. Two way valve
34. Fuel pressure regulator
35. Fuel filter
36. Fuel pump
37. Fuel tank
38. Fuel return line
39. Fuel feed line
40. Ignition coil
41. Distributor
42. Igniter with knock controller
43. Knock sensor
44. Starter injector time switch
45. Coolant temperature sensor
46. EGR valve
47. Engine

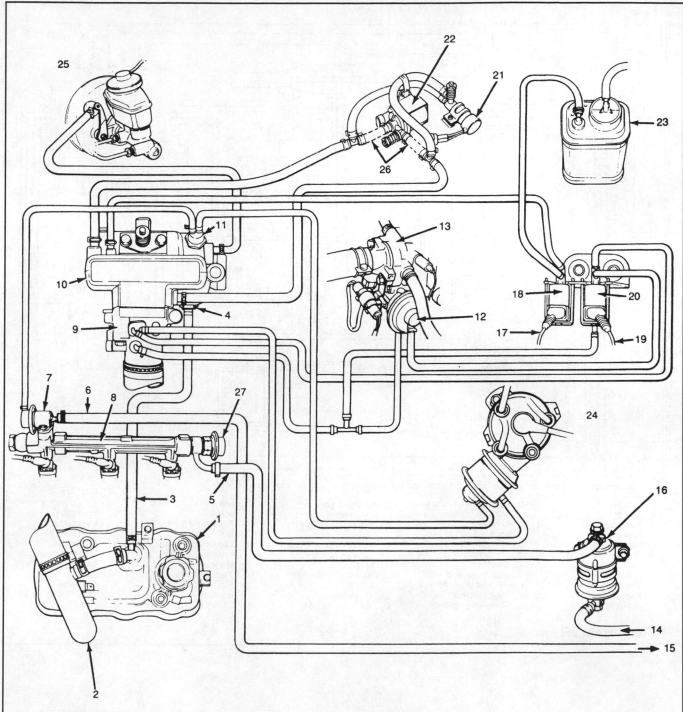

Fig. 167 1987-88 EFI Turbo system vacuum hose schematic

1. Cylinder head
2. Turbocharger intake pipe
3. PCV hose
4. PCV valve
5. Fuel feed hose
6. Fuel return hose
7. Fuel pressure regulator
8. Fuel delivery pipe

9. Throttle body
10. Surge tank
11. Gas filter
12. EGR valve
13. Intake manifold
14. From fuel pump
15. To fuel tank
16. Fuel filter
17. White/Blue and Red/Yellow wires

18. Canister vacuum switching valve
19. White/Blue and Red/green wires
20. EGR vacuum switching valve
21. Electric load idle up vacuum switching valve

22. Air conditioner idle up vacuum switching valve
23. Canister
24. Distributor
25. Brake booster
26. Only for air conditioning equipped vehicle
27. Fuel pulsation damper

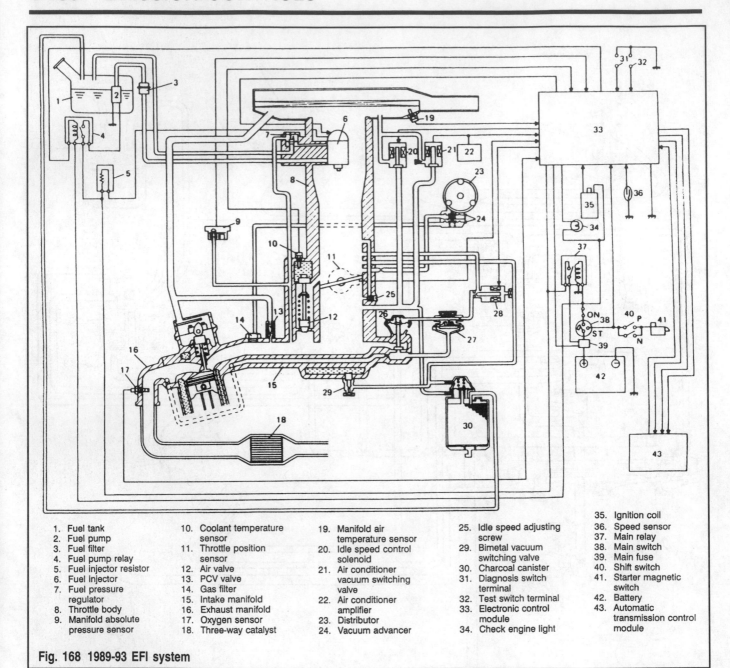

1. Fuel tank
2. Fuel pump
3. Fuel filter
4. Fuel pump relay
5. Fuel injector resistor
6. Fuel injector
7. Fuel pressure regulator
8. Throttle body
9. Manifold absolute pressure sensor
10. Coolant temperature sensor
11. Throttle position sensor
12. Air valve
13. PCV valve
14. Gas filter
15. Intake manifold
16. Exhaust manifold
17. Oxygen sensor
18. Three-way catalyst
19. Manifold air temperature sensor
20. Idle speed control solenoid
21. Air conditioner vacuum switching valve
22. Air conditioner amplifier
23. Distributor
24. Vacuum advancer
25. Idle speed adjusting screw
29. Bimetal vacuum switching valve
30. Charcoal canister
31. Diagnosis switch terminal
32. Test switch terminal
33. Electronic control module
34. Check engine light
35. Ignition coil
36. Speed sensor
37. Main relay
38. Main switch
39. Main fuse
40. Shift switch
41. Starter magnetic switch
42. Battery
43. Automatic transmission control module

Fig. 168 1989-93 EFI system

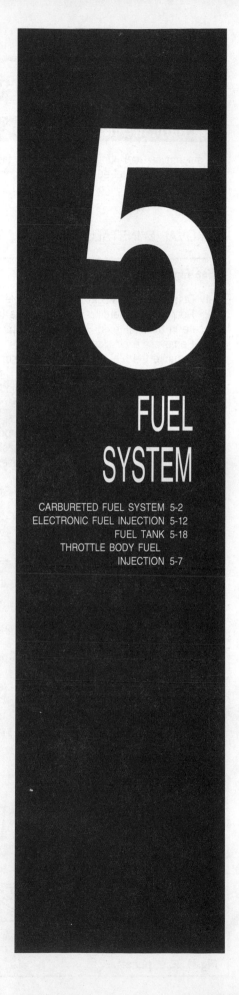

5

FUEL SYSTEM

CARBURETED FUEL SYSTEM

Mechanical Fuel Pump

A mechanical fuel pump is mounted on the cylinder head. The diaphragm in fuel pump is actuated from the cam on the engine camshaft, through a fuel pump rod and rocker arm of the fuel pump.

REMOVAL & INSTALLATION

▶ **See Figure 1**

1. Disconnect the negative battery cable.
2. Remove the fuel filler cap to release the fuel vapor pressure in the fuel tank. Reinstall the cap.
3. Remove the air cleaner
4. Remove the fuel inlet, outlet and return hoses from the fuel pump.
5. Remove the fuel pump from the cylinder head.
6. Remove the fuel pump rod from the cylinder head.

To install:

7. Lubricate and install the fuel pump rod.
8. Install the fuel pump using a new gasket.
9. Install the inlet, outlet and return hoses to the fuel pump.
10. Install the air cleaner
11. Connect the negative battery cable. Start the engine and check for leaks.

TESTING

1. Disconnect the fuel outlet hose from the fuel pump.
2. Connect a pressure gauge to the outlet hose using a T-fitting.
3. Start the engine and read the fuel pressure on the gauge.
4. Fuel pressure should be at lead 3.5 psi. If not, check for clogs or leaks in the fuel system.
5. If the fuel system hoses and pipes are clear, replace the fuel pump.

Carburetor

This 2-barrel, downdraft type carburetor has primary and secondary systems. The primary system operates under normal driving conditions and the secondary system operates under high speed-high load driving conditions. The choke valve is provided in the primary system.

The main components and their functions are as follows:

• The primary system has a mixture control solenoid valve which is operated by the electrical signals from the Electronic Control Module (ECM). The solenoid maintains the optimum air/fuel ratio of the primary slow and the primary main fuel systems at all times.

• A fuel cut solenoid valve stops fuel flow under deceleration and prevents dieseling when the engine is stopped.

• An accelerator pump system provides additional fuel for acceleration.

• The secondary system has a secondary vacuum break unit which is operated by the vacuum from the primary side and actuates the secondary throttle valve.

• The choke system is a full automatic type using a thermowax

• The switch vent solenoid valve provided on top of the float chamber is to reduce evaporative emissions.

ADJUSTMENTS

▶ **See Figures 2, 3, 4, 5, 6, 7, 8, 9, 10 and 11**

Accelerator Cable

1. Check accelerator cable for play. Move the accelerator cable up and down to determine free-play.
2. Accelerator cable free-play should not exceed 0.40-0.59 in. (10-15mm) when engine and carburetor are cold or 0.12-0.19 in. (3-5mm) when engine and carburetor are warm.
3. If out of specification loosen locknut and adjust by turning adjusting nut.

Float

1. The fuel level in float chamber should be within round mark at the center of the level gauge.

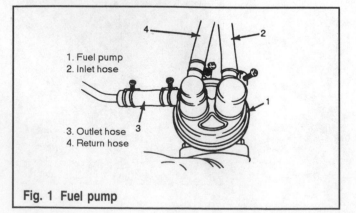

1. Fuel pump
2. Inlet hose
3. Outlet hose
4. Return hose

Fig. 1 Fuel pump

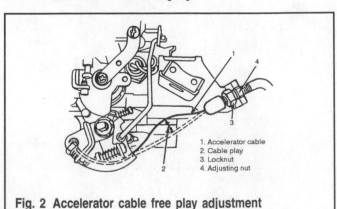

1. Accelerator cable
2. Cable play
3. Locknut
4. Adjusting nut

Fig. 2 Accelerator cable free play adjustment

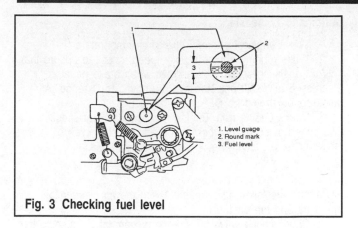

1. Level guage
2. Round mark
3. Fuel level

Fig. 3 Checking fuel level

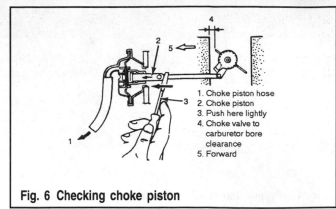

1. Choke piston hose
2. Choke piston
3. Push here lightly
4. Choke valve to carburetor bore clearance
5. Forward

Fig. 6 Checking choke piston

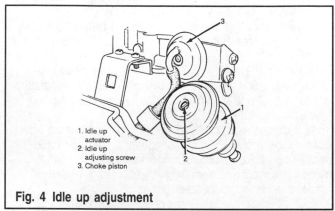

1. Idle up actuator
2. Idle up adjusting screw
3. Choke piston

Fig. 4 Idle up adjustment

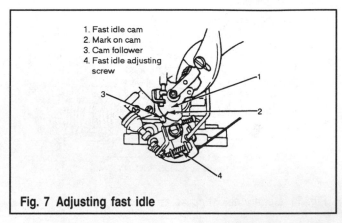

1. Fast idle cam
2. Mark on cam
3. Cam follower
4. Fast idle adjusting screw

Fig. 7 Adjusting fast idle

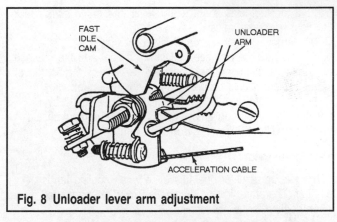

FAST IDLE CAM

UNLOADER ARM

ACCELERATION CABLE

Fig. 8 Unloader lever arm adjustment

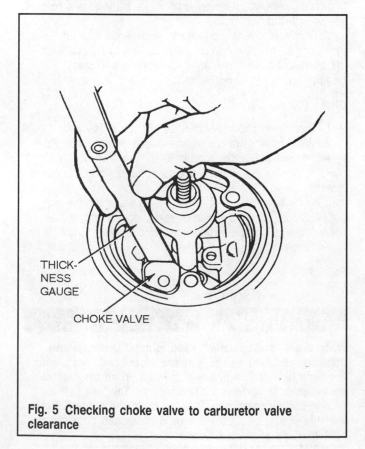

THICK-NESS GAUGE

CHOKE VALVE

Fig. 5 Checking choke valve to carburetor valve clearance

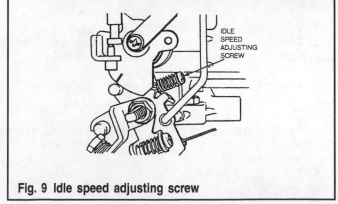

IDLE SPEED ADJUSTING SCREW

Fig. 9 Idle speed adjusting screw

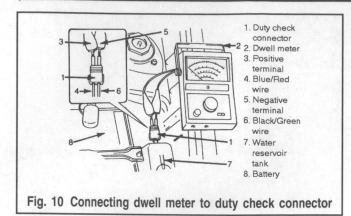

1. Duty check connector
2. Dwell meter
3. Positive terminal
4. Blue/Red wire
5. Negative terminal
6. Black/Green wire
7. Water reservoir tank
8. Battery

Fig. 10 Connecting dwell meter to duty check connector

MIXTURE ADJUSTING SCREW

Fig. 11 Mixture adjusting screw

2. If the fuel level is not found within the round mark check the float level and adjust.

3. Remove the air horn and invert it.

4. Measure the distance between the float and the surface of the choke chamber. the measured distance is the float level. Measurement should be 0.21-0.24 in. (5.3-6.3 mm).

5. If the float level is out of specification, adjust it by bending the tongue up and down. This measurement should be made without a gasket on the air horn.

Idle Up Actuator

The idle-up actuator operates even when cooling fan is running. Therefore, idle-up adjustment must be performed when cooling fan is not running.

Manual Transaxle

1. Warm engine to normal operating temperature.

2. While running engine at idle speed, check to ensure that idle up adjusting screw moves down when lights are turned **ON**.

3. With lights turned **ON** check engine rpm. Be sure that heater fan, rear defogger, engine cooling fan and air conditioner are **OFF**.

4. Engine rpm should be at specified idle speed or 50 rpm higher. If not, adjust using idle up adjusting screw located at top of idle up solenoid.

5. Check idle up system as described above with the heater fan, rear defogger, engine cooling fan and air conditioner are all operated separately.

Automatic Transaxle

1. Warm engine to normal operating temperature.

2. While running engine at idle speed, check to ensure that idle up adjusting screw moves down when brake pedal is depressed and shift selector lever is moved to **D** range. All accessories should be **OFF**.

3. Check engine rpm. Engine rpm should be at specified idle speed or 50 rpm higher. If not, adjust using idle up adjusting screw located at top of idle up solenoid.

Choke Valve

Perform the following adjustment with the air cleaner top removed and the engine cold.

1. Check choke valve for smooth movement by pushing it with a finger.

2. Make sure that choke valve is closed almost completely when ambient temperature is below 77°F (25°C) and engine is cold.

3. Check to ensure that choke valve to carburetor bore clearance is 0.004-0.019 in. (0.1-0.5mm) when air temperature is 77°F (25°C) and 0.03-0.06 in. (0.7-1.7mm) when air temperature is 95°F (35°C).

4. If clearance is not within specification, remove the air cleaner case and check strangler spring, choke piston and each link in choke system for smooth operation. Lubricate choke valve shaft and each link with lubricant if necessary. Do not remove riveted choke lever guide.

5. If the clearance is still out of specification, even after lubrication, remove carburetor from intake manifold and remove idle up actuator from carburetor.

6. Turn fast idle cam counterclockwise and insert an available pin into holes on cam and bracket to lock cam. In this state, bend the choke lever up or down with pliers. Bending up causes choke valve to close and vice-versa.

Choke Piston

1. Disconnect choke piston hose at throttle chamber.

2. With choke valve pushed down to its closing side lightly by finger pressure, apply vacuum to choke piston hose and check to ensure that choke valve to carburetor bore clearance is within 0.09-0.10 in. (2.3-2.6mm).

3. With vacuum applied, move choke piston rod toward diaphragm with small screwdriver and check to ensure that choke valve to carburetor bore clearance is within 0.16-0.18 in. (4.0-4.7mm).

Fast Idle

1. Drain the cooling system.

❋❋CAUTION

When draining the coolant, keep in mind that cats and dogs are attracted by the ethylene glycol antifreeze, and are quite likely to drink any that is left in an uncovered container or in puddles on the ground. This will prove fatal in sufficient quantity. Always drain the coolant into a sealable container. Coolant should be reused unless it is contaminated or several years old.

2. After draining, disconnect choke hoses from the carburetor thermo element holder and plug them.

3. Install radiator drain plug and refill cooling system.

4. Start engine and check hoses for leakage. After making sure that both hoses are free from leakage, warm engine to normal operating temperature.

5. With engine running at idle speed, force fast idle cam to rotate counterclockwise with pliers until mark on cam aligns with center of cam follower.

6. Check to ensure that engine speed is within 2100-2700 rpm.

7. If engine speed is not within specification, adjust by turning fast idle adjusting screw.

8. After adjusting fast idle speed, reconnect hoses.

Unloader

1. Perform this adjustment when engine is cold.
2. Remove air cleaner cover.
3. Make sure that choke valve is closed.
4. Fully open throttle valve and check choke valve to carburetor bore clearance to ensure is is within 0.10-0.12 in. (2.5-3.3mm).
5. If clearance is out of specification, adjust by bending the unloader arm.

Idle Speed

1. Check emission control system wires, accelerator cable, ignition timing and valve lash prior to setting idle speed.
2. Connect a tachometer to the engine.
3. Place transaxle in **N** and set parking brake.
4. Warm engine to normal operating temperature.
5. With lights, heater fan, rear defogger, cooling fan and air conditioner all **OFF**, check idle speed.
6. If idle speed is not within specification adjust by turning throttle screw.
7. After idle speed adjustment, check idle up system.
8. Stop engine and check accelerator cable to ensure that free-play is within specification.

Idle Mixture

The carburetor has been calibrated at the factory and should not normally need adjustment. For this reason, the mixture adjustment should never be changed from the original factory setting. However, if during diagnosis, the check indicates the carburetor to be the cause of a driver performance complaint or emission failure, or the carburetor is overhauled or replaced, the idle mixture can be adjusted using the following procedure.

1. Check the ignition timing and valve lash. Ensure the idle up actuator does not operate and the cooling fan does not run.
2. Remove the carburetor from the intake manifold following normal service procedure to again access to the mixture adjust screw pin covering the mixture adjust screw.
3. Using a 4-4.5mm drill, drill a hole in pin. After drilling, remove pin by punch or equivalent.
4. Reinstall the carburetor and air cleaner following normal service procedures. Connect emission control system hoses and lead wires. Make specified play on accelerator cable and refill cooling system.
5. Place transaxle gear shift lever in **N** and set parking brake.
6. Start engine and allow it to reach operating temperature.

7. Remove coupler on duty check connector in engine compartment and connect a dwell meter to the connector. Connect the positive terminal of dwell meter to Blue/Red wire and the negative terminal to Black/Green wire.

8. Set dwell meter to 6-cylinder position.

9. Check idle speed and adjust if not within specification.

10. Run engine at idle speed and adjust mixture screw slowly. Adjust until the desired 21-27 degrees is obtained. Allow time for dwell to stabilize after turning screw.

11. Check idle speed after setting mixture and adjust as required.

12. If adjustment cannot be made because the dwell meter does not deflect, check the feedback system.

REMOVAL & INSTALLATION

1. Disconnect the negative battery cable.
2. Drain the cooling system.

✳✳CAUTION

When draining the coolant, keep in mind that cats and dogs are attracted by the ethylene glycol antifreeze, and are quite likely to drink any that is left in an uncovered container or in puddles on the ground. This will prove fatal in sufficient quantity. Always drain the coolant into a sealable container. Coolant should be reused unless it is contaminated or several years old.

3. Remove the air cleaner element.

4. Disconnect warm air hose, cool air hose, second air hose, vacuum hose and EGR modulator from air cleaner case.

5. Remove air cleaner, accelerator cable, electric lead wires, emission control hoses, choke hoses and fuel hose.

6. Remove carburetor from intake manifold.

To install:

7. Using a new gasket, install carburetor on intake manifold.

8. Install air cleaner, accelerator cable, electric lead wires, emission control hoses, choke hoses and fuel hose.

9. Connect warm air hose, cool air hose, second air hose, vacuum hose and EGR modulator on air cleaner case.

10. Install the air cleaner element.

11. Refill the cooling system.

12. Connect the negative battery cable.

OVERHAUL

▶ **See Figure 12**

Disassembly

1. Remove air horn from float chamber after disconnecting hoses and pump lever and removing screws from air horn.

2. Remove float and needle valve from air horn and then needle valve seat and filter.

3. Remove micro switch bracket after removing springs and set screws. Do not remove micro switches from bracket.

1. Air horn
2. Float chamber
3. Throttle chamber
4. Cable bracket
5. Pump lever
6. Pump rod
7. Washer
8. Choke lever guide
9. Thermo element holder
10. Seal
11. Thermo element
12. Choke piston
13. Delay valve
14. Switch vent solenoid
15. Connector holder
16. Connector (6 terminal)
17. Connector (4 terminal)
18. Primary slow air bleeder
19. Secondary slow air bleeder
20. Mixture control solenoid valve
21. Solenoid valve seal
22. Needle valve filter
23. Needle valve gasket
24. Needle valve
25. Float
26. Air horn gasket
27. Pump piston
28. Piston return spring
29. Ball
30. Injector weight
31. Injector spring
32. Injector weight
33. Ball
34. Primary slow air bleeder
35. Primary slow jet
36. Primary main air bleeder
37. Secondary main air bleeder
38. Plug
39. Secondary slow jet
40. Idle micro switch
41. Wide open micro switch
42. Idle up actuator
43. Fuel cut solenoid valve
44. Washer
45. Level gauge seal
46. Level gauge
47. Level gauge gasket
48. Micro switch bracket
49. Primary main jet
50. Secondary main jet
51. Drain plug gasket
52. Drain plug
53. Insulator
54. Secondary diaphragm
55. Throttle adjust screw
56. Spring
57. Mixture adjust screw
58. Spring
59. Washer
60. Seal
61. Switch return spring
62. Throttle lever return spring

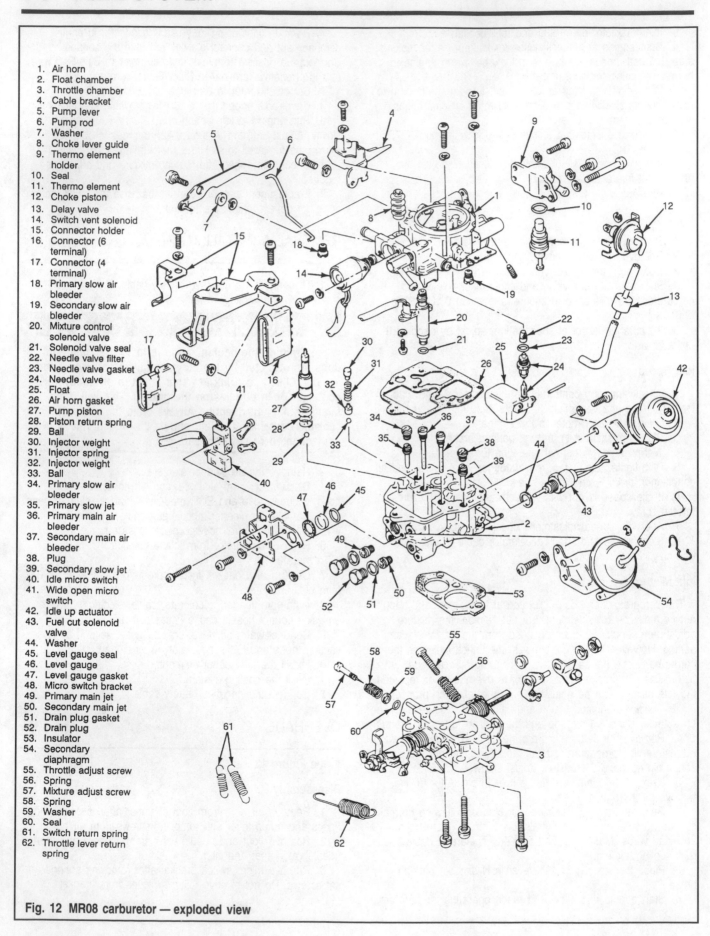

Fig. 12 MR08 carburetor — exploded view

4. Remove lockplate® and drain plugs and then primary and secondary main jets in float chamber through plug holes using a screwdriver.

5. Remove throttle chamber from float chamber after removing screws.

Cleaning

1. Wash all removable air jets and fuel jets, needle valve, valve seat, filter and float in carburetor cleaner and then dry with compressed air.

2. Blow compressed air into all passages to clean.

3. Clean bottom of float chamber.

4. Do not clean the following parts: micro switches, switch vent solenoid, fuel cut solenoid, mixture control solenoid valve, accelerator pump piston, secondary diaphragm, choke piston, idle up actuator, rubber parts and gaskets or thermo wax element.

5. Do not put drills or wires into fuel passages and metering jets for cleaning. It may cause damage in passages and jets.

6. Do not remove the mixture adjust screw pin located in front of mixture adjust screw.

Inspection

1. Check choke valve and throttle valve for smooth operation.

2. Check rubber cup of pump piston and seal of mixture control solenoid valve for deterioration and damage.

3. Check needle valve and valve seat for wear.

Assembly

1. Install the gasket on the float chamber.

2. After attaching both ends of throttle lever return spring, install throttle chamber to float chamber. Hook throttle valve side end of return spring over the boss on float chamber.

3. Two of the four washers for the throttle chamber securing screws are toothed washers and the other two are spring washers. Install each washer to the throttle chamber and tighten to 3-5 ft. lbs. (4-7 Nm).

4. Install the primary and secondary main jets.

5. Install the gaskets and drain plugs, and then lock plate after installing main jets.

6. Install level gauge seal and level gauge. When installing level gauge, direct its face with small round mark in its center toward float chamber.

7. Install micro switch bracket with micro switches and springs. Do not remove the micro switches from the bracket.

➡When bracket with micro switches has been removed from float chamber for any service and reinstalled after service work, make sure to check switches for operation and adjust if necessary.

8. Install jets, air bleeders and plug to float chamber.

9. Install balls, injector spring and weights to accelerator pump. Direct 'U' bend end side of piston return spring downward.

10. Install needle valve filter, valve seat, gasket, needle valve and float to air horn. After installing float, check for float level and adjust.

11. Install primary and secondary slow air bleeders to air horn.

12. Be sure to silicone grease to mixture control solenoid valve seal before installing air horn to float chamber.

13. Install air horn gasket to float chamber. Use new gasket.

14. Install air horn to float chamber. After installing accelerator pump lever to air horn, check the lever for smooth operation.

15. Connect hoses to carburetor.

THROTTLE BODY FUEL INJECTION

Description

▶ **See Figures 13, 14, 15, 16, 17 and 18**

Electronic throttle body fuel injection (TBI) is a fuel metering system which provides a means of fuel distribution for controlling exhaust emissions. By precisely controlling the air/fuel mixture under all operating conditions, the system provides as near as possible complete combustion.

The amount of fuel delivered by the throttle body injector is determined by a signal supplied by the Electronic Control Module (ECM). The ECM monitors various engine and vehicle conditions to calculate the fuel delivery time (pulse width) of the injector(s). The fuel pulse may be modified by the ECM to account for special operating conditions, such as cranking, cold starting, altitude, acceleration, and deceleration.

An oxygen sensor in the main exhaust stream functions to provide feedback information to the ECM as to the oxygen content, lean or rich, in the exhaust. The ECM uses this information from the oxygen sensor, and other sensors, to modify fuel delivery to achieve, as near as possible, an ideal air/fuel ratio of 14.7:1. This air/fuel ratio allows the 3-way

catalytic converter to be more efficient in the conversion process of reducing exhaust emissions while at the same time providing acceptable levels of driveability and fuel economy.

A single fuel injector is mounted on top of a throttle body, which replaces the carburetor on the intake manifold. The injector is a solenoid-operated device controlled by the ECM. The incoming fuel is directed to the lower end of the injector assembly which has a fine screen filter surrounding the injector inlet. The ECM turns on the solenoid, which lifts a normally closed ball valve off a seat. The fuel, under pressure, is injected in a conical spray pattern at the walls of the throttle body bore above the throttle valve. The excess fuel passes through a pressure regulator before being returned to the vehicle fuel tank.

The pressure regulator is a diaphragm-operated relief valve with the injector pressure on one side, and the air cleaner pressure on the other. The function of the regulator is to maintain constant pressure (approximately 11 psi) to the injector throughout the operating loads and speed ranges of the engine. If the regulator pressure is too low, below 9 psi, it can cause poor performance. Too high a pressure could cause detonation and a strong fuel odor.

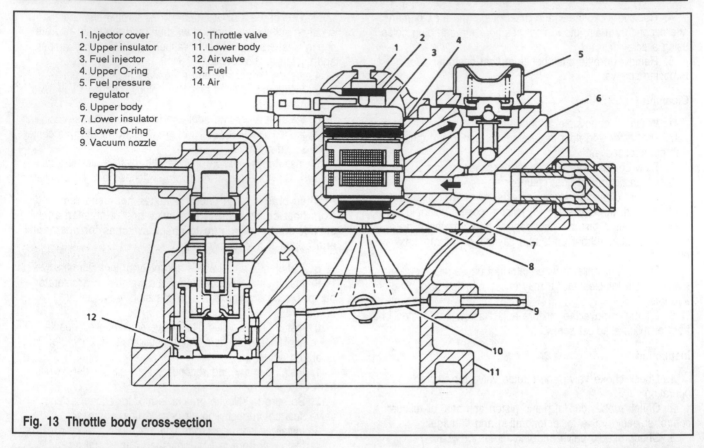

1. Injector cover
2. Upper insulator
3. Fuel injector
4. Upper O-ring
5. Fuel pressure regulator
6. Upper body
7. Lower insulator
8. Lower O-ring
9. Vacuum nozzle
10. Throttle valve
11. Lower body
12. Air valve
13. Fuel
14. Air

Fig. 13 Throttle body cross-section

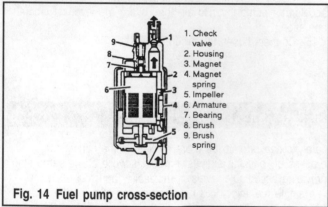

1. Check valve
2. Housing
3. Magnet
4. Magnet spring
5. Impeller
6. Armature
7. Bearing
8. Brush
9. Brush spring

Fig. 14 Fuel pump cross-section

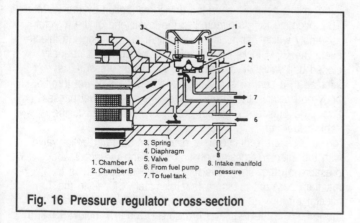

1. Chamber A
2. Chamber B
3. Spring
4. Diaphragm
5. Valve
6. From fuel pump
7. To fuel tank
8. Intake manifold pressure

Fig. 16 Pressure regulator cross-section

The fuel pump is mounted in the fuel tank. This electrically operated pump supplies sufficient pressure (25-33 psi) to

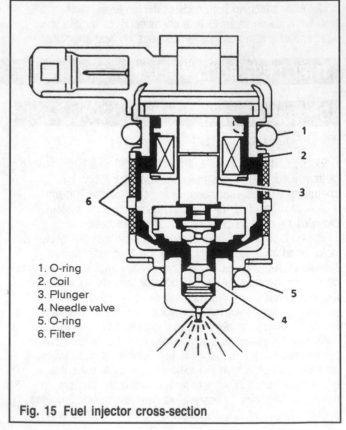

1. O-ring
2. Coil
3. Plunger
4. Needle valve
5. O-ring
6. Filter

Fig. 15 Fuel injector cross-section

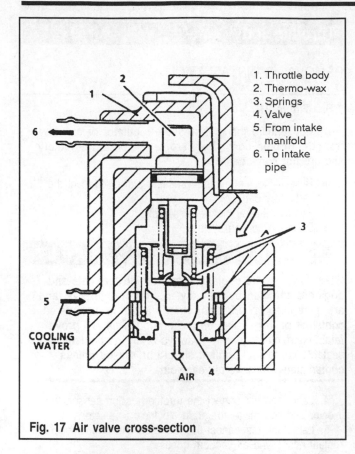

1. Throttle body
2. Thermo-wax
3. Springs
4. Valve
5. From intake manifold
6. To intake pipe

COOLING WATER

AIR

Fig. 17 Air valve cross-section

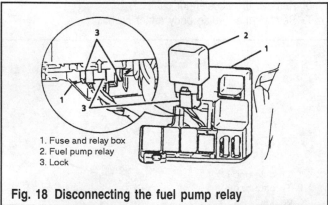

1. Fuse and relay box
2. Fuel pump relay
3. Lock

Fig. 18 Disconnecting the fuel pump relay

provide proper fuel atomization at the injector. The fuel pump also uses a check valve to hold fuel pressure within the fuel feed line when the vehicle is not running.

A relay is used to control voltage to the fuel pump. When the ignition key is turned **ON**, the ECM will initialize (start program running) and energize the fuel pump relay. The fuel pump pressurizes the system to approximately 10 psi. If the ECM does not receive a distributor reference pulse (telling the ECM the engine is turning) within 2 seconds, the ECM will then de-energize the fuel pump relay, turning off the fuel pump. If a distributor reference pulse is later received, the ECM will turn the fuel pump back on.

An air valve is used to control intake air during cold start conditions. The air valve consist of thermo-wax, springs and a valve. When the engine is cold, the thermo-wax contracts. In this state, the valve opens by the spring force, allowing the air

to be drawn into the intake manifold. Thus the amount of intake air increases even when throttle valve is at idle position and engine speed rises to the fast idle state.

Relieving Fuel System Pressure

1. Remove the gas tank cap.
2. Remove the control relay.
3. Start the engine and run at idle. Allow it to run until the engine stalls due to lack of fuel.
4. Engage the starter for a few seconds to assure relief of remaining fuel pressure.
5. Disconnect negative battery cable.
6. Connect negative battery cable after service has been completed.

Electric Fuel Pump

REMOVAL & INSTALLATION

▶ **See Figures 19 and 20**

1. Relieve the fuel system pressure.
2. Disconnect the negative battery cable.
3. Raise and support the vehicle safely.
4. Drain the fuel tank by pumping or siphoning the fuel out through the fuel feed line (tank to fuel filter line).
5. Remove the tank from the vehicle.
6. Remove the fuel feed and return clamps and hoses from the fuel pump assembly.

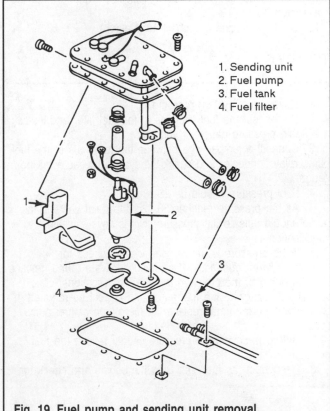

1. Sending unit
2. Fuel pump
3. Fuel tank
4. Fuel filter

Fig. 19 Fuel pump and sending unit removal

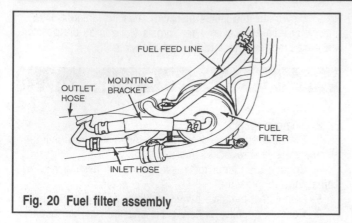

Fig. 20 Fuel filter assembly

7. Remove the 12 attaching screws from the fuel pump assembly and remove the assembly with the gasket from the fuel tank.

8. Remove the 1 mounting screw from the fuel pump motor assembly. Remove the 2 fuel pump motor connectors and remove the fuel pump motor from the fuel pump assembly.

To install:

9. Install the 2 fuel pump motor connectors. Install the fuel pump motor on the fuel pump assembly and tighten the mounting screw.

10. Install the assembly with the gasket on the fuel tank. Install the 12 attaching screws and tighten securely.

11. Install the fuel feed and return clamps and hoses on the fuel pump assembly.

12. Install the fuel tank in the vehicle.

13. Lower the vehicle and connect the negative battery cable.

14. Fill the fuel tank. Turn the ignition key **ON** and allow the fuel system to prime.

15. Start the engine and check for leaks.

TESTING

1. Relieve fuel system pressure.

2. Disconnect the fuel inlet line at the fuel filter and install a suitable pressure gauge on the line.

3. Connect a jumper wire between the terminals of the fuel pump relay connector and check the system pressure on the gauge.

4. Fuel pressure should be 25-33 lbs.

5. As the pressure reaches 33 lbs., the relief valve in the pump should pulsate the pressure so it is always within specification.

6. If the pressure is above specification, check for restrictions in the fuel lines. If no restrictions are found, replace the fuel pump. If the pressure is below specifications, check for battery voltage to the fuel pump and correct as required. If battery voltage is found, replace the fuel pump or fuel pump relay.

7. Before removing the pressure gauge, relieve the fuel pressure again.

8. Reconnect the fuel line. Start the engine and check for leaks.

Throttle Body

REMOVAL & INSTALLATION

▶ **See Figure 21**

➡ Do not remove the fuel pressure regulator or air valve from the throttle body. They are calibrated at the factory and are not serviceable.

1. Relieve the fuel system pressure and disconnect the negative battery cable.

2. Remove the air cleaner assembly.

3. Drain the cooling system.

✳✳CAUTION

When draining the coolant, keep in mind that cats and dogs are attracted by the ethylene glycol antifreeze, and are quite likely to drink any that is left in an uncovered container or in puddles on the ground. This will prove fatal in sufficient quantity. Always drain the coolant into a sealable container. Coolant should be reused unless it is contaminated or several years old.

4. Label and disconnect the throttle position sensor, fuel injector and coolant temperature electrical connectors.

5. Label and disconnect the fuel feed and return hoses, coolant hoses and all vacuum hoses.

6. Remove the accelerator cable.

7. Remove the throttle body attaching bolts.

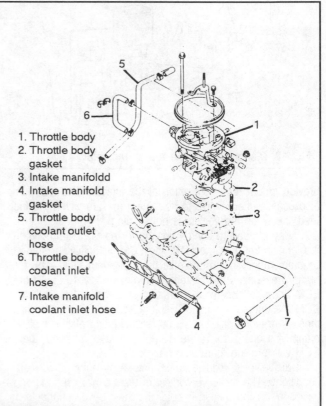

1. Throttle body
2. Throttle body gasket
3. Intake manifoldd
4. Intake manifold gasket
5. Throttle body coolant outlet hose
6. Throttle body coolant inlet hose
7. Intake manifold coolant inlet hose

Fig. 21 Throttle body and intake manifold

8. Lift the throttle body from the intake manifold.

To install:

9. Install the throttle body on the intake manifold using a new gasket.

10. Tighten throttle body bolts evenly to 17 ft. lbs. (23 Nm).

11. Remove the accelerator cable.

12. Connect the fuel feed and return hoses, coolant hoses and all vacuum hoses.

13. Connect the throttle position sensor, fuel injector and coolant temperature electrical connectors.

14. Refill the cooling system.

15. Install the air cleaner assembly.

16. Connect the negative battery cable. Start the engine and check for leaks.

INJECTOR REPLACEMENT

▶ **See Figure 22**

➡**Do not remove the fuel pressure regulator or air valve from the throttle body. They are calibrated at the factory and are not serviceable.**

1. Depressurize the fuel system, then disconnect the negative battery cable.

2. Remove the intake air hose and air cleaner.

3. Remove the injector cover and upper insulator.

4. Gently pull the injector out of the throttle body.

To install:

5. Replace both injector O-rings with new.

6. Apply a thin coat of automatic transmission fluid to the O-rings and then install the injector into the throttle body. Make sure the injector is facing the proper direction.

➡**Do not twist the injector while installing as damage or misalignment of the O-rings may occur.**

7. Install the upper insulator, cover, electrical connector and connect the negative battery cable.

8. With the ignition switch **ON** and the engine OFF, check for fuel leaks.

9. Install the air cleaner and inlet hose.

Fuel Pressure Regulator

The fuel pressure regulator is calibrated at the factory and is not serviceable. No attempt should be made to remove the regulator from the throttle body. If the regulator is defective, the throttle body must be replaced as an assembly.

Throttle Position Sensor

REMOVAL & INSTALLATION

1. Disconnect the negative battery cable.

2. Remove the air cleaner assembly

3. Remove the throttle position sensor connector.

4. Remove the retaining screws, then remove the throttle position sensor from the throttle body.

To install:

5. Install the throttle position sensor on the throttle body.

6. Adjust the throttle position sensor.

7. Tighten screws to 18 inch lbs. (2 Nm).

8. Connect the sensor connector.

9. Install the air cleaner

10. Connect the negative battery cable.

ADJUSTMENT

▶ **See Figure 23**

1. Connect a digital multimeter to the throttle position sensor terminals 1 and 2. Measure resistance.

2. Insert a 0.012 in. (0.3mm) feeler gauge between throttle stop screw and throttle lever.

1. Injector cover
2. Upper insulator
3. Fuel injector
4. Upper O-ring
5. Lower O-ring

6. Lower insulator
7. Throttle upper body
8. Gasket
9. Throttle lower body
10. Coolant temp. sensor
11. Idle speed adjusting screw cap
12. Throttle position sensor
13. Injector sub wire connector
14. O-ring
15. Clamp
16. Plate

Fig. 22 Throttle body injector assembly

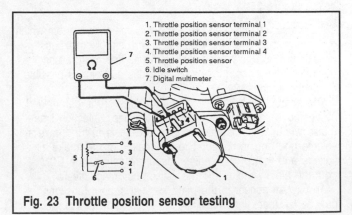

1. Throttle position sensor terminal 1
2. Throttle position sensor terminal 2
3. Throttle position sensor terminal 3
4. Throttle position sensor terminal 4
5. Throttle position sensor
6. Idle switch
7. Digital multimeter

Fig. 23 Throttle position sensor testing

3. With retaining screws loosely installed, turn throttle position sensor fully clockwise, then slowly counterclockwise until digital multimeter indicates 0 ohms (continuity).

4. Tighten screws to 18 inch lbs. (2 Nm).

5. Insert a 0.035 in. (0.9mm) feeler gauge between throttle stop screw and throttle lever. Digital multimeter should now indicate an open circuit (no continuity).

Air Valve

REMOVAL & INSTALLATION

The air valve is calibrated at the factory and is not serviceable. No attempt should be made to remove it from the throttle body. If the air valve is defective, the throttle body must be replaced as an assembly.

TESTING

▶ See Figure 24

➡ Use care not to submerse throttle body in water to prevent possible damage due to corrosion. Only the air valve should be submersed in water.

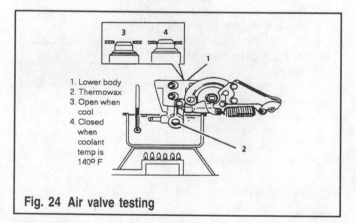

1. Lower body
2. Thermowax
3. Open when cool
4. Closed when coolant temp is 140° F

Fig. 24 Air valve testing

1. Remove the throttle body assembly.
2. Separate the throttle body halves.
3. Remove the coolant temperature sensor.
4. Immerse air valve in water.
5. Check that air valve closes as the water temperature rises. The valve should fully close at 140°F (60°C). If it does not, replace the valve.
6. Install the coolant temperature sensor.
7. Join the upper and lower halves of the throttle body using a new gasket.
8. Tighten attaching screws to 3-5 ft. lbs. (4-7 Nm).
9. Install throttle body on intake manifold using a new gasket. Tighten bolts to 17 ft. lbs. (23 Nm).

Fuel Pump Relay

REMOVAL & INSTALLATION

1. Remove the fuse and relay box cover.
2. Remove the engine coolant reservoir from its bracket.
3. Remove the screws holding the fuse and relay box.
4. Remove the connector holding the fuel pump relay and disconnect the fuel pump relay.
5. Installation is the reverse of removal.

ELECTRONIC FUEL INJECTION

Description

▶ See Figure 25

Electronic fuel injection (EFI) is a fuel metering system which provides a means of fuel distribution for controlling exhaust emissions. By precisely controlling the air/fuel mixture under all operating conditions, the system provides as near as possible complete combustion.

The amount of fuel delivered by the injectors is determined by adding several compensations to the basic injection time (pulse width) which is calculated on the basis of the intake air volume and engine speed. The information of the intake air volume and that of the engine speed are sent to the ECM from the airflow meter and the ignition coil respectively.

An oxygen sensor in the main exhaust stream functions to provide feedback information to the ECM as to the oxygen content, lean or rich, in the exhaust. The ECM uses this information from the oxygen sensor, and other sensors, to modify fuel delivery to achieve, as near as possible, an ideal air/fuel ratio of 14.7:1. This air/fuel ratio allows the 3-way catalytic converter to be more efficient in the conversion process of reducing exhaust emissions while at the same time providing acceptable levels of driveability and fuel economy.

Three individual fuel injectors are mounted on the intake manifold. The injector is a solenoid-operated device controlled by the ECM. The incoming fuel is directed to the lower end of the injector assembly which has a fine screen filter surrounding the injector inlet. The ECM turns on the solenoid, which lifts a normally closed ball valve off a seat. The fuel, under pressure, is injected in a conical spray pattern at the walls of the throttle body bore above the throttle valve. The excess fuel passes through a pressure regulator before being returned to the vehicle fuel tank.

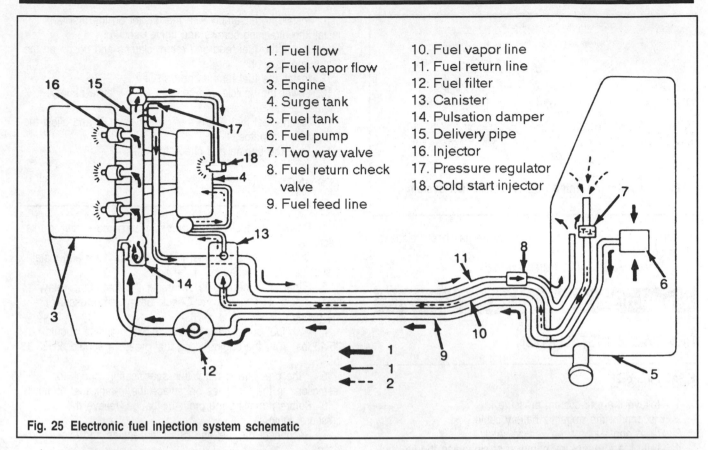

1. Fuel flow
2. Fuel vapor flow
3. Engine
4. Surge tank
5. Fuel tank
6. Fuel pump
7. Two way valve
8. Fuel return check valve
9. Fuel feed line
10. Fuel vapor line
11. Fuel return line
12. Fuel filter
13. Canister
14. Pulsation damper
15. Delivery pipe
16. Injector
17. Pressure regulator
18. Cold start injector

Fig. 25 Electronic fuel injection system schematic

The pressure regulator is a diaphragm-operated relief valve with the injector pressure on one side, and the air cleaner pressure on the other. The function of the regulator is to maintain constant pressure (approximately 11 psi) to the injector throughout the operating loads and speed ranges of the engine. If the regulator pressure is too low, below 9 psi, it can cause poor performance. Too high a pressure could cause detonation and a strong fuel odor.

The fuel pump is mounted in the fuel tank. This electrically operated pump supplies sufficient pressure (25-33 psi) to provide proper fuel atomization at the injector. The fuel pump also uses a check valve to hold fuel pressure within the fuel feed line when the vehicle is not running.

A relay is used to control voltage to the fuel pump. When the ignition key is turned **ON**, the ECM will initialize (start program running) and energize the fuel pump relay. The fuel pump pressurizes the system to approximately 10 psi. If the ECM does not receive a distributor reference pulse (telling the ECM the engine is turning) within 2 seconds, the ECM will then de-energize the fuel pump relay, turning off the fuel pump. If a distributor reference pulse is later received, the ECM will turn the fuel pump back on.

An air valve is used to control intake air during cold start conditions. The air valve consist of thermo-wax, springs and a valve. When the engine is cold, the thermo-wax contracts. In this state, the valve opens by the spring force, allowing the air to be drawn into the intake manifold. Thus the amount of intake air increases even when throttle valve is at idle position and engine speed rises to the fast idle state.

Relieving Fuel System Pressure

▶ **See Figures 26 and 27**

1. Remove the gas tank cap.
2. With engine running, remove connector of fuel pump relay and wait until the engine stops, due to a lack of fuel.

➡**The main relay and fuel pump relay are identical. The fuel pump relay lead wires are Pink, Pink/White, White/Blue, and White/Blue.**

3. Engage the starter for a few seconds to assure relief of remaining fuel pressure.
4. If fuel pressure can not be relieved in the above manner because engine failed to run, disconnect the negative battery cable, cover union bolt of high fuel pressure line with a rag

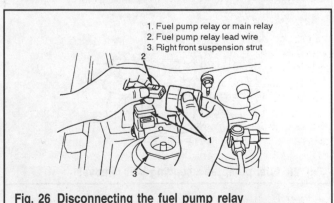

1. Fuel pump relay or main relay
2. Fuel pump relay lead wire
3. Right front suspension strut

Fig. 26 Disconnecting the fuel pump relay

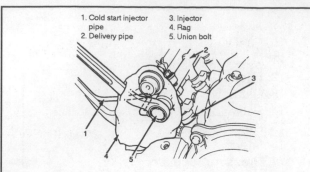

1. Cold start injector pipe
2. Delivery pipe
3. Injector
4. Rag
5. Union bolt

Fig. 27 Loosening union bolt to relieve fuel system pressure

and loosen bolt slowly. When fuel pressure has been released, retighten bolt.

5. Disconnect negative battery cable.

Electric Fuel Pump

REMOVAL & INSTALLATION

▶ **See Figure 28**

1. Relieve the fuel system pressure.
2. Disconnect the negative battery cable.
3. Raise and support the vehicle safely.
4. Drain the fuel tank by pumping or siphoning the fuel out through the fuel feed line (tank to fuel filter line).
5. Remove the tank from the vehicle.
6. Remove the fuel feed and return clamps and hoses from the fuel pump assembly.
7. Remove the attaching screws from the fuel pump assembly and remove the assembly with the gasket from the fuel tank.
8. Remove the mounting screw from the fuel pump motor assembly. Remove the fuel pump motor connectors and remove the fuel pump motor from the fuel pump assembly.

To install:

9. Install the fuel pump motor connectors. Install the fuel pump motor on the fuel pump assembly and tighten the mounting screw.

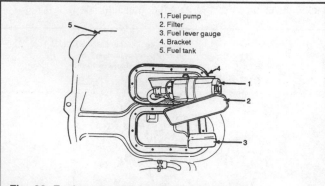

1. Fuel pump
2. Filter
3. Fuel lever gauge
4. Bracket
5. Fuel tank

Fig. 28 Fuel pump and sending unit removal

10. Install the assembly with the gasket on the fuel tank. Install the attaching screws and tighten securely.
11. Install the fuel feed and return clamps and hoses on the fuel pump assembly.
12. Install the fuel tank in the vehicle.
13. Lower the vehicle and connect the negative battery cable.
14. Fill the fuel tank. Turn the ignition key **ON** and allow the fuel system to prime.
15. Start the engine and check for leaks.

TESTING

1. Relieve the fuel system pressure as noted earlier in this Section.
2. Disconnect the fuel inlet line at the fuel filter and install a suitable pressure gauge on the line.
3. Either start the engine or jumper the fuel pump relay, using a suitable jumper wire. Check the system pressure on the gauge.
4. With fuel pump relay jumpered, fuel pressure should be 35-43 lbs. With the engine idling fuel pressure should be 25-33 lbs.
5. If the pressure is not within specification, check for restrictions in the fuel lines or replace the in-tank fuel pump.
6. Before removing the pressure gauge, relieve the fuel pressure again.
7. Reconnect the fuel line. Start the engine and check for leaks.

Throttle Body

REMOVAL & INSTALLATION

1. Disconnect the negative battery cable.
2. Drain cooling system when engine is cold.
3. Remove inlet air hose.
4. Remove throttle position sensor coupler.
5. Remove accelerator cable.
6. Remove water hoses from throttle body.
7. Label and remove vacuum hoses.
8. Remove throttle body.

To install:

9. Install throttle body using a new gasket.
10. Connect vacuum hoses.
11. Connect water hoses.
12. Connect accelerator cable and adjust free-play to 0.32-0.35 in. (8-9mm).
13. Install throttle position sensor coupler.
14. Install inlet air hose.
15. Refill the engine with coolant.
16. Connect the negative battery cable.
17. Start engine and check for leaks.

Fuel Injectors

REMOVAL & INSTALLATION

▶ **See Figures 29 and 30**

1. Relieve fuel system pressure and disconnect the negative battery cable.
2. Remove intake air hose between throttle body and intercooler.
3. Remove accelerator cable.
4. Unclamp PCV and fuel return hoses from deliver pipe.
5. Unclamp injector wiring harness.
6. Disconnect injector coupler.
7. Remove cold start injector pipe from delivery pipe.
8. Remove vacuum hose from pressure regulator.
9. Remove fuel feed hose from delivery pipe.
10. Remove pressure regulator from delivery pipe.
11. Remove delivery pipe with injectors.
12. Remove injectors from delivery pipe.

To install:
13. Replace injector O-rings and lubricate with fuel.

➡**Make sure injectors rotate smoothly. If not, probable cause is incorrect installation of O-ring.**

14. Check if insulator is scored or damaged. If it is, replace with new one.
15. Connect delivery pipe with injectors.
16. Install pressure regulator to delivery pipe using a new O-ring.
17. Install fuel feed hose to delivery pipe.
18. Install vacuum and fuel return hoses to pressure regulator and clamp securely.
19. Install cold start injector pipe to delivery pipe using new gaskets.
20. Install injector coupler. Clamp injector wiring harness.
21. Install PCV hose to cylinder head.
22. Install throttle position sensor coupler.
23. Install accelerator cable and adjust free-play.
24. Install intake air hose to throttle body and intercooler.
25. Connect the negative battery cable.
26. Start engine and check for leaks.

TESTING

▶ **See Figure 31**

1. Using a sound scope, check if injector make proper operating sounds in proportion to engine speed when engine is running or being cranked.
2. If check result is not satisfactory, it means that defect exists in injector, wiring harness, connector or ECM.
3. Remove coupler of injector and check resistance between terminals. Resistance should be 13.8 ohms at 68°F (20°C).
4. Perform injector balance test.

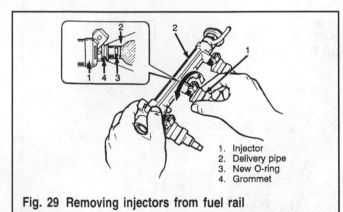

1. Injector
2. Delivery pipe
3. New O-ring
4. Grommet

Fig. 29 Removing injectors from fuel rail

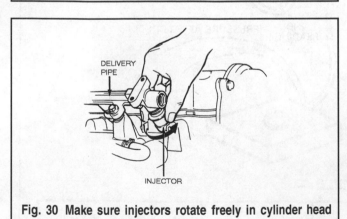

Fig. 30 Make sure injectors rotate freely in cylinder head

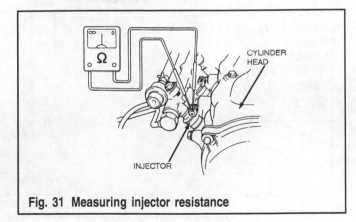

Fig. 31 Measuring injector resistance

INJECTOR BALANCE TEST

NOTE: If injectors are suspected as being dirty, they should be cleaned using an approved tool and procedure prior to performing this test. The fuel pressure test in Figure 6C20-121, should be completed prior to this test.

Step 1. If engine is at operating temperature, allow a 10 minute "cool down" period then connect fuel pressure gauge and injector tester.
1. Ignition "OFF"
2. Connect fuel pressure gauge and injector tester.
3. Ignition "ON".
4. Bleed off air in gauge. Repeat until all air is bled from gauge.

Step 2. Run test:
1. Ignition "OFF" for 10 seconds.
2. Ignition "ON". Record gauge pressure. (Pressure must hold steady, if not see the fuel system diagnosis, (Figure 6C20-121).
3. Turn injector on by depressing button on injector tester and note pressure at the instant the gauge needle stops.

Step 3.
1. Repeat step 2 on all injectors and record pressure drop on each. Retest injectors that appear faulty (Any injectors that have a 10 kPa difference, either more or less, in pressure from the average).

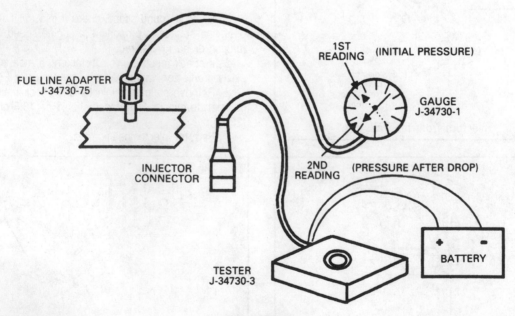

— EXAMPLE —

CYLINDER	1	2	3	4	5	6
1ST READING	225	225	225	225	225	225
2ND READING	100	100	100	90	100	115
AMOUNT OF DROP	125	125	125	135	125	110
	OK	OK	OK	FAULTY, RICH (TOO MUCH) (FUEL DROP)	OK	FAULTY, LEAN (TOO LITTLE) (FUEL DROP)

Fuel Pressure Regulator

REMOVAL & INSTALLATION

▶ **See Figure 32**

1. Relieve fuel system pressure and disconnect the negative battery cable.
2. Put ample rag under fuel pressure regulator.
3. Disconnect vacuum hose and fuel return hose from regulator.
4. Remove fuel pressure regulator from fuel delivery pipe.

To install:

5. Install the pressure regulator using a new O-ring. Tighten bolt to 6-8 ft. lbs. (8-12 Nm).
6. Connect vacuum hose and fuel return hose to regulator.
7. Start engine and check for leaks.

Throttle Position Sensor

REMOVAL & INSTALLATION

1. Disconnect the negative battery cable.
2. Remove the air cleaner assembly, as required.
3. Remove the throttle position sensor connector.
4. Remove the retaining screws, then remove the throttle position sensor from the throttle body.

To install:

5. Install the throttle position sensor on the throttle body.
6. Adjust the throttle position sensor.
7. Tighten screws to 18 inch lbs. (2 Nm).
8. Connect the sensor connector.
9. Install the air cleaner

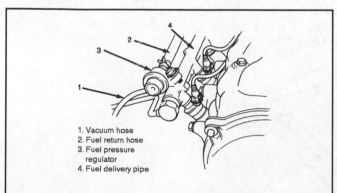

1. Vacuum hose
2. Fuel return hose
3. Fuel pressure regulator
4. Fuel delivery pipe

Fig. 32 Fuel pressure regulator assembly

10. Connect the negative battery cable.

ADJUSTMENT

▶ **See Figure 33**

1. Connect a digital multimeter to the throttle position sensor terminals IDL and E2. Measure resistance.
2. Insert a 0.024 in. (0.6mm) feeler gauge between throttle stop screw and throttle lever.
3. With retaining screws loosely installed, turn throttle position sensor fully clockwise, then slowly counterclockwise until digital multimeter indicates 0 ohms (continuity).
4. Tighten screws to 18 inch lbs. (2 Nm).
5. Insert a 0.031 in. (0.8mm) feeler gauge between throttle stop screw and throttle lever. Digital multimeter should now indicate an open circuit (no continuity).
6. Insert a 0.016 in. (0.4mm) feeler gauge between throttle stop screw and throttle lever. Digital multimeter should now indicate O ohms (continuity).

Fuel Pump Relay

REMOVAL & INSTALLATION

▶ **See Figure 26**

1. The fuel pump relay is located near the right front strut in the engine compartment.
2. The main relay and fuel pump relay are identical. The fuel pump relay lead wires are Pink, Pink/White, White/Blue, and White/Blue.
3. Simply unplug the relay from the connector.
4. Installation is the reverse of removal procedure.

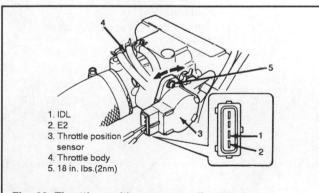

1. IDL
2. E2
3. Throttle position sensor
4. Throttle body
5. 18 in. lbs.(2nm)

Fig. 33 Throttle position sensor adjustment

FUEL TANK

Tank Assembly

REMOVAL & INSTALLATION

▶ See Figures 34 and 35

Carbureted Engine

1. Disconnect the negative battery cable.
2. Remove the fuel gauge lead wire after removing the rear seat cushion.
3. To release the pressure in the fuel tank, remove the fuel filler cap and then, reinstall it.
4. Due to absence of fuel tank drain plug, drain the fuel tank by pumping or siphoning the fuel out through the fuel feed line.
5. Raise and support the vehicle safely.
6. Remove the three hoses from pipes.
7. Remove fuel filler hose and breather hose.
8. Remove the fuel tank from the vehicle.
To install:
9. Install the fuel tank.
10. Install the fuel filler hose and breather hose.
11. Install the three hoses on the pipes.
12. Lower the vehicle.
13. Connect the fuel gauge lead wire and install the rear seat cushion.
14. Fill the fuel tank.

15. Connect the negative battery cable.
16. Turn the ignition key **ON** and allow the fuel system to prime.
17. Start the engine and check for leaks.

Fuel Injected Engine

1. Relieve the fuel system pressure and disconnect the negative battery cable.
2. Remove the fuel filler cap from the fuel tank.
3. Have a Class B fire extinguisher near the work area. Use a hand operated pump device to drain as much fuel through the fuel filler neck as possible.
4. Use a siphon to remove the remainder of the fuel in the tank by connecting the siphon to the fuel pump outlet fitting.

✴✴CAUTION

Never drain or store fuel in an open container because there is the possibility of a fire or an explosion.

5. Reinstall the fuel filler cap.
6. Remove the rear seat cushion from vehicle (if so equipped).
7. Disconnect the fuel pump motor connector and sending unit electrical connectors.
8. Disconnect the wire harness grommet and harness through the vehicle floor pan.
9. Raise and safely support the vehicle.

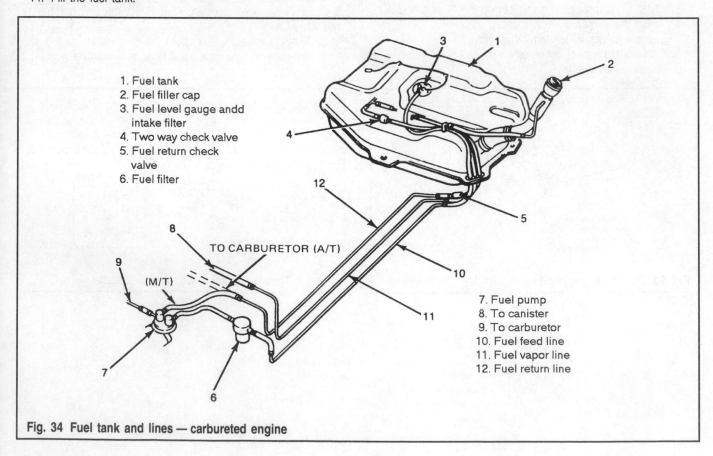

1. Fuel tank
2. Fuel filler cap
3. Fuel level gauge andd intake filter
4. Two way check valve
5. Fuel return check valve
6. Fuel filter

TO CARBURETOR (A/T)

(M/T)

7. Fuel pump
8. To canister
9. To carburetor
10. Fuel feed line
11. Fuel vapor line
12. Fuel return line

Fig. 34 Fuel tank and lines — carbureted engine

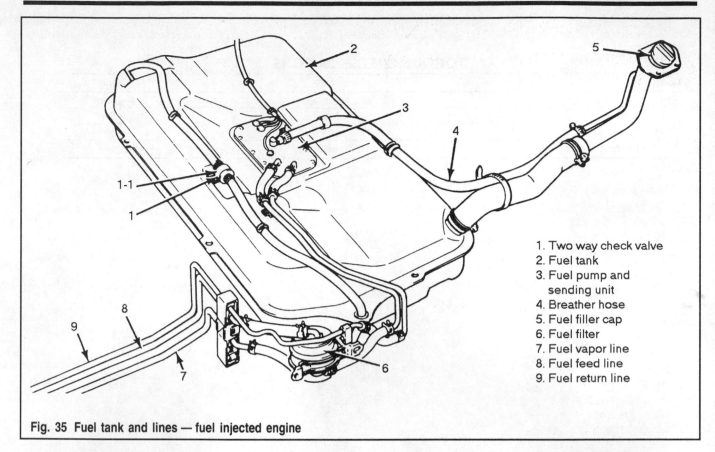

1. Two way check valve
2. Fuel tank
3. Fuel pump and
   sending unit
4. Breather hose
5. Fuel filler cap
6. Fuel filter
7. Fuel vapor line
8. Fuel feed line
9. Fuel return line

Fig. 35 Fuel tank and lines — fuel injected engine

10. Remove the fuel filler hose clamp from the filler neck assembly.

11. Remove the fuel breather hose clamp from the filler neck assembly.

12. Remove the fuel filter inlet hose clamp and hose from the filter.

➡ **A small amount of fuel may be released after the fuel hose is disconnected. In order to reduce the chance of personal injury, cover the fitting to be disconnected with a shop towel.**

13. Remove the fuel vapor clamp and hose, and fuel return hose clamps and hose from the respective fuel lines.

14. Using a suitable transaxle jack, support the fuel tank.

15. Remove the fuel tank retaining bolts and lower the tank.
    To install:

16. Reconnect all fuel hoses, lines and the fuel breather hose to the fuel tank.

17. Place the fuel tank in its proper space using the transaxle jack, Install the fuel tank retaining bolts.

18. Remove the transaxle jack.

19. Reconnect all fuel hoses, lines and the fuel breather hose to the fuel tank.

20. Install the fuel breather hose and hose clamp to the filler neck assembly.

21. Install the fuel vapor hose and hose clamps. Install the fuel return hose and hose clamp to the respective fuel lines.

22. Install the fuel filter inlet hose and hose clamp to the filter.

23. Lower the vehicle. Install the wire harness and grommet through the vehicle floor pan.

24. Connect the fuel pump motor and the sending unit connectors.

25. Install the rear seat cushion. Reconnect the negative battery cable.

TORQUE SPECIFICATIONS

Component	U.S.	Metric
Fuel Pressure Regulator	6-8 ft. lbs.	8-12 Nm
Throttle Body	17 ft. lbs.	23 Nm
Throttle Chamber	3-5 ft lbs.	4-7 Nm
Throttle Position Sensor	18 inch lbs.	2 Nm

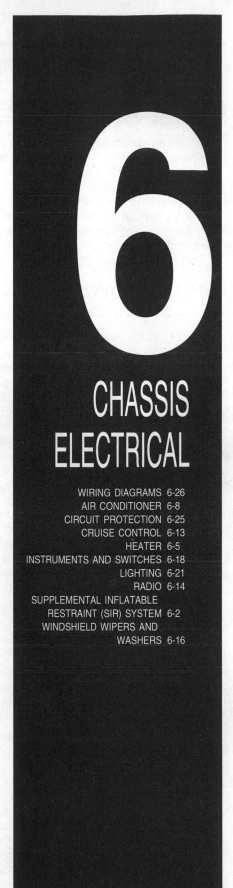

6

CHASSIS ELECTRICAL

SUPPLEMENTAL INFLATABLE RESTRAINT (SIR) SYSTEM

General Information

The air bag system used on GEO vehicles is referred to as Supplemental Inflatable Restraint (SIR) system. The SIR system provides additional protection for the driver, if a forward collision of sufficient force is encountered. The SIR assists the normal sea belt restraining system by deploying an air bag, via the steering column. A knee pad, located beneath the the driver's side instrument panel, also aid in absorbing collision impact. The steering column, as in previous design, still continues to be collapsible.

SYSTEM OPERATION

The SIR system contains a deployment loop and a Diagnostic Energy Reserve Module (DERM). The function of the deployment loop is to supply current through the inflator module in the steering wheel, which will cause air bag deployment during a severe accident. The DERM supplies the necessary power, even if the battery has been damaged.

The deployment loop is made up of the arming sensors, coil assembly, inflator module and the discriminating sensors. The inflator module is only supplied sufficient current to deploy the air bag, when the arming sensors and at least 1 of the discriminating sensors close simultaneously. The function of the DERM is to supply the deployment loop a 36 Volt Loop Reverse (36VLR) to assure air bag deployment for seconds after ignition voltage is lost during an accident.

The DERM, in conjunction with the resistors make it possible to detect circuit and component faults within the deployment loop. If the voltages monitored by the DERM fall outside expected limits, the DERM will indicate a fault code through the storage of a malfunction code and turning ON the INFLATABLE RESTRAINT lamp.

SYSTEM COMPONENTS

▶ **See Figures 1 and 2**

Diagnostic Energy Reserve Module (DERM)

The DERM is designed to perform 5 main functions. It maintains an energy reverse of 36 volts for several seconds and can maintain sufficient voltage to cause a deployment for up to 10 minutes after the ignition switch is turn **OFF** and the battery disconnected. The DERM performs diagnostic monitoring of the SIR system and records malfunction codes, which can be obtained from a hand scan tool or the INFLATABLE RESTRAINT lamp. It warns the driver of a malfunction by controlling the INFLATABLE RESTRAINT lamp and keeps a record of the SIR system during a vehicle accident.

The DERM is connected to the system with a 24 pin connector. This harness has a shorting bar across certain terminals in the contact areas. The shorting bar connects the INFLATABLE RESTRAINT lamp input to ground when the

DERM is disconnected causing the lamp to light when the ignition switch is **ON**.

The DERM does not need to be replaced after each air bag deployment. After 4 deployments the DERM will register a Code 52. The Code 52 informs that the accident memory is full and the DERM must be replaced.

Inflatable Restraint Indicator

The indicator lamp is used to verify the DERM operation by flashing 7-9 times when the ignition is first turned **ON**. It is also used to warn the driver of a SIR malfunction. For certain tests it can provide diagnostic information by flashing the fault code when the fault code diagnostic mode is enabled.

Arming Sensor

The arming sensor, mounted at the center of the upper dash panel, is a protective switch in the power feed side of the deployment loop. It is calibrated to close at low level velocity changes. This insures that the inflator module is connect to the 36VLR output of the DERM or ignition 1 voltage.

The sensor consists of a sensing element, normally open switch a diagnostic resistor and 2 steering diodes. The resistor is connected in parallel with the switch and allows a small amount of current to flow through the deployment loop during normal non-deployment operation. The DERM monitors this voltage to determine component faults.

When the arming sensor is located in the same housing as the passenger compartment discriminating sensor. The assembly is referred to as the dual sensor.

Discriminating Sensor

There are 2 discriminating sensors wired in parallel on the low side of the deployment loop. The forward sensor is located in front of the radiator. The passenger sensor is located under the console near the DERM. These sensors are located on the low side of the deployment loop and are calibrated to close with velocity changes which are sever enough to warrant air bag deployment.

The sensors consist of a sensing element, normally open switch and a diagnostic resistor. The diagnostic resistor is wired in parallel with the switch within each sensor. They provide a ground for current to pass during normal non-deployment operation. The DERM measures this current to determine component faults.

SIR Coil Assembly

The coil assembly consists of 2 current carrying coils. They are attached to the steering column and allow rotation of the steering wheel, while maintaining continuous contact of the deployment loop through the inflator module.

There is a shorting bar on the lower steering column connector, which connects the SIR coil to the SIR harness. The shorting bar shorts the circuit when the connector is disconnected. The circuit to the module is shorted in this way to help prevent unwanted deployment of the air bag, while performing service.

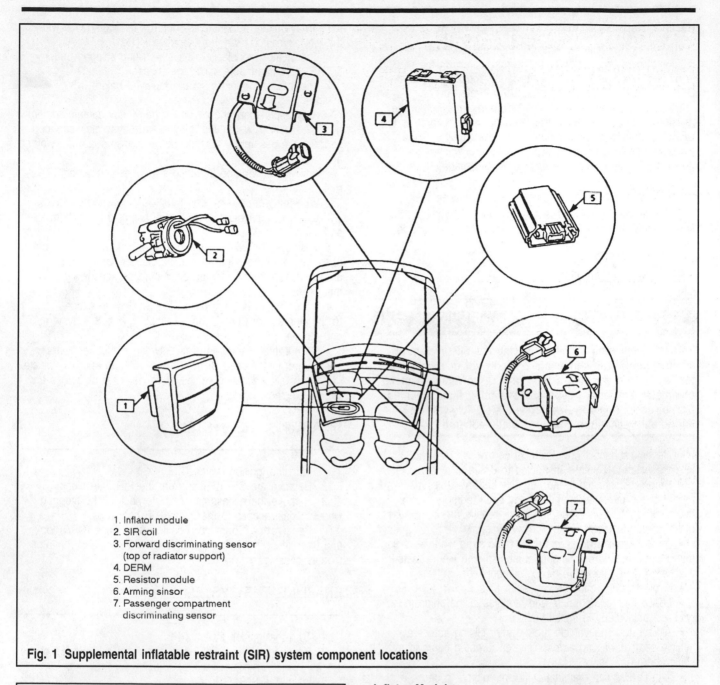

1. Inflator module
2. SIR coil
3. Forward discriminating sensor
   (top of radiator support)
4. DERM
5. Resistor module
6. Arming sinsor
7. Passenger compartment
   discriminating sensor

Fig. 1 Supplemental inflatable restraint (SIR) system component locations

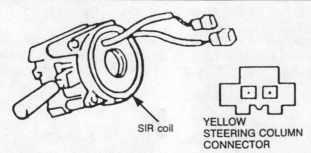

SIR coil

YELLOW
STEERING COLUMN
CONNECTOR

Fig. 2 Steering wheel connector used to disarm the system

Inflator Module

The inflator module is located in the steering wheel. It includes the air bag, inflator and initiator. When the vehicle is in an accident of sufficient force, current is passed through the deployment loop. The current passing through the deployment loop ignites the material in the inflator module and produces a gas which rapidly inflates the air bag.

There is a shorting bar on the lower steering column connector, which connects the SIR coil to the SIR harness. The shorting bar shorts the circuit when the connector is disconnected. The circuit to the module is shorted in this way to help prevent unwanted deployment of the air bag, while performing service.

Resistor Module

The resistor module is in the SIR harness between the inflator module and the DERM. The resistor allows the DERM to monitor the deployment loop for faults and also allows the DERM to detect if the air bag has been deployed.

The resistors in the resistor module are balanced with the resistors in the arming and discriminating sensors to allow the DERM to monitor voltage drops across the circuits. These resistors also help reduce the possibility of unwanted deployment in the case of wiring harness damage.

Knee Bolster

The knee bolster is used to absorb energy and control the driver's forward movement during an accident by limiting leg movement.

SERVICE PRECAUTIONS

✳✳CAUTION

To avoid deployment when servicing the SIR system or components in the immediate area, do not use electrical test equipment such as battery or A.C. powered voltmeter, ohmmeter, etc. or any type of tester other than specified. Do not use a non-powered probe tester. To avoid personal injury, all precautions must be strictly adhered to.

- Never disconnect any electrical connection with the ignition switch **ON** unless instructed to do so in a test.
- Before disconnecting the negative battery cable, make a record of the contents memorized by each memory system like the clock, audio, etc. When service or repairs are completed make certain to reset these memory system.
- Always wear a grounded wrist static strap when servicing any control module or component labeled with a Electrostatic Discharge (ESD) sensitive device symbol.
- Avoid touching module connector pins.
- Leave new components and modules in the shipping package until ready to install them.
- Always touch a vehicle ground after sliding across a vehicle seat or walking across vinyl or carpeted floors to avoid static charge damage.
- The DERM can maintain sufficient voltage to cause a deployment for up to 10 minute, even if the battery is disconnected.
- All sensors are specifically calibrated to each series vehicle's series. The sensors, mounting brackets and wiring harness must never be modified from original design.
- Never strike or jar a sensor, or deployment could happen.
- Never power up the SIR system when any sensor is not rigidly attached to the vehicle.
- Always carry an inflator module with the trim cover facing away.

- Always place an inflator module on the workbench with the trim cover up, away from loose objects.
- The inflator module is to be stored and shipped under DOT E-8236 flammable solid regulations.
- The inflator module must be deployed before it is scrapped.
- After deployment the air bag surface may contain sodium hydroxide dust. Always wear gloves and safety glasses when handling the assembly. Wash hands with mild soap and water afterwards.
- Any visible damage to sensors requires component replacement.
- Wire and connector repair must be performed using kit J-38125-A, or equivalent. Use special crimping tools, heat torch and seals.
- Absolutely no wire connector, or terminal repair is to be attempted on the arming sensor, passenger compartment discriminating sensor, forward discriminating sensor, inflator module or SIR coil assembly
- Never bake dry paint on vehicle or allow to exceed temperatures over 300°F, without disabling the SIR system and removing the inflator module.
- Do not interchange sensors between models or years.
- Do not install used SIR system parts from another vehicle.
- Never allow welding cables to lay on, near or across any vehicle electrical wiring.

DISARMING THE SYSTEM

1. Turn the ignition switch **OFF**.
2. Remove the SIR IG fuse from the SIR fuse block.
3. Remove the access cover at the back of the steering wheel to gain access to the 2-way SIR connector.
4. Remove the Connector Position Assurance (CPA) lock and disconnect the yellow 2-way connector inside the inflator module housing.

ENABLING THE SYSTEM

1. Turn the ignition switch **OFF**.
2. Reconnect the yellow 2-way connector at the back of the steering wheel and install the CPA lock.
3. Install the SIR IG fuse.
4. Refit the rear plastic access cover to the inflator module housing.
5. Turn the ignition switch **ON** and observe the inflatable restraint indicator lamp. If the lamp does not flash 7 to 9 times and then remain OFF, perform the SIR diagnostic system check.

HEATER

Blower Motor

REMOVAL & INSTALLATION

▶ **See Figures 3 and 4**

Sprint

1. Disconnect the negative battery cable.
2. Disconnect the defroster hose on the steering column side.

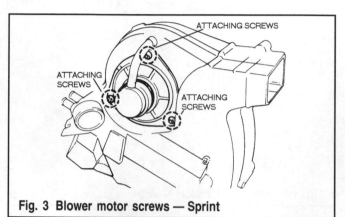

Fig. 3 Blower motor screws — Sprint

3. Disconnect the blower motor lead wire.
4. Remove the attaching screws and blower motor.
5. Installation is the reverse of removal.

Metro

1. Disconnect the negative battery cable.
2. On Metro, remove the glove compartment to access the blower motor electrical connectors.
3. Disconnect the blower motor and resistor wiring connectors.
4. Disconnect the air control cable from the blower case assembly.
5. Remove the blower case mounting bolts and case from the vehicle.
6. Remove the three motor retaining screws and blower motor. Disconnect the air hose, if equipped.

To install:

7. Install the blower motor case and secure with screws.
8. Connect the air hose to the blower motor case.
9. Install the blower motor case in the vehicle and tighten bolts to 89 inch lbs. (10 Nm).
10. Connect the air control cable. Connect the electrical connectors.
11. Install the glove compartment.
12. Connect the negative battery cable.

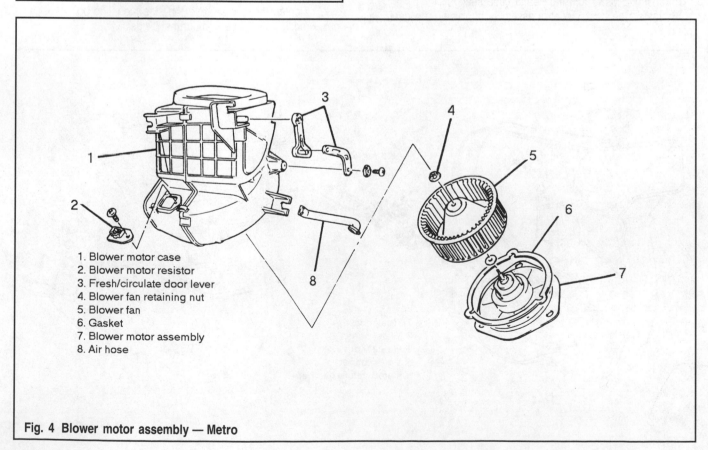

1. Blower motor case
2. Blower motor resistor
3. Fresh/circulate door lever
4. Blower fan retaining nut
5. Blower fan
6. Gasket
7. Blower motor assembly
8. Air hose

Fig. 4 Blower motor assembly — Metro

Heater Core

REMOVAL & INSTALLATION

▶ See Figures 5 and 6

Sprint

1. Drain the cooling system.
2. Remove the glove compartment.
3. Remove the defroster hoses from the heater case.
4. Disconnect the wiring connectors from the blower motor and resistor.
5. Disconnect the control cables from the heater case.
6. Pull out center vent louver.
7. Disconnect side vent ducts from center vent duct.
8. Remove center vent duct, ashtray upper plate and instrument panel member stay.
9. Remove the heater assembly attaching nuts.
10. Loosen the heater case top side mounting bolt through box wrench from glove compartment side.
11. Remove the heater control assembly by raising the dash panel.
12. Remove clips to separate the heater case into right and left sections.
13. Pull out the heater core from the heater case.
   To install:
14. Install the heater core in the heater case.
15. Install clips to join the heater case sections.
16. Install the heater control assembly by raising the dash panel.

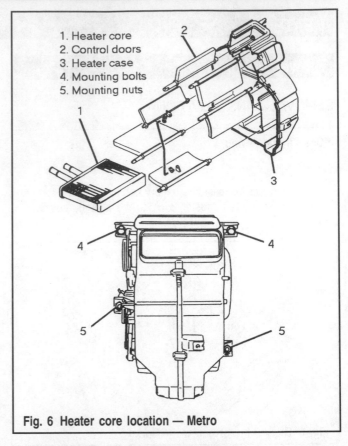

1. Heater core
2. Control doors
3. Heater case
4. Mounting bolts
5. Mounting nuts

Fig. 6 Heater core location — Metro

17. Tighten the heater case top side mounting bolt through box wrench from glove compartment side.

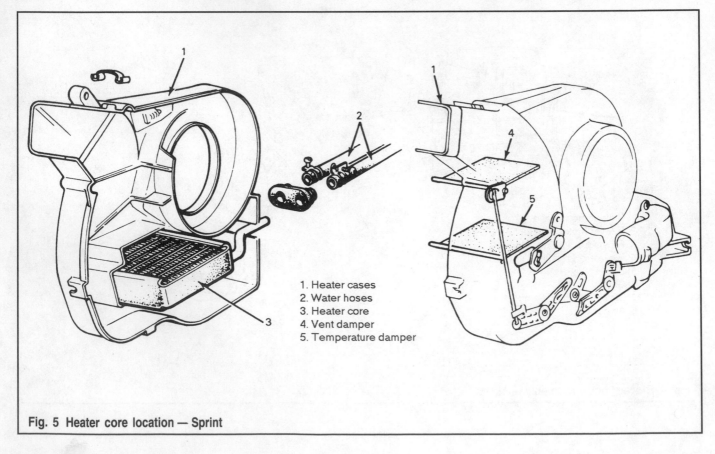

1. Heater cases
2. Water hoses
3. Heater core
4. Vent damper
5. Temperature damper

Fig. 5 Heater core location — Sprint

18. Install the heater assembly attaching nuts.
19. Install center vent duct, ashtray upper plate and instrument panel member stay.
20. Connect side vent ducts from center vent duct.
21. Install center vent louver.
22. Connect the control cables to the heater case.
23. Connect the wiring connectors to the blower motor and resistor.
24. Install the defroster hoses to the heater case.
25. Install the glove compartment.
26. Fill the cooling system.
27. Run the engine and check for leaks.

Metro

1. Disconnect the negative battery cable.
2. Drain the engine coolant.
3. Remove the instrument panel and center supports.
4. Remove the heater control assembly from the support member.
5. Disconnect all electrical connectors and cables from the heater case.
6. Disconnect the heater core hoses.
7. Remove the defrost duct and speedometer retaining bracket from the heater case.
8. Remove the fastening bolts, grommets and floor duct, if equipped, from the case and remove the case from the vehicle.
9. Separate the heater case and remove the heater core.
To install:
10. Install the core and assemble the heater case.
11. Install the fastening bolts, grommets and floor duct to the case after installation.
12. Install the defrost duct and speedometer retaining bracket to the heater case.
13. Connect the heater core hoses.
14. Connect all electrical connectors and cables to the heater case.
15. Install the center supports and instrument panel.
16. Refill the engine coolant.
17. Connect the negative battery cable.
18. Run engine and check for coolant leaks.

Control Cable

ADJUSTMENT

1. Set the temperature control lever to **HOT**.
2. Set the mode control lever to the **DEFROST** position.
3. Set the fresh/recirculate control lever to the **FRESH** position.
4. Connect and clamp each respective control cable to the heater and blower case with the heater control assembly set.

REMOVAL & INSTALLATION

▶ **See Figures 7 and 8**

1. Remove the heater control unit from the instrument panel.

2. Remove the mode and temperature control cables at the heater case. Remove the cables from the vehicle.
3. Remove the fresh/recirculate control cable at blower case and remove from vehicle.
4. Installation is the reverse of removal.
5. Adjust the cables prior to attaching at heater control unit.

Control Panel

REMOVAL & INSTALLATION

▶ **See Figure 9**

1. Disconnect the negative battery cable.
2. Pull the control knobs from the levers.
3. Release the latches at the rear of the bezel. Remove the control assembly lens and disconnect the bulb.
4. Disconnect the control cables at the blower and heater assembly.
5. Remove the control assembly fasteners.
6. Pull the control assembly out and disconnect the electrical connections.
7. Disconnect the control cables from the levers.
8. Remove the blower, air conditioning and heater switch.
To install:
9. Install the blower, air conditioning and heater switch.
10. Connect the control cables to the levers.
11. Connect the electrical connections and install the control assembly.
12. Install the control assembly fasteners.
13. Connect the control cables at the blower and heater assembly.
14. Connect the bulb and install the control assembly lens.
15. Install the control knobs.
16. Adjust the control cables.
17. Connect the negative battery cable.

Blower Switch

REMOVAL & INSTALLATION

1. Disconnect the negative battery cable.
2. Pull off control lever knobs.
3. Remove heater control lever panel plate and lever panel.
4. Remove heater control assembly attaching screws.
5. Disconnect switch connector and remove switch.
6. Installation is the reverse of removal.

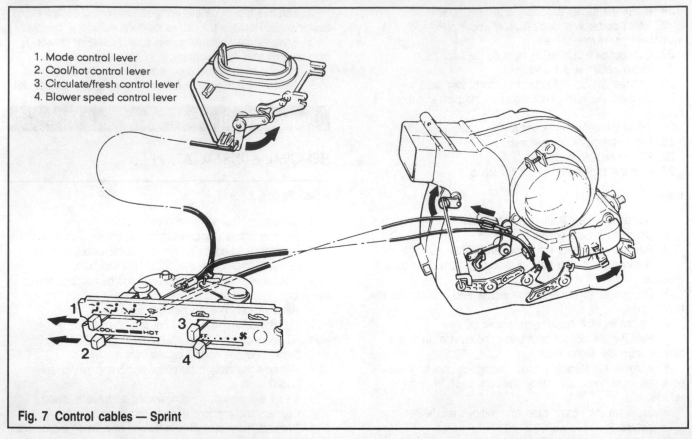

1. Mode control lever
2. Cool/hot control lever
3. Circulate/fresh control lever
4. Blower speed control lever

Fig. 7 Control cables — Sprint

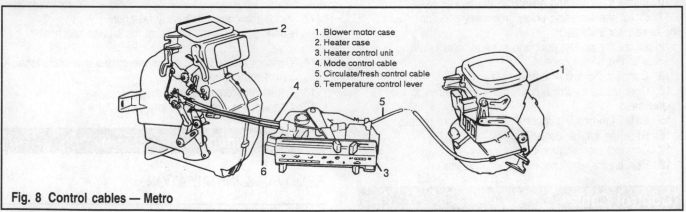

1. Blower motor case
2. Heater case
3. Heater control unit
4. Mode control cable
5. Circulate/fresh control cable
6. Temperature control lever

Fig. 8 Control cables — Metro

AIR CONDITIONER

▶ **See Figure 10**

The air conditioning compressor is driven by a drive belt from the engine crankshaft through an electromagnetic clutch. When voltage is applied to energize the clutch coil, a clutch plate and hub assembly are drawn rearward toward the pulley. As the compressor shaft turns, the compressor performs 2 functions. One is to compress the low pressure refrigerant vapor from the evaporator into a high pressure/temperature vapor. The other function is to pump refrigerant oil through the system to lubricate all components.

The condenser is mounted in front of the radiator and is comprised of small coils and cooling fins. When the high pressure/temperature vapor, from the compressor enters the condenser, heat is transferred from the refrigerant to the air passing through the front of the vehicle. The refrigerant is cooled and condensed into a liquid.

The receiver/drier is mounted on the fender and is connected to the condenser outlet and evaporator inlet. The receiver/drier is a temporary storage container for condensed liquid refrigerant, a filter which removes moisture and contaminants from the system incorporates a sight glass for checking the system's refrigerant charge.

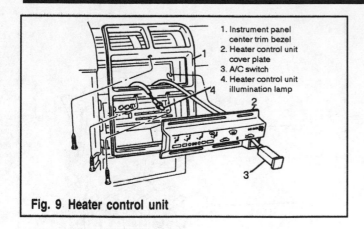

1. Instrument panel center trim bezel
2. Heater control unit cover plate
3. A/C switch
4. Heater control unit illumination lamp

Fig. 9 Heater control unit

1. Evaporator
2. Heater core
3. Blower motor
4. Expansion valve
5. Dual pressure switch
6. Receiver/dryer
7. Condenser
8. Comperssor
9. Compressor clutch
10. State of refrigerant
11. Cool air passing condenser
12. Outside air inlet
13. Recirculated air inlet

LIQUID
VAPOR
HIGH PRESSURE/HIGH TEMPERATURE VAPOR

Fig. 10 Air conditioning system major components and refrigerant flow

The expansion valve regulates the flow of liquid refrigerant into the core of the evaporator. As the condensed liquid is released through the expansion valve, the pressure is decreased and the temperature drops causing the cooling effect.

The evaporator is housed in the evaporator case, located behind the right side of the instrument panel. During the air conditioning operation, ambient air is directed through the fins of the evaporator and into the vehicle's passenger compartment. As the air passes through the evaporator fins it is cooled.

➡ R-12 refrigerant is a chlorofluorocarbon which, when released into the atmosphere, contributes to the depletion of the ozone layer in the upper atmosphere. Ozone filters out harmful radiation from the sun. DO NOT attempt to

discharge the system by merely loosening a fitting. Discharging should only be performed using an approved recovery station. Consult the laws in your area before servicing the air conditioning system. In some states it is illegal to perform repairs involving refrigerant unless the work is done by a certified technician.

Compressor

REMOVAL & INSTALLATION

▶ **See Figure 11**

1. Disconnect the negative battery cable.
2. Discharge the air conditioning system, using the proper equipment. Refer to Section 1 for proper discharging procedure.
3. Disconnect the suction, discharge hoses and electrical connector at the compressor. Plug all open hoses to prevent contamination.
4. Raise and safely support the vehicle.
5. Remove the right fender extension and oil filter. Loosen the compressor drive belt.
6. Remove the compressor mounting bolts and compressor.
To install:
7. Install the compressor and mounting bolts. Tighten compressor lower and upper mounting bolts to 21 ft. lbs. (28 Nm).
8. Install the right fender extension and oil filter. Adjust the compressor drive belt.
9. Lower the vehicle.
10. Connect the suction, discharge hoses and electrical connector at the compressor. Tighten compressor pipe fitting bolts to 18 ft. lbs. (25 Nm).
11. Evacuate and recharge the air conditioning system.
12. Connect the negative battery cable.

Condenser

REMOVAL & INSTALLATION

▶ **See Figure 12**

1. Disconnect the negative battery cable.

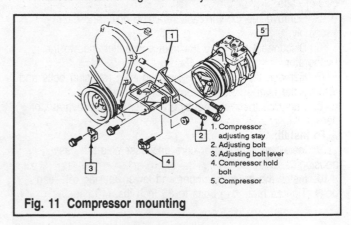

1. Compressor adjusting stay
2. Adjusting bolt
3. Adjusting bolt lever
4. Compressor hold bolt
5. Compressor

Fig. 11 Compressor mounting

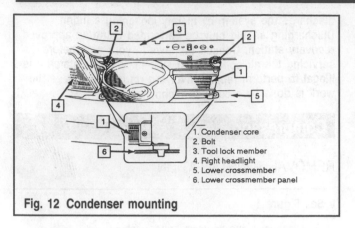

1. Condenser core
2. Bolt
3. Tool lock member
4. Right headlight
5. Lower crossmember
6. Lower crossmember panel

Fig. 12 Condenser mounting

2. Discharge the air conditioning system.
3. Remove the compressor hose. Disconnect the inlet hose to the receiver/drier. Plug all open hoses to prevent contamination.
4. Remove the hood latch and lock assembly, Metro only.
5. Disconnect the condenser cooling fan connector.
6. Remove the condenser retaining bolts, condenser, cooling fan and receiver/drier.

To install:

7. Install the condenser and cooling fan assembly. Tighten condenser mounting bolts to 15 ft. lbs. (20 Nm).
8. Add 0.7-1.0 oz. of refrigerant oil to the condenser before connecting hoses.
9. Connect the inlet and outlet hoses to the assembly. Tighten hoses to 26 ft. lbs. (35 Nm).
10. Connect the electrical connectors.
11. Install the hood latch and lock. Tighten to 11 ft. lbs. (15 Nm).
12. Evacuate and recharge the system.

Evaporator

REMOVAL & INSTALLATION

▶ See Figure 13

1. Disconnect the negative battery cable.
2. Discharge the air conditioning system.
3. Remove the glove compartment, as required.
4. Disconnect all electrical wiring and cables from the blower case.
5. Remove the blower case retaining bolts and case assembly.
6. Disconnect and plug the inlet and outlet lines to the evaporator.
7. Remove the upper and lower housing retaining bolts and remove the evaporator assembly from the vehicle.
8. Separate the case housing and remove the evaporator core.

To install:

9. Install the evaporator core and assemble the case housing.
10. Install the housing, upper and lower housing retaining bolts. Tighten mounting bolts to 89 inch lbs. (10 Nm).

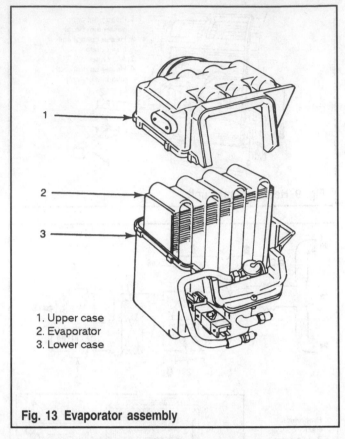

1. Upper case
2. Evaporator
3. Lower case

Fig. 13 Evaporator assembly

11. Connect the inlet and outlet lines to the evaporator. Tighten inlet pipe to 26 ft. lbs. (35 Nm) and outlet pipe to 33 ft. lbs. (45 Nm).
12. Install the blower case and retaining bolts.
13. Connect all electrical wiring and cables to the blower case.
14. Install the glove compartment, if removed.
15. Evacuate and recharge the air conditioning system.
16. Connect the negative battery cable.

Expansion Valve

REMOVAL & INSTALLATION

▶ See Figure 14

1. Disconnect the negative battery cable.
2. Discharge the air conditioning system.
3. Remove the evaporator assembly from the vehicle.
4. Remove the clamps to separate the upper and lower halves.
5. Using backup wrenches, remove the expansion valve from the evaporator.

To install:

6. Install the expansion valve on the evaporator and tighten to 18 ft. lbs. (25 Nm).
7. Install the clamps to join the upper and lower halves.
8. Install the evaporator assembly in the vehicle.
9. Evacuate and recharge the air conditioning system.
10. Connect the negative battery cable.

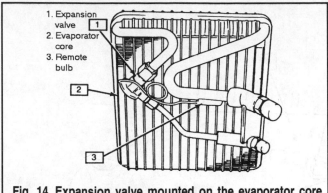

Fig. 14 Expansion valve mounted on the evaporator core

Receiver/Dryer

REMOVAL & INSTALLATION

▶ See Figures 15 and 16

1. Disconnect the negative battery cable.
2. Discharge the air conditioning system.
3. Disconnect the inlet and outlet pipe to the receiver/drier. Plug the open pipes to prevent contamination.
4. Remove the assembly from the mounting bracket.

To install:

5. Install the receiver/dryer assembly in the mounting bracket and secure in place.

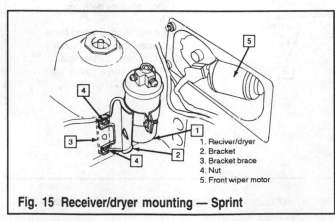

Fig. 15 Receiver/dryer mounting — Sprint

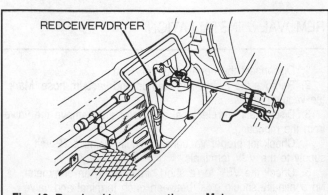

Fig. 16 Receiver/dryer mounting — Metro

6. Add 0.3 oz. (10 ml) of refrigerant oil to the inlet.
7. Connect the inlet and outlet pipe to the receiver/drier. Tighten the condenser outlet fitting to 26 ft. lbs. (35 Nm) and the receiver/dryer pipe fitting to 26 ft. lbs. (35 Nm).
8. Evacuate and recharge the air conditioning system.
9. Connect the negative battery cable.

Refrigerant Lines

REMOVAL & INSTALLATION

▶ See Figure 17

1. Disconnect the negative battery cable.
2. Discharge the air conditioning system.
3. Remove the radiator grille if removing front refrigerant lines.
4. Loosen the connector at the compressor and attaching points. Use a backup wrench on pipes with flare nut fittings.
5. Remove the pipe retaining clips.
6. Remove the pipe from the vehicle.

To install:

7. Install new replacement O-rings whenever a joint or fitting is disconnected. Lubricate pipe threads with refrigerant oil and install. Torque the $\frac{3}{8}$ in. O.D. pipes to 11-18 ft. lbs. (15-25 Nm), $\frac{1}{2}$ in. O.D. pipes to 15-22 ft. lbs. (20-30 Nm) and $\frac{5}{8}$ in. O.D. pipes to 22-29 ft. lbs. (30-40 Nm).
8. Install the pipe retaining clips.
9. Install the radiator grille if removing front refrigerant lines.
10. Install the radiator grille if removed.
11. Connect the negative battery cable.

Dual Pressure Switch

▶ See Figure 18

When the cycling refrigerant pressure drops due to leakage, a control switch stops further compressor rotation by turning off the compressor and condenser fan. The switch is located on top of the receiver/drier assembly.

REMOVAL & INSTALLATION

1. Disconnect the negative battery cable.
2. Disconnect the connector at the receiver/drier.
3. With the ignition key and air conditioning switch **ON**, disconnect the dual pressure switch connector and install a jumper wire between the 2 terminals.
4. If the compressor engages and the refrigerant pressures are normal, the switch is defective.
5. Discharge the air conditioning system.
6. Remove the switch from the receiver/drier.
7. Installation is the reverse of removal. Use thread sealing tape before installing the dual pressure switch.

Vacuum Switching Valve

At low speeds, operating the air conditioning loads the engine. To prevent stalling, the vacuum switching valve utilizes

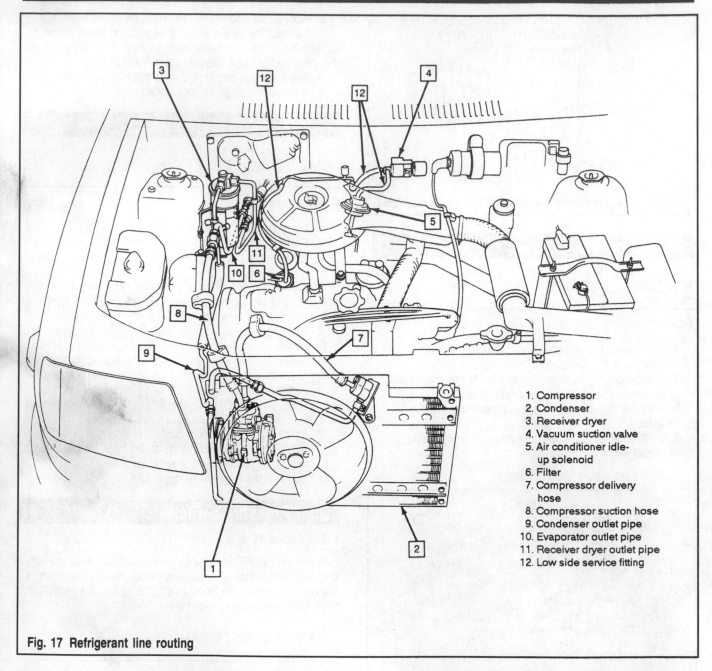

Fig. 17 Refrigerant line routing

1. Compressor
2. Condenser
3. Receiver dryer
4. Vacuum suction valve
5. Air conditioner idle-up solenoid
6. Filter
7. Compressor delivery hose
8. Compressor suction hose
9. Condenser outlet pipe
10. Evaporator outlet pipe
11. Receiver dryer outlet pipe
12. Low side service fitting

intake manifold vacuum to increase the engine idle speed. The VSV is controlled by signals from the electronic control module

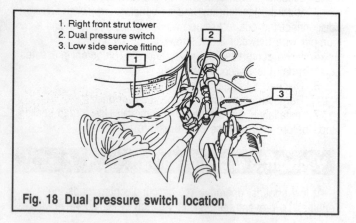

1. Right front strut tower
2. Dual pressure switch
3. Low side service fitting

Fig. 18 Dual pressure switch location

and air conditioning amplifier and is located at the bulkhead to the right of the ignition coil.

REMOVAL & INSTALLATION

1. Disconnect the negative battery cable.
2. Remove the 2 retaining clamps and vacuum hose. Mark the vacuum hoses.
3. Disconnect the electrical connector and remove the valve from the mounting.
4. Check for proper vacuum continuity using a 12 volt supply to the VSV terminals.
5. Check the VSV for a short circuit using an ohmmeter. No continuity should exist between each terminal and valve housing.

6. Check the valve for opens by measuring the resistance between the terminals; replace the valve, if any problems are found.

7. Installation is the reverse of removal.

Condenser Fan or Compressor Clutch Relay

REMOVAL & INSTALLATION

1. Disconnect the negative battery cable.

CRUISE CONTROL

▶ **See Figure 19**

The cruise control system consists of an mode control switch, electronics module, servo unit, speed sensor and wiring harness. Throttle actuation is accomplished by an electrically operated servo motor attached by cable to the vehicles throttle linkage. Maximum and minimum cruise speeds are 85 and 25 miles per hour.

The vehicle speed is provided to the electronics module by the use of a speed sensor. The sensor utilizes a magnetic reed switch which opens and closes 4 times per revolution of the speedometer cable. The sensor is located in the speedometer head.

The electronics module is the brain of the system. The module interprets the position of the servo unit, the position of the mode control switches and the output of the speed sensor. In response to these inputs, the module electrically signals the servo motor drive in or out. The electronic module is located under the dash on the driver side.

The disengagement switches, brake and clutch, are operated by the use of the brake and clutch pedals. The brake switch operates the stoplights and cancels the signal to the cruise control module when the lights are illuminated. The clutch switch disengages the cruise control if the pedal is depressed for up shifting or down shifting.

The servo consists of an electric motor with reduction gearing, electromagnetic clutch, actuating rack and a variable

2. Remove the relay from the fuse and relay box.

3. Connect a 12 volt source between terminals 1 and 3 while checking for continuity between terminals 2 and 4.

4. If no continuity exists, replace the relay.

5. Install the relay in the fuse and relay box.

6. Connect the negative battery cable.

voltage position sensor. The servo operates the throttle in response to signal from the electronics module.

✳✳CAUTION

If vehicle is equipped with an supplemental inflatable restraint system (SIR), the system must be fully disarmed before performing cruise control repairs. Failure to disarm the system could result in personal injury and/or property damage.

Brake Switch

REMOVAL & INSTALLATION

1. Disconnect the negative battery cable.

2. Remove the plastic cover from steering column, as required.

3. Disconnect the stop lamp switch electrical connector.

4. Depress the brake pedal and remove the locknut from the threaded portion of the brake light switch.

5. Remove the brake light switch.

To install:

6. Install brake light switch.

7. Adjust the switch so that the clearance between the end thread of the stoplight switch and the brake pedal contact plate is 0.02-0.04 in. (0.5-1.0mm) with the brake pedal pulled upward.

8. Depress brake pedal, install locknut and tighten to 115 inch lbs. (13 Nm).

9. Connect brake light switch electrical connector.

10. Install the plastic cover on steering column, as required.

11. Connect the negative battery cable.

Clutch Switch

REMOVAL & INSTALLATION

1. Disconnect the negative battery cable.

2. Remove the plastic cover from steering column, as required.

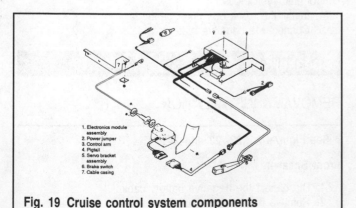

1. Electronics module assembly
2. Power jumper
3. Control arm
4. Pigtail
5. Servo bracket assembly
6. Brake switch
7. Cable casing

Fig. 19 Cruise control system components

3. Disconnect the clutch switch electrical connector.

4. Depress the clutch pedal and remove the locknut from the threaded portion of the brake light switch.

5. Remove the clutch switch.

To install:

6. Install clutch switch.

7. Rotate the clutch switch into place until the plunger bottoms out onto the pedal stopper.

8. Tighten lock nut to secure into place. Tighten locknut to 115 inch lbs. (13 Nm).

9. Connect clutch switch electrical connector.

10. Install the plastic cover on steering column, as required.

11. Connect the negative battery cable.

Electronics Module

REMOVAL & INSTALLATION

1. Locate the electronics module under the dash on the left side.

2. Disconnect the negative battery cable.

3. Disconnect the electronics module harness connector.

4. Remove the module mounting screws, then remove the module.

5. Installation is the reverse of removal.

Servo Unit

REMOVAL & INSTALLATION

1. Disconnect the negative battery cable.

2. Disconnect the servo cable from the servo unit.

RADIO

Radio Receiver

REMOVAL & INSTALLATION

▶ **See Figure 20**

1. Disconnect the negative battery cable.

2. Open the glove box. Remove the glove box open panel.

3. Remove the air conditioning switch connector and heater control unit lever knobs. Pull heater control unit cover plate from instrument panel.

4. Remove the gearshift control lever upper boot and center console.

5. Remove the ashtray.

6. Remove the instrument panel center trim bezel and radio face plate.

7. Remove the screw from the back of the radio receiver and the screws from the front face of the radio.

8. Remove the radio.

To install:

9. Install the radio. Tighten screws securely.

3. Disconnect the servo unit electrical harness.

4. Remove the servo unit attaching nut, then remove the servo unit.

To install:

5. Install the servo unit and tighten attaching nut securely.

6. Connect servo unit electrical harness.

7. Install servo cable to servo unit.

8. Connect the negative battery cable.

Servo Cable

REMOVAL & INSTALLATION

1. Disconnect the negative battery cable.

2. Disconnect the servo cable from the servo unit.

3. Disconnect the servo unit from the throttle pedal.

4. Remove the servo cable from the engine compartment side.

5. Installation is the reverse of removal.

6. Lightly secure the servo cable casing so that there is a light tension on the servo cable, but make sure not to pull the throttle off the idle setting.

7. Tighten the clamp securely.

Mode Control Switch

REMOVAL & INSTALLATION

The mode control switch is an integral part of the combination switch mounted on the steering column. Refer to "Combination Switch Removal and Installation" in this Section.

10. Install the instrument panel center trim bezel and radio face plate.

11. Install the ashtray.

12. Install the gearshift control lever upper boot and center console.

13. Pull heater control unit cover plate from instrument panel. Install the air conditioning switch connector and heater control unit lever knobs.

14. Install the glove box open panel.

15. Connect the negative battery cable.

Speakers

REMOVAL & INSTALLATION

▶ **See Figures 21, 22, 23 and 24**

Front Speakers

1. Disconnect the negative battery cable.

2. Remove the speaker grills.

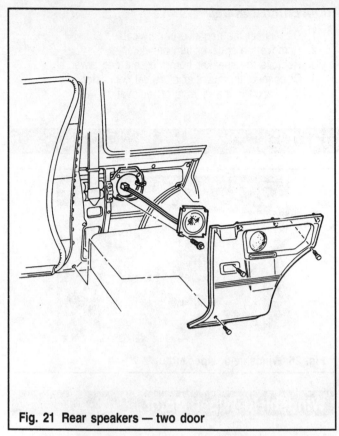

Fig. 21 Rear speakers — two door

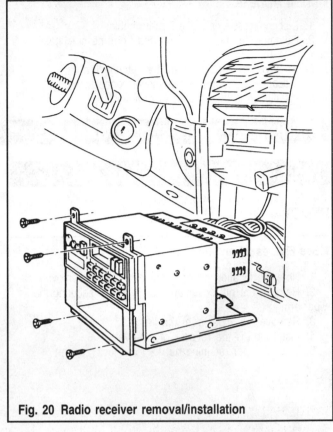

Fig. 20 Radio receiver removal/installation

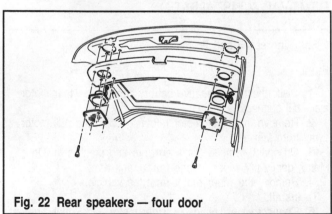

Fig. 22 Rear speakers — four door

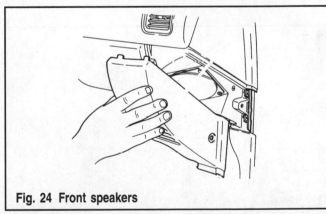

Fig. 24 Front speakers

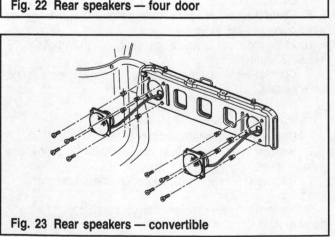

Fig. 23 Rear speakers — convertible

3. Remove the speaker retaining screws.
4. Remove the speaker from the instrument panel.
5. Disconnect the speaker electrical connector.
6. Installation is the reverse of removal.

Rear Speakers

2-DOOR MODELS

1. Disconnect the negative battery cable.
2. Remove the rear quarter trim panel.
3. Remove the speaker retaining screws.
4. Remove the speaker from the rear quarter panel.
5. Disconnect the speaker electrical connector.
6. Installation is the reverse of removal.

4-DOOR MODELS

1. Disconnect the negative battery cable.
2. Remove the speaker grilles and from the hatchback door.
3. Remove the speaker from the hatchback door.
4. Disconnect the speaker electrical connector.
5. Installation is the reverse of removal.

CONVERTIBLE MODELS

1. Disconnect the negative battery cable.
2. Remove the speaker trim panels.
3. Remove the speaker from the seat belt tower.
4. Disconnect the speaker electrical connector.
5. Installation is the reverse of removal.

WINDSHIELD WIPERS AND WASHERS

Windshield Wiper Blade and Arm

REMOVAL & INSTALLATION

▶ **See Figures 25 and 26**

1. Note the location of the wiper arm prior to removal.
2. Remove the nut cover and retaining nut securing the wiper arm.
3. Remove the wiper from the linkage
4. Installation is the reverse of removal.
5. Tighten wiper retaining nut to 15 ft. lbs. (20 Nm).

Fig. 26 Windshield wiper motor

Windshield Wiper Motor

REMOVAL & INSTALLATION

▶ **See Figures 25 and 26**

Front

1. Disconnect the negative battery cable and wiper motor electrical connectors.
2. Remove the wiper motor retaining bolts and pull motor away from firewall.
3. On sprint, remove crank arm nut and crank arm. On Metro, gently pry wiper linkage from crank arm.
4. Remove the wiper motor from the vehicle.
   To install:
5. Connect wiper linkage to wiper motor. On Sprint, tighten wiper crank arm nut to 96 inch lbs. (10 Nm).
6. Install the wiper motor to the vehicle. Tighten bolts to 15 ft. lbs. (20 Nm).
7. Connect wiper motor electrical connectors, then negative battery cable.

Rear

1. Disconnect the negative battery cable.
2. Remove the speakers from the hatchback door inner trim panel, if so equipped.
3. Remove the retaining clips and hatchback door inner trim panel from the vehicle.
4. Remove the wiper motor electrical connector and wiper motor ground screw.
5. Remove the wiper motor mounting screws and lower the wiper motor assembly.

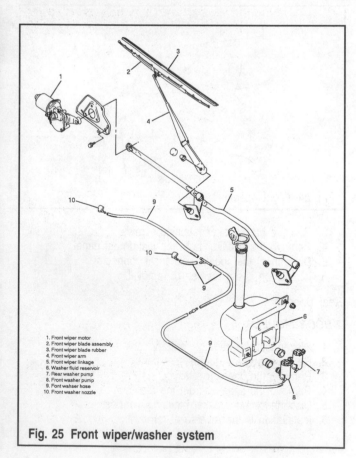

1. Front wiper motor
2. Front wiper blade assembly
3. Front wiper blade rubber
4. Front wiper arm
5. Front wiper linkage
6. Washer fluid reservoir
7. Rear washer pump
8. Front washer pump
9. Font wahser hose
10. Front washer nozzle

Fig. 25 Front wiper/washer system

6. On Sprint, remove the wiper cranking arm retaining nut from the wiper motor shaft. On Metro, pry the wiper linkage from the cranking arm.

7. Remove the rear wiper motor.

To install:

8. Connect wiper linkage to wiper motor. On Sprint, tighten wiper crank arm nut to 96 inch lbs. (10 Nm).

9. Install the wiper motor to the vehicle. Tighten bolts to 15 ft. lbs. (20 Nm).

10. Install the wiper motor electrical connector and wiper motor ground screw.

11. Install the retaining clips and hatchback door inner trim panel.

12. Install the speakers in the hatchback door inner trim panel, if so equipped.

13. Connect the negative battery cable.

Wiper Linkage

REMOVAL & INSTALLATION

▶ **See Figures 25 and 27**

Front

1. Disconnect the negative battery cable.
2. Remove the wiper arm.
3. Remove the cowl vent grilles.
4. Remove the wiper linkage assembly retaining nuts.
5. Remove the wiper motor.

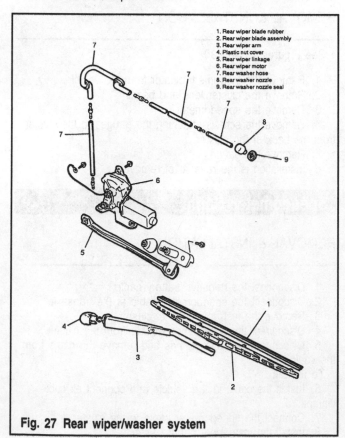

1. Rear wiper blade rubber
2. Rear wiper blade assembly
3. Rear wiper arm
4. Plastic nut cover
5. Rear wiper linkage
6. Rear wiper motor
7. Rear washer hose
8. Rear washer nozzle
9. Rear washer nozzle seal

Fig. 27 Rear wiper/washer system

6. Slide the wiper linkage assembly through the wiper motor opening.

To install:

7. Install the wiper linkage assembly through the wiper motor opening.

8. Install the wiper motor.

9. Install the wiper linkage assembly retaining nuts and tighten to 11 ft. lbs. (15 Nm).

10. Install the cowl vent grilles.

11. Install the wiper arm.

12. Connect the negative battery cable.

Rear

1. Disconnect the negative battery cable.
2. Remove the rear wiper arm.
3. Remove the speakers and interior door trim from the hatchback.
4. Gently pry rear wiper linkage from motor crank arm.
5. Remove the rear wiper linkage assembly retaining bolts and slide the linkage out of the door.

To install:

6. Slide the linkage into the door and install the rear wiper linkage assembly retaining bolts. Tighten bolts to 15 ft. lbs. (20 Nm).

7. Install the rear wiper linkage on motor crank arm.

8. Install the speakers and interior door trim on the hatchback.

9. Install the rear wiper arm.

10. Connect the negative battery cable.

Windshield Washer Reservoir

A single reservoir feeds both front and rear washer systems. The reservoir is located on the left wheel housing in the engine compartment.

REMOVAL & INSTALLATION

▶ **See Figure 25**

1. Disconnect the negative battery cable.
2. Disconnect the washer pump electrical connectors.
3. Remove the screws and clips attaching the reservoir to the wheel housing.
4. Remove the attaching nuts and the washer fluid reservoir from the vehicle.

To install:

5. Install the washer fluid reservoir on the vehicle.
6. Install the screws and clips attaching the reservoir to the wheel housing.
7. Connect the washer pump electrical connectors.
8. Connect the negative battery cable.

Windshield Washer Pump

Dual washer pumps are located on the washer reservoir. One feeds the front windshield washer system, the other feeds the rear windshield washer. Removal and installation procedures are the same for both pumps.

REMOVAL & INSTALLATION

▶ See Figures 25 and 27

1. Disconnect the negative battery cable.
2. Disconnect the washer pump electrical connectors.
3. Remove the screws and clips attaching the reservoir to the wheel housing.
4. Remove the attaching nuts and the washer fluid reservoir from the vehicle.

5. Remove the washer pumps from the reservoir.
To install:
6. Install the washer pumps on the reservoir.
7. Install the washer fluid reservoir on the vehicle.
8. Install the screws and clips attaching the reservoir to the wheel housing.
9. Connect the washer pump electrical connectors.
10. Connect the negative battery cable.

INSTRUMENTS AND SWITCHES

Instrument Panel Cluster Trim Bezel

REMOVAL & INSTALLATION

1. Disable the SIR (air bag) system.
2. Disconnect the negative battery cable.
3. Remove the lower steering column trim panel.
4. Loosen the upper steering column and lower steering support to gain clearance for bezel removal.
5. Remove the instrument panel cluster trim bezel.
6. Disconnect the electrical connectors.
To install:
7. Connect the electrical connectors.
8. Install the instrument panel cluster trim bezel.
9. Tighten the upper steering column and lower steering support to 10 ft. lbs. (14 Nm).
10. Install the lower steering column trim panel.
11. Connect the negative battery cable.
12. Enable the SIR (air bag) system.

Instrument Cluster

REMOVAL & INSTALLATION

▶ See Figures 28 and 29

1. Disconnect the negative battery cable.
2. Remove the instrument panel trim bezel.
3. Disconnect the retaining clip and the speedometer cable at the transaxle to ease cluster removal.
4. Remove the cluster assembly from the instrument panel.
5. Disconnect the speedometer cable and all electrical connectors from the back of the cluster assembly.
To install:
6. Connect the speedometer cable and all electrical connectors to the back of the cluster assembly.
7. Install the cluster assembly in the instrument panel.
8. Connect the retaining clip and the speedometer cable at the transaxle.
9. Install the instrument panel trim bezel.
10. Connect the negative battery cable.

Speedometer

REMOVAL & INSTALLATION

▶ See Figures 28 and 30

1. Remove the instrument cluster from the vehicle.
2. Remove the cluster lens and bezel.
3. Remove the screws attaching the speedometer to the cluster from the back of the cluster.
4. Remove the speedometer.
5. Installation is the reverse of removal.

Tachometer and Gauges

REMOVAL & INSTALLATION

▶ See Figures 28 and 30

1. Remove the instrument cluster from the vehicle.
2. Remove the cluster lens and bezel.
3. Remove the speedometer.
4. Remove the screws attaching the gauges to the cluster from the back of the cluster.
5. Remove the gauges.
6. Installation is the reverse of removal.

Speedometer Cable

REMOVAL & INSTALLATION

1. Disconnect the negative battery cable.
2. Disconnect the speedometer cable at the transaxle.
3. Remove the instrument panel cluster.
4. Disconnect the speedometer cable from the cluster.
5. Disconnect all cable clamps and remove the cable from the vehicle.
To install:
6. Install the cable in the vehicle and connect all cable clamps.
7. Connect the speedometer cable to the cluster.
8. Install the instrument panel cluster.
9. Connect the speedometer cable at the transaxle.

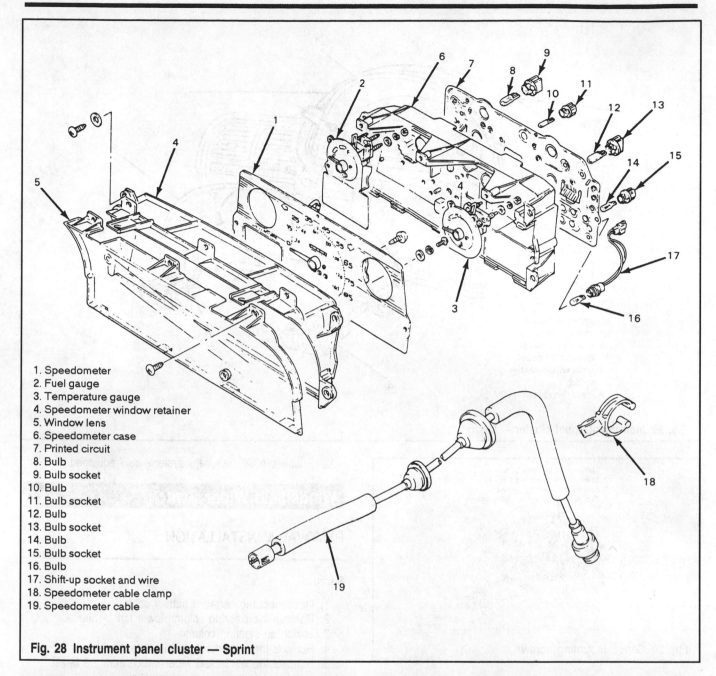

1. Speedometer
2. Fuel gauge
3. Temperature gauge
4. Speedometer window retainer
5. Window lens
6. Speedometer case
7. Printed circuit
8. Bulb
9. Bulb socket
10. Bulb
11. Bulb socket
12. Bulb
13. Bulb socket
14. Bulb
15. Bulb socket
16. Bulb
17. Shift-up socket and wire
18. Speedometer cable clamp
19. Speedometer cable

Fig. 28 Instrument panel cluster — Sprint

10. Connect the negative battery cable.

Combination Switch

REMOVAL & INSTALLATION

▶ **See Figures 31 and 32**

Sprint

On the Sprint, the combination switch integrates the functions of the turn signal switch and the dimmer switch.
1. Place the ignition switch in the **LOCK** position.
2. Disconnect the negative battery cable.
3. Remove the steering wheel and steering column covers.
4. Disconnect all electrical connectors.

5. Remove the screws retaining the combination switch and remove from the steering column.
To install:
6. Install the switch assembly on the steering column.
7. Connect all electrical connectors.
8. Install the steering wheel and tighten nut to 24 ft. lbs. (33 Nm). Install the steering column covers.
9. Connect the negative battery cable.

Metro

On the Metro, the combination switch integrates the functions of the headlight/dimmer switch, turn signal switch and windshield wiper/washer switch.
1. Place the ignition switch in the **LOCK** position. Disable the SIR (air bag) system, as if equipped.
2. Disconnect the negative battery cable.
3. Remove the steering wheel and steering column covers.

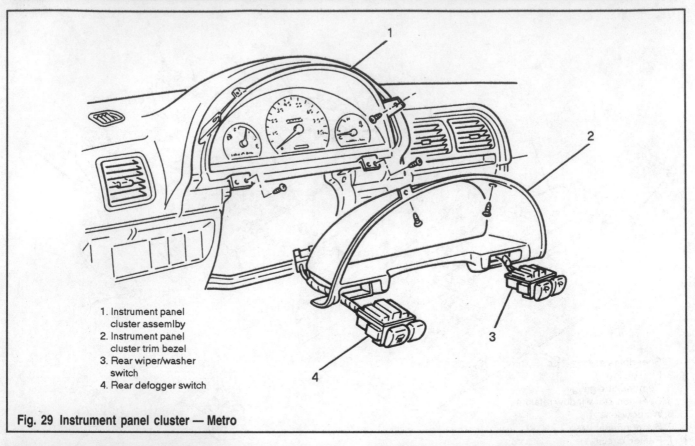

1. Instrument panel cluster assemlby
2. Instrument panel cluster trim bezel
3. Rear wiper/washer switch
4. Rear defogger switch

Fig. 29 Instrument panel cluster — Metro

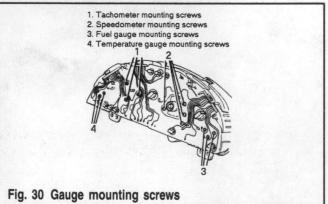

1. Tachometer mounting screws
2. Speedometer mounting screws
3. Fuel gauge mounting screws
4. Temperature gauge mounting screws

Fig. 30 Gauge mounting screws

4. Disconnect all electrical connectors.

5. Remove the screws retaining the air bag coil and turn signal/dimmer switch assembly.

➥**The coil assembly will become uncentered if the steering column is separated from the steering gear and it is allowed to rotate.**

6. Remove the switch assembly from the steering column.

To install:

7. Install the switch assembly on the steering column.

8. Install the screws retaining the air bag coil and turn signal/dimmer switch assembly.

9. Connect all electrical connectors.

10. Install the steering wheel and tighten nut to 24 ft. lbs. (33 Nm). Install the steering column covers.

11. Connect the negative battery cable.

12. Enable the SIR (air bag) system, as if equipped.

Windshield Wiper Switch

REMOVAL & INSTALLATION

Sprint

1. Disconnect the negative battery cable.
2. Remove the steering column lower trim panel.
3. Lower the steering column.
4. Remove the instrument panel cluster bezel.
5. Remove the windshield wiper switch from the bezel.
6. Installation is the reverse of removal.

Metro

The windshield wiper switch used on the Metro is an integral part of the combination switch. See "Combination Switch Removal and Installation" in this Section.

Rear Windshield Wiper Switch

The rear windshield wiper/washer switch is located in the instrument panel cluster bezel.

REMOVAL & INSTALLATION

1. Disconnect the negative battery cable.
2. Remove the instrument panel cluster bezel.

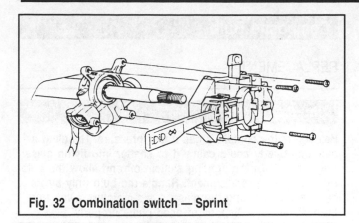
Fig. 32 Combination switch — Sprint

3. Disconnect the electrical connector.
4. Remove the switch from the bezel.
5. Installation is the reverse of removal.

Headlight Switch

REMOVAL & INSTALLATION

Sprint

1. Disconnect the negative battery cable.
2. Remove the steering column lower trim panel.
3. Lower the steering column.
4. Remove the instrument panel cluster bezel.
5. Remove the headlight switch from the bezel.
6. Installation is the reverse of removal.

Metro

The headlight switch used on the Metro is an integral part of the combination switch. See "Combination Switch Removal and Installation" in this Section.

LIGHTING

Headlamp Assembly

REMOVAL & INSTALLATION

▶ **See Figures 33, 34, 35 and 36**

Sealed Beam Headlamp Assembly

1. Disconnect the negative battery cable.
2. Remove the trim bezel.
3. Remove the retaining ring.
4. Disconnect the headlamp bulb electrical connector.
5. Remove the headlamp from the vehicle.
6. Installation is the reverse of removal.

Composite Headlamp Assembly

1. Disconnect the negative battery cable.
2. Remove the composite headlamp bulb from the headlamp lens assembly.

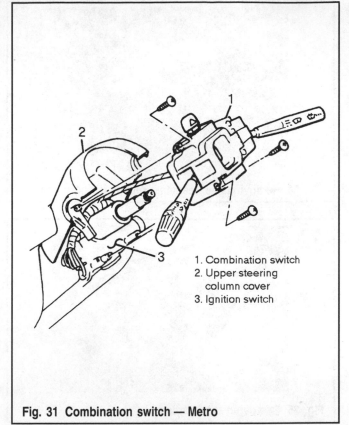

1. Combination switch
2. Upper steering column cover
3. Ignition switch

Fig. 31 Combination switch — Metro

Fig. 33 Removing the headlamp bezel screws

3. Remove the parking lamp housing.
4. Remove the plastic retaining clips and screw from the wheel housing. Pull the wheel housing back to gain access to the mounting nuts.
5. Remove the rubber retaining strap and air cleaner resonator, as required.

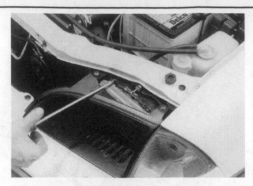

Fig. 34 Removing the headlamp retaining ring screws

Fig. 35 Removing the headlamp

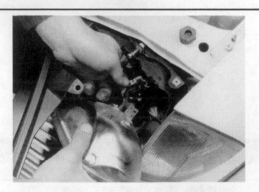

Fig. 36 Disconnecting the headlamp connector

6. Remove the retaining nuts and then remove the composite headlamp assembly.

To install:

7. Install the composite headlamp assembly and tighten retaining nuts to 89 inch lbs. (10 Nm).

8. Install the rubber retaining strap and air cleaner resonator, as required.

9. Install the plastic retaining clips and screw in the wheel housing.

10. Install the parking lamp housing.

11. the composite headlamp bulb from the headlamp lens assembly.

12. Connect the negative battery cable.

Composite Bulb

REPLACEMENT

❊❊CAUTION

Halogen bulbs contain a gas under pressure. Handling a bulb improperly could cause it to shatter into flying glass fragments. Turn the lighting system off and allow the bulb to cool prior to replacement. Handle the bulb only by its base, avoid touching the glass. Keep moisture away from the bulb. Always dispose of used bulbs properly.

1. Disconnect the negative battery cable.
2. Disconnect the composite bulb electrical connector.
3. Loosen the bulb locking cap by rotating counterclockwise.
4. Pull the bulb with lock cap from the housing.
5. Installation is the reverse of removal.

HEADLAMP AIMING

➡A professional headlamp aiming is recommended. This headlamp alignment procedure is given as an aid to adjusting grossly misadjusted lamps.

1. Place the vehicle on level ground facing a wall or garage door.
2. At dusk, shine the low beams onto the garage door or wall 2-3 feet away.
3. Place a horizontal mark on the top edges of the bright spot (center) on the door or wall.
4. Move the car about 25 feet straight back. The top of the low beam should shine no higher than the marks on the door or wall.
5. Make the necessary adjustments using the adjustment screws at the side and top or bottom of the headlamp. These screws are accessible without removing any hardware.

Parking Lamps

REMOVAL & INSTALLATION

▶ See Figures 37, 38, 39 and 40

Front Turn Signal and Parking Lights

1. Disconnect the negative battery cable.
2. Remove the screws from the parking lamp assembly.
3. Remove the parking lamp assembly.
4. Remove the socket from the lamp assembly.
5. Remove the bulb from the socket.
6. Installation is the reverse of removal.

Front Turn Signal Lamps

1. Disconnect the negative battery cable.
2. Remove the screws from the turn signal lamp assembly.
3. Remove the turn signal lamp assembly.

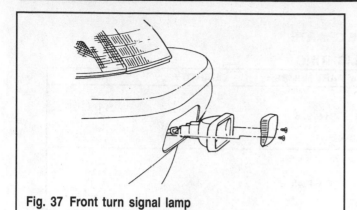

Fig. 37 Front turn signal lamp

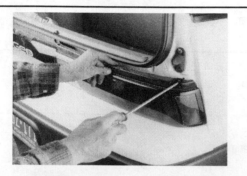

Fig. 38 Removing the rear combination lamp attaching screws

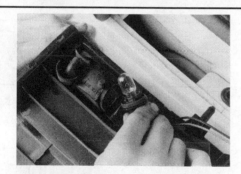

Fig. 40 Remove the bulb socket from the lamp assembly by turning counterclockwise

4. Remove the socket from the lamp assembly.
5. Remove the bulb from the socket.
6. Installation is the reverse of removal.

License Plate Lamps

1. Disconnect the negative battery cable.

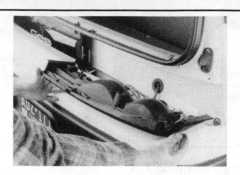

Fig. 39 Pull the combination lamp assembly away from the vehicle.

2. Remove the screws from the license plate lamp assembly.
3. Remove the license plate lamp assembly.
4. Remove the socket from the lamp assembly.
5. Remove the bulb from the socket.
6. Installation is the reverse of removal.

Rear Combination Lamp

The rear combination lamp assembly contains the backup lights, rear parking lights and brake lights.
1. Disconnect the negative battery cable.
2. Remove the rear garnish from vehicle.
3. Remove the rear combination lamp assembly attaching screws and pull the lamp assembly away from the end panel.
4. Remove the four bulb sockets from the lamp assembly.
5. Remove the lamp assembly, then remove the bulbs from the sockets.
6. Installation is the reverse of removal.

Dome Lamp

1. Disconnect the negative battery cable.
2. Gently pry dome lamp lens from lamp assembly.
3. Remove dome lamp bulb.
4. Installation is the reverse of removal.

Instrument Panel Cluster Lamps

1. Disconnect the negative battery cable.
2. Remove the instrument cluster from the vehicle.
3. Remove the bulb sockets from the back of the cluster assembly.
4. Remove the bulbs from the sockets.
5. Installation is the reverse of removal.

BULB USAGE CHARTS

EXTERIOR LIGHTING

USE	TRADE NUMBER	GM PART NUMBER	QUANTITY	ART
BACKUP LAMPS	921	9441956	2	
CENTER HIGH-MOUNTED STOPLAMP (CONVERTIBLE)	46	96064245	2	
CENTER HIGH-MOUNTED STOPLAMP (HARDTOP)	921	9441956	1	
FRONT SIDE MARKER LAMPS	168	9425542	2	
FRONT TURN SIGNAL LAMPS	1156	96061988	2	
HEADLAMPS (COMPOSITE)	9004	96055351	2	
HEADLAMPS (SEALED-BEAM)	6052	96063670	2	
LICENSE PLATE ILLUMINATION LAMPS	168	9425542	2	
REAR SIDE MARKER LAMPS	194	9421330	2	
STOP/TAILLAMPS	1157	9428902	2	
REAR TURN SIGNAL LAMPS	1156	96061988	2	

INTERIOR LIGHTING

USE	TRADE NUMBER	GM PART NUMBER	QUANTITY	ART
DOME LAMP	—	96051559	1	

CIRCUIT PROTECTION

♦ See Figures 41, 42 and 43

Fuses

All electrical circuits are protected against excessive loads which might occur because of shorts or overloads in the wiring system. Such protection is provided by a fuses. The fuse box is located under the left side of the dash. Additional fuses are located in the fuse and relay box in the engine compartment

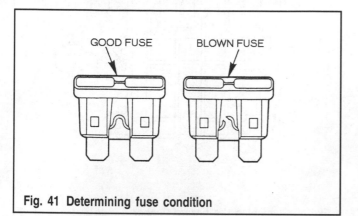

Fig. 41 Determining fuse condition

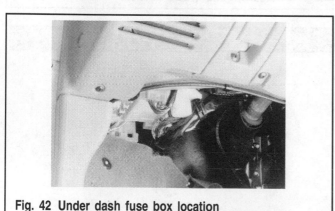

Fig. 42 Under dash fuse box location

Fig. 43 Engine compartment fuse/relay box location

REPLACEMENT

To replace a blown fuse, simply remove the fuse box cover and locate the blown fuse. Remove the fuse from the box by gently pulling and replace with a fuse of the same amperage rating.

➡**Prior to replacing the fuse, inspect the circuit covered by the fuse to find the problem that caused the fuse to blow.**

Fusible Links

In addition to fuses, some circuits use fusible links to protect the wiring. Like fused, fusible links are one time protection devices that will melt and create an open circuit.

➡**Not all fusible link open circuits can be detected by observation. Always inspect that there is battery voltage past the fusible link to verify continuity.**

Fusible links are used instead of a fuse in wiring circuits that are not normally fused, such as the ignition circuit. Each fusible link is four wire gage sizes smaller than the cable it is designed to protect. Links are marked on the insulation with wire gage size because the heavy insulation makes the link appear to be a heavier gage than it actually is. The same wire size fusible link must be used when replacing an open fusible link.

REPLACEMENT

♦ See Figure 44

To replace a damaged fusible link, disconnect the negative battery cable, cut the link off beyond the splice and replace with a repair link. When connecting the repair link, strip the wire and use staking type pliers to crimp the splice securely in two places.

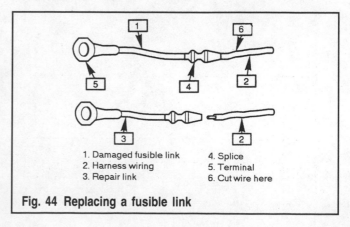

1. Damaged fusible link
2. Harness wiring
3. Repair link
4. Splice
5. Terminal
6. Cut wire here

Fig. 44 Replacing a fusible link

Flashers

REPLACEMENT

▶ **See Figure 45**

The hazard/turn signal relay (flasher) is located on top the the under dash fuse box. To replace the flasher, remove the fuse box retaining bolts and locate the flasher at the right rear corner. Pull gently to remove the flasher. Replace the one of like kind.

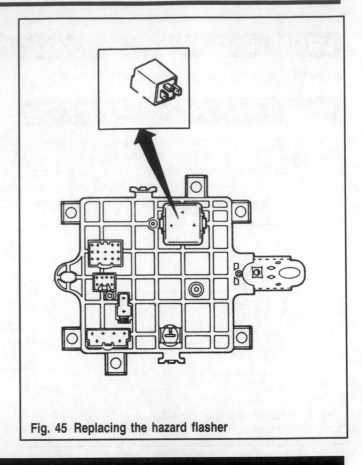

Fig. 45 Replacing the hazard flasher

WIRING DIAGRAMS

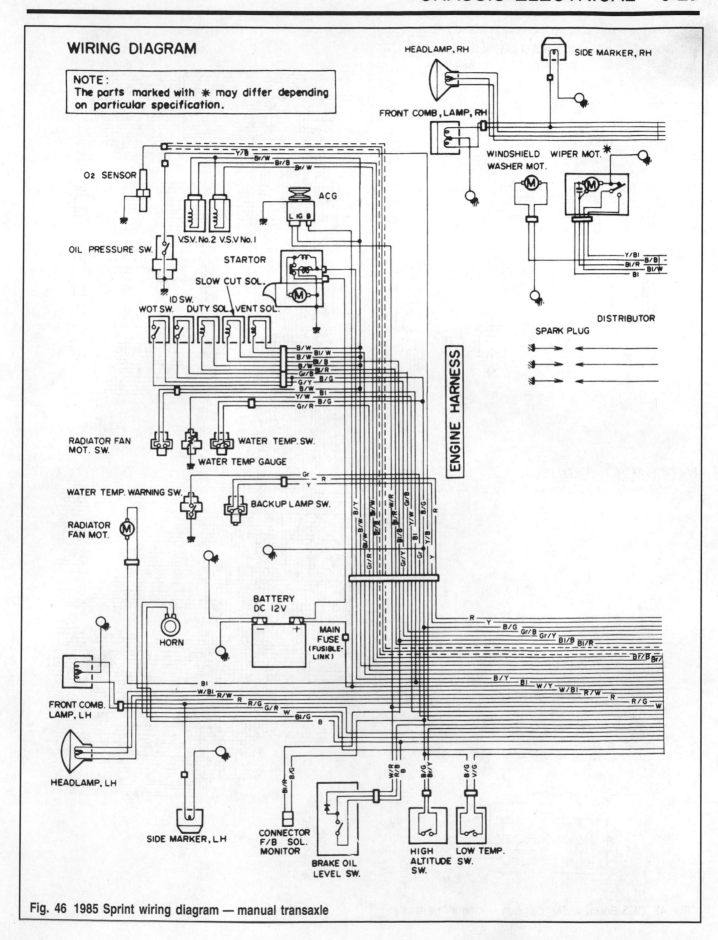

WIRING DIAGRAM

NOTE:
The parts marked with ✻ may differ depending on particular specification.

Fig. 46 1985 Sprint wiring diagram — manual transaxle

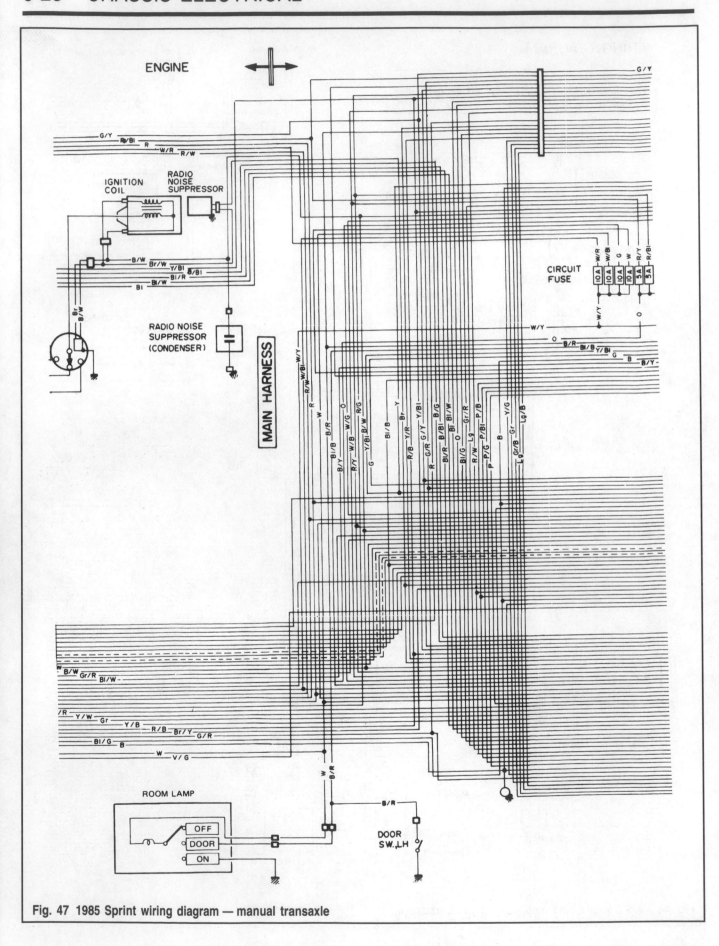

Fig. 47 1985 Sprint wiring diagram — manual transaxle

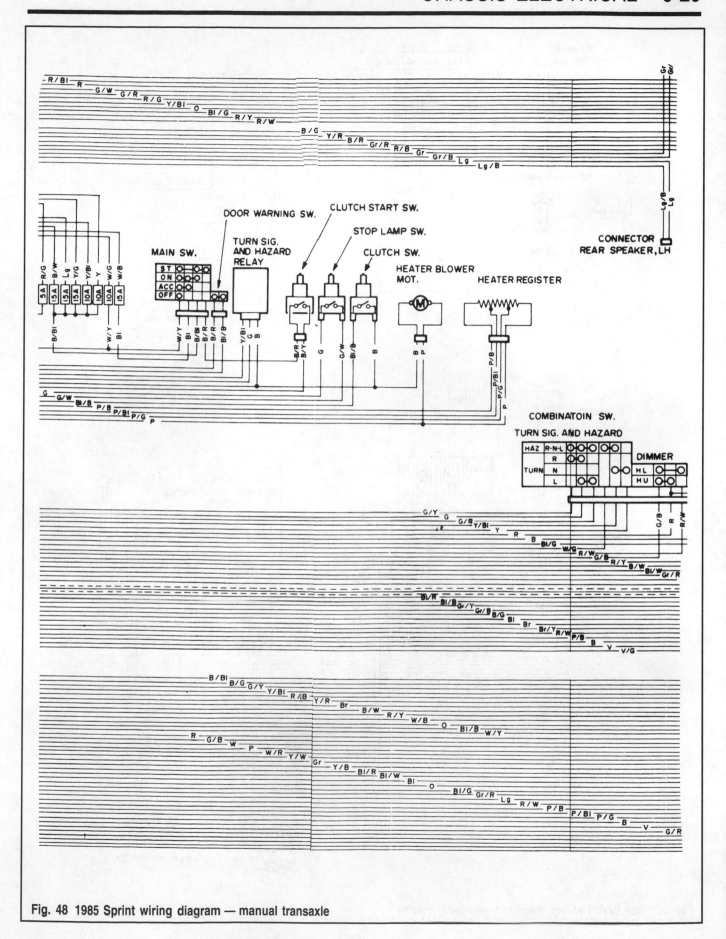

Fig. 48 1985 Sprint wiring diagram — manual transaxle

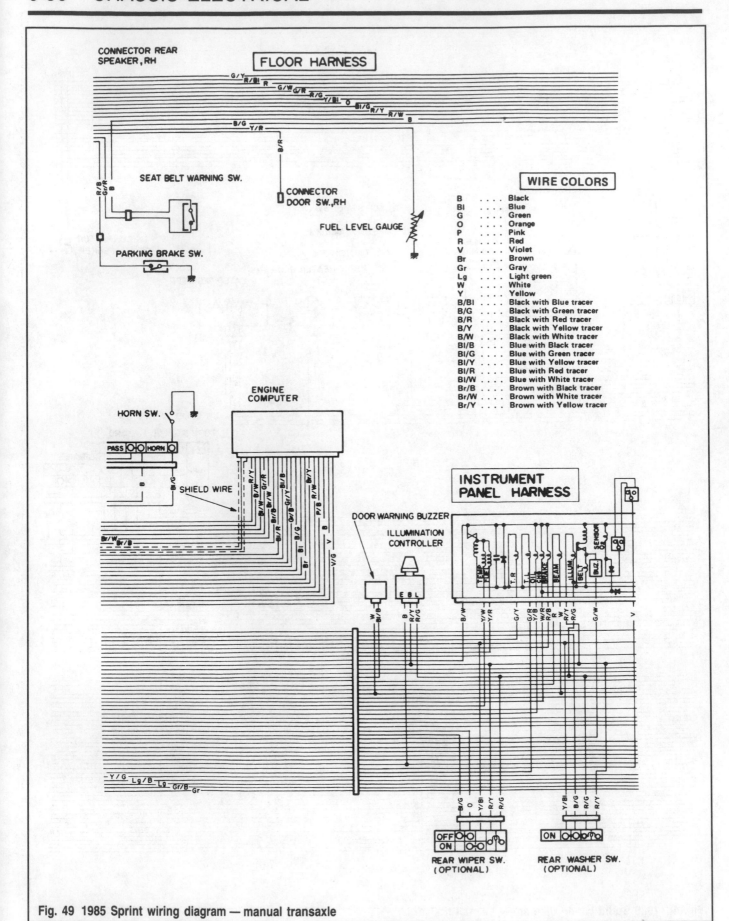

Fig. 49 1985 Sprint wiring diagram — manual transaxle

REAR WASHER MOT.
(OPTIONAL)

G/B	. . . .	Green with Black tracer
G/R	. . . .	Green with Red tracer
G/W	. . . .	Green with White tracer
G/Y	. . . .	Green with Yellow tracer
Gr/B	. . . .	Gray with Black tracer
Gr/Y	. . . .	Gray with Yellow tracer
P/B	. . . .	Pink with Black tracer
P/Bl	. . . .	Pink with Blue tracer
P/G	. . . .	Pink with Green tracer
R/B	. . . .	Red with Black tracer
R/Bl	. . . .	Red with Blue tracer
R/G	. . . .	Red with Green tracer
R/Y	. . . .	Red with Yellow tracer
R/W	. . . .	Red with White tracer
V/G	. . . .	Violet with Green tracer
W/B	. . . .	White with Black tracer
W/Bl	. . . .	White with Blue tracer
W/G	. . . .	White with Green tracer
W/R	. . . .	White with Red tracer
W/Y	. . . .	White with Yellow tracer
Y/B	. . . .	Yellow with Black tracer
Y/Bl	. . . .	Yellow with Blue tracer
Y/G	. . . .	Yellow with Green tracer
Y/R	. . . .	Yellow with Red tracer
Y/W	. . . .	Yellow with White tracer

LAMP BULB DATA	
Item	C.P. or W.
Head Lamp	55/65 W
Park & Directional Signal	3/32 cp
Front Side Marker	2 cp
Tail & Stop	3/32 cp
Rear Side Marker	3 cp
License Illumination	4 cp
Back up	32 cp
Interior (Dome)	5 W

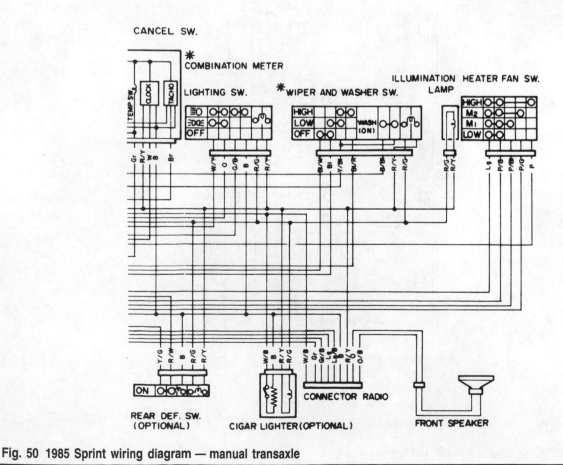

Fig. 50 1985 Sprint wiring diagram — manual transaxle

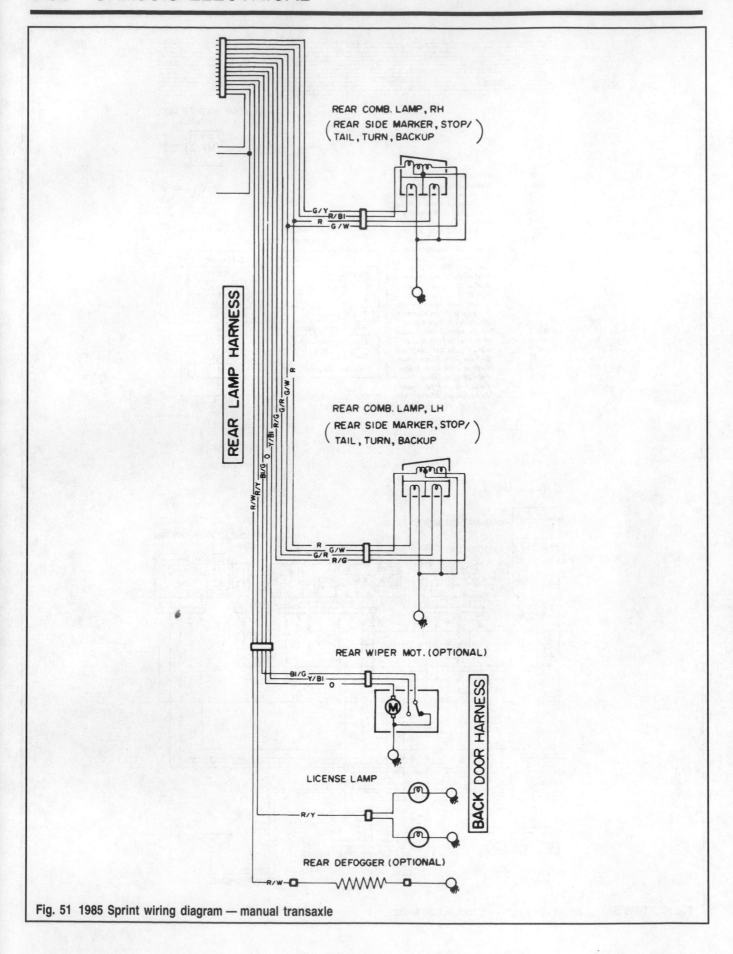

Fig. 51 1985 Sprint wiring diagram — manual transaxle

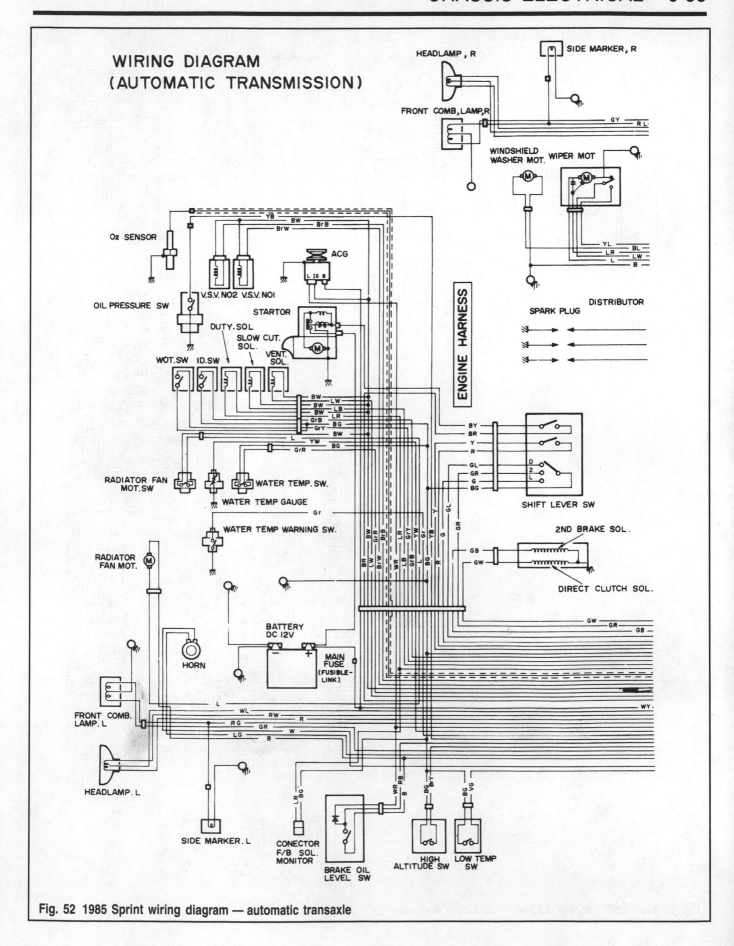

Fig. 52 1985 Sprint wiring diagram — automatic transaxle

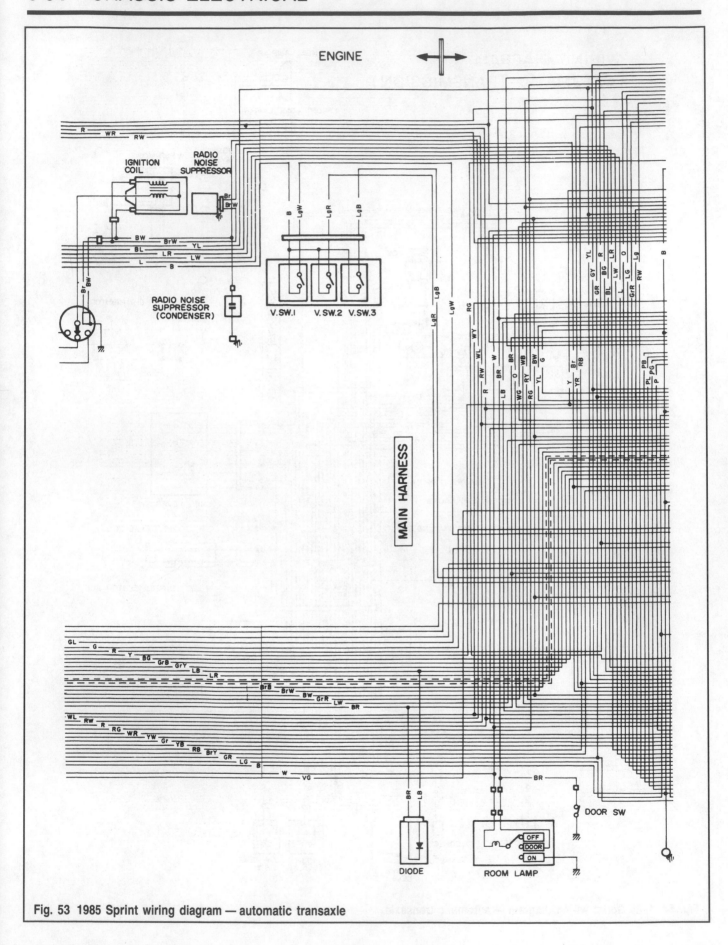

Fig. 53 1985 Sprint wiring diagram—automatic transaxle

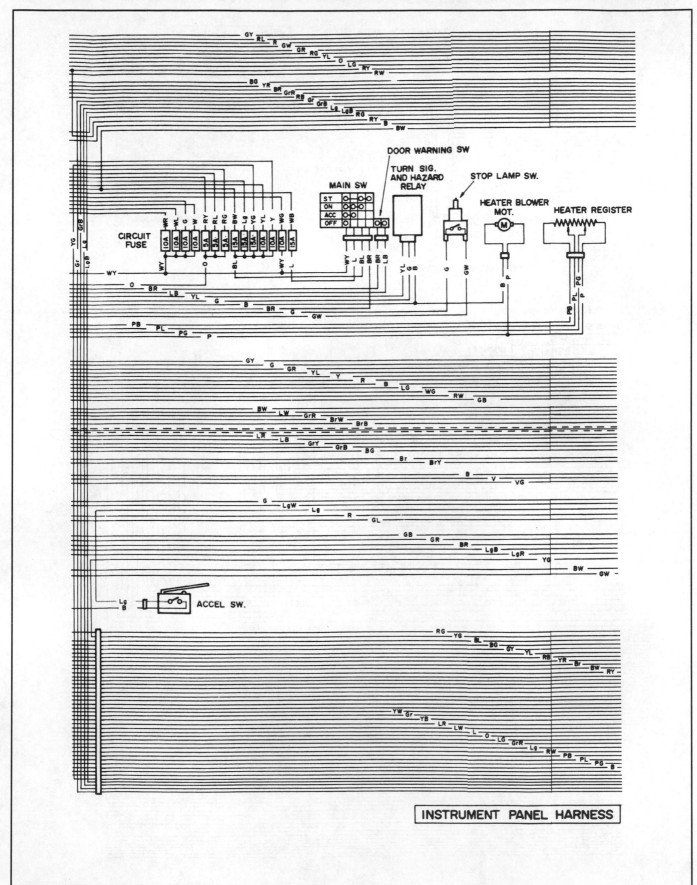

Fig. 54 1985 Sprint wiring diagram — automatic transaxle

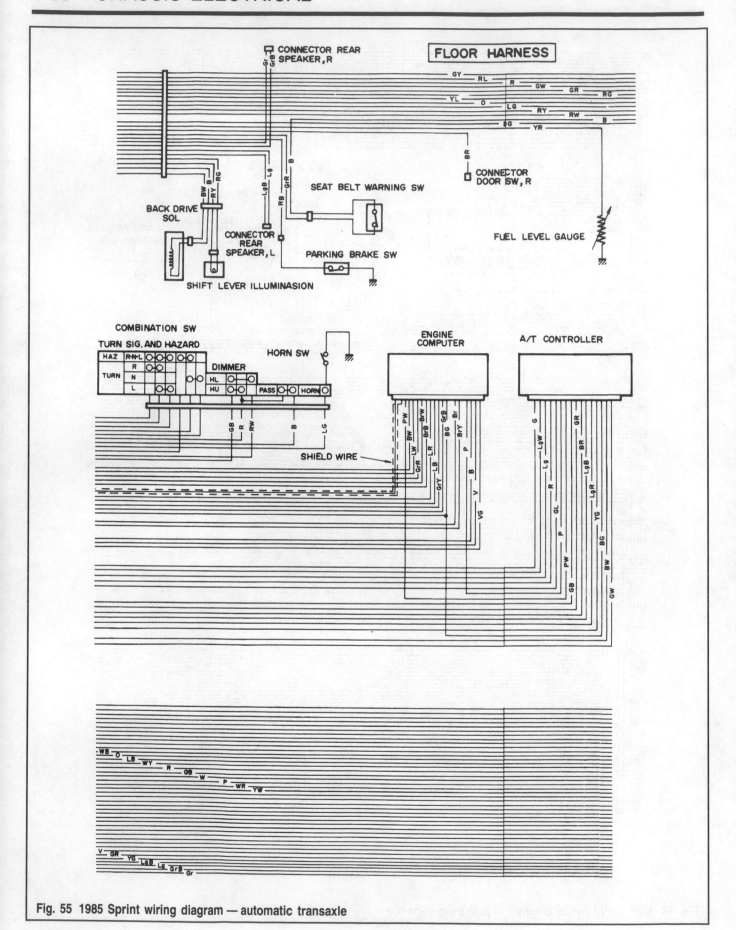

Fig. 55 1985 Sprint wiring diagram — automatic transaxle

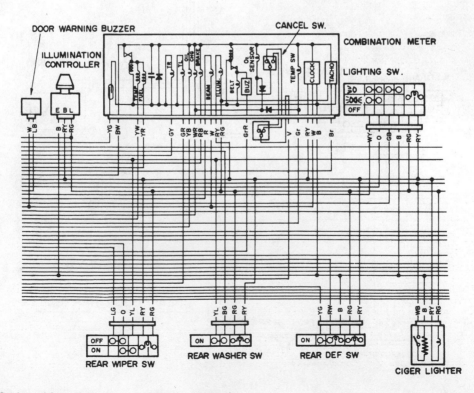

Fig. 56 1985 Sprint wiring diagram — automatic transaxle

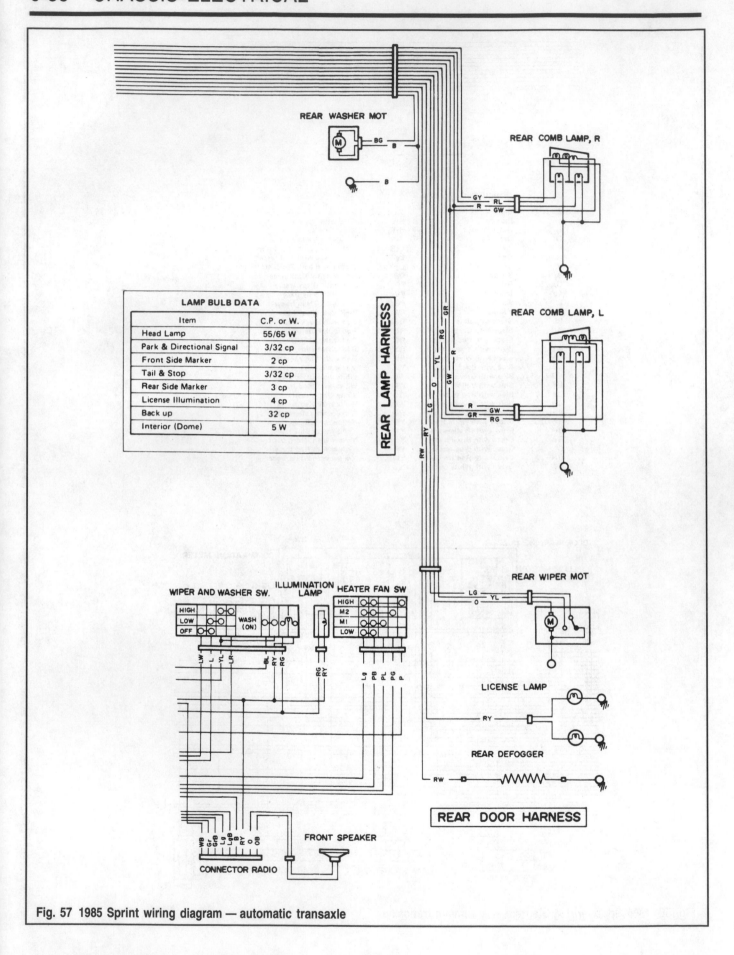

Fig. 57 1985 Sprint wiring diagram — automatic transaxle

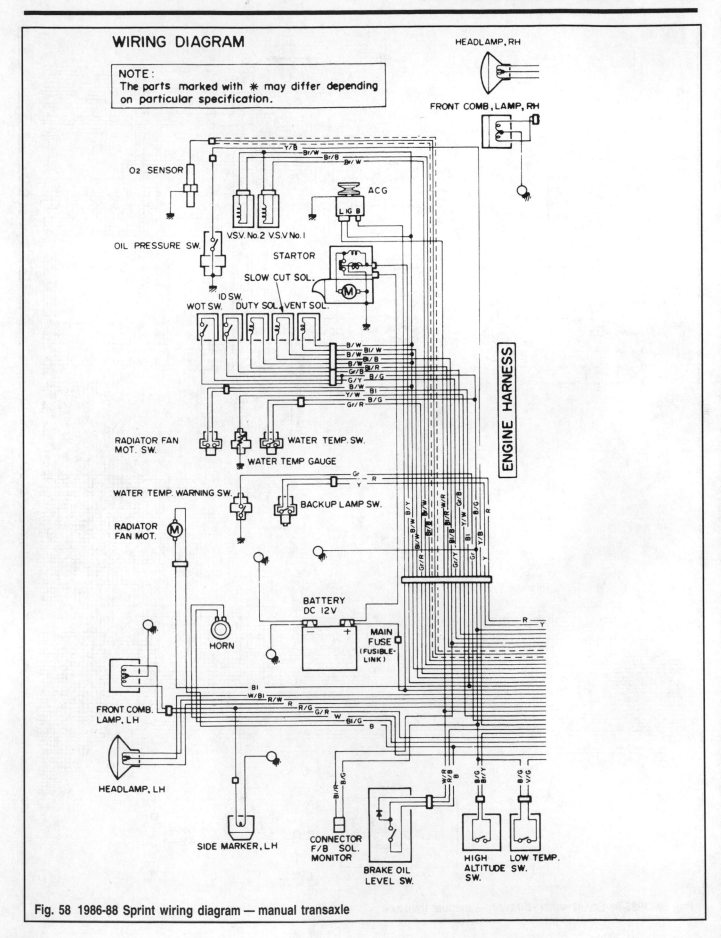

WIRING DIAGRAM

NOTE:
The parts marked with ✳ may differ depending on particular specification.

Fig. 58 1986-88 Sprint wiring diagram — manual transaxle

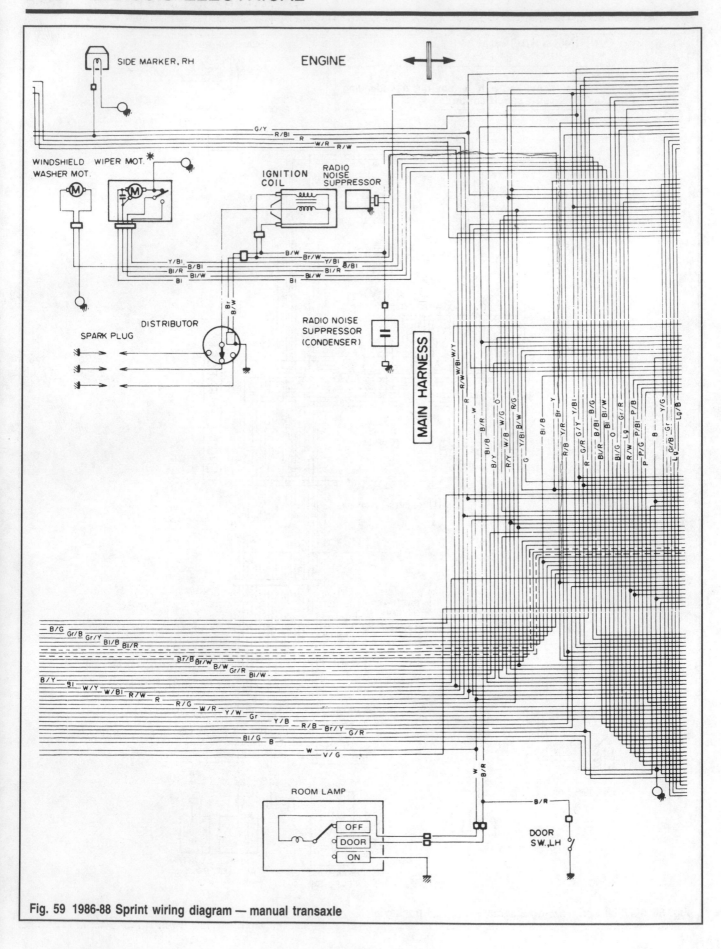

Fig. 59 1986-88 Sprint wiring diagram — manual transaxle

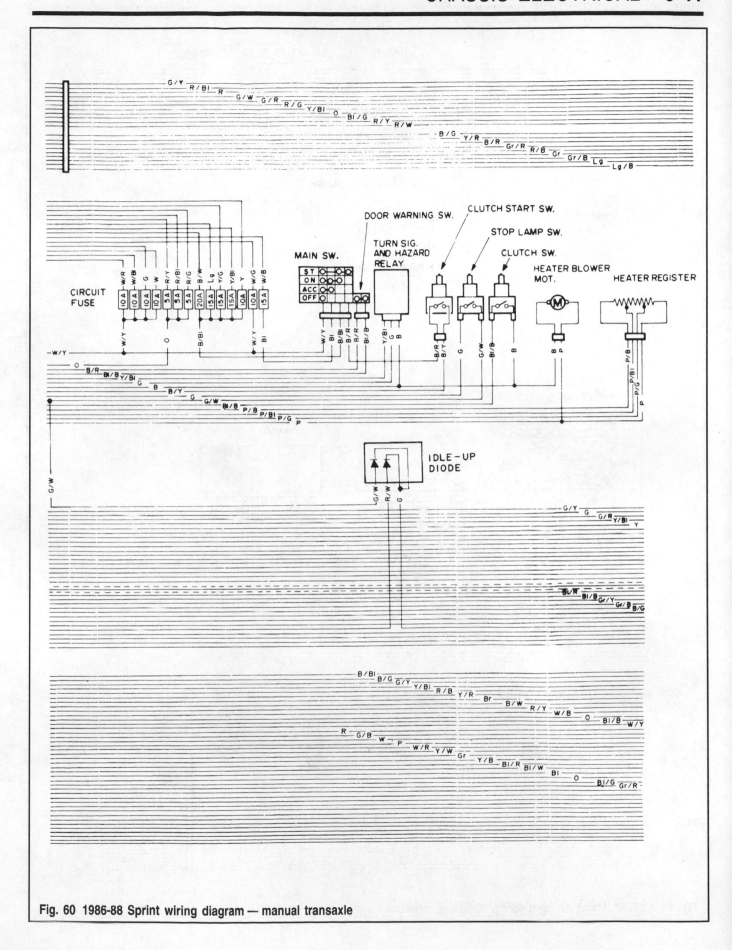

Fig. 60 1986-88 Sprint wiring diagram — manual transaxle

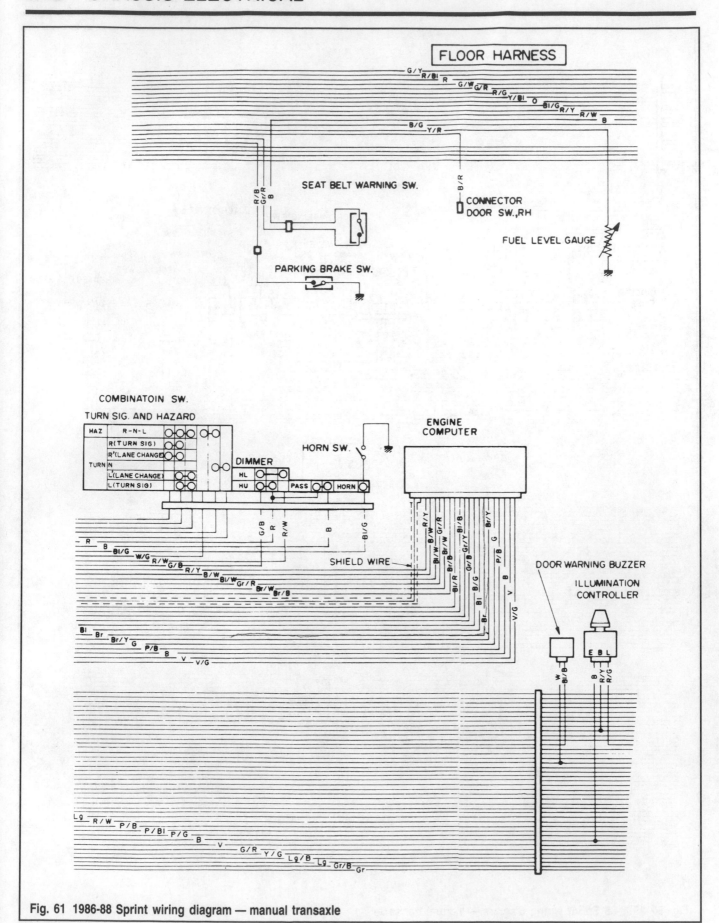

Fig. 61 1986-88 Sprint wiring diagram — manual transaxle

WIRE COLORS

B	Black	G/B	Green with Black tracer
Bl	Blue	G/R	Green with Red tracer
G	Green	G/W	Green with White tracer
O	Orange	G/Y	Green with Yellow tracer
P	Pink	Gr/B	Gray with Black tracer
R	Red	Gr/Y	Gray with Yellow tracer
V	Violet	P/B	Pink with Black tracer
Br	Brown	P/Bl	Pink with Blue tracer
Gr	Gray	P/G	Pink with Green tracer
Lg	Light green	R/B	Red with Black tracer
W	White	R/Bl	Red with Blue tracer
Y	Yellow	R/G	Red with Green tracer
B/Bl	Black with Blue tracer	R/Y	Red with Yellow tracer
B/G	Black with Green tracer	R/W	Red with White tracer
B/R	Black with Red tracer	V/G	Violet with Green tracer
B/Y	Black with Yellow tracer	W/B	White with Black tracer
B/W	Black with White tracer	W/Bl	White with Blue tracer
Bl/B	Blue with Black tracer	W/G	White with Green tracer
Bl/G	Blue with Green tracer	W/R	White with Red tracer
Bl/Y	Blue with Yellow tracer	W/Y	White with Yellow tracer
Bl/R	Blue with Red tracer	Y/B	Yellow with Black tracer
Bl/W	Blue with White tracer	Y/Bl	Yellow with Blue tracer
Br/B	Brown with Black tracer	Y/G	Yellow with Green tracer
Br/W	Brown with White tracer	Y/R	Yellow with Red tracer
Br/Y	Brown with Yellow tracer	Y/W	Yellow with White tracer

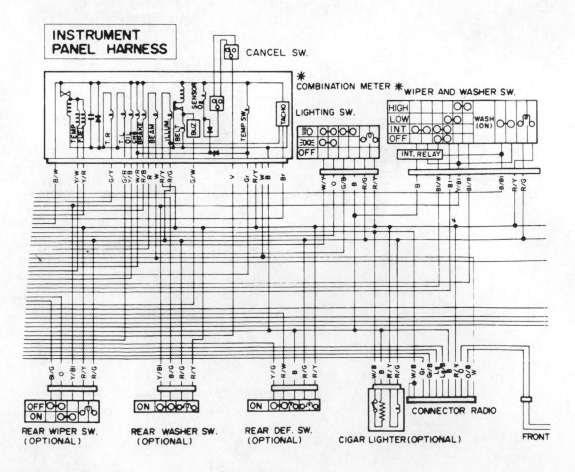

Fig. 62 1986-88 Sprint wiring diagram — manual transaxle

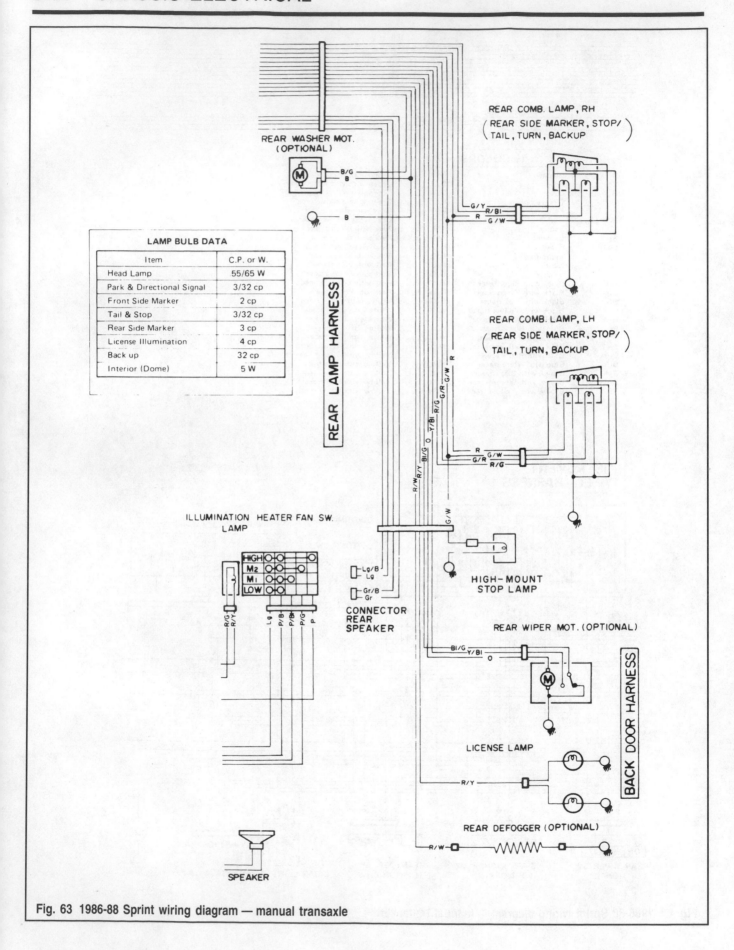

LAMP BULB DATA

Item	C.P. or W.
Head Lamp	55/65 W
Park & Directional Signal	3/32 cp
Front Side Marker	2 cp
Tail & Stop	3/32 cp
Rear Side Marker	3 cp
License Illumination	4 cp
Back up	32 cp
Interior (Dome)	5 W

Fig. 63 1986-88 Sprint wiring diagram — manual transaxle

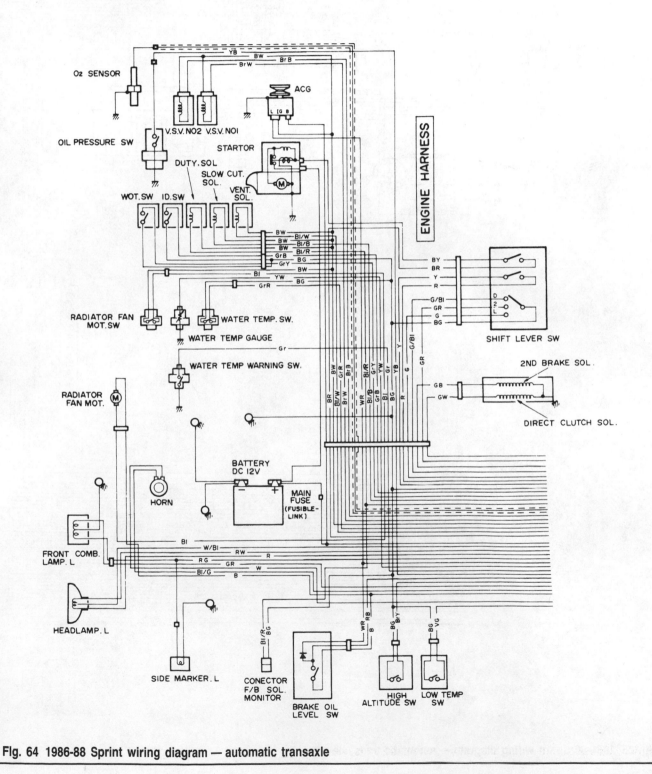

Fig. 64 1986-88 Sprint wiring diagram — automatic transaxle

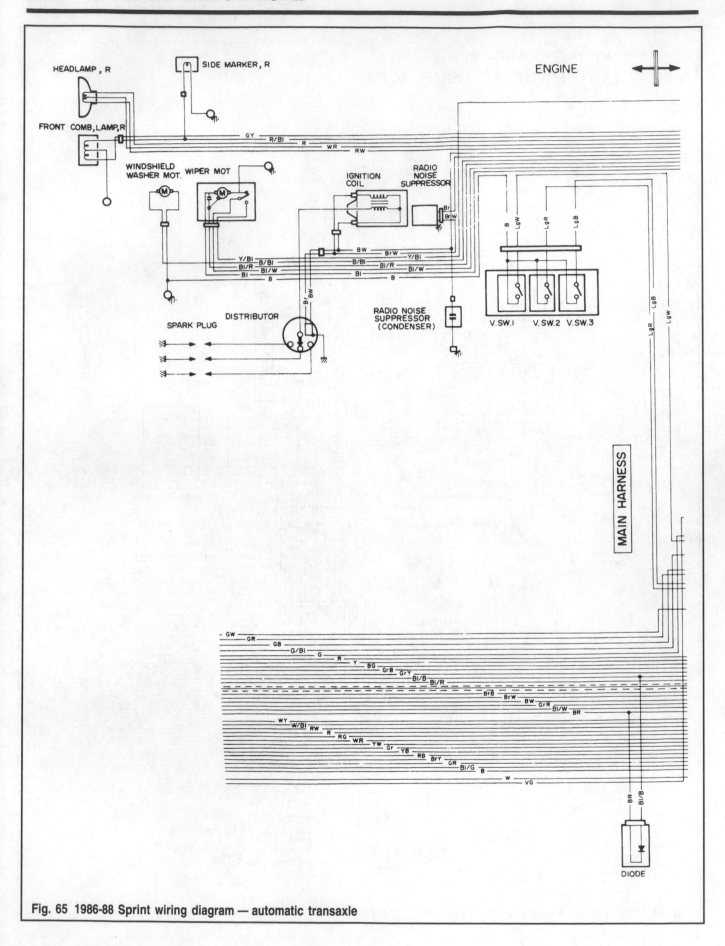

Fig. 65 1986-88 Sprint wiring diagram — automatic transaxle

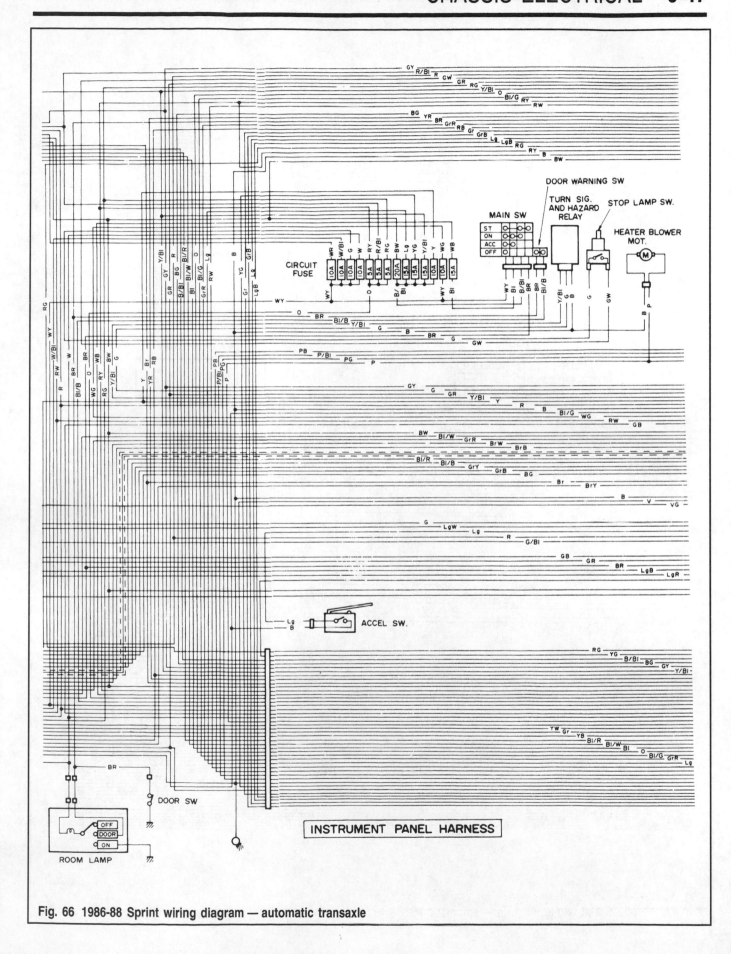

Fig. 66 1986-88 Sprint wiring diagram — automatic transaxle

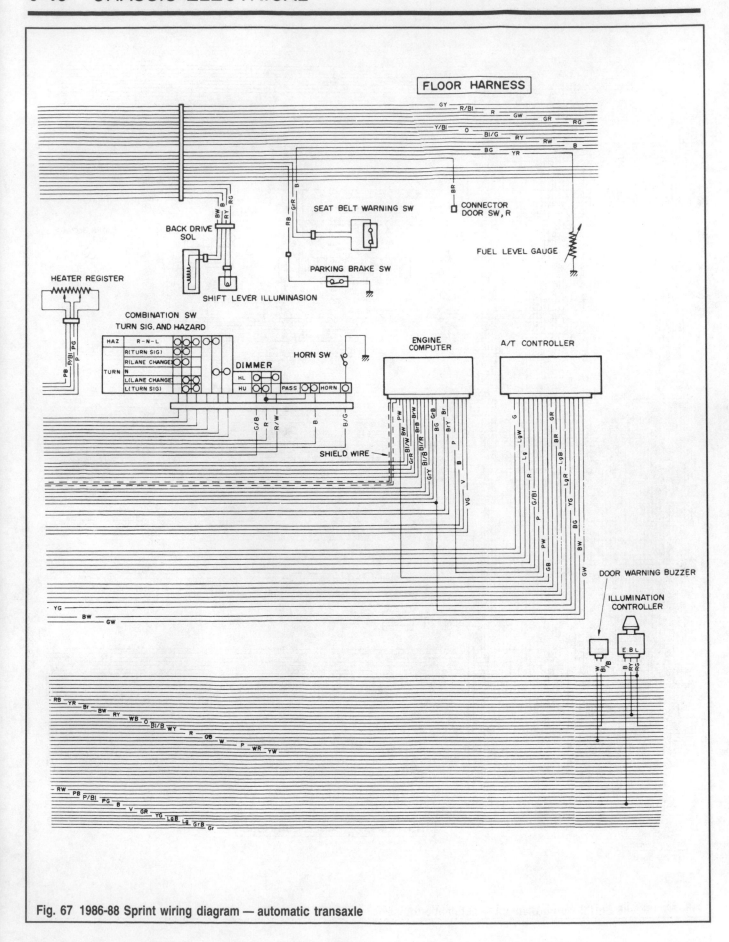

Fig. 67 1986-88 Sprint wiring diagram — automatic transaxle

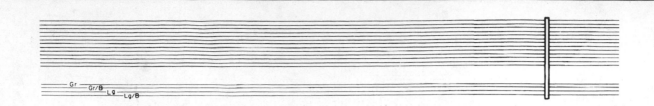

WIRE COLORS

B	Black	GY	Green with Yellow tracer
Bl	Blue	GrB	Gray with Black tracer
G	Green	GrR	Gray with Red tracer
O	Orange	GrY	Gray with Yellow tracer
P	Pink	LgB	Light green with Black tracer
R	Red	LgR	Light green with Red tracer
V	Violet	LgW	Light green with White tracer
Br	Brown	OB	Orange with Black tracer
Gr	Gray	PB	Pink with Black tracer
Lg	Light green	P/Bl	Pink with Blue tracer
W	White	PG	Pink with Green tracer
Y	Yellow	PW	Pink with White tracer
B/Bl	Black with Blue tracer	RB	Red with Black tracer
BG	Black with Green tracer	R/Bl	Red with Blue tracer
BR	Black with Red tracer	RG	Red with Green tracer
BY	Black with Yellow tracer	RY	Red with Yellow tracer
BW	Black with White tracer	RW	Red with White tracer
Bl/B	Blue with Black tracer	VG	Violet with Green tracer
Bl/G	Blue with Green tracer	WB	White with Black tracer
Bl/Y	Blue with Yellow tracer	W/Bl	White with Blue tracer
Bl/R	Blue with Red tracer	WG	White with Green tracer
Bl/W	Blue with White tracer	WR	White with Red tracer
BrB	Brown with Black tracer	WY	White with Yellow tracer
BrW	Brown with White tracer	YB	Yellow with Black tracer
BrY	Brown with Yellow tracer	Y/Bl	Yellow with Blue tracer
GB	Green with Black tracer	YG	Yellow with Green tracer
G/Bl	Green with Blue tracer	YR	Yellow with Red tracer
GR	Green with Red tracer	YW	Yellow with White tracer
GW	Green with White tracer		

LAMP BULB DATA

Item	C.P. or W.
Head Lamp	55/65 W
Park & Directional Signal	3/32 cp
Front Side Marker	2 cp
Tail & Stop	3/32 cp
Rear Side Marker	3 cp
License Illumination	4 cp
Back up	32 cp
Interior (Dome)	5 W

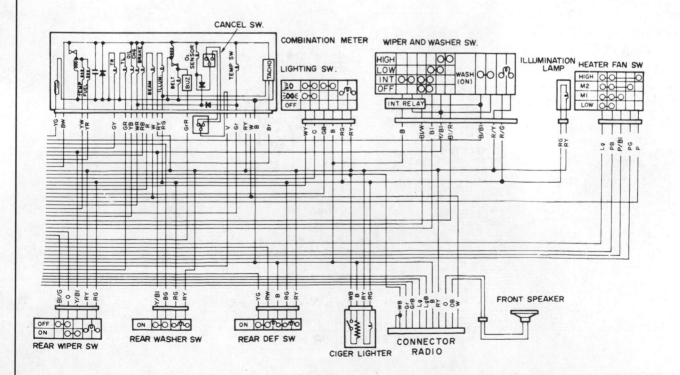

Fig. 68 1986-88 Sprint wiring diagram — automatic transaxle

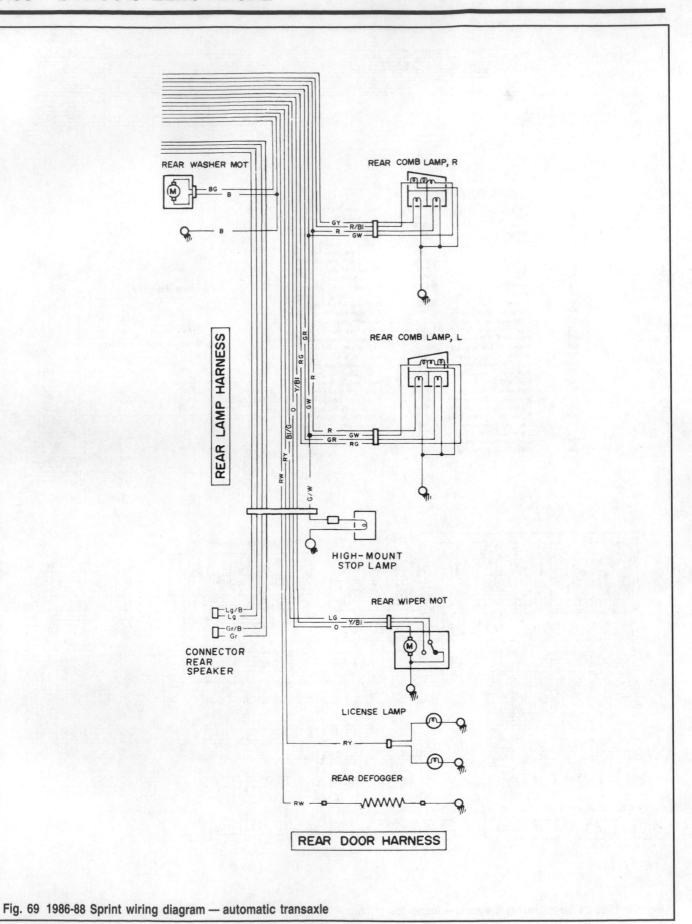

Fig. 69 1986-88 Sprint wiring diagram — automatic transaxle

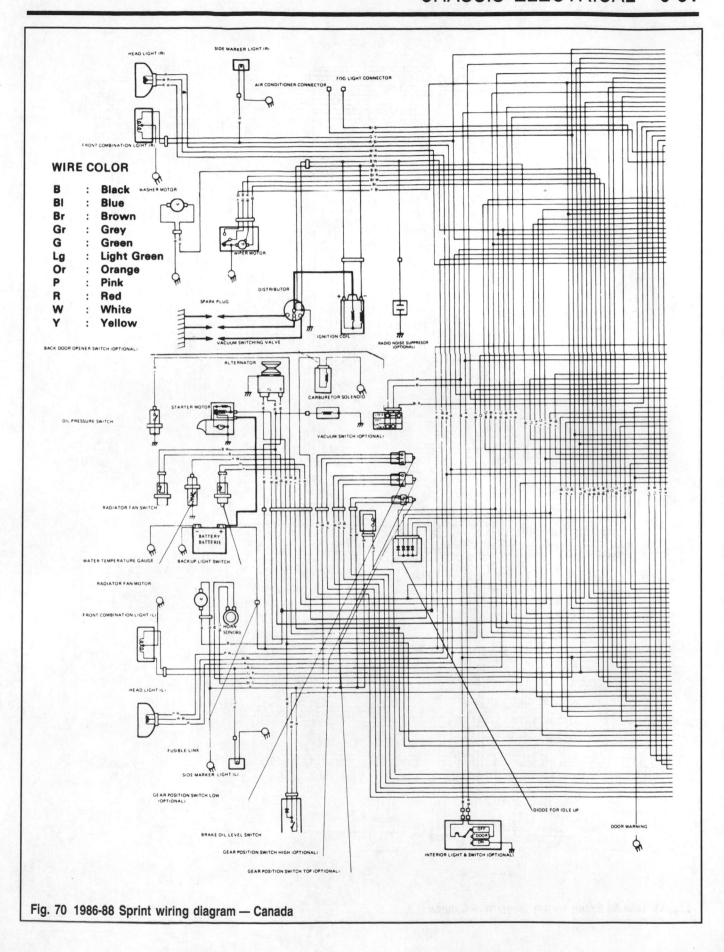

WIRE COLOR

B	:	Black
Bl	:	Blue
Br	:	Brown
Gr	:	Grey
G	:	Green
Lg	:	Light Green
Or	:	Orange
P	:	Pink
R	:	Red
W	:	White
Y	:	Yellow

Fig. 70 1986-88 Sprint wiring diagram — Canada

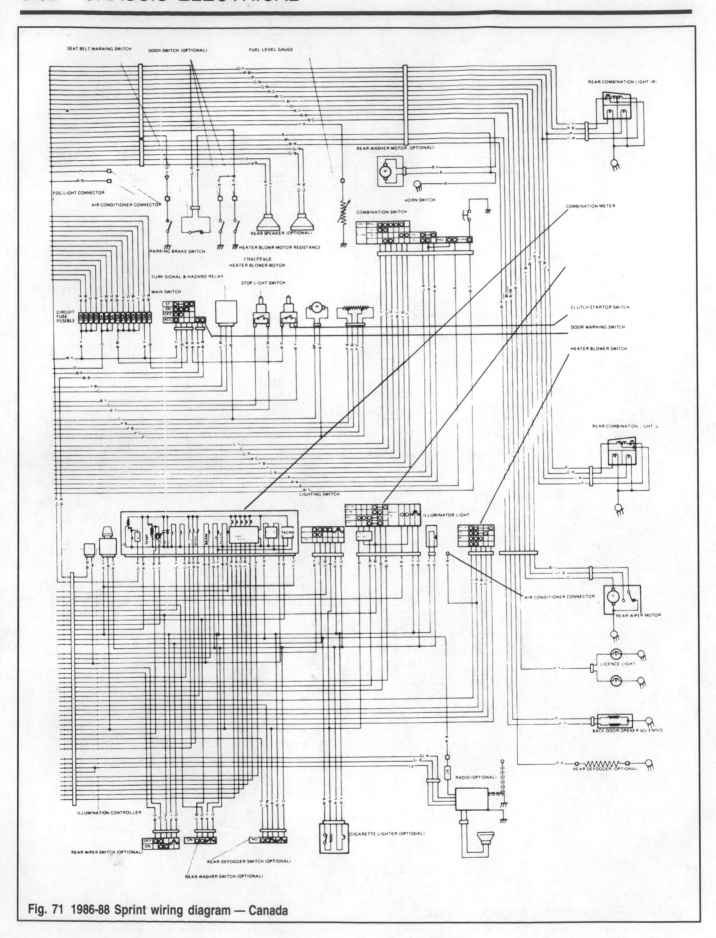

Fig. 71 1986-88 Sprint wiring diagram — Canada

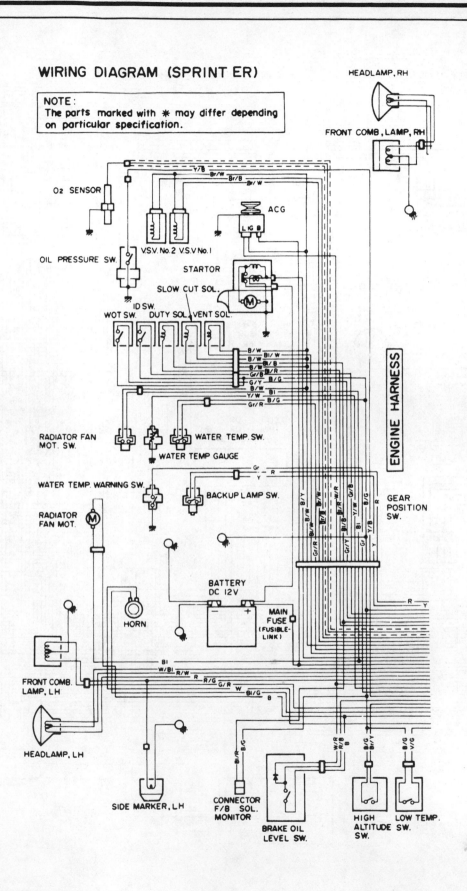

WIRING DIAGRAM (SPRINT ER)

NOTE :
The parts marked with ✳ may differ depending on particular specification.

HEADLAMP, RH

FRONT COMB. LAMP, RH

O₂ SENSOR

ACG

OIL PRESSURE SW.

V.S.V. No.2 V.S.V No.I

STARTOR

SLOW CUT SOL.

ID SW.

WOT SW.   DUTY SOL. VENT SOL.

ENGINE HARNESS

RADIATOR FAN MOT. SW.

WATER TEMP. SW.

WATER TEMP GAUGE

WATER TEMP. WARNING SW.

BACKUP LAMP SW.

GEAR POSITION SW.

RADIATOR FAN MOT.

BATTERY DC 12V

MAIN FUSE (FUSIBLE-LINK)

HORN

FRONT COMB. LAMP, LH

HEADLAMP, LH

SIDE MARKER, LH

CONNECTOR F/B SOL. MONITOR

BRAKE OIL LEVEL SW.

HIGH ALTITUDE SW.

LOW TEMP. SW.

Fig. 72 1986-88 Sprint wiring diagram

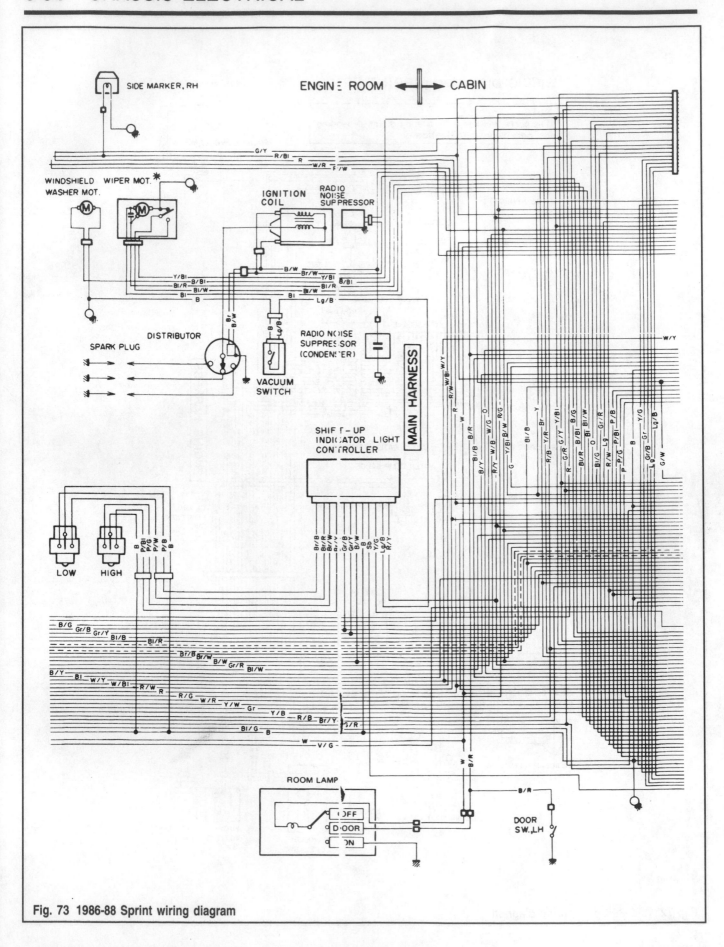

Fig. 73 1986-88 Sprint wiring diagram

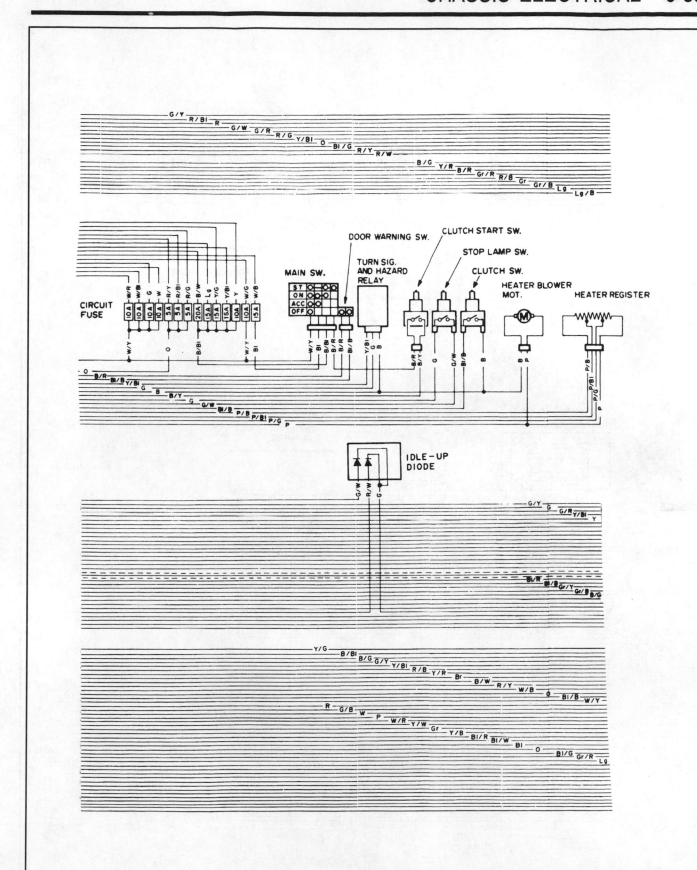

Fig. 74 1986-88 Sprint wiring diagram

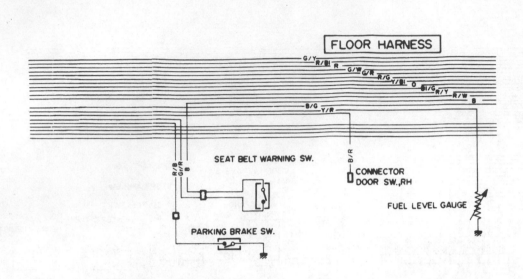

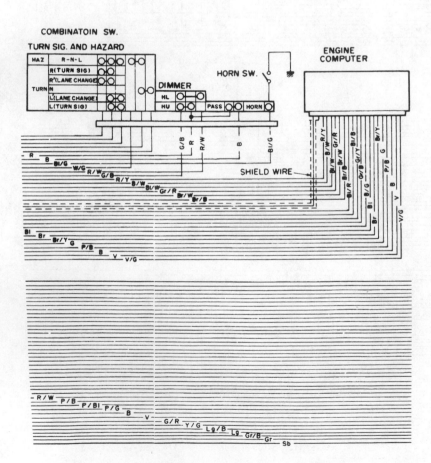

Fig. 75 1986-88 Sprint wiring diagram

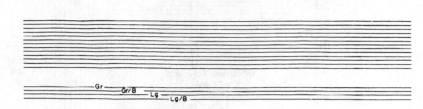

WIRE COLORS

B	.... Black	G/B	....	Green with Black tracer
Bl	.... Blue	G/R	....	Green with Red tracer
G	.... Green	G/W	....	Green with White tracer
O	.... Orange	G/Y	....	Green with Yellow tracer
P	.... Pink	Gr/B	....	Gray with Black tracer
R	.... Red	Gr/Y	....	Gray with Yellow tracer
V	.... Violet	Lg/B	....	Light green with Black tracer
Br	.... Brown	P/B	....	Pink with Black tracer
Gr	.... Gray	P/Bl	....	Pink with Blue tracer
Lg	.... Light green	P/G	....	Pink with Green tracer
Sb	.... Skyblue	P/W	....	Pink with White tracer
W	.... White	R/B	....	Red with Black tracer
Y	.... Yellow	R/Bl	....	Red with Blue tracer
B/Bl	.... Black with Blue tracer	R/G	....	Red with Green tracer
B/G	.... Black with Green tracer	R/Y	....	Red with Yellow tracer
B/R	.... Black with Red tracer	R/W	....	Red with White tracer
B/Y	.... Black with Yellow tracer	V/G	....	Violet with Green tracer
B/W	.... Black with White tracer	W/B	....	White with Black tracer
Bl/B	.... Blue with Black tracer	W/Bl	....	White with Blue tracer
Bl/G	.... Blue with Green tracer	W/G	....	White with Green tracer
Bl/Y	.... Blue with Yellow tracer	W/R	....	White with Red tracer
Bl/R	.... Blue with Red tracer	W/Y	....	White with Yellow tracer
Bl/W	.... Blue with White tracer	Y/B	....	Yellow with Black tracer
Br/B	.... Brown with Black tracer	Y/Bl	....	Yellow with Blue tracer
Br/R	.... Brown with Red tracer	Y/G	....	Yellow with Green tracer
Br/W	.... Brown with White tracer	Y/R	....	Yellow with Red tracer
Br/Y	.... Brown with Yellow tracer	Y/W	....	Yellow with White tracer

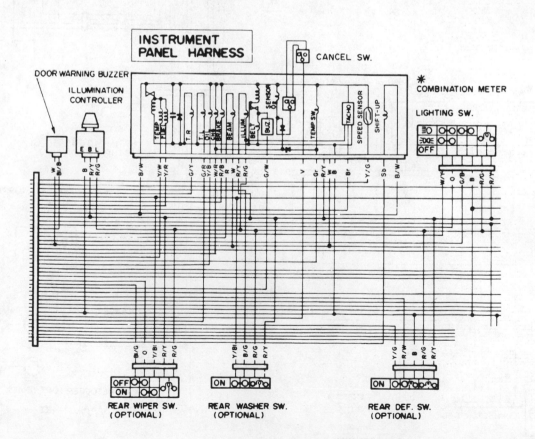

Fig. 76 1986-88 Sprint wiring diagram

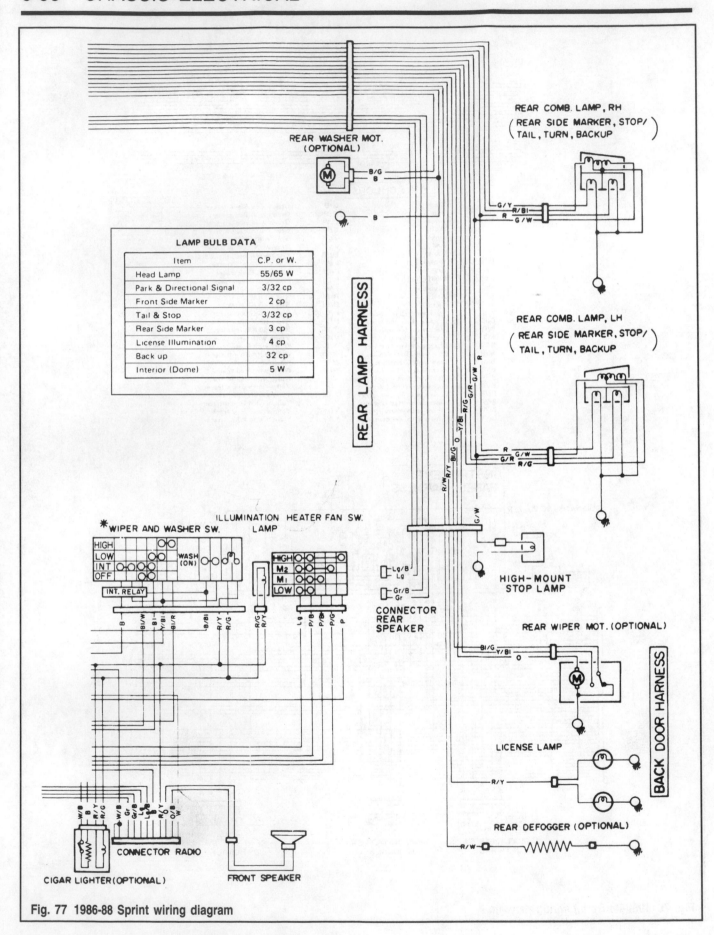

Fig. 77 1986-88 Sprint wiring diagram

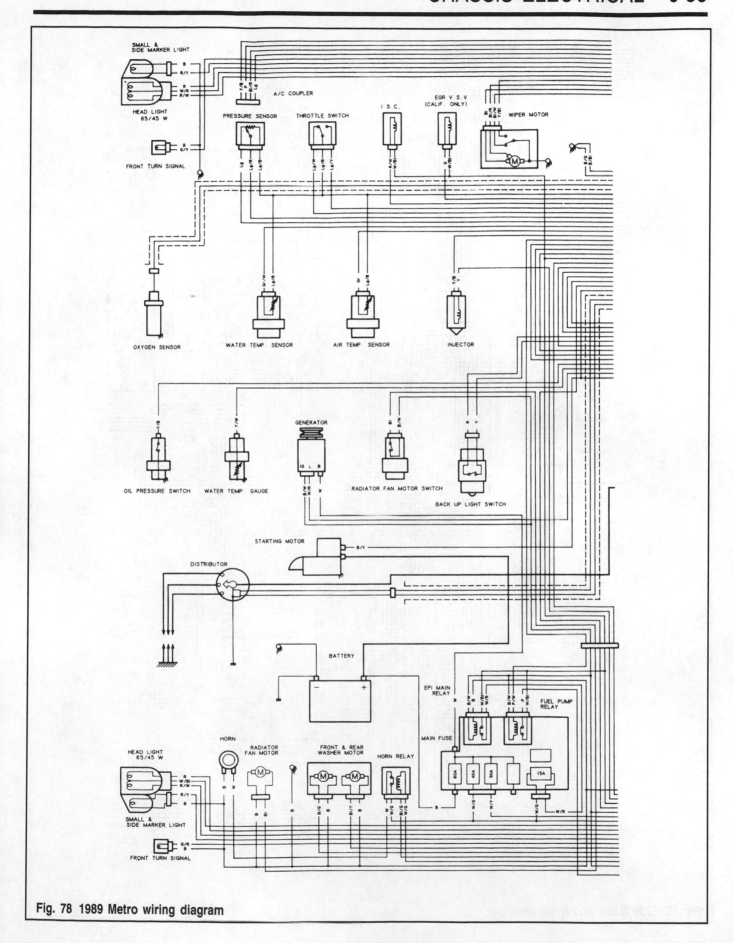

Fig. 78 1989 Metro wiring diagram

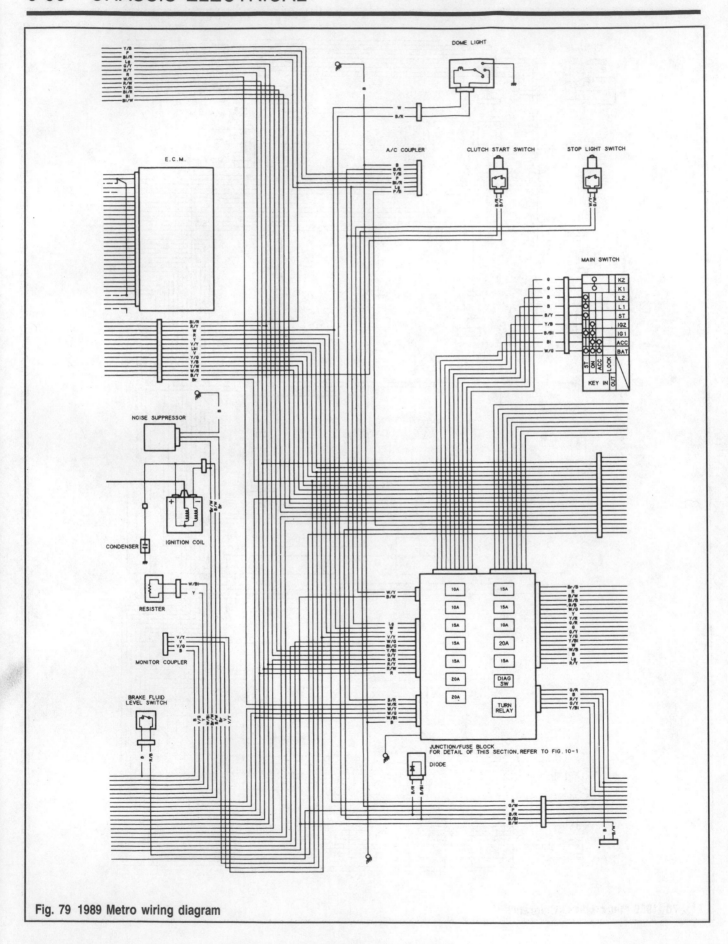

Fig. 79 1989 Metro wiring diagram

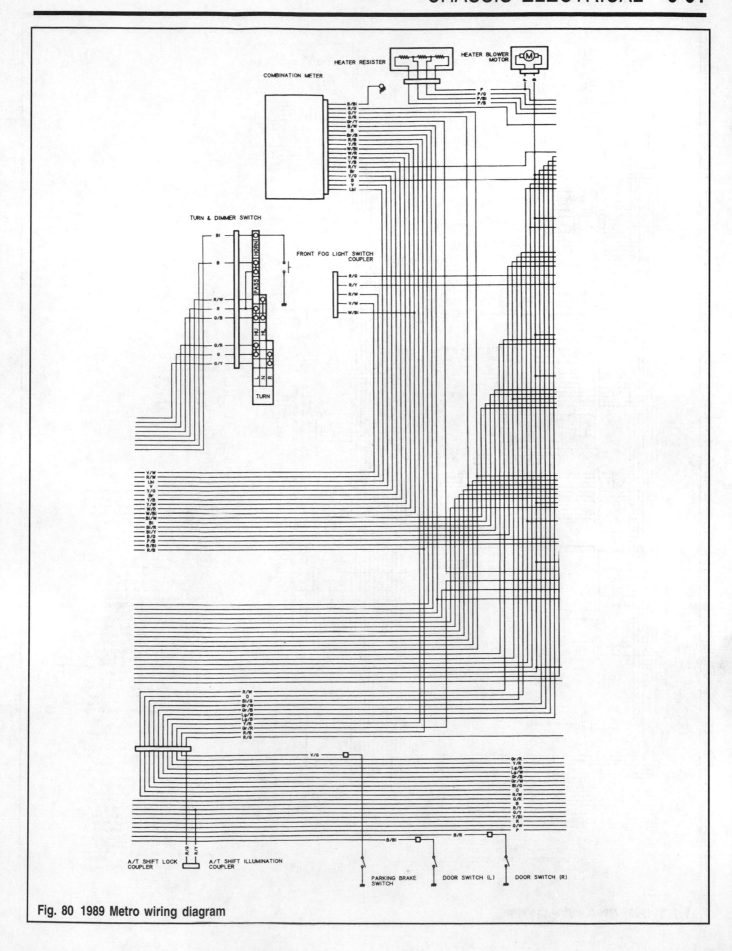

Fig. 80 1989 Metro wiring diagram

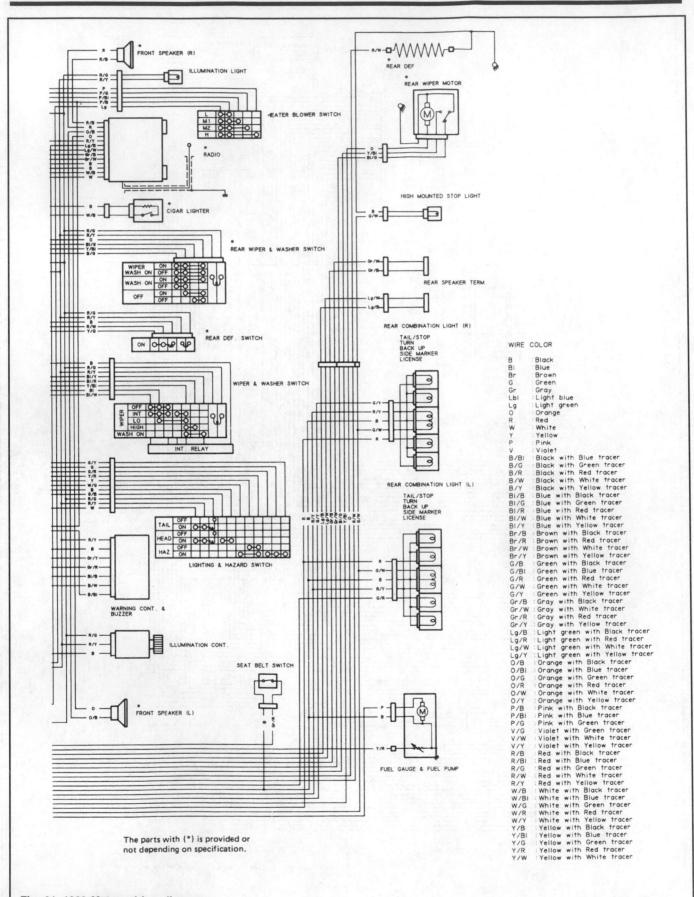

Fig. 81 1989 Metro wiring diagram

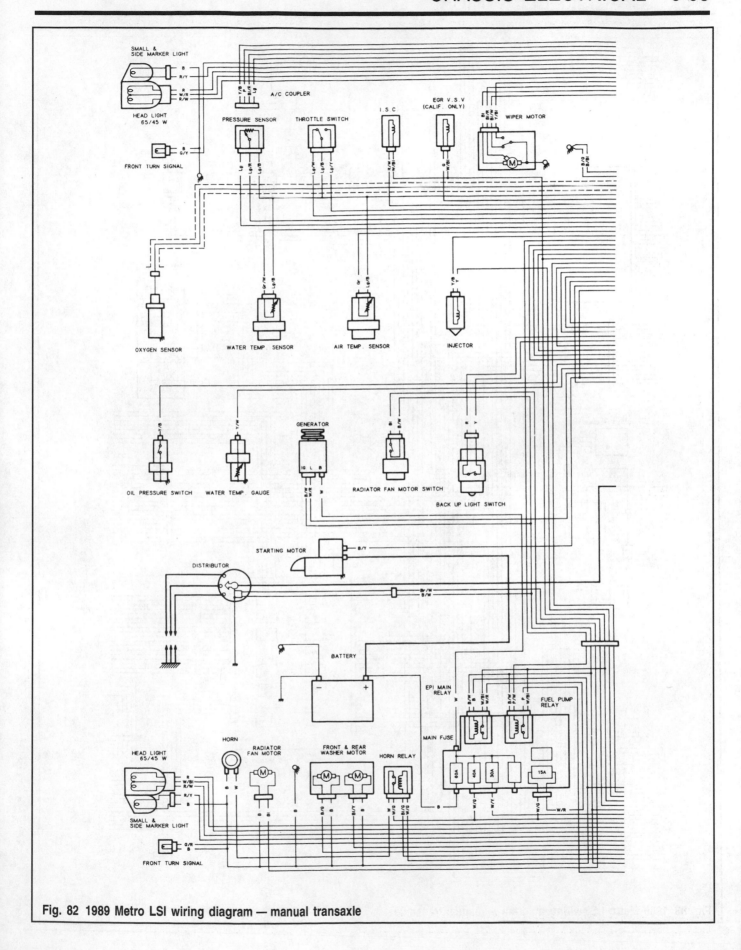

Fig. 82 1989 Metro LSI wiring diagram — manual transaxle

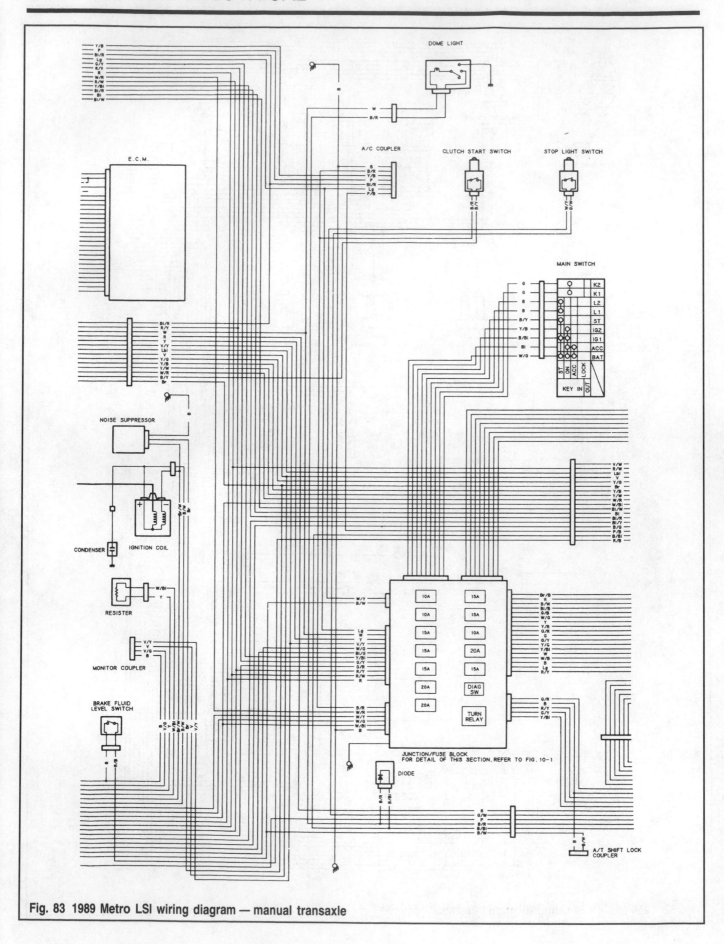

Fig. 83 1989 Metro LSI wiring diagram — manual transaxle

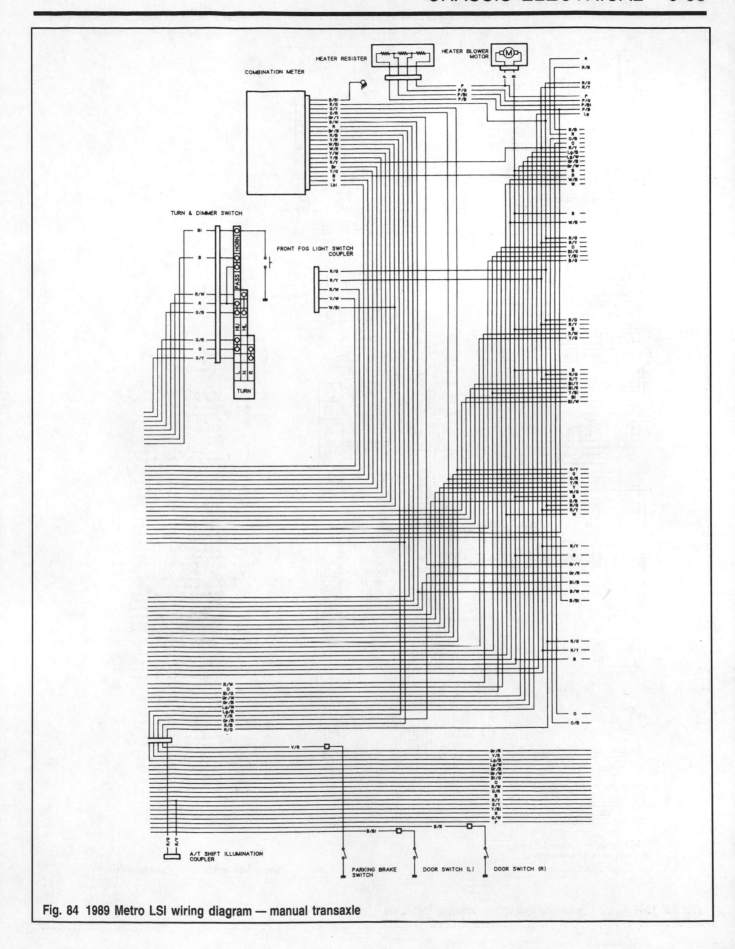

Fig. 84 1989 Metro LSI wiring diagram — manual transaxle

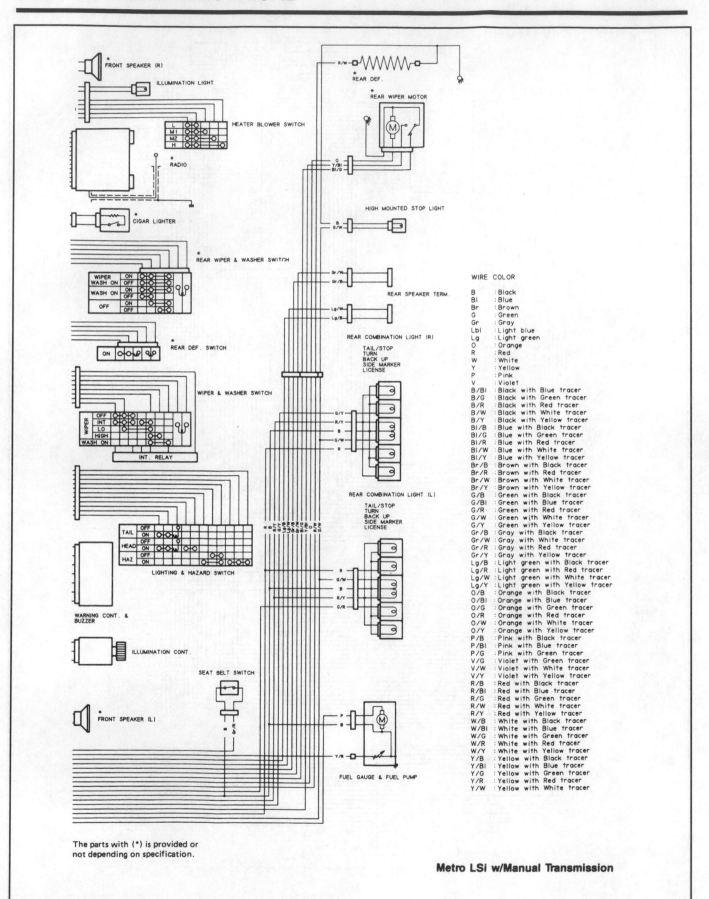

The parts with (*) is provided or
not depending on specification.

Metro LSi w/Manual Transmission

Fig. 85 1989 Metro LSI wiring diagram — manual transaxle

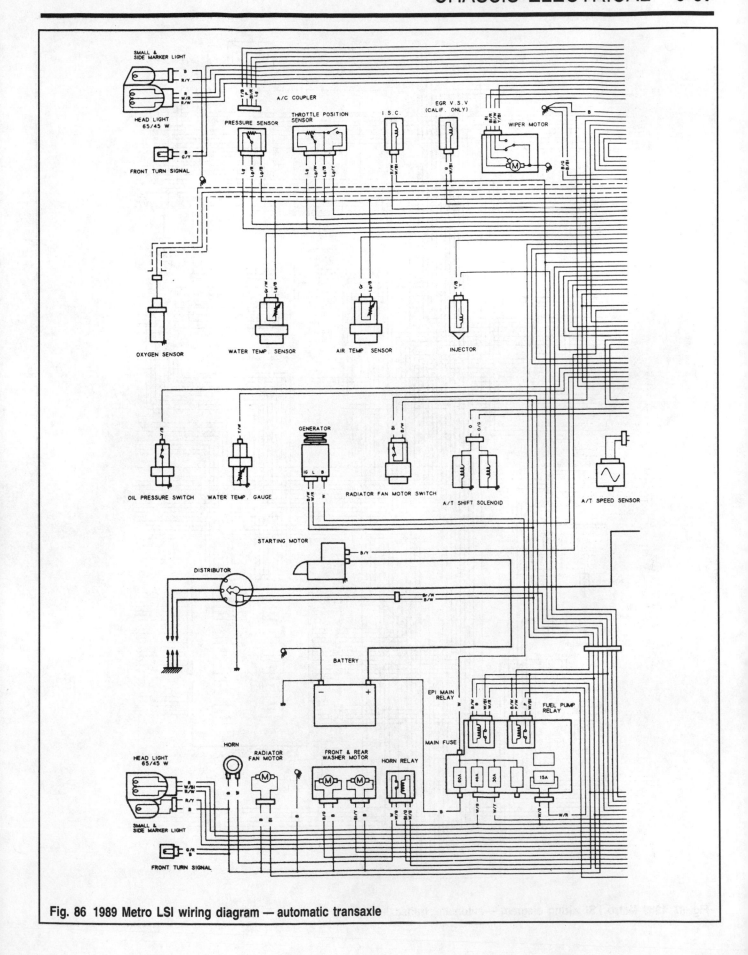

Fig. 86 1989 Metro LSI wiring diagram — automatic transaxle

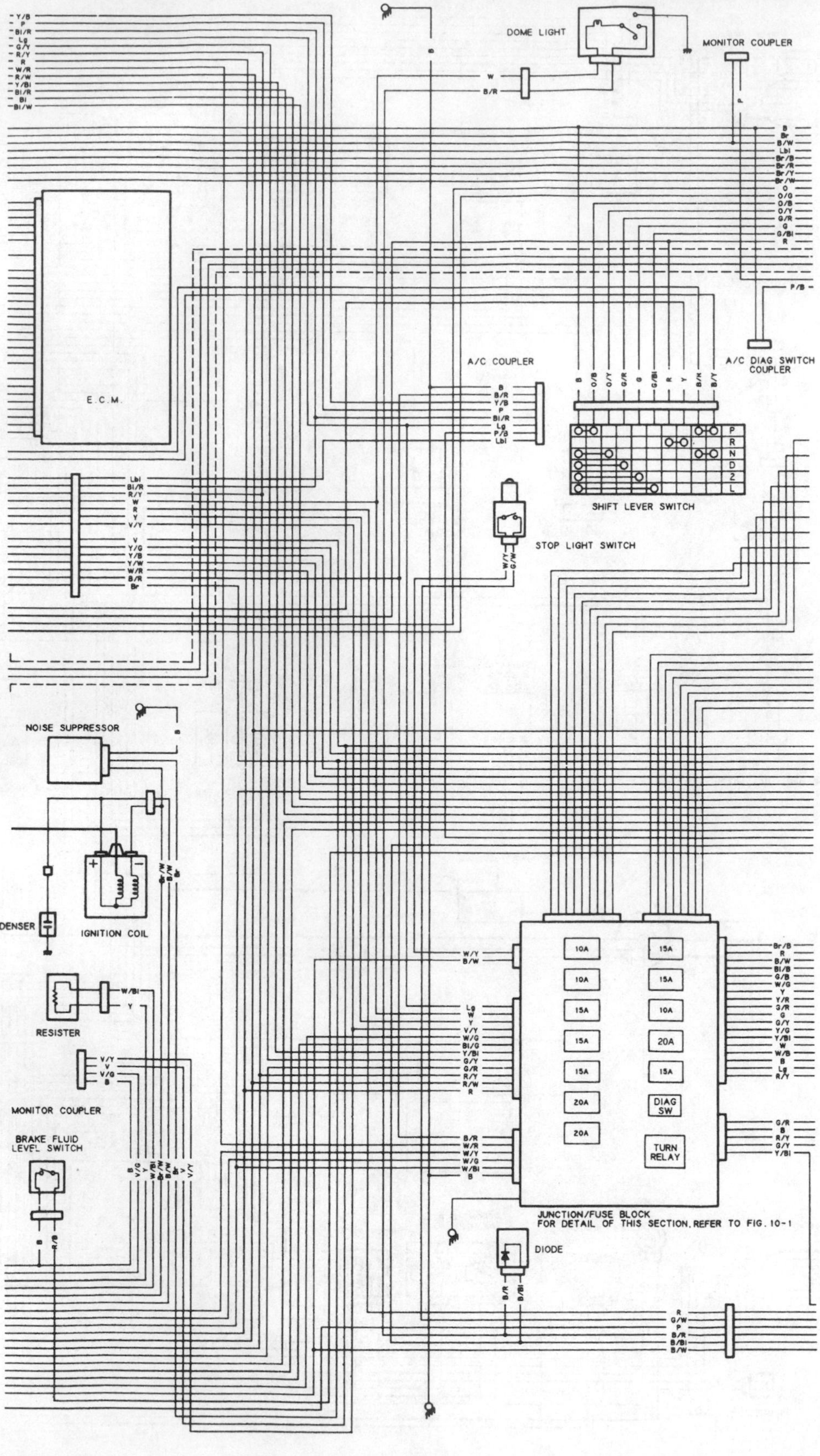

Fig. 87 1989 Metro LSI wiring diagram — automatic transaxle

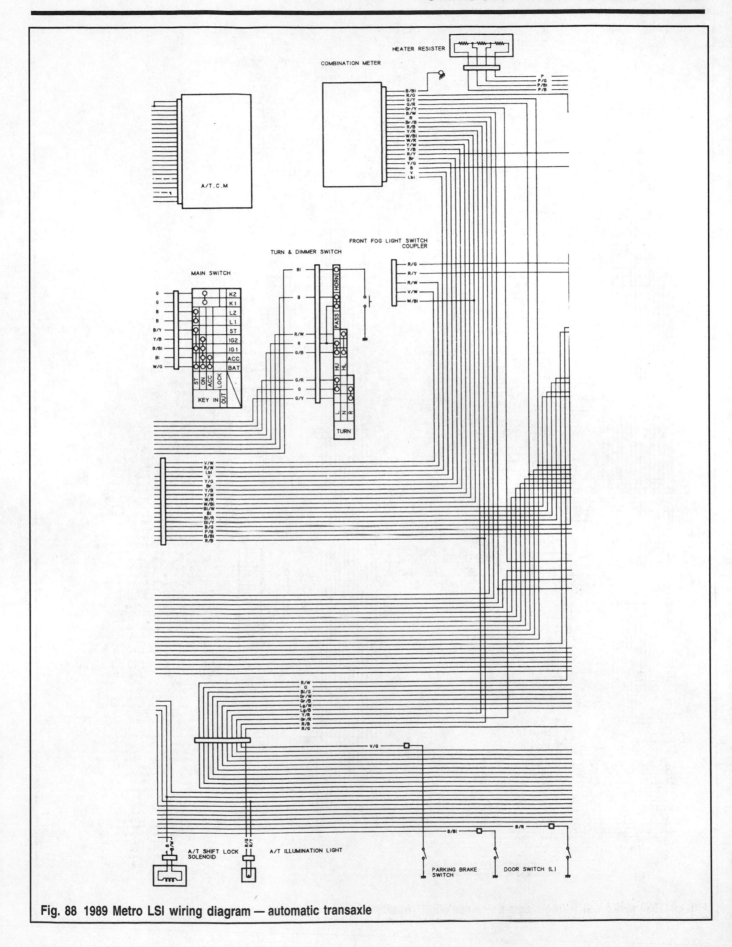

Fig. 88 1989 Metro LSI wiring diagram — automatic transaxle

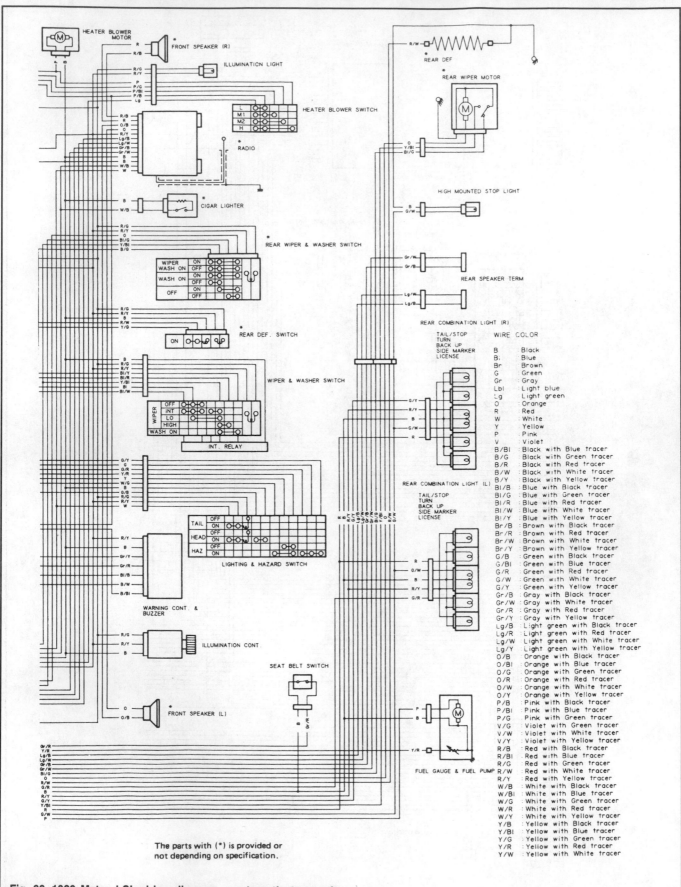

Fig. 89 1989 Metro LSI wiring diagram — automatic transaxle

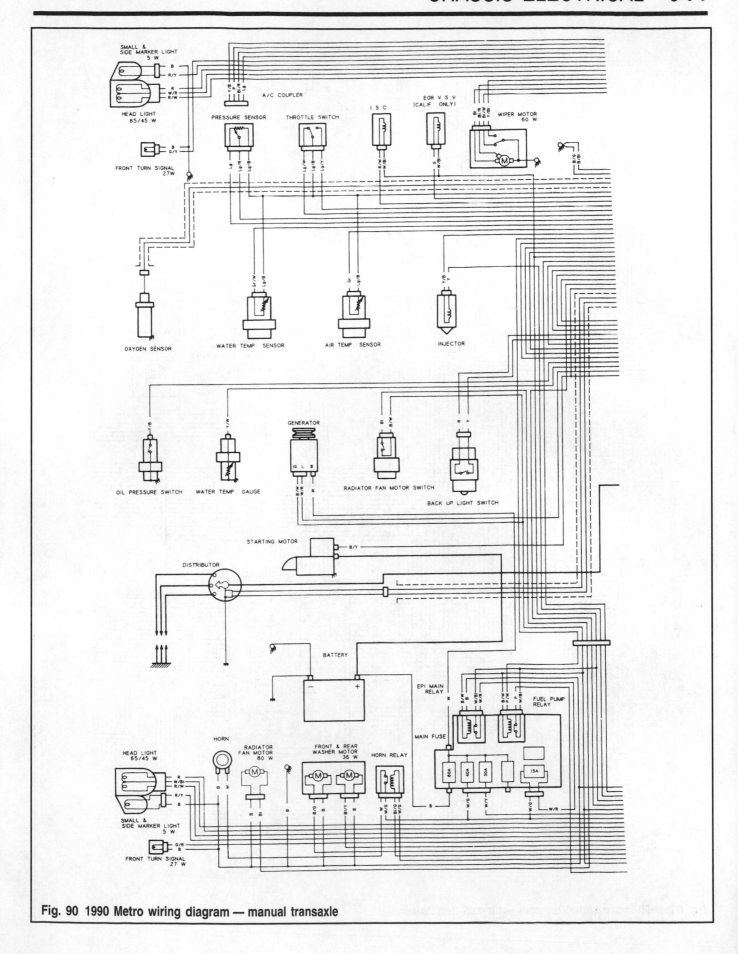

Fig. 90 1990 Metro wiring diagram — manual transaxle

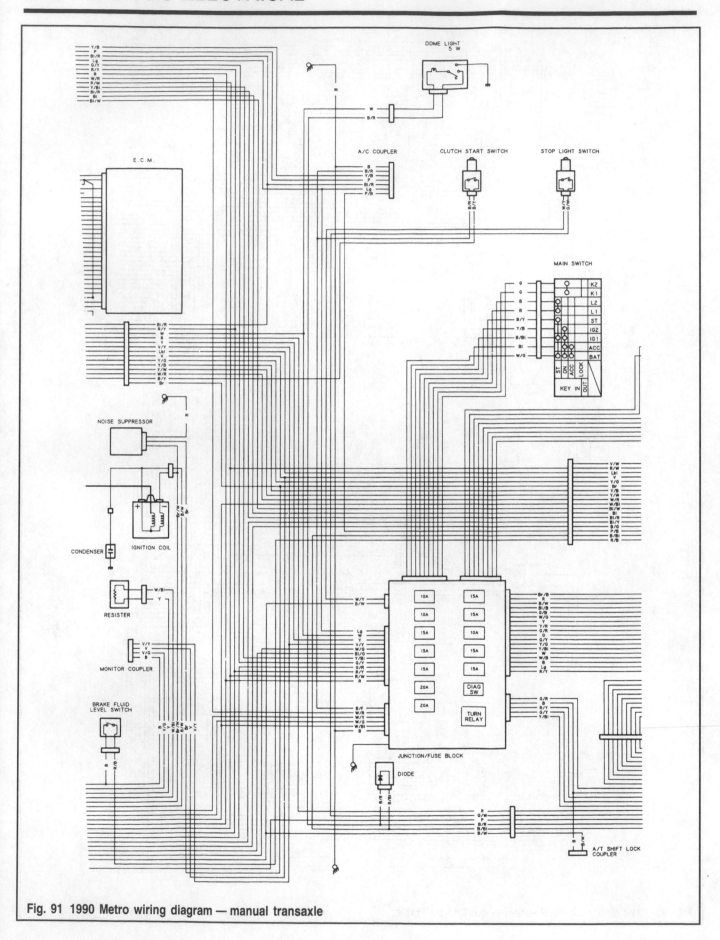

Fig. 91 1990 Metro wiring diagram — manual transaxle

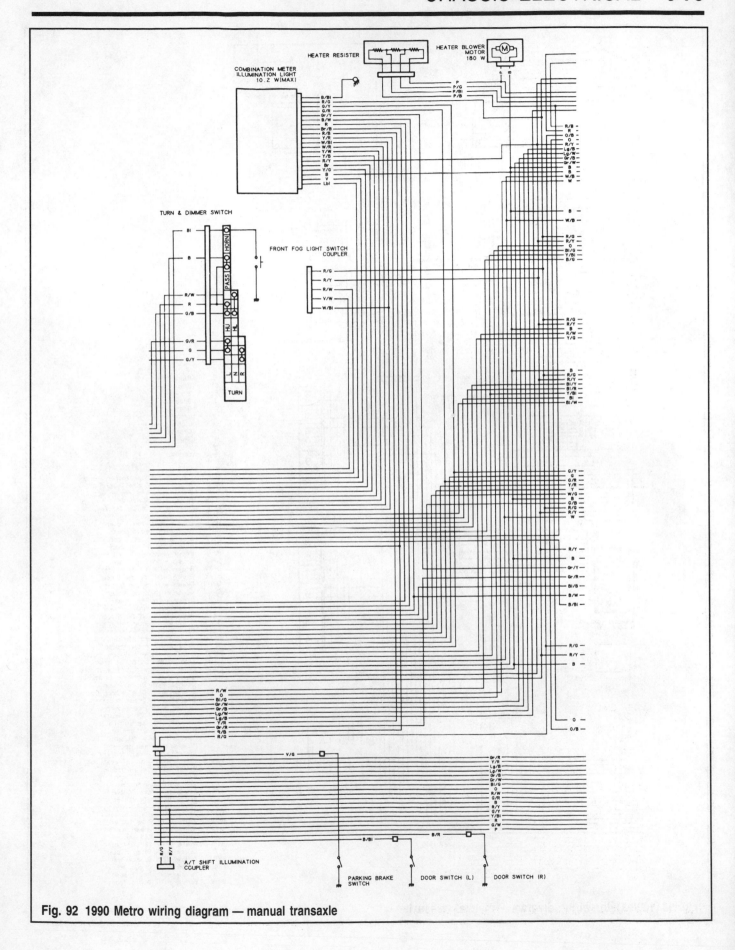

Fig. 92 1990 Metro wiring diagram — manual transaxle

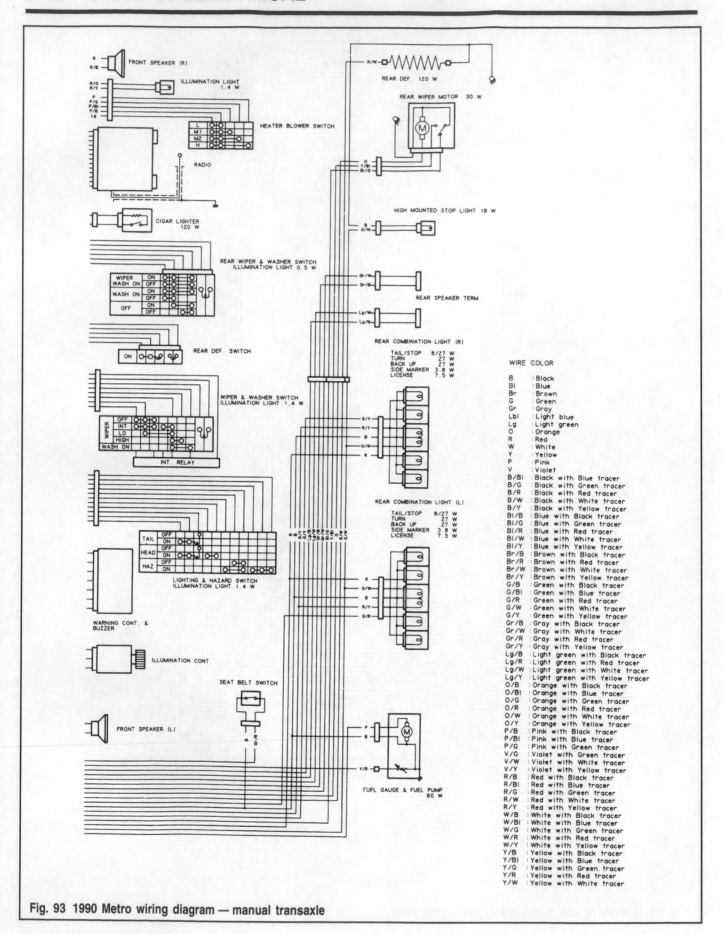

Fig. 93 1990 Metro wiring diagram — manual transaxle

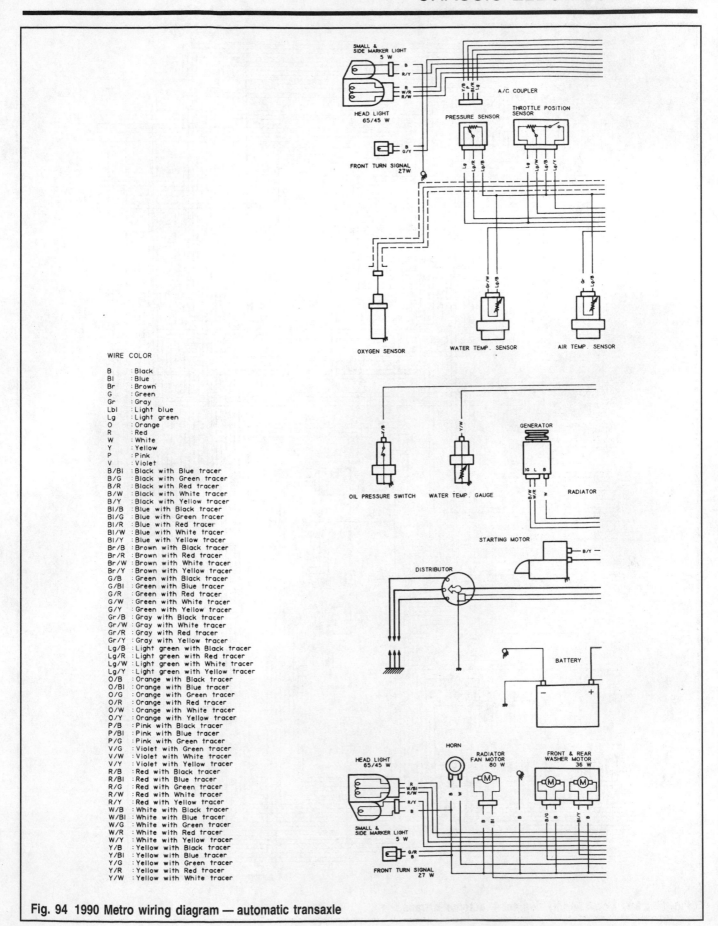

Fig. 94 1990 Metro wiring diagram — automatic transaxle

WIRE COLOR

B	: Black
Bl	: Blue
Br	: Brown
G	: Green
Gr	: Gray
Lbl	: Light blue
Lg	: Light green
O	: Orange
R	: Red
W	: White
Y	: Yellow
P	: Pink
V	: Violet
B/Bl	: Black with Blue tracer
B/G	: Black with Green tracer
B/R	: Black with Red tracer
B/W	: Black with White tracer
B/Y	: Black with Yellow tracer
Bl/B	: Blue with Black tracer
Bl/G	: Blue with Green tracer
Bl/R	: Blue with Red tracer
Bl/W	: Blue with White tracer
Bl/Y	: Blue with Yellow tracer
Br/B	: Brown with Black tracer
Br/R	: Brown with Red tracer
Br/W	: Brown with White tracer
Br/Y	: Brown with Yellow tracer
G/B	: Green with Black tracer
G/Bl	: Green with Blue tracer
G/R	: Green with Red tracer
G/W	: Green with White tracer
G/Y	: Green with Yellow tracer
Gr/B	: Gray with Black tracer
Gr/W	: Gray with White tracer
Gr/R	: Gray with Red tracer
Gr/Y	: Gray with Yellow tracer
Lg/B	: Light green with Black tracer
Lg/R	: Light green with Red tracer
Lg/W	: Light green with White tracer
Lg/Y	: Light green with Yellow tracer
O/B	: Orange with Black tracer
O/Bl	: Orange with Blue tracer
O/G	: Orange with Green tracer
O/R	: Orange with Red tracer
O/W	: Orange with White tracer
O/Y	: Orange with Yellow tracer
P/B	: Pink with Black tracer
P/Bl	: Pink with Blue tracer
P/G	: Pink with Green tracer
V/G	: Violet with Green tracer
V/W	: Violet with White tracer
V/Y	: Violet with Yellow tracer
R/B	: Red with Black tracer
R/Bl	: Red with Blue tracer
R/G	: Red with Green tracer
R/W	: Red with White tracer
R/Y	: Red with Yellow tracer
W/B	: White with Black tracer
W/Bl	: White with Blue tracer
W/G	: White with Green tracer
W/R	: White with Red tracer
W/Y	: White with Yellow tracer
Y/B	: Yellow with Black tracer
Y/Bl	: Yellow with Blue tracer
Y/G	: Yellow with Green tracer
Y/R	: Yellow with Red tracer
Y/W	: Yellow with White tracer

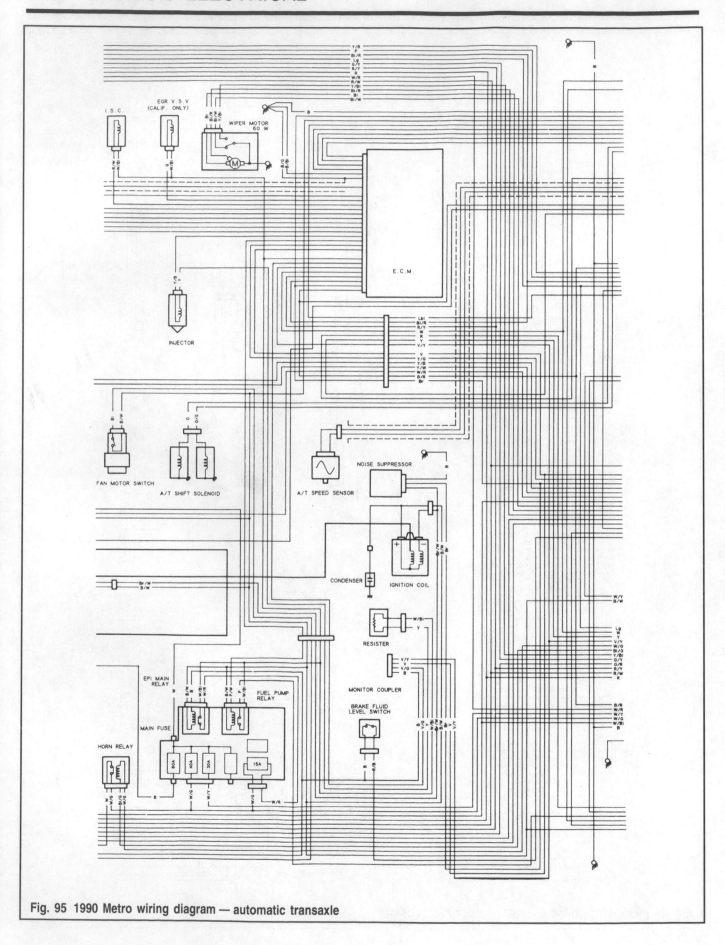

Fig. 95 1990 Metro wiring diagram — automatic transaxle

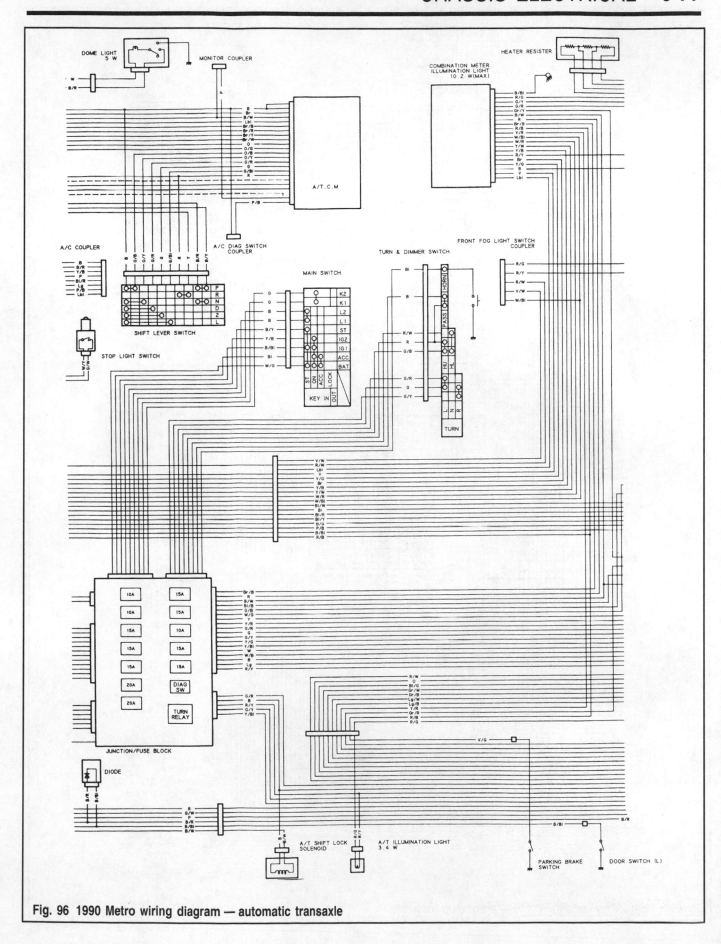

Fig. 96 1990 Metro wiring diagram — automatic transaxle

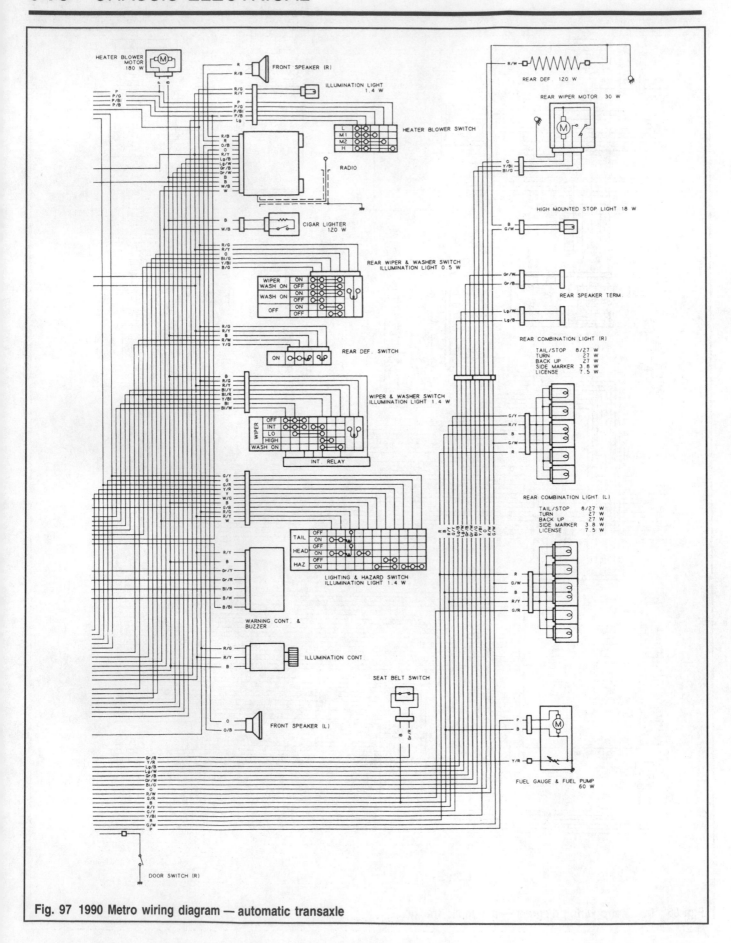

Fig. 97 1990 Metro wiring diagram — automatic transaxle

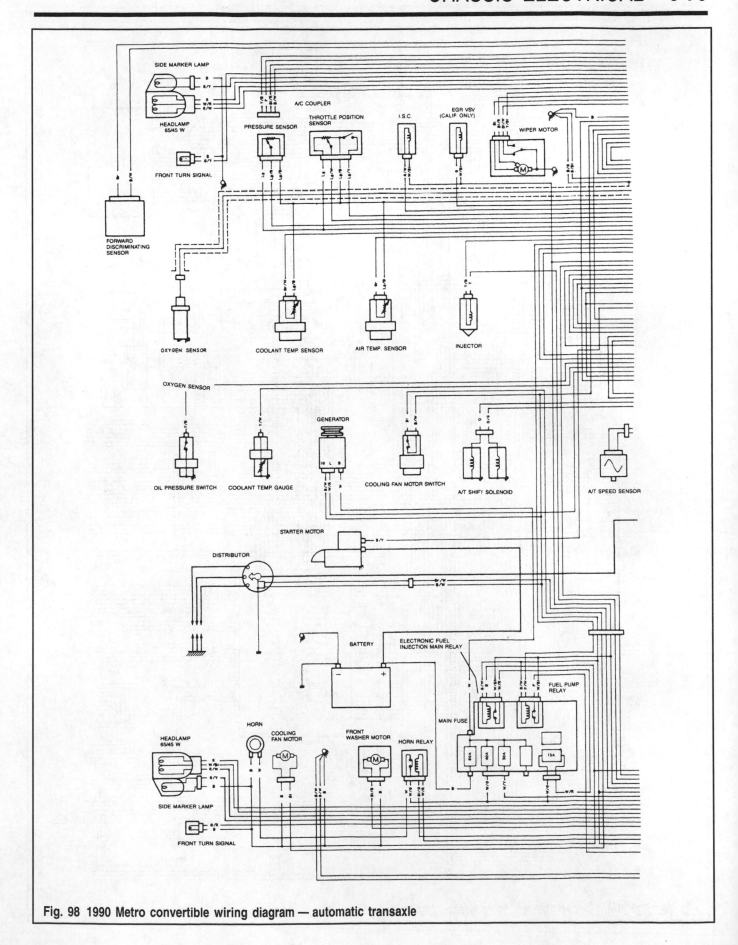

Fig. 98 1990 Metro convertible wiring diagram — automatic transaxle

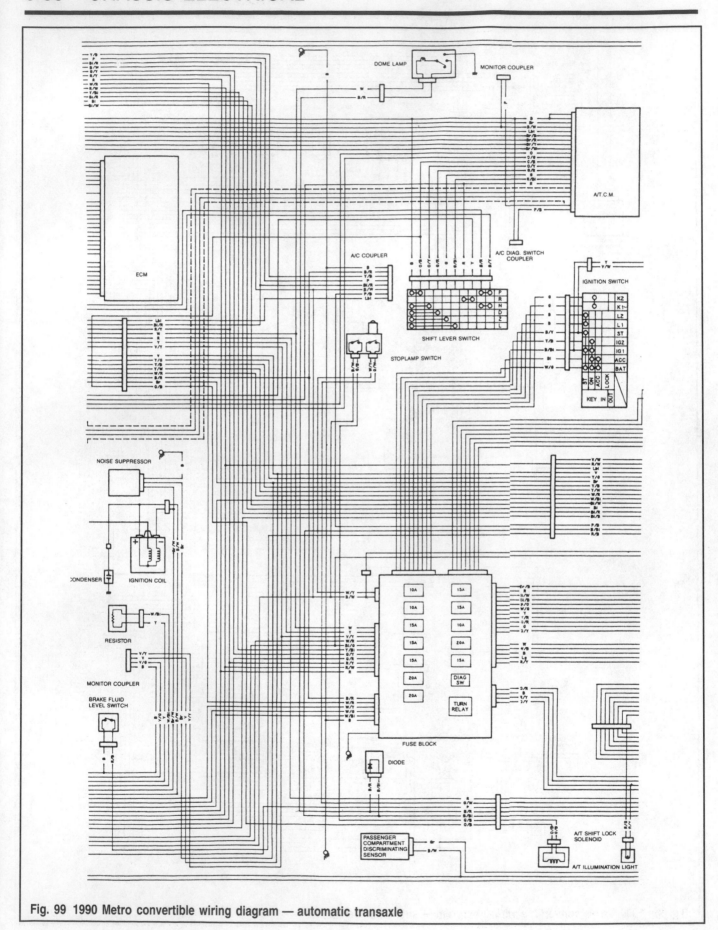

Fig. 99 1990 Metro convertible wiring diagram — automatic transaxle

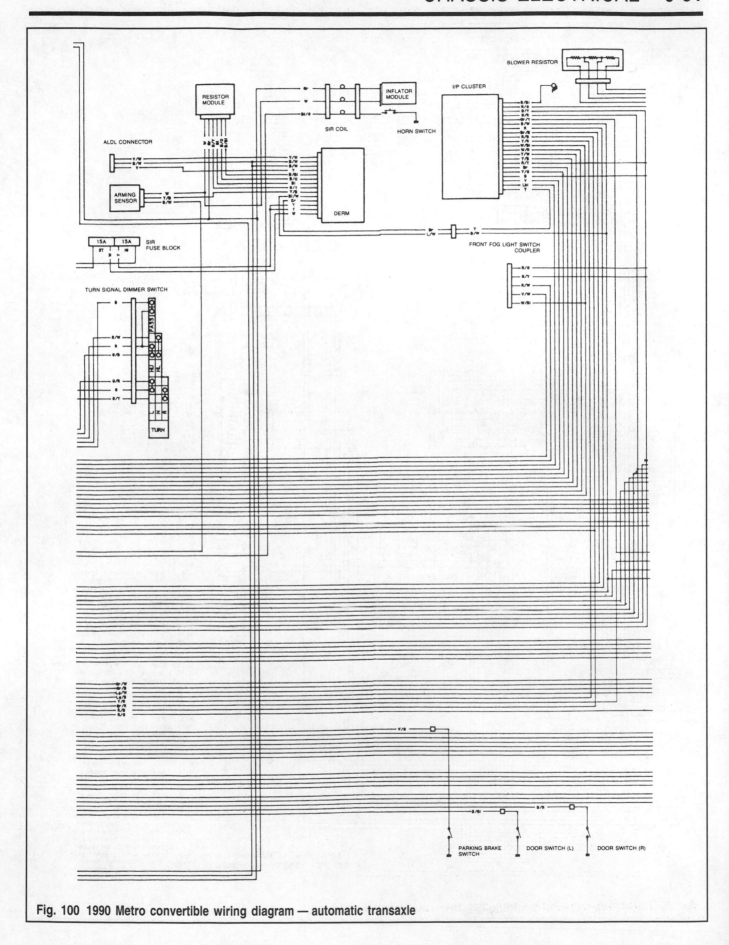

Fig. 100 1990 Metro convertible wiring diagram — automatic transaxle

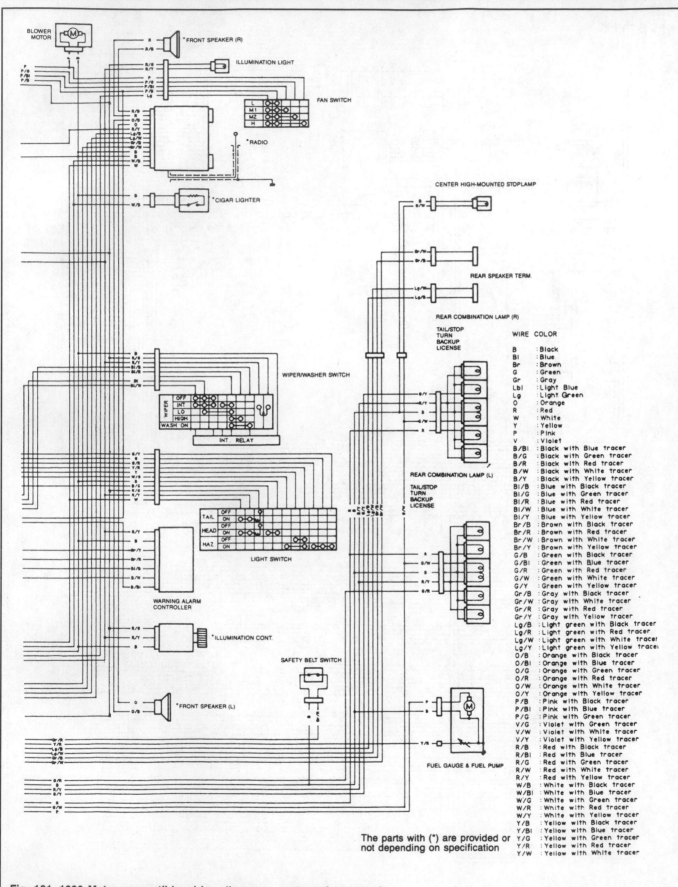

Fig. 101 1990 Metro convertible wiring diagram — automatic transaxle

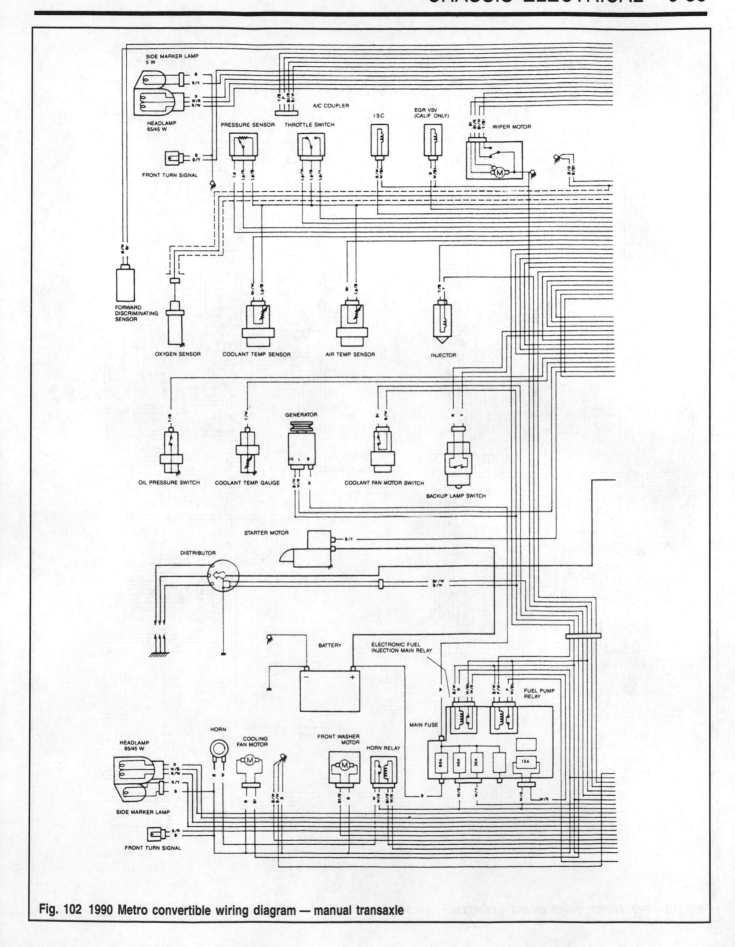

Fig. 102 1990 Metro convertible wiring diagram — manual transaxle

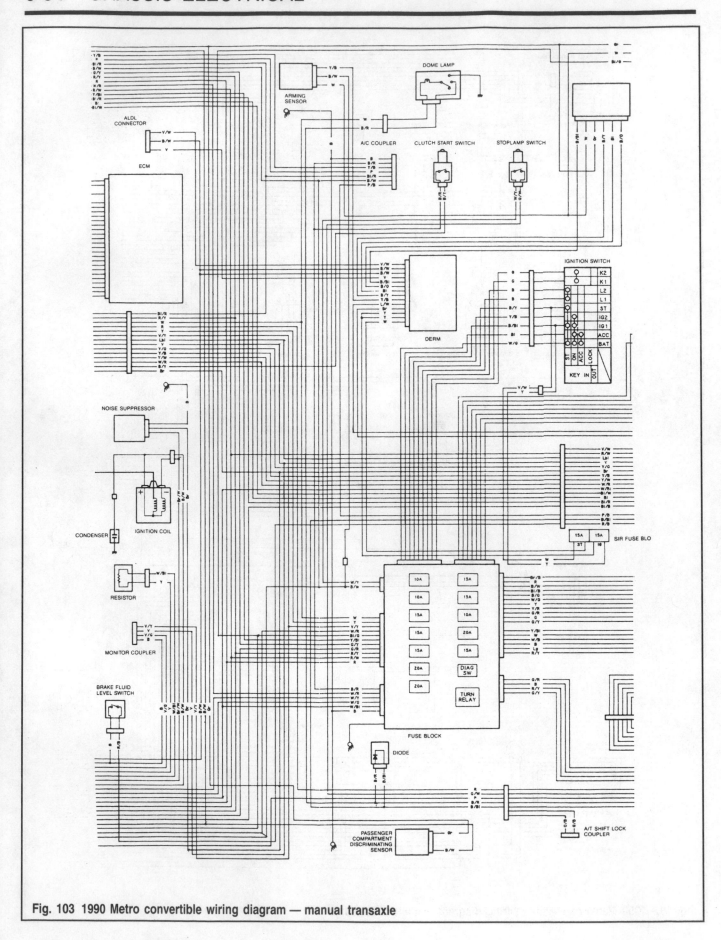

Fig. 103 1990 Metro convertible wiring diagram — manual transaxle

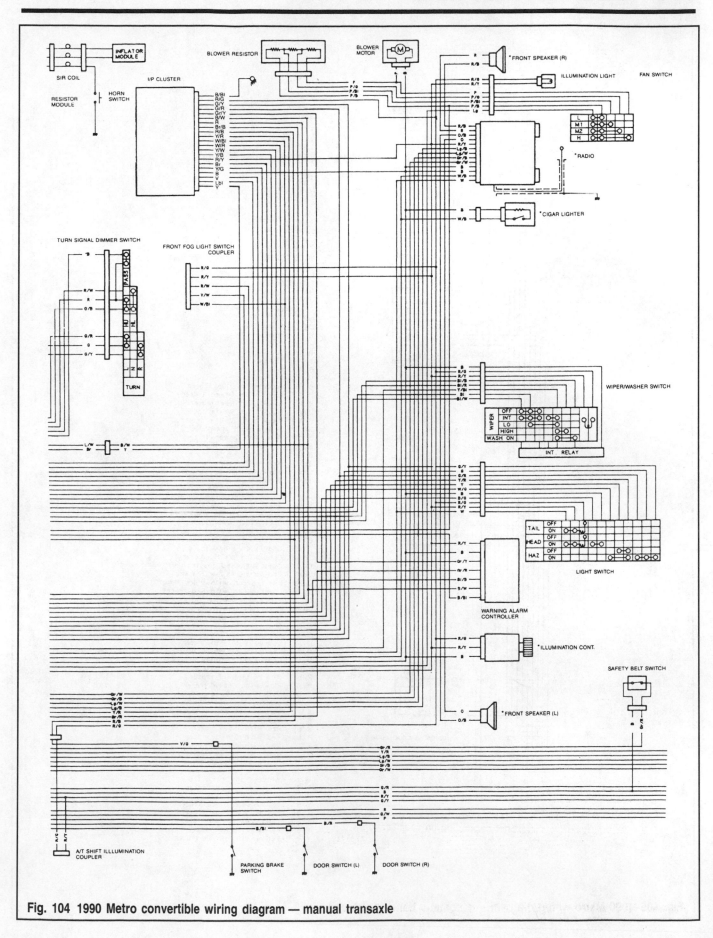

Fig. 104 1990 Metro convertible wiring diagram — manual transaxle

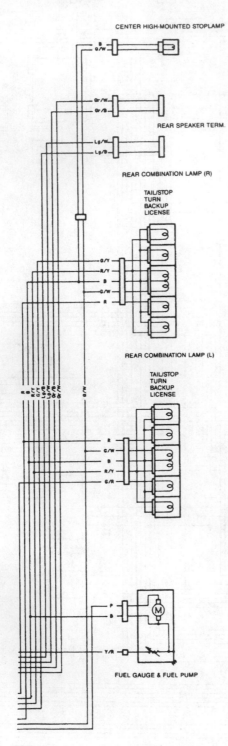

WIRE COLOR

B : Black
Bl : Blue
Br : Brown
G : Green
Gr : Gray
Lbl : Light Blue
Lg : Light Green
O : Orange
R : Red
W : White
Y : Yellow
P : Pink
V : Violet
B/Bl : Black with Blue tracer
B/G : Black with Green tracer
B/R : Black with Red tracer
B/W : Black with White tracer
B/Y : Black with Yellow tracer
Bl/B : Blue with Black tracer
Bl/G : Blue with Green tracer
Bl/R : Blue with Red tracer
Bl/W : Blue with White tracer
Bl/Y : Blue with Yellow tracer
Br/B : Brown with Black tracer
Br/R : Brown with Red tracer
Br/W : Brown with White tracer
Br/Y : Brown with Yellow tracer
G/B : Green with Black tracer
G/Bl : Green with Blue tracer
G/R : Green with Red tracer
G/W : Green with White tracer
G/Y : Green with Yellow tracer
Gr/B : Gray with Black tracer
Gr/W : Gray with White tracer
Gr/R : Gray with Red tracer
Gr/Y : Gray with Yellow tracer
Lg/B : Light green with Black tracer
Lg/R : Light green with Red tracer
Lg/W : Light green with White tracer
Lg/Y : Light green with Yellow tracer
O/B : Orange with Black tracer
O/Bl : Orange with Blue tracer
O/G : Orange with Green tracer
O/R : Orange with Red tracer
O/W : Orange with White tracer
O/Y : Orange with Yellow tracer
P/B : Pink with Black tracer
P/Bl : Pink with Blue tracer
P/G : Pink with Green tracer
V/G : Violet with Green tracer
V/W : Violet with White tracer
V/Y : Violet with Yellow tracer
R/B : Red with Black tracer
R/Bl : Red with Blue tracer
R/G : Red with Green tracer
R/W : Red with White tracer
R/Y : Red with Yellow tracer
W/B : White with Black tracer
W/Bl : White with Blue tracer
W/G : White with Green tracer
W/R : White with Red tracer
W/Y : White with Yellow tracer
Y/B : Yellow with Black tracer
Y/Bl : Yellow with Blue tracer
Y/G : Yellow with Green tracer
Y/R : Yellow with Red tracer
Y/W : Yellow with White tracer

The parts with (*) are provided or
not depending on specification.

Fig. 105 1990 Metro wiring diagram — automatic transaxle, Canada

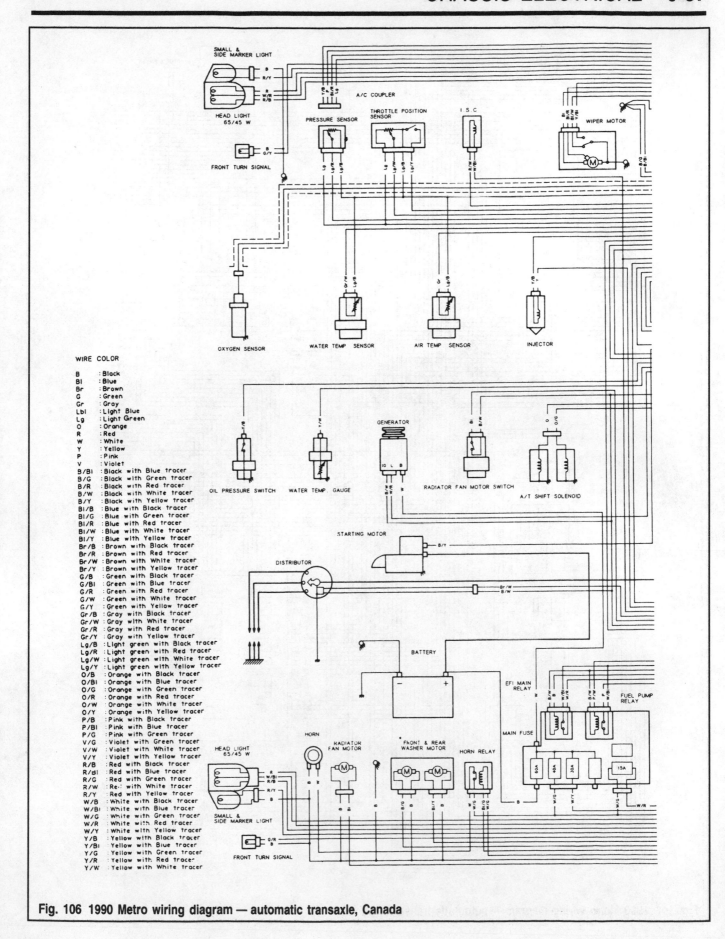

Fig. 106 1990 Metro wiring diagram — automatic transaxle, Canada

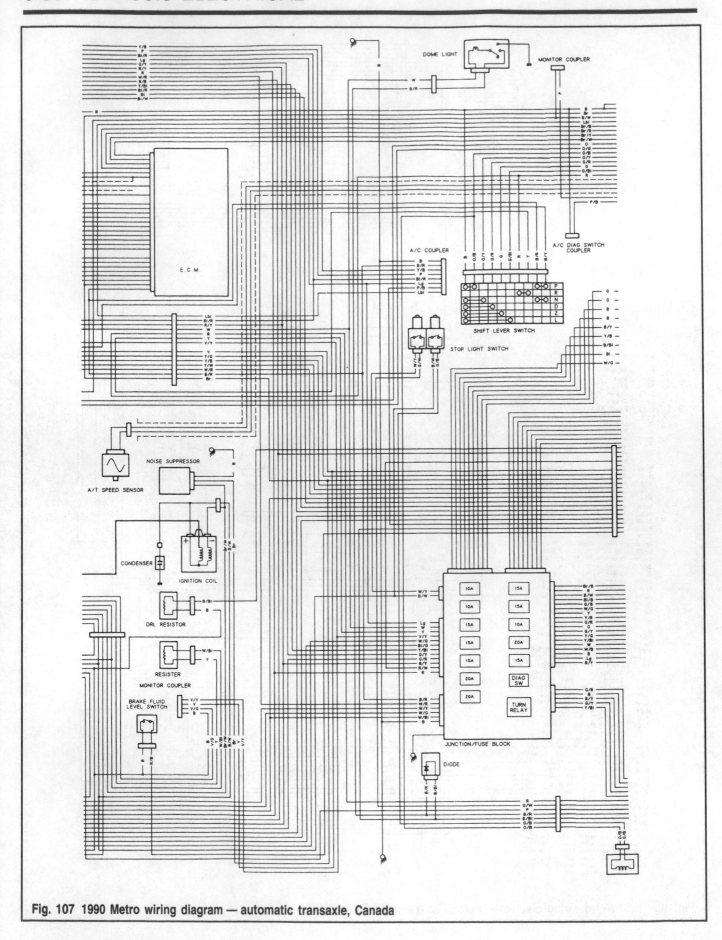

Fig. 107 1990 Metro wiring diagram — automatic transaxle, Canada

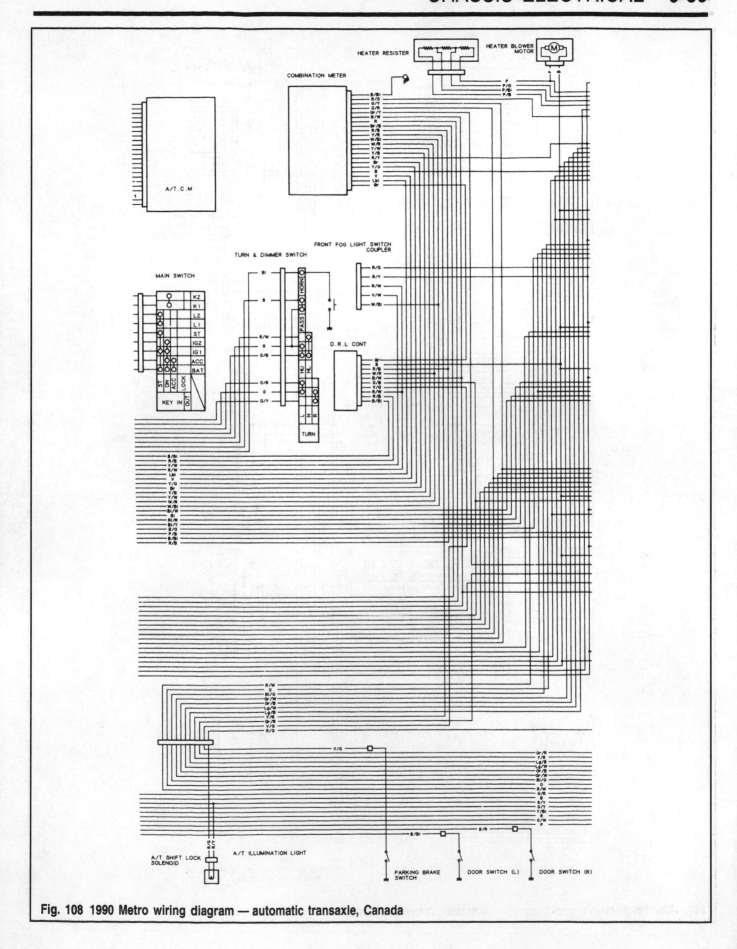

Fig. 108 1990 Metro wiring diagram — automatic transaxle, Canada

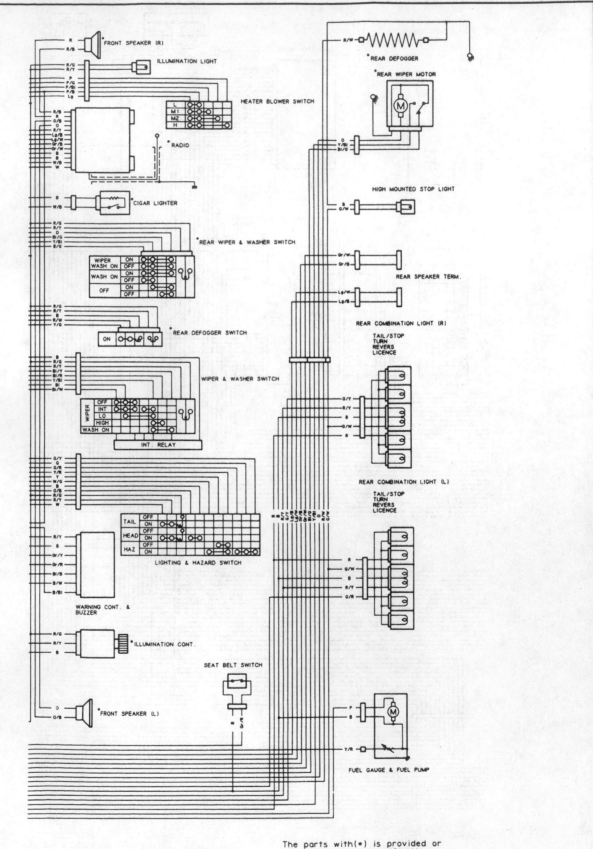

Fig. 109 1990 Metro wiring diagram — automatic transaxle, Canada

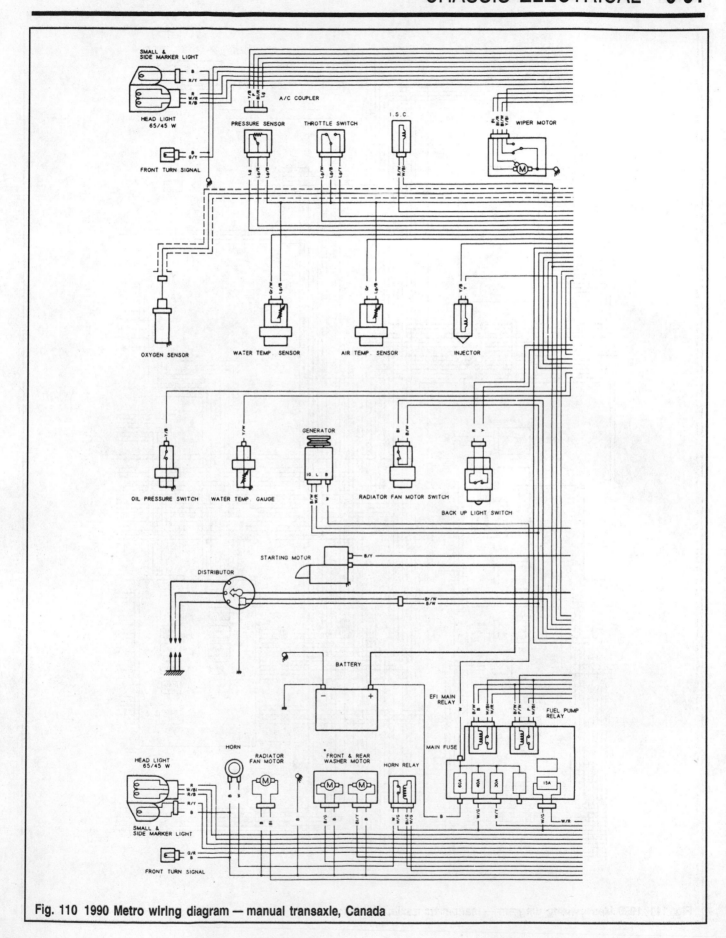

Fig. 110 1990 Metro wiring diagram — manual transaxle, Canada

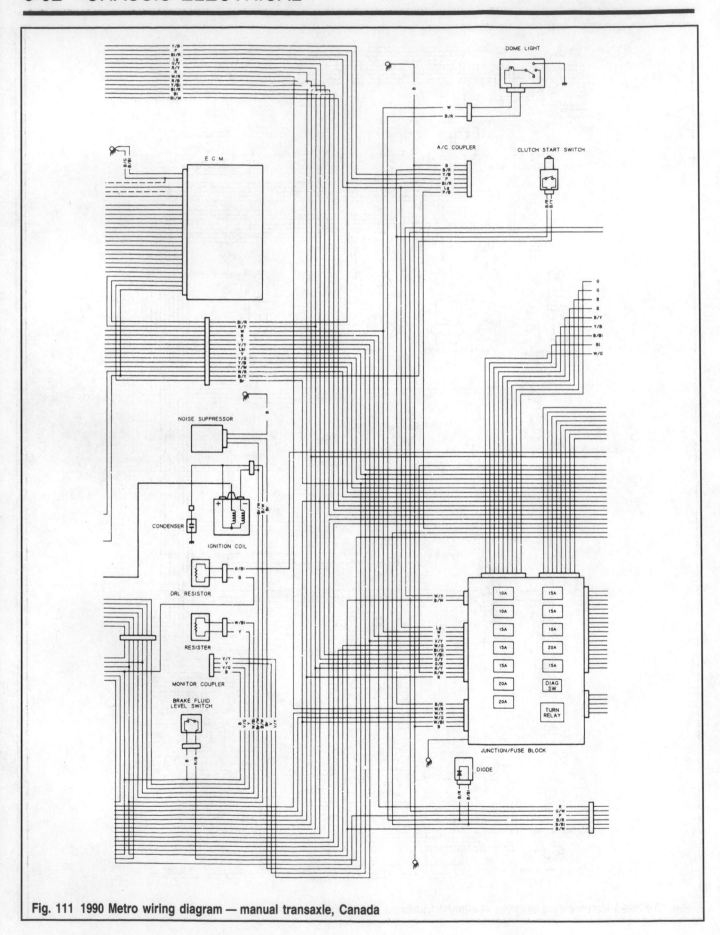

Fig. 111 1990 Metro wiring diagram — manual transaxle, Canada

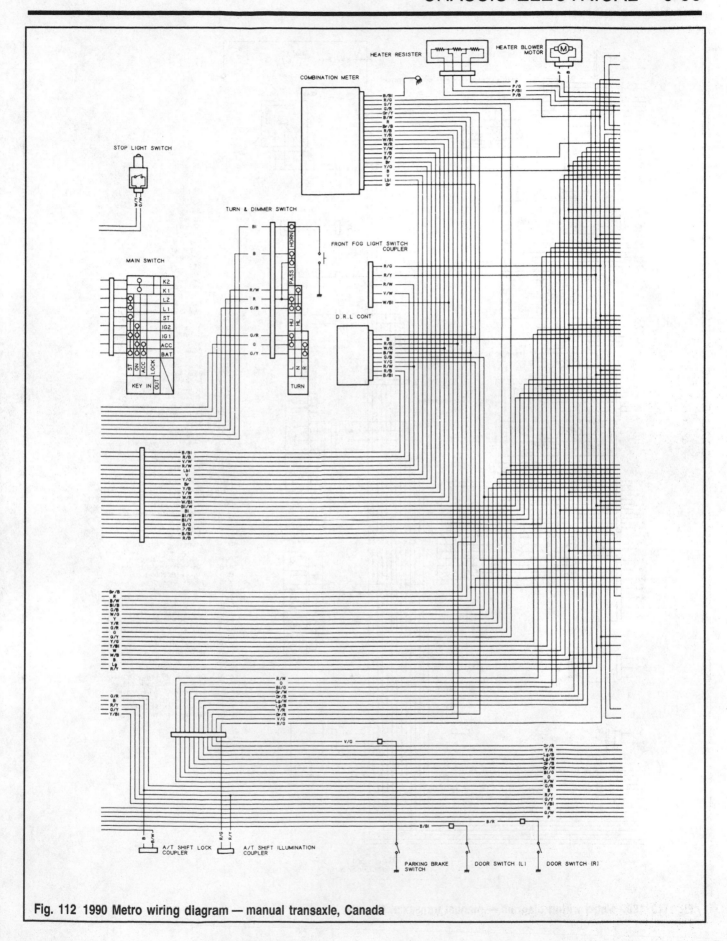

Fig. 112 1990 Metro wiring diagram — manual transaxle, Canada

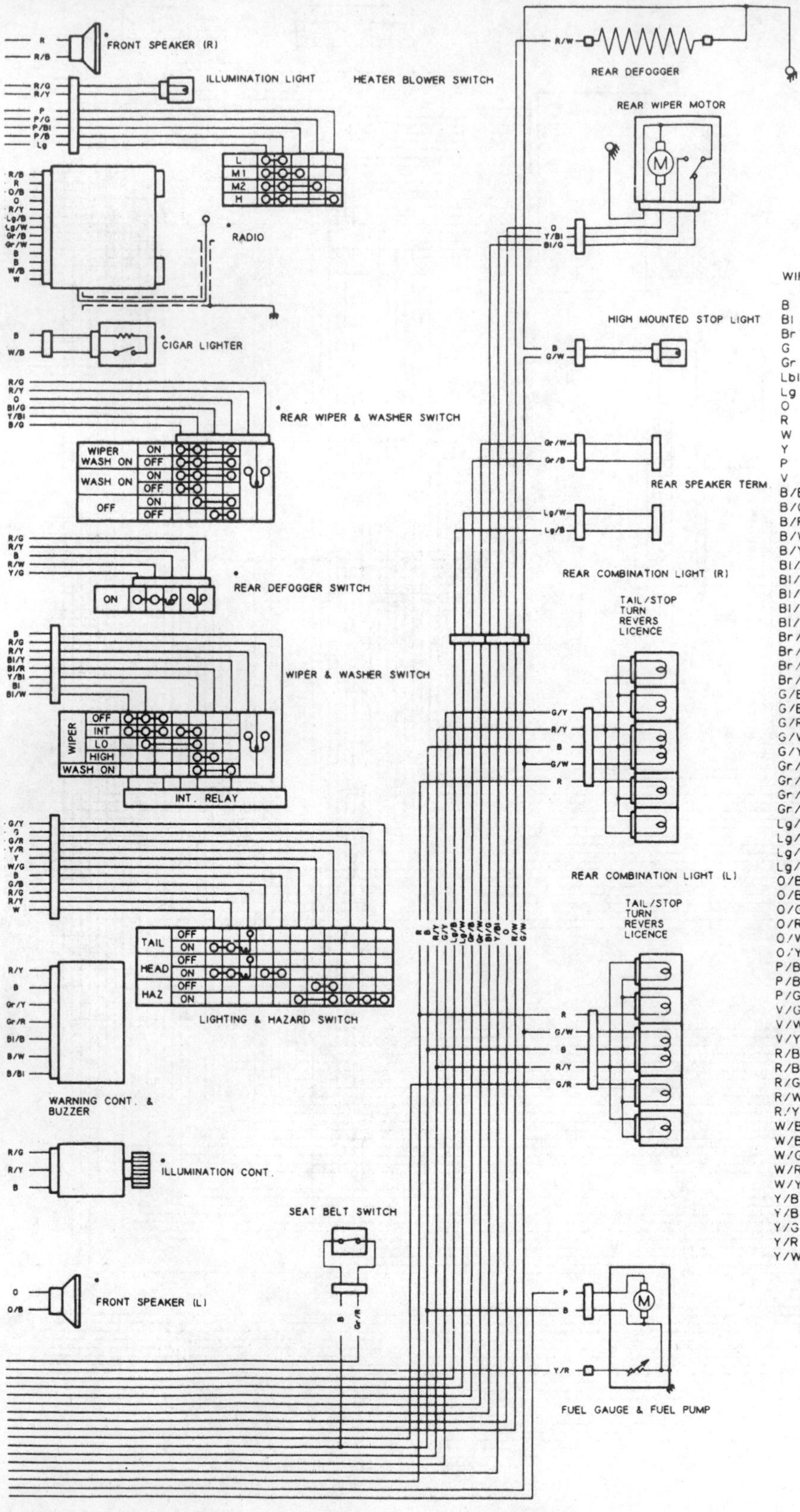

Fig. 113 1990 Metro wiring diagram — manual transaxle, Canada

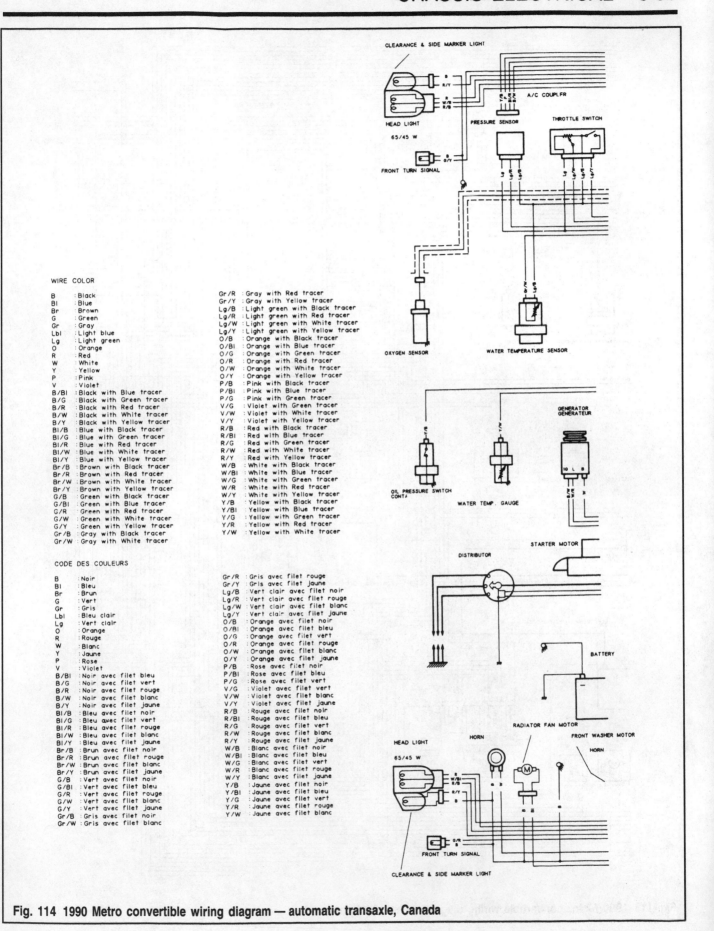

Fig. 114 1990 Metro convertible wiring diagram — automatic transaxle, Canada

WIRE COLOR

B	: Black	Gr/R	: Gray with Red tracer
Bl	: Blue	Gr/Y	: Gray with Yellow tracer
Br	: Brown	Lg/B	: Light green with Black tracer
G	: Green	Lg/R	: Light green with Red tracer
Gr	: Gray	Lg/W	: Light green with White tracer
Lbl	: Light blue	Lg/Y	: Light green with Yellow tracer
Lg	: Light green	O/B	: Orange with Black tracer
O	: Orange	O/Bl	: Orange with Blue tracer
R	: Red	O/G	: Orange with Green tracer
W	: White	O/R	: Orange with Red tracer
Y	: Yellow	O/W	: Orange with White tracer
P	: Pink	O/Y	: Orange with Yellow tracer
V	: Violet	P/B	: Pink with Black tracer
B/Bl	: Black with Blue tracer	P/Bl	: Pink with Blue tracer
B/G	: Black with Green tracer	P/G	: Pink with Green tracer
B/R	: Black with Red tracer	V/G	: Violet with Green tracer
B/W	: Black with White tracer	V/W	: Violet with White tracer
B/Y	: Black with Yellow tracer	V/Y	: Violet with Yellow tracer
Bl/B	: Blue with Black tracer	R/B	: Red with Black tracer
Bl/G	: Blue with Green tracer	R/Bl	: Red with Blue tracer
Bl/R	: Blue with Red tracer	R/G	: Red with Green tracer
Bl/W	: Blue with White tracer	R/W	: Red with White tracer
Bl/Y	: Blue with Yellow tracer	R/Y	: Red with Yellow tracer
Br/B	: Brown with Black tracer	W/B	: White with Black tracer
Br/R	: Brown with Red tracer	W/Bl	: White with Blue tracer
Br/W	: Brown with White tracer	W/G	: White with Green tracer
Br/Y	: Brown with Yellow tracer	W/R	: White with Red tracer
G/B	: Green with Black tracer	W/Y	: White with Yellow tracer
G/Bl	: Green with Blue tracer	Y/B	: Yellow with Black tracer
G/R	: Green with Red tracer	Y/Bl	: Yellow with Blue tracer
G/W	: Green with White tracer	Y/G	: Yellow with Green tracer
G/Y	: Green with Yellow tracer	Y/R	: Yellow with Red tracer
Gr/B	: Gray with Black tracer	Y/W	: Yellow with White tracer
Gr/W	: Gray with White tracer		

CODE DES COULEURS

B	: Noir	Gr/R	: Gris avec filet rouge
Bl	: Bleu	Gr/Y	: Gris avec filet jaune
Br	: Brun	Lg/B	: Vert clair avec filet noir
G	: Vert	Lg/R	: Vert clair avec filet rouge
Gr	: Gris	Lg/W	: Vert clair avec filet blanc
Lbl	: Bleu clair	Lg/Y	: Vert clair avec filet jaune
Lg	: Vert clair	O/B	: Orange avec filet noir
O	: Orange	O/Bl	: Orange avec filet bleu
R	: Rouge	O/G	: Orange avec filet vert
W	: Blanc	O/R	: Orange avec filet rouge
Y	: Jaune	O/W	: Orange avec filet blanc
P	: Rose	O/Y	: Orange avec filet jaune
V	: Violet	P/B	: Rose avec filet noir
B/Bl	: Noir avec filet bleu	P/Bl	: Rose avec filet bleu
B/G	: Noir avec filet vert	P/G	: Rose avec filet vert
B/R	: Noir avec filet rouge	V/G	: Violet avec filet vert
B/W	: Noir avec filet blanc	V/W	: Violet avec filet blanc
B/Y	: Noir avec filet jaune	V/Y	: Violet avec filet jaune
Bl/B	: Bleu avec filet noir	R/B	: Rouge avec filet noir
Bl/G	: Bleu avec filet vert	R/Bl	: Rouge avec filet bleu
Bl/R	: Bleu avec filet rouge	R/G	: Rouge avec filet vert
Bl/W	: Bleu avec filet blanc	R/W	: Rouge avec filet blanc
Bl/Y	: Bleu avec filet jaune	R/Y	: Rouge avec filet jaune
Br/B	: Brun avec filet noir	W/B	: Blanc avec filet noir
Br/R	: Brun avec filet rouge	W/Bl	: Blanc avec filet bleu
Br/W	: Brun avec filet blanc	W/G	: Blanc avec filet vert
Br/Y	: Brun avec filet jaune	W/R	: Blanc avec filet rouge
G/B	: Vert avec filet noir	W/Y	: Blanc avec filet jaune
G/Bl	: Vert avec filet bleu	Y/B	: Jaune avec filet noir
G/R	: Vert avec filet rouge	Y/Bl	: Jaune avec filet bleu
G/W	: Vert avec filet blanc	Y/G	: Jaune avec filet vert
G/Y	: Vert avec filet jaune	Y/R	: Jaune avec filet rouge
Gr/B	: Gris avec filet noir	Y/W	: Jaune avec filet blanc
Gr/W	: Gris avec filet blanc		

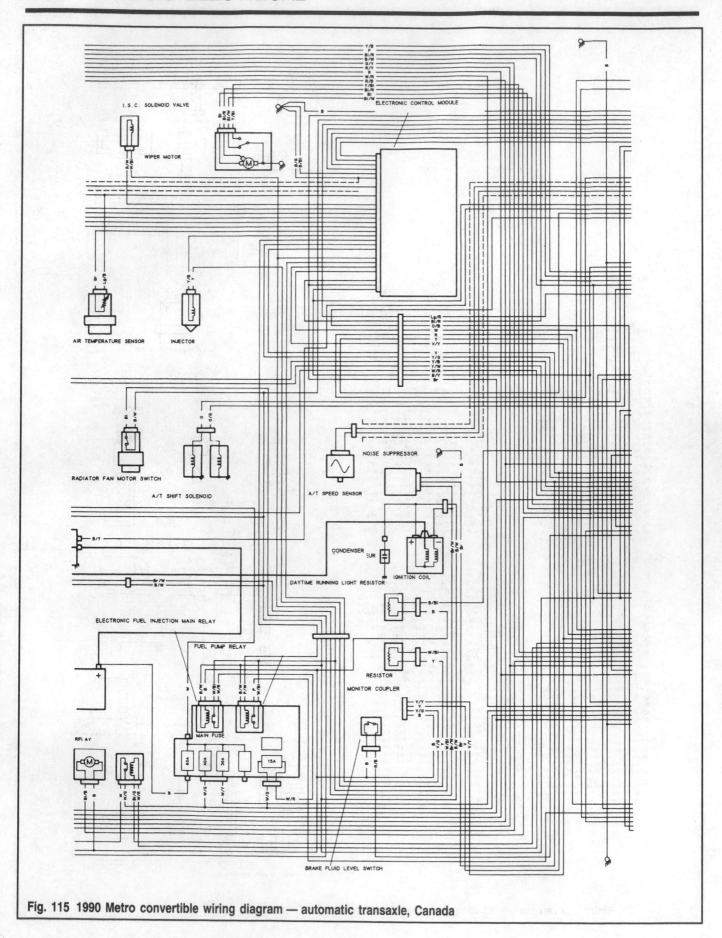

Fig. 115 1990 Metro convertible wiring diagram — automatic transaxle, Canada

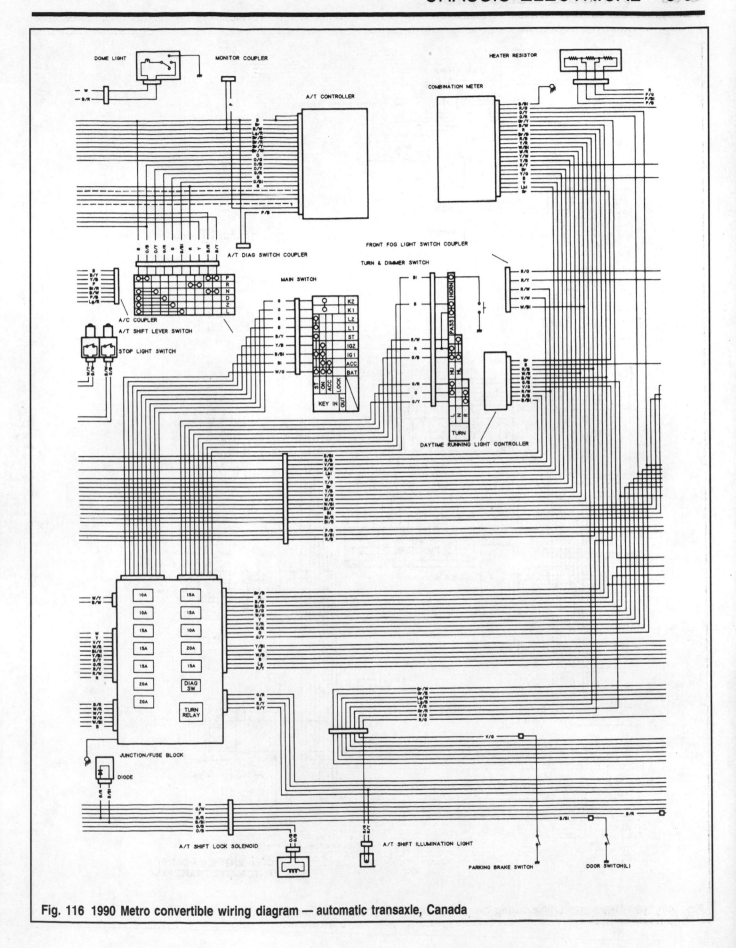

Fig. 116 1990 Metro convertible wiring diagram — automatic transaxle, Canada

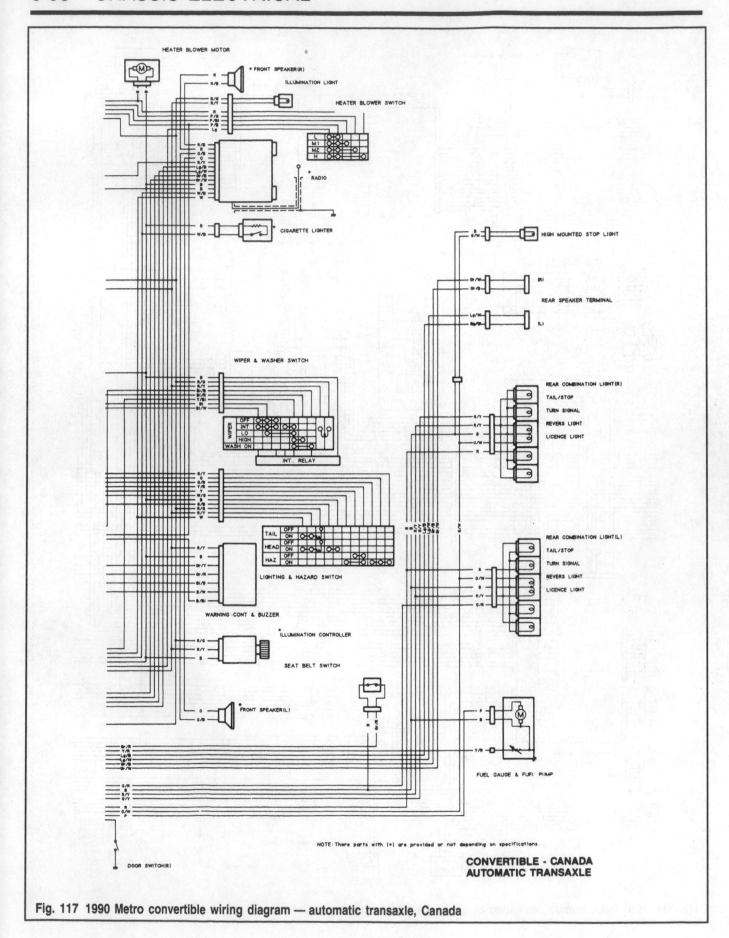

Fig. 117 1990 Metro convertible wiring diagram — automatic transaxle, Canada

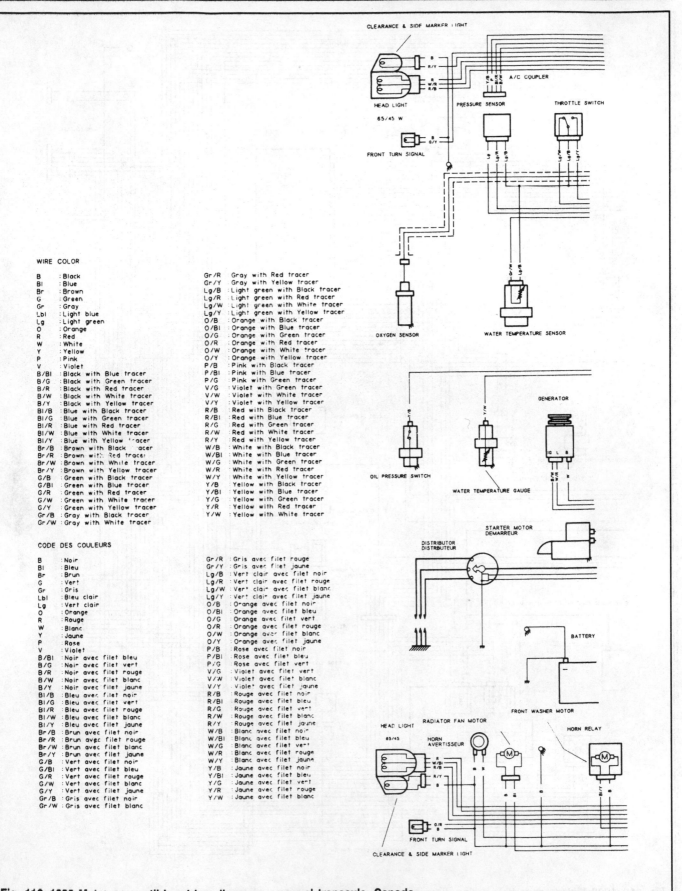

WIRE COLOR

B	: Black	Gr/R	: Gray with Red tracer
Bl	: Blue	Gr/Y	: Gray with Yellow tracer
Br	: Brown	Lg/B	: Light green with Black tracer
G	: Green	Lg/R	: Light green with Red tracer
Gr	: Gray	Lg/W	: Light green with White tracer
Lbl	: Light blue	Lg/Y	: Light green with Yellow tracer
Lg	: Light green	O/B	: Orange with Black tracer
O	: Orange	O/Bl	: Orange with Blue tracer
R	: Red	O/G	: Orange with Green tracer
W	: White	O/R	: Orange with Red tracer
Y	: Yellow	O/W	: Orange with White tracer
P	: Pink	O/Y	: Orange with Yellow tracer
V	: Violet	P/B	: Pink with Black tracer
B/Bl	: Black with Blue tracer	P/Bl	: Pink with Blue tracer
B/G	: Black with Green tracer	P/G	: Pink with Green tracer
B/R	: Black with Red tracer	V/G	: Violet with Green tracer
B/W	: Black with White tracer	V/W	: Violet with White tracer
B/Y	: Black with Yellow tracer	V/Y	: Violet with Yellow tracer
Bl/B	: Blue with Black tracer	R/B	: Red with Black tracer
Bl/G	: Blue with Green tracer	R/Bl	: Red with Blue tracer
Bl/R	: Blue with Red tracer	R/G	: Red with Green tracer
Bl/W	: Blue with White tracer	R/W	: Red with White tracer
Bl/Y	: Blue with Yellow tracer	R/Y	: Red with Yellow tracer
Br/B	: Brown with Black tracer	W/B	: White with Black tracer
Br/R	: Brown with Red tracer	W/Bl	: White with Blue tracer
Br/W	: Brown with White tracer	W/G	: White with Green tracer
Br/Y	: Brown with Yellow tracer	W/R	: White with Red tracer
G/B	: Green with Black tracer	W/Y	: White with Yellow tracer
G/Bl	: Green with Blue tracer	Y/B	: Yellow with Black tracer
G/R	: Green with Red tracer	Y/Bl	: Yellow with Blue tracer
G/W	: Green with White tracer	Y/G	: Yellow with Green tracer
G/Y	: Green with Yellow tracer	Y/R	: Yellow with Red tracer
Gr/B	: Gray with Black tracer	Y/W	: Yellow with White tracer
Gr/W	: Gray with White tracer		

CODE DES COULEURS

B	: Noir	Gr/R	: Gris avec filet rouge
Bl	: Bleu	Gr/Y	: Gris avec filet jaune
Br	: Brun	Lg/B	: Vert clair avec filet noir
G	: Vert	Lg/R	: Vert clair avec filet rouge
Gr	: Gris	Lg/W	: Vert clair avec filet blanc
Lbl	: Bleu clair	Lg/Y	: Vert clair avec filet jaune
Lg	: Vert clair	O/B	: Orange avec filet noir
O	: Orange	O/Bl	: Orange avec filet bleu
R	: Rouge	O/G	: Orange avec filet vert
W	: Blanc	O/R	: Orange avec filet rouge
Y	: Jaune	O/W	: Orange avec filet blanc
P	: Rose	O/Y	: Orange avec filet jaune
V	: Violet	P/B	: Rose avec filet noir
B/Bl	: Noir avec filet bleu	P/Bl	: Rose avec filet bleu
B/G	: Noir avec filet vert	P/G	: Rose avec filet vert
B/R	: Noir avec filet rouge	V/G	: Violet avec filet vert
B/W	: Noir avec filet blanc	V/W	: Violet avec filet blanc
B/Y	: Noir avec filet jaune	V/Y	: Violet avec filet jaune
Bl/B	: Bleu avec filet noir	R/B	: Rouge avec filet noir
Bl/G	: Bleu avec filet vert	R/Bl	: Rouge avec filet bleu
Bl/R	: Bleu avec filet rouge	R/G	: Rouge avec filet vert
Bl/W	: Bleu avec filet blanc	R/W	: Rouge avec filet blanc
Bl/Y	: Bleu avec filet jaune	R/Y	: Rouge avec filet jaune
Br/B	: Brun avec filet noir	W/B	: Blanc avec filet noir
Br/R	: Brun avec filet rouge	W/Bl	: Blanc avec filet bleu
Br/W	: Brun avec filet blanc	W/G	: Blanc avec filet vert
Br/Y	: Brun avec filet jaune	W/R	: Blanc avec filet rouge
G/B	: Vert avec filet noir	W/Y	: Blanc avec filet jaune
G/Bl	: Vert avec filet bleu	Y/B	: Jaune avec filet noir
G/R	: Vert avec filet rouge	Y/Bl	: Jaune avec filet bleu
G/W	: Vert avec filet blanc	Y/G	: Jaune avec filet vert
G/Y	: Vert avec filet jaune	Y/R	: Jaune avec filet rouge
Gr/B	: Gris avec filet noir	Y/W	: Jaune avec filet blanc
Gr/W	: Gris avec filet blanc		

Fig. 118 1990 Metro convertible wiring diagram — manual transaxle, Canada

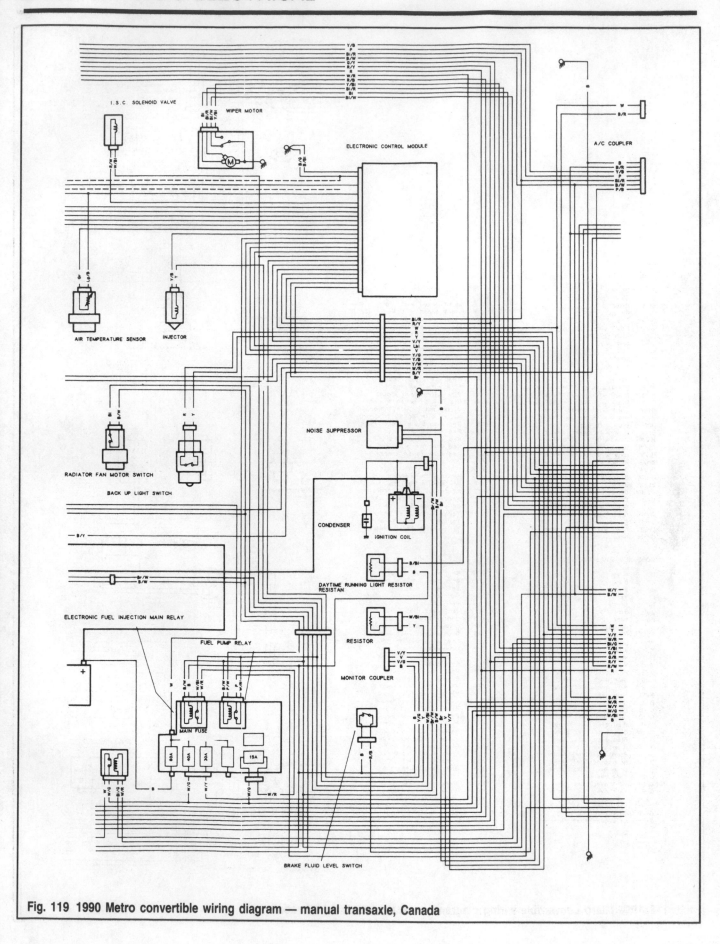

Fig. 119 1990 Metro convertible wiring diagram — manual transaxle, Canada

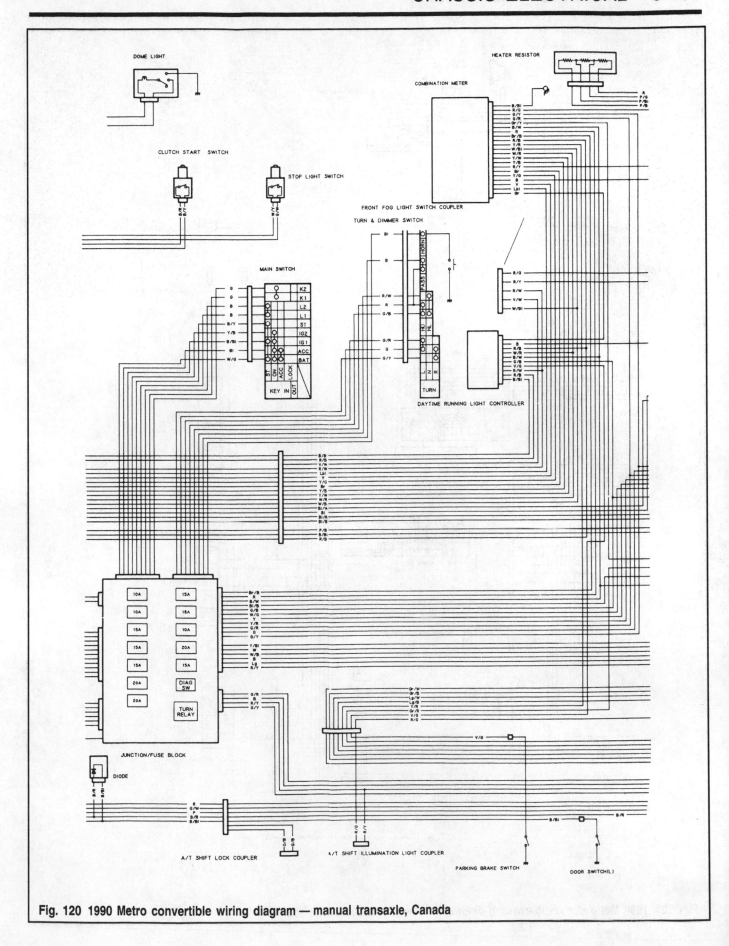

Fig. 120 1990 Metro convertible wiring diagram — manual transaxle, Canada

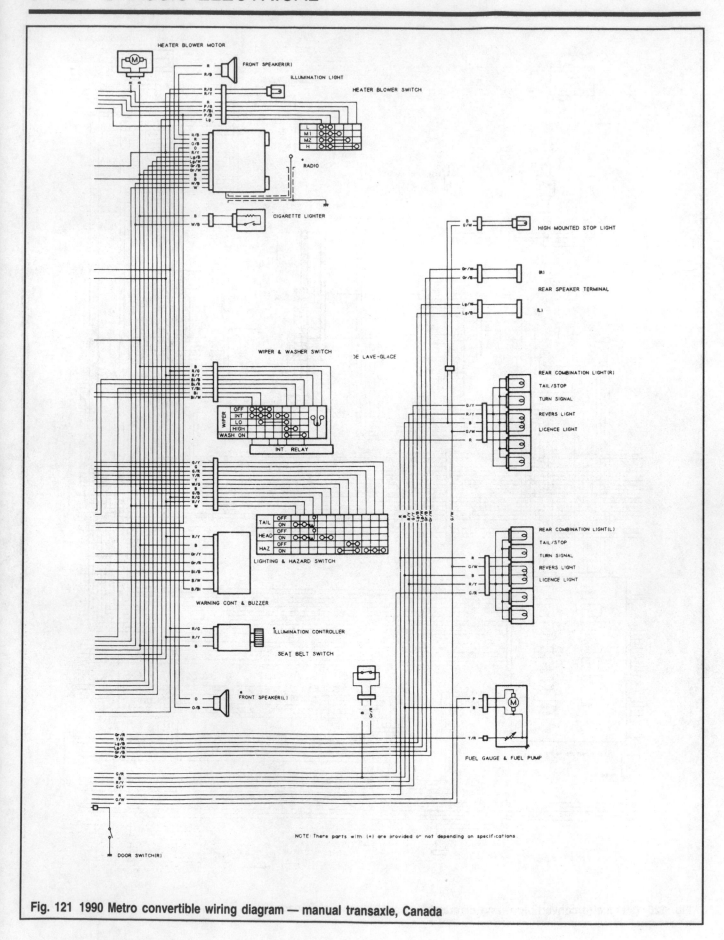

Fig. 121 1990 Metro convertible wiring diagram — manual transaxle, Canada

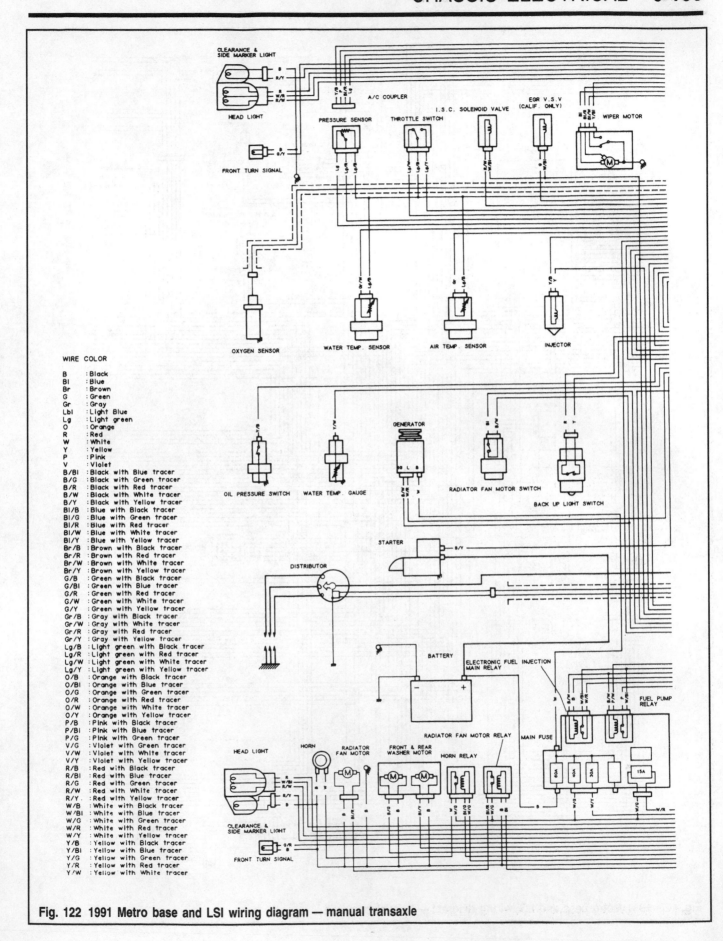

WIRE COLOR

B : Black
Bl : Blue
Br : Brown
G : Green
Gr : Gray
Lbl : Light Blue
Lg : Light green
O : Orange
R : Red
W : White
Y : Yellow
P : Pink
V : Violet
B/Bl : Black with Blue tracer
B/G : Black with Green tracer
B/R : Black with Red tracer
B/W : Black with White tracer
B/Y : Black with Yellow tracer
Bl/B : Blue with Black tracer
Bl/G : Blue with Green tracer
Bl/R : Blue with Red tracer
Bl/W : Blue with White tracer
Bl/Y : Blue with Yellow tracer
Br/B : Brown with Black tracer
Br/R : Brown with Red tracer
Br/W : Brown with White tracer
Br/Y : Brown with Yellow tracer
G/B : Green with Black tracer
G/Bl : Green with Blue tracer
G/R : Green with Red tracer
G/W : Green with White tracer
G/Y : Green with Yellow tracer
Gr/B : Gray with Black tracer
Gr/W : Gray with White tracer
Gr/R : Gray with Red tracer
Gr/Y : Gray with Yellow tracer
Lg/B : Light green with Black tracer
Lg/R : Light green with Red tracer
Lg/W : Light green with White tracer
Lg/Y : Light green with Yellow tracer
O/B : Orange with Black tracer
O/Bl : Orange with Blue tracer
O/G : Orange with Green tracer
O/R : Orange with Red tracer
O/W : Orange with White tracer
O/Y : Orange with Yellow tracer
P/B : Pink with Black tracer
P/Bl : Pink with Blue tracer
P/G : Pink with Green tracer
V/G : Violet with Green tracer
V/W : Violet with White tracer
V/Y : Violet with Yellow tracer
R/B : Red with Black tracer
R/Bl : Red with Blue tracer
R/G : Red with Green tracer
R/W : Red with White tracer
R/Y : Red with Yellow tracer
W/B : White with Black tracer
W/Bl : White with Blue tracer
W/G : White with Green tracer
W/R : White with Red tracer
W/Y : White with Yellow tracer
Y/B : Yellow with Black tracer
Y/Bl : Yellow with Blue tracer
Y/G : Yellow with Green tracer
Y/R : Yellow with Red tracer
Y/W : Yellow with White tracer

CLEARANCE & SIDE MARKER LIGHT

HEAD LIGHT

FRONT TURN SIGNAL

A/C COUPLER

PRESSURE SENSOR

THROTTLE SWITCH

I.S.C. SOLENOID VALVE

EGR V.S.V (CALIF. ONLY)

WIPER MOTOR

OXYGEN SENSOR

WATER TEMP. SENSOR

AIR TEMP. SENSOR

INJECTOR

OIL PRESSURE SWITCH

WATER TEMP. GAUGE

GENERATOR

RADIATOR FAN MOTOR SWITCH

BACK UP LIGHT SWITCH

STARTER

DISTRIBUTOR

BATTERY

ELECTRONIC FUEL INJECTION MAIN RELAY

RADIATOR FAN MOTOR RELAY

MAIN FUSE

FUEL PUMP RELAY

HEAD LIGHT

HORN

RADIATOR FAN MOTOR

FRONT & REAR WASHER MOTOR

HORN RELAY

CLEARANCE & SIDE MARKER LIGHT

FRONT TURN SIGNAL

Fig. 122 1991 Metro base and LSI wiring diagram — manual transaxle

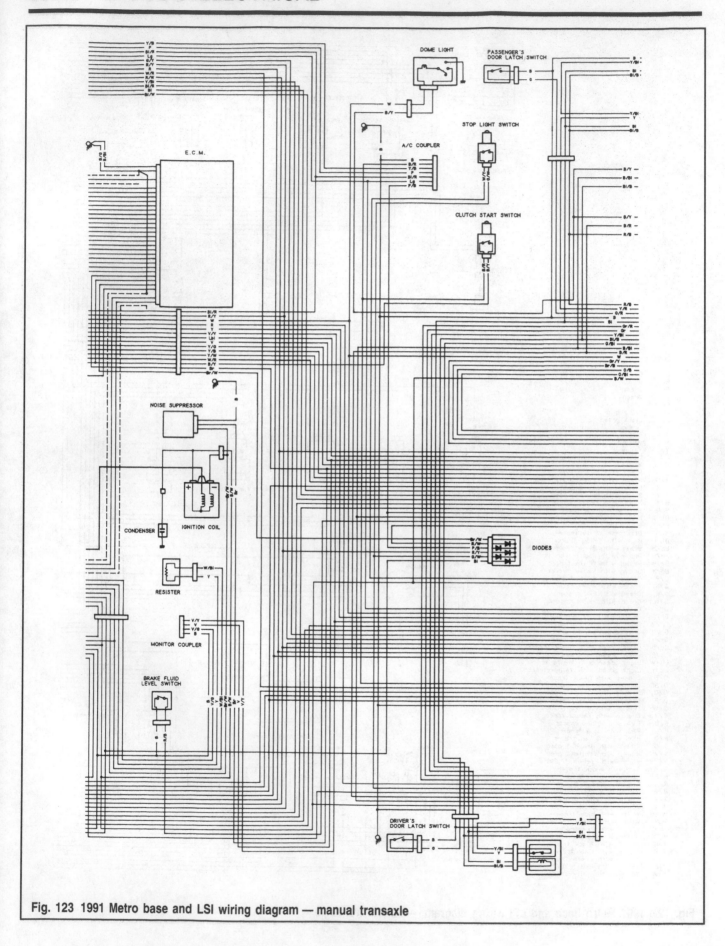

Fig. 123 1991 Metro base and LSI wiring diagram — manual transaxle

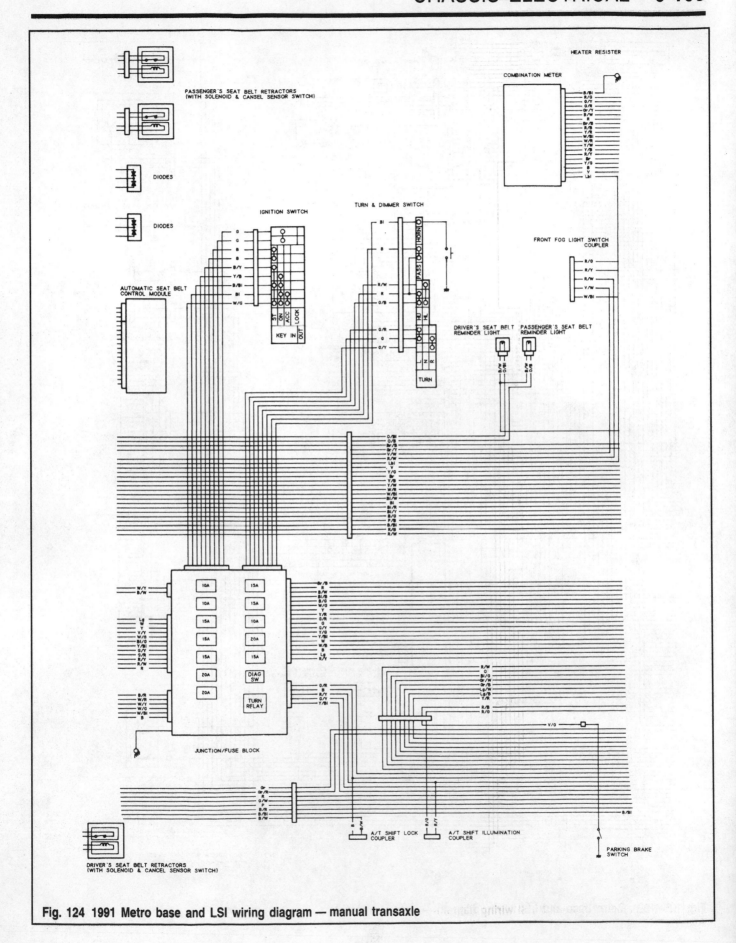

Fig. 124 1991 Metro base and LSI wiring diagram — manual transaxle

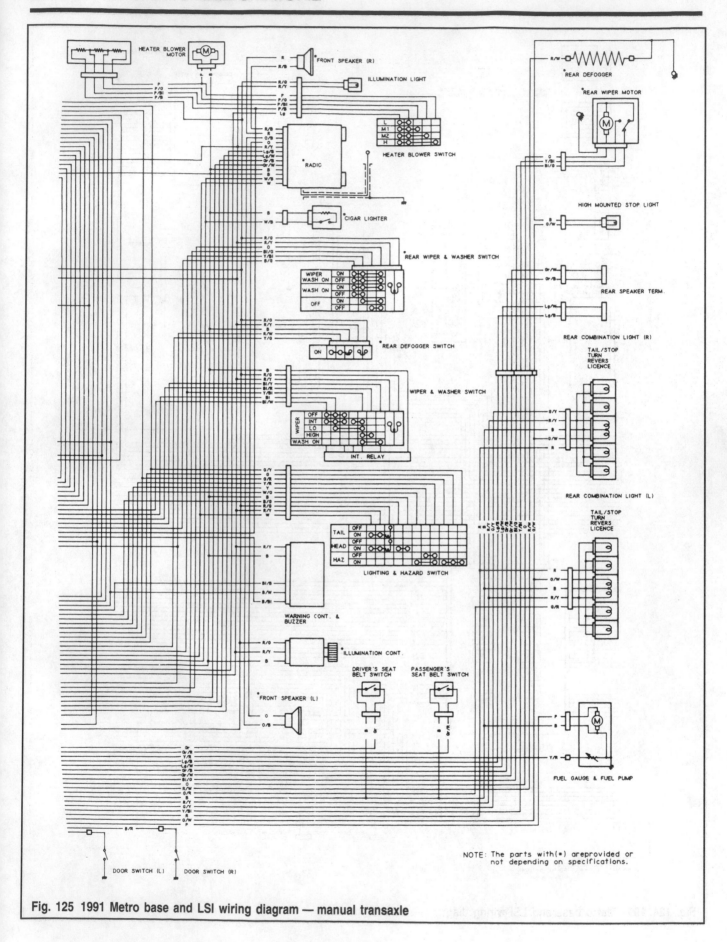

Fig. 125 1991 Metro base and LSI wiring diagram — manual transaxle

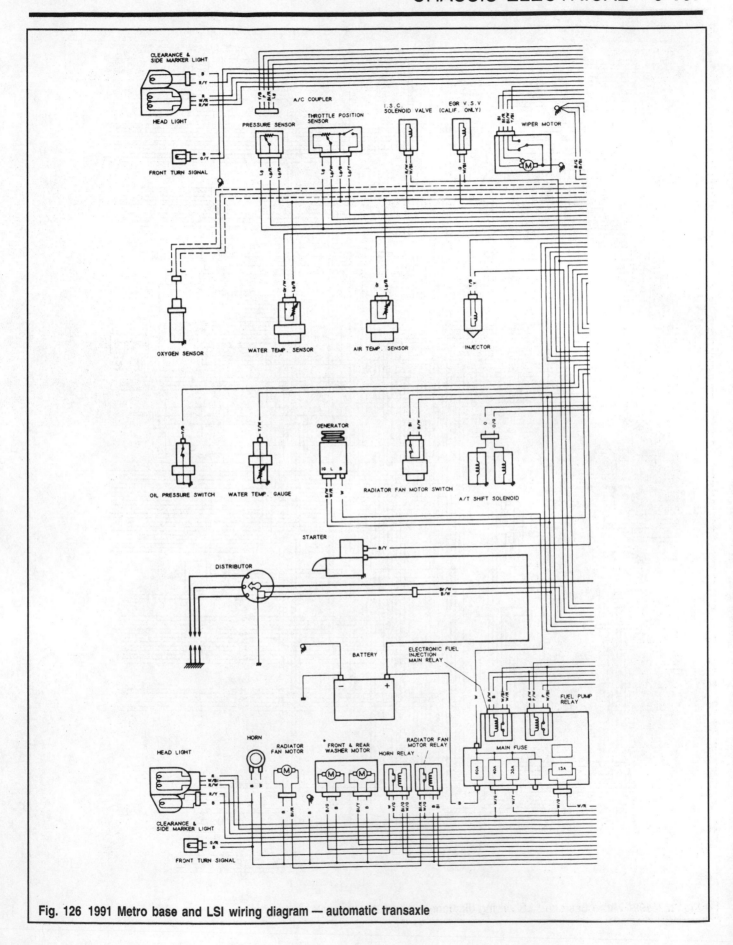

Fig. 126 1991 Metro base and LSI wiring diagram — automatic transaxle

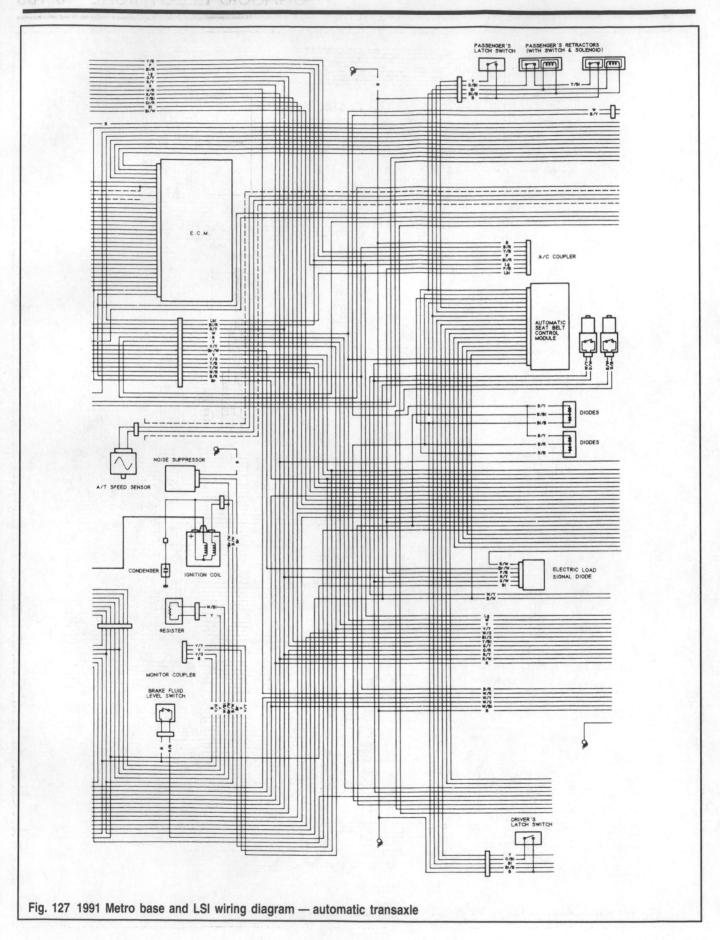

Fig. 127 1991 Metro base and LSI wiring diagram — automatic transaxle

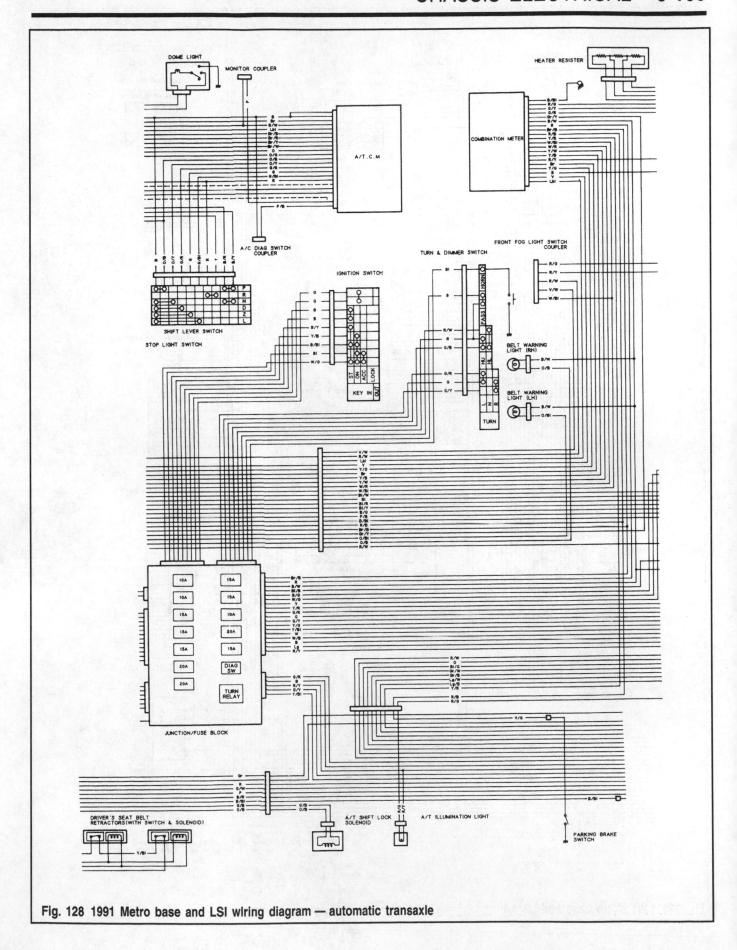

Fig. 128 1991 Metro base and LSI wiring diagram — automatic transaxle

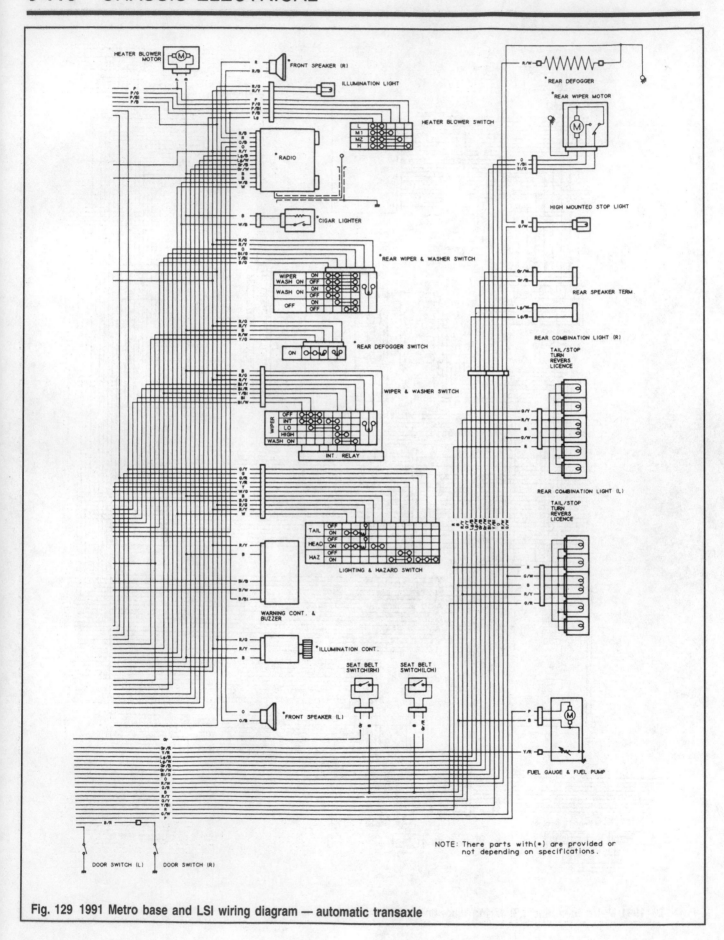

Fig. 129 1991 Metro base and LSI wiring diagram — automatic transaxle

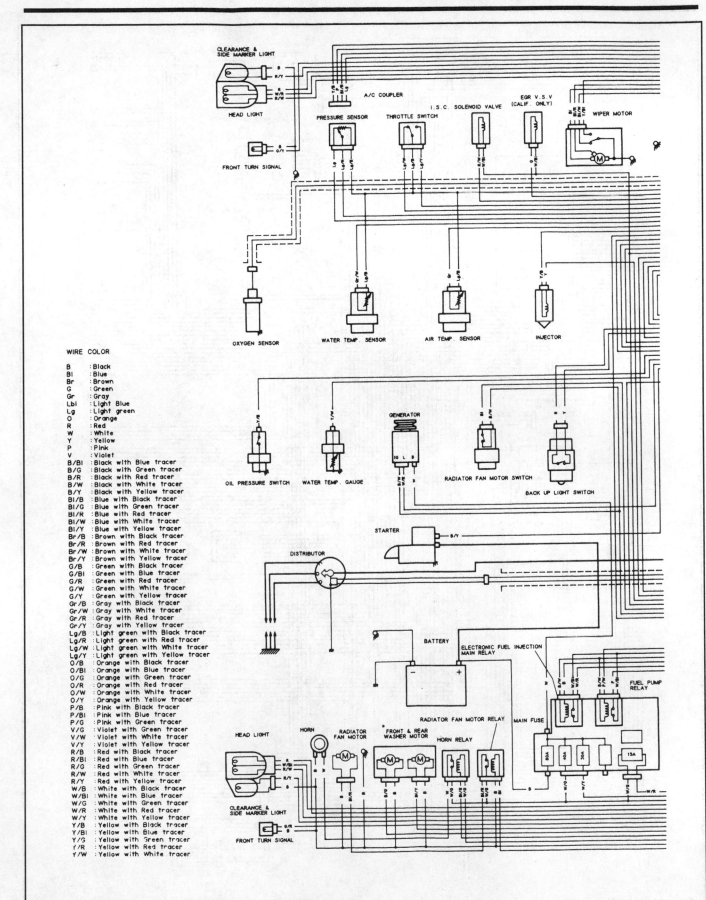

Fig. 130 1991 Metro XFI wiring diagram — manual transaxle

WIRE COLOR

B : Black
Bl : Blue
Br : Brown
G : Green
Gr : Gray
Lbl : Light Blue
Lg : Light green
O : Orange
R : Red
W : White
Y : Yellow
P : Pink
V : Violet
B/Bl : Black with Blue tracer
B/G : Black with Green tracer
B/R : Black with Red tracer
B/W : Black with White tracer
B/Y : Black with Yellow tracer
Bl/B : Blue with Black tracer
Bl/G : Blue with Green tracer
Bl/R : Blue with Red tracer
Bl/W : Blue with White tracer
Bl/Y : Blue with Yellow tracer
Br/B : Brown with Black tracer
Br/R : Brown with Red tracer
Br/W : Brown with White tracer
Br/Y : Brown with Yellow tracer
G/B : Green with Black tracer
G/Bl : Green with Blue tracer
G/R : Green with Red tracer
G/W : Green with White tracer
G/Y : Green with Yellow tracer
Gr/B : Gray with Black tracer
Gr/W : Gray with White tracer
Gr/R : Gray with Red tracer
Gr/Y : Gray with Yellow tracer
Lg/B : Light green with Black tracer
Lg/R : Light green with Red tracer
Lg/W : Light green with White tracer
Lg/Y : Light green with Yellow tracer
O/B : Orange with Black tracer
O/Bl : Orange with Blue tracer
O/G : Orange with Green tracer
O/R : Orange with Red tracer
O/W : Orange with White tracer
O/Y : Orange with Yellow tracer
P/B : Pink with Black tracer
P/Bl : Pink with Blue tracer
P/G : Pink with Green tracer
V/G : Violet with Green tracer
V/W : Violet with White tracer
V/Y : Violet with Yellow tracer
R/B : Red with Black tracer
R/Bl : Red with Blue tracer
R/G : Red with Green tracer
R/W : Red with White tracer
R/Y : Red with Yellow tracer
W/B : White with Black tracer
W/Bl : White with Blue tracer
W/G : White with Green tracer
W/R : White with Red tracer
W/Y : White with Yellow tracer
Y/B : Yellow with Black tracer
Y/Bl : Yellow with Blue tracer
Y/G : Yellow with Green tracer
Y/R : Yellow with Red tracer
Y/W : Yellow with White tracer

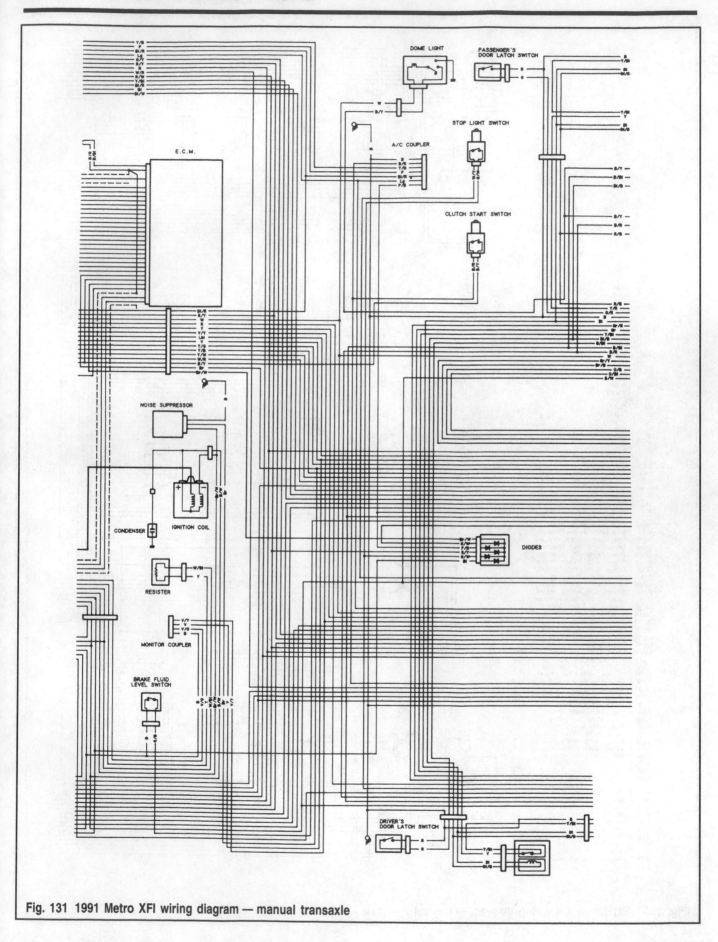

Fig. 131 1991 Metro XFI wiring diagram — manual transaxle

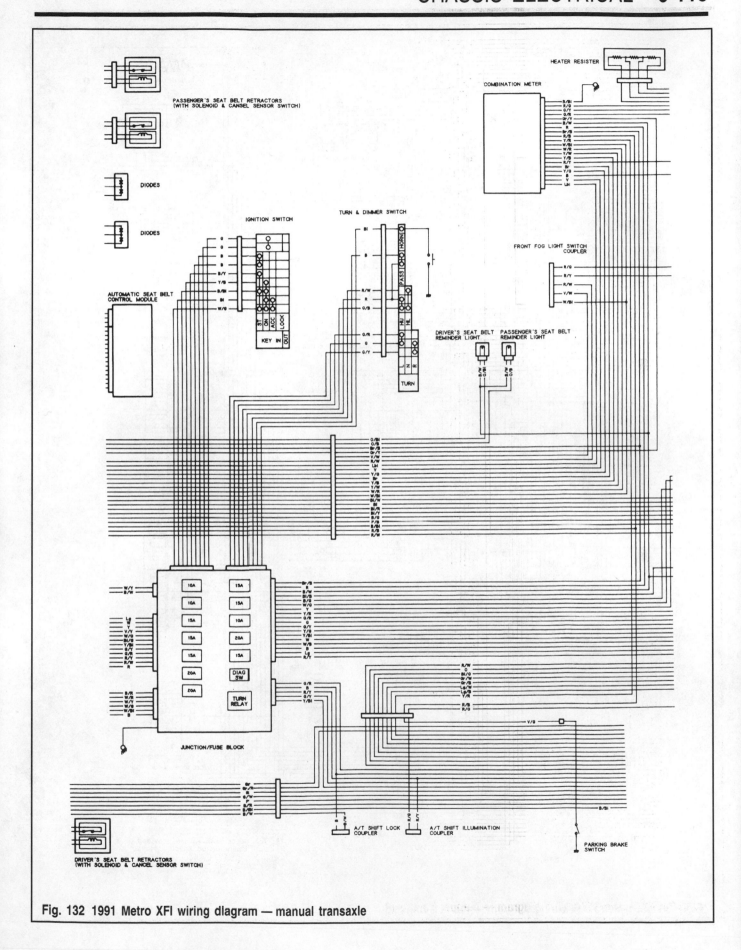

Fig. 132 1991 Metro XFI wiring diagram — manual transaxle

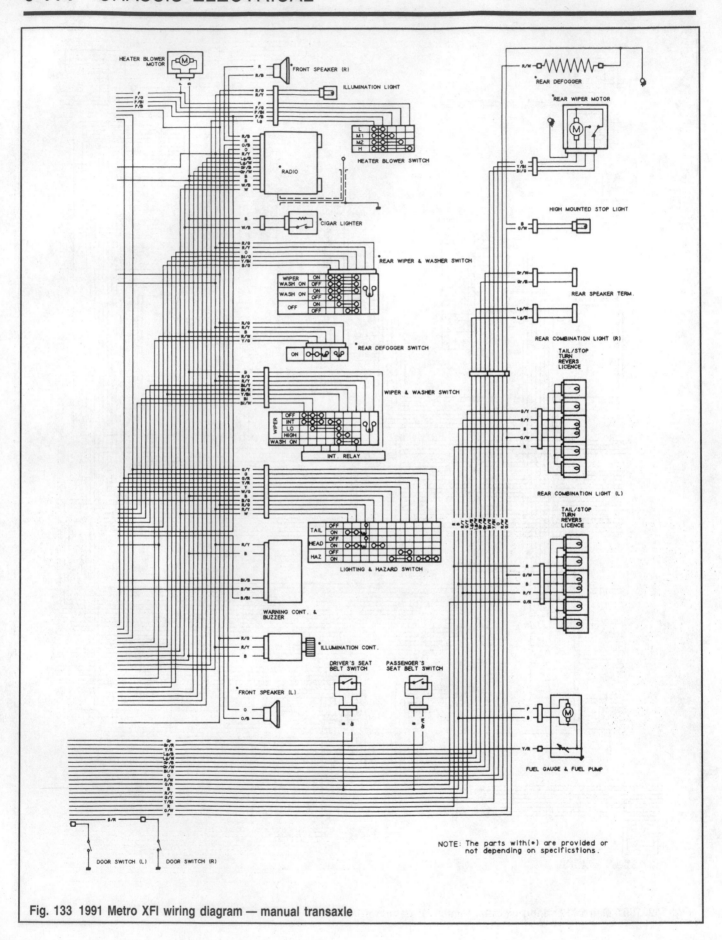

Fig. 133 1991 Metro XFi wiring diagram — manual transaxle

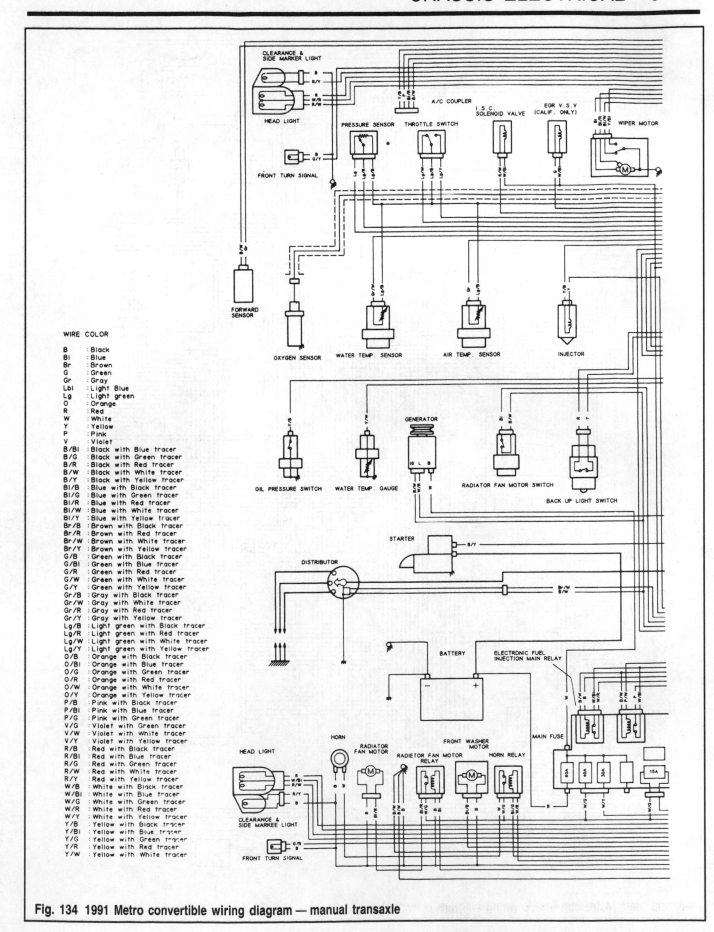

Fig. 134 1991 Metro convertible wiring diagram — manual transaxle

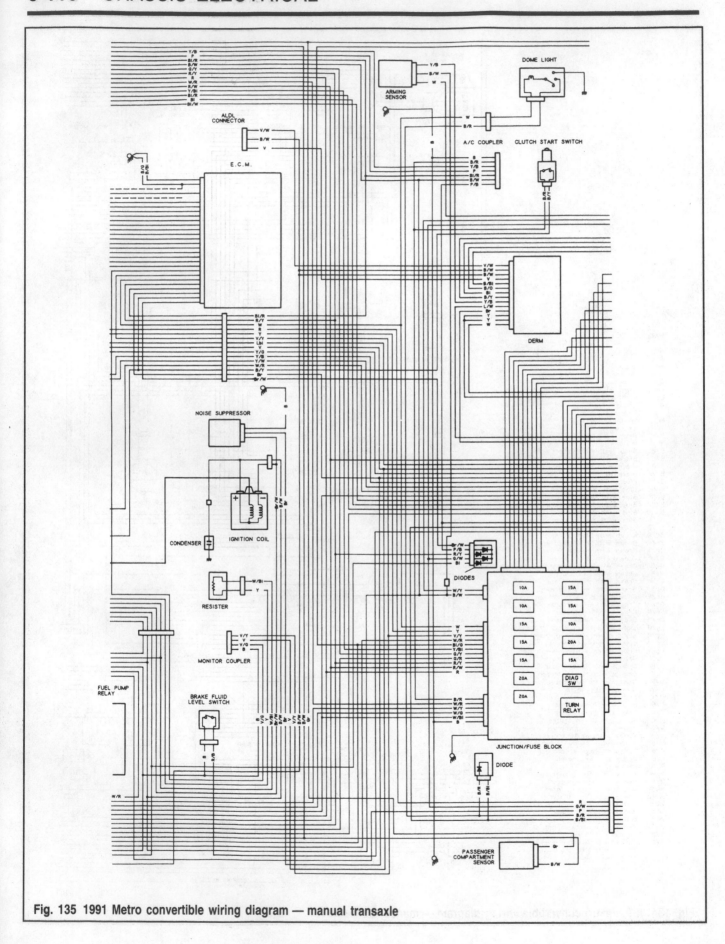

Fig. 135 1991 Metro convertible wiring diagram — manual transaxle

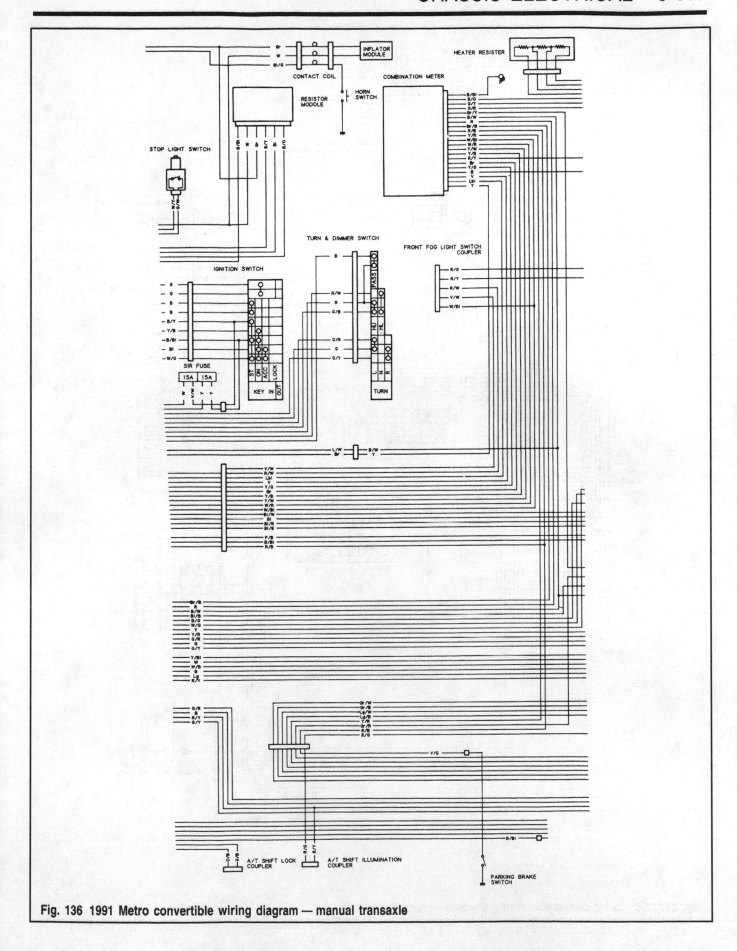

Fig. 136 1991 Metro convertible wiring diagram — manual transaxle

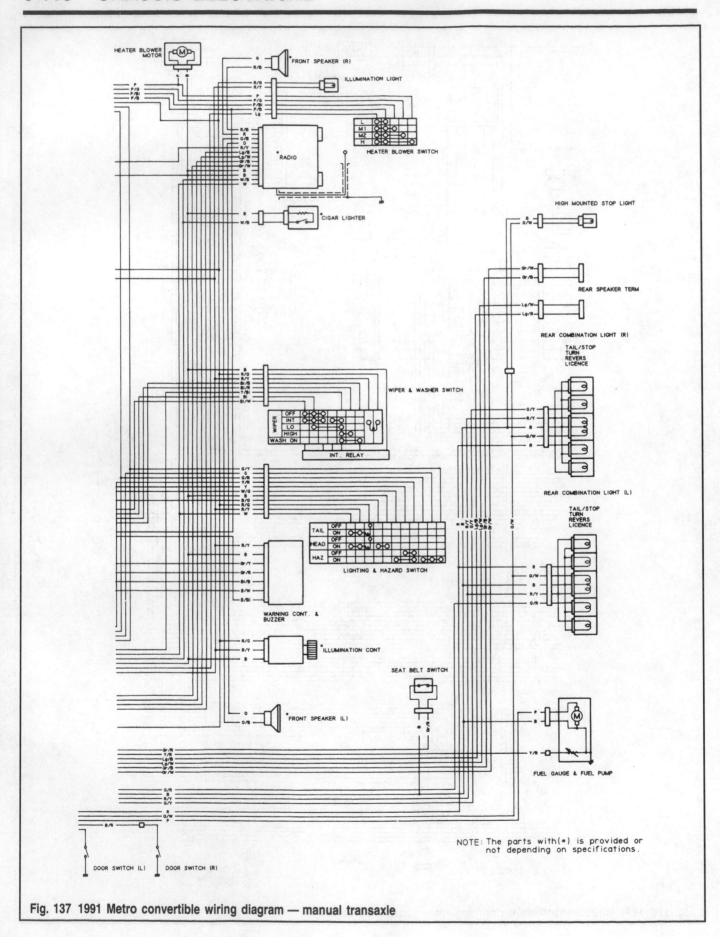

Fig. 137 1991 Metro convertible wiring diagram — manual transaxle

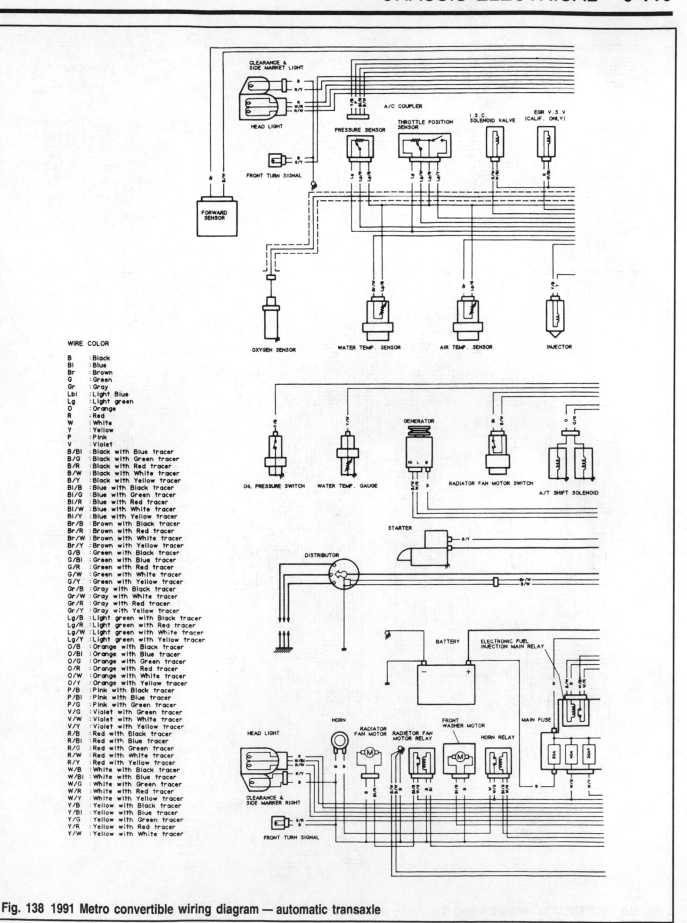

WIRE COLOR

B : Black
Bl : Blue
Br : Brown
G : Green
Gr : Gray
Lbl : Light Blue
Lg : Light green
O : Orange
R : Red
W : White
Y : Yellow
P : Pink
V : Violet
B/Bl : Black with Blue tracer
B/G : Black with Green tracer
B/R : Black with Red tracer
B/W : Black with White tracer
B/Y : Black with Yellow tracer
Bl/B : Blue with Black tracer
Bl/G : Blue with Green tracer
Bl/R : Blue with Red tracer
Bl/W : Blue with White tracer
Bl/Y : Blue with Yellow tracer
Br/B : Brown with Black tracer
Br/R : Brown with Red tracer
Br/W : Brown with White tracer
Br/Y : Brown with Yellow tracer
G/B : Green with Black tracer
G/Bl : Green with Blue tracer
G/R : Green with Red tracer
G/W : Green with White tracer
G/Y : Green with Yellow tracer
Gr/B : Gray with Black tracer
Gr/W : Gray with White tracer
Gr/R : Gray with Red tracer
Gr/Y : Gray with Yellow tracer
Lg/B : Light green with Black tracer
Lg/R : Light green with Red tracer
Lg/W : Light green with White tracer
Lg/Y : Light green with Yellow tracer
O/B : Orange with Black tracer
O/Bl : Orange with Blue tracer
O/G : Orange with Green tracer
O/R : Orange with Red tracer
O/W : Orange with White tracer
O/Y : Orange with Yellow tracer
P/B : Pink with Black tracer
P/Bl : Pink with Blue tracer
P/G : Pink with Green tracer
V/G : Violet with Green tracer
V/W : Violet with White tracer
V/Y : Violet with Yellow tracer
R/B : Red with Black tracer
R/Bl : Red with Blue tracer
R/G : Red with Green tracer
R/W : Red with White tracer
R/Y : Red with Yellow tracer
W/B : White with Black tracer
W/Bl : White with Blue tracer
W/G : White with Green tracer
W/R : White with Red tracer
W/Y : White with Yellow tracer
Y/B : Yellow with Black tracer
Y/Bl : Yellow with Blue tracer
Y/G : Yellow with Green tracer
Y/R : Yellow with Red tracer
Y/W : Yellow with White tracer

Fig. 138 1991 Metro convertible wiring diagram — automatic transaxle

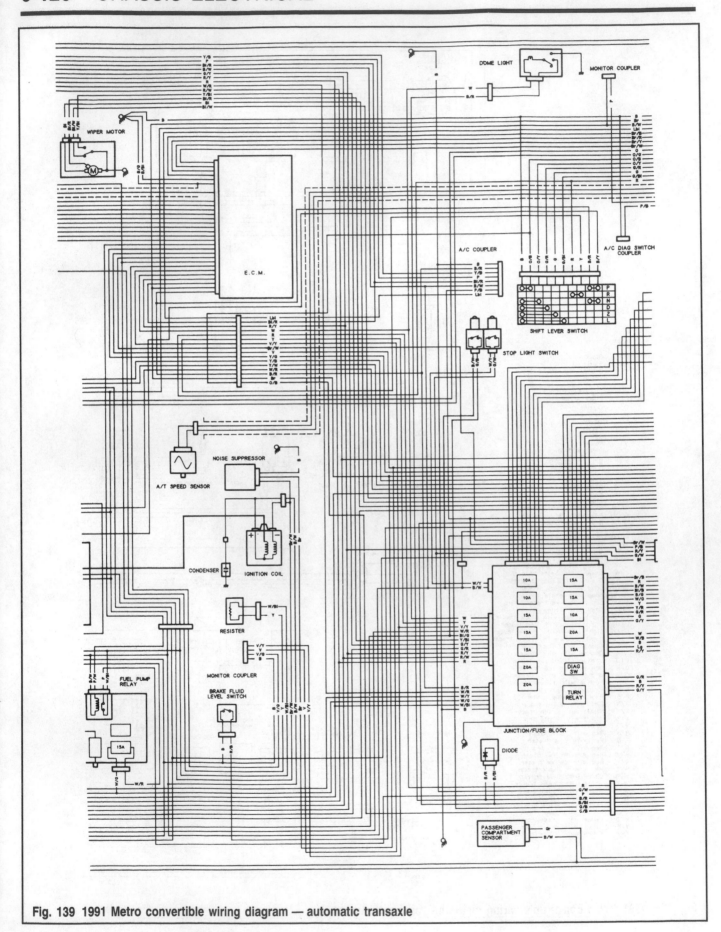

Fig. 139 1991 Metro convertible wiring diagram — automatic transaxle

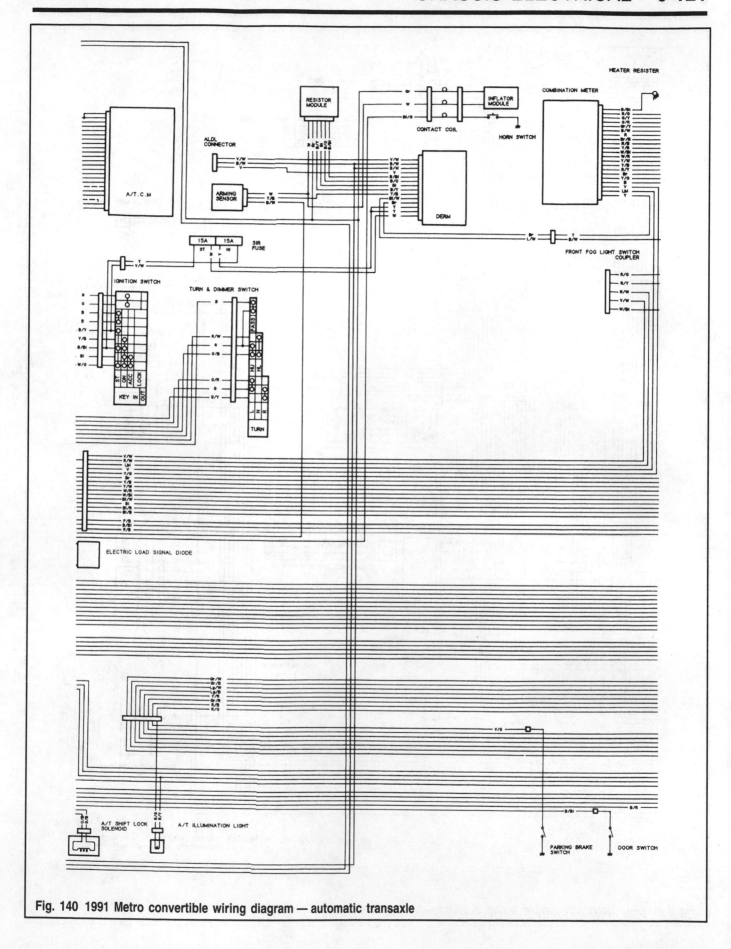

Fig. 140 1991 Metro convertible wiring diagram — automatic transaxle

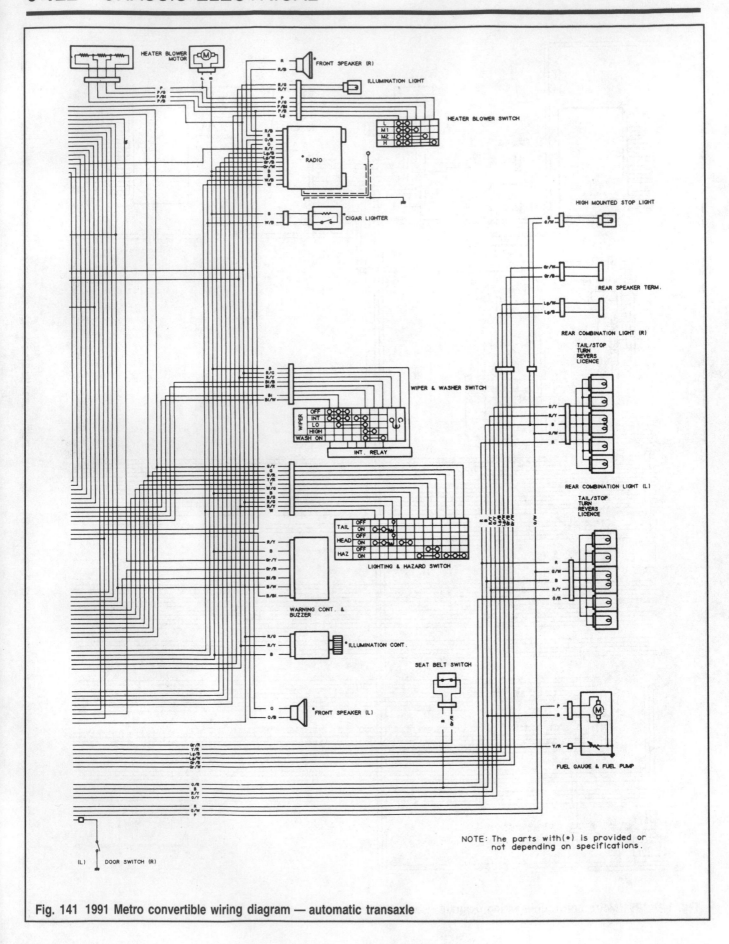

Fig. 141 1991 Metro convertible wiring diagram — automatic transaxle

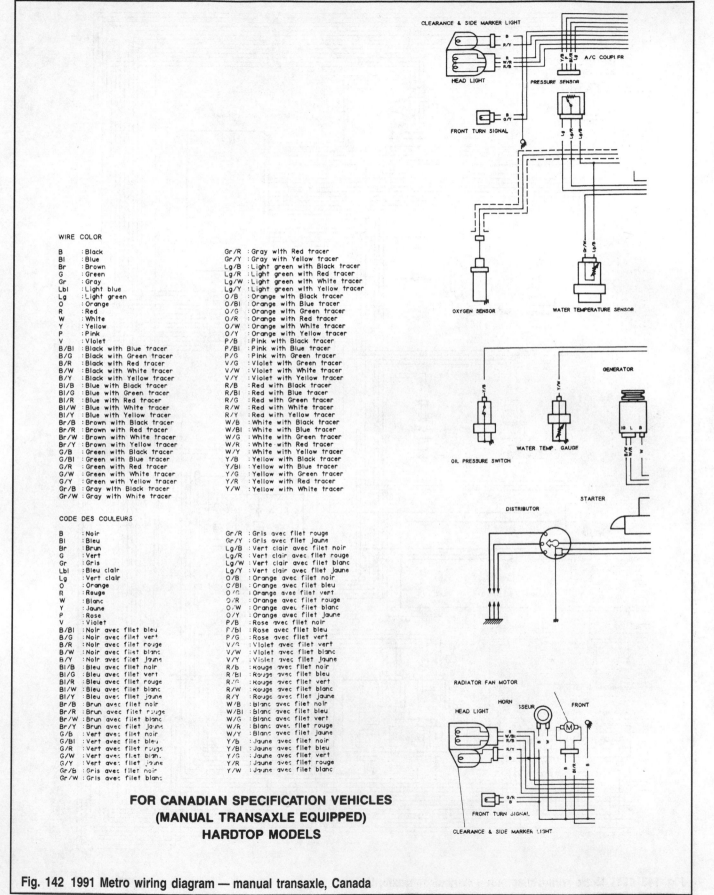

WIRE COLOR

B	: Black	Gr/R	: Gray with Red tracer
Bl	: Blue	Gr/Y	: Gray with Yellow tracer
Br	: Brown	Lg/B	: Light green with Black tracer
G	: Green	Lg/R	: Light green with Red tracer
Gr	: Gray	Lg/W	: Light green with White tracer
Lbl	: Light blue	Lg/Y	: Light green with Yellow tracer
Lg	: Light green	O/B	: Orange with Black tracer
O	: Orange	O/Bl	: Orange with Blue tracer
R	: Red	O/G	: Orange with Green tracer
W	: White	O/R	: Orange with Red tracer
Y	: Yellow	O/W	: Orange with White tracer
P	: Pink	O/Y	: Orange with Yellow tracer
V	: Violet	P/B	: Pink with Black tracer
B/Bl	: Black with Blue tracer	P/Bl	: Pink with Blue tracer
B/G	: Black with Green tracer	P/G	: Pink with Green tracer
B/R	: Black with Red tracer	V/G	: Violet with Green tracer
B/W	: Black with White tracer	V/W	: Violet with White tracer
B/Y	: Black with Yellow tracer	V/Y	: Violet with Yellow tracer
Bl/B	: Blue with Black tracer	R/B	: Red with Black tracer
Bl/G	: Blue with Green tracer	R/Bl	: Red with Blue tracer
Bl/R	: Blue with Red tracer	R/G	: Red with Green tracer
Bl/W	: Blue with White tracer	R/W	: Red with White tracer
Bl/Y	: Blue with Yellow tracer	R/Y	: Red with Yellow tracer
Br/B	: Brown with Black tracer	W/B	: White with Black tracer
Br/R	: Brown with Red tracer	W/Bl	: White with Blue tracer
Br/W	: Brown with White tracer	W/G	: White with Green tracer
Br/Y	: Brown with Yellow tracer	W/R	: White with Red tracer
G/B	: Green with Black tracer	W/Y	: White with Yellow tracer
G/Bl	: Green with Blue tracer	Y/B	: Yellow with Black tracer
G/R	: Green with Red tracer	Y/Bl	: Yellow with Blue tracer
G/W	: Green with White tracer	Y/G	: Yellow with Green tracer
G/Y	: Green with Yellow tracer	Y/R	: Yellow with Red tracer
Gr/B	: Gray with Black tracer	Y/W	: Yellow with White tracer
Gr/W	: Gray with White tracer		

CODE DES COULEURS

B	: Noir	Gr/R	: Gris avec filet rouge
Bl	: Bleu	Gr/Y	: Gris avec filet jaune
Br	: Brun	Lg/B	: Vert clair avec filet noir
G	: Vert	Lg/R	: Vert clair avec filet rouge
Gr	: Gris	Lg/W	: Vert clair avec filet blanc
Lbl	: Bleu clair	Lg/Y	: Vert clair avec filet jaune
Lg	: Vert clair	O/B	: Orange avec filet noir
O	: Orange	O/Bl	: Orange avec filet bleu
R	: Rouge	O/G	: Orange avec filet vert
W	: Blanc	O/R	: Orange avec filet rouge
Y	: Jaune	O/W	: Orange avec filet blanc
P	: Rose	O/Y	: Orange avec filet jaune
V	: Violet	P/B	: Rose avec filet noir
B/Bl	: Noir avec filet bleu	P/Bl	: Rose avec filet bleu
B/G	: Noir avec filet vert	P/G	: Rose avec filet vert
B/R	: Noir avec filet rouge	V/G	: Violet avec filet vert
B/W	: Noir avec filet blanc	V/W	: Violet avec filet blanc
B/Y	: Noir avec filet jaune	V/Y	: Violet avec filet jaune
Bl/B	: Bleu avec filet noir	R/b	: Rouge avec filet noir
Bl/G	: Bleu avec filet vert	R/Bl	: Rouge avec filet bleu
Bl/R	: Bleu avec filet rouge	R/G	: Rouge avec filet vert
Bl/W	: Bleu avec filet blanc	R/W	: Rouge avec filet blanc
Bl/Y	: Bleu avec filet jaune	R/Y	: Rouge avec filet jaune
Br/B	: Brun avec filet noir	W/B	: Blanc avec filet noir
Br/R	: Brun avec filet rouge	W/Bl	: Blanc avec filet bleu
Br/W	: Brun avec filet blanc	W/G	: Blanc avec filet vert
Br/Y	: Brun avec filet jaune	W/R	: Blanc avec filet rouge
G/B	: Vert avec filet noir	W/Y	: Blanc avec filet jaune
G/Bl	: Vert avec filet bleu	Y/b	: Jaune avec filet noir
G/R	: Vert avec filet rouge	Y/Bl	: Jaune avec filet bleu
G/W	: Vert avec filet blanc	Y/G	: Jaune avec filet vert
G/Y	: Vert avec filet jaune	Y/R	: Jaune avec filet rouge
Gr/B	: Gris avec filet noir	Y/W	: Jaune avec filet blanc
Gr/W	: Gris avec filet blanc		

**FOR CANADIAN SPECIFICATION VEHICLES
(MANUAL TRANSAXLE EQUIPPED)
HARDTOP MODELS**

Fig. 142 1991 Metro wiring diagram — manual transaxle, Canada

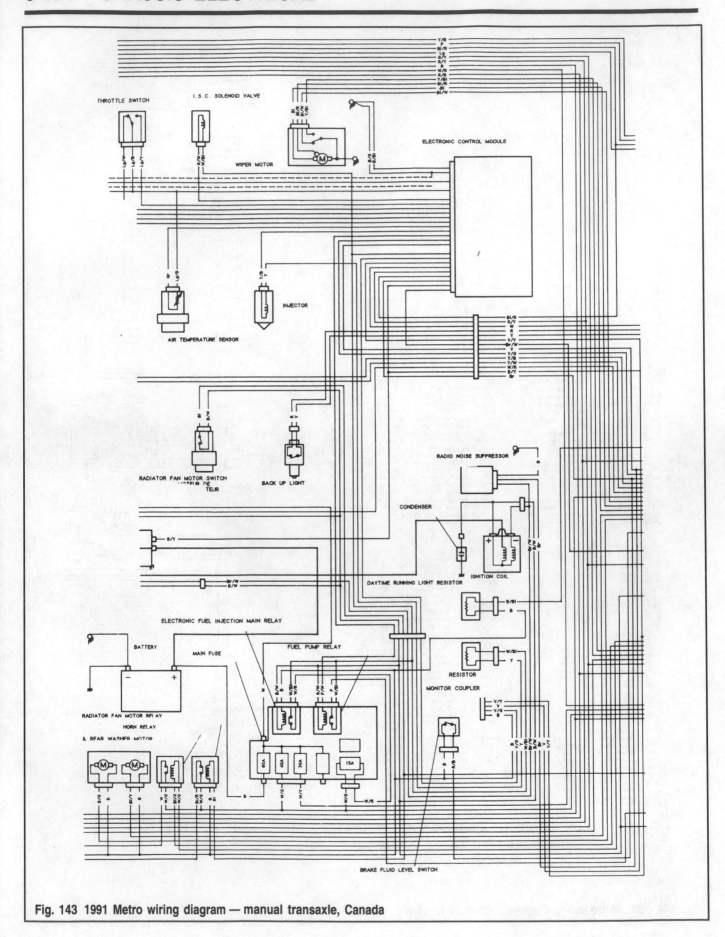

Fig. 143 1991 Metro wiring diagram — manual transaxle, Canada

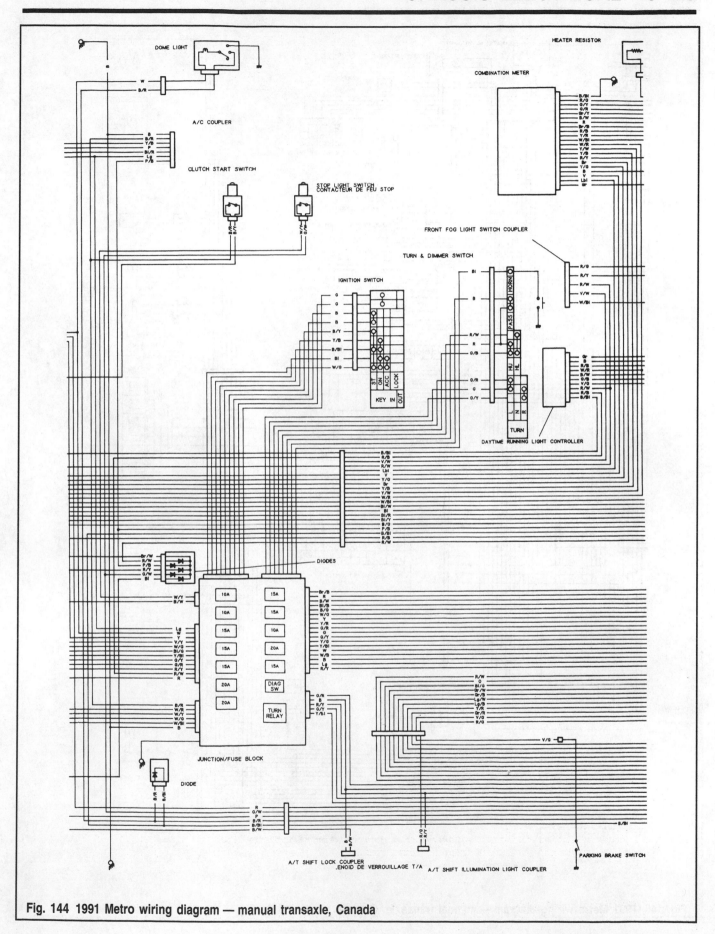

Fig. 144 1991 Metro wiring diagram — manual transaxle, Canada

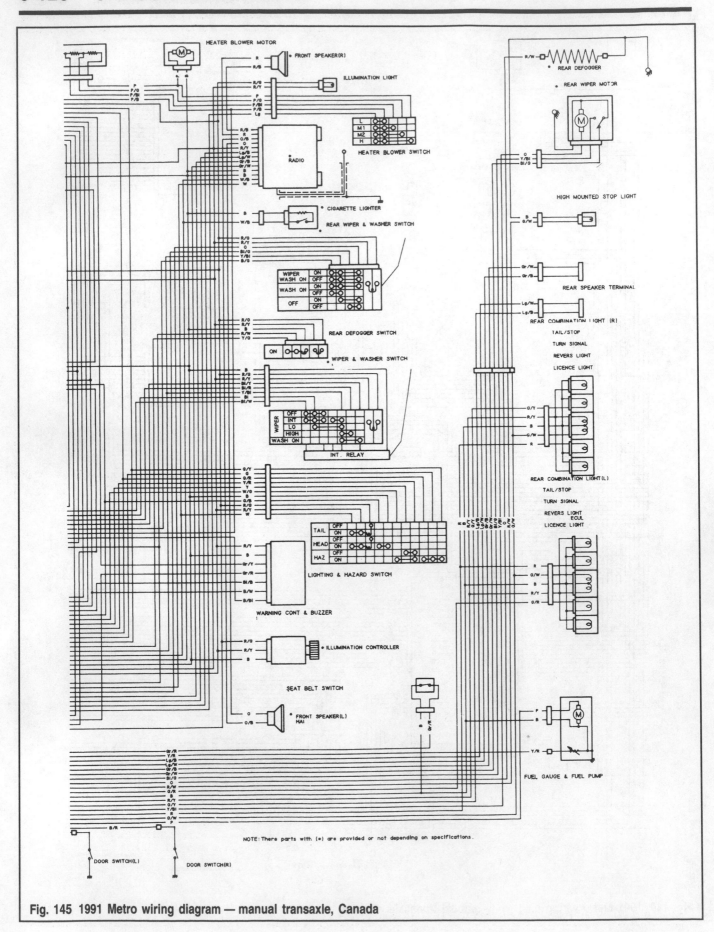

Fig. 145 1991 Metro wiring diagram — manual transaxle, Canada

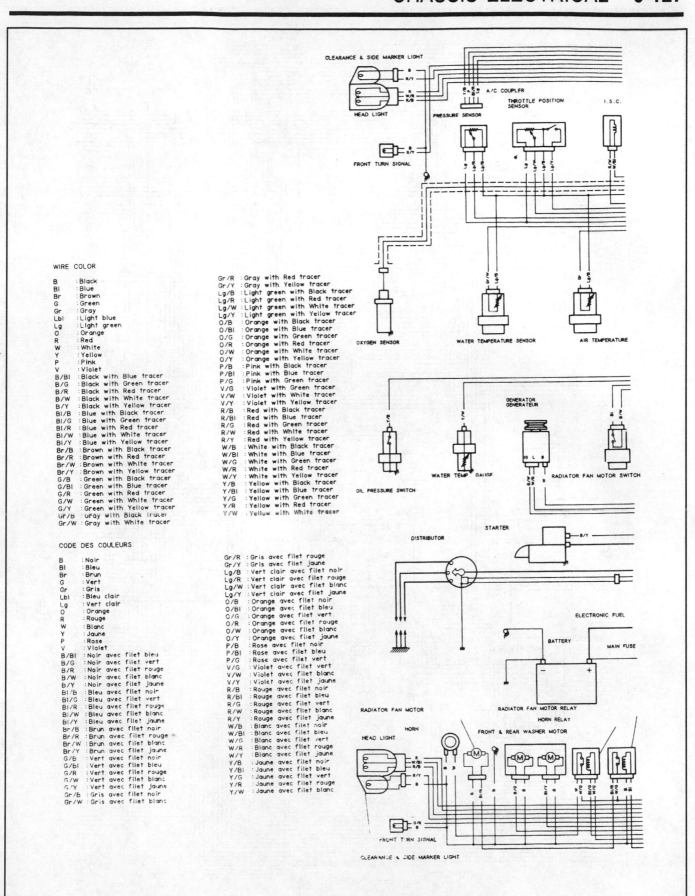

WIRE COLOR

B	: Black
Bl	: Blue
Br	: Brown
G	: Green
Gr	: Gray
Lbl	: Light blue
Lg	: Light green
O	: Orange
R	: Red
W	: White
Y	: Yellow
P	: Pink
V	: Violet
B/Bl	: Black with Blue tracer
B/G	: Black with Green tracer
B/R	: Black with Red tracer
B/W	: Black with White tracer
B/Y	: Black with Yellow tracer
Bl/B	: Blue with Black tracer
Bl/G	: Blue with Green tracer
Bl/R	: Blue with Red tracer
Bl/W	: Blue with White tracer
Bl/Y	: Blue with Yellow tracer
Br/B	: Brown with Black tracer
Br/R	: Brown with Red tracer
Br/W	: Brown with White tracer
Br/Y	: Brown with Yellow tracer
G/B	: Green with Black tracer
G/Bl	: Green with Blue tracer
G/R	: Green with Red tracer
G/W	: Green with White tracer
G/Y	: Green with Yellow tracer
Gr/B	: Gray with Black tracer
Gr/W	: Gray with White tracer

Gr/R	: Gray with Red tracer
Gr/Y	: Gray with Yellow tracer
Lg/B	: Light green with Black tracer
Lg/R	: Light green with Red tracer
Lg/W	: Light green with White tracer
Lg/Y	: Light green with Yellow tracer
O/B	: Orange with Black tracer
O/Bl	: Orange with Blue tracer
O/G	: Orange with Green tracer
O/R	: Orange with Red tracer
O/W	: Orange with White tracer
O/Y	: Orange with Yellow tracer
P/B	: Pink with Black tracer
P/Bl	: Pink with Blue tracer
P/G	: Pink with Green tracer
V/G	: Violet with Green tracer
V/W	: Violet with White tracer
V/Y	: Violet with Yellow tracer
R/B	: Red with Black tracer
R/Bl	: Red with Blue tracer
R/G	: Red with Green tracer
R/W	: Red with White tracer
R/Y	: Red with Yellow tracer
W/B	: White with Black tracer
W/Bl	: White with Blue tracer
W/G	: White with Green tracer
W/R	: White with Red tracer
W/Y	: White with Yellow tracer
Y/B	: Yellow with Black tracer
Y/Bl	: Yellow with Blue tracer
Y/G	: Yellow with Green tracer
Y/R	: Yellow with Red tracer
Y/W	: Yellow with White tracer

CODE DES COULEURS

B	: Noir
Bl	: Bleu
Br	: Brun
G	: Vert
Gr	: Gris
Lbl	: Bleu clair
Lg	: Vert clair
O	: Orange
R	: Rouge
W	: Blanc
Y	: Jaune
P	: Rose
V	: Violet
B/Bl	: Noir avec filet bleu
B/G	: Noir avec filet vert
B/R	: Noir avec filet rouge
B/W	: Noir avec filet blanc
B/Y	: Noir avec filet jaune
Bl/B	: Bleu avec filet noir
Bl/G	: Bleu avec filet vert
Bl/R	: Bleu avec filet rouge
Bl/W	: Bleu avec filet blanc
Bl/Y	: Bleu avec filet jaune
Br/B	: Brun avec filet noir
Br/R	: Brun avec filet rouge
Br/W	: Brun avec filet blanc
Br/Y	: Brun avec filet jaune
G/B	: Vert avec filet noir
G/Bl	: Vert avec filet bleu
G/R	: Vert avec filet rouge
G/W	: Vert avec filet blanc
G/Y	: Vert avec filet jaune
Gr/B	: Gris avec filet noir
Gr/W	: Gris avec filet blanc

Gr/R	: Gris avec filet rouge
Gr/Y	: Gris avec filet jaune
Lg/B	: Vert clair avec filet noir
Lg/R	: Vert clair avec filet rouge
Lg/W	: Vert clair avec filet blanc
Lg/Y	: Vert clair avec filet jaune
O/B	: Orange avec filet noir
O/Bl	: Orange avec filet bleu
O/G	: Orange avec filet vert
O/R	: Orange avec filet rouge
O/W	: Orange avec filet blanc
O/Y	: Orange avec filet jaune
P/B	: Rose avec filet noir
P/Bl	: Rose avec filet bleu
P/G	: Rose avec filet vert
V/G	: Violet avec filet vert
V/W	: Violet avec filet blanc
V/Y	: Violet avec filet jaune
R/B	: Rouge avec filet noir
R/Bl	: Rouge avec filet bleu
R/G	: Rouge avec filet vert
R/W	: Rouge avec filet blanc
R/Y	: Rouge avec filet jaune
W/B	: Blanc avec filet noir
W/Bl	: Blanc avec filet bleu
W/G	: Blanc avec filet vert
W/R	: Blanc avec filet rouge
W/Y	: Blanc avec filet jaune
Y/B	: Jaune avec filet noir
Y/Bl	: Jaune avec filet bleu
Y/G	: Jaune avec filet vert
Y/R	: Jaune avec filet rouge
Y/W	: Jaune avec filet blanc

Fig. 146 1991 Metro wiring diagram — automatic transaxle, Canada

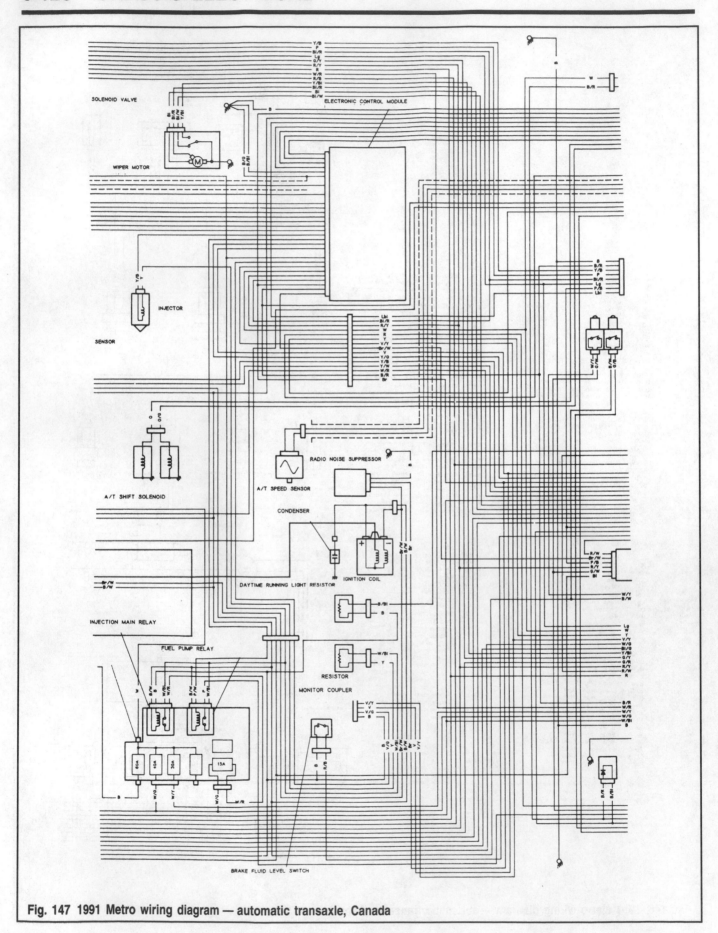

Fig. 147 1991 Metro wiring diagram — automatic transaxle, Canada

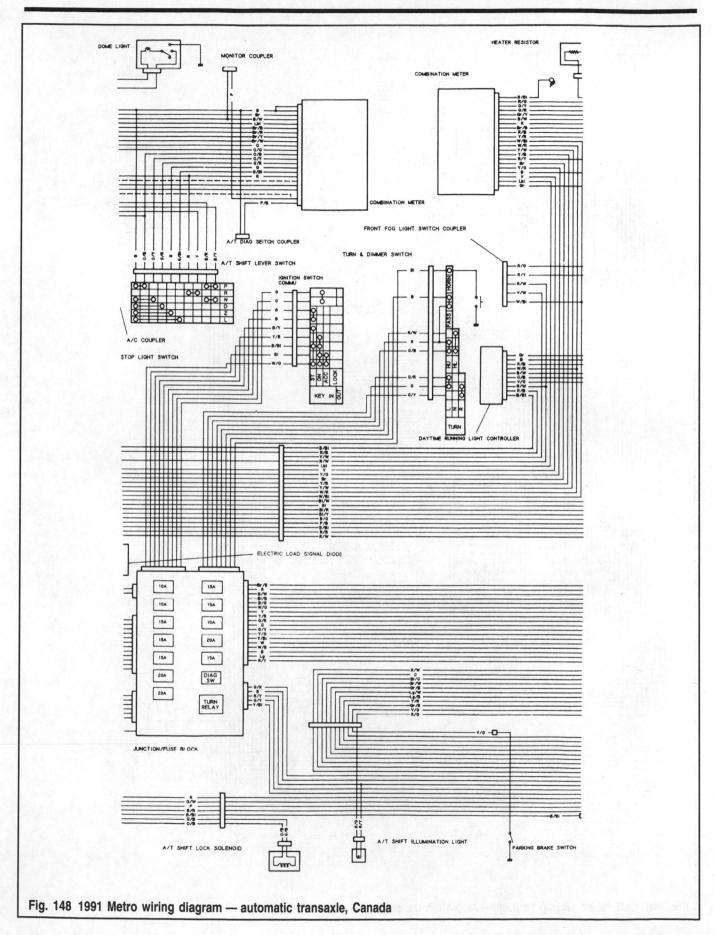

Fig. 148 1991 Metro wiring diagram — automatic transaxle, Canada

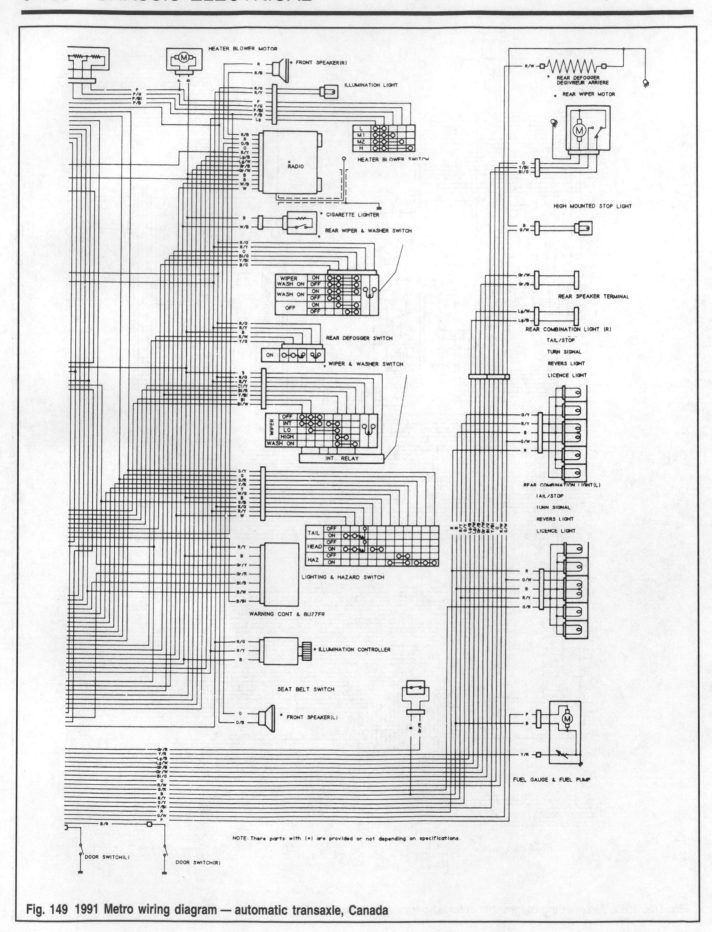

Fig. 149 1991 Metro wiring diagram — automatic transaxle, Canada

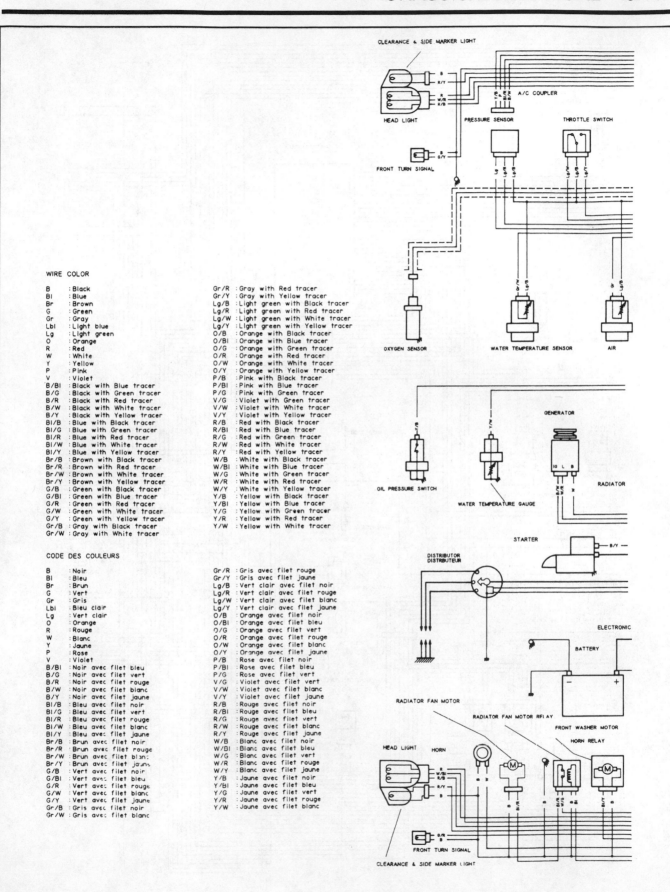

WIRE COLOR

B	: Black	Gr/R	: Gray with Red tracer
Bl	: Blue	Gr/Y	: Gray with Yellow tracer
Br	: Brown	Lg/B	: Light green with Black tracer
G	: Green	Lg/R	: Light green with Red tracer
Gr	: Gray	Lg/W	: Light green with White tracer
Lbl	: Light blue	Lg/Y	: Light green with Yellow tracer
Lg	: Light green	O/B	: Orange with Black tracer
O	: Orange	O/Bl	: Orange with Blue tracer
R	: Red	O/G	: Orange with Green tracer
W	: White	O/R	: Orange with Red tracer
Y	: Yellow	O/W	: Orange with White tracer
P	: Pink	O/Y	: Orange with Yellow tracer
V	: Violet	P/B	: Pink with Black tracer
B/Bl	: Black with Blue tracer	P/Bl	: Pink with Blue tracer
B/G	: Black with Green tracer	P/G	: Pink with Green tracer
B/R	: Black with Red tracer	V/G	: Violet with Green tracer
B/W	: Black with White tracer	V/W	: Violet with White tracer
B/Y	: Black with Yellow tracer	V/Y	: Violet with Yellow tracer
Bl/B	: Blue with Black tracer	R/B	: Red with Black tracer
Bl/G	: Blue with Green tracer	R/Bl	: Red with Blue tracer
Bl/R	: Blue with Red tracer	R/G	: Red with Green tracer
Bl/W	: Blue with White tracer	R/W	: Red with White tracer
Bl/Y	: Blue with Yellow tracer	R/Y	: Red with Yellow tracer
Br/B	: Brown with Black tracer	W/B	: White with Black tracer
Br/R	: Brown with Red tracer	W/Bl	: White with Blue tracer
Br/W	: Brown with White tracer	W/G	: White with Green tracer
Br/Y	: Brown with Yellow tracer	W/R	: White with Red tracer
G/B	: Green with Black tracer	W/Y	: White with Yellow tracer
G/Bl	: Green with Blue tracer	Y/B	: Yellow with Black tracer
G/R	: Green with Red tracer	Y/Bl	: Yellow with Blue tracer
G/W	: Green with White tracer	Y/G	: Yellow with Green tracer
G/Y	: Green with Yellow tracer	Y/R	: Yellow with Red tracer
Gr/B	: Gray with Black tracer	Y/W	: Yellow with White tracer
Gr/W	: Gray with White tracer		

CODE DES COULEURS

B	: Noir	Gr/R	: Gris avec filet rouge
Bl	: Bleu	Gr/Y	: Gris avec filet jaune
Br	: Brun	Lg/B	: Vert clair avec filet noir
G	: Vert	Lg/R	: Vert clair avec filet rouge
Gr	: Gris	Lg/W	: Vert clair avec filet blanc
Lbl	: Bleu clair	Lg/Y	: Vert clair avec filet jaune
Lg	: Vert clair	O/B	: Orange avec filet noir
O	: Orange	O/Bl	: Orange avec filet bleu
R	: Rouge	O/G	: Orange avec filet vert
W	: Blanc	O/R	: Orange avec filet rouge
Y	: Jaune	O/W	: Orange avec filet blanc
P	: Rose	O/Y	: Orange avec filet jaune
V	: Violet	P/B	: Rose avec filet noir
B/Bl	: Noir avec filet bleu	P/Bl	: Rose avec filet bleu
B/G	: Noir avec filet vert	P/G	: Rose avec filet vert
B/R	: Noir avec filet rouge	V/G	: Violet avec filet vert
B/W	: Noir avec filet blanc	V/W	: Violet avec filet blanc
B/Y	: Noir avec filet jaune	V/Y	: Violet avec filet jaune
Bl/B	: Bleu avec filet noir	R/B	: Rouge avec filet noir
Bl/G	: Bleu avec filet vert	R/Bl	: Rouge avec filet bleu
Bl/R	: Bleu avec filet rouge	R/G	: Rouge avec filet vert
Bl/W	: Bleu avec filet blanc	R/W	: Rouge avec filet blanc
Bl/Y	: Bleu avec filet jaune	R/Y	: Rouge avec filet jaune
Br/B	: Brun avec filet noir	W/B	: Blanc avec filet noir
Br/R	: Brun avec filet rouge	W/Bl	: Blanc avec filet bleu
Br/W	: Brun avec filet blanc	W/G	: Blanc avec filet vert
Br/Y	: Brun avec filet jaune	W/R	: Blanc avec filet rouge
G/B	: Vert avec filet noir	W/Y	: Blanc avec filet jaune
G/Bl	: Vert avec filet bleu	Y/B	: Jaune avec filet noir
G/R	: Vert avec filet rouge	Y/Bl	: Jaune avec filet bleu
G/W	: Vert avec filet blanc	Y/G	: Jaune avec filet vert
G/Y	: Vert avec filet jaune	Y/R	: Jaune avec filet rouge
Gr/B	: Gris avec filet noir	Y/W	: Jaune avec filet blanc
Gr/W	: Gris avec filet blanc		

Fig. 150 1991 Metro convertible wiring diagram — manual transaxle, Canada

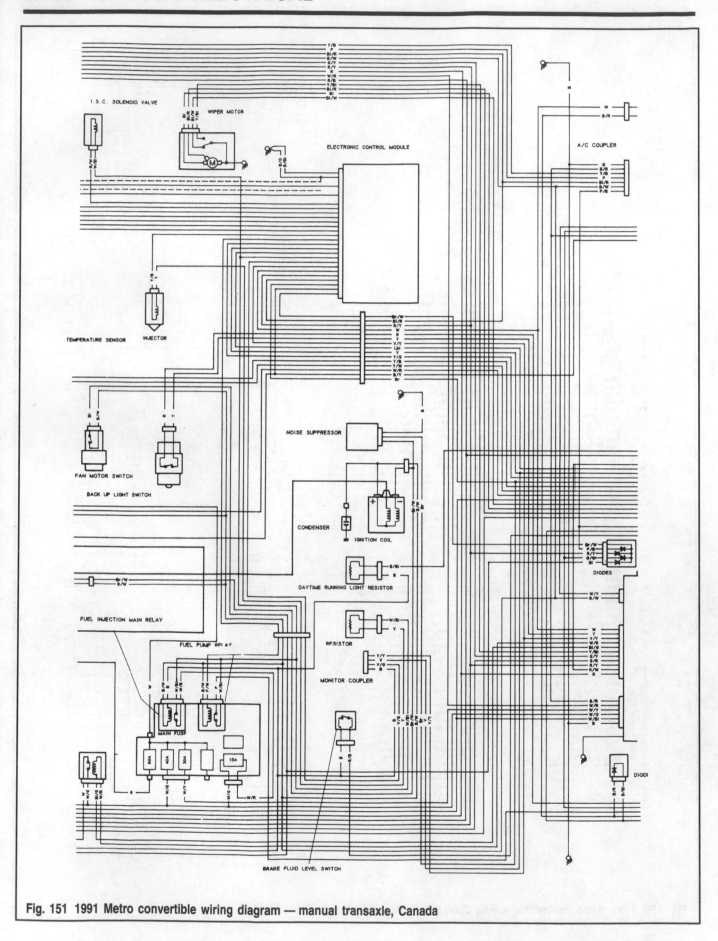

Fig. 151 1991 Metro convertible wiring diagram — manual transaxle, Canada

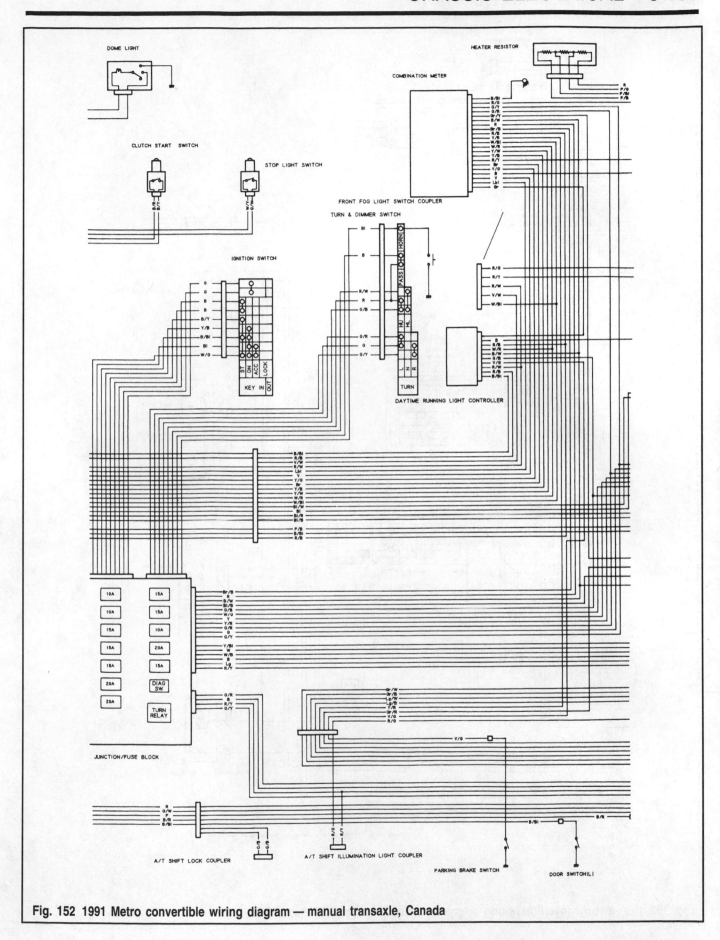

Fig. 152 1991 Metro convertible wiring diagram — manual transaxle, Canada

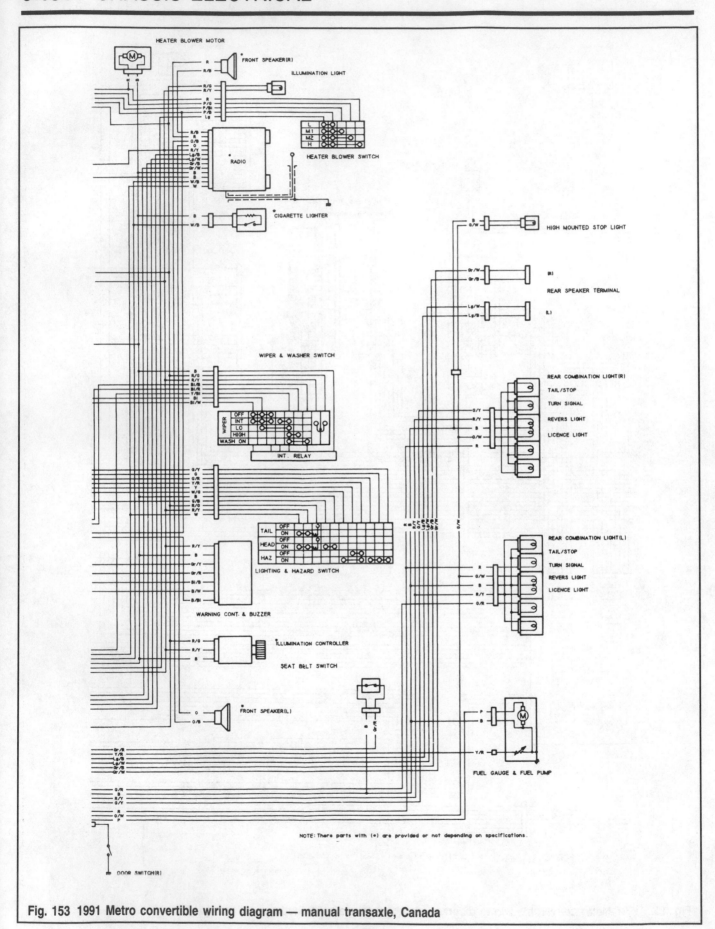

Fig. 153 1991 Metro convertible wiring diagram — manual transaxle, Canada

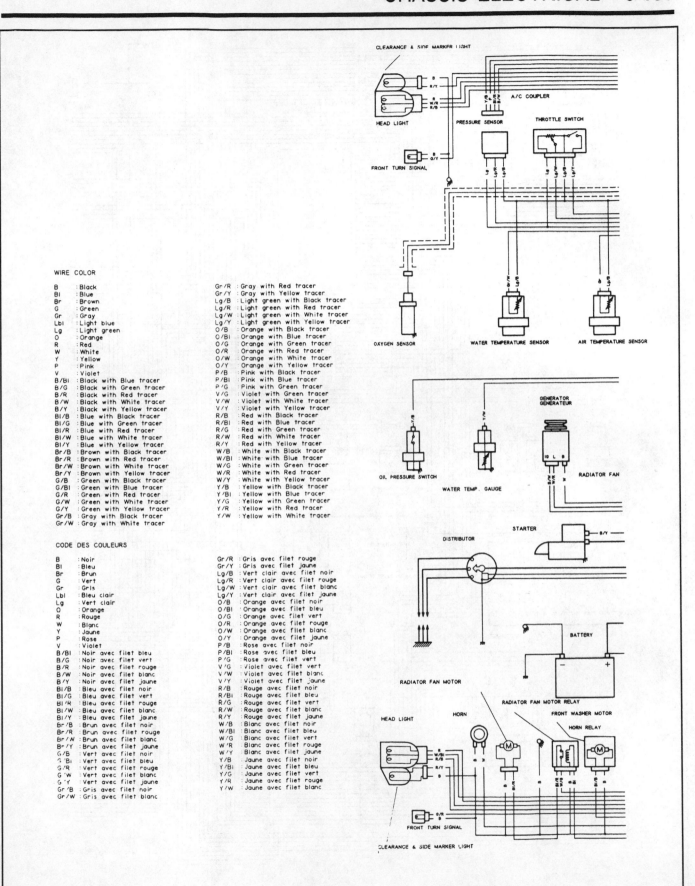

WIRE COLOR

B : Black	Gr/R : Gray with Red tracer
Bl : Blue	Gr/Y : Gray with Yellow tracer
Br : Brown	Lg/B : Light green with Black tracer
G : Green	Lg/R : Light green with Red tracer
Gr : Gray	Lg/W : Light green with White tracer
Lbl : Light blue	Lg/Y : Light green with Yellow tracer
Lg : Light green	O/B : Orange with Black tracer
O : Orange	O/Bl : Orange with Blue tracer
R : Red	O/G : Orange with Green tracer
W : White	O/R : Orange with Red tracer
Y : Yellow	O/W : Orange with White tracer
P : Pink	O/Y : Orange with Yellow tracer
V : Violet	P/B : Pink with Black tracer
B/Bl : Black with Blue tracer	P/Bl : Pink with Blue tracer
B/G : Black with Green tracer	P/G : Pink with Green tracer
B/R : Black with Red tracer	V/G : Violet with Green tracer
B/W : Black with White tracer	V/W : Violet with White tracer
B/Y : Black with Yellow tracer	V/Y : Violet with Yellow tracer
Bl/B : Blue with Black tracer	R/B : Red with Black tracer
Bl/G : Blue with Green tracer	R/Bl : Red with Blue tracer
Bl/R : Blue with Red tracer	R/G : Red with Green tracer
Bl/W : Blue with White tracer	R/W : Red with White tracer
Bl/Y : Blue with Yellow tracer	R/Y : Red with Yellow tracer
Br/B : Brown with Black tracer	W/B : White with Black tracer
Br/R : Brown with Red tracer	W/Bl : White with Blue tracer
Br/W : Brown with White tracer	W/G : White with Green tracer
Br/Y : Brown with Yellow tracer	W/R : White with Red tracer
G/B : Green with Black tracer	W/Y : White with Yellow tracer
G/Bl : Green with Blue tracer	Y/B : Yellow with Black tracer
G/R : Green with Red tracer	Y/Bl : Yellow with Blue tracer
G/W : Green with White tracer	Y/G : Yellow with Green tracer
G/Y : Green with Yellow tracer	Y/R : Yellow with Red tracer
Gr/B : Gray with Black tracer	Y/W : Yellow with White tracer
Gr/W : Gray with White tracer	

CODE DES COULEURS

B : Noir	Gr/R : Gris avec filet rouge
Bl : Bleu	Gr/Y : Gris avec filet jaune
Br : Brun	Lg/B : Vert clair avec filet noir
G : Vert	Lg/R : Vert clair avec filet rouge
Gr : Gris	Lg/W : Vert clair avec filet blanc
Lbl : Bleu clair	Lg/Y : Vert clair avec filet jaune
Lg : Vert clair	O/B : Orange avec filet noir
O : Orange	O/Bl : Orange avec filet bleu
R : Rouge	O/G : Orange avec filet vert
W : Blanc	O/R : Orange avec filet rouge
Y : Jaune	O/W : Orange avec filet blanc
P : Rose	O/Y : Orange avec filet jaune
V : Violet	P/B : Rose avec filet noir
B/Bl : Noir avec filet bleu	P/Bl : Rose avec filet bleu
B/G : Noir avec filet vert	P/G : Rose avec filet vert
B/R : Noir avec filet rouge	V/G : Violet avec filet vert
B/W : Noir avec filet blanc	V/W : Violet avec filet blanc
B/Y : Noir avec filet jaune	V/Y : Violet avec filet jaune
Bl/B : Bleu avec filet noir	R/B : Rouge avec filet noir
Bl/G : Bleu avec filet vert	R/Bl : Rouge avec filet bleu
Bl/R : Bleu avec filet rouge	R/G : Rouge avec filet vert
Bl/W : Bleu avec filet blanc	R/W : Rouge avec filet blanc
Bl/Y : Bleu avec filet jaune	R/Y : Rouge avec filet jaune
Br/B : Brun avec filet noir	W/B : Blanc avec filet noir
Br/R : Brun avec filet rouge	W/Bl : Blanc avec filet bleu
Br/N : Brun avec filet blanc	W/G : Blanc avec filet vert
Br/Y : Brun avec filet jaune	W/R : Blanc avec filet rouge
G/B : Vert avec filet noir	W/Y : Blanc avec filet jaune
G/Bl : Vert avec filet bleu	Y/B : Jaune avec filet noir
G/R : Vert avec filet rouge	Y/Bl : Jaune avec filet bleu
G/W : Vert avec filet blanc	Y/G : Jaune avec filet vert
G/Y : Vert avec filet jaune	Y/R : Jaune avec filet rouge
Gr/B : Gris avec filet noir	Y/W : Jaune avec filet blanc
Gr/W : Gris avec filet blanc	

Fig. 154 1991 Metro convertible wiring diagram — automatic transaxle, Canada

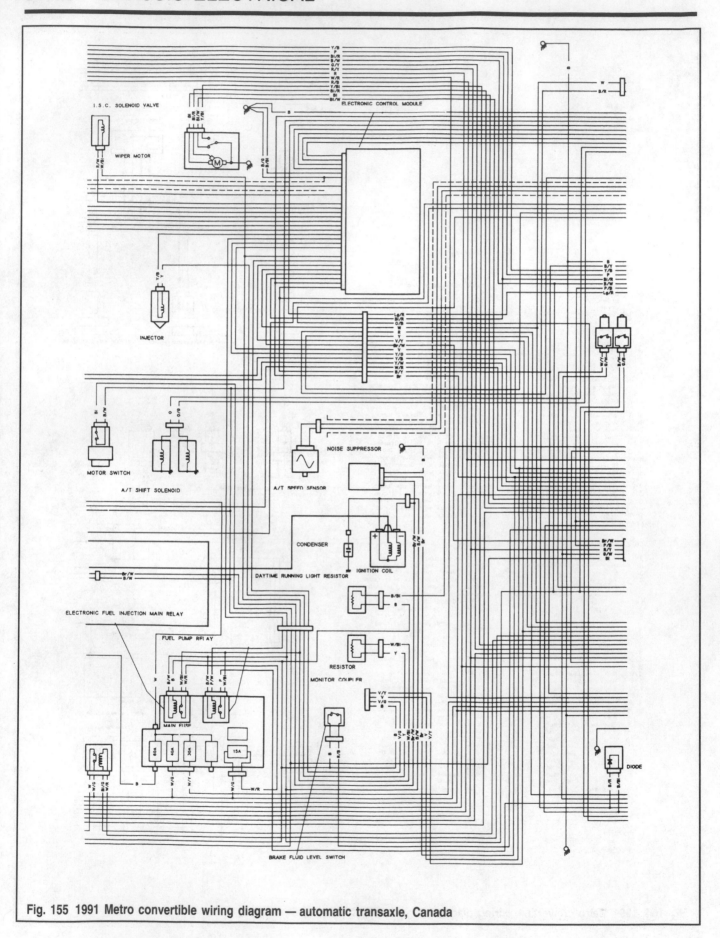

Fig. 155 1991 Metro convertible wiring diagram — automatic transaxle, Canada

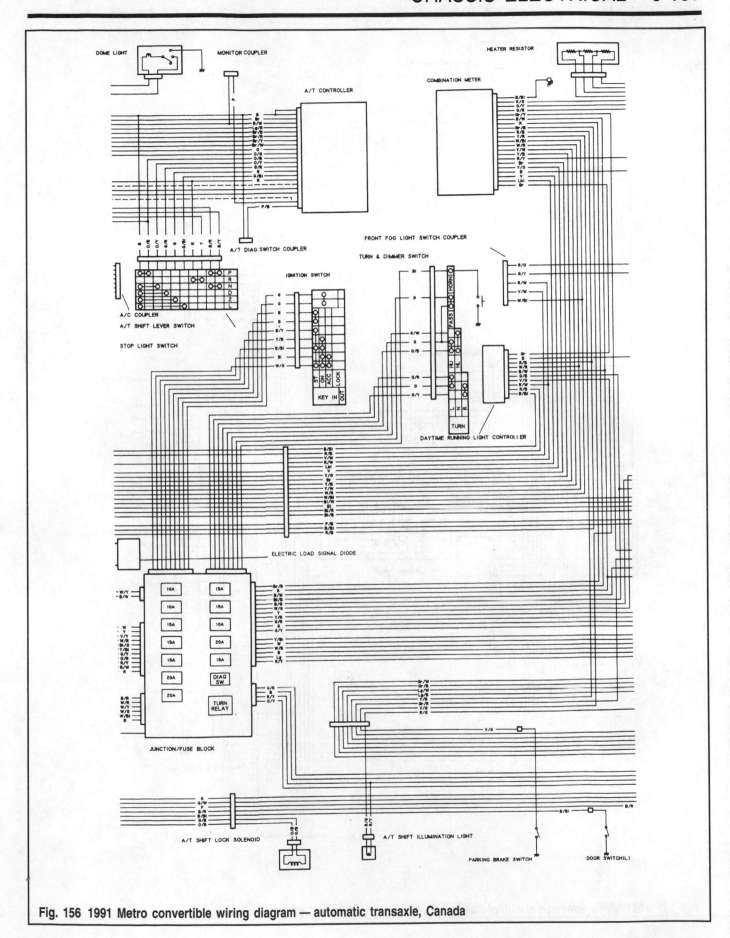

Fig. 156 1991 Metro convertible wiring diagram — automatic transaxle, Canada

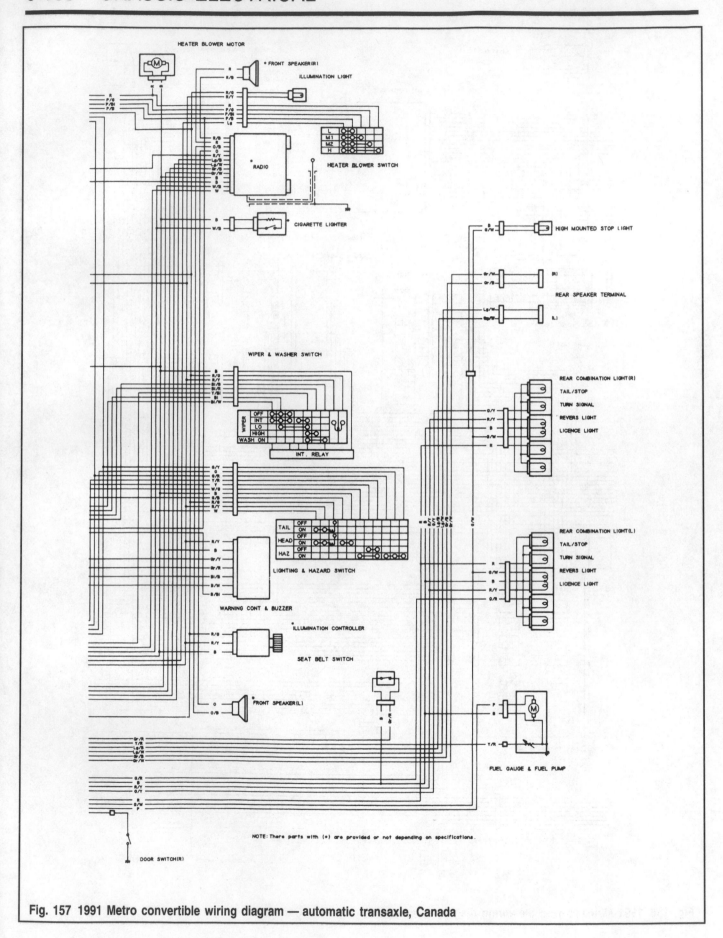

Fig. 157 1991 Metro convertible wiring diagram — automatic transaxle, Canada

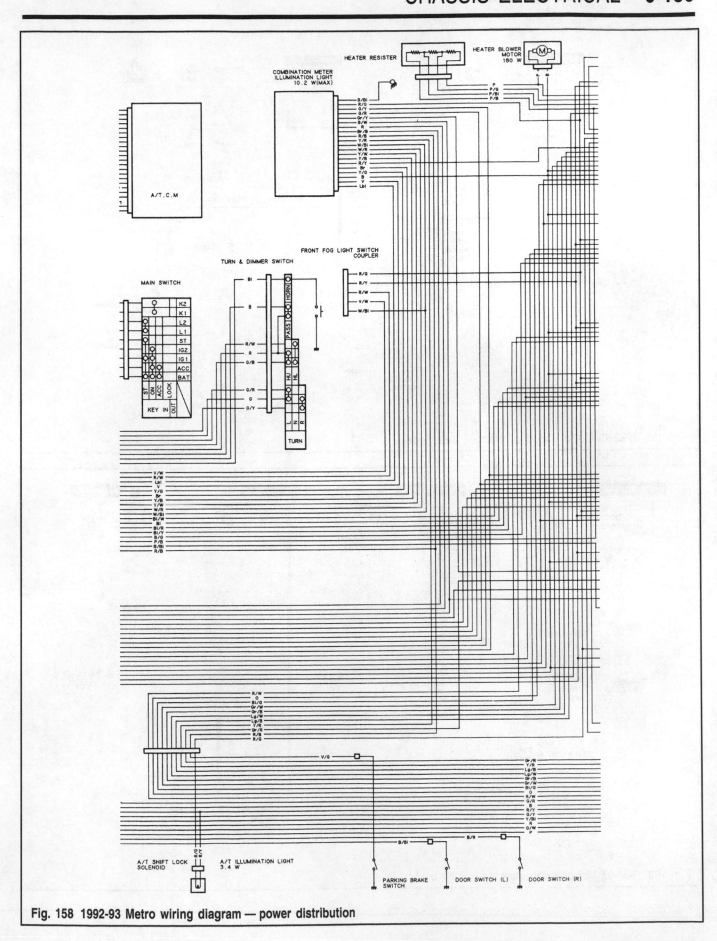

Fig. 158 1992-93 Metro wiring diagram — power distribution

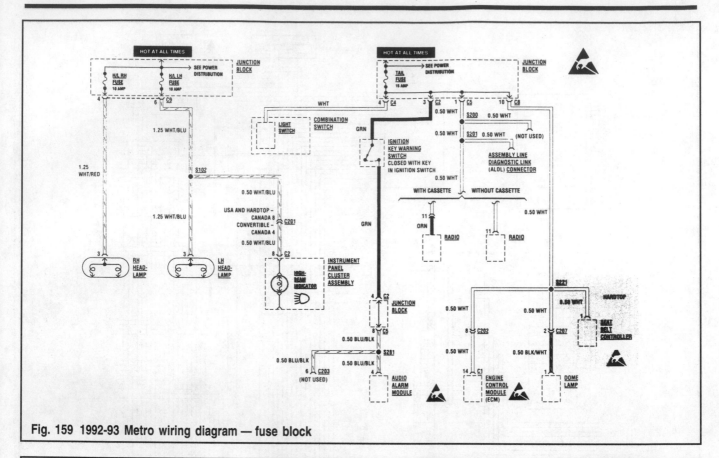

Fig. 159 1992-93 Metro wiring diagram — fuse block

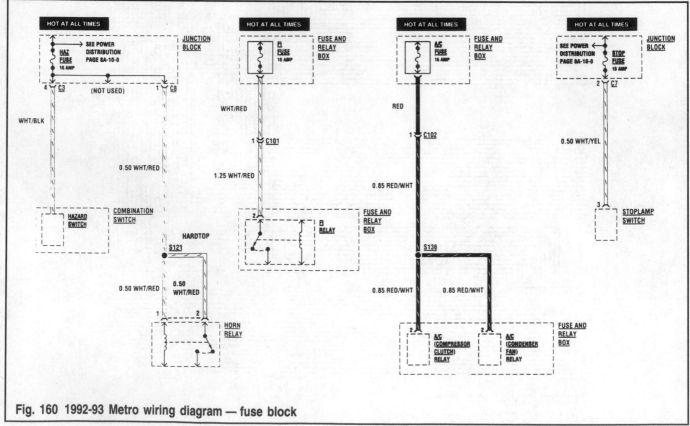

Fig. 160 1992-93 Metro wiring diagram — fuse block

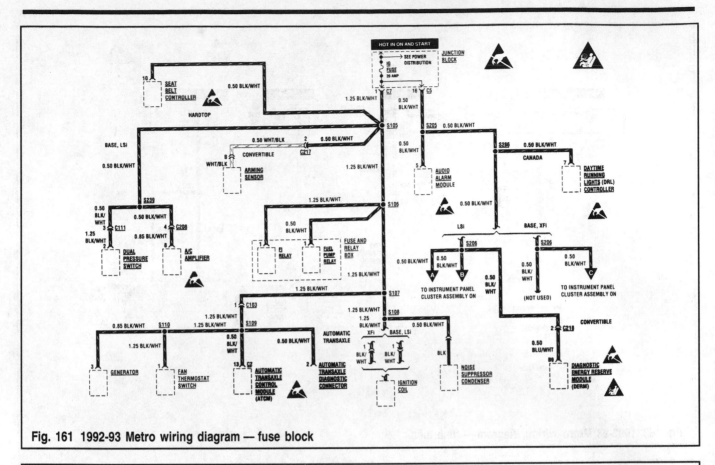

Fig. 161 1992-93 Metro wiring diagram — fuse block

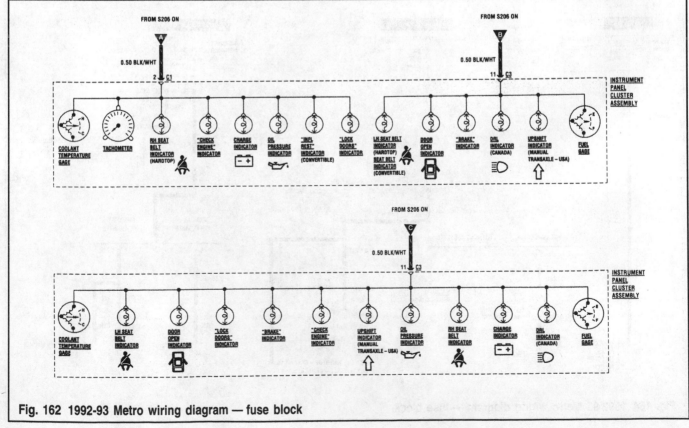

Fig. 162 1992-93 Metro wiring diagram — fuse block

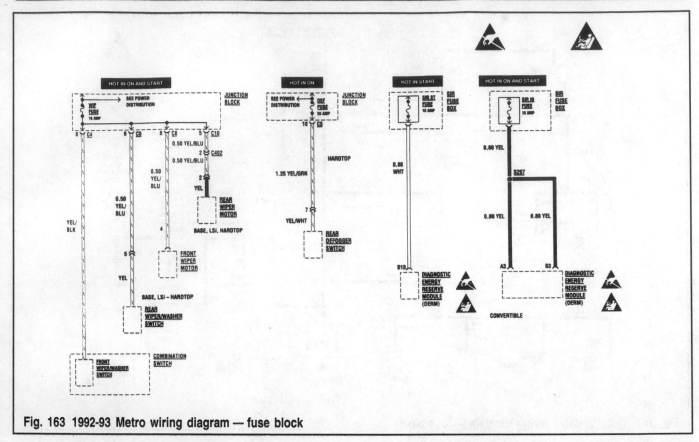

Fig. 163 1992-93 Metro wiring diagram — fuse block

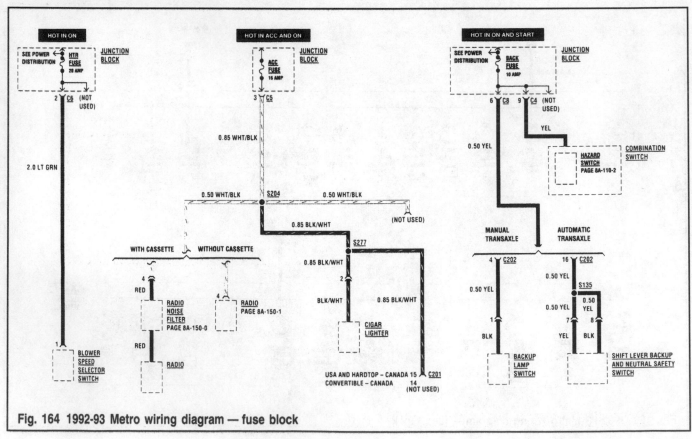

Fig. 164 1992-93 Metro wiring diagram — fuse block

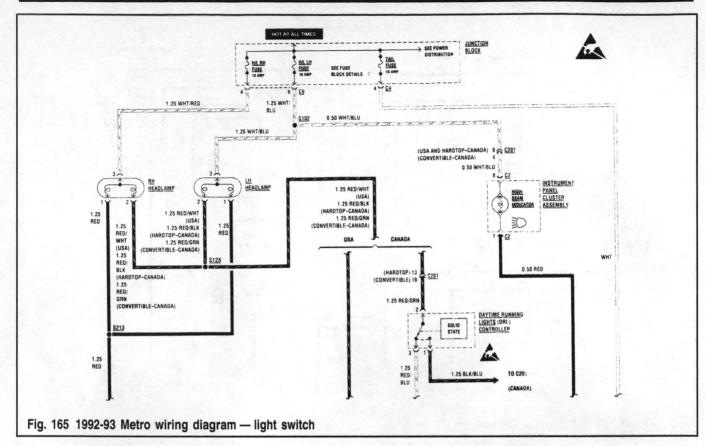

Fig. 165 1992-93 Metro wiring diagram — light switch

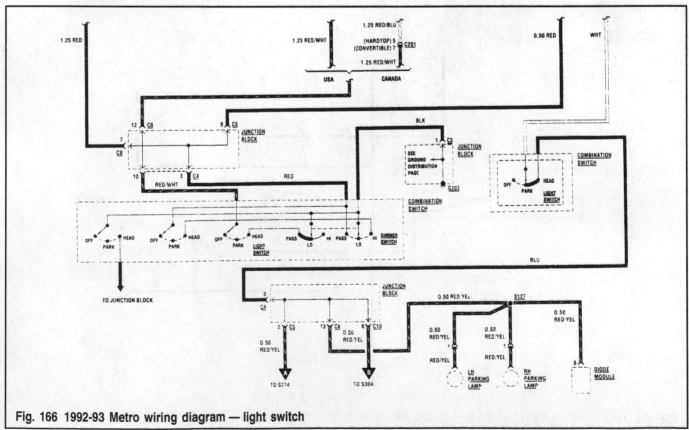

Fig. 166 1992-93 Metro wiring diagram — light switch

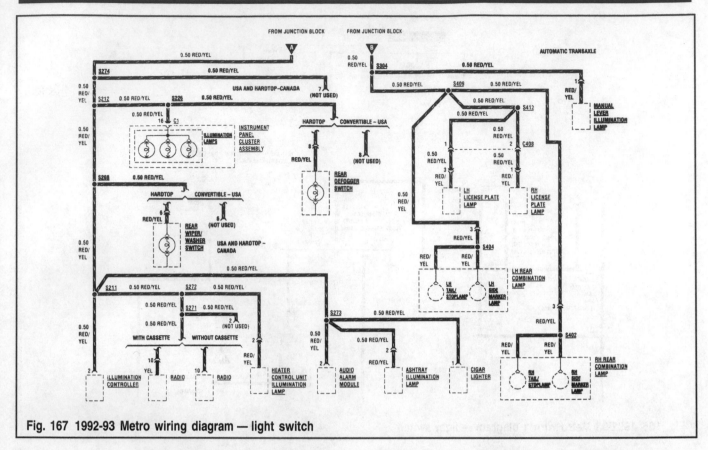

Fig. 167 1992-93 Metro wiring diagram — light switch

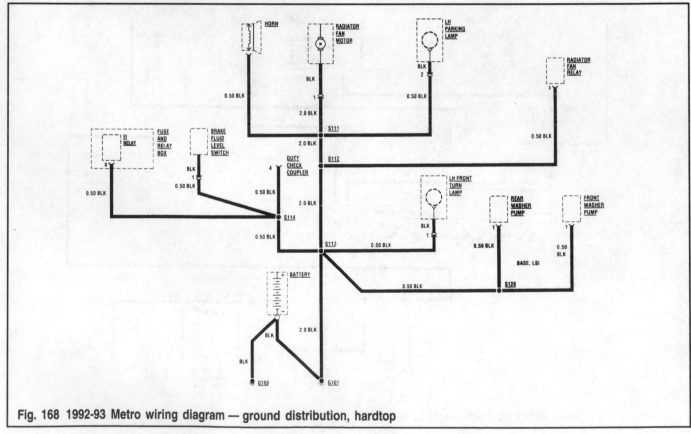

Fig. 168 1992-93 Metro wiring diagram — ground distribution, hardtop

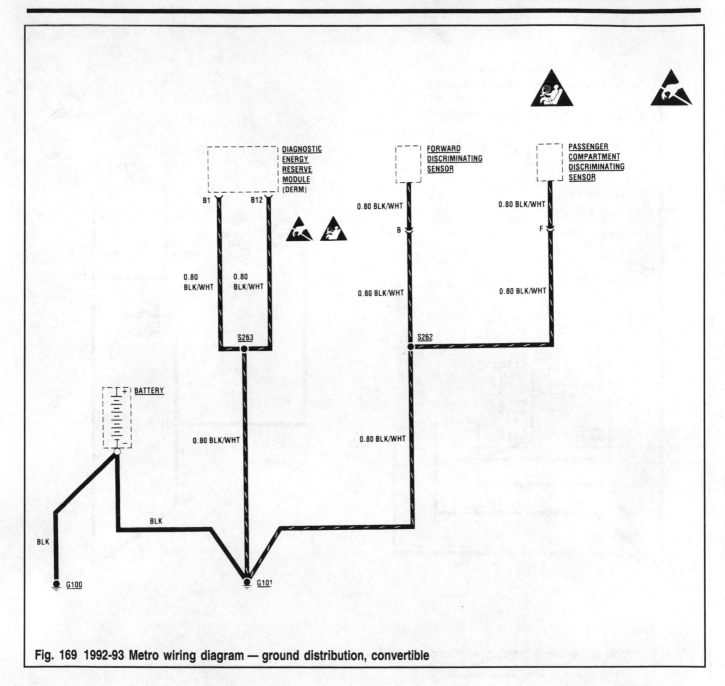

Fig. 169 1992-93 Metro wiring diagram — ground distribution, convertible

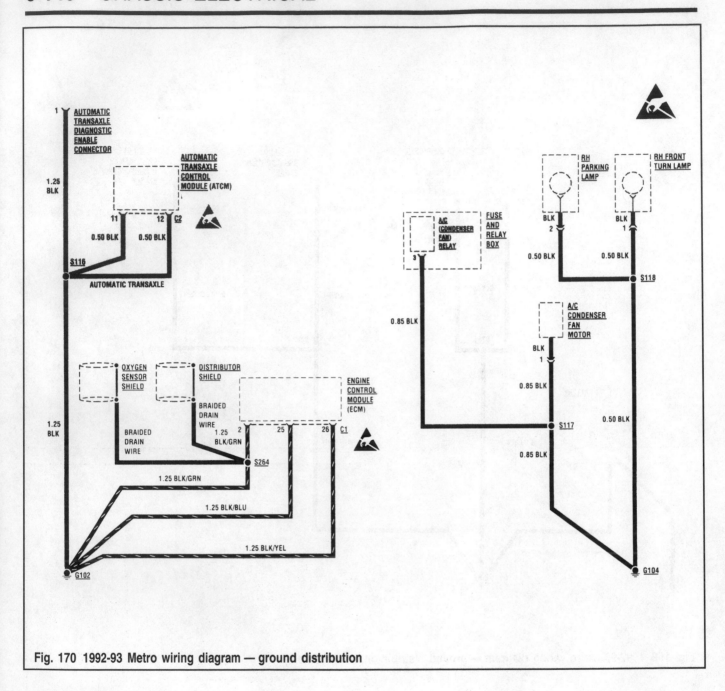

Fig. 170 1992-93 Metro wiring diagram — ground distribution

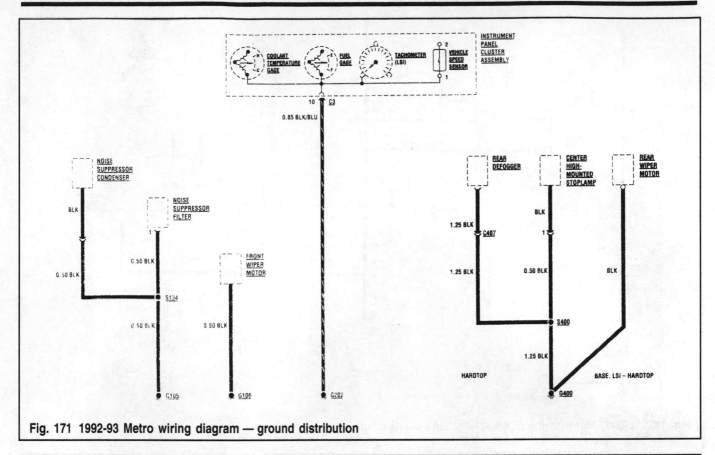

Fig. 171 1992-93 Metro wiring diagram — ground distribution

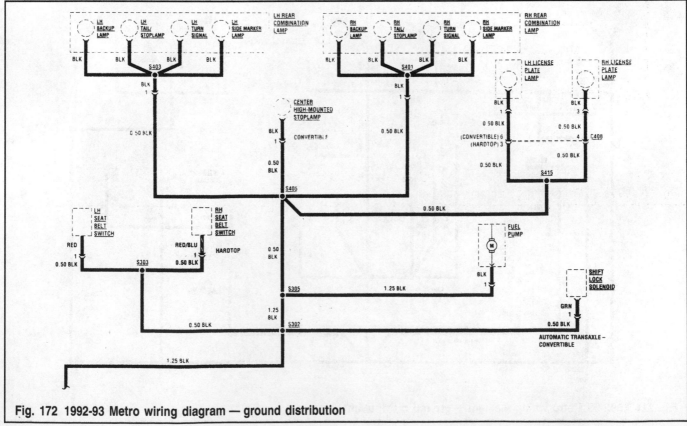

Fig. 172 1992-93 Metro wiring diagram — ground distribution

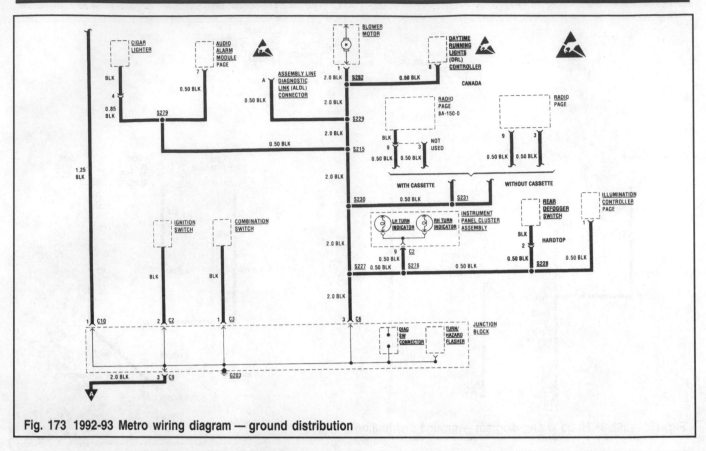

Fig. 173 1992-93 Metro wiring diagram — ground distribution

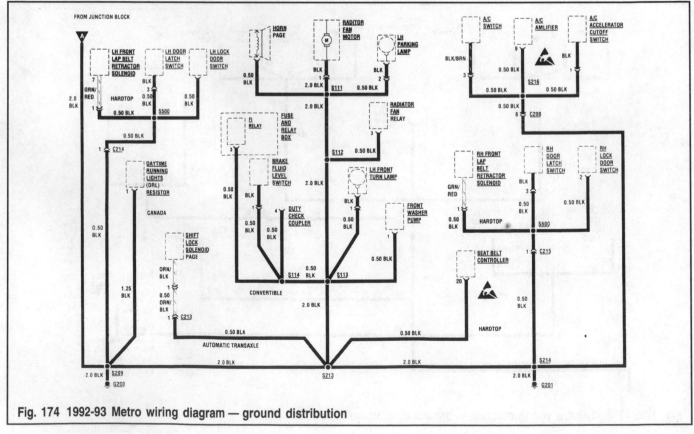

Fig. 174 1992-93 Metro wiring diagram — ground distribution

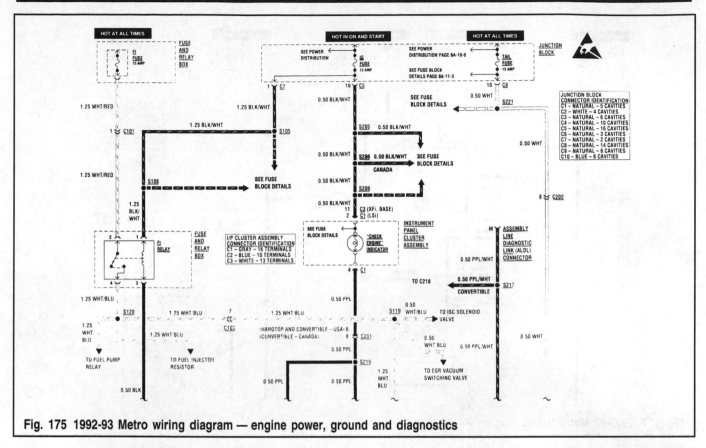

Fig. 175 1992-93 Metro wiring diagram — engine power, ground and diagnostics

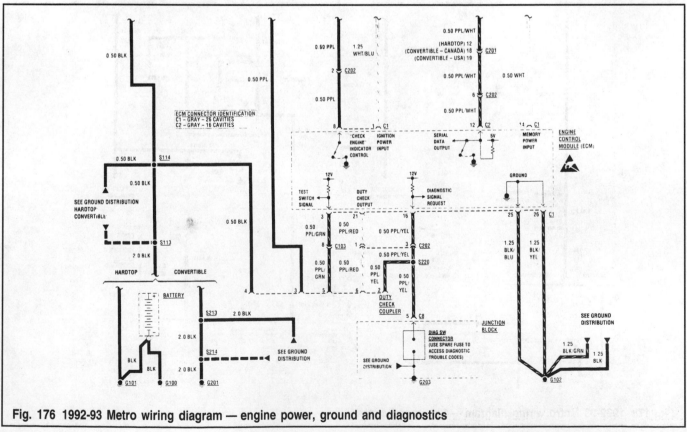

Fig. 176 1992-93 Metro wiring diagram — engine power, ground and diagnostics

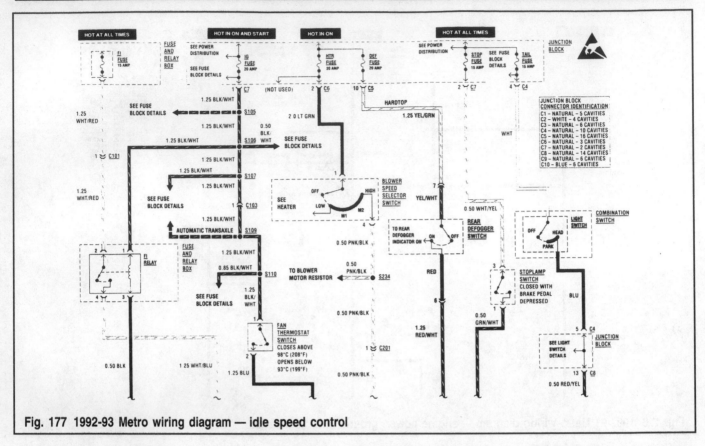

Fig. 177 1992-93 Metro wiring diagram — idle speed control

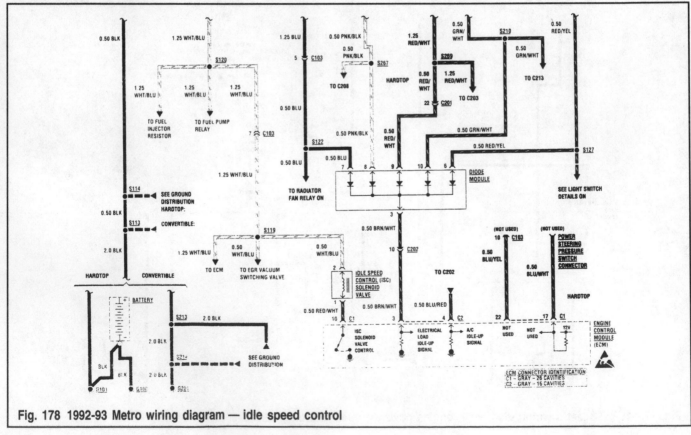

Fig. 178 1992-93 Metro wiring diagram — idle speed control

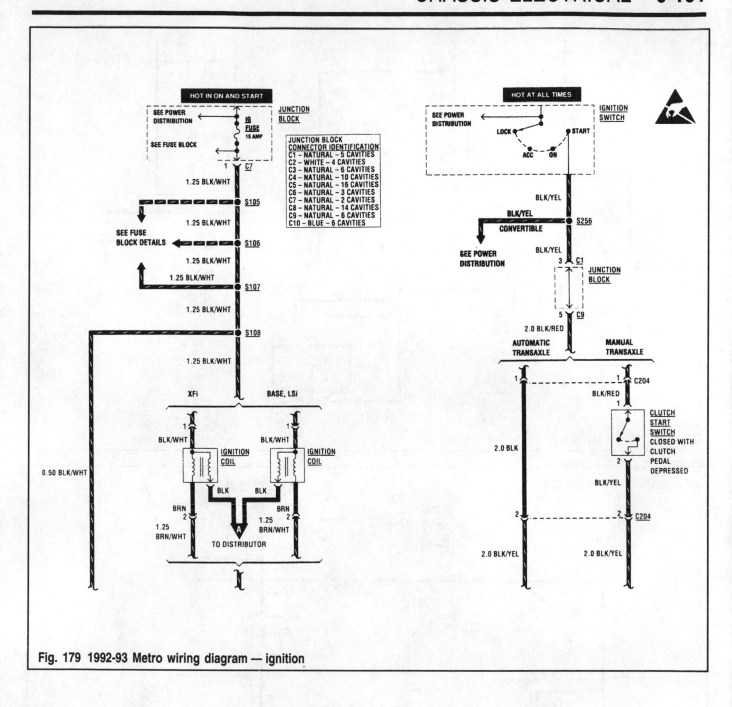

Fig. 179 1992-93 Metro wiring diagram — ignition

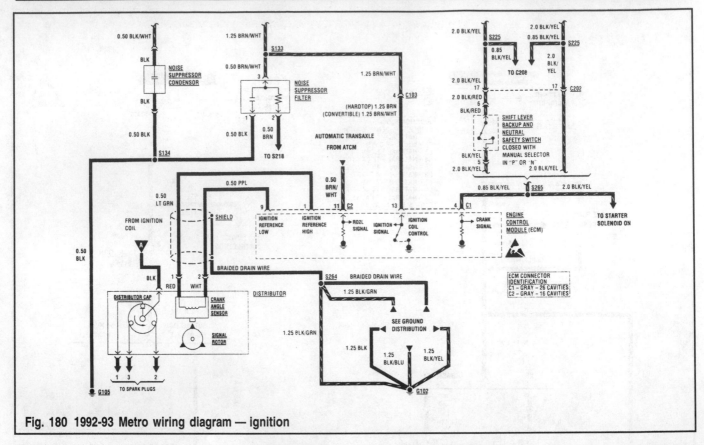

Fig. 180 1992-93 Metro wiring diagram — ignition

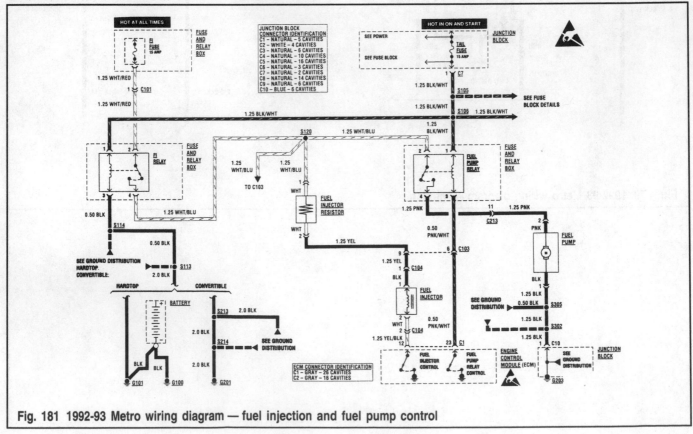

Fig. 181 1992-93 Metro wiring diagram — fuel injection and fuel pump control

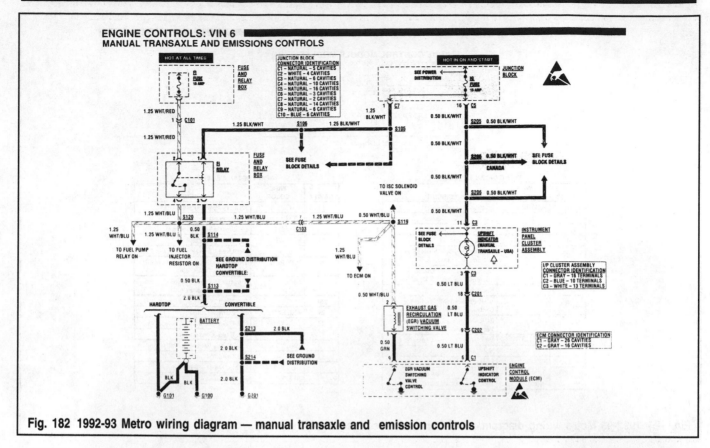

Fig. 182 1992-93 Metro wiring diagram — manual transaxle and emission controls

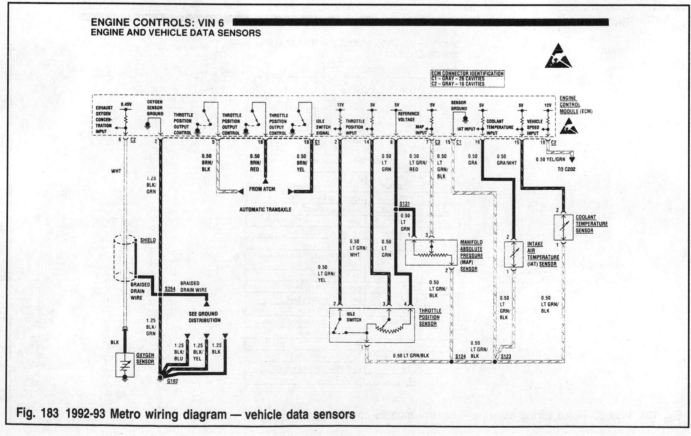

Fig. 183 1992-93 Metro wiring diagram — vehicle data sensors

ENGINE CONTROLS: VIN 6

ENGINE CONTROL MODULE MODULE (ECM)
CONNECTOR C1

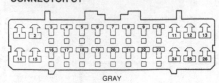

GRAY

	WIRING DETAIL LEGEND	
CAVITY	WIRE COLOR	CIRCUIT
1	WHT/BLU	Ignition Power Input
2	BLK/GRN	Oxygen Sensor Ground
3	PPL/GRN	Test Switch Signal
4	BLK/YEL	Crank Signal
5	BRN/BLK	Throttle Position Output Control (Automatic Transaxle)
6	LT BLU	Upshift Indicator Control (Manual Transaxle – USA)
7	—	Not Used
8	PPL	"CHECK ENGINE" Indicator Control
9	GRN	EGR Vacuum Switching Valve Control
10	RED/WHT	ISC Solenoid Valve Control
11	—	Not Used
12	YEL/BLK	Fuel Injector Control
13	BRN	Ignition Coil Control (Hardtop)
	BRN/WHT	Ignition Coil Control (Convertible)

	WIRING DETAIL LEGEND	
CAVITY	WIRE COLOR	CIRCUIT
14	WHT	Memory Power Input
15	LT GRN/BLK	Sensor Ground
16	PPL/YEL	Diagnostic Request Signal
17	BLU/WHT	Not Used (Hardtop)
	—	Not Used (Convertible)
18	BRN/RED	Throttle Position Output Control (Automatic Transaxle)
19	BRN/YEL	Throttle Position Output Control (Automatic Transaxle)
20	—	Not Used
21	PPL/RED	Duty Check Output
22	BLU/YEL	Not Used (Hardtop)
	—	Not Used (Convertible)
23	PNK/WHT	Fuel Pump Relay Control
24	—	Not Used
25	BLK/BLU	ECM Ground – G102
26	BLK/YEL	ECM Ground – G102

Fig. 184 1992-93 Metro wiring diagram — control module connector c1

ENGINE CONTROLS: VIN 6

ENGINE CONTROL MODULE MODULE (ECM)
CONNECTOR C2

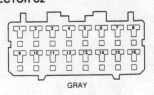

GRAY

	WIRING DETAIL LEGEND	
CAVITY	WIRE COLOR	CIRCUIT
1	LT GRN	Ignition Reference High
2	LT GRN/YEL	Idle Switch Signal
3	BRN/WHT	Electrical Load Idle-Up Signal
4	BLU/RED	A/C Idle-Up Signal
5	—	Not Used
6	WHT	Exhaust Oxygen Concentration Input
7	LT GRN/RED	MAP Input
8	LT GRN	Reference Voltage (5V)
9	PPL	Ignition Reference Low
10	YEL/GRN	Vehicle Speed Input
11	BRN/WHT	RD2L Signal (Automatic Transaxle)
12	PPL/WHT	Serial Data Output
13	—	Not Used
14	LT GRN/WHT	Throttle Position Input
15	GRA/WHT	Coolant Temperature Input
16	GRA	IAT Input

Fig. 185 1992-93 Metro wiring diagram — control module connector c2

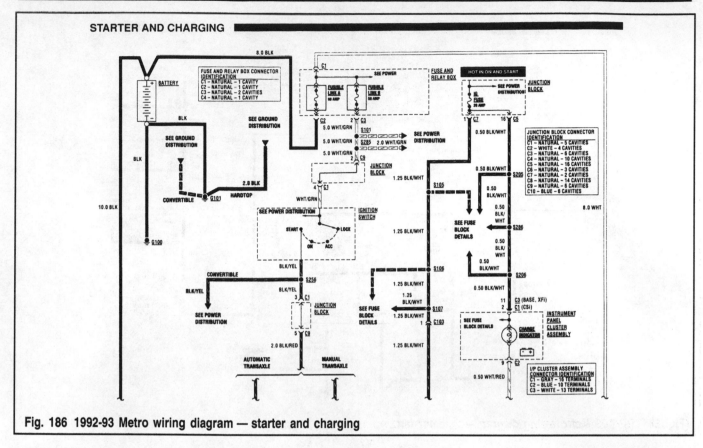

Fig. 186 1992-93 Metro wiring diagram — starter and charging

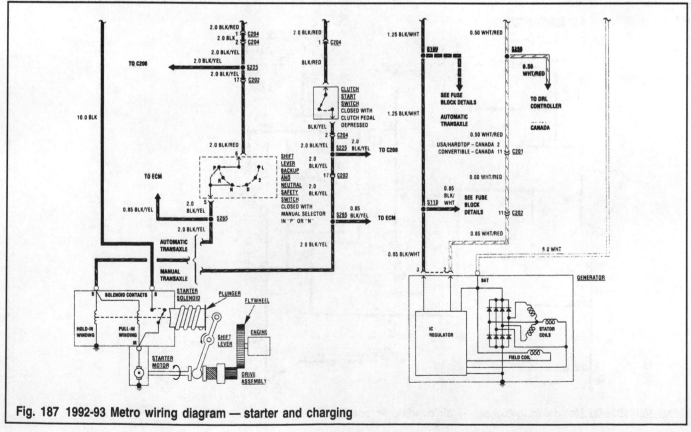

Fig. 187 1992-93 Metro wiring diagram — starter and charging

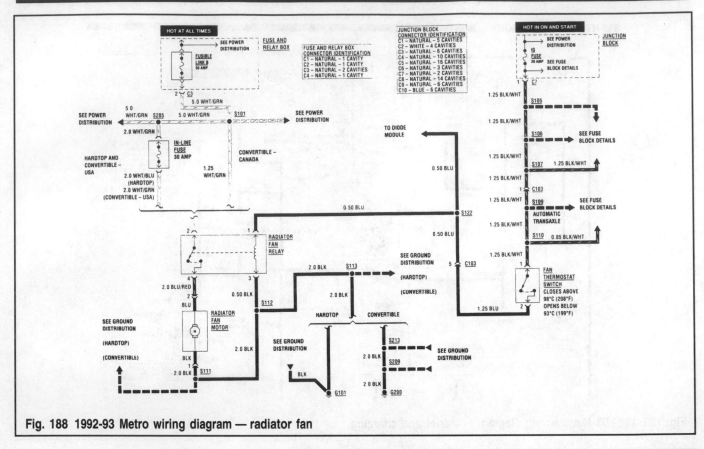

Fig. 188 1992-93 Metro wiring diagram — radiator fan

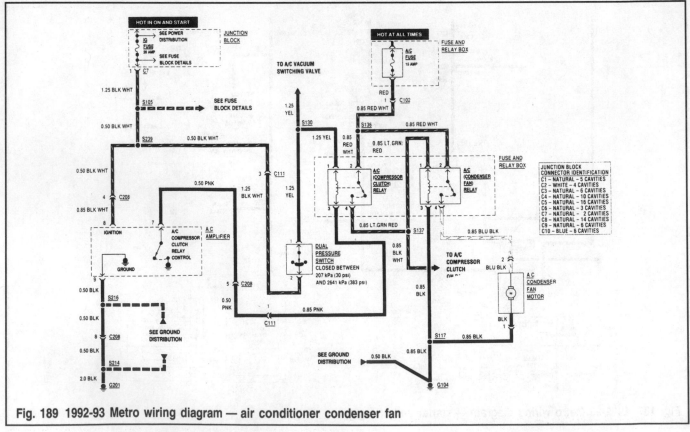

Fig. 189 1992-93 Metro wiring diagram — air conditioner condenser fan

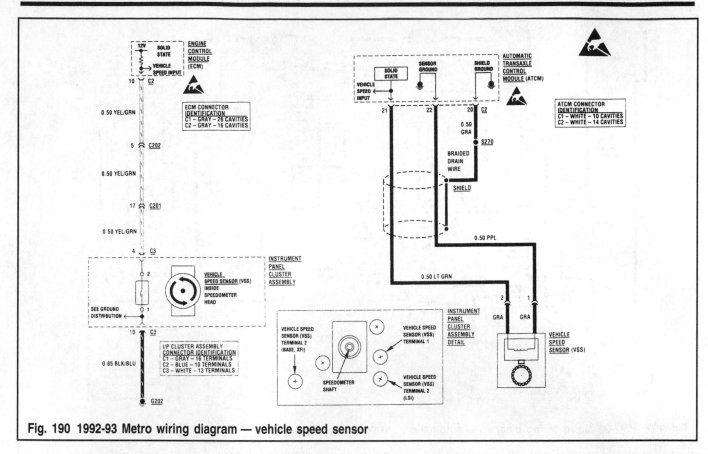

Fig. 190 1992-93 Metro wiring diagram — vehicle speed sensor

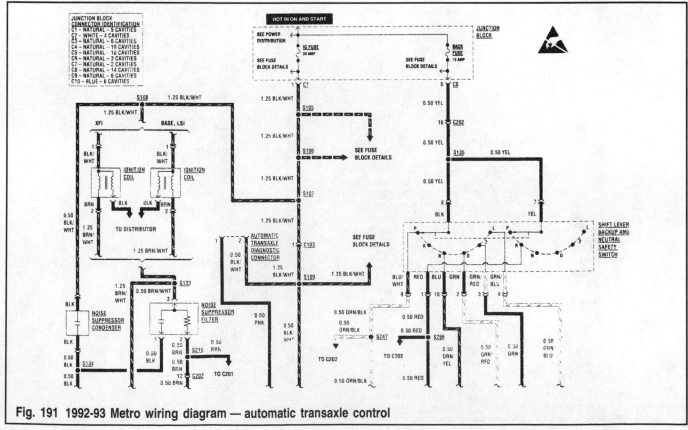

Fig. 191 1992-93 Metro wiring diagram — automatic transaxle control

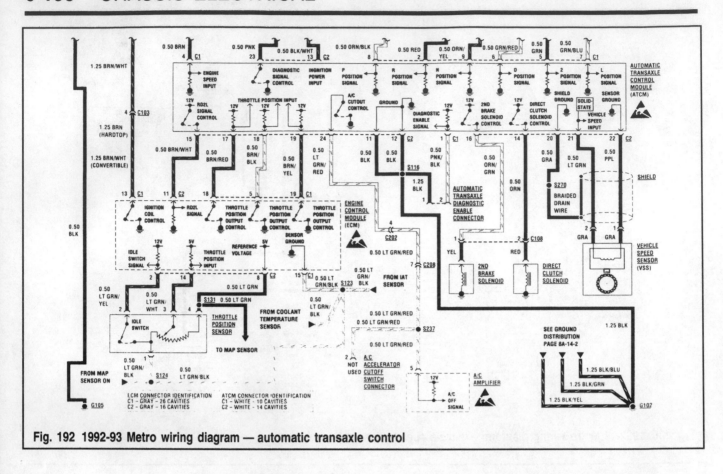

Fig. 192 1992-93 Metro wiring diagram — automatic transaxle control

AUTOMATIC TRANSAXLE CONTROL MODULE (ATCM) CONNECTOR C1

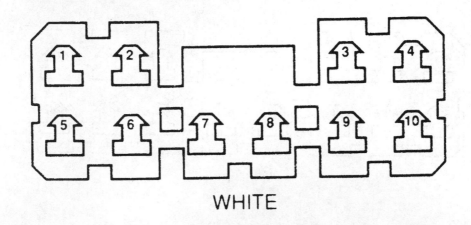

WHITE

WIRING DETAIL LEGEND

CAVITY	WIRE COLOR	CIRCUIT
1	PNK/BLK	Diagnostic Enable Signal
2	RED	R Position Signal
3	—	Not Used
4	BRN	Engine Speed Input
5	GRN	2 Position Signal
6	GRN/RED	D Position Signal
7	GRN/BLU	L Position Signal
8	ORN/BLK	P Position Signal
9	ORN/YEL	N Position Signal
10	—	Not Used

Fig. 193 1992-93 Metro wiring diagram — automatic transaxle control module connector c1

AUTOMATIC TRANSAXLE CONTROL MODULE (ATCM) CONNECTOR C2

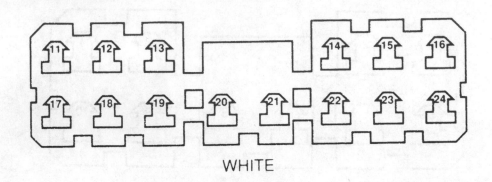

WHITE

WIRING DETAIL LEGEND

CAVITY	WIRE COLOR	CIRCUIT
11	BLK	Ground -- G102
12	BLK	Ground -- G102
13	BLK/WHT	Ignition Power Input
14	ORN	Direct Clutch Solenoid Control
15	BRN/WHT	RD2L Signal Control
16	ORN/GRN	2nd Brake Solenoid Control
17	BRN/RED	Throttle Position Input
18	BRN/BLK	Throttle Position Input
19	BRN/YEL	Throttle Position Input
20	GRA	Vehicle Speed Sensor Shield Ground
21	LT GRN	Vehicle Speed Input
22	PPL	Vehicle Speed Sensor Ground
23	PNK	Diagnostic Signal Control
24	LT GRN/RED	A/C Cutout Control

Fig. 194 1992-93 Metro wiring diagram — automatic transaxle control module connector c2

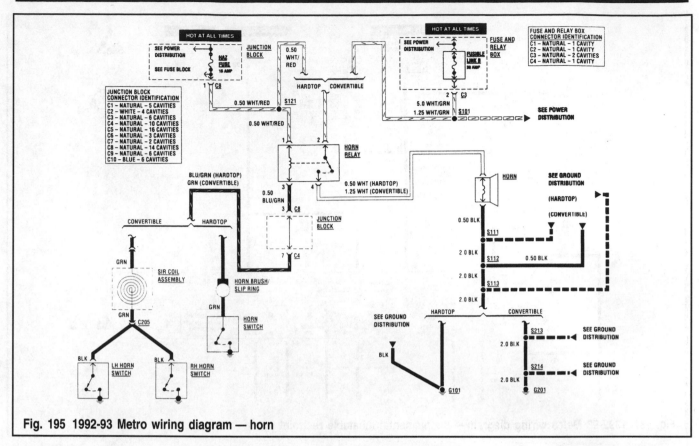

Fig. 195 1992-93 Metro wiring diagram — horn

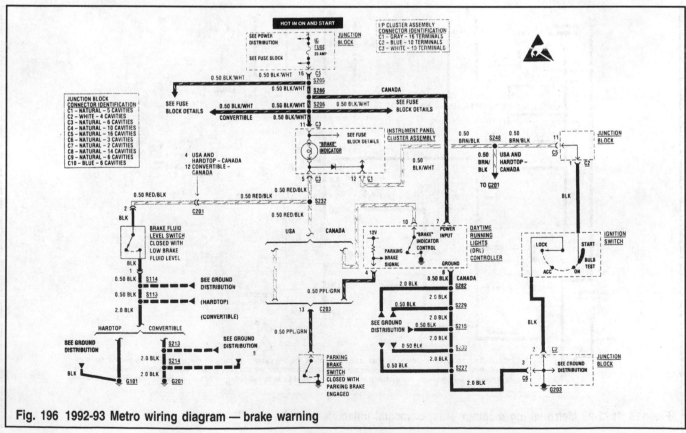

Fig. 196 1992-93 Metro wiring diagram — brake warning

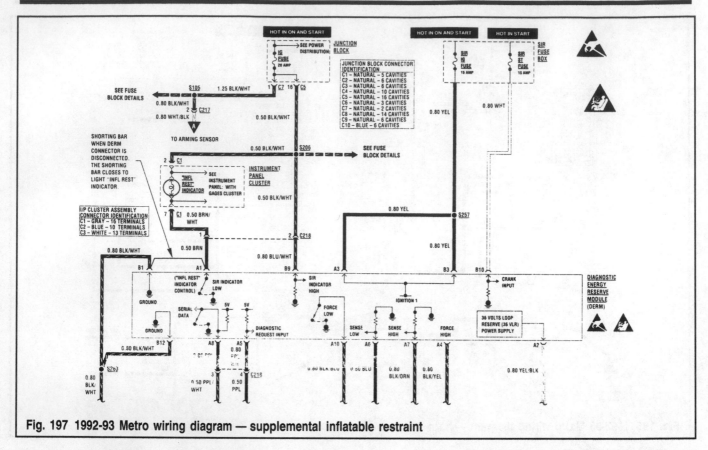

Fig. 197 1992-93 Metro wiring diagram — supplemental inflatable restraint

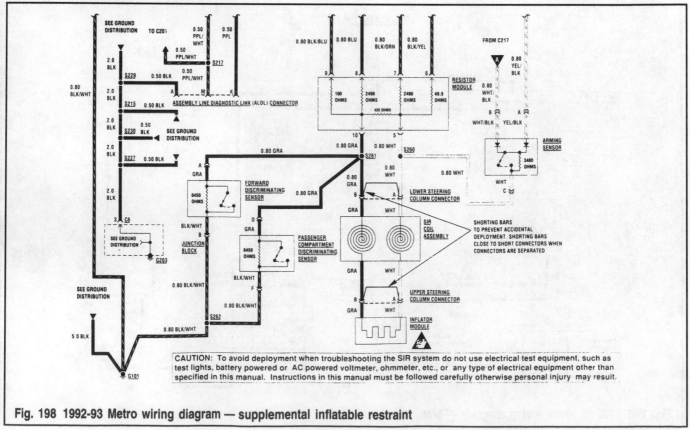

Fig. 198 1992-93 Metro wiring diagram — supplemental inflatable restraint

DIAGNOSTIC ENERGY RESERVE MODULE
(DERM) CONNECTOR

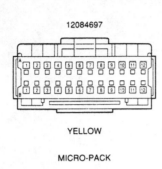

12084697

YELLOW

MICRO-PACK

WIRING DETAIL LEGEND

CAVITY	WIRE COLOR	CIRCUIT
A1	BRN	SIR Indicator Low
A2	YEL/BLK	36 Volt Loop Reserve (36 VLR) Power Supply
A3	YEL	Ignition 1
A4	BLK/YEL	Force High
A5	PPL/WHT	Diagnostic Request Input
A6	BLU	Sense Low
A7	BLK/ORN	Sense High
A8	PPL	Serial Data
A9	—	Not Used
A10	BLK/BLU	Force Low
A11	—	Not Used
A12	—	Not Used
B1	BLK/WHT	Ground – G101
B2	—	Not Used
B3	YEL	Ignition 1
B4	—	Not Used
B5	—	Not Used
B6	—	Not Used
B7	—	Not Used
B8	—	Not Used
B9	BLU/WHT	SIR Indicator High
B10	WHT	Crank Input
B11	—	Not Used
B12	BLK/WHT	Ground – G101

Fig. 199 1992-93 Metro wiring diagram — diagnostic energy reserve module connector

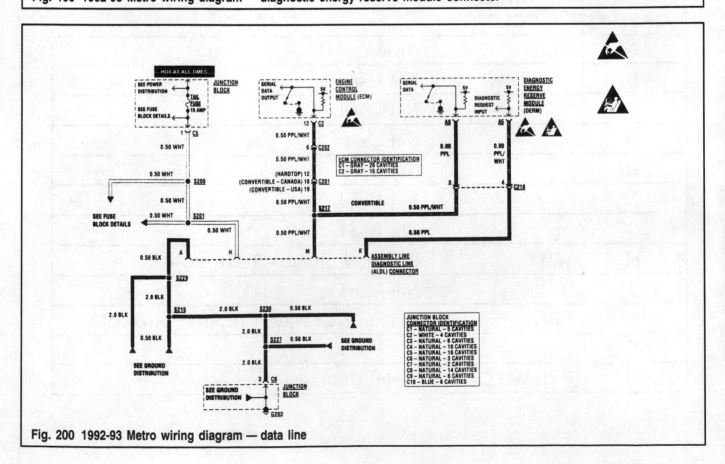

Fig. 200 1992-93 Metro wiring diagram — data line

ASSEMBLY LINE DIAGNOSTIC LINK (ALDL) CONNECTOR

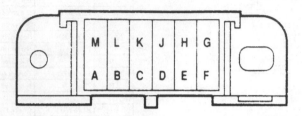

BLACK

WIRING DETAIL LEGEND

CAVITY	WIRE COLOR	CIRCUIT
A	BLK	Ground – G203
B	—	Not Used
C	—	Not Used
D	—	Not Used
E	—	Not Used
F	—	Not Used
G	—	Not Used
H	WHT	Battery Voltage – TAIL Fuse
J	—	Not Used
K	PPL	Diagnostic Request Input (Convertible)
L	—	Not Used
M	PPL/WHT	Serial Data

Fig. 201 1992-93 Metro wiring diagram — assembly line diagnostic link connector

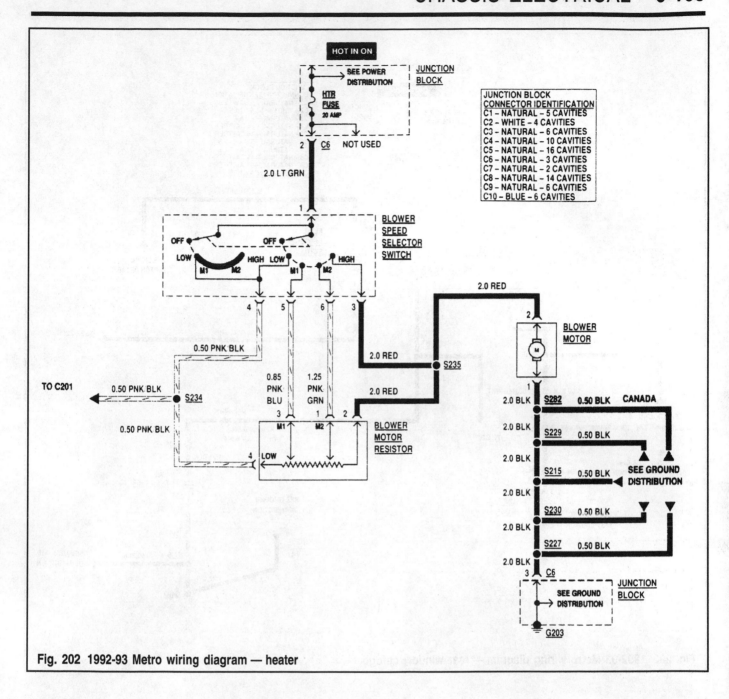

Fig. 202 1992-93 Metro wiring diagram — heater

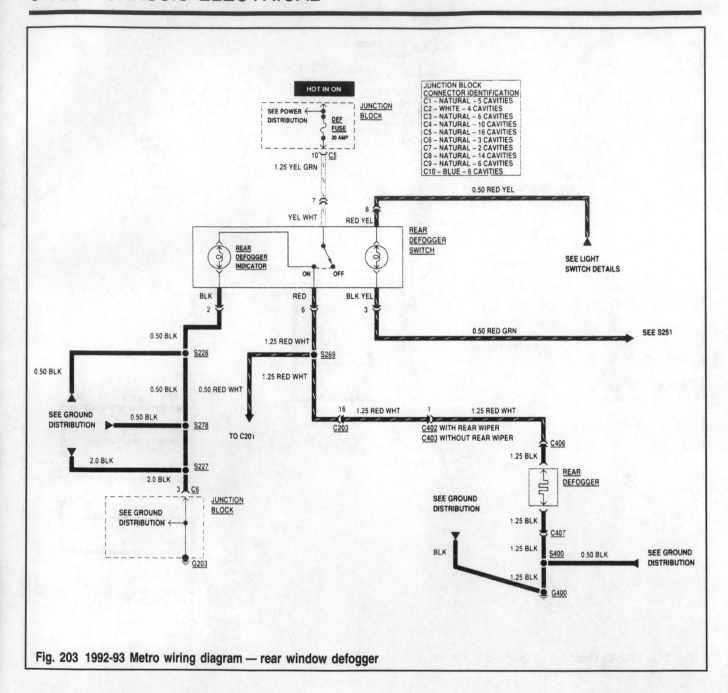

Fig. 203 1992-93 Metro wiring diagram — rear window defogger

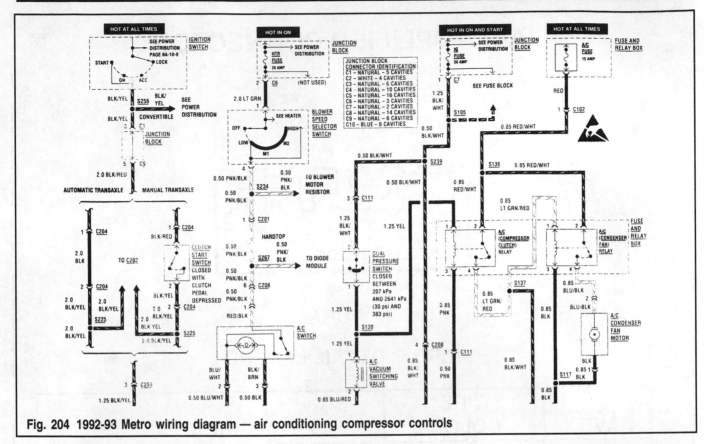

Fig. 204 1992-93 Metro wiring diagram — air conditioning compressor controls

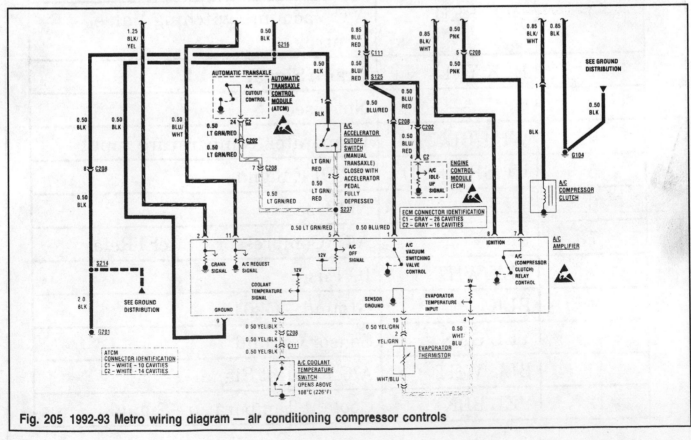

Fig. 205 1992-93 Metro wiring diagram — air conditioning compressor controls

A/C AMPLIFIER CONNECTOR

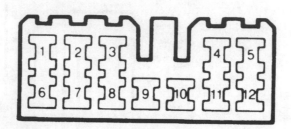

NATURAL

WIRING DETAIL LEGEND

CAVITY	WIRE COLOR	CIRCUIT
1	BLU/RED	A/C Vacuum Switching Valve Control
2	BLK/YEL	Crank Signal
3	—	Not Used
4	WHT/BLU	Evaporator Temperature Input
5	LT GRN/RED	AC OFF Signal
6	—	Not Used
7	PNK	A/C (Compressor Clutch) Relay
8	BLK/WHT	IG Fuse
9	BLK	Ground – G201
10	YEL/GRN	Sensor Ground
11	BLU/WHT	A/C Request Signal
12	YEL/BLK	Coolant Temperature Signal

Fig. 206 1992-93 Metro wiring diagram — air conditioner amplifier connector

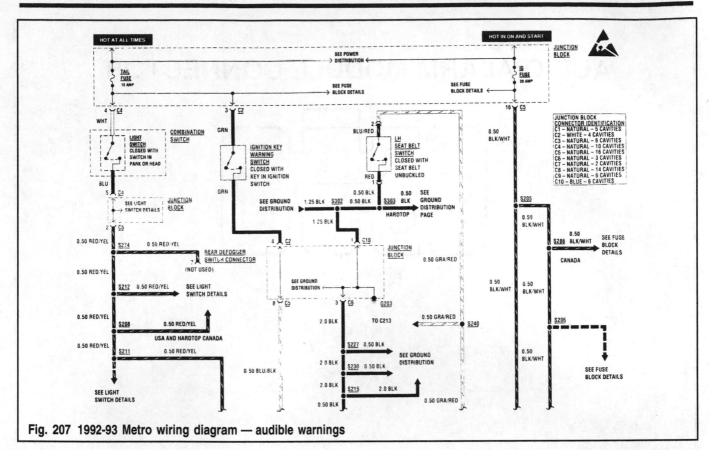

Fig. 207 1992-93 Metro wiring diagram — audible warnings

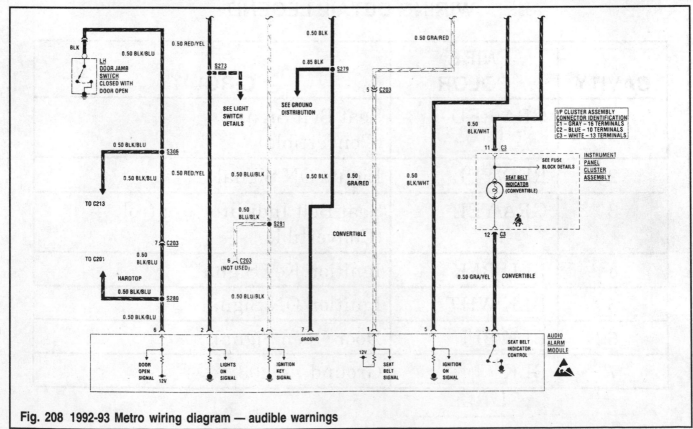

Fig. 208 1992-93 Metro wiring diagram — audible warnings

AUDIO ALARM MODULE CONNECTOR

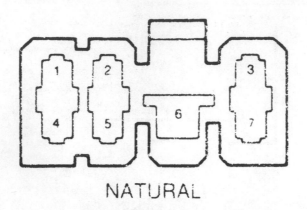

NATURAL

WIRING DETAIL LEGEND

CAVITY	WIRE COLOR	CIRCUIT
1	GRA/RED	Seat Belt Signal (Convertible)
2	RED/YEL	Lights ON Signal
3	GRA/YEL	Seat Belt Indicator Control (Convertible)
4	BLU/BLK	Ignition Key Signal
5	BLK/WHT	Ignition ON Signal
6	BLK/BLU	Door Open Signal
7	BLK	Ground – G203

Fig. 209 1992-93 Metro wiring diagram — audio audible warning connector

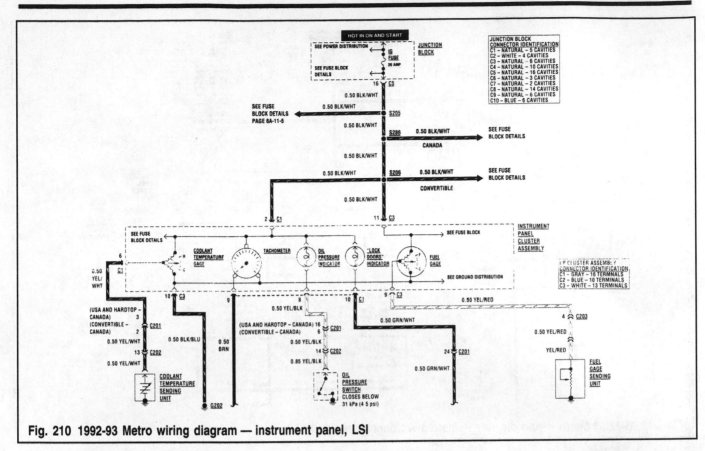

Fig. 210 1992-93 Metro wiring diagram — instrument panel, LSI

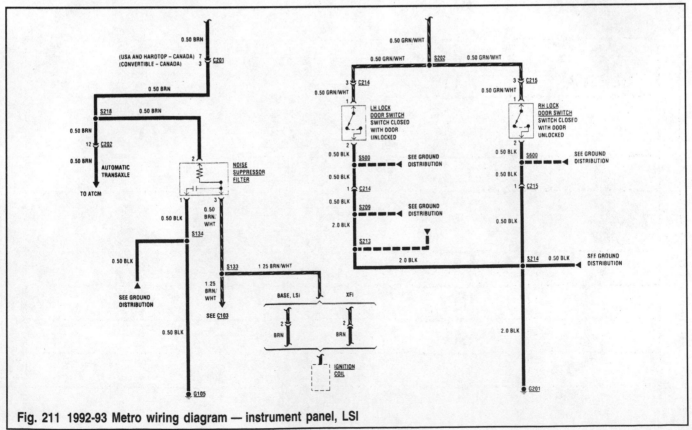

Fig. 211 1992-93 Metro wiring diagram — instrument panel, LSI

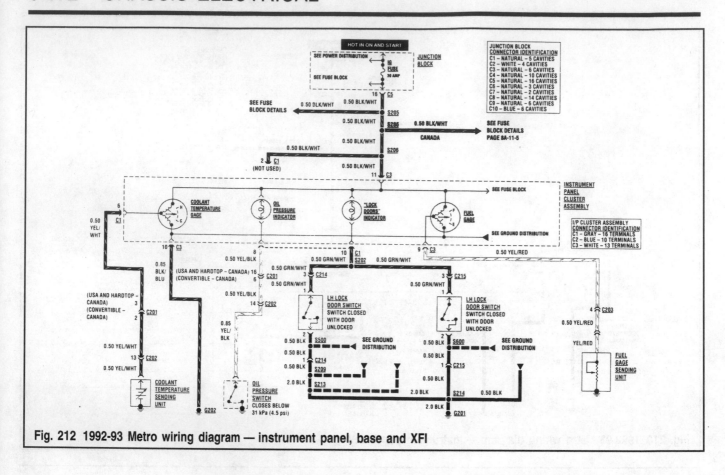

Fig. 212 1992-93 Metro wiring diagram — instrument panel, base and XFI

INSTRUMENT PANEL CLUSTER CONNECTOR: C1

GRAY

WIRING DETAIL LEGEND

TERMINAL	WIRE COLOR	CIRCUIT
1	WHT/RED	Generator
2	BLK/WHT	IG Fuse
3	ORN/BLK	Seat Belt Controller (Hardtop – USA)
	--	Not Used (Canada and Convertible – USA)
4	PPL	ECM – "CHECK ENGINE" Indicator
5	—	Not Used
6	YEL/WHT	Coolant Temperature Sending Unit
7	BRN/WHT	Diagnostic Energy Reserve Module (DERM) – (Convertible)
	—	Not Used
8	YEL/BLK	Oil Pressure Switch
9	BRN	Ignition Coil – Tachometer Input (LSi)
	—	Not Used (Base, XFi)
10	GRN/WHT	(RH) (LH) Lock Door Switches
11	—	Not Used
12	BRN/BLK	Ignition Switch
13	—	Not Used
14	—	Not Used
15	RED/GRN	Ilumination Controller
16	RED/YEL	Light Switch

INSTRUMENT PANEL CLUSTER CONNECTOR: C2

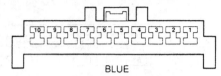

BLUE

WIRING DETAIL LEGEND

TERMINAL	WIRE COLOR	CIRCUIT
1	--	Not Used
2	—	Not Used
3	—	Not Used
4	—	Not Used
5	—	Not Used
6	—	Not Used
7	WHT/BLU	H/L LH Fuse
8	RED	Dimmer Switch – High-Beam Indicator
9	BLK	Ground – G203
10	GRN/YEL	Combination Switch – RH Turn Signal

Fig. 213 1992-93 Metro wiring diagram — instrument panel connectors

INSTRUMENT PANEL CLUSTER CONNECTOR: C3

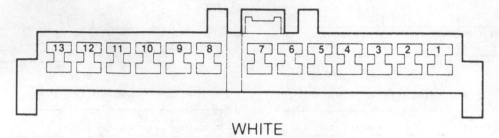

WHITE

WIRING DETAIL LEGEND

TERMINAL	WIRE COLOR	CIRCUIT
1	GRN/RED	Combination Switch – LH Turn Signal
2	—	Not Used
3	LT BLU	ECM – Upshift Signal (Manual Transaxle)
	—	Not Used (Automatic Transaxle)
4	YEL/GRN	ECM – Vehicle Speed Input
5	RED/BLK	Parking Brake Switch/Brake Fluid Level Switch
6	GRA/YEL	Seat Belt Controller (Hardtop)
	—	Not Used (Convertible)
7	—	Not Used
8	—	Not Used
9	YEL/RED	Fuel Gage Sending Unit
10	BLK/BLU	Ground – G202
11	BLK/WHT	IG Fuse
12	ORN/BLU	Seat Belt Controller (Hardtop)
	GRN/YEL	Audio Alarm Module (Convertible)
13	—	Not Used

Fig. 214 1992-93 Metro wiring diagram — instrument panel connectors

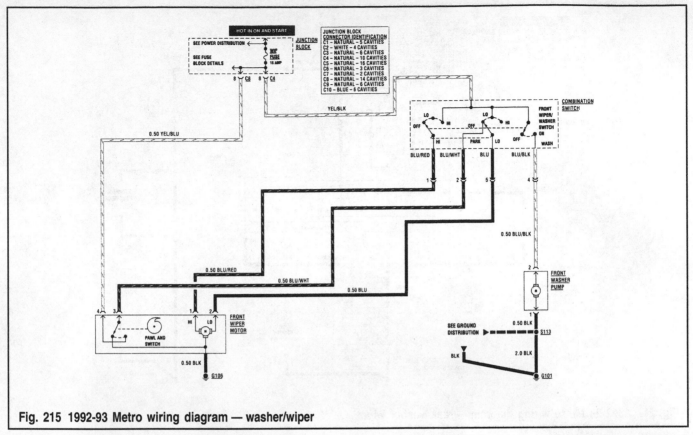

Fig. 215 1992-93 Metro wiring diagram — washer/wiper

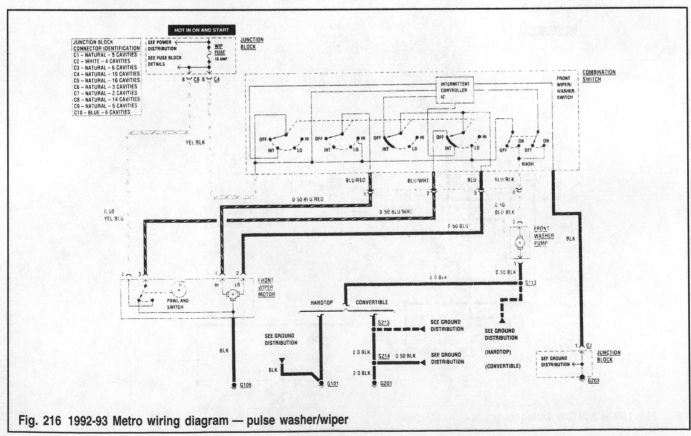

Fig. 216 1992-93 Metro wiring diagram — pulse washer/wiper

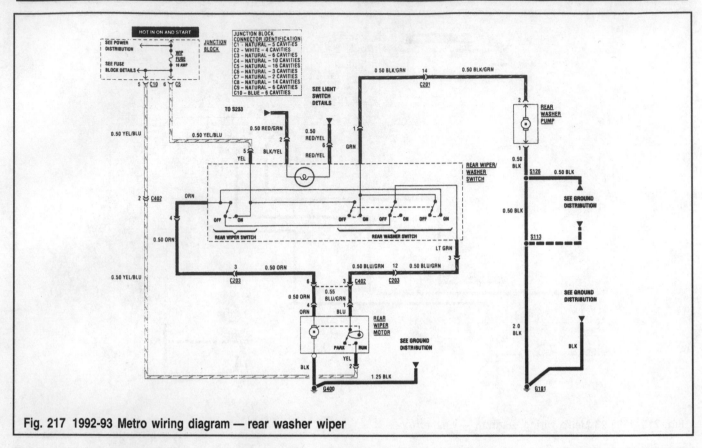

Fig. 217 1992-93 Metro wiring diagram — rear washer wiper

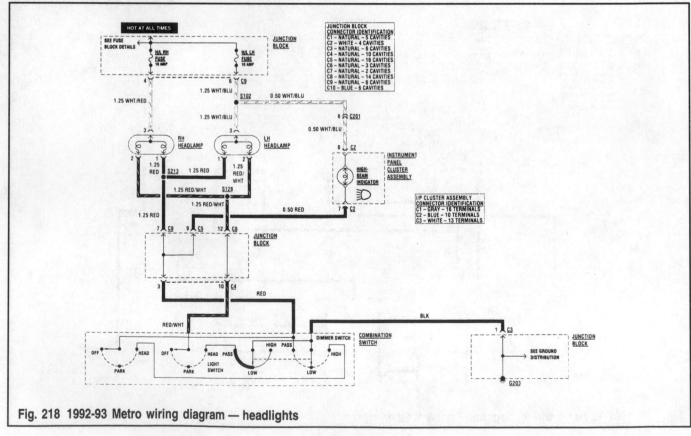

Fig. 218 1992-93 Metro wiring diagram — headlights

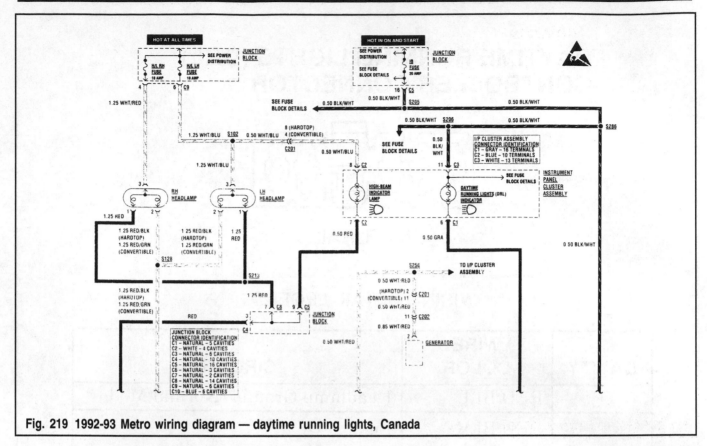

Fig. 219 1992-93 Metro wiring diagram — daytime running lights, Canada

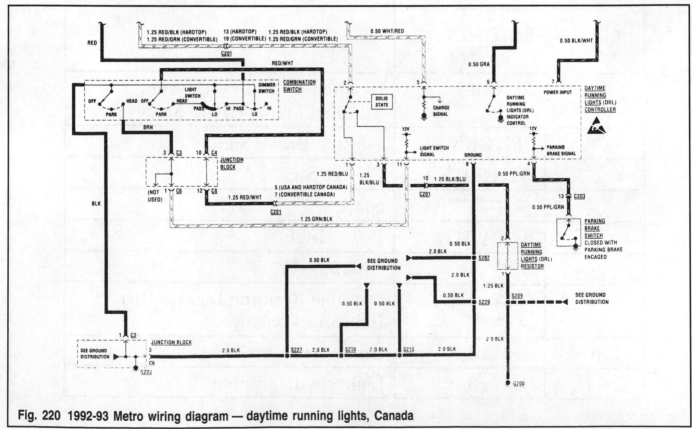

Fig. 220 1992-93 Metro wiring diagram — daytime running lights, Canada

DAYTIME RUNNING LIGHTS (DRL) CONTROLLER CONNECTOR

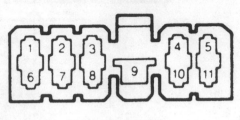

NATURAL

WIRING DETAIL LEGEND

CAVITY	WIRE COLOR	CIRCUIT
1	RED/BLU	Headlamp Ground (Normal Mode)
2	RED/BLK (Hardtop)	Light Switch
	RED/GRN (Convertible)	
3	BLK/BLU	Headlamp Ground (Daytime Running Lights (DRL) Mode)
4	PPL/GRN	Parking Brake Signal
5	WHT/RED	Charge Signal
6	---	Not Used
7	BLK/WHT	Power Input
8	BLK	Ground – G203
9	GRA	Daytime Running Lights (DRL) Indicator Control
10	RED/BLK	Brake Indicator Control
11	GRN/BLK	Light Switch Signal

Fig. 221 1992-93 Metro wiring diagram — daytime running lights controller connector, Canada

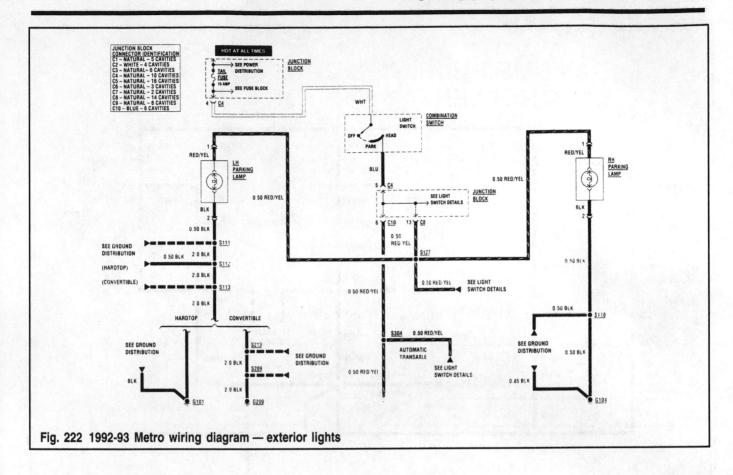

Fig. 222 1992-93 Metro wiring diagram — exterior lights

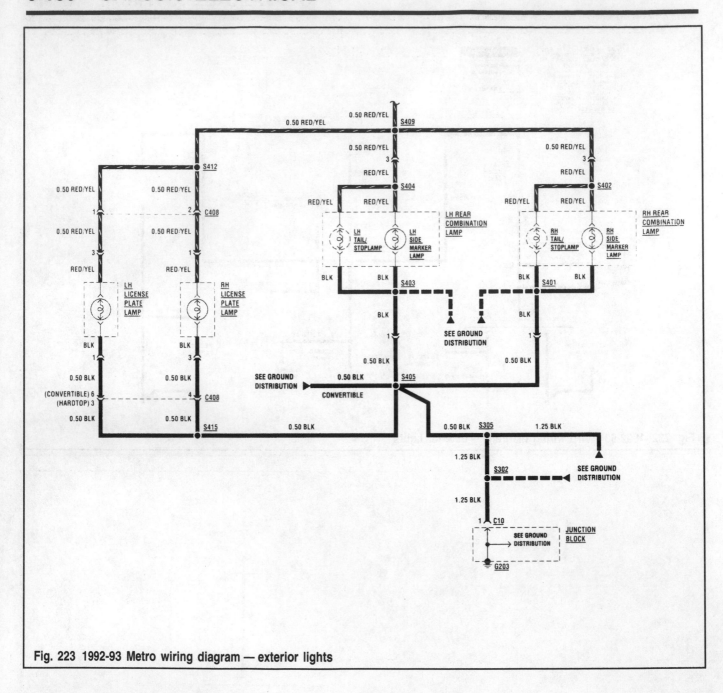

Fig. 223 1992-93 Metro wiring diagram — exterior lights

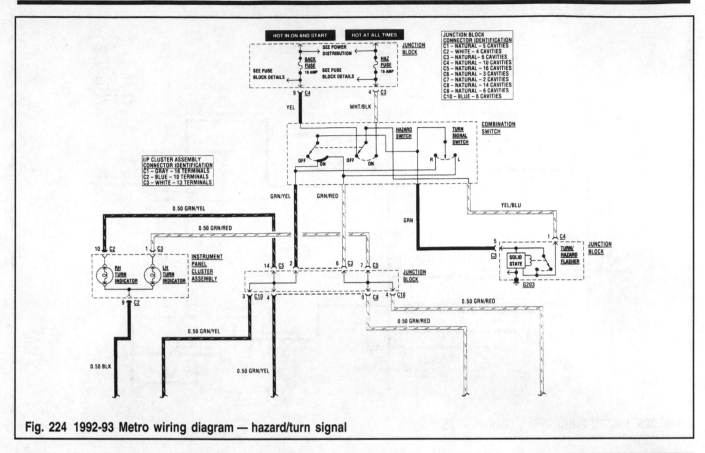

Fig. 224 1992-93 Metro wiring diagram — hazard/turn signal

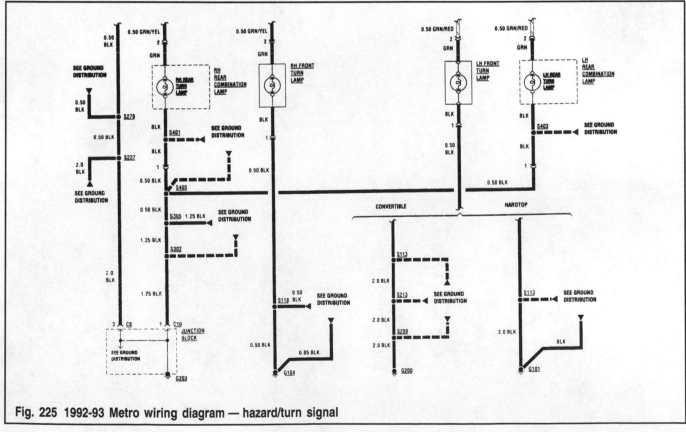

Fig. 225 1992-93 Metro wiring diagram — hazard/turn signal

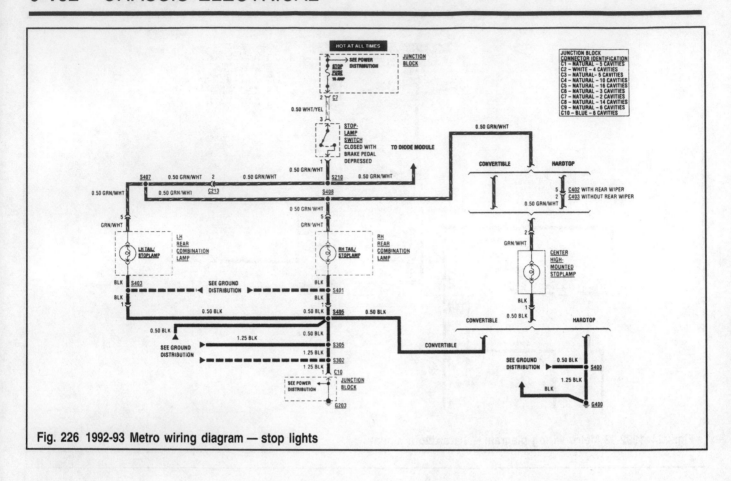

Fig. 226 1992-93 Metro wiring diagram — stop lights

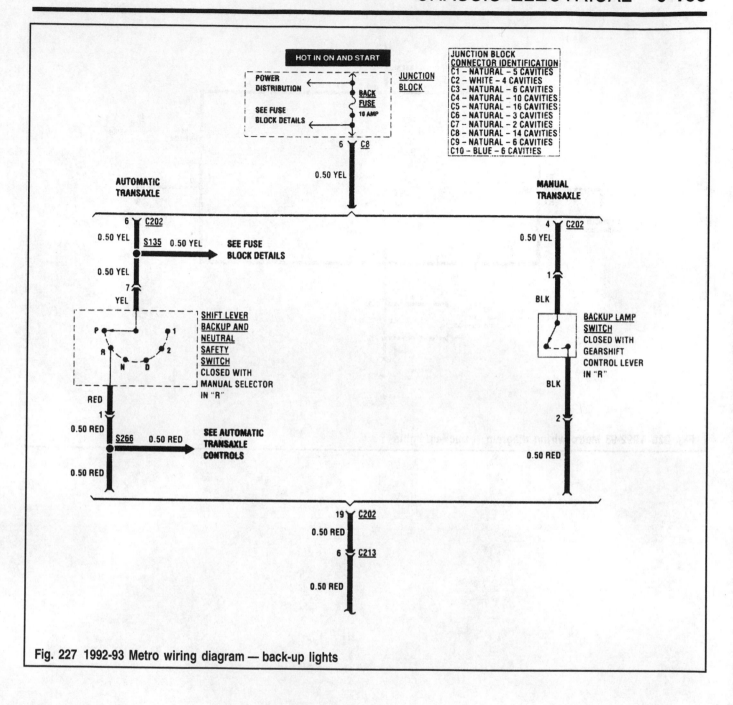

Fig. 227 1992-93 Metro wiring diagram — back-up lights

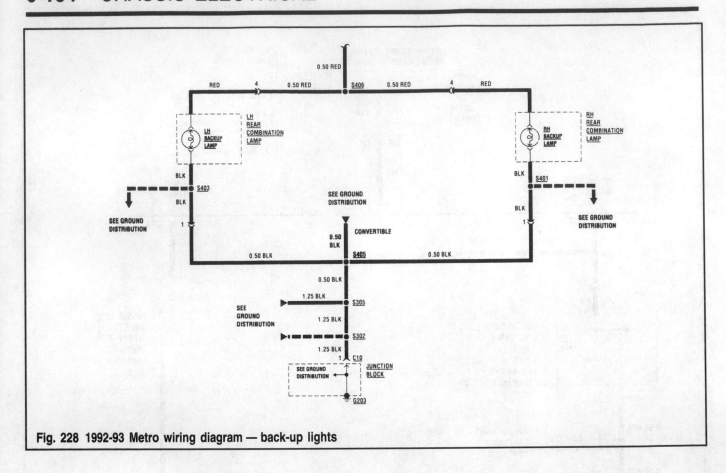

Fig. 228 1992-93 Metro wiring diagram — back-up lights

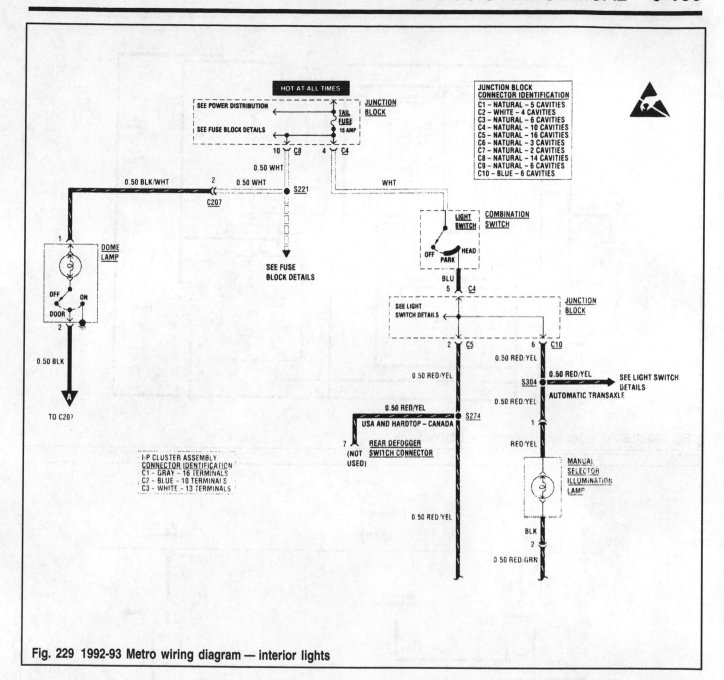

Fig. 229 1992-93 Metro wiring diagram — interior lights

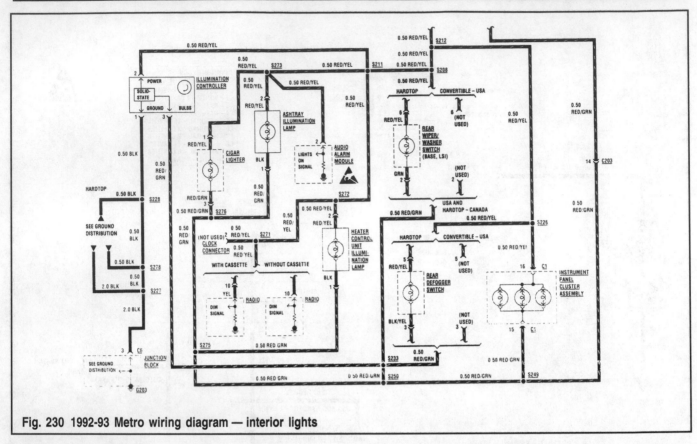

Fig. 230 1992-93 Metro wiring diagram — interior lights

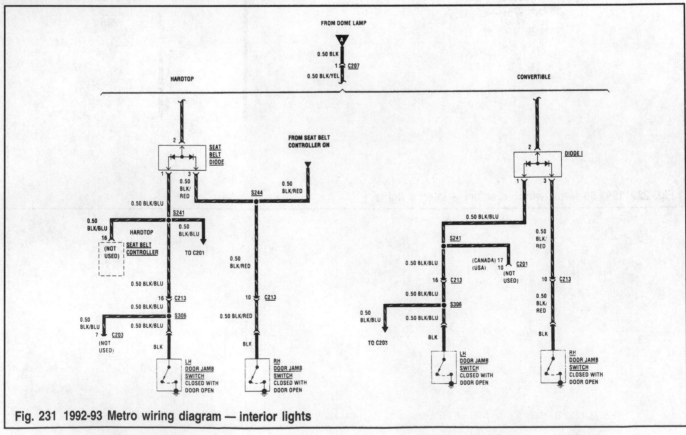

Fig. 231 1992-93 Metro wiring diagram — interior lights

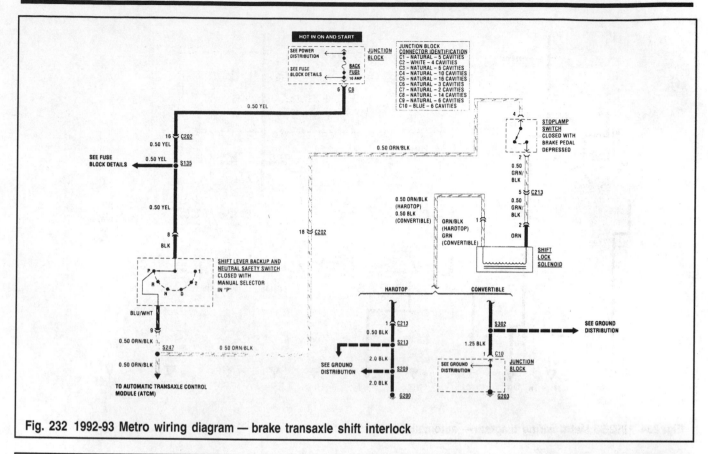

Fig. 232 1992-93 Metro wiring diagram — brake transaxle shift interlock

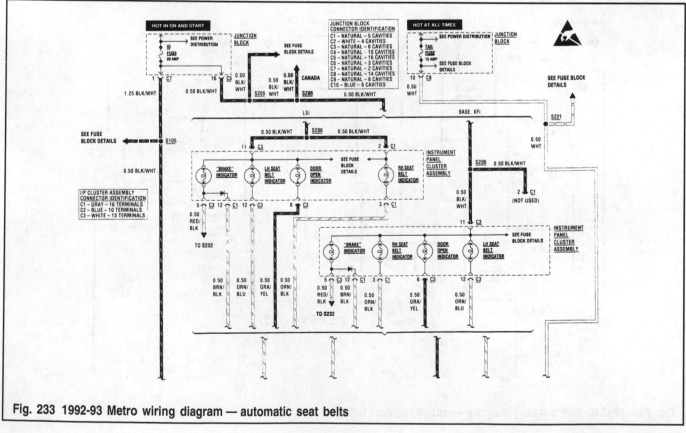

Fig. 233 1992-93 Metro wiring diagram — automatic seat belts

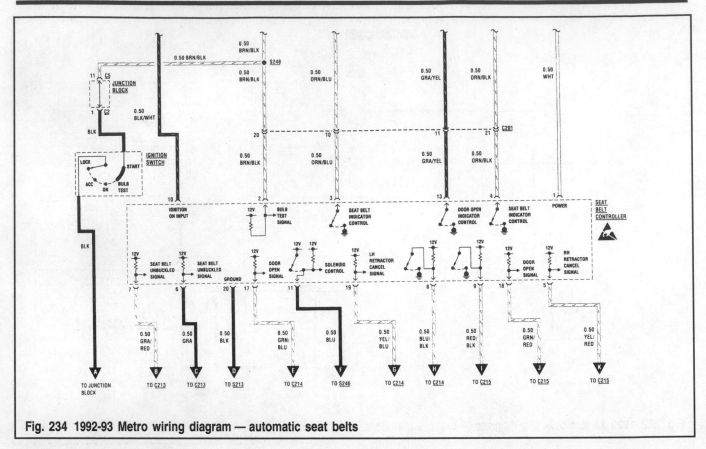

Fig. 234 1992-93 Metro wiring diagram — automatic seat belts

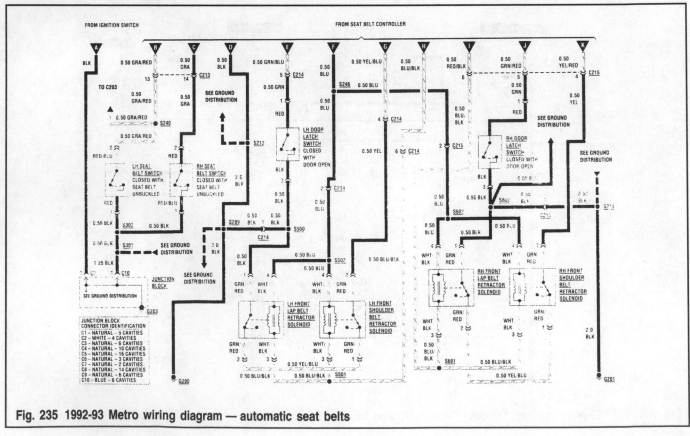

Fig. 235 1992-93 Metro wiring diagram — automatic seat belts

SEAT BELT CONTROLLER CONNECTOR

WIRING DETAIL LEGEND

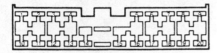

WHITE

CAVITY	WIRE COLOR	CIRCUIT
1	WHT	TAIL Fuse
2	BRN/BLK	Bulb Test Signal
3	ORN/BLK	RH Seat Belt Indicator
4	ORN/BLU	LH Seat Belt Indicator
5	YEL/RED	RH Retractor Cancel Signal
6	GRA	RH Seat Belt Unbuckled Signal
7	GRA/RED	LH Seat Belt Unbuckled Signal
8	BLU/BLK	LH Retractor Solenoid Ground
9	RED/BLK	RH Retractor Solenoid Ground
10	BLK/WHT	IG Fuse
11	BLU	Retractor Solenoid Power
12	—	Not Used
13	GRA/YEL	Door Open Indicator Control
14	BLK/RED	Seat Belt Diode/RH Door Switch
15	—	Not Used
16	BLK/BLU	Seat Belt Diode/LH Door Switch
17	GRN/BLU	LH Door Open Signal
18	GRN/RED	RH Door Open Signal
19	YEL/BLU	LH Retractor Cancel Signal
20	BLK	Ground – G200

Fig. 236 1992-93 Metro wiring diagram — seat belt controller connector

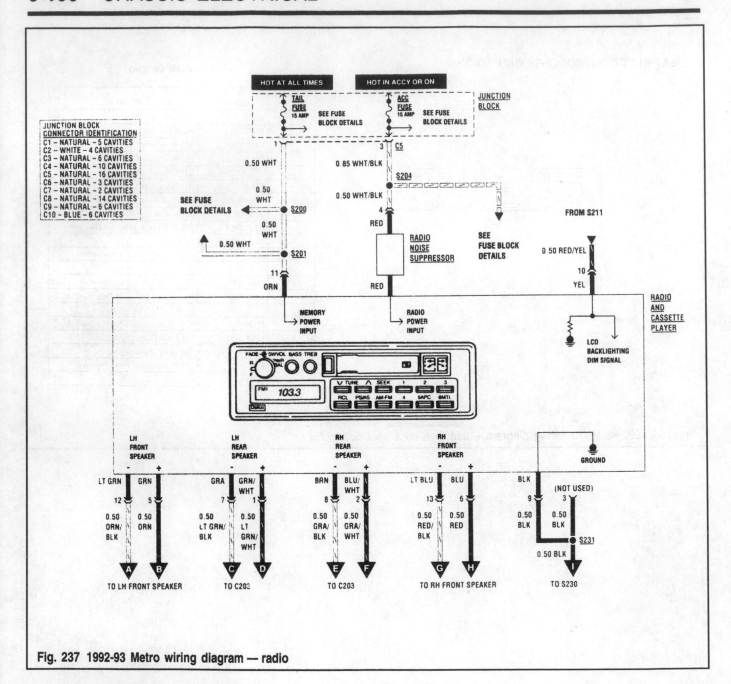

Fig. 237 1992-93 Metro wiring diagram — radio

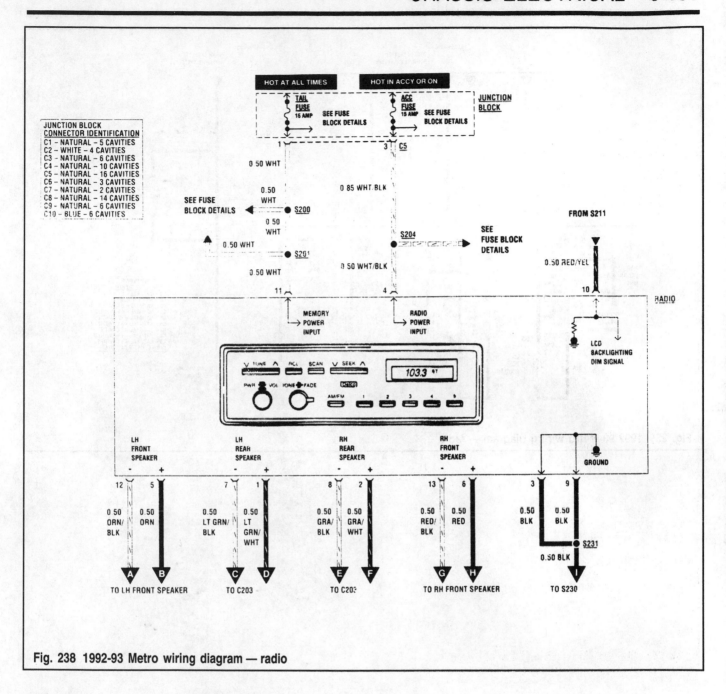

Fig. 238 1992-93 Metro wiring diagram — radio

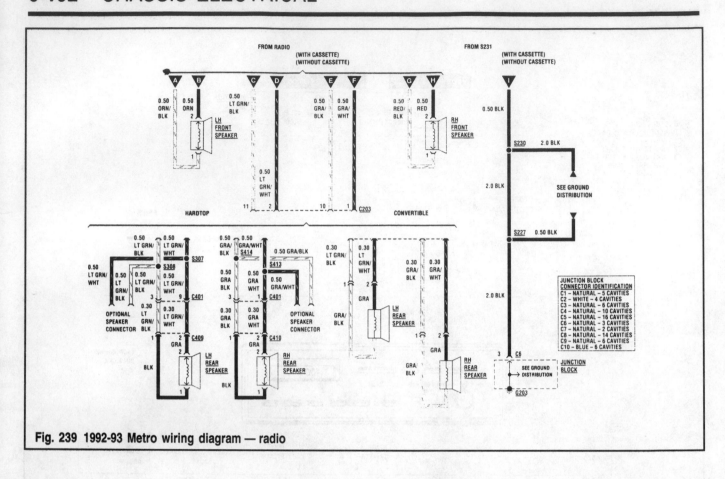

Fig. 239 1992-93 Metro wiring diagram — radio

RADIO CONNECTOR

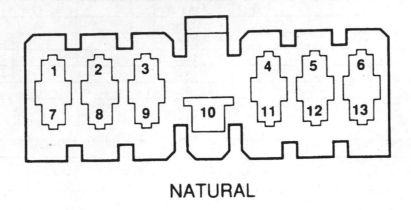

NATURAL

WIRING DETAIL LEGEND

CAVITY	WIRE COLOR	CIRCUIT
1	LT GRN/WHT	LH Rear Speaker (+)
2	GRA/WHT	RH Rear Speaker (+)
3	BLK	Ground – G203 (without Cassette)
	—	Not Used (with Cassette)
4	WHT/BLK	Radio Power
5	ORN	LH Front Speaker (+)
6	RED	RH Front Speaker (+)
7	LT GRN/BLK	LH Rear Speaker (-)
8	GRA/BLK	RH Rear Speaker (-)
9	BLK	Ground – G203
10	RED/YEL	Illumination Dim Signal
11	WHT	Memory Power
12	ORN/BLK	LH Front Speaker (-)
13	RED/BLK	RH Front Speaker (-)

Fig. 240 1992-93 Metro wiring diagram — radio connector

TORQUE SPECIFICATIONS

Component	U.S.	Metric
Blower case bolts	89 inch lbs.	(10 Nm)
Brake switch	115 inch lbs.	(13 Nm)
Clutch switch	115 inch lbs.	(13 Nm)
Compressor bolts	21 ft. lbs.	(28 Nm)
Compressor pipe fitting	18 ft. lbs.	(25 Nm)
Condenser bolts	15 ft. lbs.	(20 Nm)
Condenser hose fitting	26 ft. lbs.	(35 Nm)
Evaporator core:		
Inlet pipe	26 ft. lbs.	(35 Nm)
Outlet pipe	33 ft. lbs.	(45 Nm)
Expansion valve	18 ft. lbs.	(25 Nm)
Headlamp assembly	89 inch lbs.	(10 Nm)
Receiver/dryer pipe	26 ft. lbs.	(35 Nm)
Refrigerant lines:		
3/8 in. O.D. pipes	11–18 ft. lbs.	(15–25 Nm)
1/2 in. O.D. pipes	15–22 ft. lbs.	(20–30 Nm)
5/8 in. O.D. pipes	22–29 ft. lbs.	(30–40 Nm)
Steering column support	10 ft. lbs.	(14 Nm)
Steering wheel	24 ft. lbs.	(33 Nm)
Windshield wiper:		
Wiper arm nut	15 ft. lbs.	(20 Nm)
Wiper crank arm nut	96 inch lbs.	(10 Nm)
Wiper motor	15 ft. lbs.	(20 Nm)
Wiper linkage	11 ft. lbs.	(15 Nm)

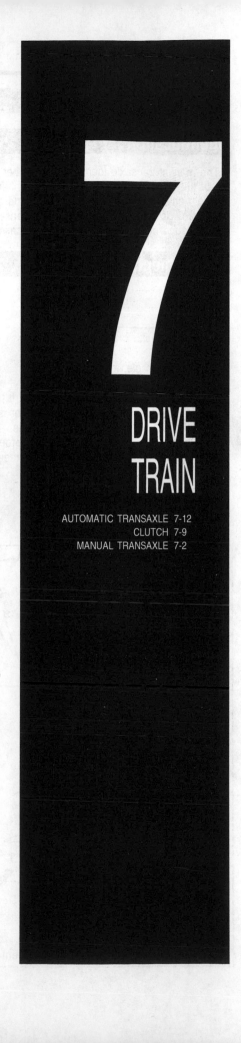

7

DRIVE
TRAIN

MANUAL TRANSAXLE

Identification

The manual transaxle identification number is located on the top of the right case. This seven digit number is stamped into the right case and refers to model year and serial number sequence. On some models, additional transaxle identification can be found on the service parts identification label.

Adjustments

LINKAGE

▶ **See Figure 1**

1. At the console, loosen the gear shift control housing nuts and the guide plate bolts.
2. Adjust the guide plate by displacing it toward the front and rear so that the gear shift control lever is brought in the middle of the guide plate at the right angle.
3. Once the guide plate is positioned properly, tighten the guide plate bolts to 7 ft. lbs. (9 Nm) and then the housing nuts to 4 ft. lbs. (5 Nm).

CLUTCH SWITCH

▶ **See Figure 2**

1. Disconnect the clutch switch electrical connector.
2. Depress the clutch pedal to the floor and return to within 0.6-0.12 in. of its travel from the floor.
3. Attach a ohmmeter to the clutch switch connector.
4. Adjust the clutch switch until continuity is obtained.
5. Tighten the clutch switch to 115 inch lbs. (13 Nm).
6. Connect the electrical connector.

Back-up Light Switch

REMOVAL & INSTALLATION

▶ **See Figure 3**

1. Disconnect the negative battery cable.
2. Remove the back-up lamp switch electrical connector.
3. Remove the back-up lamp switch wire from retaining clamp.
4. Remove back-up lamp switch from case.
To install:
5. Using a new O-ring, install the back-up lamp switch. Tighten to 17 ft. lbs. (23 Nm).

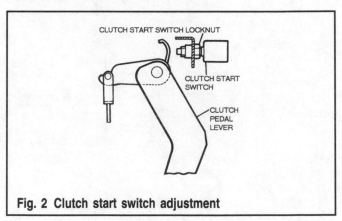

Fig. 2 Clutch start switch adjustment

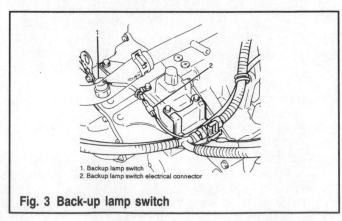

Fig. 3 Back-up lamp switch

1. Gearshift control housing nut
2. Guide plate bolt
3. Guide plate
4. Gearshift control lever
5. Right angle
6. Front side

Fig. 1 Gearshift control lever adjustment

6. Install the back-up lamp switch wire retaining clamp.
7. Install the back-up lamp switch electrical connector.
8. Connect the negative battery cable.

Transaxle

REMOVAL & INSTALLATION

1. Disconnect the negative battery cable and the ground strap at the transaxle.
2. Remove the clutch cable adjusting nuts, retaining clip from the cable and cable from the bracket.
3. Disconnect and tag all the wiring harness clamps and connectors involved with the transaxle removal.
4. Remove the speedometer cable boot, speedometer case clip and speedometer cable from the case.
5. Remove the transaxle retaining bolts.
6. Remove the starter assembly and starter motor plate.
7. Remove the vacuum hose from the pressure sensor.
8. Install the engine support to prevent the engine from lowering excessively.
9. Raise and support the vehicle safely. Drain the transaxle oil.
10. Remove the gear shaft control shaft bolt and nut and detach the control shaft from the gear shift shaft.
11. Extension rod nut and remove the rod with washers.
12. Remove the exhaust pipe front and rear flange bolts.
13. Remove the clutch housing lower plate.
14. Remove the left front wheel.
15. Remove the left tie rod end.
16. Remove the left ball joint by removing the joint stud bolt.
17. Remove both halfshafts at the transaxle.
18. Support the transaxle with a suitable jack and remove the transaxle retaining bolts and nuts.
19. Remove the 2 rear engine mounting bolts.
20. Remove the 3 bolts and 2 nuts from the transaxle mounting left hand bracket, remove the left hand bracket.
21. Lower the transaxle with the engine attached in order to detach it from the stud bolt at the engine rear mounting portion. Pull the transaxle straight out toward the left side to disconnect the input shaft from the clutch cover, lower and remove the transaxle assembly.

To install:
22. While the transaxle is being raised into its correct position, install the right hand halfshaft into the differential.
23. Install the transaxle along with the transaxle to engine nuts and bolts. Install the left hand bracket with its 3 bolts and 2 nuts. Torque them to 37 ft. lbs. (50 Nm).
24. Install the 2 rear engine mounting nuts and torque them to 37 ft. lbs. (50 Nm).
25. Lower the transaxle supporting jack. Torque the transaxle to engine bolt and nut to 37 ft. lbs. (50 Nm).
26. Install the left hand halfshaft to the transaxle. Be sure to push each driveaxle in fully to engage the snaprings with the differential gear.
27. Install the left ball joint and ball joint stud bolt. Torque the ball joint bolt and nut to 44 ft. lbs. (60 Nm).
28. Install the left tie rod end, castle nut and cotter pin. Torque the castle nut to 32 ft. lbs. (43 Nm).
29. Install the left front wheel.

30. Install the clutch housing lower plate.
31. Install the exhaust pipe front and rear flange nuts.
32. Install the extension rod nut and washers. Torque the rod nut to 24 ft. lbs. (33 Nm).
33. Install the control shaft to gear shift and install the gear shift control shaft bolt and nut. Torque the gear shift control shaft bolt and nut to 13 ft. lbs. (18 Nm).
34. Refill the transaxle with the recommended lubricant.
35. Lower the vehicle.
36. Remove the engine support fixture.
37. Install the vacuum hose to the pressure sensor.
38. Install the starter, starter motor plate and 2 bolts.
39. Install the transaxle retaining bolts. Torque the retaining bolts to 37 ft. lbs. (50 Nm).
40. Install the speedometer cable to case, speedometer case clip and speedometer cable boot.
41. Install the clutch cable bracket, retaining clip to cable and clutch cable adjusting nut. Adjust the clutch free-play as necessary.
42. Install the negative battery cable and the ground strap to the transaxle.

OVERHAUL

▶ **See Figures 4, 5, 6, 7, 8 and 9**

➡ **Special tools are required for transaxle overhaul. Without these tools, measurement for bearing shim thickness and transaxle preload can not be made.**

Transaxle Assembly

DISASSEMBLY

1. Remove the backup lamp switch.
2. Remove the bolts from the side case and remove the side case.
3. Remove the snapring and hub plate from the input shaft.
4. Remove the shift fork screw and guide ball from the 5th gear shift fork.
5. With the transaxle in neutral, remove the roll pin from the 5th gear shift fork.
6. Push in on the gear shift shaft to engage transaxle into gear. Slide the 5th gear synchronizer sleeve down to engage 5th gear. This will lock the transaxle in two gears allowing for removal of the 5th gear retaining nut. The retaining nut is staked to the countershaft. Remove the stake mark prior to removing the retaining nut.
7. Remove 5th gear shift fork, sleeve, hub, synchronizer ring, spring and keys as an assembly from the input shaft.
8. Remove 5th gear, bearing, spacer and washer from the input shaft.
9. Remove 5th gear from the countershaft.
10. Remove screws retaining the bearing/shim retainer plate to the left case and remove plate and shims. Mark or tag shims for the input shaft and countershaft for reference during assembly.
11. Remove bolts retaining left case cap and remove the cap.
12. Remove the roll pin retaining the gear shift yoke to the gear shift/selector shaft.

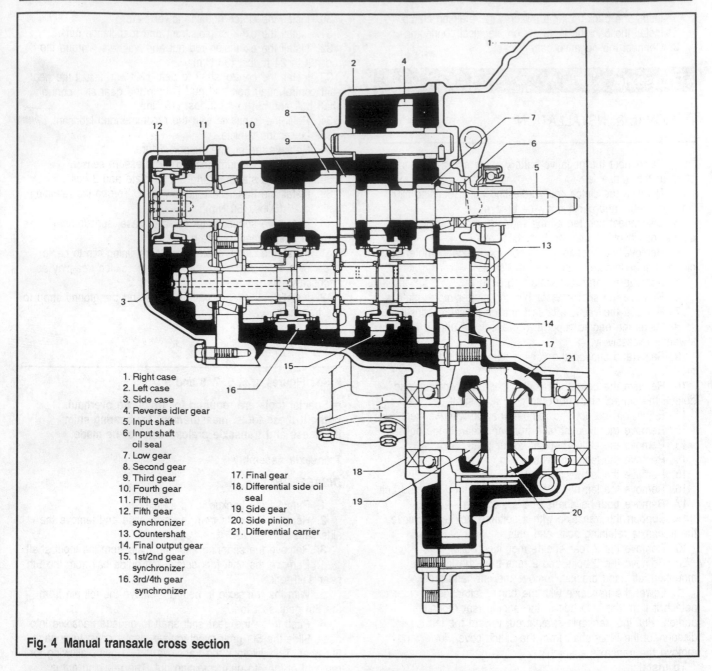

1. Right case
2. Left case
3. Side case
4. Reverse idler gear
5. Input shaft
6. Input shaft oil seal
7. Low gear
8. Second gear
9. Third gear
10. Fourth gear
11. Fifth gear
12. Fifth gear synchronizer
13. Countershaft
14. Final output gear
15. 1st/2nd gear synchronizer
16. 3rd/4th gear synchronizer
17. Final gear
18. Differential side oil seal
19. Side gear
20. Side pinion
21. Differential carrier

Fig. 4 Manual transaxle cross section

13. Install a drift into the roll pin hole in the gear shift/selector shaft and raise the shaft for removal of the yoke and roll pin.

14. Remove the bolt retaining the reverse spring and detent ball. Remove the spring and ball from the case.

15. Remove the locating bolt for the gear shift/selector shaft.

16. Remove the bolts retaining the detent balls and springs for the shift fork shafts.

17. Remove the bolts retaining the case halves.

18. Insert a prybar into the slots between the case halves, pry or lift to separate case halves.

19. Remove the left case. All inner parts such as input shaft, countershaft and differential should remain on the right case.

20. Raise 5th and reverse shift shafts to gain clearance for removal of the reverse gear and shaft.

21. Remove bolts retaining reverse idler shift lever to the case and remove lever.

22. Remove 5th and reverse gear shift shafts together as an assembly.

23. Remove the input shaft, countershaft, 1st/2nd and 3rd/4th shift shafts together as an assembly. It may be necessary to raise the differential assembly to gain clearance for removal of the above components.

24. Remove the differential assembly from the right case.

25. Remove the input shaft and counter shaft bearing cups from the right case using puller tool J29369-2, or equivalent, with a slide hammer.

26. Remove the input shaft seal from the right case using the same tool.

27. Remove the differential side oil seals from the right and left case.

28. Remove the roll pin from the gear shift arm. Position the gear shift arm just above the square recess of the right case by moving the shift shaft. Using a drift, drive the pin out.

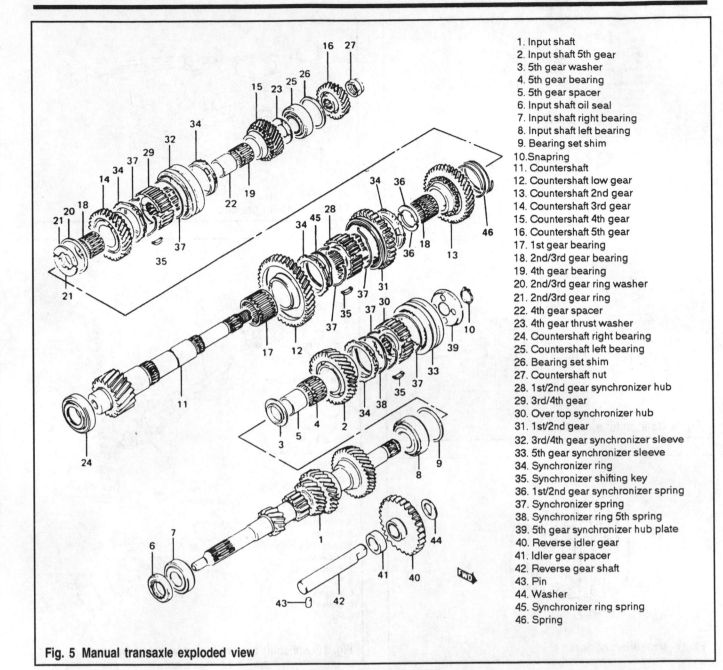

1. Input shaft
2. Input shaft 5th gear
3. 5th gear washer
4. 5th gear bearing
5. 5th gear spacer
6. Input shaft oil seal
7. Input shaft right bearing
8. Input shaft left bearing
9. Bearing set shim
10. Snapring
11. Countershaft
12. Countershaft low gear
13. Countershaft 2nd gear
14. Countershaft 3rd gear
15. Countershaft 4th gear
16. Countershaft 5th gear
17. 1st gear bearing
18. 2nd/3rd gear bearing
19. 4th gear bearing
20. 2nd/3rd gear ring washer
21. 2nd/3rd gear ring
22. 4th gear spacer
23. 4th gear thrust washer
24. Countershaft right bearing
25. Countershaft left bearing
26. Bearing set shim
27. Countershaft nut
28. 1st/2nd gear synchronizer hub
29. 3rd/4th gear
30. Over top synchronizer hub
31. 1st/2nd gear
32. 3rd/4th gear synchronizer sleeve
33. 5th gear synchronizer sleeve
34. Synchronizer ring
35. Synchronizer shifting key
36. 1st/2nd gear synchronizer spring
37. Synchronizer spring
38. Synchronizer ring 5th spring
39. 5th gear synchronizer hub plate
40. Reverse idler gear
41. Idler gear spacer
42. Reverse gear shaft
43. Pin
44. Washer
45. Synchronizer ring spring
46. Spring

Fig. 5 Manual transaxle exploded view

29. Remove the retaining bolt for the shifter shaft detent ball and spring. Remove ball and spring from case.

30. Slide the shifter shaft out and remove the arm, roll pin and shifter shaft from case.

31. Remove the shifter shaft boot from the flange of the oil seal.

32. Remove the input shaft and countershaft bearing cups from the left case.

Input Shaft

DISASSEMBLY

➡Third and fourth gears should not be removed from the input shaft. If the gears are damaged or excessively worn, replace the input shaft.

1. Remove the right bearing (small) from the input shaft using a bearing separator and hydraulic press.

2. Remove the left bearing (large) from the input shaft using a bearing separator and hydraulic press.

Countershaft

DISASSEMBLY

➡The countershaft right bearing cage protrudes beyond the countershaft end face. Use care not to place the countershaft with the right bearing on a work bench or damage to the bearing cage may occur.

1. Remove the right bearing from the countershaft using a bearing separator and hydraulic press.

2. Remove the left bearing from the countershaft using a bearing separator and hydraulic press.

3. Remove the 4th gear thrust washer, 4th gear, bearing, spacer, 4th gear synchronizer hub and sleeve assembly. Next remove 3rd gear synchronizer ring, 3rd gear and bearing.

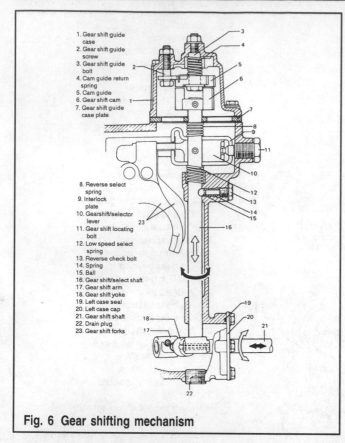

1. Gear shift guide case
2. Gear shift guide screw
3. Gear shift guide bolt
4. Cam guide return spring
5. Cam guide
6. Gear shift cam
7. Gear shift guide case plate
8. Reverse select spring
9. Interlock plate
10. Gearshift/selector lever
11. Gear shift locating bolt
12. Low speed select spring
13. Reverse check bolt
14. Spring
15. Ball
16. Gear shift/select shaft
17. Gear shift arm
18. Gear shift yoke
19. Left case seal
20. Left case cap
21. Gear shift shaft
22. Drain plug
23. Gear shift forks

Fig. 6 Gear shifting mechanism

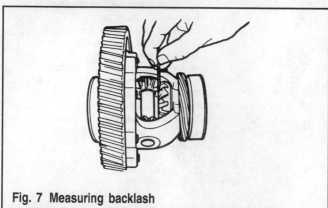

Fig. 7 Measuring backlash

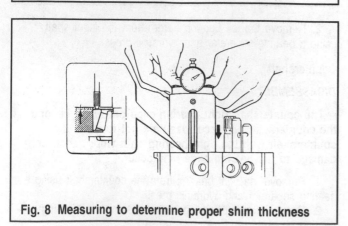

Fig. 8 Measuring to determine proper shim thickness

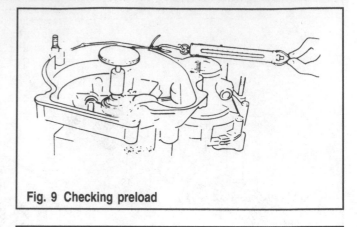

Fig. 9 Checking preload

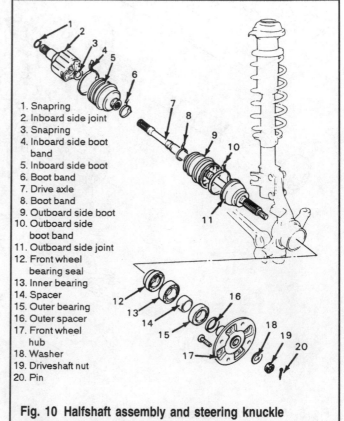

1. Snapring
2. Inboard side joint
3. Snapring
4. Inboard side boot band
5. Inboard side boot
6. Boot band
7. Drive axle
8. Boot band
9. Outboard side boot
10. Outboard side boot band
11. Outboard side joint
12. Front wheel bearing seal
13. Inner bearing
14. Spacer
15. Outer bearing
16. Outer spacer
17. Front wheel hub
18. Washer
19. Driveshaft nut
20. Pin

Fig. 10 Halfshaft assembly and steering knuckle

4. Remove the ring washer from 2nd gear retaining ring halves. Remove the two ring halves, 2nd gear, bearing and 2nd gear synchronizer ring.

5. Remove 1st/2nd gear synchronizer assembly retaining ring halves. Remove 1st/2nd synchronizer hub and sleeve assembly, 1st gear synchronizer ring, 1st gear and bearing.

Differential Case

DISASSEMBLY

1. Remove the side bearings using a gear puller and a plug to protect the gearing bore.

2. Remove the speedometer drive gear using a puller.

3. Remove the roll pin retaining the pinion shaft.

4. Remove the pinion shaft, pinion gears and side gears from the case.

5. Remove the ring gear retaining bolts and then remove the ring gear.

Cleaning and Inspection

Wash all parts thoroughly in clean solvent. Be sure all old lubricant, metallic particles, dirt or foreign material are removed from the surfaces of every part.

Apply compressed air to each oil feed port and channel in each case half to remove any obstructions or cleaning solvent residue. Inspect the case halves for cracks, porosity, damaged mating surfaces, stripped bolt threads or distortion. Replace any part that exhibits these conditions.

Inspect all gear teeth for signs of excessive wear or damage and check all gear splines for burrs, nicks, wear or damage. Remove minor nicks or scratches on an oil stone. Replace any part exhibiting excessive wear or damage.

Inspect all thrust washer for evidence of excessive wear, distortion or damage. Replace any of these parts if they exhibit these conditions.

Inspect the condition of the needle, roller and thrust bearings. Wash bearings thoroughly in a cleaning solvent. Apply compressed air to dry.

➡**Do not allow bearings to spin while applying compressed air. Spinning bearings may damage the rollers.**

Lubricate bearings with light oil and check for roughness by slowly turning the race by hand.

Inspect shift forks and shift shafts for evidence of excessive wear, distortion or damage. Replace any of these parts if they exhibit these conditions.

The synchronizer hubs and sliding sleeves are a selected assembly and should be kept together as originally assembled, but the keys, springs and rings may be replaced if worn or broken.

Assemble the low and high speed synchronizer spring to the hubs. Insert one end of the spring in the spring setting hole on the hub, directing the springs on each hub in opposition to each other so that the load is evenly applied to the synchronizer keys.

Input Shaft

ASSEMBLY

1. Install the right bearing (small) on the input shaft using a bearing driver and hydraulic press.
2. Install the left bearing (large) on the input shaft using a bearing driver and hydraulic press.

Countershaft

DISASSEMBLY

1. Apply clean transaxle fluid to the sliding surfaces of all parts prior to assembly.
2. Install the low gear bearing and then the gear on the shaft.
3. Install the low gear synchronizer ring and ring spring.
4. Install the 1st/2nd gear synchronizer assembly on the shaft. When installing the hub to the countershaft, align the oil groove on the hub with the oil hole onto he shaft.
5. Install the low speed synchronizer hub rings. Fit the two rings into the groove on the countershaft.

6. Install the 2nd gear bearing and then the gear on the shaft. Install the two rings with the protrusion of the ring into the hole on the countershaft.
7. Install the ring washer.
8. Install the spring to 2nd gear.
9. Install the 3rd gear bearing and then the gear on the shaft.
10. Install the 3rd/4th gear synchronizer assembly on the shaft. Install the hub on the countershaft in such a way that oil groove of the hub meets the oil hole of the shaft.
11. Install the 4th gear and then the thrust washer. The oil grooves on the washer goes against 4th gear.
12. Install the left and right bearings on the shaft.

Differential Case

ASSEMBLY

1. Apply clean transaxle oil to the sliding surfaces of all parts prior to assembly.
2. Install side washers and then side gears.
3. Install the pinion washers and pinion gears.
4. Install the pinion gear shaft.
5. Measure the backlash of the side pinions and side gears with a feeler gauge. If backlash exceeds 0-0.009 in., adjust it by varying the thickness of the side gear washers.
6. Install the pinion shaft roll pin.
7. Install the ring gear and retaining bolts. Tighten bolts to 58-72 ft. lbs. (80-100 Nm).
8. Install the speedometer gear.
9. Install the right and left side bearings. Install the bearing with the seal side facing the differential case.

Transaxle

ASSEMBLY

1. Apply grease to the lips of the input shaft seal and differential side oil seals after installation. Apply clean transaxle oil to the sliding surfaces of all parts prior to assembly.
2. Install the input shaft seal in the right case.
3. Install the input shaft bearing cup in the right case.
4. Install the countershaft bearing cup in the right case.
5. Install the right and left case differential oil seals.
6. Install the reverse gear shift lever. Apply thread locking cement to the bolts prior to installing. Torque bolts to 14-20 ft. lbs. (18-28 Nm).
7. Install gear shift shaft oil seal. After installation, apply grease to the lip of the seal.
8. Install gear shift shaft boot. Apply grease to the shaft prior to installing.
9. Install the shift shaft detent ball, spring, gasket and bolt.
10. Install the gear shift arm and roll pin tot he gear shift shaft.
11. Install the differential assembly into the right case.
12. Install the 5th and reverse gear shift and guide shaft to the right case.
13. Install the input shaft, countershaft, 1st/2nd and 3rd/4th gear shift shafts to the right case.
14. Install the idler gear, shaft, pin, spacer and washer to the right case.
15. Install the case magnet to the right case.
16. Apply Loctite® 518 or equivalent, uniformly to the mating surface of the left case.

17. Place the left case on the right case and install the retaining bolts. tighten bolts to 14-20 ft. lbs. (18-28 Nm). After tightening bolts, check the input shaft and countershaft for smooth rotation by running them by hand.

18. Install the shift fork shaft detent balls, springs, gaskets and bolts. Tighten bolts to 8-11 ft. lbs. (10-16 Nm).

19. Install the gear shift yoke on the gear shift arm. Install the gear shift/select shaft assembly, guiding the shaft into the hole in the gear shift yoke. Align the hole in the yoke with the hole in the shaft and install a new roll pin to retain it.

20. Install the gearshift locating bolt and washer. Tighten to 30-43 ft. lbs. (40-60 Nm).

21. Install the reverse check ball, spring, washer and bolt.

22. Install the case cap with a new O-ring to the left case. In stall the retaining bolts.

23. Measure and determine the bearing shim size for the input shaft and countershaft as follows:

   a. Install the left bearing cups for the input shaft and countershaft.

   b. Using finger pressure, press countershaft left bearing cup against the bearing rollers.

   c. Rotate the countershaft three or four times by hand to seat the bearing. Install the nut from installation tool J34858 on the shaft and then install the countershaft nut and torque to 44-58 ft. lbs. (60-80 Nm).

   d. Install a dial gauge on J34858 shim selector tool. Place the shim selector on a flat surface and zero the gauge.

   e. Place the shim selector on the countershaft and left case. Press down on the shim selector and read the dial indicator. The reading on the dial gauge will indicate the size shim required.

   f. The shim stock is available in twelve selective thickness. Each shim has the thickness stamped on the side. Select the shim required and install it on the back side of the left countershaft bearing cup.

   g. Repeat the above steps for measuring the input shaft.

   h. Select the shim required and install it on the back side of the left input shaft bearing cup.

24. Install the case . Fit the protrusion of the case plate joint the groove of the gear shift guide shaft. Apply thread locking cement to the threads of the screws and install.

25. Check the preload of the transaxle. Install tool J34852 on the input shaft. Connect a spring balance to the wire on the tool and pull the spring balance. Check the preload in **N** and in 4th gear. If the preload is not 3-15 Nm, the shims will have to be changed on the input shaft or countershaft.

26. With the transaxle in 4th gear, install 5th gear on the input shaft and countershaft. Engage the synchronizer so the transaxle will be locked in two gears.

27. Install the countershaft nut. After tightening, stake the nut with a chisel. If a crack is found at the staked portion, replace the nut.

28. Disengage 5th gear synchronizer and shift the transaxle into **N**.

29. Install the shift guide ball and shift fork screw to the shift fork. After tightening the screw, stake it in place.

30. Install a new roll pin to 5th and reverse gear shift shaft.

31. Install the synchronizer hub plate and a new snapring.

32. Apply Loctite® 518, or equivalent, to the mating surface of the side case. Install the side case. Fit the oil receiver cup

in the side case into the hole of the input shaft. Install the bolts 14-20 ft. lbs. (18-28 Nm).

33. Install the back-up light switch.

Halfshafts

REMOVAL & INSTALLATION

◆ **See Figure 10**

1. Remove the grease cap, the cotter pin and the halfshaft nut from both front wheels.
2. Loosen the wheel nuts.
3. Raise and support the vehicle safely.
4. Remove the front wheels.
5. Drain the transaxle fluid.
6. Using a prybar, pry on the inboard joints of the right and left hand halfshafts to detach the halfshafts from the snaprings of the differential side gears.
7. Remove the stabilizer bar mounting bolts and the ball joint stud bolt. Pull down on the stabilizer bar and remove the ball joint stud from the steering knuckle.
8. Pull the halfshafts out of the transaxle's side gear, first, and then from the steering knuckles.

➡**To prevent the halfshaft boots from becoming damaged, be careful not to bring them into contact with any parts. If any malfunction is found in the either of the joints, replace the joints as an assembly.**

To install:

9. To install, snap the halfshaft into the transaxle, first, and then into the steering knuckle.
10. Install ball joint and tighten nut to 44 ft. lbs. (60 Nm). Install the cotter pin.
11. Install the stabilizer bar and tighten mount bolts to 32 ft. lbs. (43 Nm).
12. Install the halfshaft nut and tighten to 129 ft. lbs. (175 Nm).
13. Fill the transaxle with fluid.
14. Install the front wheels.
15. Lower the vehicle.

CV-JOINT OVERHAUL

◆ **See Figure 11**

➡**Do not disassemble the wheel side (outboard joint). If damaged, replace it as an assembly. Do not disassemble the spider of the differential side joint. If damaged, replace the differential side joint assembly.**

Disassembly

1. Remove the boot band from the differential side joint
2. Remove the housing from the differential side joint.
3. Remove the snapring and then spider from shaft.
4. Remove inside and outside boots from shaft.

Inspection and Cleaning

1. Check the boots for tears or deterioration. Replace as necessary.

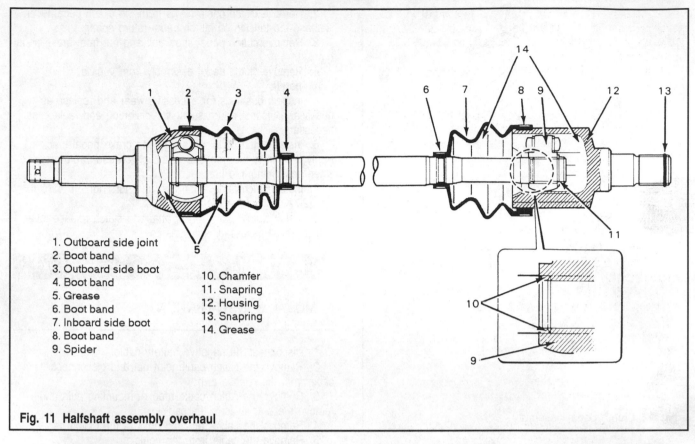

Fig. 11 Halfshaft assembly overhaul

1. Outboard side joint
2. Boot band
3. Outboard side boot
4. Boot band
5. Grease
6. Boot band
7. Inboard side boot
8. Boot band
9. Spider
10. Chamfer
11. Snapring
12. Housing
13. Snapring
14. Grease

2. Check the circlip, snapring, and boot bands for breakage or deformation. Replace as necessary.

3. Wash the disassembled parts in degreaser. After washing dry with compressed air.

4. Clean boots with a rag. Do not wash the boots in solvent.

5. Clean the spider of the differential side joint with a clean towel to prevent the needle bearing of the spider from being degreased. Do not wash the spider in solvent.

Assembly

1. Liberally apply the joint grease to the wheel side joint. Use the back joint grease in the tube included in the wheel side boot set or wheel side joint assembly.

2. Fit the wheel side boot on the shaft. Fill the inside of the boot with the joint grease then fix the boot bands.

3. Fit the differential side boot on the shaft.

4. Liberally apply the joint grease to the differential side joint. Use the yellow joint grease in the tube included in the differential side boot set or the differential side joint assembly.

5. Install the spider of the differential side joint on the shaft, facing its chamfered side to the wheel side joint.

6. After installing the spider, fit the snapring in the groove of the shaft.

7. Fill the inside of the differential side boot with the joint grease, then install the housing. Fix the boot to the housing with a boot band.

8. Check boots for distortion or dents and correct as necessary.

CLUTCH

✳✳CAUTION

The clutch driven disc contains asbestos, which has been determined to be a caner causing agent. Never clean clutch surfaces with compressed air. Avoid inhaling any dust from any clutch surface. When cleaning clutch surfaces, use a commercially available brake cleaning fluid.

Adjustments

RELEASE ARM PLAY

▶ **See Figure 12**

1. At the transaxle, move the clutch release arm to check the free-play, it should be 0.08-0.16 in. on Sprint and 0.06-0.08 in. on Metro.

2. If necessary, turn the clutch cable joint nut to adjust the cable length.

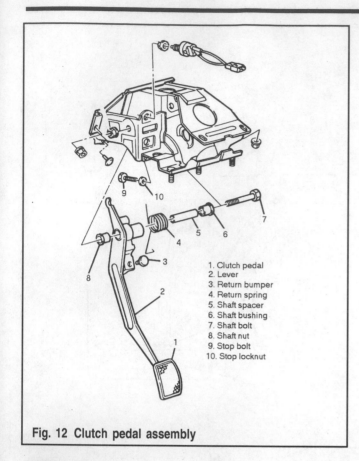

1. Clutch pedal
2. Lever
3. Return bumper
4. Return spring
5. Shaft spacer
6. Shaft bushing
7. Shaft bolt
8. Shaft nut
9. Stop bolt
10. Stop locknut

Fig. 12 Clutch pedal assembly

PEDAL HEIGHT

The clutch pedal height should be adjusted so the clutch pedal is the exact same height as the brake pedal. The pedal is adjusted at the stop bolt on the upper end of the pedal pivot.

CLUTCH START SWITCH

1. Apply the parking brake firmly and place the gear shift lever in **N** position.
2. Disconnect the lead wire at the switch.
3. Loosen the locknut and screw the switch out.
4. Depress clutch pedal all the way to the floor and then return it back 0.4-1.1 in. along its travel from the floor.
5. Connect an ohmmeter to the switch and slowly screw the switch in until the switch is **ON**. Hold the switch at this position and tighten the locknut to 8-11 ft. lbs. (10-15 Nm).
6. Connect the lead wire.

Clutch Pedal

REMOVAL & INSTALLATION

▶ See Figure 12

1. Remove clutch cable adjustment nut from the clutch cable end at the release lever

2. Remove clutch cable clevis from the clutch pedal lever. Release the tension on clutch pedal return spring.
3. Remove clutch pedal shaft bolt and nut from brake pedal bracket.
4. Remove clutch pedal assembly from vehicle.
   To install:
5. Inspect bushings for excessive wear and replace as necessary. Inspect return spring for distortion and replace as necessary.
6. Install clutch pedal assembly into brake pedal bracket. Apply tension to the free end of the clutch pedal return spring when positioning into bracket.
7. Install clutch pedal shaft bolt and nut. Tighten to 15 ft. lbs. (20 Nm).
8. Install clutch cable clevis, attach to clutch release lever and make all necessary adjustments.

Clutch Cable

REMOVAL & INSTALLATION

1. Disconnect the negative battery cable.
2. Remove the clutch cable joint nut and disconnect the cable from the release arm.
3. Remove the clutch cable bracket mounting nuts and remove the bracket from the cable.
4. Remove the cable retaining bolts at the clutch pedal.
5. Remove the cable from the vehicle.
   To install:
6. Before installation, apply grease to the hook and pin end of the cable.
7. Connect the cable to the clutch pedal and install the retaining bolts.
8. Install the clutch cable bracket on the cable.
9. Position the bracket on the transaxle and install the mounting bolts.
10. Connect the cable to the release lever and install the joint nut on the cable.
11. Adjust the pedal free-play as previously outlined and connect the negative battery cable.

Clutch Disc and Clutch Cover

REMOVAL & INSTALLATION

▶ See Figure 13

1. Remove the transaxle.
2. Install pilot tool J-34860 for Sprint or J-37761 for Metro into the pilot bearing to support the clutch assembly.
3. Matchmark the clutch cover and flywheel for installation reference.
4. Loosen the clutch cover-to-flywheel bolts, one turn at a time (evenly) until the spring pressure is released.
5. Remove the clutch disc and clutch cover.

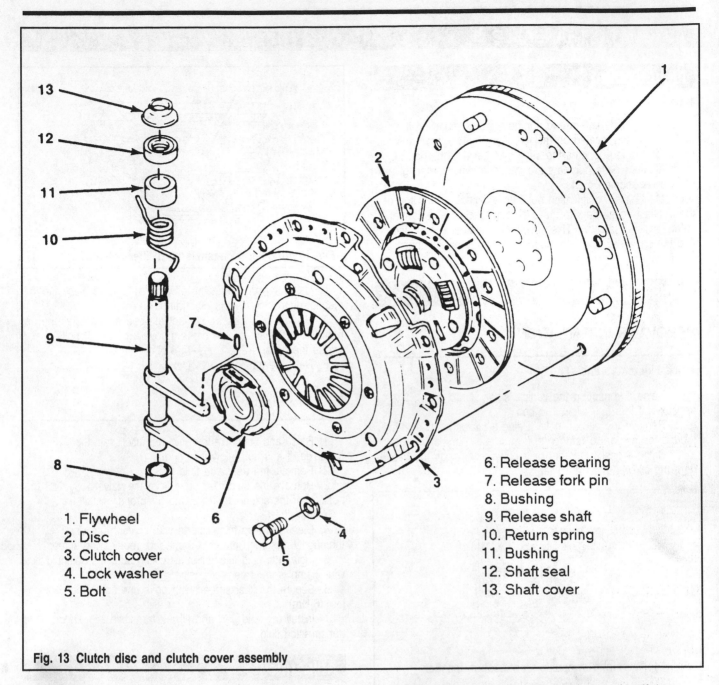

1. Flywheel
2. Disc
3. Clutch cover
4. Lock washer
5. Bolt

6. Release bearing
7. Release fork pin
8. Bushing
9. Release shaft
10. Return spring
11. Bushing
12. Shaft seal
13. Shaft cover

Fig. 13 Clutch disc and clutch cover assembly

To install:

6. Clean the flywheel mating surfaces of all oil, grease and metal deposits. Inspect flywheel for cracks, heat checking or other defects and replace or resurface as necessary.

7. Check the wear on the facings of the clutch disc by measuring the depth of each rivet head depression. Replace clutch disc when rivet heads are 0.02 in. below surface of clutch surface.

8. Check diaphragm spring and pressure plate for wear or damage. If the spring or plate is excessively worn, replace the clutch cover assembly.

9. Check the pilot bearing for smooth operation. If the bearing does not spin freely, replace it.

10. Position the clutch disc and clutch cover with the matchmarks aligned and support with pilot tool.

11. Install the clutch cover bolts and tighten evenly to 18 ft. lbs. (23 Nm). Remove the pilot tool.

12. Lightly lubricate the splines, pilot bearing surface of the input shaft and release bearing with grease.

13. Install the transaxle.

14. Adjust the clutch cable.

AUTOMATIC TRANSAXLE

Identification

▶ See Figure 14

On Sprint, code letters and numbers are stamped on the identification tag located on the left side (front) of the transaxle housing. The tag denotes the serial number and the date of manufacture. These numbers are important when ordering service replacement parts.

On Metro, the identification number is located on the top of the transaxle case next to the shift lever backup and neutral safety switch assembly. This seven digit number is stamped into the case and refers to model year and serial number sequence.

Fluid Pan

REMOVAL & INSTALLATION

▶ See Figures 15 and 16

1. Raise and support the vehicle safely. Drain the transaxle; if it is hot, allow it to cool.
2. Remove the oil pan bolts. Using a plastic hammer, tap around the oil pan to remove it; do not use a prybar.
3. Using a gasket scraper or a putty knife, clean the gasket from the oil pan and transaxle.

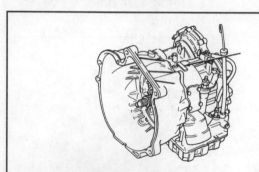

Fig. 14 Automatic transaxle identification location — Metro

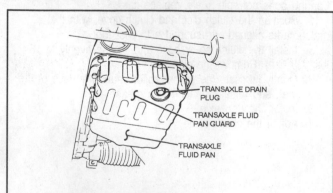

Fig. 15 Automatic transaxle fluid pan

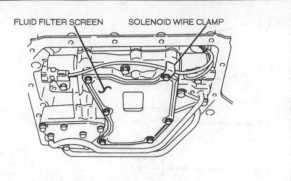

Fig. 16 Automatic transaxle fluid filter screen

4. Using solvent, clean the oil pan; be sure to place the magnet directly below the oil strainer.
5. Using a new gasket, sealant (if necessary), install the oil pan. Using sealant on the cross grooved (on head) bolts, torque the bolts to 3-4 ft. lbs. (4-6 Nm).
6. Refill the transaxle with Dexron®II transmission fluid.

FILTER SERVICE

1. Raise and support the vehicle safely. Drain the transaxle; if it is hot, allow it to cool.
2. Remove the transaxle fluid pan.
3. Remove the fluid filter bolts from the valve body. Not the position of the solenoid wire clamp for proper installation.
   To install:
4. Clean the fluid filter screen with solvent and dry thoroughly. If screen mesh is damaged, replace the screen.
5. Install the fluid filter screen making sure the solenoid wire clamp is in its correct position.
6. Secure the filter screen with bolts and tighten to 53 inch lbs. (6 Nm).
7. Install the fluid pan and fill the transaxle with Dexron®II transmission fluid.

Adjustments

SHIFT LINKAGE

▶ See Figure 17

1. Place the shift lever in the **N** position.
2. Turn the adjusting nut in until it contacts the manual select cable joint.
3. Tighten the locknut.
4. To adjust the interlock cable (back drive cable), use the following procedure:
   a. Shift the selector to the **P** position.
   b. Loosen the adjusting and locknut on the interlock cable.

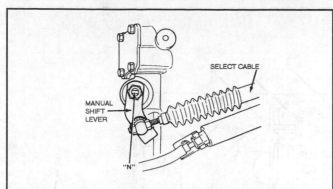

Fig. 17 Automatic transaxle shift linkage adjustment

c. Pull the outer wire (interlock cable) forward so there is no deflection on the inner wire, tighten the adjusting nut hand tight only and then tighten the locknut.

➡**After tightening the nuts, make sure that with the shifter lever shifted to the PARK position, the ignition key can be turned from the ACC to the LOCK position and the key can be removed from the ignition switch. With the selector lever shifted to any range other than the PARK position, the ignition key can not be turned from the ACC to LOCK position.**

5. On the Metro adjust the shift lock solenoid so that it will operate as follows:

a. When the ignition switch is turned **OFF**, the solenoid is not operated.

b. When the ignition switch is turned **ON**, and the brake pedal is depressed, the solenoid is operated and the lock plate is positioned properly.

c. There is no clearance between the lock plate and the guide plate.

d. If the manual release knob is pulled when the ignition switch is turned **OFF**, the selector lever can be shifted from the **P** range to any other range.

➡**After tightening the solenoid retaining nuts, make sure that with the shifter lever shifted to the PARK position, the ignition key can be turned from the ACC to the LOCK position and the key can be removed from the ignition switch.**

OIL PRESSURE CONTROL CABLE

1. Inspect and/or adjust the accelerator cable play by performing the following procedures:

a. At the carburetor, check the amount of play in the accelerator cable; it should be 0.40-0.59 in. (10-15mm) cold or 0.12-0.19 in. (3-5mm) warm.

b. If necessary to adjust, loosen the locknut and turn the adjustment nut until the correct specifications are met.

c. After adjustment, tighten the locknut.

2. Operate the engine until normal operating temperatures are reached and allow the engine to idle; make sure the carburetor is not on the fast idle step.

3. From near transaxle's dipstick tube, remove the oil pressure control cable cover. Using a feeler gauge, check that

the boot-to-inner cable stopper clearance is 0-0.02 in. (0-0.5mm).

4. If the clearance is not within specifications, perform the following procedures:

a. Loosen the adjusting nuts (engine side of bracket) and turn them to adjust the clearance.

b. If the adjustment (engine side) fails to establish the clearance, tighten the nuts and move the other side (dipstick side) of the bracket.

c. Loosen the adjusting nuts (dipstick side of bracket) and turn them to adjust the clearance.

d. After adjustment is complete, tighten the adjusting nuts, recheck adjustment and install the cover.

INTERLOCK (BACK DRIVE) CABLE

▶ **See Figure 18**

1. Place the shift selector into the **P** position.
2. Loosen both back drive cable nuts.
3. Pull the outer wire forward so there is no deflection on the inner wire and tighten both nuts (hand tight); tighten the nut farthest from the clevis end first and then tighten the other nut.
4. After tightening the nuts, check the following situations:

a. With the shift selector in the **P** position, the ignition key can be turned from **ACC** to **LOCK** position and removed from the ignition switch.

b. With the shift selector in any position, other than **P**, the ignition key cannot be turned from **ACC** to **LOCK** position.

THROTTLE VALVE (TV) CABLE

▶ **See Figure 19**

1. Inspect the accelerator cable for play and adjust if necessary.
2. Star the engine and allow it to reach normal operating temperature.
3. Remove the TV cable adjustment cover.
4. Measure the TV cable boot to inner cable stopper clearance with a feeler gauge. If clearance is more than 0.02 in. adjust the cable.
5. Adjust the clearance by turning the TV cable adjustment nuts until proper clearance is reached.
6. The accelerator cable nuts may also be used to adjust the TV cable if no further adjustment on the TV cable is available.

Back-up and Neutral Safety Switch

REMOVAL & INSTALLATION

▶ **See Figure 20**

1. Disconnect the negative battery cable.
2. Remove the electrical connector at the engine wiring harness.
3. Remove the harness from the retaining clamps.
4. Remove the switch from the transaxle.

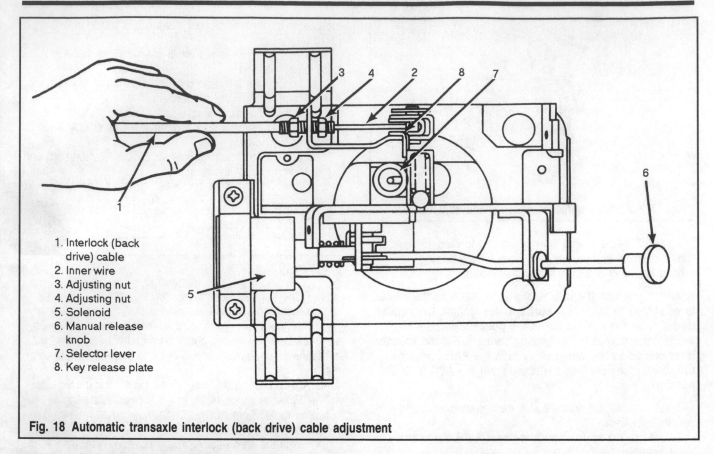

1. Interlock (back drive) cable
2. Inner wire
3. Adjusting nut
4. Adjusting nut
5. Solenoid
6. Manual release knob
7. Selector lever
8. Key release plate

Fig. 18 Automatic transaxle interlock (back drive) cable adjustment

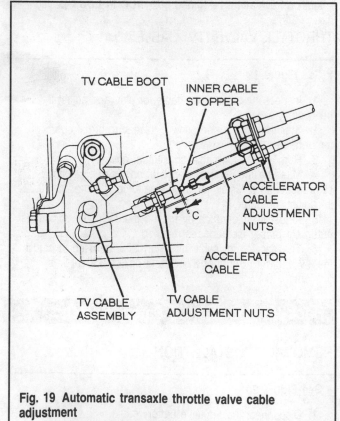

TV CABLE BOOT

INNER CABLE STOPPER

ACCELERATOR CABLE ADJUSTMENT NUTS

ACCELERATOR CABLE

TV CABLE ASSEMBLY

TV CABLE ADJUSTMENT NUTS

Fig. 19 Automatic transaxle throttle valve cable adjustment

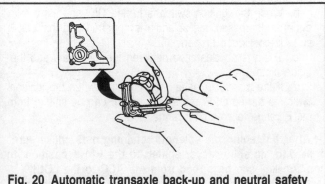

Fig. 20 Automatic transaxle back-up and neutral safety switch adjustment

To install:

5. Place the transaxle in the **N** position.

6. Turn the shift switch assembly joint clockwise or counterclockwise until a distinct click noise is heard.

7. Install the switch and tighten the bolt to 17 ft. lbs. (23 Nm).

8. Install the harness retaining clips and connect the electrical connector.

9. Connect the negative battery cable.

10. Ensure the starter motor operates only when the transaxle shift lever is in the **P** or **N** positions and does not operate when in the **D**, **2**, **L** or **R** positions.

Transaxle

REMOVAL & INSTALLATION

1. From the air cleaner, remove the air suction guide.
2. Disconnect both cables from the battery and the negative cable from the transaxle. Remove the battery and the battery tray.
3. From the transaxle, disconnect the solenoid coupler, the shift lever switch coupler and the wiring harness.
4. Separate the oil pressure control cable from the accelerator cable. From the transaxle, disconnect the accelerator cable and the shift selector cable.
5. Remove the starter motor. Place a catch pan under the transaxle and drain the fluid.
6. Disconnect and plug the oil cooler tubes at the transaxle.
7. Raise and support the vehicle safely. Remove the exhaust pipe and the lower clutch housing plate.

➡**Before removing the torque converter-to-drive plate bolts, make alignment marks on the torque converter and drive plate for assembly purposes.**

8. Using a prybar, insert it through the notch (underside of transaxle) to lock the drive plate gear. Remove the torque converter-to-drive plate bolts.
9. To remove the left halfshaft, perform the following procedures:
   a. From the wheel hub, remove the center cap, the split pin and the driveshaft nut.
   b. Remove the lug nuts and the front wheels.
   c. Using a prybar, position it between the differential case and the halfshaft's inboard joint, pry the joint until the snapring disconnects from the side gear.
   d. Remove both stabilizer bar-to-chassis brackets and the ball stud-to-steering knuckle bolt. Pull the stabilizer bar downward to disconnect the ball joint from the steering knuckle.
   e. Carefully remove the halfshaft from the differential case and the steering knuckle to prevent tearing the boots.
10. Using a prybar, disconnect the right halfshaft from the differential case.
11. Remove the transaxle mounting member bolts and the member. Using a floor jack and a piece of wood, support the transaxle.
12. Remove the left transaxle mount.
13. Remove the transaxle-to-engine bolts. Slide the transaxle from the engine (to prevent damaging the crankshaft, drive plate or torque converter) and lower it from the vehicle.
   To install:
14. Using grease, lubricate the cup around the center of the torque converter.

15. Measure the distance between the torque converter and the transaxle housing; it should be at least 0.85 in. (21.4mm). If the distance is less than specified, the torque converter is improperly installed; remove and reinstall it.
16. When installing the transaxle, guide the right halfshaft into the differential case; make sure the snapring seats in the differential gear.
17. To install the left halfshaft, perform the following procedures:
   a. Clean and lubricate the halfshaft splines with grease.
   b. Carefully install the halfshaft into the steering knuckle and the differential case to prevent tearing the boots; make sure the snapring seats in the differential gear.
   c. Install the ball joint stud into the steering knuckle and torque the bolt to 36-50 ft. lbs. (50-70 Nm).
   d. Install the stabilizer bar-to-chassis brackets and torque the bolts to 22-39 ft. lbs. (30-55 Nm).
   e. Torque the halfshaft hub nut to 108-195 ft. lbs. (150-270 Nm) and install the split pin (to the shaft) and the center cap.
   f. Torque the lug nuts to 29-50 ft. lbs. (40-70 Nm).
18. Torque the transaxle housing-to-engine bolts to 12-16.5 ft. lbs. (16-23 Nm), the mounting member-to-chassis bolts to 40 ft. lbs. (55 Nm), the mounting member-to-transaxle nuts to 33 ft. lbs. (45 Nm) and the transaxle-to-mount bolts to 40 ft. lbs. (55 Nm).
19. Using a prybar, insert it through the notch (underside of transaxle) to lock the drive plate gear and torque the torque converter-to-drive plate bolts to 13-14 ft. lbs. (18-19 Nm).
20. Install the oil cooler lines and the starter.
21. After connecting the oil pressure control cable to the accelerator cable, check and/or adjust the cable play.
22. Connect the wiring harness, the shift lever switch coupler and the solenoid coupler to the transaxle.
23. Install and adjust the select cable and shift switch.
24. Install the battery tray and the battery. Connect the battery cables to the battery and the negative battery cable to the transaxle.
25. Install the air suction guide to the air cleaner.
26. Refill and check the fluid level.

Halfshaft

REMOVAL & INSTALLATION

Halfshaft servicing procedures for the automatic transaxle are the same as for the manual transaxle. Refer to Halfshafts in the Manual Transaxle portion of this Section.

TORQUE SPECIFICATIONS

Component	U.S.	Metric
Automatic Transaxle:		
Backup/neutral safety switch	17 ft. lbs.	23 Nm
Crossmember-to-chassis	40 ft. lbs.	55 Nm
Crossmember-to-transaxle	33 ft. lbs.	45 Nm
Filter screen	53 inch lbs.	6 Nm
Mount-to-transaxle	40 ft. lbs.	55 Nm
Oil pan	3–4 ft. lbs.	4–6 Nm
Torque converter	13–14 ft. lbs.	18–19 Nm
Transaxle-to-engine	12–16.5 ft. lbs.	16–23 Nm
Backup lamp switch	17 ft. lbs.	23 Nm
Ball joint nut	44 ft. lbs.	60 Nm
Clutch cover	18 ft. lbs.	23 Nm
Clutch pedal shaft bolt	15 ft. lbs.	20 Nm
Clutch switch	115 inch lbs.	13 Nm
Halfshaft nut	129 ft. lbs.	175 Nm
Manual transaxle:		
Case half retaining bolts	14–20 ft. lbs.	18–28 Nm
Countershaft nut	44–58 ft. lbs.	60–80 Nm
Extension rod nut	24 ft. lbs.	33 Nm
Gearshift locating bolts	30–43 ft. lbs.	40–60 Nm
Left mounting bracket	37 ft. lbs.	50 Nm
Rear mounting nuts	37 ft. lbs.	50 Nm
Reverse gear shift lever	14–20 ft. lbs.	18–28 Nm
Ring gear retaining bolts	58–72 ft. lbs.	80–100 Nm
Shift fork	8–11 ft. lbs.	10–16 Nm
Shift linkage guide plate	7 ft. lbs.	9 Nm
Shifter control shaft	13 ft. lbs.	18 Nm
Shifter housing nuts	4 ft. lbs.	5 Nm
Side case bolts	14–20 ft. lbs.	18–28 Nm
Transaxle-to-engine	37 ft. lbs.	50 Nm
Stabilizer bar	32 ft. lbs.	43 Nm
Tie Rod nut	32 ft. lbs.	43 Nm

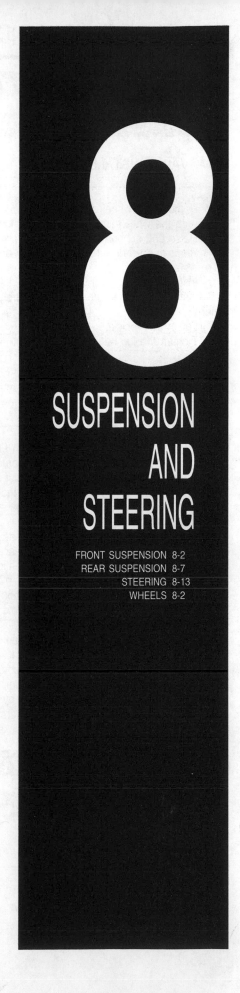

8

SUSPENSION AND STEERING

WHEELS

Wheels

REMOVAL & INSTALLATION

1. Remove the wheel covers.
2. With the wheels still on the ground, loosen the lug nuts.
3. Raise and support the vehicle safely.
4. Remove the lug nuts and the wheel and tire assembly.

To install:

5. Install the wheel and tire assembly.
6. Install and tighten the lug nuts securely using a star pattern.
7. Lower the vehicle.
8. Tighten the lug nuts to 44 ft. lbs. (60 Nm) using a star pattern.
9. Install the wheel cover.

INSPECTION

The original equipment tires have built-in tread wear indicators to show when tires need replacement. These indicators will appear as 0.47 in. wide bands when the tire tread depth becomes 0.063 in. When the indicators appear in 3 or more grooves at 6 locations, tire replacement is recommended.

Irregular and premature tire wear has many causes. Some of them are: incorrect inflation pressures, lack of regular rotation, driving habits, or improper wheel alignment. If wheel alignment is reset due to tire wear condition, always reset toe as close to zero degrees as the specification allows.

If the following conditions are noted, rotate the tires:

- Front tire wear is different from rear.
- Left and right front tire wear is unequal.
- Left and right rear tire wear is unequal.

Check wheel alignment if the following conditions are noted:

- Left and right front tire wear is unequal.
- Wear is uneven across the tread of any front tire.
- Front tire treads have a scuffed appearance with feather edges on one side of the tread ribs or blocks.

Wheel Lug Studs

REPLACEMENT

▶ See Figure 1

1. Raise and support the vehicle safely.
2. Remove the wheel and tire assembly.
3. On the rear, remove the brake drum assembly.
4. On the front, remove the hub/rotor assembly.
5. Using a press, remove the wheel lug studs.

To install:

6. Press the new wheel stud into the brake drum or hub/rotor assembly.

➡**Use care to align the splines on the stud and brake drum/hub**

7. On the rear, install the brake drum assembly.
8. On the front, install the hub/rotor assembly.
9. Install the wheel and tire assembly.
10. Lower the vehicle.

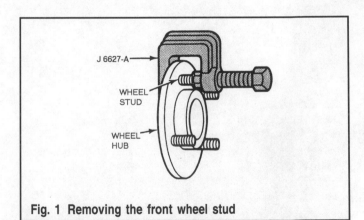

Fig. 1 Removing the front wheel stud

FRONT SUSPENSION

MacPherson Strut

REMOVAL & INSTALLATION

▶ See Figure 2

1. Raise and support the vehicle safely.
2. Remove the tire and wheel assembly.
3. Remove the brake hose clip, then the hose from the strut.

4. Remove the upper strut support nuts from the engine compartment.
5. Remove the strut-to-steering knuckle bolts, then the strut assembly from the vehicle.

To install:

6. Install the strut assembly onto the vehicle. Install the upper support nuts loosely. Then install the strut-to-steering knuckle bolts and tighten to 59 ft. lbs. (80 Nm).
7. Tighten the upper strut support nuts to 20 ft. lbs. (27 Nm).
8. Install the brake hose clip.
9. Install the tire and wheel assembly.
10. Lower the vehicle.

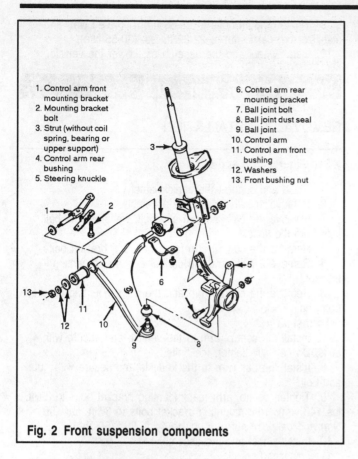

1. Control arm front mounting bracket
2. Mounting bracket bolt
3. Strut (without coil spring, bearing or upper support)
4. Control arm rear bushing
5. Steering knuckle
6. Control arm rear mounting bracket
7. Ball joint bolt
8. Ball joint dust seal
9. Ball joint
10. Control arm
11. Control arm front bushing
12. Washers
13. Front bushing nut

Fig. 2 Front suspension components

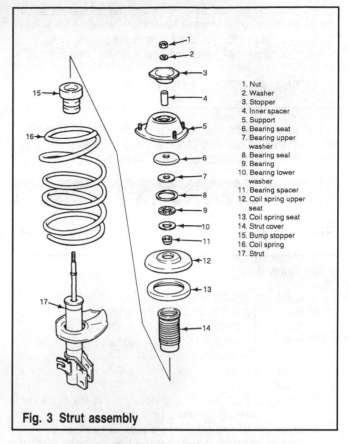

1. Nut
2. Washer
3. Stopper
4. Inner spacer
5. Support
6. Bearing seat
7. Bearing upper washer
8. Bearing seal
9. Bearing
10. Bearing lower washer
11. Bearing spacer
12. Coil spring upper seat
13. Coil spring seat
14. Strut cover
15. Bump stopper
16. Coil spring
17. Strut

Fig. 3 Strut assembly

11. Check front end alignment.

OVERHAUL

▶ **See Figure 3**

1. Remove the strut from the vehicle.
2. Mount the strut in a suitable spring compressor.
3. Compress the strut spring slowly and evenly to approximately half is height after initial contact with top cap. Never bottom spring.
4. Remove the retainer nut from the strut shaft.
5. Remove the strut from the assembly.
6. Disassemble the strut components and inspect for damage or wear. Replace worn or damaged components as required.

To assemble:

7. Mount strut on spring compressor.
8. Position spring on strut and ensure spring is properly seated on spring plate.
9. Install all shields, bumpers and insulators on shaft. Install spring seat on top of spring.
10. Lower the compressor to capture spring seat and pull up strut rod to full extension.
11. Compress spring and guide the strut rod through bearing cap.

➡ **During compression of the spring be sure to guide the shaft through the exact center of the bearing. If the threads of the strut rod catch on the bearing cap and**

prevent the shaft from passing cleanly through the bearing, stop compressing immediately. Decompress the spring and begin again.

12. Compress spring until approximately 1 inch of the damper rod protrudes through the bearing cap. Do not compress the spring any further. Install and tighten nut to 29 ft. lbs. (40 Nm).
13. Apply grease to strut nut and threads.
14. Back off spring compressor and remove strut assembly.
15. Install the strut into the vehicle and tighten the fasteners to specifications.
16. Inspect the front alignment.

Lower Ball Joints

INSPECTION

Ball joints must be replace if any looseness is detected in the joint or if the ball joint seal is cut.

To inspect ball joints, raise and support the vehicle safely. Grasp the top and bottom of the tire and move the top of the tire with an in-and-out motion. Observe for any horizontal movement of the steering knuckle relative to the control arm.

If the ball joint is disconnected from the knuckle and any looseness is detected, or if the ball joint can be twisted in its socket using finger pressure, replace the ball joint.

Ball joint tightness in the knuckle boss should also be checked when inspecting the ball joint. This may be done by shaking the wheel and feeling for movement of the stud end or castle nut at the knuckle boss. Checking the fastener torque at the castle nut is an alternative method of inspecting for wear. A loose nut can indicate a bend stud in the knuckle boss. Worn or damaged ball joints and knuckles must be replaced.

REMOVAL & INSTALLATION

The lower ball joint is an integral part of the lower control arm. Therefore, if ball joint replacement is necessary, the lower control arm must be replaced as an assembly.

Stabilizer Bar

REMOVAL & INSTALLATION

▶ See Figure 4

1. Raise and support the vehicle safely.
2. Remove the wheel and tire assemblies.
3. Remove the stabilizer bar mount bushing brackets.
4. Remove the castle nut, washer and bushing from the stabilizer at the lower control arm.
5. Remove the stabilizer bar from the vehicle.

To install:

6. Install the stabilizer bar and loosely install the castle nut, washer and bushing at the lower control arm.
7. Install the stabilizer bar mount bushing brackets.
8. Position stabilizer bar so that paint marks on the bar are centered between the mount bushings.

9. Tighten mount bolts to 29-65 ft. lbs. (40-90 Nm) and stabilizer bar castle nut to 22-39 ft. lbs. (30-55 Nm).
10. Install wheel and tire assemblies. Lower the vehicle.

Lower Control Arm

REMOVAL & INSTALLATION

▶ See Figures 2, 5 and 6

1. Raise and support the vehicle safely.
2. Remove the wheel and tire assembly.
3. Remove the ball joint nut and bolt. Separate the ball joint from the knuckle.
4. Remove the control arm front mounting bracket bolts.
5. Remove 2 bolts and the control arm rear mounting bracket.
6. Remove the control arm and the front mounting bracket from the vehicle.

To install:

7. Install the control arm to the vehicle and secure with 4 bolts. Do not fully tighten the bolts.
8. Install the ball joint to the knuckle and secure with nut and bolt.
9. Tighten control arm rear mounting bracket bolts to 32 ft. lbs. (43 Nm); front mounting bracket bolts to 66 ft. lbs. (90 Nm) and ball joint nut and bolt to 44 ft. lbs. (60 Nm).
10. Install wheel and tire assembly.
11. Lower the vehicle.
12. Check front wheel alignment.

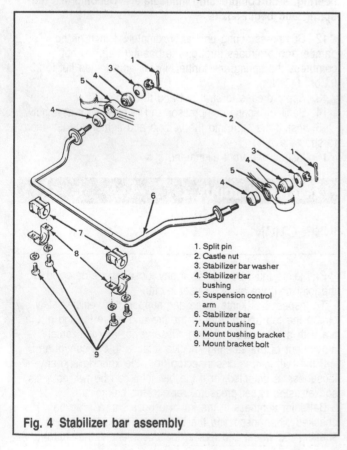

1. Split pin
2. Castle nut
3. Stabilizer bar washer
4. Stabilizer bar bushing
5. Suspension control arm
6. Stabilizer bar
7. Mount bushing
8. Mount bushing bracket
9. Mount bracket bolt

Fig. 4 Stabilizer bar assembly

Fig. 5 Front control arm front bushing

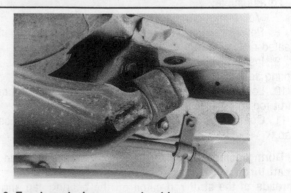

Fig. 6 Front control arm rear bushing

Knuckle and Spindle

REMOVAL & INSTALLATION

▶ **See Figure 7**

1. Raise and support the vehicle safely.
2. Remove the wheel and tire assembly.
3. Remove the hub from the steering knuckle, as outlined in this Section.
4. Remove the tie rod end cotter pin and nut.
5. Remove the ball joint bolt from the steering knuckle.
6. Using the ball joint removal tool J-21687-02 or equivalent, remove the ball joint from the steering knuckle.
7. Remove the strut-to-steering knuckle bolts.
8. Remove the steering knuckle from the vehicle. Support the axle shaft with a jackstand to prevent damage to the CV-joint.
9. Using a brass drift, drive the inner and outer wheel bearings from the steering knuckle.
10. Remove the spacer and clean the steering knuckle cavity.

To install:

11. Lubricate the new bearings and the steering knuckle cavity.
12. Using the installation tool J-34856, drive the new bearings, with the internal seals facing outward, into the steering knuckle.
13. Using the seal installation tool J-34881, drive the new seal into the steering knuckle, grease the seal lip.

14. Install the steering knuckle on the vehicle.
15. Install the strut-to-steering knuckle bolts. Tighten the strut-to-steering knuckle bolts to 59 ft. lbs. (80 Nm).
16. Install the ball joint bolt through the steering knuckle.
17. Install the ball joint nut and tighten to 44 ft. lbs. (60 Nm).
18. Install the tie rod end cotter pin and nut. Tighten nut to 32 ft. lbs. (43 Nm).
19. Install the hub on the steering knuckle. Tighten axle shaft castle nut to 129 ft. lbs. (175 Nm).
20. Install the wheel and tire assembly.

Front Hub

REMOVAL & INSTALLATION

▶ **See Figure 7**

1. Raise and support the vehicle safely.
2. Remove the wheel and tire assembly.
3. Remove the brake caliper.
4. Unstake and remove the drive axle nut and washer.
5. Remove the hub retaining nuts.
6. Using a slide hammer, remove the hub from the vehicle.
7. Remove the brake rotor.

To install:

8. Install the brake rotor.
9. Apply a light coat of grease to the outside of the hub shaft.
10. Install the hub and outer spacer to the knuckle.

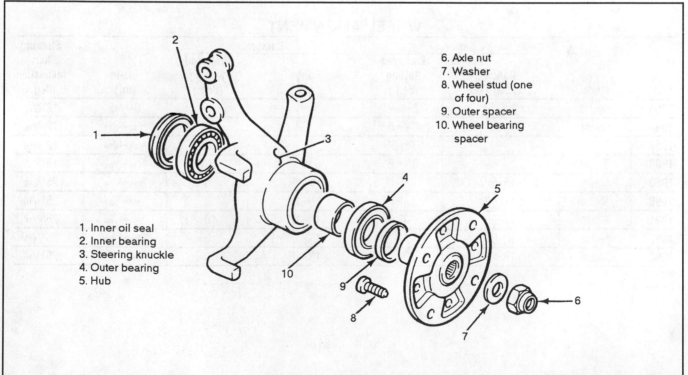

1. Inner oil seal
2. Inner bearing
3. Steering knuckle
4. Outer bearing
5. Hub

6. Axle nut
7. Washer
8. Wheel stud (one of four)
9. Outer spacer
10. Wheel bearing spacer

Fig. 7 Steering knuckle, hub and bearing assembly

11. Install the hub retaining bolts and tighten to 37 ft. lbs. (50 Nm).

12. Install the drive axle nut and tighten to 129 ft. lbs. (137 Nm).

13. Install the caliper.

14. Install the wheel and tire assembly.

15. Lower the vehicle.

Front End Alignment

The do-it-yourself mechanic should not attempt to perform any wheel alignment procedures. Expensive, highly-specialized alignment tools are needed and making these adjustments blindly would most likely result in damage. The 4-wheel alignment should be performed by a certified alignment technician using the proper alignment tools.

The front suspension on these vehicles provides no adjustment for caster or camber. The only adjustment possible is toe-in.

CASTER

Caster is the tilting of the upper most point of the steering axis either forward or backward from the vertical (when viewed from the side of the vehicle). A backward tilt is positive and a forward tilt is negative. Caster influences directional control of the steering, but does not affect tire wear.

Caster is affected by vehicle height; therefore, it is important to keep the body at its designed height. Overloading the vehicle or a weak or sagging spring will affect the caster. When the rear of the vehicle is lower than its normal designated trim height, the front suspension move to a more positive caster. If the rear of the vehicle is higher than its designated trim height, the front suspension move to a less positive caster.

CAMBER

Camber is the tilting of the wheels from the vertical when viewed from the front of the vehicle. When the wheels tilt outward at the top, the camber is positive. When the wheels tilt inward, the camber is negative. The amount of tilt measured in degrees from the vertical is the camber angle. Camber influences both directional control and tire wear.

TOE-IN

Toe is a measurement of how much the front of the wheels are turned in or out from the geometric centerline/thrust line. When the wheels are turned in (toe-in), toe is positive. When the wheels are turned out (toe-out), the toe is negative. The actual amount of toe is normally only a fraction of a degree. The purpose of toe is to ensure that the wheels roll parallel.

WHEEL ALIGNMENT

Year	Model	Caster Range (deg.)	Caster Preferred Setting (deg.)	Camber Range (deg.)	Camber Preferred Setting (deg.)	Toe-in (in.)	Steering Axis Inclination (deg.)
1985	Sprint	—	$3^3/_{16}$P	—	1P	0–$^5/_{32}$	$12^{13}/_{16}$
1986	Sprint	—	$3^3/_{16}$P	—	1P	$^5/_{32}$–$^5/_{32}$	$12^{13}/_{16}$
1987	Sprint	—	$3^3/_{16}$P	—	$^1/_4$P	$^5/_{64}$–$^5/_{64}$	$12^{13}/_{16}$
1988	Sprint	—	$3^3/_{16}$P	—	$^1/_4$P	$^5/_{64}$–$^5/_{64}$	$12^{13}/_{16}$
1989	Metro	1P–5P	3P	1N–1P	0	$^5/_{64}$–$^5/_{64}$	$25^{11}/_{16}$
1990	Metro	1P–5P	3P	1N–1P	0	$^5/_{64}$–$^5/_{64}$	$25^{11}/_{16}$
1991	Metro	1P–5P	3P	1N–1P	0	$^5/_{64}$–$^5/_{64}$	$25^{11}/_{16}$
1992	Metro	1P–5P	3P	1N–1P	0	$^5/_{64}$–$^5/_{64}$	$25^{11}/_{16}$
1993	Metro	1P–5P	3P	1N–1P	0	$^5/_{64}$–$^5/_{64}$	$25^{11}/_{16}$

N—Negative
P—Positive

REAR SUSPENSION

Shock Absorbers

REMOVAL & INSTALLATION

1985-88 Sprint

▶ **See Figure 8**

1. Raise and safely support the vehicle. Remove the wheels.
2. Support the rear axle assembly using jackstands.
3. Remove the upper shock absorber locknut and absorber nut.
4. Remove the lower shock mount bolt.
5. Remove the shock absorber from the vehicle.

To install:
6. Install the shock absorber.
7. Install the lower shock mount bolt and tighten to 32-50 ft. lbs. (45-70 Nm).
8. Install the upper shock locknut and absorber nut. Tighten to 13-20 ft. lbs. (18-28 Nm).
9. Remove the jackstand and lower the vehicle.

1989-93 Metro

▶ **See Figure 9**

1. Raise and safely support the vehicle. Remove the wheel and tire assembly.

2. Place a jackstand under the suspension arm for support when it lowers.
3. Remove the shock support nuts and push the shock down.
4. Remove the lower shock-to-knuckle bolt.

➡**Do not open the knuckle slit wider than necessary. Do not lower the jack more than necessary during the strut removal to prevent the coil spring from coming off, or a brake flexible hose from stretching.**

5. Remove the shock from the knuckle. Compress the shock as short as possible for removal. If the shock is hard to remove, open the slit of the knuckle by inserting a wedge.

To install:
6. Install the shock absorber in the vehicle. Position the bottom of the alignment projection inside the knuckle opening.
7. Install the upper support nuts and tighten to 24 ft. lbs. (30 Nm).
8. Install shock absorber-to-knuckle bolt and tighten to 44 ft. lbs. (60 Nm).
9. Install the wheel and tire assembly.
10. Remove the jackstand and lower the vehicle.

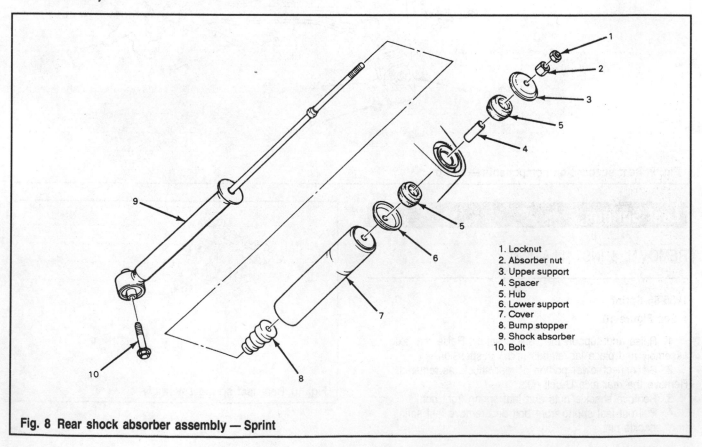

1. Locknut
2. Absorber nut
3. Upper support
4. Spacer
5. Hub
6. Lower support
7. Cover
8. Bump stopper
9. Shock absorber
10. Bolt

Fig. 8 Rear shock absorber assembly — Sprint

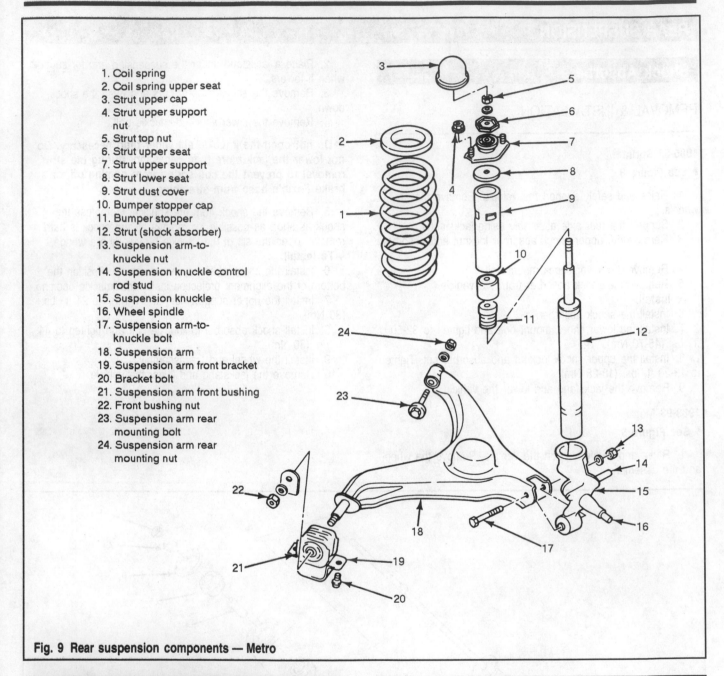

1. Coil spring
2. Coil spring upper seat
3. Strut upper cap
4. Strut upper support nut
5. Strut top nut
6. Strut upper seat
7. Strut upper support
8. Strut lower seat
9. Strut dust cover
10. Bumper stopper cap
11. Bumper stopper
12. Strut (shock absorber)
13. Suspension arm-to-knuckle nut
14. Suspension knuckle control rod stud
15. Suspension knuckle
16. Wheel spindle
17. Suspension arm-to-knuckle bolt
18. Suspension arm
19. Suspension arm front bracket
20. Bracket bolt
21. Suspension arm front bushing
22. Front bushing nut
23. Suspension arm rear mounting bolt
24. Suspension arm rear mounting nut

Fig. 9 Rear suspension components — Metro

Leaf Springs

REMOVAL & INSTALLATION

1985-86 Sprint

♦ **See Figure 10**

1. Raise and support the vehicle safely. Raise rear axle assembly and place jackstands under suspension.

2. Disconnect lower portion of rear shock, as required. Remove the rear axle U-bolt nuts.

3. Remove shackle nuts and leaf spring front nut.

4. Pull out leaf spring front bolt and remove leaf spring from shackle pin.

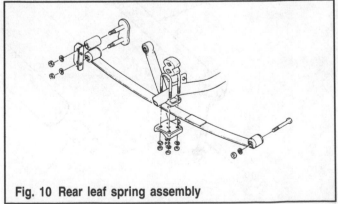

Fig. 10 Rear leaf spring assembly

To install:

5. Install front bolt and shackle pins with the threads facing outward. Tighten shackle pin nuts to 22-39 ft. lbs. (30-55 Nm). Tighten front bolt to 33-50 ft. lbs. (45-70 Nm).

6. Position axle on spring by aligning leaf spring pin with hole in underside of axle.

7. Install bump stopper.

8. Align leaf spring underside pin with hole in spring seat. Install U-bolts from bump stopper side towards spring seat side and tighten to 22-32 ft. lbs. (30-45 Nm).

9. Install lower portion of shock, if removed.

10. Inspect all components for tightness and proper alignment. Lower the vehicle.

Coil Springs

REMOVAL & INSTALLATION

1987-88 Sprint

▶ See Figure 11

1. Raise and support the vehicle safely.
2. Place a jack under the rear axle and raise it slightly.
3. As required, disconnect the brake pipes and parking brake cable.
4. Remove the rear shock absorbers.
5. Disconnect the lateral rod.
6. Lower the rear axle until all tension is remove from the springs.

7. Remove the springs from the vehicle.

To install:

8. Install the springs in the vehicle with the flat side upward. Ensure the bottom of the spring is properly seated in the spring pocket on the rear axle.

9. Raise the rear axle to tension the springs.

10. Install the lateral rod and tighten bolt to 32-50 ft. lbs. (45-70 Nm).

11. Install the shock absorbers. Tighten lower bolt to 32-50 ft. lbs. (45-70 Nm). Tighten upper nut to 13-20 ft. lbs. (18-28 Nm).

12. Connect the brake pipes and parking brake cable, as required.

13. Remove the jack under the rear axle and lower the vehicle.

1989-93 Metro

▶ See Figure 9

1. Raise and support the vehicle safely.

➡**To facilitate the toe-in adjustment after reinstallation, confirm which one of the lines stamped on the washer is in the closest alignment with the stamped line on the control rod. If not marked, add the alignment marks.**

2. Remove the control rod inside bolt (body center side).

3. Remove the outside (wheel side) of the control rod from the rear knuckle stud bolt.

4. Loosen the rear mount not on the suspension arm, but do not remove the bolt.

5. Loosen the front nut of the suspension arm.

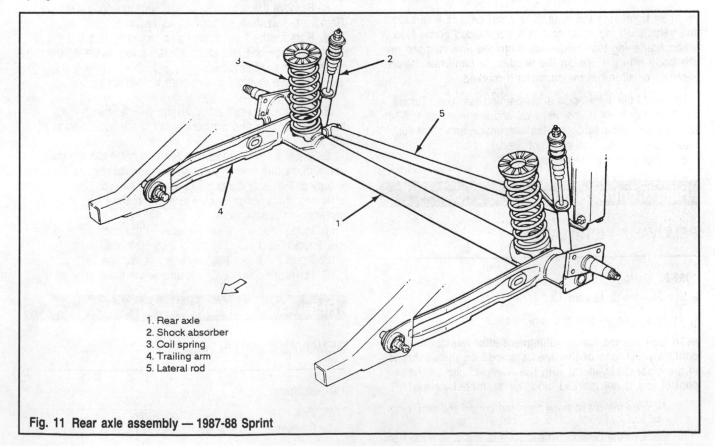

1. Rear axle
2. Shock absorber
3. Coil spring
4. Trailing arm
5. Lateral rod

Fig. 11 Rear axle assembly — 1987-88 Sprint

6. Loosen the lower mount nut on the knuckle. Place a jack under the suspension arm to prevent it from lowering and remove the lower mount nut on the knuckle.

7. Raise the jack placed under the suspension arm enough to allow the removal of the lower mount bolt of the knuckle.

8. Move the brake drum/backing plate toward the outside of the vehicle body so as to separate the lower mount of the knuckle from the suspension arm. Then lower the jack gradually and remove the coil spring.

9. Remove the suspension arm.

To install:

10. Install the 4 mounting bracket bolts. Torque the mounting bracket bolts to 33 ft. lbs. (45 Nm).

11. Install the rear and front mounting nuts, but do not torque them at this time.

➡Make sure that the front mounting washer is installed in the proper direction.

12. Place the jack under the suspension arm.

13. Install the coil spring on the spring seat of the suspension arm then raise the suspension arm. When seating the coil spring, mate the spring end with the stepped part of the suspension arm spring.

14. Install the lower knuckle mount bolt. Torque the bolt to 37 ft. lbs. (50 Nm).

15. Remove the jack from under the suspension arm.

16. Install the inside and outside control rod bolts, but do not tighten them at this time.

17. Install the wheel assemblies and lower the vehicle.

18. Install the control rod inside and outside nut and torque them to 59 ft. lbs. (80 Nm).

➡When tightening the nuts, it is most desirable to have the vehicle off the hoist and in a non-loaded state. Also when tightening the inside nut, align the line stamped on the body with the line on the washer as confirmed before removal or align the matchmarks if marked.

19. Install the suspension arm front and rear nuts. Torque the front nuts to 44 ft. lbs. (60 Nm) and the rear nuts to 37 ft. lbs. (50 Nm). After tightening the suspension arm outer nut, make sure that the washer is not tilted.

20. Check the rear wheel alignment.

Rear Control Arms

REMOVAL & INSTALLATION

1989-93 Metro

▶ **See Figures 9, 12 and 13**

1. Raise and support the vehicle safely.

➡To facilitate the toe-in adjustment after reinstallation, confirm which one of the lines stamped on the washer is in the closest alignment with the stamped line on the control rod. If not marked, add the alignment marks.

2. Remove the brake hose from the control rod by pulling off the E-ring.

3. Remove the outside (wheel side) of the control rod from the rear knuckle stud bolt.

Fig. 12 Rear control arm front bushing

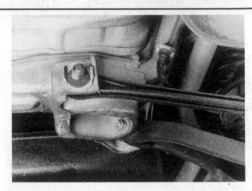

Fig. 13 Rear control arm rear bushing

4. Remove the rear spring.

5. Remove the outermost control arm mounting bolts. Remove the washer and bushing as required.

6. Remove the inner control arm mounting bolt and nut. Hold the inside bolt with another wrench to prevent it from turning as the nut is turned.

7. Remove the control arm from the vehicle.

To install:

8. Install the control arm onto the vehicle. Install the bushing assembly and mounting bolts to the outer portion of the arm.

9. Install the inner mounting bolt and nut. Hold the inside bolt with another wrench to prevent it from turning as the nut is turned. Tighten mounting bolt to 59 ft. lbs. (80 Nm).

10. Install the lower knuckle to arm mounting bolt and nut, tightening to specifications.

11. Install the outside (wheel side) of the control rod to the rear knuckle stud bolt. Tighten bolt to 59 ft. lbs. (80 Nm).

12. Install the brake hose and secure with the E-ring.

13. Lower the vehicle. Check and adjust the rear alignment.

Rear Axle Assembly

REMOVAL & INSTALLATION

1985-86 Sprint

1. Raise and support the vehicle safely.
2. Remove the rear wheels and brake drums.

3. Remove the brake line at the flex hose. Remove the flex hose and brake line retainers.

4. Remove the brake hose pipe from bracket on the axle assembly.

5. Plug the brake flex hose to prevent loss of brake fluid and system contamination due to moisture.

6. Remove brake backing plate nuts, then remove backing plate.

7. If necessary, disconnect the parking brake cables and reposition out of the way.

8. Remove U-bolt nuts, U-bolts and jounce stop.

9. Remove the rear axle assembly from the vehicle.

To install:

10. Place axle on leaf spring by aligning pin on the top of the leaf spring with hole in underside of axle. Then fit pin on underside of leaf spring in hole of spring seat and tighten U-bolt nut to 22-32 ft. lbs. (30-45 Nm).

11. Apply watertight sealant to joint seam of axle and brake backing plate and tighten brake backing plate nuts to 13-20 ft. lbs. (18-28 Nm).

12. Install flex hose in bracket and secure with retainer. Install brake line at flex hose.

13. Install the brake drum and wheel.

14. Bleed the brake system and adjust the rear brakes as necessary.

1987-88 Sprint

▶ **See Figure 11**

1. Raise and support the vehicle safely.

2. Remove the wheel and brake drum.

3. Remove the brake hose attaching clip at the trailing arm bracket. Disconnect the brake pipe from the wheel cylinder and remove the brake hose/pipe from the trailing arm.

4. Remove the rear brakes and disconnect the parking brake from the brake shoe.

5. Remove the parking brake cable from the backing plate.

6. Remove the backing plate from the rear axle.

7. Support the center of the rear axle with a floor jack.

8. Remove the lateral rod body side bolt.

9. Remove the shock absorber lower mounting nut.

10. Lower the rear axle gradually until tension of suspension spring is relieved, then remove spring.

11. Remove trailing arm front bolts and remove rear axle from vehicle.

To install:

12. Raise the rear axle into the vehicle and loosely install the trailing arm front bolts.

13. Install coil spring on rear axle spring seat with flat face upward. Seat lower spring end with stepped part of rear axle seat.

14. Raise floor jack slightly and install shock absorber lower mounting bolt. Tighten to 32-50 ft. lbs. (45-70 Nm).

15. Install lateral rod and tighten nut to 32-50 ft. lbs. (45-70 Nm).

16. Tighten trailing arm nut to 50-65 ft. lbs. (70-90 Nm).

17. Apply watertight sealant to joint seam of axle and brake backing plate. Install backing plate and tighten bolts to 13-20 ft. lbs. (18-28 Nm).

18. Put brake hose/pipe through hole in bracket on trailing arm and install pipe flare nut to wheel cylinder. Tighten to 10-13 ft. lbs. (14-18 Nm).

19. Secure brake pipe/hose to bracket with E-clip.

20. Apply water tight sealant to parking brake cable and install on backing plate. Attach cable end to brake shoe.

21. Install rear brake shoes and brake drum. Install the wheel assembly.

22. Bleed brake system and adjust rear brakes.

23. Lower the vehicle.

Lateral Rod

REMOVAL & INSTALLATION

▶ **See Figure 14**

1. Raise and support the vehicle safely. Support the rear axle with a floor jack.

2. Remove the lateral rod attaching bolts, then remove the lateral rod.

3. Installation is the reverse of removal. Tighten lateral rod bolts to 32-50 ft. lbs. (45-70 Nm)

Rear Spindle/Knuckle Assembly

REMOVAL & INSTALLATION

1985-88 Sprint

The 1985-88 Sprint uses a solid rear axle assembly. The rear spindle assembly is an integral part of the rear axle assembly. If the spindle is damaged, the rear axle assembly must be replace. The rear bearing and seal are located inside of the hub of the brake drum, which is then mounted to the spindle. Refer to Rear Axle removal and installation procedure in this Section for more information.

1989-93 Metro

▶ **See Figure 9**

The Metro uses an independent rear suspension. The rear wheels are mounted on knuckles much like the front wheels.

1. Raise and safely support the vehicle.

2. Remove the tire and wheel assemblies, then the brake line, retaining clip and flexible hose from the center of the rear axle.

Fig. 14 Lateral rod attaching point

3. Remove the tension spring from the rear axle, disconnect the parking brake cable from the turn buckle and the cable joint.

4. Remove the brake backing plate from the knuckle after removing the 4 plate retaining bolts.

5. Using a suitable jack, support under the lower suspension arm to prevent it from lowering.

➡**As a preparatory step for this removal, check the stamped line on the washer to use for a guide in the reinstallation.**

6. Remove the lower strut mounting bolt.

7. Remove the lower knuckle mounting bolt.

8. Remove the knuckle (spindle) from the suspension arm and from the strut.

➡**If it is hard to remove the knuckle from the strut, open the slit in the knuckle by inserting a wedge. Do not open the slit wider than necessary.**

To install:

9. Install the knuckle assembly onto the lower end of the strut. Align the projection on the strut against the slit of the knuckle and push the strut into the knuckle until it is properly positioned.

10. Install the lower strut retaining bolt and tighten to a torque of 44 ft. lbs. (60 Nm).

11. Install the lower mount end of the knuckle to suspension arm. Torque the nut to 44 ft. lbs. (60 Nm).

12. Remove the jack from under the suspension arm.

13. Torque the knuckle lower mount nut to 37 ft. lbs. (50 Nm).

14. Install the backing plate and secure with the retaining bolts. Torque the retaining bolts to 17 ft. lbs. (23 Nm).

15. Install the brake hose bracket to the knuckle. Install the brake line to the wheel cylinder and tighten the line to 12 ft. lbs. (16 Nm).

16. Install the breather plug cap to the breather plug. Install the brake drum assembly.

17. Install the control rod and control rod nuts. Torque the nuts to 59 ft. lbs. (80 Nm).

18. Confirm that all removed components are installed and securely in place.

19. Adjust the rear brakes and bleed the system.

Rear Wheel Bearings

REMOVAL & INSTALLATION

1. Raise and support the vehicle safely.

2. Remove the wheel assembly.

3. Remove the dust cap, the cotter pin, the castle nut and the washer.

4. Loosen the adjusting nuts of the parking brake cable.

5. Remove the plug from the rear of the backing plate. Insert a suitable tool through the hole, making contact with the shoe hold-down spring, then push the spring to release the parking brake shoe lever.

6. Using a slide hammer tool and a brake drum remover tool, pull the brake drum from the halfshaft.

7. Using a brass drift and a hammer, drive the rear wheel bearings from the brake drum.

➡**When installing the wheel bearings, face the sealed sides (numbered sides) outward. Fill the wheel bearing cavity with bearing grease.**

8. Drive the new bearings into the brake drum with the bearing installation tool.

9. To install, use a new seal and reverse the removal procedures. Tighten the hub castle nut to 41 ft. lbs. (55 Nm) for vehicles through 1991, or to 74 ft. lbs. (100 Nm) for 1992-93 vehicles. Stake the nut in place. Bleed the brake system, then operate the brakes 3-5 times to obtain the proper drum-to-shoe clearance and adjust the parking brake cable.

Rear Wheel Alignment

The rear suspension on Sprint provides no adjustment for caster, camber or toe-in. The rear suspension on the Metro provides no adjustment for caster or camber. The only adjustment possible is toe-in.

CASTER

Caster is the tilting of the upper most point of the steering axis either forward or backward from the vertical (when viewed from the side of the vehicle). A backward tilt is positive and a forward tilt is negative. Caster influences directional control of the steering, but does not affect tire wear.

Caster is affected by vehicle height; therefore, it is important to keep the body at its designed height. Overloading the vehicle or a weak or sagging spring will affect the caster. When the rear of the vehicle is lower than its normal designated trim height, the front suspension move to a more positive caster. If the rear of the vehicle is higher than its designated trim height, the front suspension move to a less positive caster.

CAMBER

Camber is the tilting of the wheels from the vertical when viewed from the front of the vehicle. When the wheels tilt outward at the top, the camber is positive. When the wheels tilt inward, the camber is negative. The amount of tilt measured in degrees from the vertical is the camber angle. Camber influences both directional control and tire wear.

TOE-IN

Toe-in is a measurement of how much the front of the wheels are turned in or out from the geometric centerline/thrust line. When the wheels are turned in (toe-in), toe is positive. When the wheels are turned out (toe-out), the toe is negative. The actual amount of toe is normally only a fraction of a degree. The purpose of toe is to ensure that the wheels roll parallel.

STEERING

Steering Wheel

✳✳CAUTION

On vehicles equipped with an air bag, the air bag system must be disarmed before working around the steering wheel or instrument panel. Failure to do so may result in deployment of the air bag and possible personal injury. Refer to the Air Bag Disarming procedures later in this Section.

REMOVAL & INSTALLATION

▶ **See Figures 15 and 16**

1. If equipped, with an air bag system, disable the air bag system as follows:
   a. Turn the ignition switch to the **OFF** position.
   b. Remove the **SIR IG** fuse in the supplemental inflatable restraint fuse block.
   c. Remove the rear plastic access cover to the air bag module.
   d. Disconnect the yellow 2-way connector and connector position assurance (CPA) inside the inflator module housing.
2. Disconnect the negative battery cable.
3. Remove the air bag module attaching screws, then the air bag assembly from the vehicle.

✳✳CAUTION

When carrying a live air bag module, make sure that the bag and trim cover are pointed away from you. Never carry the air bag module by the wires or the connector on the underside of the air bag module. In case of an accidental deployment, the bag will then deploy with minimal chance of injury. When placing a live air bag module on a bench or other surface, always face the bag and trim cover in the up position, away from the surface. Never rest a steering column assembly on the steering wheel with the air bag module face down and the column vertical. This is necessary so that a free space is provided to allow the air bag to expand in the unlikely event of accidental deployment. Otherwise, personal injury could result.

➡The air bag system coil assembly is easily damaged if the correct steering wheel puller tools are not used.

4. Remove the steering wheel attaching nut, then using a suitable puller, remove the steering wheel.
5. Disconnect the electrical connectors from the steering wheel, then the rear steering wheel cover.
   To install:
6. Reverse procedure to install. Torque steering nut to 25 ft. lbs. (34 Nm) and the air bag module attaching screws to 44 inch lbs. (5 Nm).
7. Reactivate the air bag system as follows:
   a. Turn the ignition switch to the **OFF** position.

b. Connect the yellow 2-way connector and connector position assurance (CPA) inside the inflator module housing.
   c. Install the **SIR IG** fuse in the supplemental inflatable restraint fuse block.
   d. Install the rear plastic access cover to the air bag module.
   e. Turn the ignition switch to the **RUN** position. Observe the **INFLATABLE RESTRAINT** indicator lamp. If the lamp does not flash 7 to 9 times and then remain off, there is a problem in the air bag system and further diagnostic testing of the system is needed.

Combination Switch

REMOVAL & INSTALLATION

▶ **See Figures 15 and 16**

1. On vehicles equipped with an air bag, the air bag system must be disarmed before working around the steering wheel or instrument panel.
2. Remove the steering wheel.
3. Remove the lower steering column trim cover.
4. Loosen the steering column mounting nuts and lower column slightly.
5. Remove upper and lower steering column covers.
6. Disconnect combination switch electrical connector.
7. Remove switch from column.
   To install:
8. Install switch to column.
9. Connect combination switch electrical connector.
10. Install upper and lower steering column covers.
11. Tighten the steering column mounting nuts to 10 ft. lbs. (14 Nm).
12. Install the lower steering column trim cover.
13. Install the steering wheel.

Ignition Switch

REMOVAL & INSTALLATION

1. Remove the steering column from the vehicle and mount in a table vise.
2. Remove ignition switch mounting bolts. Using a hammer and chisel, create slots on the top of the mounting bolts, then remove the bolts with a screwdriver.
3. Turn key in ignition switch to **ON** and remove switch from steering column.
   To install:
4. Position the oblong hole in the steering shaft so that it is visible thorough, and in the center of the hole in the steering column.
5. Install ignition switch to column with the ignition key still in the **ON** position.
6. Turn the key to the **LOCK** position and remove the key from the ignition switch.

7. Align the ignition switch hub with the oblong hole in the steering shaft. Rotate the shaft to ensure that the steering shaft is locked.

8. Install new break-away head bolts to ignition switch and tighten until break-away heads break off.

9. Turn ignition key to **ON** position and check that the shaft rotates smoothly. Remove the column from vise.

10. Install steering column in vehicle.

Steering Column

REMOVAL & INSTALLATION

▶ **See Figures 15 and 16**

➡The steering column is very susceptible to damage once it has been removed from the vehicle. The vehicle's wheels must be in a straight ahead position and the key must be in the LOCK position when removing or installing the steering column. Failure to do so may cause the air bag coil assembly to become off centered and may result in unneeded air bag system damage. In the event air bay deployment has occurred, inspect the coil assembly for any signs of scorching, melting or other damage due to excessive heat. If the coil has been damaged, replace it. The steering column should never be supported by only the lower support bracket, damage to the column lower bearing adapter could result.

1. If equipped with an air bag system, disable the air bag system as follows:

a. Turn the ignition switch to the **OFF** position.

b. Remove the **SIR IG** fuse in the supplemental inflatable restraint fuse block.

c. Remove the rear plastic access cover to the air bag module.

d. Disconnect the yellow 2-way connector and connector position assurance (CPA) inside the inflator module housing.

2. Disconnect the negative battery cable.

3. Remove the air bag module attaching screws, then the air bag assembly from the vehicle.

❊❊CAUTION

When carrying a live air bag module, make sure that the bag and trim cover are pointed away from you. Never carry the air bag module by the wires or the connector on the underside of the air bag module. In case of an accidental deployment, the bag will then deploy with minimal chance of injury. When placing a live air bag module on a bench or other surface, always face the bag and trim cover in the up position, away from the surface. Never rest a steering column assembly on the steering wheel with the air bag module face down and the column vertical. This is necessary so that a free space is provided to allow the air bag to expand in the unlikely event of accidental deployment. Otherwise, personal injury could result.

➡The air bag system coil assembly is easily damaged if the correct steering wheel puller tools are not used.

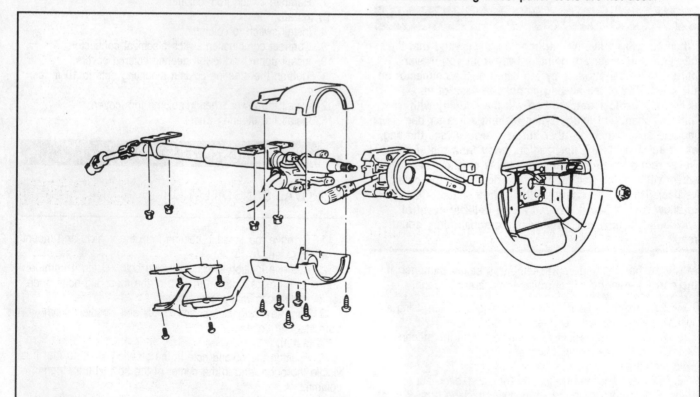

Fig. 15 Steering column assembly — Metro

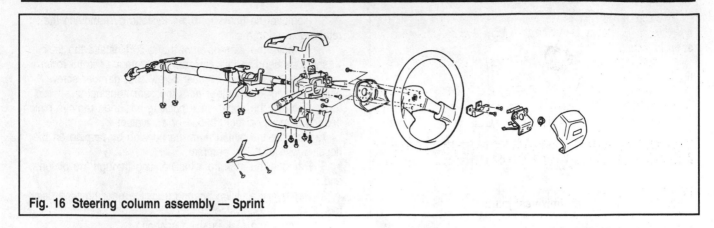

Fig. 16 Steering column assembly — Sprint

4. Remove the steering wheel attaching nut, then using a suitable puller, remove the steering wheel.

5. Disconnect the electrical connectors from the steering wheel, then the rear steering wheel cover.

6. Remove the steering shaft trim panel. Remove the lower steering column trim panel and the steering column reinforcement plate.

7. Disconnect the steering column electrical connectors. Remove the brake transaxle shift interlock cable from the ignition switch.

8. Remove the steering column to steering shaft joint pinch bolt. Remove the upper and lower steering column mounting nuts and remove the steering column from the vehicle.

To install:

9. Installation is the reverse order of the removal procedure. Torque the steering column upper and lower mounting nuts to 10 ft. lbs. (14 Nm). Torque the steering column to steering shaft joint pinch bolt to 18 ft. lbs. (25 Nm).

10. Reactivate the air bag system as follows:

a. Turn the ignition switch to the **OFF** position.

b. Connect the yellow 2-way connector and connector position assurance (CPA) inside the inflator module housing.

c. Install the **SIR IG** fuse in the supplemental inflatable restraint fuse block.

d. Install the rear plastic access cover to the air bag module.

e. Turn the ignition switch to the **RUN** position. Observe the **INFLATABLE RESTRAINT** indicator lamp. If the lamp does not flash 7 to 8 times and then remain off, there is a problem in the air bag system and further diagnostic testing of the system is needed.

Steering Linkage

REMOVAL & INSTALLATION

Tie Rod End

▶ **See Figure 17**

1. Raise and support the vehicle safely.
2. Remove the front wheel and tire assembly.
3. Remove the cotter pin and castle nut from the ball joint.
4. Remove the tie rod end from the knuckle using a ball joint separator.
5. Loosen the locknut on the threaded end of the tie rod.

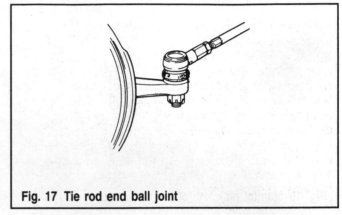

Fig. 17 Tie rod end ball joint

6. Unscrew the tie rod end from the tie rod. Note the number of turns necessary for removal.

To install:

7. Screw the new tie rod end onto the tie rod the exact number of turns necessary to remove the old tie rod end. This will allow the alignment to be close enough to drive the vehicle to the alignment shop.

8. Tighten the locknut to 32 ft. lbs. (43 Nm).

9. Install the castle nut and tighten to 32 ft. lbs. (43 Nm). Install the cotter pin.

10. Install the front wheel and tire assembly.

11. Lower the vehicle.

12. Check and adjust the front wheel alignment.

Manual Rack and Pinion

REMOVAL & INSTALLATION

▶ **See Figures 18 and 19**

1. Slide the driver's seat back as far as possible.
2. Pull off the front part of the floor mat on the driver's side and remove the steering shaft joint cover.
3. Loosen the steering shaft upper joint bolt, but do not remove.
4. Remove the steering shaft lower joint bolt and disconnect the lower joint from the pinion.
5. Raise and support the vehicle safely.
6. Remove the tie rod ends from the steering knuckles. Mark the left and right tie rods accordingly.

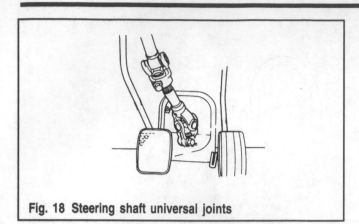

Fig. 18 Steering shaft universal joints

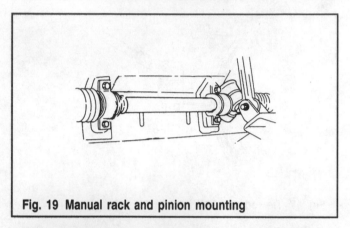

Fig. 19 Manual rack and pinion mounting

7. From under the dash, remove the steering joint cover.

8. Remove the lower steering shaft-to-steering gear clinch bolt and separate the steering shaft from the steering gear.

9. Remove the steering gear mounting bolts, the brackets and the steering gear case from the vehicle.

To install:

10. Install the steering gear, brackets and mounting bolts. Tighten bolts to 18 ft. lbs. (25 Nm).

11. Connect the steering shaft to the steering gear. Install the lower steering shaft-to-steering gear clinch bolt and tighten to 18 ft. lbs. (25 Nm).

12. Install the steering joint cover.

13. Install the tie rod ends to the steering knuckles. Tighten tie rod end-to-steering knuckle nut to 32 ft. lbs. (43 Nm).

14. Lower the vehicle.

15. Connect the lower joint to the pinion. Install the steering shaft lower joint bolt and tighten to 18 ft. lbs. (25 Nm).

16. Tighten the steering shaft upper joint bolt to 18 ft. lbs. (25 Nm).

17. Install the steering shaft joint cover.

18. Check and adjust the front wheel alignment.

OVERHAUL

▶ **See Figure 20**

Disassembly

1. Remove the rack from the vehicle.

2. Matchmark the tie rod end threads for installation reference and remove the tie rod ends.

3. Remove the boots from the tie rods by removing the retaining wires and clips.

4. Remove the tie rods from the rack. Unstake the lock washers by bending flat. Unscrew and remove the tie rods.

5. Remove the rack damper screw cap, damper screw, plunger spring and plunger from the gear housing.

6. Remove the upper case packing and then remove pinion bearing plug using tool J39534 or equivalent.

7. Remove the pinion from the housing by tapping on the housing with a plastic hammer.

8. Remove the rack from the housing through the pinion end.

9. Remove the pinion bearing from the gear housing using tool J34839, or equivalent.

10. Remove the rack bushing snapring.

11. Remove the rack bushing using tools J34869 and J239075, or equivalent.

Cleaning and Inspection

1. Clean dirt and grease from all steering gear parts using an appropriate solvent.

2. Inspect steering rack boots for wear, deterioration or tears. Replace if even the smallest sign of wear is evident.

3. Inspect tie rod end ball stud dust seal for deterioration, wear or tears. Replace if even the smallest sign of wear is evident. Coat the inside of the seal with grease prior to installation.

4. Inspect rack plunger and spring for wear or damage. Replace as necessary.

5. Inspect pinion, pinion gasket and pinion oil seal for wear or damage. Replace any part found to be defective.

6. Inspect pinion needle bearing for wear and rotational smoothness. Replace if defective.

7. Inspect steering rack bushing for damage or wear. Replace if defective.

8. Check steering rack run-out using V-blocks and a dial indicator. Run-out should not exceed 0.016 in. (40 mm).

Assembly

1. Coat entire surface of rack bushing with a thin layer of manual steering gear lubricant and install bushing into housing using tool J34868 and J7079-2, or equivalent. Install the snapring.

➡ **The inside of the bushing has a fragile, special coating. Be sure to use the correct tool when installing the bushing, using care not to damage the special coating.**

2. Apply manual steering gear lubricant to pinion bearing rollers. Install bearing to housing using tool J34840, or equivalent and a hammer. Following installation, check roller for proper operation.

3. Apply manual steering gear lubricant to steering rack toothed surface. Install rack into housing from the pinion end.

4. Apply manual steering gear lubricant to pinion gears, needle bearings and gear case oil seal lip. Install pinion bearing plug using Loctite® 414 on the bearing plug threads. Tighten plug to 70 ft. lbs. (95 Nm). Install upper case packing.

5. Apply manual steering gear lubricant to sliding surface of rack plunger. Install plunger, spring and damper screw. Tighten screw until it is snug.

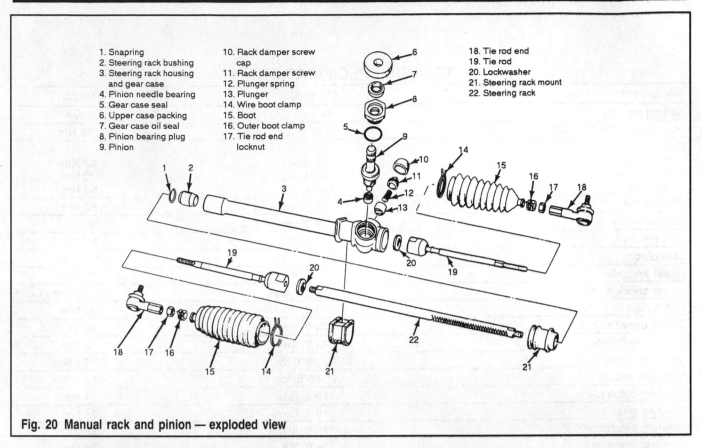

1. Snapring
2. Steering rack bushing
3. Steering rack housing and gear case
4. Pinion needle bearing
5. Gear case seal
6. Upper case packing
7. Gear case oil seal
8. Pinion bearing plug
9. Pinion
10. Rack damper screw cap
11. Rack damper screw
12. Plunger spring
13. Plunger
14. Wire boot clamp
15. Boot
16. Outer boot clamp
17. Tie rod end locknut
18. Tie rod end
19. Tie rod
20. Lockwasher
21. Steering rack mount
22. Steering rack

Fig. 20 Manual rack and pinion — exploded view

6. Measure rotation resistance using a torque wrench and tool J34871. If observed torque is greater than specification, back off the rack damper screw (up to ¼ turn) until specified torque is 10.6 inch lbs. (1.2 Nm).

7. If observed pinion rotational torque is less than specification, tighten the plunger damper screw until specification is reached.

8. Install rack damper screw cap as deeply as possible.

9. Install the tie rods to the rack, positioning lock washers in between. Align flats on washers with flats on rack. Tighten tie rod to 63 ft. lbs. (85 Nm) and stake lockwasher over each tie rod ball nut.

10. Apply manual steering gear lubricant to inside portion of the outer end of each steering gear boot. Position boots on grooves of the steering gear housing and secure with new wires. Secure the outer end of each boot with clamp. Make sure boots are free from twists and properly fastened.

11. Install tie rod end and locknut. Align locknuts with marks make on tie rod threads during removal. Tighten locknuts to 32 ft. lbs. (43 Nm).

12. Install manual steering gear assembly to vehicle.

TORQUE SPECIFICATIONS

Component	U.S.	Metric
Air bag module	44 inch lbs.	5 Nm
Axle shaft castle nut (front)	129 ft. lbs.	175 Nm
Control arm:		
Rear mount	32 ft. lbs.	43 Nm
Front mount	66 ft. lbs.	90 Nm
Ball joint	44 ft. lbs.	60 Nm
Control rod	59 ft. lbs.	80 Nm
Damper rod locknut	29 ft. lbs.	40 Nm
Hub retaining nut	37 ft. lbs.	50 Nm
Lateral rod	32-50 ft. lbs.	45-70 Nm
Lower knuckle	37 ft. lbs.	50 Nm
Lower shock mount	32-50 ft. lbs.	45-70 Nm
Lug nuts	44 ft. lbs.	60 Nm
Shock upper support	24 ft. lbs.	30 Nm
Shock-to-knuckle	44 ft. lbs.	60 Nm
Stabilizer castle nut	22-39 ft. lbs.	30-55 Nm
Stabilizer mount	29-65 ft. lbs.	40-90 Nm
Steering column	10 ft. lbs.	14 Nm
Steering gear	18 ft. lbs.	25 Nm
Steering pinch bolt	18 ft. lbs.	25 Nm
Steering wheel nut	25 ft. lbs.	34 Nm
Strut to knuckle	59 ft. lbs.	80 Nm
Suspension arm:		
Front	44 ft. lbs.	60 Nm
Rear	37 ft. lbs.	50 Nm
Tie rod end	32 ft. lbs.	43 Nm
Upper shock mount	13-20 ft. lbs.	18-28 Nm
Upper strut support	20 ft. lbs.	27 Nm
Wheel cylinder	12 ft. lbs.	16 Nm

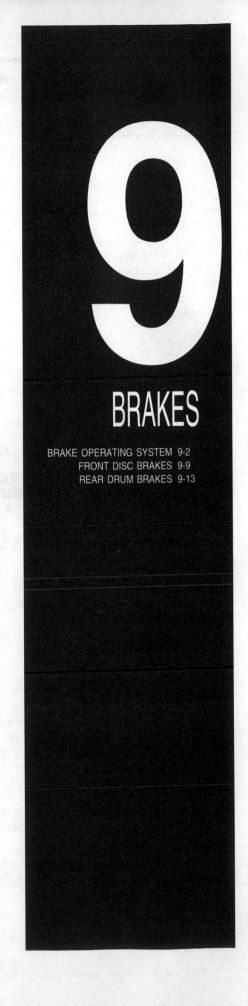

9

BRAKES

BRAKE OPERATING SYSTEM

Adjustments

DRUM BRAKES

The rear brakes have a self-adjusting mechanism that does not require adjustment for proper drum to shoe clearance when brake shoe has been replaced or brake drum has been removed for some other service.

Adjustment is automatically accomplished by depressing brake pedal 3-5 times after all parts are installed. Then check brake drum for dragging and brake system for proper performance.

BRAKE PEDAL

Brake pedal height is determined by brake pedal booster pushrod length and brake light switch adjustment. Brake pedal height is normal if the brake pedal is as high as the clutch pedal. If brake pedal height is not normal, check brake pedal booster pushrod length and brake light switch adjustments.

Brake Light Switch

REMOVAL & INSTALLATION

▶ See Figure 1

1. Disconnect the negative battery cable.
2. Remove the plastic cover from steering column, as required.
3. Disconnect the brake light switch electrical connector.
4. Depress the brake pedal and remove the locknut from the threaded portion of the brake light switch.
5. Remove the brake light switch.
To install:
6. Install brake light switch.
7. Adjust the switch so that the clearance between the end thread of the brake light switch and the brake pedal contact plate is 0.02-0.04 in. (0.5-1.0mm) with the brake pedal fully upward.
8. Depress brake pedal, install locknut and tighten to 115 inch lbs. (13 Nm).
9. Connect brake light switch electrical connector.
10. Install the plastic cover on steering column, as required.
11. Connect the negative battery cable.

Brake Pedal

REMOVAL & INSTALLATION

▶ See Figure 2

1. Remove cover from steering column, as required.

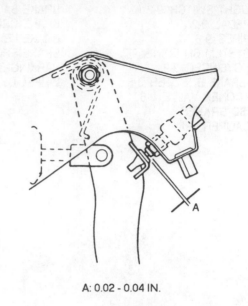

A: 0.02 - 0.04 IN.

Fig. 1 Adjusting brake light switch

2. Remove cotter pin and clevis pin from brake booster pushrod.
3. Release brake pedal return spring tension.
4. Remove brake pedal shaft bolt and nut.
5. Remove brake pedal from vehicle.
To install:
6. Inspect brake pedal bushings for wear and replace as necessary.
7. Install brake pedal to vehicle and secure with shaft bolt and nut. Tighten bolt to 17 ft. lbs. (20 Nm).
8. Reposition and tension pedal return spring.
9. Install cotter pin and clevis pin to brake booster pushrod.
10. Install cover on steering column, as required.

Master Cylinder

REMOVAL & INSTALLATION

▶ See Figure 3

➡Be careful not to spill brake fluid on the painted surfaces of the vehicle; it will damage the finish.

1. Disconnect the negative battery cable. Clean around the reservoir cap and take some of the fluid out with a syringe.
2. Disconnect and plug the brake tubes from the master cylinder.
3. Remove the mounting nuts and washers.

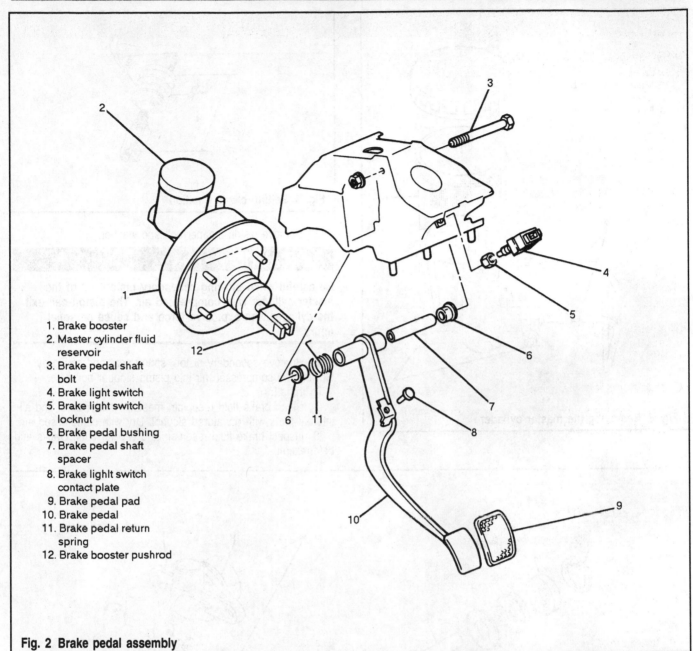

1. Brake booster
2. Master cylinder fluid reservoir
3. Brake pedal shaft bolt
4. Brake light switch
5. Brake light switch locknut
6. Brake pedal bushing
7. Brake pedal shaft spacer
8. Brake lighlt switch contact plate
9. Brake pedal pad
10. Brake pedal
11. Brake pedal return spring
12. Brake booster pushrod

Fig. 2 Brake pedal assembly

4. Remove the master cylinder.
To install:
5. If a new master cylinder is to be installed, bleed as follows:

   a. Install the master cylinder in a holding fixture, taking precautions to protect the cylinder body from damage.

   b. Fill the fluid reservoir with clean brake fluid meeting DOT 3 recommendations.

   c. Position a container under the outlet fittings. Depress the cylinder piston slowly through it's full travel. Cover both outlets and let the piston return to normal resting position.

   d. Wait 5 seconds and then repeat the operation until the fluid exiting the master cylinder fittings is free of air bubbles.
6. Install the master cylinder. Tighten mounting bolts to 8-12 ft. lbs. (11-16 Nm).
7. Connect the brake tubes to the master cylinder. Tighten to 10-13 ft. lbs. (14-18 Nm).

8. Fill the master cylinder with clean brake fluid and bleed the brake system.
9. Connect the negative battery cable.

OVERHAUL

▶ **See Figure 4**

1. Remove the master cylinder from the vehicle.
2. Remove the brake fluid reservoir from the master cylinder by driving out brake fluid reservoir connector pin and removing from grommets.
3. Remove the snapring from the master cylinder shaft using snapring pliers.
4. Remove the primary piston stopper, cylinder cup and plate, and primary piston.

1. Master cylinder body
2. Brake pipe nuts
3. Brake fluid reservoir cap
4. Brake fluid reservoir
5. Master cylinder mounting nuts

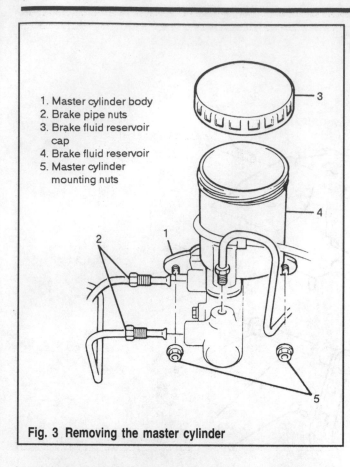

Fig. 3 Removing the master cylinder

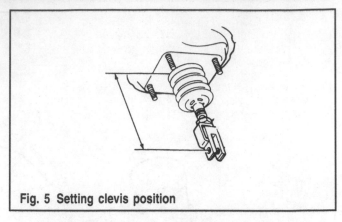

Fig. 5 Setting clevis position

5. Remove piston stopper bolt and washer.

✳✳CAUTION

Be careful when blowing secondary piston out of the master cylinder with compressed air. The piston can exit the cylinder with explosive force and cause personal injury.

6. Remove secondary piston, spring seat and spring by blowing dry compressed air into piston stopper bolt hole.
To install:
7. Clean brake fluid reservoir, master cylinder body and all internal parts with denatured alcohol. Dry with compressed air.
8. Inspect brake fluid reservoir and cap for cuts, cracks and deformation.

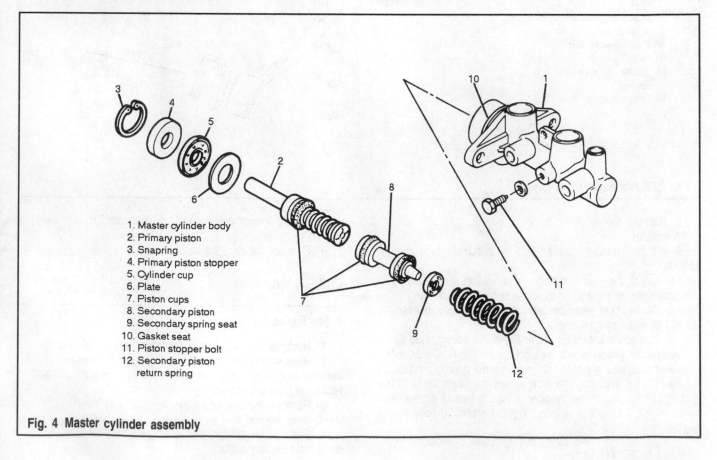

1. Master cylinder body
2. Primary piston
3. Snapring
4. Primary piston stopper
5. Cylinder cup
6. Plate
7. Piston cups
8. Secondary piston
9. Secondary spring seat
10. Gasket seat
11. Piston stopper bolt
12. Secondary piston return spring

Fig. 4 Master cylinder assembly

9. Inspect master cylinder body for scoring or corrosion. If these conditions are noted, replace the master cylinder.

10. Inspect master cylinder internal parts for wear and replace as necessary.

➡**Internal replacement parts are available only as a complete piston set. Should any of the master cylinder internal parts need to be replaced, replace them all.**

11. Coat all parts with clean brake fluid.

12. Install the secondary piston spring, spring seat and piston.

13. Install the primary piston stopper, cylinder cup and plate, and primary piston.

14. Compress pistons and install snapring using snapring pliers.

15. Install piston stopper washer and bolt with pistons pushed all the way in. Tighten piston stopper bolt to 89 inch lbs. (10 Nm).

16. Coat the brake fluid reservoir grommets with clean brake fluid and install in master cylinder. Make sure that grommets seat properly.

17. Install brake fluid reservoir on master cylinder and secure by driving reservoir connector pin in using a drift.

18. Install master cylinder on vehicle.

Power Brake Booster

REMOVAL & INSTALLATION

1. Disconnect the negative battery cable.
2. Remove the master cylinder.
3. Disconnect the pushrod clevis pin from the brake pedal arm.
4. Disconnect the vacuum hose from the brake booster.
5. Remove the mounting nuts from under the dash, then remove the booster.

To install:

6. Install the booster and tighten mounting nuts to 14-20 ft. lbs. (19-27 Nm).
7. Connect the vacuum hose from the brake booster.
8. Connect the pushrod clevis pin from the brake pedal arm.
9. Adjust the brake booster piston-to-master cylinder primary piston clearance.
10. Install the master cylinder.
11. Connect the negative battery cable.

ADJUSTMENT

▶ **See Figures 5, 6 and 7**

Booster Piston Rod Clearance

1. The brake booster piston-to-master cylinder primary piston clearance should be 0 in. (0mm). In other words, they should be touching each other without exerting any force.

2. Using a booster piston rod gauge PN J39567 or equivalent, lower the pin of the gauge until its tip touches the end of the master cylinder primary piston. Perform this step with the master cylinder gasket in place.

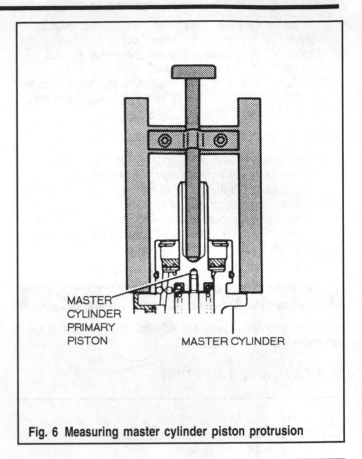

Fig. 6 Measuring master cylinder piston protrusion

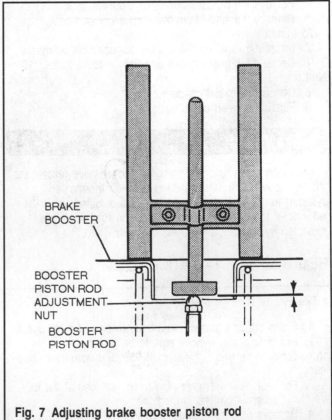

Fig. 7 Adjusting brake booster piston rod

3. Remove the gauge from the master cylinder, invert it, and place it on the front of the brake booster assembly.

4. Measure the clearance between the master cylinder primary piston and the booster piston.

5. Adjust booster piston rod length until the rod touches the master cylinder primary piston by turning the adjustment nut at the end of the piston rod.

Clevis Position

1. Remove the power brake booster from the vehicle.

2. Measure the distance between the brake booster mounting surface and the center of the clevis rod hole. Make measurement with gasket removed.

3. Measurement should be 4.51-4.55 in. (114.5-115.5mm).

4. Adjust clevis as required and tighten adjustment nut to 18 ft. lbs. (25 Nm).

5. Install brake booster.

Proportioner Valve

The proportioner valve is located along the right side of the engine compartment bulkhead.

REMOVAL & INSTALLATION

1. Clean dirt and foreign material from pipes and fittings.
2. Disconnect the proportioner valve electrical connector.
3. Disconnect the brake hoses.
4. Remove the proportioner valve mounting bolts.
5. Remove the valve from the engine compartment.
To install:
6. Install the valve on the engine compartment bulkhead.
7. Connect the brake hoses and tighten to 12 ft. lbs. (16 Nm).
8. Connect electrical connector.
9. Flush and bleed brake system.

Brake Pipes

The brake pipes run from the proportioner valve (except the left front brake pipe, which runs directly off the master cylinder) to the wheels. The rear pipes are routed under the left side of the vehicle and along with the fuel pipes, are protected by metal guard plates.

REMOVAL & INSTALLATION

▶ See Figure 8

1. Clean dirt and foreign material from pipes and fittings.
2. For front pipes, remove pipe to be replaced at proportioner valve and/or master cylinder and from brake hose fitting.
3. For rear pipes, remove pipe to be replaced at the four way junction and from the proportioner valve.
4. Remove pipe from guide brackets and clamps.
To install:
5. Prepare hose ends using the double flare method.

6. Install new pipes and tighten connections to 12 ft. lbs. (16 Nm).
7. Tighten brake pipe clamps to 124 inch lbs. (14 Nm).
8. Flush and bleed brake system.

BRAKE PIPE FLARING

▶ See Figure 9

Use only brake line tubing approved for automotive use; never use copper tubing. Whenever possible, try to work with brake lines that are already cut to the length needed. These lines are available at most auto parts stores and have machine made flares, the quality of which is hard to duplicate with most of the available inexpensive flaring kits.

When the brakes are applied, there is a great amount of pressure developed in the hydraulic system. An improperly formed flare can leak with resultant loss of stopping power. If you have never formed a double-flare, take time to familiarize yourself with the flaring kit; practice forming double-flares on scrap tubing until you are satisfied with the results.

The following procedure applies to most commercially available double-flaring kits. If these instructions differ in any way from those in your kit, follow the instructions in the kit.

1. Obtain the recommended tubing and steel fitting nuts of the correct size.
2. Cut tubing to correct length. Correct length can be determined by measuring the old pipe using a string and adding 0.125 in. for each double flare.

➡**Do not use single flaring tools. Double flares must be used to produce a flare strong enough to hold the system pressure. Using single lap flaring tools could cause system failure.**

3. Square the end of the tube with a file and chamfer the edges.
4. Insert the tube into the proper size hole in the bar until the end of the tube sticks out the thickness of the single flare adapter. Tighten the bar wing nuts tightly so the tube cannot move.
5. Place the single flare adapter into the tube and slide the bar into the yoke.
6. Position the yoke screw over the single flare adapter and tighten it until the bar is locked in the yoke. Continue tightening the yoke screw until the adapter bottoms on the bar. This should form the single flare.

➡**Make sure the tube is not forced out of the hole in the bar during the single flare operation. If it is, the single flare will not be formed properly and the procedure must be repeated from Step 1.**

7. Loosen the yoke screw and remove the single flare adapter.
8. Position the yoke screw over the tube and tighten until the taper contacts the single flare and the bar is locked in the yoke. Continue tightening to form the double flare.

➡**Make sure the tube is not forced out of the hole in the bar during the double flare operation. If it is, the double flare will not be formed properly and the procedure must be repeated from Step 1.**

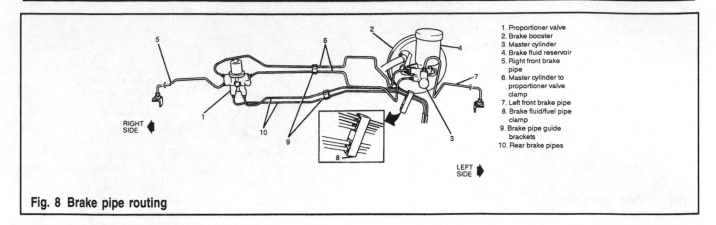

Fig. 8 Brake pipe routing

1. Proportioner valve
2. Brake booster
3. Master cylinder
4. Brake fluid reservoir
5. Right front brake pipe
6. Master cylinder to proportioner valve clamp
7. Left front brake pipe
8. Brake fluid/fuel pipe clamp
9. Brake pipe guide brackets
10. Rear brake pipes

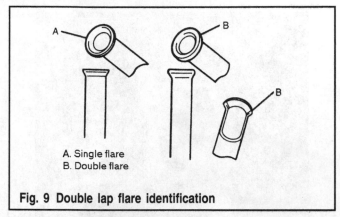

A. Single flare
B. Double flare

Fig. 9 Double lap flare identification

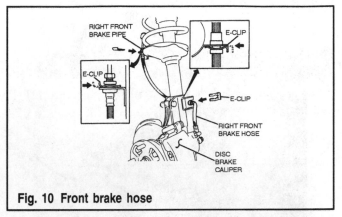

Fig. 10 Front brake hose

9. Loosen the screw and remove the bar from the yoke. Remove the tube from the bar.

10. Check the flare for cracks or uneven flaring. If the flare is not perfect, cut it off and begin again at Step 1.

Brake Hoses

Coated steel brake pipes thread into a flexible brake hose near each wheel. This design provides needed flexibility with moving suspension components.

REMOVAL & INSTALLATION

▶ See Figures 10 and 11

1. Raise and support the vehicle safely.
2. Remove the wheel and tire.
3. Clean dirt and foreign material from pipes and fittings.
4. Remove the E-clip and hose from brake hose bracket.
5. Remove hose at brake hose pipe and caliper by removing union bolt.

To install:

6. Install brake hose at brake pipe and caliper. Tighten brake pipe fitting to 12 ft. lbs. (16 Nm) and union bolt to 17 ft. lbs. (23 Nm).

7. Install hose on brake hose bracket and secure with E-clip.

8. Install wheel and tire. Lower vehicle.
9. Flush and bleed brake system.

Brake System Bleeding

▶ See Figures 12 and 13

1. Clean the bleeder screw at each wheel.
2. Start with the wheel farthest from the master cylinder (right rear).
3. Attach a rubber hose to the bleeder screw and place the end in a clear container of brake fluid.
4. Fill the master cylinder with brake fluid. Have an assistant slowly pump up the brake pedal and hold the pressure.
5. Open the bleed screw about ¼ turn, press the brake pedal to the floor, close the bleed screw and slowly release the pedal. Continue until no more air bubbles are forced from the cylinder on application of the brake pedal.
6. Repeat procedure on remaining wheel cylinders and calipers, still working from the cylinder/caliper farthest from the master cylinder.

➡Master cylinders equipped with bleed screws may be bled independently. When bleeding the master cylinder, it is necessary to cap 1 reservoir section while bleeding the other to prevent pressure loss through the cap vent hole.

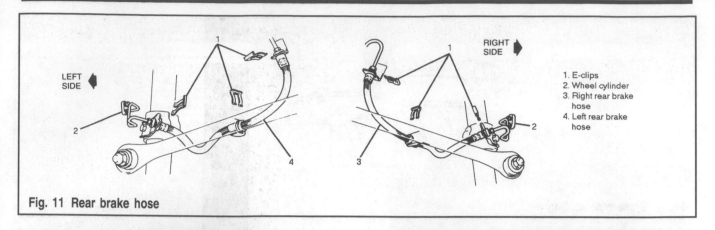

Fig. 11 Rear brake hose

LEFT SIDE

RIGHT SIDE

1. E-clips
2. Wheel cylinder
3. Right rear brake hose
4. Left rear brake hose

Fig. 13 Bleeding the rear brakes

Fig. 12 Bleeding the front brakes

FRONT DISC BRAKES

Disc Brake Pads

REMOVAL & INSTALLATION

▶ See Figures 14, 15, 16, 17, 18, 19, 20, 21, 22 and 23

✳✳CAUTION

Brake shoes contain asbestos, which has been determined to be a cancer causing agent. Never clean the brake surfaces with compressed air! Avoid inhaling any dust from any brake surface! When cleaning brake surfaces, us a commercially available brake cleaning fluid!

1. Raise and safely support the front of the vehicle. Set the parking brake and block the rear wheels.
2. Siphon a sufficient quantity of brake fluid from the master cylinder reservoir to prevent the brake fluid from overflowing from the master cylinder when removing or installing the brake pads. This is necessary as the piston must be forced into the cylinder bore to provide sufficient clearance to install the pads.
3. Remove the wheel, then reinstall 2 lug nuts finger tight to hold the disc in place.

➡**Disassemble brakes one wheel at a time. This will prevent parts confusion and also prevent the opposite caliper piston from popping out during pad installation.**

Fig. 14 Front disc brake assembly

Fig. 15 Removing caliper mounting bolts

Fig. 16 Removing the caliper from the rotor

4. Remove the 2 caliper mounting bolts and then remove the caliper from the mounting bracket. Position the caliper out of the way and support it with wire so it doesn't hang by the brake line.

➡**It may be necessary to rock the caliper back and forth a bit in order to reposition the piston so it will clear the brake pads.**

5. Remove the brake pads, the wear indicators, the anti-squeal shims, the support plates and the anti squeal springs (if so equipped). Disassemble slowly and take note of how the parts fit together. This will save much time during reassembly.

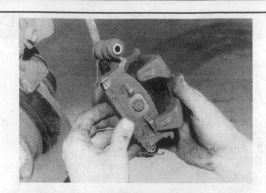

Fig. 17 Removing the outside brake pad

Fig. 18 Removing the inside brake pad

Fig. 19 The inside brake pad is attached to the caliper piston with a spring clip

6. Inspect the brake disc (both sides) for scoring or gouging. Measure the disc for both thickness and run-out. Complete inspection procedures are given later in this section.

7. Inspect the pads for remaining thickness and condition. Any sign of uneven wear, cracking, heat checking or spotting is cause for replacement. Compare the wear of the inner pad to the outer pad. While they will not wear at exactly the same rate, the remaining thickness should be about the same on both pads. If one is heavily worn and the other is not, suspect either a binding caliper piston or dirty slides in the caliper mount.

8. Examine the 2 caliper retaining bolts and the slide bushings in which they run. Everything should be clean and dry. If cleaning is needed, use spray solvents and a clean cloth. Do not wire brush or sand the bolts-this will cause

grooves in the metal which will trap more dirt. Check the condition of the rubber dust boots and replace them if damaged.

To install:

9. Install the pad support plates onto the mounting bracket.

10. Install new pad wear indicators onto each pad, making sure the arrow on the tab points in the direction of disc rotation.

11. Install new anti-squeal pads to the back of the pads.

12. Install the pads into the mounting bracket and install the anti-squeal springs.

13. Use a caliper compressor, or a C-clamp to slowly press the caliper piston back into the caliper. If the piston is frozen, or if the caliper is leaking hydraulic fluid, the caliper must be overhauled or replaced.

14. Install the caliper assembly to the mounting plate. Before installing the retaining bolts, apply a thin, even coating of anti-seize compound to the threads and slide surfaces. Don't use grease or spray lubricants; they will not hold up under the extreme temperatures generated by the brakes. Tighten the bolts to specification.

15. Remove the 2 lugs holding the disc in place and install the wheel.

16. Lower the vehicle to the ground. Check the level of the brake fluid in the master cylinder reservoir; it should be at least to the middle of the reservoir.

17. Depress the brake pedal several times and make sure that the movement feels normal. The first brake pedal application may result in a very 'long' pedal due to the pistons being retracted. Always make several brake applications before

Fig. 20 Disc brake system hardware. Inside pad is at top and outside pad is on bottom. Note wear indicator springs protruding from sides of outside pad

Fig. 21 Removing the anti-squeal springs from the caliper wear indicators

Fig. 22 Using a C-clamp to compress the caliper piston

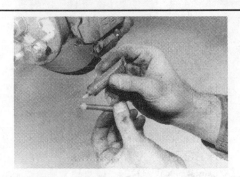

Fig. 23 Coat the caliper mounting bolts with anti-seize during installation

starting the vehicle. Bleeding is not usually necessary after pad replacement.

18. Recheck the fluid level and add to the 'MAX' line if necessary.

➡ **Braking should be moderate for the first 5 miles or so until the new pads seat correctly. The new pads will bed best if put through several moderate heating and cooling cycles. Avoid hard braking until the brakes have experienced several long, slow stops with time to cool in between. Taking the time to properly bed the brakes will yield quieter operation, more efficient stopping and contribute to extended brake life.**

Brake Caliper

REMOVAL & INSTALLATION

▸ **See Figures 14, 15, 16, 17, 18, 19, 20, 21, 22 and 23**

1. Raise and safely support the front of the vehicle. Set the parking brake and block the rear wheels.
2. Siphon a sufficient quantity of brake fluid from the master cylinder reservoir to prevent the brake fluid from overflowing the master cylinder when removing or installing the calipers. This is necessary as the piston must be forced into the cylinder bore to provide sufficient clearance to install the caliper.
3. Remove the wheel, then reinstall 2 lug nuts finger tight to hold the disc in place.

➡ **Disassemble brakes one wheel at a time. This will prevent parts confusion and also prevent the opposite caliper piston from popping out during installation. Mark the relationship between the wheel and the axle hub before removing the tire and wheel assembly.**

4. Disconnect the hose union at the caliper. Use a pan to catch any spilled fluid and immediately plug the disconnected hose.
5. Remove the 2 caliper mounting bolts and then remove the caliper from the mounting bracket.

To install:

6. Use a caliper compressor, a C-clamp or large pair of pliers to slowly press the caliper piston back into the caliper.
7. Install the caliper assembly to the mounting plate. Before installing the retaining bolts, apply a thin, even coating of anti-seize compound to the threads and slide surfaces. Don't use grease or spray lubricants; they will not hold up under the extreme temperatures generated by the brakes. Tighten the bolts.
8. Install the brake hose to the caliper. Always use a new gasket and tighten the union.
9. Bleed the brake system.
10. Remove the 2 lugs holding the disc in place and install the wheel.
11. Lower the vehicle to the ground. Check the level of brake fluid in the master cylinder reservoir; it should be at least to the middle of the reservoir.

OVERHAUL

▸ **See Figure 24**

1. Remove the brake caliper from the vehicle.
2. Clean the exterior of the brake caliper with brake fluid.
3. Remove the piston boot retaining ring and boot from the caliper by prying off with a flat bladed tool.

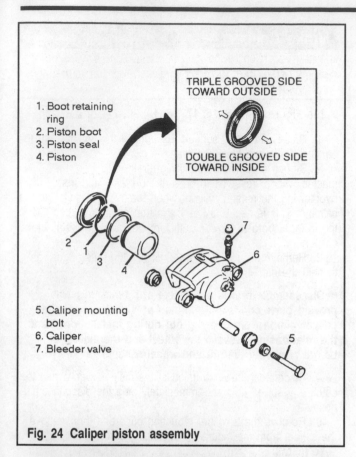

1. Boot retaining ring
2. Piston boot
3. Piston seal
4. Piston

TRIPLE GROOVED SIDE TOWARD OUTSIDE

DOUBLE GROOVED SIDE TOWARD INSIDE

5. Caliper mounting bolt
6. Caliper
7. Bleeder valve

Fig. 24 Caliper piston assembly

4. Remove the piston from caliper using compressed air. Apply air gradually to the brake hose union bolt hole. Cover piston with a shop rag to absorb its momentum.

☀☀CAUTION

The piston can exit the caliper with explosive force. Apply compressed air gradually and keep fingers out of the way.

5. Remove the piston seal from caliper using a thin bladed tool.
6. Remove the bleeder valve and cap from the caliper.
7. Clean all parts in denatured alcohol.
8. Dry all parts and blow out all passages in caliper housing and bleeder valve with compressed air.
9. Inspect the piston for scoring, nicks, corrosion or wear. Replace as necessary.
10. Inspect caliper bore and seal for scoring, nicks, corrosion and wear. Replace components as necessary.
11. Inspect caliper upper and lower slide bushings and boots for wear and corrosion.
12. Install piston seal and boot with clean brake fluid.
13. Install bleeder valve and cap. Tighten bleeder valve to 89 inch lbs. (10 Nm).
14. Install new piston seal into groove on caliper housing. Make sure the seal is not twisted.
15. Install new boot to piston. Install with the double grooved side toward the piston and the triple grooved side outward.

16. Install the piston and boot to caliper. Seat piston boot onto caliper. Position piston so it protrudes from the caliper 0.40 in. (10mm).
17. Install piston boot retaining ring.
18. Install caliper on vehicle.

Brake Rotor

REMOVAL & INSTALLATION

▶ **See Figures 25, 26, 27 and 28**

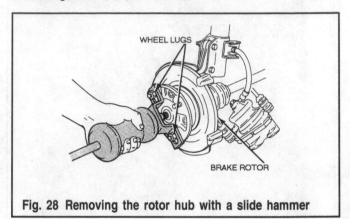

WHEEL LUGS

BRAKE ROTOR

Fig. 28 Removing the rotor hub with a slide hammer

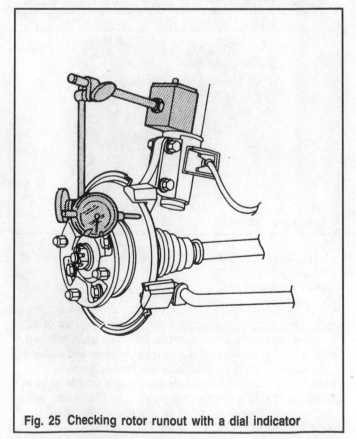

Fig. 25 Checking rotor runout with a dial indicator

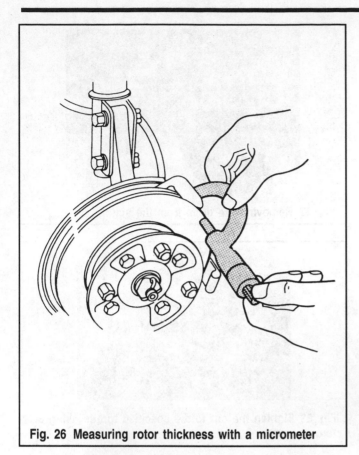

Fig. 26 Measuring rotor thickness with a micrometer

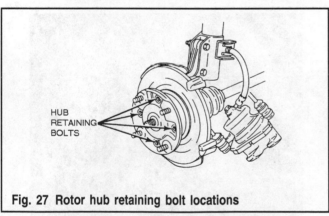

Fig. 27 Rotor hub retaining bolt locations

HUB
RETAINING
BOLTS

1. Elevate and safely support the vehicle. If only the front end is supported, set the parking brake and block the rear wheels.

2. Remove the wheel.

3. Remove the brake caliper from its mount and suspend it out of the way. Don't disconnect the hose and don't let the caliper hang by the hose. Remove the brake pads with all the clips, shims, etc.

4. Install all the lug nuts to hold the rotor in place. If the nuts are open at both ends, it is helpful to install them backwards (tapered end out) to secure the disc. Tighten the nuts a bit tighter than finger tight, but make sure all are at approximately the same tightness.

5. Check the run-out and thickness measurements of the rotor.

6. Remove the 2 bolts holding the caliper mounting bracket to the steering knuckle. These bolts will be tight. Remove the 4 lug nuts holding the rotor.

7. Remove the bracket from the knuckle. Before removing the rotor, make a mark on the rotor indexing one wheel stud to one hole in the rotor. This assures the rotor will be re-installed in its original position, serving to eliminate minor vibrations in the brake system.

To install:

8. When reinstalling, make certain the rotor is clean and free of any particles of rust or metal from resurfacing. Observe the index mark made earlier and fit the rotor over the wheel lugs. Install 2 lug nuts to hold it in place.

9. Install the caliper mounting bracket in position and tighten the bolts.

10. Install the brake pads and the hardware.

11. Install the caliper. Tighten the mounting bolts.

12. Install the wheel and lower the vehicle to the ground.

REAR DRUM BRAKES

Brake Drums

REMOVAL & INSTALLATION

▶ **See Figures 29, 30, 31, 32, 33 and 34**

1. Raise and support the vehicle safely.
2. Remove the tire and wheel assembly.

3. Remove the spindle cap without damaging the sealing portion of the cap.

4. Unfasten the staked portion of the nut using a suitable chisel.

5. Remove the castle nut and washer.

6. Slacken the parking brake cable by loosening its adjusting nuts.

7. Remove the backing plate plug, located on the back side of the backing plate.

Fig. 29 Rear drum brake assembly

Fig. 32 Removing the drum from the spindle

Fig. 30 Removing the spindle cap

Fig. 33 Tighten the nut to the specified torque using a torque wrench

Fig. 31 Unstake the nut using a suitable chisel

Fig. 34 Staking the nut in place

8. Insert a suitable tool into the plug until its tip contacts the shoe hold-down and push the spring in the direction of the leading shoe. The allows a greater clearance between the shoes and the drum.

9. Remove the drum from the spindle.

To install:

10. Install the drum on the spindle.

11. Install the castle nut and washer.

12. Tighten castle nut   then stake in place.

13. Install the spindle cap.

14. Install the wheel and tire, then lower the vehicle.

Brake Shoes

REMOVAL & INSTALLATION

▶ See Figures 35, 36, 37, 38, 39, 40, 41, 42, 43, 44, 45 and 46

✳✳CAUTION

Brake shoes contain asbestos, which has been determined to be a cancer causing agent. Never clean the brake surfaces with compressed air! Avoid inhaling any dust from any brake surface! When cleaning brake surfaces, us a commercially available brake cleaning fluid!

1. Disconnect the battery negative cable.

Fig. 35 Removing the lower brake shoe return spring

Fig. 36 Removing the anti-rattle spring

Fig. 37 Removing the brake shoe hold down springs

Fig. 38 Removing the parking brake lever from the cable

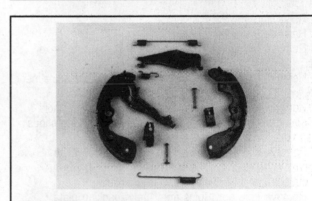

Fig. 39 Rear brake shoe assembly

Fig. 40 Lubricating the contact points with grease

Fig. 41 Installing the brake shoe hold down springs

Fig. 42 Installing the brake adjustment strut

2. Raise and support the vehicle safely.
3. Remove the brake drum.
4. Remove the upper and lower springs from the brake shoes.
5. Remove the anti rattle spring and brake shoe adjustment strut.
6. Remove the primary and secondary brake shoe hold down springs by turning hold down pins and removing shoes from vehicle.
7. Remove clip securing parking brake shoe lever to secondary shoe.
8. Remove parking brake cable from lever.
9. Remove hold down pins from brake backing plate.

Fig. 43 Installing the anti-rattle spring

Fig. 44 Installing the upper return spring

To install:
10. Inspect all components for damage from heat and stress. Replace components as necessary. Lubricate all contact points on the backing plate with grease.
11. Install the hold down pins on the backing plate.
12. Install the parking brake cable to parking brake shoe lever.
13. Install clip securing parking brake shoe lever to secondary shoe.
14. Install primary and secondary brake shoes to vehicle and secure with hold down springs. Position hold down spring on hold down pins and turn pins downward.
15. Install brake adjustment strut and anti-rattle spring.
16. Install upper and lower return springs to primary and secondary brake shoes.
17. Install brake drum and tighten spindle nut then stake in place.
18. Install wheel and tire.
19. Lower vehicle.
20. Press brake pedal 3-5 times to adjust the brake shoe clearance.
21. Check to ensure the brake drum is free from dragging and proper braking is obtained.

Wheel Cylinder

REMOVAL & INSTALLATION

▶ See Figure 46

1. Disconnect the battery negative cable.

Fig. 45 Installing the lower return spring

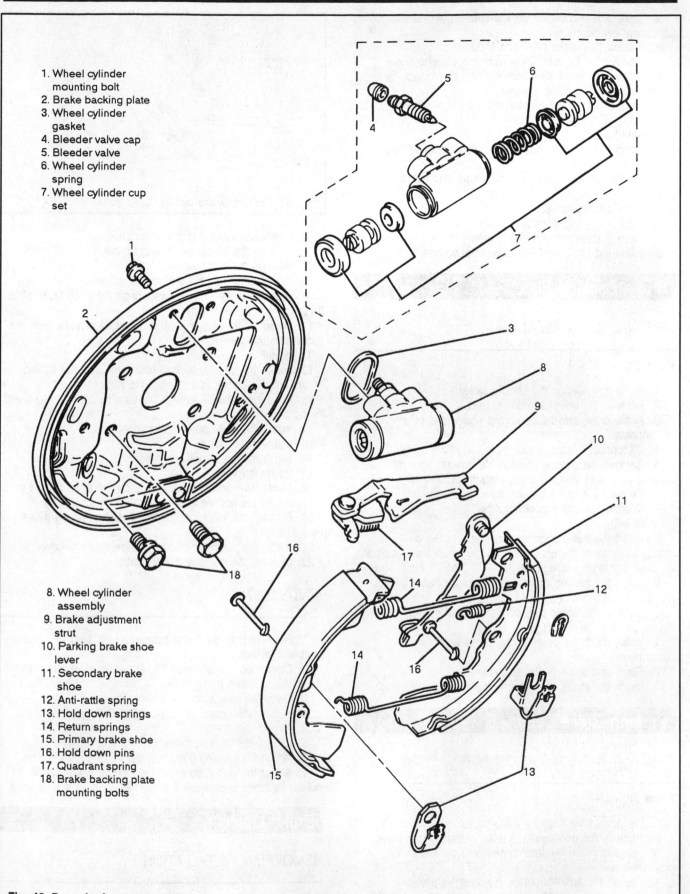

1. Wheel cylinder mounting bolt
2. Brake backing plate
3. Wheel cylinder gasket
4. Bleeder valve cap
5. Bleeder valve
6. Wheel cylinder spring
7. Wheel cylinder cup set

8. Wheel cylinder assembly
9. Brake adjustment strut
10. Parking brake shoe lever
11. Secondary brake shoe
12. Anti-rattle spring
13. Hold down springs
14. Return springs
15. Primary brake shoe
16. Hold down pins
17. Quadrant spring
18. Brake backing plate mounting bolts

Fig. 46 Drum brake components

2. Raise and support the vehicle safely, then remove the tire and wheel assembly.

3. Remove the brake drum and shoes.

4. Remove the bleeder screw from the wheel cylinder.

5. Loosen the brake pipe flare nut and disconnect the brake pipe from the wheel cylinder.

6. Remove the wheel cylinder attaching bolts and the wheel cylinder from the backing plate.

To install:

7. Install the wheel cylinder and tighten mounting bolts to 115 inch lbs. (13 Nm).

8. Connect brake pipe to wheel cylinder and tighten to 12 ft. lbs. (16 Nm).

9. Install bleeder valve.

10. Install the brake drum and shoes.

11. Flush and bleed the brake system.

12. Install the wheel and tire. Lower the vehicle.

Brake Backing Plate

REMOVAL & INSTALLATION

▶ **See Figure 46**

1. Raise and support the vehicle safely.

2. Remove the wheel and tire assembly.

3. Remove the brake drum, brake shoes and other components.

4. Disconnect the brake pipe from the wheel cylinder.

5. Remove the parking brake cable retainer from the backing plate and feed the cable through to remove.

6. Remove the brake backing plate mounting bolts.

7. Remove the brake backing plate.

To install:

8. Install the brake backing plate using sealer on the mating surfaces of the brake backing plate and the suspension knuckle. Tighten mounting bolts to 17 ft. lbs. (23 Nm).

9. Install the parking brake cable from the backing plate and secure with retainer.

10. Connect the brake pipe from the wheel cylinder and tighten to 12 ft. lbs. (16 Nm).

11. Install the brake drum, brake shoes and other components.

12. Flush and bleed the brake system.

13. Install the wheel and tire assembly. Lower the vehicle.

Parking Brake Cable

REMOVAL & INSTALLATION

▶ **See Figure 47**

1. Disconnect the negative battery cable.

2. Remove the parking brake lever assembly trim cover.

3. Disconnect the electrical connector from the parking brake switch.

4. Loosen the adjuster nut on the lever assembly.

5. Remove the parking brake cables from the equalizer plate.

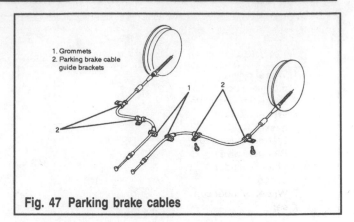

Fig. 47 Parking brake cables

6. Raise and support the vehicle safely.

7. Remove the wheel and tire assembly.

8. Remove the brake drum.

9. Remove the rear brakes and components.

10. Disconnect the parking brake cable from the brake shoe lever and the backing plate.

11. Remove the cable(s) from the chassis mounts, then the cable from the vehicle.

To install:

12. Install the cable(s) to the chassis mounts and tighten mount attaching bolts to 11 ft. lbs. (15 Nm).

13. Feed the cable(s) through the backing plate and connect to the brake shoe lever.

14. Install the rear brakes and components.

15. Install the brake drum.

16. Install the wheel and tire assembly.

17. Lower the vehicle.

18. Install the parking brake cables on the equalizer plate.

19. Adjust the parking brake lever assembly.

20. Connect the electrical connector to the parking brake switch.

21. Install the parking brake lever assembly trim cover.

22. Connect the negative battery cable.

ADJUSTMENT

1. Remove both door seal plates and the seat belt buckle bolts at the floor.

2. Disconnect the shoulder harness bolts at the floor and the interior, bottom trim panels.

3. Raise the rear seat cushion.

4. Pull up the carpet to gain access to the parking brake lever.

5. Loosen the parking brake cable adjusting nuts.

6. Adjust the parking brake cables, so they work evenly.

7. Adjust the cable, so when the parking brake handle is pulled, its travel is between 5-8 notches, with 44 lbs. of force.

Brake Lever

REMOVAL & INSTALLATION

▶ **See Figure 48**

➡**Do not disassemble the parking brake assembly. It must be replaced as an assembly only.**

1. Disconnect the negative battery cable.
2. Remove the parking brake lever assembly trim cover.
3. Disconnect the electrical connector from the parking brake switch.
4. Loosen the adjuster nut on the lever assembly.
5. Remove the parking brake cables from the equalizer plate.
6. Remove the parking brake lever assembly mounting bolts.

7. Remove the parking brake assembly from the vehicle.

To install:

8. Install the parking brake assembly in the vehicle.
9. Install the parking brake lever assembly mounting bolts and tighten to 11 ft. lbs. (15 Nm).
10. Install the parking brake cables on the equalizer plate.
11. Adjust the parking brake assembly.
12. Connect the electrical connector from the parking brake switch.
13. Install the parking brake lever assembly trim cover.
14. Connect the negative battery cable.

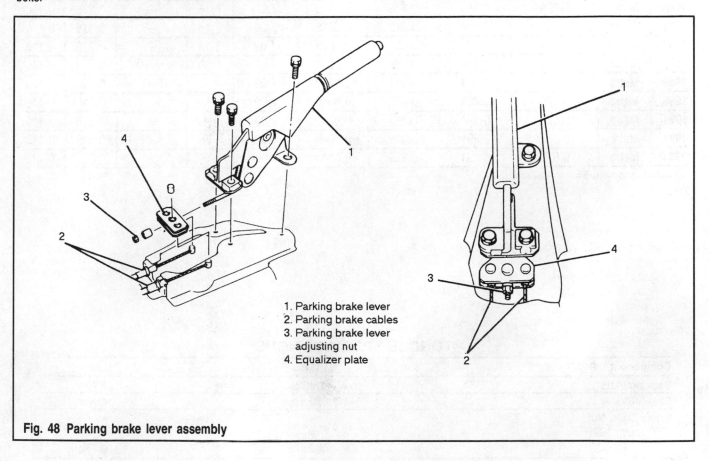

1. Parking brake lever
2. Parking brake cables
3. Parking brake lever adjusting nut
4. Equalizer plate

Fig. 48 Parking brake lever assembly

BRAKE SPECIFICATIONS

All measurements in inches unless noted.

Year	Model	Master Cylinder Bore	Brake Disc			Brake Drum Diameter			Minimum Lining Thickness	
			Original Thickness	Minimum Thickness	Maximum Runout	Original Inside Diameter	Max. Wear Limit	Maximum Machine Diameter	Front	Rear
1985	Sprint	0.825	0.394	0.315	0.0028	7.09	7.16	—	0.315	0.110
1986	Sprint	0.825	0.394	0.315	0.0028	7.09	7.16	—	0.315	0.110
1987	Sprint	0.825	0.394	0.315	0.0028	7.09	7.16	—	0.315	0.110
1988	Sprint	0.825	0.394	0.315	0.0028	7.09	7.16	—	0.315	0.110
1989	Metro	0.825	0.394	0.315	0.0040	7.09	7.16	—	0.315	0.110
1990	Metro	0.825	0.394	0.315	0.0040	7.09	7.16	—	0.315	0.110
1991	Metro	0.825	0.394	0.315	0.0040	7.09	7.16	—	0.315	0.110
1992	Metro	0.825	0.394	0.315	0.0040	7.09	7.16	—	0.315	0.110
1993	Metro	0.825	0.394	0.315	0.0040	7.09	7.16	—	0.315	0.110

① All brake pad measurements include shoe and lining

TORQUE SPECIFICATIONS

Component	U.S.	Metric
Backing Plate	17 ft. lbs.	23 Nm
Bleeder Valve	89 inch lbs.	10 Nm
Brake Drum Nut		
Through 1991	41 ft. lbs.	55 Nm
1992-93	74 ft. lbs.	100 Nm
Brake Hoses	12 ft. lbs.	16 Nm
Brake Light Switch	115 inch lbs.	13 Nm
Brake Pedal	17 ft. lbs.	20 Nm
Brake Pipe Clamps	124 inch lbs.	14 Nm
Brake Pipes	10-13 ft. lbs.	14-18 Nm
Caliper Union Bolt	17 ft. lbs.	23 Nm
Clevis Nut	18 ft. lbs.	25 Nm
Master Cylinder	8-12 ft. lbs.	11-16 Nm
Parking Brake Lever	11 ft. lbs.	15 Nm
Piston Stopper Bolt	89 inch lbs.	10 Nm
Power Brake Booster	14-20 ft. lbs.	19-27 Nm
Wheel Cylinder	115 inch lbs.	13 Nm

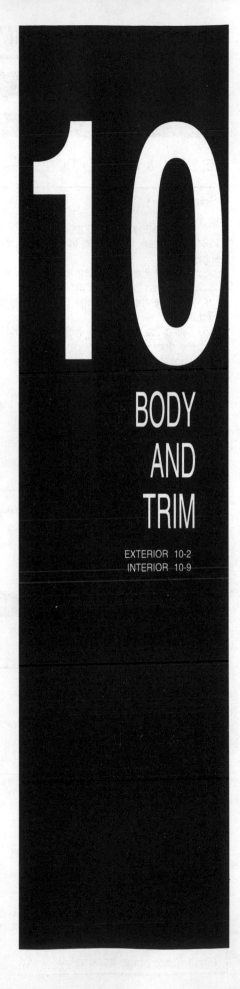

10

BODY AND TRIM

EXTERIOR

Doors

REMOVAL & INSTALLATION

▶ **See Figure 1**

1. Remove the door stopper pin.
2. Matchmark the hinges to the body for installation reference.
3. Support the door using a floor jack with a piece of wood placed between the jack and panel.
4. Remove the door hinge bolts and then remove the door.

To install:

5. Using the jack, position the door and install hinge bolts. Align the door to the reference marks.
6. Loosely tighten the hinge bolts and close the door lightly to check alignment.
7. Align door and tighten hinge bolts to 25 ft. lbs. (34 Nm).
8. As necessary, align door striker by loosening the screws and adjusting.
9. Install the door stopper pin.

ADJUSTMENT

Door adjustment is made by loosening the mounting bolts and/or striker and adjusting position as required. Position the door so that a clearance of 0.20-0.26 in. exists between the door and the rocker panel, fender or other door. The door should be flush within 0.04 in.

Hood

REMOVAL & INSTALLATION

▶ **See Figure 2**

1. Raise hood and suitably support.
2. Install protective covers over fenders to prevent paint damage.

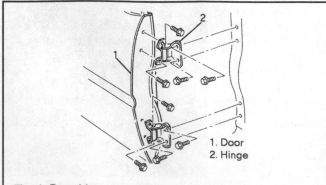

1. Door
2. Hinge

Fig. 1 Door hinge assembly

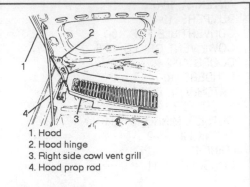

1. Hood
2. Hood hinge
3. Right side cowl vent grill
4. Hood prop rod

Fig. 2 Hood hinge assembly

3. Mark the position of the hinges to the hood for installation reference.

➡ **A helper is necessary to hold the hood during removal.**

4. Remove the hinge bolts and lift the hood from the vehicle.

To install:

5. Align the hood with the marks made during removal.
6. Install the hinge bolts but do not tighten fully.
7. Adjust the hood to obtain the proper clearances.
8. Tighten hood hinge bolts to 20 ft. lbs. (27 Nm).

ADJUSTMENT

Hood adjustment is made by loosening the mounting bolts slightly and repositioning the hood. Always use an assistant during this procedure. The hood, when loosened, may come in contact with other painted surfaces and cause damage to their finish. Position the hood so that a clearance of 0.60 in. exists between the hood and cowl vent grille, a clearance of 0.20 in. exists between the hood and head lamps, and a clearance of 0.15 in. exists between the hood and fenders. The hood should be flush within 0.04 in.

Trunk Lid

REMOVAL & INSTALLATION

▶ **See Figure 3**

Convertible Models

1. Disconnect the negative battery cable.
2. Raise and support the deck lid.
3. Remove the screws securing center high mounted stop lamp to the deck lid.
4. Pull stop lamp from deck lid and disconnect the electrical connector.
5. Remove stop light wiring from deck lid by removing grommets and feeding wiring through deck lid.
6. Remove the screw securing each deck lid side reveal molding to the deck lid.

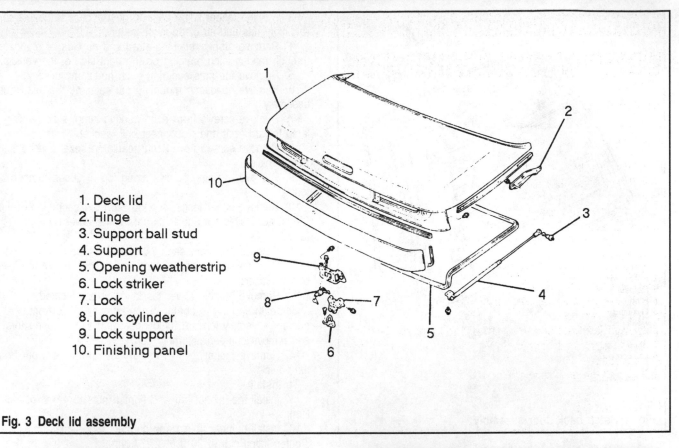

1. Deck lid
2. Hinge
3. Support ball stud
4. Support
5. Opening weatherstrip
6. Lock striker
7. Lock
8. Lock cylinder
9. Lock support
10. Finishing panel

Fig. 3 Deck lid assembly

7. Remove the screws securing each deck lid support to the deck lid.

➡**A helper is necessary to hold the hood during removal.**

8. Remove the bolts securing the deck lid to each hinge and remove the deck lid from the vehicle.

To install:

9. Install the deck lid and secure with bolts.
10. Align deck lid and tighten bolts to 33 ft. lbs. (45 Nm).
11. Install the deck lid supports and secure with screws.
12. Install the screws to the deck lid reveal molding.
13. Feed wiring through deck lid and install grommets.
14. Connect the center high mounted stop light electrical connector.
15. Install the center high mounted stop lamp to the deck lid and secure with screw.
16. Lower deck lid and check adjustment.
17. Connect the negative battery cable.

ADJUSTMENT

Position the deck lid so that a clearance of 0.26 in. exists between the deck lid and the quarter panel. The deck lid should be flush within 0.04 in.

Hatchback Door

REMOVAL & INSTALLATION

▶ **See Figure 4**

Hardtop Models

1. Disconnect the negative battery cable.
2. Raise and support the hatchback door.
3. Remove the screw securing each speaker grille and speaker to hatchback door.
4. Lower speakers and disconnect electrical connectors.
5. Remove plastic retaining clips and hatchback door interior trim panel.
6. Remove rear wiper motor, rear defogger, and center high mounted stop light electrical connectors.
7. Remove grommet from the upper right side of the hatchback door and feed wires through the opening.
8. Remove washer hose from the upper left side of the hatchback door.
9. Remove the screws from the hatchback door support and lower supports.
10. Mark position of hinges on door for installation reference.

➡**A helper is necessary to hold the door during removal.**

11. Remove bolts from door hinge and lift hatchback door from vehicle.

To install:

12. Align the door hinges to the marks and install the hatchback door. Tighten hinge bolts to 33 ft. lbs. (45 Nm).

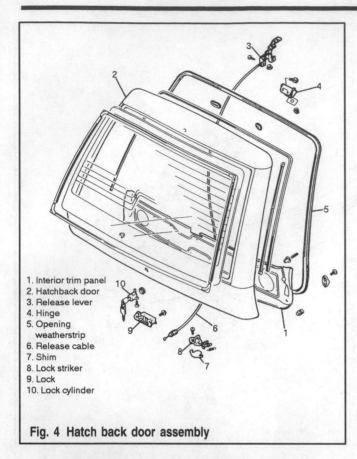

1. Interior trim panel
2. Hatchback door
3. Release lever
4. Hinge
5. Opening weatherstrip
6. Release cable
7. Shim
8. Lock striker
9. Lock
10. Lock cylinder

Fig. 4 Hatch back door assembly

13. Install the door supports and washer hose.
14. Feed door wires through opening in hatchback door and install grommet.
15. Install rear wiper motor, rear window defogger and center high mounted stop light electrical connectors.
16. Install hatchback door interior trim panel.
17. Connect speaker electrical connectors and install speakers in place.
18. Lower hatchback door gently to check for proper alignment. Adjust as necessary.

ADJUSTMENT

Position the hatchback door so that a clearance of 0.22 in. exists between the door and the quarter panel and a clearance of 0.34 in. exists between the door and the roof. The door should be flush within 0.04 in.

Bumpers

REMOVAL & INSTALLATION

▶ **See Figures 5 and 6**

Front

1. Disconnect the negative battery cable.
2. Remove the screws and retaining clips from each front fender lining.

3. Pull the fender lining back to gain access to headlamp retaining nuts and air cleaner resonator.
4. Remove rubber retaining strap and air cleaner resonator through fender lining opening on the right side of the vehicle.
5. Remove the nuts securing each headlamp assembly.
6. Remove headlamp mounting nut securing the headlamp assembly.
7. Remove screws from each parking lamp, slide parking lamp toward front and disconnect bulb socket.
8. Remove screws from each headlamp bezel and bezels from vehicle.
9. Remove retaining screws along top of upper bumper fascia.
10. Remove upper fascia support nut from each side of the fascia, accessible through the front for the lower bumper fascia.
11. Remove bolt from each lower fascia brace
12. Remove screws accessible through the front of the lower bumper fascia.
13. Remove bumper lower fascia fitting bolt located underneath and in the center of the bumper. Slide front bumper assembly forward, disconnect turn signal connectors and remove bumper assembly from vehicle.
14. Remove mounting nuts and remove the impact bar from the vehicle.
   To install:
15. Install the impact bar and tighten nuts to 44 ft. lbs. (60 Nm).
16. Install bumper fascia and connect turn signal lamps. Tighten fitting bolt to 20 ft. lbs. (27 Nm).
17. Install screws accessible through the front of the lower bumper fascia.
18. Install bolt for each lower fascia brace. Tighten to 15 ft. lbs. (20 Nm).
19. Install upper fascia support nut for each side of the fascia, accessible through the front of the lower bumper fascia. Tighten to 15 ft. lbs. (20 Nm).
20. Install retaining screws along top of upper bumper fascia.
21. Install screws for each headlamp bezel and bezels on vehicle.
22. Connect bulb socket. Install screws from each parking lamp, slide parking lamp into front of vehicle.
23. Install headlamp mounting nut securing the headlamp assembly.
24. Install the nuts securing each headlamp assembly.
25. Install rubber retaining strap and air cleaner resonator through fender lining opening on the right side of the vehicle.
26. Install the screws and retaining clips for each front fender lining.
27. Connect the negative battery cable.

Rear Bumper

1. Disconnect the negative battery cable.
2. Remove retaining screws and license plate bracket.
3. Remove retaining screws and rear center garnish.
4. Remove retaining screws from combination lamp assembly, pull assembly away from vehicle and disconnect bulb sockets from lamp. Remove rear combination lamp assemblies.

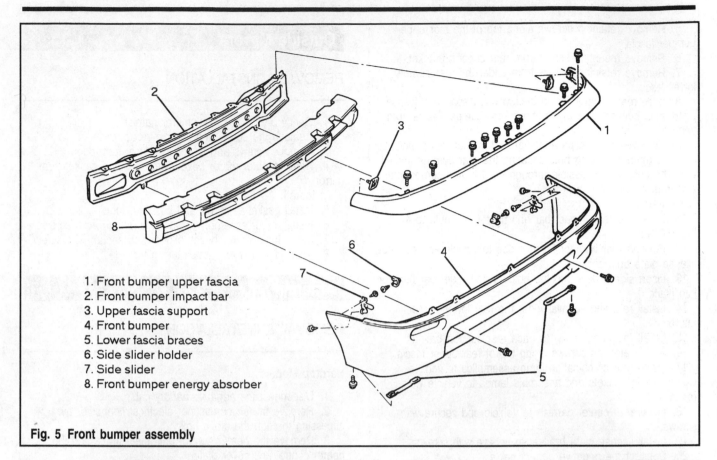

1. Front bumper upper fascia
2. Front bumper impact bar
3. Upper fascia support
4. Front bumper
5. Lower fascia braces
6. Side slider holder
7. Side slider
8. Front bumper energy absorber

Fig. 5 Front bumper assembly

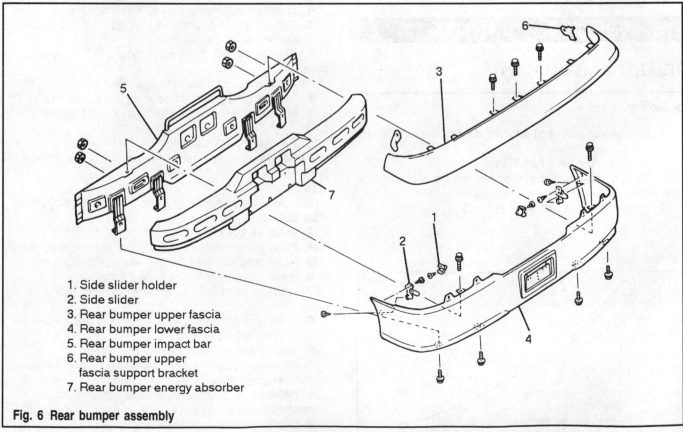

1. Side slider holder
2. Side slider
3. Rear bumper upper fascia
4. Rear bumper lower fascia
5. Rear bumper impact bar
6. Rear bumper upper
   fascia support bracket
7. Rear bumper energy absorber

Fig. 6 Rear bumper assembly

5. Remove retaining screws along top of the rear upper bumper fascia.

6. Remove mounting screw from rear support bracket.

7. Remove retaining screws from under the rear bumper lower fascia.

8. Slide rear bumper fascia backwards, disconnect license plate lamp bulb sockets and remove rear bumper fascia from vehicle.

9. Remove plastic clips and rear end interior trim panel.

10. Remove mounting nuts securing the rear bumper impact bar. The nuts are accessible through the luggage compartment and from under the vehicle.

To install:

11. Install the rear impact bar and tighten the nuts to 44 ft. lbs. (60 Nm).

12. Position rear bumper fascia close to vehicle and connect license plate bulb sockets.

13. Insert side sliders into the holders and slide rear bumper into place.

14. Install retaining screws under the rear lower bumper fascia.

15. Install mounting screw to each rear support bracket.

16. Install retaining screws along top of rear upper fascia.

17. Install rear combination lamp assemblies to vehicle. Connect bulb sockets and assemble lamps to vehicle with retaining screws.

18. Install rear center garnish to vehicle and secure with screws.

19. Install license plate bracket to vehicle with screws.

20. Connect the negative battery cable.

Cowl Vent Grille

REMOVAL & INSTALLATION

▶ **See Figure 7**

1. Remove nut cover and retaining nut securing each wiper arm.

2. Remove wiper arms from linkage.

3. Remove plastic retaining clips securing the cowl vent and remove the vent.

4. Installation is the reverse of removal.

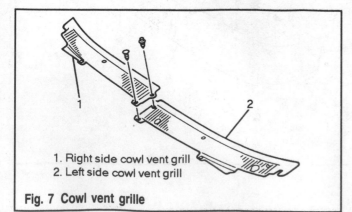

1. Right side cowl vent grill
2. Left side cowl vent grill

Fig. 7 Cowl vent grille

Outside Mirrors

REMOVAL & INSTALLATION

1. Gently pry off the inner mirror garnish.

2. Remove the screw and inner mirror garnish.

3. Remove screws and mirror assembly from door.

4. Remove outer mirror bezel from door and gasket from mirror.

To install:

5. Install gasket to mirror and bezel to door.

6. Install mirror assembly to door and secure with screws.

7. Install inner mirror bezel to door and secure with screw.

8. Snap inner mirror garnish into place.

Antenna

REMOVAL & INSTALLATION

Hardtop Models

1. Disconnect the negative battery cable.

2. Remove the air conditioner electrical connector by accessing through the glove box.

3. Remove the heater control unit lever knobs and the heater control unit cover plate.

4. Remove the illumination lamp from cover plate.

5. Remove gearshift control lever upper boot and console on manual transaxle models.

6. Remove the instrument panel bezel and front radio face panel.

7. Remove the radio from the instrument panel.

8. Remove radio antenna lead and electrical connectors.

9. Remove antenna cable from clips under instrument panel.

10. Remove left kick panel.

11. Remove antenna mast screws and guide antenna wire through hole.

To install:

12. Guide antenna wire through hole and install antenna mast screws.

13. Install left kick panel.

14. Install antenna cable on clips under instrument panel.

15. Install radio antenna lead and electrical connectors.

16. Install the radio in the instrument panel.

17. Install the instrument panel bezel and front radio face panel.

18. Install gearshift control lever upper boot and console on manual transaxle models.

19. Install the illumination lamp on cover plate.

20. Install the heater control unit lever knobs and the heater control unit cover plate.

21. Install the air conditioner electrical connector by accessing through the glove box.

22. Connect the negative battery cable.

Convertible Models

1. Remove the inner wheel housing.

2. Remove the antenna mast from ground base.

3. Remove antenna ground base mounting nut.

4. Remove antenna cable connector located behind wheel housing.

5. Remove antenna ground base assembly and cable from vehicle.

To install:

6. Install antenna ground base assembly and cable in vehicle.

7. Install antenna cable connector located behind wheel housing.

8. Install antenna ground base mounting nut and tighten to 11 ft. lbs. (15 Nm).

9. Install the antenna mast from ground base.

10. Install the inner wheel housing.

Fenders

REMOVAL & INSTALLATION

▶ **See Figure 8**

1. Disconnect the negative battery cable.

2. Remove the parking lamp and slide away from fender. Disconnect bulb socket.

3. Raise and support the vehicle safely.

4. Remove tire and wheel.

5. Remove wheel housing.

6. Remove antenna from right fender, as required.

7. Remove fender bolts at door pillar.

8. Remove inner fender bolt.

9. Remove upper fender bolts.

10. Remove support nut securing fender to bumper fascia.

11. Remove retaining bolt from fender brace.

12. Slide fender off bumper side slider and remove.

To install:

13. Slide fender on bumper side slider and install.

14. Install retaining bolt on fender brace. Tighten to 15 ft. lbs. (20 Nm).

15. Install support nut securing fender to bumper fascia. Tighten to 15 ft. lbs. (20 Nm).

16. Install upper fender bolts. Tighten to 15 ft. lbs. (20 Nm).

17. Install inner fender bolt. Tighten to 15 ft. lbs. (20 Nm).

18. Install fender bolts at door pillar. Tighten to 15 ft. lbs. (20 Nm).

19. Install antenna on right fender, as required.

20. Install wheel housing.

21. Install tire and wheel.

22. Lower vehicle.

23. Connect bulb socket and install the parking lamp.

24. Connect the negative battery cable.

Convertible Top

REMOVAL & INSTALLATION

▶ **See Figure 9**

1. Unlatch the folding top at the windshield header. Raise top halfway and support.

2. Remove screws and header seal retainer from header.

3. Detach folded top edge of top material from header.

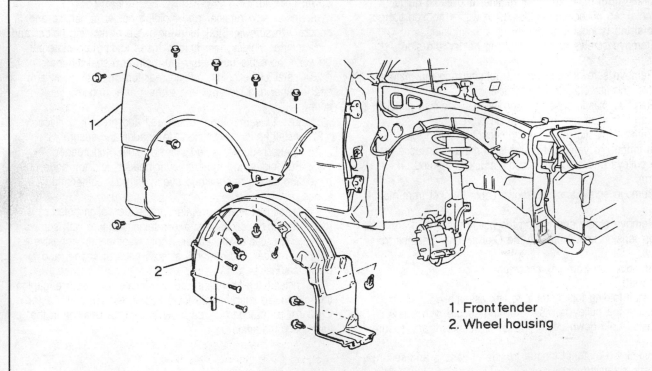

1. Front fender
2. Wheel housing

Fig. 8 Front fender assembly

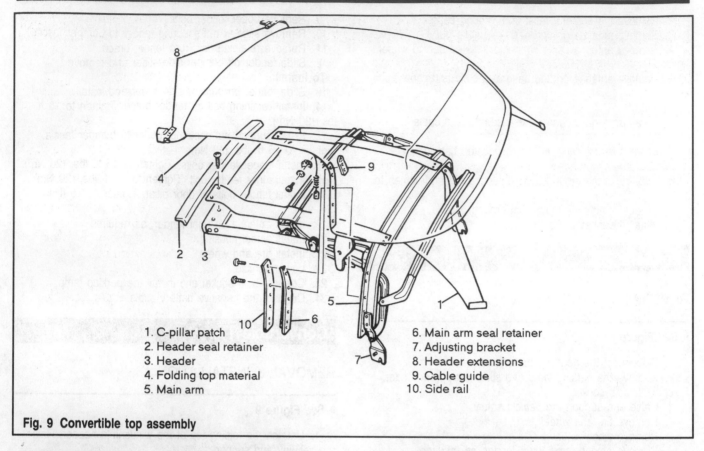

1. C-pillar patch
2. Header seal retainer
3. Header
4. Folding top material
5. Main arm
6. Main arm seal retainer
7. Adjusting bracket
8. Header extensions
9. Cable guide
10. Side rail

Fig. 9 Convertible top assembly

4. Remove screws from header extension.

5. Remove screws securing side rail, main arm seal retainer, top material and cable guide to main arm. Separate top material from main arm seal retainer and cable guide. Bend metal tab of molding holder down with a hooked tip tool. The metal tab is located under the quarter molding.

6. Remove screws securing molding holder and side retainer.

7. Remove screws securing rear retainer and top material to vehicle and lift retainer from vehicle.

8. Remove plastic clips securing interior side trim panel to vehicle and position trim panel outside of vehicle.

9. Remove plastic retaining clip securing folding top material tongue to vehicle. Pull top material to gain access to the top pulleys and hold down cable brackets located on the main arm.

10. Remove screw and hold down cable bracket from main arm.

11. Remove screw and folding top pulley from main arm. Unfasten tension belt. Unfasten the C-pillar inner patches from rear bow.

12. Remove top from link assembly.

To install:

13. Install folding top material to link assembly.

14. Install top pulley to main arm and secure with screw.

15. Install hold down cable bracket to main arm and secure with screw.

16. Install top material tongue to side of vehicle and secure with plastic retaining clip.

17. Install interior side trim panel into position and secure with retaining clips.

18. Install rear retainer to vehicle and secure with screws. Lower deck lid.

19. Install side retainer and molding holder to vehicle and secure with screws. Straighten metal tab of molding holder and slide quarter molding into holder. Insert folding top material between the cable guide and the main arm seal retainer.

20. Install cable guide, folding rear top material, main arm seal retainer and side rail to the main arm. Secure with screws.

21. Install weather strip to side rail and press into place.

22. Install header extensions to header and secure with screws. Attach double sided tape to folding top header.

23. Pull folding top material over header, fold top edge of material onto the header and attach with a weatherstrip adhesive.

24. Install header seal retainer to header, align holes of folding top material, header and retainer. Secure with screws starting from center of header. Apply weatherstrip adhesive between header and material at both ends of header and press material securely into place.

25. Install latch to folding top to windshield header engaging the folding top latch handle lock. Fasten tension belt. Fasten C-pillar inner patches to rear bow to remove wrinkles in the folding top material.

INTERIOR

Instrument Panel and Pad

REMOVAL & INSTALLATION

▶ **See Figures 10 and 11**

✳✳CAUTION

The Supplemental Inflatable Restraint (SIR) system must be disabled prior to performing this service. Refer to Section 6 for SIR disabling procedure.

1. Disconnect the negative battery cable.
2. On convertible models, remove the inflator module from the steering wheel.
3. Remove the lower steering column trim panel.
4. On convertible models, remove the steering wheel.
5. On convertible models, remove the SIR coil/combination switch assembly.
6. On hardtop models, remove the combination switch from the steering wheel.
7. Remove the right and left kick panels by removing a plastic retaining nut and clip from each panel.
8. Remove the right and left speaker grilles from instrument panel by removing screws and plastic retaining clip from each grille.

9. On convertible models, remove the retaining clip securing instrument panel to each door jamb.
10. Remove the right and left from speakers from instrument panel by removing screws and one electrical connector from each speaker.
11. Remove the glove box inner panel.
12. Remove the A/C switch electrical connector through the glove box.
13. Remove the heater control unit lever knobs and pull the heater control unit from the instrument panel.
14. Disconnect the heater control unit illumination lamp from cover plate.
15. On manual transmission vehicles, remove the gearshift control lever upper boot from console, then remove the console.
16. Remove the ashtray.
17. Remove the center console trim bezel and instrument panel center trim bezel. Remove the radio.
18. Remove the electrical connectors from the cluster trim bezel mounted switches.
19. Remove the retaining clip and speedometer cable at transaxle to ease cluster assembly removal.
20. Remove cluster assembly from instrument panel.
21. Remove the speedometer cable and all electrical connectors from back of cluster assembly, then remove cluster assembly from vehicle.
22. Remove ashtray illumination lamp electrical connector.
23. Remove electrical connector from rear of cigar lighter then, remove retaining ring from rear of cigar lighter.

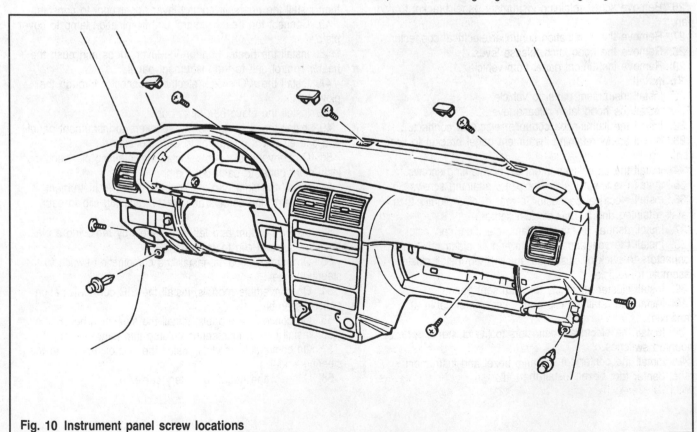

Fig. 10 Instrument panel screw locations

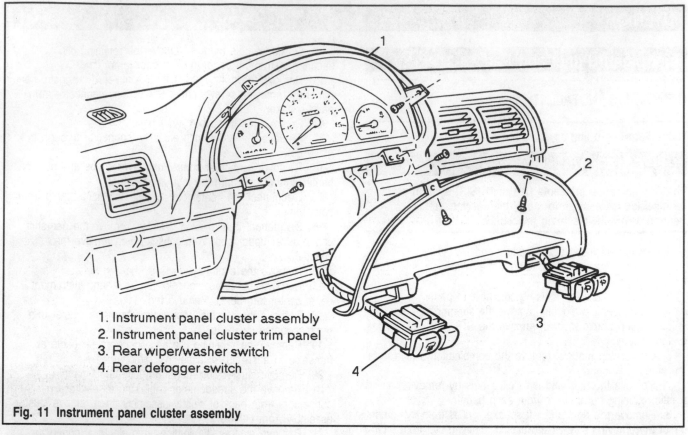

1. Instrument panel cluster assembly
2. Instrument panel cluster trim panel
3. Rear wiper/washer switch
4. Rear defogger switch

Fig. 11 Instrument panel cluster assembly

24. Remove the lower instrument panel retaining screws.
25. Remove the upper instrument panel retaining screws.
26. Remove screw retaining instrument panel bracket to floor pan.
27. Remove the illumination controller electrical connector.
28. Remove the hood latch release lever.
29. Remove instrument panel from vehicle.

To install:
30. Install instrument panel to vehicle.
31. Install the hood latch release lever.
32. Install the illumination controller electrical connector.
33. Install screw retaining instrument panel bracket to floor pan.
34. Install the upper instrument panel retaining screws.
35. Install the lower instrument panel retaining screws.
36. Install electrical connector to rear of cigar lighter then, install retaining ring to rear of cigar lighter.
37. Install ashtray illumination lamp electrical connector.
38. Install the speedometer cable and all electrical connectors to back of cluster assembly, then install cluster assembly to vehicle.
39. Install cluster assembly to instrument panel.
40. Install the retaining clip and speedometer cable at transaxle.
41. Install the electrical connectors to the cluster trim bezel mounted switches.
42. Install the center console trim bezel and instrument panel center trim bezel. install the radio.

43. Install the ashtray.
44. On manual transmission vehicles, install the console, then install the gearshift control lever upper boot to console.
45. Connect the heater control unit illumination lamp to cover plate.
46. Install the heater control unit lever knobs and push the heater control unit to the instrument panel.
47. Install the A/C switch electrical connector through the glove box.
48. Install the glove box inner panel.
49. Install the right and left to speakers to instrument panel and one electrical connector to each speaker.
50. On convertible models, install the retaining clip securing instrument panel to each door jamb.
51. Install the right and left speaker grilles to instrument panel by removing screws and plastic retaining clip to each grille.
52. Install the right and left kick panels by removing a plastic retaining nut and clip to each panel.
53. On hardtop models, install the combination switch to the steering wheel.
54. On convertible models, install the SIR coil/combination switch assembly.
55. On convertible models, install the steering wheel.
56. Install the lower steering column trim panel.
57. On convertible models, install the inflator module to the steering wheel.
58. Connect the negative battery cable.

Console

REMOVAL & INSTALLATION

▶ **See Figure 12**

1. Remove the gearshift control lever upper boot from console.
2. Remove screws securing console to vehicle.
3. Remove console from vehicle.
4. Installation is the reverse of removal.

Door Panels

REMOVAL & INSTALLATION

▶ **See Figure 13**

1. Remove the inside door handle bezel and gently pull from door trim.
2. Remove screws from armrest handle garnish.
3. Remove plastic screw covers from door armrest.
4. Remove screws and armrest from door.
5. Remove regulator handle using a cloth to remove snapring.
6. Gently pry door panel away from door, disengaging retaining clips.

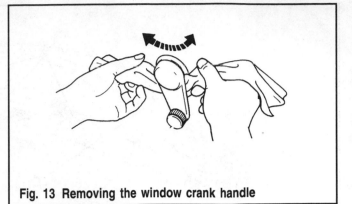

Fig. 13 Removing the window crank handle

To install:

7. Install door panel to door and press retaining clips into place.
8. Install snapring to window regulator handle and install handle.
9. Install armrest to door.
10. Install screws and plastic screw covers.
11. Install screw and armrest handle garnish.
12. Install inside door handle bezel.

Headliner

REMOVAL & INSTALLATION

▶ **See Figure 14**

1. Disconnect the negative battery cable.
2. Remove the dome lamp bezel and dome lamp assembly.
3. Remove the inside rearview mirror.
4. Remove the sunshades and inner support.
5. Remove the door opening laces.
6. Remove the screws and assist handles.
7. Remove the A-pillar trim panels.
8. Remove the drip rail weather-strips.
9. On 4-door models, remove the B-pillar upper trim panel from vehicle.

➡ **The front listing wire is longer than the other wires.**

10. Remove the headliner and listing wires from vehicle.
11. Remove the adhesive tape from the roof flange.
To install:
12. Install 2-sided bondable tape to upper side of each roof flange. Tape should be applied no further than 10 mm from the end of roof flange.
13. Install the listing wires and headliner to vehicle. Pull headliner tight and secure it to the 2-sided bondable tape on the roof flanges. This will help to eliminate any wrinkles in the headlining. Be sure to eliminate wrinkles around center pillars when installing headlining material.
14. Install the dome lamp bezel and dome lamp assembly.
15. On 4-door models, install the B-pillar upper trim panel to vehicle.
16. Install the rear quarter window interior trim panel, hatchback door opening weatherstrip and drip rail weatherstrip on both sides of the vehicle.

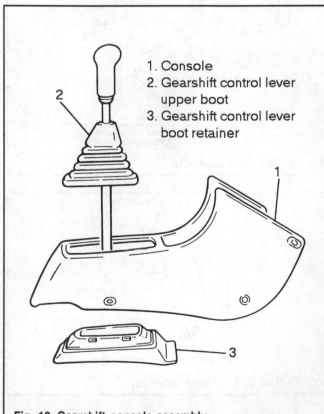

1. Console
2. Gearshift control lever upper boot
3. Gearshift control lever boot retainer

Fig. 12 Gearshift console assembly

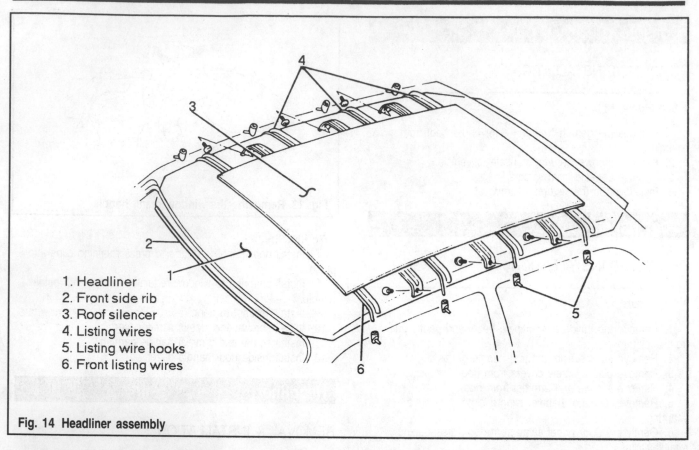

1. Headliner
2. Front side rib
3. Roof silencer
4. Listing wires
5. Listing wire hooks
6. Front listing wires

Fig. 14 Headliner assembly

17. Remove the A-pillar trim panels.
18. Install the assist handles and screws.
19. Install the sunshade inner supports and sunshades.
20. Install the rear view mirror.
21. Install the dome lamp and bezel.
22. Use an infrared lamp to warm the roof lining for 30-60 seconds. The heat will help remove the wrinkles that may develop.
23. Connect the negative battery cable.

Door Locks

REMOVAL & INSTALLATION

▶ See Figures 15 and 16

Striker Assembly

1. Disconnect the negative battery cable.
2. Remove the door panel and unclip the outer sealing strip from door.
3. Remove the door trim bracket.
4. Disconnect the seat belt retractor electrical connector.
5. Remove the seat belt retractor and seat belt assembly from the door.
6. Remove the water deflector.
7. Remove the door glass.
8. Remove the rear window guide channel as required.
9. Remove the lock assembly switch electrical connector.
10. Remove the handle rod and lock rod from the door lock.
11. Remove the door lock assembly from the door.

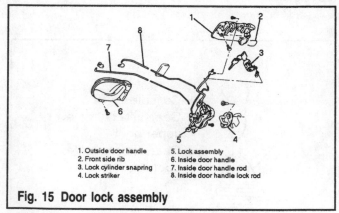

1. Outside door handle
2. Front side rib
3. Lock cylinder snapring
4. Lock striker
5. Lock assembly
6. Inside door handle
7. Inside door handle rod
8. Inside door handle lock rod

Fig. 15 Door lock assembly

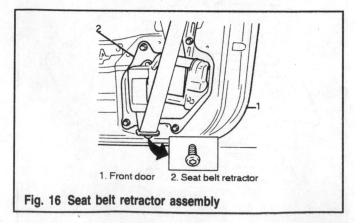

1. Front door
2. Seat belt retractor

Fig. 16 Seat belt retractor assembly

12. Remove the lock striker from the door panel.

To install:

13. Install the lock striker and secure with screws. Adjust the lock striker to door distance to 0.51-0.59 in. (13-15 mm) by installing or removing shims.

14. Install the door lock assembly and secure with screws. Adjust the striker up and down measurement so that the striker shaft aligns with the center of the door lock.

15. Install the outside handle rod and outside handle lock rod. Adjust the lock rod distance to 0-0.08 in. (0-2 mm).

16. Connect the lock assembly switch electrical connector.

17. Install the rear window guide channel as required.

18. Install the door glass.

19. Install the water deflector.

20. Install the seat belt retractor and seat belt assembly to the door. Tighten seat belt retractor assembly nut, bolts and seat belt anchor to 33 ft. lbs. (45 Nm).

21. Connect the seat belt retractor electrical connector.

22. Install the door trim bracket.

23. Install the door panel and attach the outer sealing strip to door.

24. Connect the negative battery cable.

Lock Cylinder

1. Disconnect the negative battery cable.

2. Remove the door panel and pull water deflector far enough away from door to gain access to lock cylinder.

3. Remove lock rod from lock cylinder.

4. Remove retaining clip and lock cylinder from door.

To install:

5. Install lock cylinder and retaining clip.

6. Install lock rod to lock cylinder.

7. Install water deflector and door panel.

8. Connect the negative battery cable.

Hatchback/Deck Lid Lock

REMOVAL & INSTALLATION

▶ **See Figures 17 and 18**

Striker Assembly

1. Remove the rear end interior trim panel.

2. Remove the lock striker from the vehicle.

3. Installation is the reverse of removal.

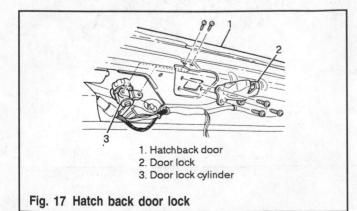

1. Hatchback door
2. Door lock
3. Door lock cylinder

Fig. 17 Hatch back door lock

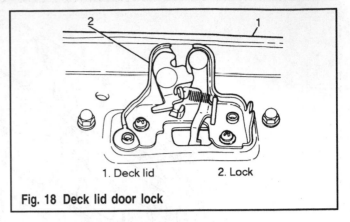

1. Deck lid   2. Lock

Fig. 18 Deck lid door lock

4. Adjust the striker by loosening the screws and move the striker into position for proper alignment.

Lock Cylinder

1. On hatchback doors, remove the speaker grills and speakers. Lower speakers and disconnect electrical connectors.

2. On hatchback doors, remove the door interior trim panel.

3. Remove the door lock from the door.

4. Installation is the reverse of removal.

Door Glass

REMOVAL & INSTALLATION

▶ **See Figures 19 and 20**

Hardtop Models

1. Remove the front door trim and inner mirror garnish.

2. Remove the inner mirror garnish.

3. Unclip the outer sealing strip from the door. Pull the water deflector far enough away from the door to gain access to the bottom channel-to-regulator screws.

4. Remove the window bottom channel-to-regulator retaining screws.

5. Remove the window assembly from the door.

6. Remove the window from the bottom channel.

To install:

7. Install the window to the bottom channel. Coat the bottom channel with soapy water to ease installation.

8. Install the window assembly to the door. Align the window bottom channel so that the distance from the bottom channel rear screw to the rear edge of the window is 11.95 in. on 2-door models or 9.96 in. on 4-door models.

9. Install the window bottom channel-to-regulator retaining screws. Tighten screws to 44 inch lbs. (5 Nm).

➡**Overtightening screws may break window.**

10. Adjust regulator screws so that measurements between the front door window and the front door window frame are equal at the front and rear of the top edge.

11. Inspect window for correct front/rear and left/right position.

12. Place water deflector in its normal position.

13. Clip outer sealing strip onto door.

14. Install inner mirror garnish to door and install door panel.

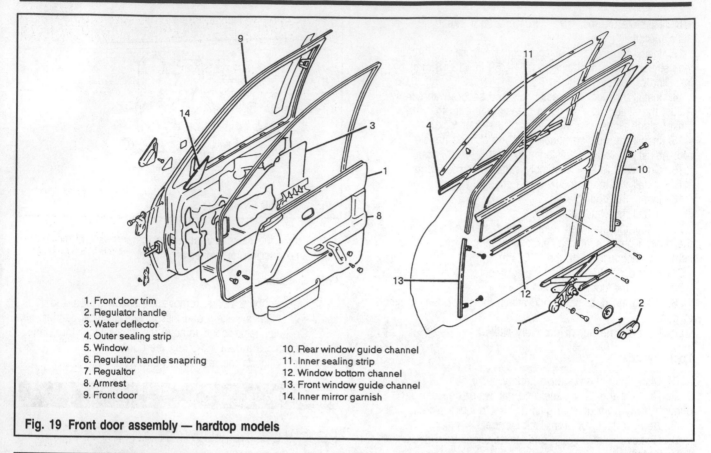

1. Front door trim
2. Regulator handle
3. Water deflector
4. Outer sealing strip
5. Window
6. Regulator handle snapring
7. Regualtor
8. Armrest
9. Front door
10. Rear window guide channel
11. Inner sealing strip
12. Window bottom channel
13. Front window guide channel
14. Inner mirror garnish

Fig. 19 Front door assembly — hardtop models

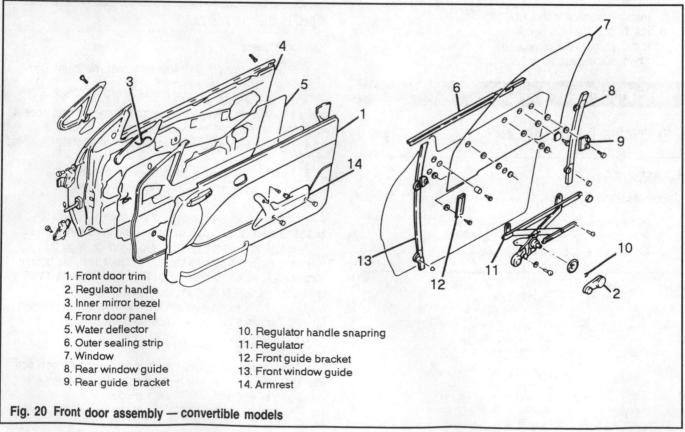

1. Front door trim
2. Regulator handle
3. Inner mirror bezel
4. Fronr door panel
5. Water deflector
6. Outer sealing strip
7. Window
8. Rear window guide
9. Rear guide bracket
10. Regulator handle snapring
11. Regulator
12. Front guide bracket
13. Front window guide
14. Armrest

Fig. 20 Front door assembly — convertible models

Convertible Models

1. Remove the front door trim and inner mirror garnish.
2. Remove the inner mirror bezel. Pull the water deflector far enough away from the door to gain access to the bottom channel-to-regulator screws.
3. Remove the door trim support.
4. Remove the window regulator mounting nuts.
5. Remove the window assembly from the door.
6. Remove the regulator bottom bolts from the window, the window male stopper, the window male stabilizer and the front and rear guide brackets.

To install:

7. Loosen upper and lower front and rear window guide mounting nuts.
8. Install front and rear guide bracket to window and secure with bolts. Tighten bolts to 44 inch lbs. (5 Nm).
9. Install male stabilizer and stopper to window and secure with bolts. Tighten bolts to 44 inch lbs. (5 Nm).
10. Install regulator bottom bolts and tighten to 44 inch lbs. (5 Nm).

➡**Overtightening screws may break window.**

11. Install window assembly to door.
12. Install regulator-to-window bolts and tighten to 44 inch lbs. (5 Nm).
13. Install door trim supports and secure with screw. Clip outer sealing strip to door.
14. Tighten front and rear window guide upper and lower mounting nuts at the center of the oblong holes in the door panel to 115 inch lbs. (13 Nm).
15. Raise window to its fully closed position. Inspect window for correct front/rear and left/right position. If window is not properly positioned, correct by loosening the front and rear window guide mounting nuts and adjusting the front and rear window guides.
16. Adjust regulator equalizer screws so that measurements between the top stack link and the front door window are equal at the front and rear of the window top.
17. Install the water deflector, inner mirror bezel and door panel.

Window Regulator

REMOVAL & INSTALLATION

▶ **See Figures 19 and 20**

1. Remove the window.
2. Pull water deflector far enough away from door to gain access to the regulator retaining screws.
3. Remove retaining screws from the regulator.
4. Remove the regulator through the large opening in the door.

To install:

5. Apply a multipurpose grease to all lubrication and sliding points.
6. Install regulator to door and secure with screws. Position water deflector back to its normal position.
7. Install the window.

Windshield Glass

REMOVAL & INSTALLATION

▶ **See Figures 21 and 22**

1. Remove the A-pillar trim.
2. Remove the inside rearview mirror and dome lamp.
3. Remove the sunshades.
4. Remove the cowl vent grille.
5. Remove the windshield stoppers, cowl vent grille and windshield wipers.
6. Punch a hole through adhesive with an awl and slip piano wire through hole. Cut adhesive around window keeping piano wire as close to the window as possible to avoid body damage.
7. Remove windshield from vehicle.

To install:

8. Using a knife cleaned with alcohol smooth remaining adhesive around body side so that it is uniform in thickness.
9. Remove adhesive from window if it is to be reused. Use care to not damage primer coated surface.
10. Install headliner, sunshades, dome lamp assembly and rear view mirror.
11. Install windshield stoppers and secure with screws.
12. Install reveal molding to window.
13. Clean surface of window, peel paper from one side of new windshield spacer which is included in the new molding set and adhere to windshield.

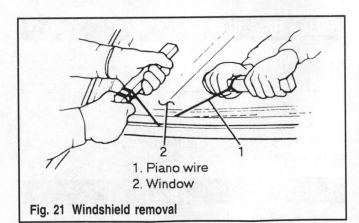

1. Piano wire
2. Window

Fig. 21 Windshield removal

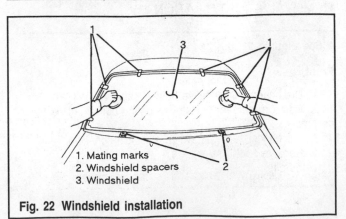

1. Mating marks
2. Windshield spacers
3. Windshield

Fig. 22 Windshield installation

14. Install windshield to body. Position window so that the distance between the upper end of the window and the body is about 0.24 in. and the distance between each side of the window and the body are even.

15. Using a wax pencil, mark points on window and body. Remove window.

16. Apply primer to body surface where windshield is to be adhered. Apply primer to edge of windshield and reveal molding.

17. Using a cartridge type caulking gun, apply a smooth continuous bead of urethane adhesive around primed surface edge of the windshield.

18. Using rubber suction cups, install the windshield, aligning mating marks.

19. Press windshield firmly into adhesive using care not to excessively squeeze adhesive out. Wipe around edge of window to ensure a watertight seal and apply more adhesive if necessary.

20. Install cowl vent grille and windshield wiper arms. Tighten wiper arm nuts to 15 ft. lbs. (20 Nm).

21. Water test windshield after adhesive is set.

Stationary Glass

REMOVAL & INSTALLATION

Stationary glass is removed and installed using the same procedure as the windshield. Refer to Windshield Glass Removal and Installation.

Inside Rear View Mirror

REMOVAL & INSTALLATION

1. Remove the dome lamp bezel.
2. Remove the rear view mirror mounting screws.
3. Remove the rear view mirror from the vehicle.
4. Installation is the reverse of removal.

Seats

REMOVAL & INSTALLATION

▶ **See Figures 23 and 24**

Front

1. Disconnect the negative battery cable.
2. Remove the seat adjuster mounting bolts from seat assembly.
3. Disconnect seat belt switch electrical connector.
4. Remove seat from vehicle.
To install:
5. Install seat in vehicle.

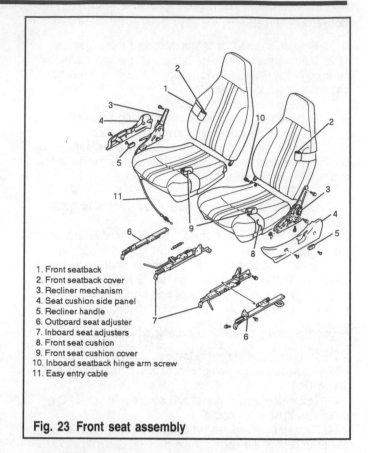

1. Front seatback
2. Front seatback cover
3. Recliner mechanism
4. Seat cushion side panel
5. Recliner handle
6. Outboard seat adjuster
7. Inboard seat adjusters
8. Front seat cushion
9. Front seat cushion cover
10. Inboard seatback hinge arm screw
11. Easy entry cable

Fig. 23 Front seat assembly

6. Connect seat belt switch electrical connector.
7. Install the seat adjuster mounting bolts and tighten to 13 ft. lbs. (18 Nm).
8. Connect the negative battery cable.

Rear

1. Remove luggage compartment security shelf strings from hooks and lift the shelf out of the vehicle.
2. Disengage plastic snaps securing luggage compartment carpet to floor at rear of luggage compartment.
3. Remove plastic retaining clips along forward edge of luggage compartment floor.
4. Place rear seat back in folded position.
5. Lift carpet over the rear seat back to gain access to rear retaining clips which secure the rear seat cushion to the floor pan. Remove the screws and raise seat cushion at front edge disengaging front retaining slips.
6. Slide seat cushion over seat belt buckles and remove from vehicle.
To install:
7. Install seat cushion to vehicle, feed seat belt buckles through seat cushion and engage front retaining clips.
8. Secure each rear retaining clip to floor pan with one screw.
9. Place seat back in upright position and reinstall luggage compartment carpet.
10. Install luggage compartment security shelf into vehicle and attach security shelf strings to security shelf string hooks.

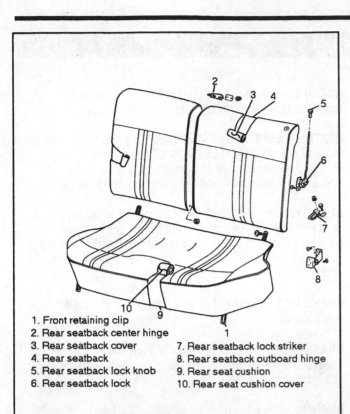

1. Front retaining clip
2. Rear seatback center hinge
3. Rear seatback cover
4. Rear seatback
5. Rear seatback lock knob
6. Rear seatback lock
7. Rear seatback lock striker
8. Rear seatback outboard hinge
9. Rear seat cushion
10. Rear seat cushion cover

Fig. 24 Rear seat assembly

Seat Belts

REMOVAL & INSTALLATION

▶ See Figure 25

Hardtop Model

1. Disconnect the negative battery cable.
2. Remove the front door panel.
3. Remove the seat belt guide loop bracket from window.
4. Pull rubber window channel from window and remove screws and window frame shoulder bracket.
5. Disconnect seat belt retractor assembly electrical connector.
6. Remove mounting bolts and seat belt retractor.

To install:

7. Install seat belt retractor and tighten mounting bolts to 33 ft. lbs. (45 Nm).
8. Connect seat belt retractor assembly electrical connector.
9. Install window frame shoulder bracket.
10. Install the seat belt guide loop bracket to window and tighten bolt to 33 ft. lbs. (45 Nm).
11. Install front door panel and connect negative battery cable.

Convertible Model

1. Disconnect the negative battery cable.

2. Remove the anchor bolt securing the seat belt to the floor.
3. Remove the plastic retaining clips and rear speaker panel.
4. Remove the plastic retaining clips and the passenger compartment quarter trim panel.
5. Remove the plastic cover and anchor bolt securing seat belt guide loop to vehicle.
6. Remove the anchor bolt and seat belt retractor assembly from the vehicle.
7. Remove the anchor bolt and remove the seat belt buckle from the vehicle.

To install:

8. Install the seat belt buckle and tighten bolt to 33 ft. lbs. (45 Nm).
9. Install the seat belt retractor and tighten bolt to 33 ft. lbs. (45 Nm).
10. Install the seat belt guide loop and tighten bolt to 33 ft. lbs. (45 Nm).
11. Install the plastic retaining clips and the passenger compartment quarter trim panel.
12. Install the plastic retaining clips and rear speaker panel.
13. Install the anchor bolt securing the seat belt to the floor. Tighten bolt to 33 ft. lbs. (45 Nm).
14. Connect the negative battery cable.

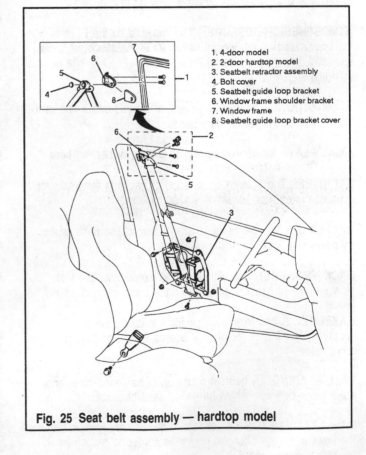

1. 4-door model
2. 2-door hardtop model
3. Seatbelt retractor assembly
4. Bolt cover
5. Seatbelt guide loop bracket
6. Window frame shoulder bracket
7. Window frame
8. Seatbelt guide loop bracket cover

Fig. 25 Seat belt assembly — hardtop model

GLOSSARY

AIR/FUEL RATIO: The ratio of air to gasoline by weight in the fuel mixture drawn into the engine.

AIR INJECTION: One method of reducing harmful exhaust emissions by injecting air into each of the exhaust ports of an engine. The fresh air entering the hot exhaust manifold causes any remaining fuel to be burned before it can exit the tailpipe.

ALTERNATOR: A device used for converting mechanical energy into electrical energy.

AMMETER: An instrument, calibrated in amperes, used to measure the flow of an electrical current in a circuit. Ammeters are always connected in series with the circuit being tested.

AMPERE: The rate of flow of electrical current present when one volt of electrical pressure is applied against one ohm of electrical resistance.

ANALOG COMPUTER: Any microprocessor that uses similar (analogous) electrical signals to make its calculations.

ARMATURE: A laminated, soft iron core wrapped by a wire that converts electrical energy to mechanical energy as in a motor or relay. When rotated in a magnetic field, it changes mechanical energy into electrical energy as in a generator.

ATMOSPHERIC PRESSURE: The pressure on the Earth's surface caused by the weight of the air in the atmosphere. At sea level, this pressure is 14.7 psi at 32{248}F (101 kPa at 0{248}C).

ATOMIZATION: The breaking down of a liquid into a fine mist that can be suspended in air.

AXIAL PLAY: Movement parallel to a shaft or bearing bore.

BACKFIRE: The sudden combustion of gases in the intake or exhaust system that results in a loud explosion.

BACKLASH: The clearance or play between two parts, such as meshed gears.

BACKPRESSURE: Restrictions in the exhaust system that slow the exit of exhaust gases from the combustion chamber.

BAKELITE: A heat resistant, plastic insulator material commonly used in printed circuit boards and transistorized components.

BALL BEARING: A bearing made up of hardened inner and outer races between which hardened steel balls roll.

BALLAST RESISTOR: A resistor in the primary ignition circuit that lowers voltage after the engine is started to reduce wear on ignition components.

BEARING: A friction reducing, supportive device usually located between a stationary part and a moving part.

BIMETAL TEMPERATURE SENSOR: Any sensor or switch made of two dissimilar types of metal that bend when heated or cooled due to the different expansion rates of the alloys. These types of sensors usually function as an on/off switch.

BLOWBY: Combustion gases, composed of water vapor and unburned fuel, that leak past the piston rings into the crankcase during normal engine operation. These gases are removed by the PCV system to prevent the buildup of harmful acids in the crankcase.

BRAKE PAD: A brake shoe and lining assembly used with disc brakes.

BRAKE SHOE: The backing for the brake lining. The term is, however, usually applied to the assembly of the brake backing and lining.

BUSHING: A liner, usually removable, for a bearing; an anti-friction liner used in place of a bearing.

CALIPER: A hydraulically activated device in a disc brake system, which is mounted straddling the brake rotor (disc). The caliper contains at least one piston and two brake pads. Hydraulic pressure on the piston(s) forces the pads against the rotor.

CAMSHAFT: A shaft in the engine on which are the lobes (cams) which operate the valves. The camshaft is driven by the crankshaft, via a belt, chain or gears, at one half the crankshaft speed.

CAPACITOR: A device which stores an electrical charge.

CARBON MONOXIDE (CO): A colorless, odorless gas given off as a normal byproduct of combustion. It is poisonous and extremely dangerous in confined areas, building up slowly to toxic levels without warning if adequate ventilation is not available.

CARBURETOR: A device, usually mounted on the intake manifold of an engine, which mixes the air and fuel in the proper proportion to allow even combustion.

CATALYTIC CONVERTER: A device installed in the exhaust system, like a muffler, that converts harmful byproducts of combustion into carbon dioxide and water vapor by means of a heat-producing chemical reaction.

CENTRIFUGAL ADVANCE: A mechanical method of advancing the spark timing by using flyweights in the distributor that react to centrifugal force generated by the distributor shaft rotation.

CHECK VALVE: Any one-way valve installed to permit the flow of air, fuel or vacuum in one direction only.

CHOKE: A device, usually a moveable valve, placed in the intake path of a carburetor to restrict the flow of air.

CIRCUIT: Any unbroken path through which an electrical current can flow. Also used to describe fuel flow in some instances.

CIRCUIT BREAKER: A switch which protects an electrical circuit from overload by opening the circuit when the current flow exceeds a predetermined level. Some circuit breakers must be reset manually, while most reset automatically

COIL (IGNITION): A transformer in the ignition circuit which steps up the voltage provided to the spark plugs.

COMBINATION MANIFOLD: An assembly which includes both the intake and exhaust manifolds in one casting.

COMBINATION VALVE: A device used in some fuel systems that routes fuel vapors to a charcoal storage canister instead of venting them into the atmosphere. The valve relieves fuel tank pressure and allows fresh air into the tank as the fuel level drops to prevent a vapor lock situation.

COMPRESSION RATIO: The comparison of the total volume of the cylinder and combustion chamber with the piston at BDC and the piston at TDC.

CONDENSER: 1. An electrical device which acts to store an electrical charge, preventing voltage surges.
  2. A radiator-like device in the air conditioning system in which refrigerant gas condenses into a liquid, giving off heat.

CONDUCTOR: Any material through which an electrical current can be transmitted easily.

CONTINUITY: Continuous or complete circuit. Can be checked with an ohmmeter.

COUNTERSHAFT: An intermediate shaft which is rotated by a mainshaft and transmits, in turn, that rotation to a working part.

CRANKCASE: The lower part of an engine in which the crankshaft and related parts operate.

CRANKSHAFT: The main driving shaft of an engine which receives reciprocating motion from the pistons and converts it to rotary motion.

CYLINDER: In an engine, the round hole in the engine block in which the piston(s) ride.

CYLINDER BLOCK: The main structural member of an engine in which is found the cylinders, crankshaft and other principal parts.

CYLINDER HEAD: The detachable portion of the engine, fastened, usually, to the top of the cylinder block, containing all or most of the combustion chambers. On overhead valve engines, it contains the valves and their operating parts. On overhead cam engines, it contains the camshaft as well.

DEAD CENTER: The extreme top or bottom of the piston stroke.

DETONATION: An unwanted explosion of the air/fuel mixture in the combustion chamber caused by excess heat and compression, advanced timing, or an overly lean mixture. Also referred to as "ping".

DIAPHRAGM: A thin, flexible wall separating two cavities, such as in a vacuum advance unit.

DIESELING: A condition in which hot spots in the combustion chamber cause the engine to run on after the key is turned off.

DIFFERENTIAL: A geared assembly which allows the transmission of motion between drive axles, giving one axle the ability to turn faster than the other.

DIODE: An electrical device that will allow current to flow in one direction only.

DISC BRAKE: A hydraulic braking assembly consisting of a brake disc, or rotor, mounted on an axle, and a caliper assembly containing, usually two brake pads which are activated by hydraulic pressure. The pads are forced against the sides of the disc, creating friction which slows the vehicle.

DISTRIBUTOR: A mechanically driven device on an engine which is responsible for electrically firing the spark plug at a predetermined point of the piston stroke.

DOWEL PIN: A pin, inserted in mating holes in two different parts allowing those parts to maintain a fixed relationship.

DRUM BRAKE: A braking system which consists of two brake shoes and one or two wheel cylinders, mounted on a fixed backing plate, and a brake drum, mounted on an axle, which revolves around the assembly.

DWELL: The rate, measured in degrees of shaft rotation, at which an electrical circuit cycles on and off.

ELECTRONIC CONTROL UNIT (ECU): Ignition module, module, amplifier or igniter. See Module for definition.

ELECTRONIC IGNITION: A system in which the timing and firing of the spark plugs is controlled by an electronic control unit, usually called a module. These systems have no points or condenser.

ENDPLAY: The measured amount of axial movement in a shaft.

ENGINE: A device that converts heat into mechanical energy.

EXHAUST MANIFOLD: A set of cast passages or pipes which conduct exhaust gases from the engine.

FEELER GAUGE: A blade, usually metal, of precisely predetermined thickness, used to measure the clearance between two parts.

FIRING ORDER: The order in which combustion occurs in the cylinders of an engine. Also the order in which spark is distributed to the plugs by the distributor.

FLOODING: The presence of too much fuel in the intake manifold and combustion chamber which prevents the air/fuel mixture from firing, thereby causing a no-start situation.

FLYWHEEL: A disc shaped part bolted to the rear end of the crankshaft. Around the outer perimeter is affixed the ring gear. The starter drive engages the ring gear, turning the flywheel, which rotates the crankshaft, imparting the initial starting motion to the engine.

FOOT POUND (ft.lb. or sometimes, ft. lbs.): The amount of energy or work needed to raise an item weighing one pound, a distance of one foot.

FUSE: A protective device in a circuit which prevents circuit overload by breaking the circuit when a specific amperage is present. The device is constructed around a strip or wire of a lower amperage rating than the circuit it is designed to protect. When an amperage higher than that stamped on the fuse is present in the circuit, the strip or wire melts, opening the circuit.

GEAR RATIO: The ratio between the number of teeth on meshing gears.

GENERATOR: A device which converts mechanical energy into electrical energy.

HEAT RANGE: The measure of a spark plug's ability to dissipate heat from its firing end. The higher the heat range, the hotter the plug fires.

HUB: The center part of a wheel or gear.

HYDROCARBON (HC): Any chemical compound made up of hydrogen and carbon. A major pollutant formed by the engine as a byproduct of combustion.

HYDROMETER: An instrument used to measure the specific gravity of a solution.

INCH POUND (in.lb. or sometimes, in. lbs.): One twelfth of a foot pound.

INDUCTION: A means of transferring electrical energy in the form of a magnetic field. Principle used in the ignition coil to increase voltage.

INJECTOR: A device which receives metered fuel under relatively low pressure and is activated to inject the fuel into the engine under relatively high pressure at a predetermined time.

INPUT SHAFT: The shaft to which torque is applied, usually carrying the driving gear or gears.

INTAKE MANIFOLD: A casting of passages or pipes used to conduct air or a fuel/air mixture to the cylinders.

JOURNAL: The bearing surface within which a shaft operates.

KEY: A small block usually fitted in a notch between a shaft and a hub to prevent slippage of the two parts.

MANIFOLD: A casting of passages or set of pipes which connect the cylinders to an inlet or outlet source.

MANIFOLD VACUUM: Low pressure in an engine intake manifold formed just below the throttle plates. Manifold vacuum is highest at idle and drops under acceleration.

MASTER CYLINDER: The primary fluid pressurizing device in a hydraulic system. In automotive use, it is found in brake and hydraulic clutch systems and is pedal activated, either directly or, in a power brake system, through the power booster.

MODULE: Electronic control unit, amplifier or igniter of solid state or integrated design which controls the current flow in the ignition primary circuit based on input from the pick-up coil. When the module opens the primary circuit, the high secondary voltage is induced in the coil.

NEEDLE BEARING: A bearing which consists of a number (usually a large number) of long, thin rollers.

OHM:(Ω) The unit used to measure the resistance of conductor to electrical flow. One ohm is the amount of resistance that limits current flow to one ampere in a circuit with one volt of pressure.

OHMMETER: An instrument used for measuring the resistance, in ohms, in an electrical circuit.

OUTPUT SHAFT: The shaft which transmits torque from a device, such as a transmission.

OVERDRIVE: A gear assembly which produces more shaft revolutions than that transmitted to it.

OVERHEAD CAMSHAFT (OHC): An engine configuration in which the camshaft is mounted on top of the cylinder head and operates the valve either directly or by means of rocker arms.

OVERHEAD VALVE (OHV): An engine configuration in which all of the valves are located in the cylinder head and the camshaft is located in the cylinder block. The camshaft operates the valves via lifters and pushrods.

OXIDES OF NITROGEN (NOx): Chemical compounds of nitrogen produced as a byproduct of combustion. They combine with hydrocarbons to produce smog.

OXYGEN SENSOR: Used with the feedback system to sense the presence of oxygen in the exhaust gas and signal the computer which can reference the voltage signal to an air/fuel ratio.

PINION: The smaller of two meshing gears.

PISTON RING: An open ended ring which fits into a groove on the outer diameter of the piston. Its chief function is to form a seal between the piston and cylinder wall. Most automotive pistons have three rings: two for compression sealing; one for oil sealing.

PRELOAD: A predetermined load placed on a bearing during assembly or by adjustment.

PRIMARY CIRCUIT: Is the low voltage side of the ignition system which consists of the ignition switch, ballast resistor or resistance wire, bypass, coil, electronic control unit and pick-up coil as well as the connecting wires and harnesses.

PRESS FIT: The mating of two parts under pressure, due to the inner diameter of one being smaller than the outer diameter of the other, or vice versa; an interference fit.

RACE: The surface on the inner or outer ring of a bearing on which the balls, needles or rollers move.

REGULATOR: A device which maintains the amperage and/or voltage levels of a circuit at predetermined values.

RELAY: A switch which automatically opens and/or closes a circuit.

RESISTANCE: The opposition to the flow of current through a circuit or electrical device, and is measured in ohms. Resistance is equal to the voltage divided by the amperage.

RESISTOR: A device, usually made of wire, which offers a preset amount of resistance in an electrical circuit.

RING GEAR: The name given to a ring-shaped gear attached to a differential case, or affixed to a flywheel or as part a planetary gear set.

ROLLER BEARING: A bearing made up of hardened inner and outer races between which hardened steel rollers move.

ROTOR: 1. The disc-shaped part of a disc brake assembly, upon which the brake pads bear; also called, brake disc.
2. The device mounted atop the distributor shaft, which passes current to the distributor cap tower contacts.

SECONDARY CIRCUIT: The high voltage side of the ignition system, usually above 20,000 volts. The secondary includes the ignition coil, coil wire, distributor cap and rotor, spark plug wires and spark plugs.

SENDING UNIT: A mechanical, electrical, hydraulic or electromagnetic device which transmits information to a gauge.

SENSOR: Any device designed to measure engine operating conditions or ambient pressures and temperatures. Usually electronic in nature and designed to send a voltage signal to an on-board computer, some sensors may operate as a simple on/off switch or they may provide a variable voltage signal (like a potentiometer) as conditions or measured parameters change.

SHIM: Spacers of precise, predetermined thickness used between parts to establish a proper working relationship.

SLAVE CYLINDER: In automotive use, a device in the hydraulic clutch system which is activated by hydraulic force, disengaging the clutch.

SOLENOID: A coil used to produce a magnetic field, the effect of which is produce work.

SPARK PLUG: A device screwed into the combustion chamber of a spark ignition engine. The basic construction is a conductive core inside of a ceramic insulator, mounted in an outer conductive base. An electrical charge from the spark plug wire travels along the conductive core and jumps a preset air gap to a grounding point or points at the end of the conductive base. The resultant spark ignites the fuel/air mixture in the combustion chamber.

SPLINES: Ridges machined or cast onto the outer diameter of a shaft or inner diameter of a bore to enable parts to mate without rotation.

TACHOMETER: A device used to measure the rotary speed of an engine, shaft, gear, etc., usually in rotations per minute.

THERMOSTAT: A valve, located in the cooling system of an engine, which is closed when cold and opens gradually in response to engine heating, controlling the temperature of the coolant and rate of coolant flow.

TOP DEAD CENTER (TDC): The point at which the piston reaches the top of its travel on the compression stroke.

TORQUE: The twisting force applied to an object.

TORQUE CONVERTER: A turbine used to transmit power from a driving member to a driven member via hydraulic action, providing changes in drive ratio and torque. In automotive use, it links the driveplate at the rear of the engine to the automatic transmission.

TRANSDUCER: A device used to change a force into an electrical signal.

TRANSISTOR: A semi-conductor component which can be actuated by a small voltage to perform an electrical switching function.

TUNE-UP: A regular maintenance function, usually associated with the replacement and adjustment of parts and components in the electrical and fuel systems of a vehicle for the purpose of attaining optimum performance.

TURBOCHARGER: An exhaust driven pump which compresses intake air and forces it into the combustion chambers at higher than atmospheric pressures. The increased air pressure allows more fuel to be burned and results in increased horsepower being produced.

VACUUM ADVANCE: A device which advances the ignition timing in response to increased engine vacuum.

VACUUM GAUGE: An instrument used to measure the presence of vacuum in a chamber.

VALVE: A device which control the pressure, direction of flow or rate of flow of a liquid or gas.

VALVE CLEARANCE: The measured gap between the end of the valve stem and the rocker arm, cam lobe or follower that activates the valve.

VISCOSITY: The rating of a liquid's internal resistance to flow.

VOLTMETER: An instrument used for measuring electrical force in units called volts. Voltmeters are always connected parallel with the circuit being tested.

WHEEL CYLINDER: Found in the automotive drum brake assembly, it is a device, actuated by hydraulic pressure, which, through internal pistons, pushes the brake shoes outward against the drums.

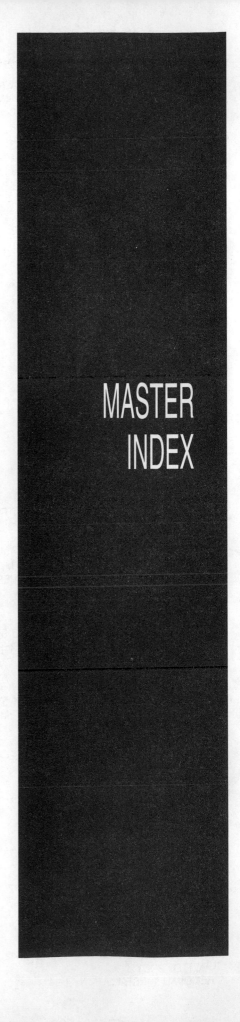

MASTER

INDEX

Total Car Care, continued

Sentra/Pulsar/NX 1982-96
PART NO. 8263/52700

Stanza/200SX/240SX 1982-92
PART NO. 8262/52750

240SX/Altima 1993-98
PART NO. 52752

Datsun/Nissan Z and ZX 1970-88
PART NO. 8846/52800

RENAULT
Coupes/Sedans/Wagons 1975-85
PART NO. 58300

SATURN
Coupes/Sedans/Wagons 1991-98
PART NO. 8419/62300

SUBARU
ff-1/1300/1400/1600/1800/Brat 1970-84
PART NO. 8790/64300

Coupes/Sedans/Wagons 1985-96
PART NO. 8259/64302

SUZUKI
Samurai/Sidekick/Tracker 1986-98
PART NO. 66500

TOYOTA
Camry 1983-96
PART NO. 8265/68200

Celica/Supra 1971-85
PART NO. 68250

Celica 1986-93
PART NO. 8413/68252

Corolla 1970-87
PART NO. 8586/68300

Corolla 1988-97
PART NO. 8414/68302

Cressida/Corona/Crown/MkII 1970-82
PART NO. 68350

Cressida/Van 1983-90
PART NO. 68352

Toyota Trucks 1970-88
PART NO. 8578/68600

Pick-Ups/Land Cruiser/4Runner 1989-96
PART NO. 8163/68602

Previa 1991-98
PART NO. 68640

Tercel 1984-94
PART NO. 8595/68700

VOLKSWAGEN
Air-Cooled 1949-69
PART NO. 70200

Air-Cooled 1970-81
PART NO. 70202

Front Wheel Drive 1974-89
PART NO. 8663/70400

Golf/Jetta/Cabriolet 1990-93
PART NO. 8429/70402

VOLVO
Coupes/Sedans/Wagons 1970-89
PART NO. 8786/72300

Coupes/Sedans/Wagons 1990-98
PART NO. 8428/72302

Total Service Series

Auto Detailing
PART NO. 8394

Auto Body Repair
PART NO. 7898

Automatic Transmission Repair 1980-84
PART NO. 7890

Automatic Transmissions/ Transaxles Diagnosis and Repair
PART NO. 8944

Brake System Diagnosis and Repair
PART NO. 8945

Chevrolet Engine Overhaul Manual
PART NO. 8794

Easy Car Care
PART NO. 8042

Engine Code Manual
PART NO. 8851

Ford Engine Overhaul Manual
PART NO. 8793

Fuel Injection and Feedback Carburetors 1977-85
PART NO. 7488

Fuel Injection Diagnosis and Repair
PART NO. 8946

Motorcycle Repair
PART NO. 9099

Small Engine Repair (Up to 20 Hp)
PART NO. 8325

Collector's Hard-Cover Manuals

Auto Repair Manual 1993-97
PART NO. 7919

Auto Repair Manual 1988-92
PART NO. 7906

Auto Repair Manual 1980-87
PART NO. 7670

Auto Repair Manual 1972-79
PART NO. 6914

Auto Repair Manual 1964-71
PART NO. 5974

Auto Repair Manual 1954-63
PART NO. 5652

Auto Repair Manual 1940-53
PART NO. 5631

Import Car Repair Manual 1993-97
PART NO. 7920

Import Car Repair Manual 1988-92
PART NO. 7907

Import Car Repair Manual 1980-87
PART NO. 7672

Truck and Van Repair Manual 1993-97
PART NO. 7921

Truck and Van Repair Manual 1991-95
PART NO. 7911

Truck and Van Repair Manual 1986-90
PART NO. 7902

Truck and Van Repair Manual 1979-86
PART NO. 7655

Truck and Van Repair Manual 1971-78
PART NO. 7012

Truck Repair Manual 1961-71
PART NO. 6198

Motorcycle and ATV Repair Manual 1945-85
PART NO. 7635

System-Specific Manuals

Guide to Air Conditioning Repair and Service 1982-85
PART NO. 7580

Guide to Automatic Transmission Repair 1984-89
PART NO. 8054

Guide to Automatic Transmission Repair 1984-89 Domestic cars and trucks
PART NO. 8053

Guide to Automatic Transmission Repair 1980-84 Domestic cars and trucks
PART NO. 7891

Guide to Automatic Transmission Repair 1974-80 Import cars and trucks
PART NO. 7645

Guide to Brakes, Steering, and Suspension 1980-87
PART NO. 7819

Guide to Fuel Injection and Electronic Engine Controls 1984-88

Guide to Electronic Engine Controls 1978-85
PART NO. 7535

Guide to Engine Repair and Rebuilding
PART NO. 7643

Guide to Vacuum Diagrams 1980-86 Domestic cars and trucks
PART NO. 7821

Multi-Vehicle Spanish Repair Manuals

Auto Repair Manual 1992-96
PART NO. 8947

Import Repair Manual 1992-96
PART NO. 8948

Truck and Van Repair Manual 1992-96
PART NO. 8949

Auto Repair Manual 1987-91
PART NO. 8138

Auto Repair Manual 1980-87
PART NO. 7795

Auto Repair Manual 1976-83
PART NO. 7476